BUILD YOUR OWN

FLIGHT SIM IN C++

PROGRAMMING A 3D FLIGHT SIMULATOR USING OOP

MICHAEL RADTKE
CHRISTOPHER LAMPTON

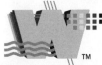

Waite Group Press™
A Division of Sams Publishing
Corte Madera, CA

Publisher: *Mitchell Waite*
Editor-in-Chief: *Charles Drucker*

Acquisitions Editor: *Jill Pisoni*

Editorial Director: *John Crudo*
Managing Editor: *Andrea Rosenberg*
Content Editor: *Harry Henderson*
Copy Editor: *Tynan Northrop*
Technical Reviewer: *André LaMothe*

Production Director: *Julianne Ososke*
Production Manager: *Cecile Kaufman*
Cover Design: *Sestina Quarequio*
Cover Illustration: © *Westlight*
Chapter Opener Art: © *Westlight*
Illustrations: *Ben Long, Larry Wilson*
Production: *Christi Fryday, Judith Levinson*

Waite Group Press™ is a division of Sams Publishing.

Waite Group Press™ is distributed to bookstores and book wholesalers by Publishers Group West, Box 8843, Emeryville, CA 94662, 1-800-788-3123 (in California 1-510-658-3453).

Printed in the United States of America
96 97 98 99 • 10 9 8 7 6 5 4 3 2 1

Library of Congress Cataloging-in-Publication Data
Radtke, Michael.
     Build your own flight sim in C++ / Michael Radtke, Chris Lampton.
       p.   cm.
     Rev. ed. of: Flights of fantasy. 1993.
     Includes bibliographical references and index.
     ISBN: 1-57169-022-0 : $39.99
     1. Flight simulators--Computer programs.   2. C++ (Computer program language)   I. Lampton, Christopher.
II. Lampton, Christopher. Flights of fantasy.   III.Title.
TL712.5.R32   1996
794.8' 75--dc20
                                         69-11089
                                         CIP

Dedication

To the continued free exchange of ideas on the net.

Message from the
Publisher

WELCOME TO OUR NERVOUS SYSTEM

Some people say that the World Wide Web is a graphical extension of the information superhighway, just a network of humans and machines sending each other long lists of the equivalent of digital junk mail.

I think it is much more than that. To me the Web is nothing less than the nervous system of the entire planet—not just a collection of computer brains connected together, but more like a billion silicon neurons entangled and recirculating electro-chemical signals of information and data, each contributing to the birth of another CPU and another Web site.

Think of each person's hard disk connected at once to every other hard disk on earth, driven by human navigators searching like Columbus for the New World. Seen this way the Web is more of a super entity, a growing, living thing, controlled by the universal human will to expand, to be more. Yet, unlike a purposeful business plan with rigid rules, the Web expands in a nonlinear, unpredictable, creative way that echoes natural evolution.

We created our Web site not just to extend the reach of our computer book products but to be part of this synaptic neural network, to experience, like a nerve in the body, the flow of ideas and then to pass those ideas up the food chain of the mind. Your mind. Even more, we wanted to pump some of our own creative juices into this rich wine of technology.

TASTE OUR DIGITAL WINE

And so we ask you to taste our wine by visiting the body of our business. Begin by understanding the metaphor we have created for our Web site—a universal learning center, situated in outer space in the form of a space station. A place where you can journey to study any topic from the convenience of your own screen. Right now we are focusing on computer topics, but the stars are the limit on the Web.

If you are interested in discussing this Web site or finding out more about the Waite Group, please send me email with your comments and I will be happy to respond. Being a programmer myself, I love to talk about technology and find out what our readers are looking for.

Sincerely,

Mitchell Waite

Mitchell Waite, C.E.O. and Publisher

200 Tamal Plaza
Corte Madera CA 94925
415 924 2575
415 924 2576 fax

Internet email:
mwaite@waite.com

Website:
http://www.waite.com/waite

CREATING THE HIGHEST QUALITY COMPUTER BOOKS IN THE INDUSTRY

Waite Group Press
Waite Group New Media

About the Authors

Michael Radtke has worked with Waite Group Press for three years in various capacities: technical editor, programmer and bug shooter. He holds a degree in both Human Organizational Processes and Mathematics from Montclair State University in New Jersey. Involved in software development since 1982, he has programmed and/or designed various shrink-wrapped software products for entertainment, home productivity, and business. When he is not programming, brainstorming, or pulling someone's leg, he plays piano for his own enjoyment.

Christopher Lampton is the author of more than 80 books for readers young and old. These include 20 books on microcomputers and computer programming, including introductory books on BASIC, Pascal, and assembly language programming, and four books on computer graphics and animation programming. He has also written books on topics as diverse as biotechnology, airline safety, underwater archaeology, sound, astronomy, dinosaurs, the origin of the universe, and predicting the course of epi-

demics. He holds a degree in broadcast communications from the University of Maryland, College Park, and has worked both as a disk jockey and as a producer of television commercials for a Maryland TV station. When he is not writing, programming, or indulging in his hobby as a fanatic computer gamer, he serves as Associate Sysop (system operator) of the Game Publishers Forums (GAMPUB) on the CompuServe Information Service. He is also the author of Waite Group Press's *Flights of Fantasy, Nanotechnology Playhouse*, and *Gardens of Imagination*.

Contents

Table of Contents

Acknowledgments

This is a book of synergy, and as such, its sum has many parts to be appreciated. First of all, the publisher, Waite Group Press, has continued to pursue visions which excite computer aficionados. Everyone at Waite is supportive of techno-cyber-compu-babbling writers, and their efforts make it easy to get the job done. It was the Waite webmaster who introduced me to them. Thanks, drdrax1@waite.com! And a tip of my virtual hat goes to Mitch and his keen eye for the cutting edge of technology. Coordinating the entire hodgepodge, Andrea Rosenberg provided *const* declarations for us global modules, including Harry Henderson, André LaMothe, and the contributing programmers and authors.

The entire experience was an excellent demonstration of class inheritance. The first version of the program, *Flights of Fantasy*, had a considerable list of contributors. Christopher Lampton and Mark Betz wrote the lion's share of code in that version, and it would be a disservice not to give them tremendous kudos here. If their code has been changed, the design lives on in a revised form. It is also noteworthy to mention the other contributors listed by Chris Lampton in the first edition: Hans Peter Rushworth, John Dlugosz, and Hal Raymond. I do not know *exactly* what they did, but first edition references alluded to many late night phone calls while working out flight algorithms.

The new version of the program was enlightened by Dale Sather's excellent shading implementation and examples. Keith Weiner and Erik Lorenzen intoned two separate sets of sound code, one of FM sound effects and the other using music by David Schultz. Check out Appendix C for a version of the flight simulator which uses the DiamondWare Sound ToolKit, a shareware sound library.

Foreword

Since the dawn of time humankind has dreamt of flying among the birds in the skies above. This dream became clearer and took form as the ages passed. The great artist, sculptor, and scholar Leonardo da Vinci was one of the first to try to create a flying machine. His renderings show some of the first visualizations of what we now know as the airplane and helicopter.

As time marched on, the drawings of Leonardo came to life one winter day in the epic first flight of the Wright Brothers. The day that "The Flyer" rose above the Earth and flew would have a profound effect on humankind in the near and distant future.

Today we have begun to create modern aircraft that finally realize the machines that we have so longed to see in action. Fighters that look like something out of *Star Wars*. Experimental planes made of new materials and flown by computers at many times the speed of sound.

However, these flights of fantasy have always been privy to those chosen few with the access to these amazing machines. True, but not for long. As the aircraft industry was humming forward at mach speed, so was the computer industry. Two men, Evans and Sutherland, laid much of the groundwork for 3D visualization that could be used to create synthetic cockpits and simulate flight in the virtual cyberspace of the computer. Alas, this new technology was again for the elite. Those who owned or had access to supercomputers and custom hardware needed to perform the millions of operations per second to create the illusion of flight. Then something happened. The computer industry, in particular the personal computer industry, started making quantum leaps in processor power and soon the PC had as much computing power as a minicomputer. The dream of flight simulation had become a reality to the home user.

We have all played flight simulators on our PCs in awe of the worlds we flew above. However, the underlying magical technology was still out of reach for most, except, of course, for the students

The Wright Brothers' epic first flight

of computer science and higher mathematics. Then Christopher Lampton along with Waite Group Press published the first book on flight simulation for the PC. The book was an instant success and best-seller.

Many moons have passed since the first printing of *Flights of Fantasy* and now it's time to move forward. *Build Your Own Flight Sim in C++* is the next step in evolution of this genre. The authors have added and expanded the original material to cover texture mapping, advanced lighting, synthesized sound, and more. Along with these additions, the code of the book has been rewritten in C++ with classes and object-oriented techniques. This book completes Chris's original conquest of the skies in cyberspace and gives you the tools to take the next step. So strap in, engage the engines, taxi down the runway, and lift off with this new flight of fantasy…

André LaMothe

Preface

Once upon a time, an insightful programming author named Christopher Lampton sat down to write a book on flight simulators. Chris had observed the computer-gaming world's infatuation with these flight-simulation programs. It was a phenomenon that propelled many titles onto software best-selling lists year after year. These products use state-of-the-art techniques for rendering animated, three-dimensional images onto the computer monitor. Chris and other armchair pilots were able to fly an airplane with aerodynamical realism and thrills, but without the expense of paying for fuel or airplane maintenance. His book, *Flights of Fantasy,* presented a guided tour of computer flight-simulator components, from the creation of images on the video screen to the prototype of an airplane's flight. It included an operational flight simulator with source code—the first of its kind and a smashing success.

This book is a revision of that work. It is meant for programmers who want to write a flight simulator. It covers, in depth, the major problems of such a task. In the pages that follow, all aspects of flight-simulation programming are presented: input device control, creation of three-dimensional shapes, sound effects, light sources, shadowing, a viewing system, and a model for flight simulation which imitates actual airplanes. The concepts are defined, explored, and often accompanied by a simple demonstration program as illustration.

A program is usually a growing work and the original *Flights of Fantasy* flight simulator is no exception. Simply put, much of the original code was written in C and compiled under C++; the strength of the C++ programming language was not used to its fullest. In revising the flight simulator, the code was first taxied into the hangar where it was changed—updated and organized with more C++ classes. The many example programs which demonstrate the elements of three-dimensional programming were altered to use C++ methodology: the *iostream* methods replaced *printf* calls; *new* and *delete* replaced *malloc* and *free,* etc. Time was spent debugging the original code.

As the current book has been renamed to better depict its content, so too, the program has received a new name to differentiate the versions. The new version, *FSIM,* now uses many classes developed in the first 15 chapters of the book. Some of the original routines formed naturally into their own classes, while other parts had to be induced under coding surgery. It has been compiled under Borland version 4.5 and resides on the CD for your exploits. Examine it. Tweak, twist, and supercharge it. Most of all though, have fun.

With the program's metamorphosis, the text was changed to reflect these code improvements. Chapters were added, expanded, and/or replaced. Code listings and figures were revamped.

At the time of this writing, the book is finished and another pass is being made to the code presented in the book. Any and all code is included on the accompanying CD as long as it was done at the time the CD was put to bed (publisher's jargon for sent to the presses). As was said previously, a program is a growing work. The book and CD are snapshots of that work at one point in time. For this reason, on the CD, there is a file called README.TXT that documents any major changes or bugs unearthed since the book was completed. Smaller changes are documented within the source files. Revision notes preface all code changes along with comments noting the reason for the change and action taken.

To reflect the dynamic nature of the evolving code in this book, the latest code is available on the Internet at www.waite.com. Again, the README.TXT file will map any changes or anomalies since the CD version. The site for the continued development of the flight simulator was changed from a CompuServe forum to provide a common area for those net-using readers who don't have a CompuServe account. Now, straight net shooters and AOL folk can partake in ongoing development along with CompuServants since all three can access the Internet.

Michael Radtke
Berkeley, CA

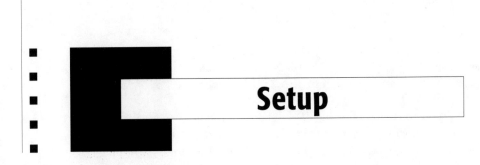

Setup

The accompanying *Build Your Own Flight Sim in C++* CD contains the flight simulator built throughout this book and the example source code. It also includes an installation program to copy these files to your hard disk.

Requirements

To install all the files, you will need approximately 10.5MB of free space on your hard disk. The installation program creates a directory called **BYOFS**, then creates the following subdirectories within **BYOFS**:

```
3DWIRE
FRAC
FSIM
FSIM_BYOFS
FSIM_STK
GENERAL
GOURAUD
LIGHTING
MOUNTAIN
OPTIMIZE
POLYGON
SOUND
TEXTURE
WALKMAN2
WIREFRAM
```

The files are then copied into the appropriate subdirectory. The **FSIM** subdirectory contains the full flight simulator. Other subdirectories contain code modules developed within several chapters throughout the book.

Installation

There is nothing magical about the installation process. It is totally understandable that you may only want to install certain source modules to save hard disk space. We have included an installation program on the CD called SOURCE.EXE which lets you select the modules you wish to copy to your hard disk. An alternate batch file named INSTALL will copy ALL of the source code using the DOS XCOPY command. Or alternately, you may want to use your own tools to select which files you copy to your hard disk.

We'll assume that you're installing the CD from drive E:. (If not, replace E: with the correct CD drive letter.) To begin, place the *Build Your Own Flight Sim in C++* CD in the E: drive. Switch to the root directory of the E: drive at the DOS prompt by typing

```
E:
CD\
```

Start the SOURCE installation program by typing

```
SOURCE
```

After a moment, the main screen appears. The source projects are listed in the same order as they appear in this book. The main features of this SOURCE program are

- the list which allows you to highlight and select items for copying
- the menu which determines what action to take for selected items
- a system display for various statistics such as how much disk space is available

Select and Copy Projects

To copy a project to your hard disk:

1. Move the highlight to the list by using the tab key.
2. Locate the project you want to copy and press F to flag the project for copying. If you want to select all the projects in the list, press A.
3. The SOURCE program normally creates a directory on the C: drive called **BYOFS**. If you prefer a different destination, press D, then enter the drive and directory you like better.
4. To begin copying the selected projects, press C. The program creates the directory on the destination drive if it does not exist, and the projects are copied into subdirectories.

Flash Copy

If you only want to copy one project, you can Flash Copy it to your hard disk. As long as no items have been flagged for copying, the Flash Copy option is available to you. To do this, simply highlight the desired item, then press C.

Do-It-Yourself Install

If you want to install files yourself, go for it. We have taken care to group all necessary source files within their own subdirectories. To do this, first create a destination directory on the desired drive. For this example, we'll call it FLYER. Then copy the desired files from the CD drive. For example, to install the Walkman2 project files to the F: drive type:

```
E:
CD\
MD F:\FLYER
XCOPY /S WALKMAN2 F:\FLYER
```

CONFIGURATION

The program project files which are included with the installed files are configured to a Borland C++ version 4.5 compiler which was installed on `C:\BC45`. The path to the compiler libraries and header files may be different on your computer! In this case, the typical error message will be "Unable to open include file IOSTREAM.H" (or some different header file name). To change these paths from our default, open one of the projects, then click on Options - Project. The displayed Directories dialog allows you to change the paths to match your computer. Enter the correct path if necessary and save the project using the Options - Save menu selection.

Borland 4.5 was used to create the make files in each directory. If you are going to use these .MAK files to build the program, you may also need to change the path to your compiler from our default (`C:\BC45`). A DOS error message similar to the above IDE error message will result if this is the case. Use an ASCII editor to adjust the paths for your computer environment. The paths are located in the Options section of the individual make files.

The older version of Turbo project files (ending in .PRJ) have been updated and tested along with the .IDE project versions. Older version users will likewise have to adjust the project directories if they are different from our default (`C:\BORLANDC`).

CHAPTER

1

A Graphics Primer

In the late 1970s, Bruce Artwick changed the course of microcomputer gaming history. The computer arcade games of that era were making the transition from the simplicity of *Pong* and *Breakout* to the relative complexity of *Asteroids* and *Pac Man*, but Artwick's ambitions went beyond even sophisticated two-dimensional animations. He wanted to create a world inside his microcomputer and to show animated images of that world on the video display.

To that end, he developed a set of three-dimensional animation routines tailor-made for the limited capabilities of 8-bit microcomputers. With the encouragement of a friend who flew small planes, Artwick used these animation techniques to write a game called *Flight Simulator*, which ran in low-resolution graphics on the Apple II and TRS-80 Model I computers.

Released commercially in 1979 by Artwick's company, SubLOGIC Inc., *Flight Simulator* allowed the player to fly a small airplane over a rectangular patch of land bisected by a river and bordered on two sides by mountains. If the player wished, he or she could declare war and dogfight with a squadron of World War I biplanes. Despite the low-resolution graphics, the game drew raves from players and reviewers alike because it did something no microcomputer game had done before: It created a fully three-dimensional world in which the player could move about freely—and depicted that world graphically on the video display of the computer.

Even so, *Flight Simulator* is memorable more for what it became than for what it was. Over the next three years, Artwick wrote a sequel, *Flight Simulator 2,* which was first marketed in 1982 by the Microsoft Corporation for the IBM PC. *FS2* was a quantum jump beyond Artwick's first simulator. Although the original *FS* was still embedded within it as "World War I Flying Ace," the meat of the new game was a huge database of scenery that let the player fly over much of Illinois (Artwick's home), northwest Washington State (site of Microsoft), Southern California, and the New York-to-Boston corridor—all in high-resolution color graphics.

The Descendants of *Flight Simulator*

Flight Simulator 2 was an immediate hit. Weekly newsmagazines carried articles about it and celebrities gushed over it. Over the next few years, it was translated to almost every popular computing platform of the period: the Commodore 64 and Amiga, the Atari 800 and ST, the Apple II and Macintosh. Artwick has upgraded the program several times: The current version of *Flight Simulator* is 5.1, and undoubtedly there is a version 6 in the development hangar.

The phenomenal success of Artwick's *Flight Simulator* did not go unnoticed. Following the publication of *FS2,* flight simulator games evolved into a genre of computer games. One entire company, Microprose Software, sprang up around a line of flight simulators (though it later diversified into other kinds of simulations). Other companies, such as Spectrum Holobyte, soon joined the fray. Although Artwick's *FS2* remained state-of-the-art for several years (an unusual feat in the fast-moving world of entertainment software), his competitors eventually produced equally impressive games. The list of flight simulator games provides a chronology of game software: Microprose's *F-19 Stealth Fighter*; Spectrum Holobyte's *Falcon* (version 3.0 shown in Figure 1-1); Sierra Dynamix's *Red Baron, Aces Over the Pacific,* and *Aces Over Europe,* now packaged together as *Aces Complete Collector's Edition*; Three-Sixty Pacific's *Megafortress*; LucasArts's *BattleHawks* and *Secret Weapons of the Luftwaffe*; Electronic

Figure 1-1 Falcon 3.0 is one of the most realistic and complex flight simulators on the market

Arts's *Chuck Yeager* series and *U.S. Navy Fighters*; Velocity Development's *Jetfighter* series; and Looking Glass Technologies' *Flight Unlimited*. Not only winged aircraft but helicopter simulators, such as Interactive Magic's *Apache* and Nova Logic's *Comanche,* can be found in software kiosks.

What these games have in common, aside from a large and enthusiastic following among computer game aficionados and armchair pilots, is that they all use computer graphics to create the illusion of a three-dimensional world inside the computer. Most of these games rely on a technique known as *polygon-fill graphics* to render images of mountains, buildings, rivers, coastlines, and occasionally human beings. When done well, the effect is almost magical: The player is transported into the world of the flight simulator as though it were real.

Although the effect that they produce seems like magic, the techniques used to render the three-dimensional world of a flight simulator aren't magical at all. For years they were hidden in the pages of esoteric programming texts, where programmers without a background in advanced mathematics and computer theory have found it difficult to apply them. Until now.

To illustrate how these techniques work, we'll build a number of demonstration programs in later chapters, culminating in a working flight simulator.

For the benefit of programmers with no PC graphics-programming experience, though, we'll start with an overview of the basic concepts of computer graphics in general and IBM PC graphics in particular. Programmers who have already mastered two-dimensional graphics techniques may wish to skim the rest of this chapter, though skipping it entirely is not recommended—at the very least, I hope you'd find it entertaining.

Graphics and Games

At the heart of every great computer game is a picture, or, more likely, two or three or a thousand pictures.

At one time it was possible to publish a major computer game that didn't use graphics. In the 1980s, Infocom Inc. published a wonderful series of text adventures with no graphics capabilities whatsoever. But game buyers in the 1990s demand state-of-the-art graphics, even if the visual images have little or nothing to do with the game. (One of the most popular arcade games ever, Spectrum Holobyte's version of *Tetris,* features background scenes from the former Soviet Union that are completely unrelated to the action of the game.) Great game design and play balance are also essential to a top-notch game, of course, but neither can save a game with lousy graphics from commercial oblivion.

Thus, a programmer who wants to produce games for the IBM PC must understand the graphics capabilities of that computer. And a programmer who wants to produce three-dimensional animation must have an acute understanding of PC graphics.

Text versus Graphics

The images on a video display fall loosely into two categories: text and graphics. At any given time, the video display of a PC-compatible microcomputer is either in text mode or graphics mode. A text mode display consists of alphanumeric characters, while a graphics mode display is made up of pictures.

The distinction isn't always that obvious, though. Sometimes what looks like text is really graphics and what looks like graphics is really text. The Microsoft Windows operating system, for instance, uses graphics mode to produce all of its text output. (See Figure 1-2.) And the IBM character set (see Figure 1-3) includes graphics characters that can be used to render crude pictures in text mode.

In fact, the two display modes have one important characteristic in common. Whether in text or graphics mode, everything on the video display is made up of a matrix of dots called pixels, short for "pictorial elements." The pixel is the atomic component out of which all computer images are constructed. If you look closely at the display screen of your microcomputer, you may be able to discern the individual pixels.

The Programmer's View

The most obvious differences between text mode and graphics mode lie on the programming level. When a PC is in text mode, the programmer must specify what appears on the video display in terms of a predefined character set consisting of 256

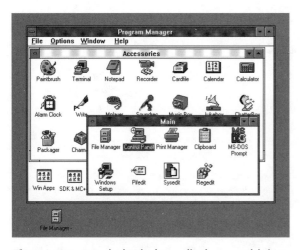

Figure 1-2 A typical Windows display, combining graphic images with text characters, created using graphics techniques

Figure 1-3 The IBM PC text mode character set. Notice the graphics characters that can be used to construct a crude image

different characters. Any of these characters can be placed in any of 2,000 different positions on the video display. But the individual pixels within the characters cannot be altered, nor can a character be positioned on the display any more precisely than the 2,000 available positions allow. Thus, the text characters must line up in neat rows and columns across the display. (See Figure 1-4.)

When a PC is in graphics mode, on the other hand, the programmer has direct control over every pixel on the display. There is no predefined character set in graphics mode. The programmer is free to invent pixel images and place them anywhere on the video display.

Since graphics mode offers the programmer that kind of power, you might wonder why any programmer would choose to work in text mode. The answer is that graphics

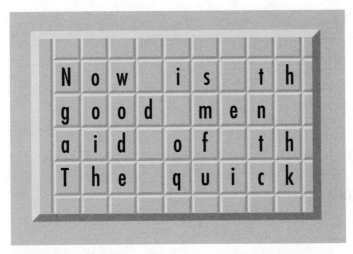

Figure 1-4 Each character on a text mode display fits into a rigidly defined "box" on the screen

mode, while offering considerable power and freedom, isn't easy to use. If all you need to do is display text characters on the video screen, it's much easier to use the predefined character set.

A game programmer really doesn't have that choice. Game buyers demand state-of-the-art graphics when they purchase software, and there's no way to produce state-of-the-art graphics in text mode. So for the rest of this chapter I'll look at the graphics capabilities of the video graphics array (VGA), the graphics adapter sold with the vast majority of PC-compatible microcomputers.

Inside the VGA

The VGA adapter includes a multitude of text and graphics modes, each of which has different characteristics and is programmed in a different way. The reasons for this are at least partly historical; the VGA is designed to be compatible with software written for earlier IBM graphics adapters. Looking at the various video modes of the VGA adapter is like walking through a museum full of exhibits showing how programming was done in the (not so distant) past.

In the beginning, there *were* no graphics on the IBM PC. When International Business Machines released its first microcomputer in the fall of 1981, there was only one video adapter available for the new computer. Called the monochrome display adapter (MDA), it was incapable of producing images on the computer's video display that were not constructed from the 256 characters of the IBM character set.

It didn't take long for IBM to realize that this was a mistake. Almost immediately after the introduction of the PC, the color graphics adapter (CGA) was released. The text characters it displayed were fuzzier than the ones produced by the MDA, but the CGA offered something that the MDA did not—color images, in which every pixel was under the programmer's control.

Unfortunately, the color images produced by the CGA weren't especially good, particularly in comparison with those produced by other computers on the market at the time. This didn't stop people from buying IBM microcomputers by the millions, but it was an obstacle for game programmers. Few major games were designed on the IBM PC in the early 1980s (*FS2* was a notable exception) and games translated for the IBM from other computers were usually graphically inferior to the original versions.

IBM Graphics Improve

In 1984, IBM introduced the enhanced graphics adapter (EGA). Graphics produced on the EGA improved a quantum leap beyond those produced by the CGA, but they still lagged behind the screen images of other 16-bit computers debuting at about that time. Few IBM users bought the EGA in the years immediately after its introduction and game designers still ignored the PC. Then, two or three years later, the price of the EGA adapter went down and sales went up. Slowly, game designers began to discover the PC.

Finally, introducing the PS/2 line in 1987, IBM surprised the gaming world with VGA, which could output startlingly vivid images to the PC's video display. The VGA made the IBM a viable gaming machine for the first time. As the 1990s dawned, game players who owned other machines moved to the IBM and compatibles in droves and game programmers in the United States began designing games first, and often exclusively, for the PC.

Why was the VGA responsible for such a dramatic revolution? It was capable of placing 256 colors on the video display at one time. Compare this to the capability of other gaming computers popular in 1987: the Commodore 64 and the Atari ST could display 16 colors at one time and the Commodore Amiga could display 32. (Actually, the Amiga is capable of displaying 4,096 colors at one time, but the programming restrictions on the manner these colors can be displayed are so severe that few game designers have embraced this capability.)

Video Modes Galore

When the first CGA rolled out of the factory in 1981, it supported seven official video modes: four could only display text characters and three were capable of displaying pixel graphics. The EGA, which was intended by IBM to be upwardly compatible with the CGA, supported all of these modes and added several more. In all, the EGA supported 16 official video modes, 7 of which were graphics modes.

The VGA expanded the list to 24 different modes, 9 of them graphics modes. Most of these modes are of historical interest only. They exist so that programs written for earlier IBM video adapters will still run on the VGA adapter. And the so-called super VGA (SVGA) adapters offer additional modes. SVGA is not a label for a standard. This name is more an invention of the marketplace to signify there are higher resolution modes on the card than found on the VGA card. Higher resolution modes among many different manufacturers are not the same.

There are also several unofficial graphics modes available on the VGA adapter. They're called unofficial because the video controller chips are altered directly, bypassing the BIOS. Deep-diving programmers will modify the CRT controller and timer/sequencer to create new resolutions. Thus, there is a notorious "mode X" which has its own publicity agent and alters the resolution to 320x240. (Only kidding about the publicity agent.) Anyone interested in these types of soft modes can learn more about them in the *Black Art of 3D Game Programming*, (LaMothe, Waite Group Press, 1995) or the *LINUX Video_Driver_HOW_TO* (various, Open Software Foundation [via Slackware], 1995).

From another direction comes the Video Electronics Standards Association (VESA) mode. There are programmers who swear by the VESA mode, but alas, it is a driver which hooks the video interrupt and standardizes a set of extended video commands.

The VESA interface does make life easier for getting high-performance graphics out of a multitude of different SVGA cards. Since the standard is well supported, any designer using VESA can be assured that the majority of users will have VESA drivers. Copies of the standard can be obtained by writing to VESA, 2150 N. First Street, San Jose, CA 95131-2020.

What are the differences among the standard VGA modes? Obviously, some of them are text modes and some are video modes. We've already looked at the difference between text modes and video modes. But what could be the difference between one text mode and another text mode? Or between one video mode and another video mode? In both cases, the answer is the same.

Resolution and Color Depth

Modes differ from one another in the number of pixels that can be placed on the display at one time and in the number of colors those pixels can display. The first of these attributes is called resolution, the second is sometimes referred to as color depth. These attributes in turn affect the amount of detail that can be displayed on the screen in graphics modes and the number of characters that can appear on the screen in text modes.

Figure 1-5(a) shows a low-resolution text mode. The text characters are large and blocky; only 40 can be displayed horizontally. This mode was included in early IBM PCs because some users were expected to use a standard television as a video output device and the large characters were more readable on a TV screen. Few people took this option, however, and the mode was only retained in later graphics adapters to accommodate those programs that had been written to use it.

Figure 1-5(b) shows a high-resolution text mode. The text characters are smaller and sharper looking. Because 80 characters can be displayed horizontally, this mode is ideal for applications that need to present a large amount of text to the user all at once—for instance, word processors or spreadsheets.

The graphics modes shown in Figure 1-6 are similarly divided between low-resolution modes and high-resolution modes. The lowest-resolution graphics modes available on the standard VGA adapter feature a matrix of 320 pixels horizontally and 200 pixels (300x200) vertically. The highest-resolution modes feature a matrix of 720x400 pixels (for text modes) and 640x480 pixels (for graphics modes). The lowest color-depth modes offer only two different colors of pixel on the display at one time; the highest color-depth modes offer pixels in 256 colors at one time. As a general rule, the greater the color depth, the smaller the number of pixels that can be displayed on the screen at one time.

For our purposes as game programmers, only two of the standard VGA graphics modes are of real importance: mode 12h, which can display a matrix of 640x480 pixels in 16 different colors, and mode 13h, which can display a matrix of 320x200 pixels in 256 colors. Most games currently on the market use one of these two modes or

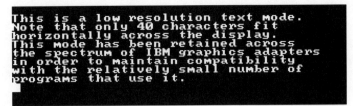

Figure 1-5 A comparison of low-resolution and high-resolution text modes

(a) A low-resolution text mode. Note that only 40 characters can be printed horizontally across the display

(b) A high-resolution text mode. Note that 80 characters can be printed horizontally across the display in this mode

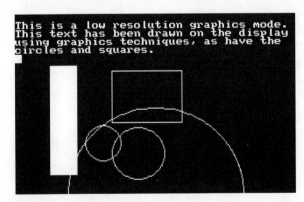

Figure 1-6 A low-resolution graphics mode, showing both text and graphics on the display. This mode supports 320 pixels horizontally and 200 pixels vertically

variations on them as discussed above. A 640x480 resolution has an edge on popularity in modern software titles. This mode is probably a proprietary altered mode since the games do not require a VESA driver, have more than the 16 colors that mode 12h provides, and the companies themselves zip their lip when questioned. The other games use mode 13h because of its greater color depth. Thus, that's the mode that we'll use for the programs in this book. And that's the mode I'll describe in detail in the remainder of this chapter.

The Memory Connection

We've now looked briefly at the graphics modes offered by the VGA adapter and focused on mode 13h for further discussion. Now let's get down to the real nitty-gritty. Let's look at how a programmer goes about creating patterns of pixels on the video display of a PC-compatible microcomputer. (For now, I'll talk about this in theoretical terms. In Chapter 3, I'll give specific programming examples showing how images are placed on the computer display.)

You can think of the VGA adapter as a miniature television transmitter, sending a video signal from the computer to the video monitor much as a television station sends a picture to the television set in your bedroom, as shown in Figure 1-7. The main difference between the VGA adapter and a television transmitter is that the television transmitter sends its signal as electromagnetic waves that travel through space to an antenna while the VGA adapter sends its signal through a cable as an electric current. And, with the growing popularity of cable television, even that difference is starting to disappear. (There are also some technical differences between the form that the VGA signal takes and the form taken by a standard television transmission, but those differences need not concern us here.)

A television picture has to originate somewhere—usually from a video camera in a television studio or from a videotape player similar to the VCR you probably have hooked up to your television. There's obviously no television studio or videotape player inside your computer, so where does the VGA picture originate?

The answer is video memory. Before I discuss video memory, though, I want to digress for a moment and talk about computer memory in general.

Bits, Bytes, and Binary

If you've been using microcomputers for a while, you probably have a good idea of what their memory is. Internally, it's the part of the computer that holds data and computer programs to which the computer's central processing unit (CPU) needs instantaneous access. (There are also external memory storage devices, such as hard disks and CD-ROMs, which hold data and computer programs to which the CPU eventually will need access.)

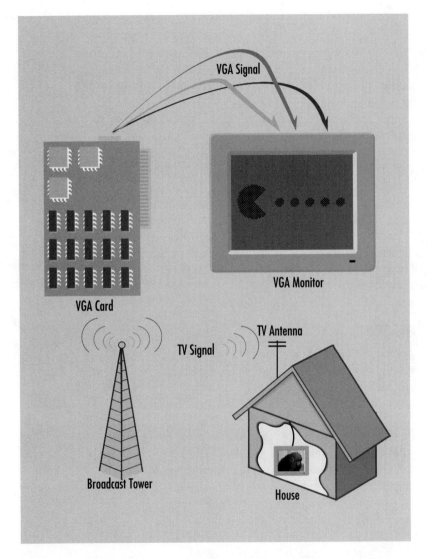

Figure 1-7 The VGA sends a signal to the VGA monitor much like a television station transmits a signal to your television set

More specifically, internal memory is a sequence of miniaturized circuits that can hold numeric values in the form of electrical voltages. In a PC-compatible microcomputer, each of these circuits holds the equivalent of an 8-digit binary number, otherwise known as a byte.

A binary number is a number made up of only two kinds of digits: zeroes and ones. So, some 8-digit binary numbers would be 10010011, 01101110, and 11101000. Like the decimal numbers that we ordinarily use for counting (which use 10 different digits, 0 through 9), binary numbers can represent any possible integer numeric value—that is, any possible whole number. An 8-digit binary number, however, can only represent numbers that fall into the range 00000000 to 11111111, which in decimal is 0 to 255. Thus, each computer memory circuit holds an electronic representation of a number in that range.

At the most primitive level, most of the work performed by a computer program involves storing numeric values in memory circuits, retrieving them from those circuits, performing arithmetic operations on them, and putting the result of those operations back into memory circuits. If you program microcomputers in a high-level language, such as C, you may not be aware of the degree to which these memory circuits figure into your algorithms because high-level languages are designed to hide the details of the CPU's interactions with memory. But if you program in a low-level language, such as assembly language, you'll often find yourself making direct reference to the computer's memory circuitry.

Memory Addresses

Every memory circuit in the computer has an identifying number called an address, which makes it easier for the numeric values stored in that circuit to be retrieved at a later time. In a computer with 1 megabyte (or meg) of memory, there are 1,048,576 separate memory circuits, arranged in sequence so that the first circuit has address 0 and the last circuit has address 1,048,575. Usually, we represent these addresses in the hexadecimal numbering system, which uses 16 different digits—from 0 to 9, plus the first six letters of the alphabet—to represent numeric values. Although this might seem to complicate matters somewhat, the mathematical relationship between hexadecimal and binary actually makes it simpler to represent numbers in this manner than in decimal. In hexadecimal, the memory circuits in a 1-meg computer have addresses 0x00000 to 0xFFFFF. (In C, the 0x prefix is used to identify a hexadecimal number. Sometimes I will also use the assembly language convention of identifying hexadecimal numbers with a trailing "h," as in FFFFFh.)

Because of the way in which the IBM PC's memory is referenced by the earlier processors in the 80X86 series, it's traditional (and usually necessary) to reference addresses in the PC's memory using two numbers rather than one, like this: 5000:018A. The first of these numbers is called the segment, the second is the offset. To obtain an absolute address (that is, the sort of address discussed in the previous paragraph) from a segment:offset address, you multiply the segment by 16 and add it to the offset. Fortunately, this is easy to do in hexadecimal, in which multiplying by 16 is similar to multiplying by 10 in decimal. To multiply a hexadecimal number by 16, simply shift every digit in the number one position to the left and add a 0 in the least significant digit position (i.e., at the right end of the number). For instance, 0x5000 multiplied by 16 is 0x50000, so the address 5000:018A is equivalent to the absolute address 0x50018A.

If we want to store a number in the computer's memory and retrieve it later, we can store the number in a specific memory address, note that address, then retrieve that number later from the same address (assuming we haven't turned the machine off or otherwise erased the contents of memory in the meantime). And, in fact, this is exactly what we are doing when we use variables in a high-level language such as C. The variable represents a memory address and the statement that assigns a value to the variable stores a numeric value at that address. Of course, we never need to know exactly what memory address the value was stored at; it's the job of the C compiler to worry about that. Even in assembly language, we generally give symbolic names to memory addresses and let the assembler worry about what addresses those names represent.

Pointing at Memory

There are occasions, though, when we need to store a value in (or retrieve a value from) a specific memory address, especially when we are dealing with video memory—which I'll discuss in more detail in just a moment. In C, we can do this with the help of pointers. A pointer is a variable that "points" at a value somewhere in the computer's memory. The pointer itself is equal to the address at which the value is stored, but we can dereference the pointer using the *indirection operator* (*) to obtain the value stored at that address. Here's a short program that demonstrates the use of pointers:

```
#include <iostream.h>

void main()
{
        int intvar;
        int *pointvar=&intvar;
        *pointvar=3;

        cout << "\n\nThe value of INTVAR is " << intvar << endl;
        cout << "The value of *POINTVAR is " << *pointvar << endl;
        cout << "The address at which POINTVAR is pointing is " << pointvar << endl;
        cout << "The address represented by the variable is " << &intvar << endl;

        char c;
        cin.get(c);
}
```

The first line in the main() function creates an integer variable called *intvar*. The second line creates a pointer to type int called *pointvar* and uses the address operator ("&") to set this pointer equal to the address of *intvar*.

Finally, the program prints out the value of the variable *intvar* (to which you'll notice we have not yet directly assigned a value), the value pointed to by *pointvar* (using the dereference operator), and the actual value of *pointvar*—that is, the address to which *pointvar* is pointing. So that the program doesn't end and return to Windows or the Borland IDE, the last line waits for you to press a key. You could type this program and compile it with Borland C++ to find out what values are pointed out (or you can read ahead and find out the easy way), but can you predict in advance what values each of these will have? (Don't worry if you can't figure out the address to which *pointvar* is pointing, since this is arbitrary and unpredictable.)

When I ran this program, the results were as follows:

The value of INTVAR is 3.
The value of *POINTVAR is 3.
The address at which POINTVAR is pointing is 0x11eb0ffe.
The address represented by the variable INTVAR is 0x11eb0ffe.

Notice that *intvar* has taken on the same value as *pointvar*. That's because, as far as C++ is concerned, these are the same variables. When we use the dereference operator in front of the name of *POINTVAR,* it tells the compiler to treat *pointvar* as though it were a variable stored at the address currently stored in *pointvar*—in this case, 0x11eb0ffe. Since this is the same address represented by *intvar* (as you'll notice above), setting *pointvar* equal to 3 is equivalent to setting *intvar* (without a dereference operator) equal to 3.

Near and Far

There are two types of pointers in most 80X86 PC versions of C and C++: near pointers and far pointers. Near pointers can only point at values within a 64K range; far pointers can point at values anywhere in the first megabyte of the computer's memory. When compiling programs in certain memory models, such as the large model (which we'll use on all programs in this book), all pointers are automatically made far pointers. That's fortunate because our graphics functions in this book often require far pointers. Of course, it's best not to rely on the compiler to make a pointer into a far pointer. You can use the FAR keyword, which goes in the variable declaration, to make a pointer a far pointer, as you will sometimes see in our code, for emphasis:

```
void far *farpointer;
```

To assign a specific address to a far pointer in Borland C++, we use the MK_FP (MaKe Far Pointer) macro, defined in the header file DOS.H. For instance, to point a pointer at a char value in memory address 5000:018A, we would write

```
char far *charpointer=MK_FP(0x5000,0x018A);
```

We pass two values to the MK_FP macro: the segment and the offset of the memory location to which we wish the pointer to point. In the above example, the variable *charpointer* is pointed at segment 5000 and offset 018a. Now we can use the dereference operator on this pointer to examine and alter the contents of memory location 5000:018A. For instance, to print out the current contents of that location as a decimal number, we could write:

```
cout << "The current contents of address 5000:018A is " << *charpointer << endl ;
```

To change the contents of the location to a value of 176, we could write:

```
*charpointer=(char) 176;
```

We've used the typecast (char) here to tell the compiler that we wish the value 176 to be a single-byte value rather than a 2-byte integer. (A typecast, which consists of a C++ variable type in parentheses, tells the compiler to treat a data item of one type as though it were of another type.) This isn't strictly necessary since the C++ compiler will automatically convert this integer into a byte value, but it helps to make the code clearer.

Now that we have a general idea of how PC memory works, let's take a closer look at video memory in particular.

How Bitmaps Work

A moment ago, I asked where the video image transmitted to the monitor by the VGA adapter originates. The answer is video memory. What is video memory? The VGA circuitry is constantly scanning a certain set of memory addresses in your PC and interpreting the contents of those memory addresses as the symbolic representation of a picture. It then renders this picture as an electronic video signal and outputs that signal to the monitor, which in turn converts the signal into a full-color image. See Figure 1-8 for an illustration of this process.

What form does this "symbolic representation of a picture" take? That depends (as you might guess) on what video mode the VGA board is currently in. If it is in a text mode, the contents of video memory are interpreted as a series of code numbers representing the 256 characters in the IBM character set, interspersed with attribute bytes that determine the colors in which the characters are displayed.

In graphics mode, on the other hand, the contents of video memory take the form of a bitmap, which is one of the most important concepts in computer graphics programming. Though we usually treat the contents of the computer's memory as a series of bytes, in a bitmap we must view those bytes in terms of the individual binary digits (zeroes and ones) that make them up. In a bitmap, specific patterns of zeroes and ones represent specific patterns of pixels.

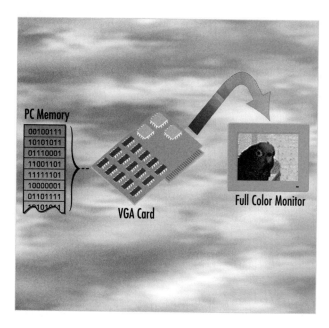

Figure 1-8 The VGA card scans a particular section of the computer's memory and converts what it finds there into a video signal

A Two-Color Bitmap

In the simplest kind of bitmap, one that represents a video image containing only two colors, the value of each bit in each byte represents the state of a pixel in the image. The zeroes usually represent pixels set to the background color while the ones represent pixels set to the foreground color.

For instance, in Figure 1-9, there is a simple, two-color bitmap of the letter Z. This bitmap consists of eight bytes of data, which would normally be arranged sequentially in the computer's memory. We have displayed it, however, as though the bits in those bytes were arranged in a rectangle, with eight pixels on a side. Bitmaps are almost always arranged in rectangular fashion on the video display.

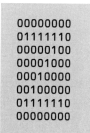

Figure 1-9 A simple, two-color bitmap of the letter Z

Two-color computer graphics displays, once quite common, are rapidly becoming obsolete. Sixteen- and 256-color displays are now far more typical. And inexpensive graphics boards are already available that will put 16 million colors—or as many of these colors as will fit—on a VGA display.

How do we represent multicolor displays with a bitmap? It's necessary to increase the number of bits per pixel. With a 4-color display, for instance, 2 bits represent a single pixel. There are four possible combinations of 2 bits—00, 01, 10, and 11— so 4 bits can represent 4 possible colors. Similarly, 4 bits can represent 16 possible colors.

Mode 13h supports 256 colors, so 8 bits (an entire byte) are required to represent each pixel in the mode 13h bitmap. This is a fortunate coincidence. Since the CPU naturally accesses memory values eight bits at a time, this makes it quite easy to manipulate the mode 13h bitmap. In effect, the mode 13h display is a bytemap rather than a bitmap (though for technical reasons the term bitmap is still used).

Mode 13h Memory

Every video adapter for PC compatibles contains a certain amount of memory. Most standard VGA adapters contain 256K (262,144 bytes) of memory, though this memory only occupies 64K (65,536) of memory addresses. What happens to the other 192K of memory? Fortunately, you don't need to worry about that. In mode 13h, we can only use 64K of memory; the rest goes untouched, so you don't need to know where it is. (Most SVGA adapters now ship with 1MB or more of Video memory. A lot of today's animation now uses paging techniques to speed and smooth the animation process.)

When the VGA adapter is installed in a computer, all graphics bitmaps reside between memory addresses A000:0000 and A000:FFFF. Many video modes allow the bitmap to be moved around within this range, but mode 13h does not. Because there are 64,000 pixels on the mode 13h display—that's 320 columns of pixels times 200 rows of pixels—and each of these pixels is represented in the bitmap by a byte, the mode 13h bitmap is 64,000 (0xFA00) bytes long. It always occupies addresses A000:0000 through A000:F9FF.

To put a picture on the mode 13h screen, the programmer must change the values in this video memory area until they represent the bitmap for that picture. We'll look at some working code that does precisely this in Chapter 3.

The Color Palette

When we say that a certain video mode has a color depth of 2 or 4 or 16 or 256 colors, we mean that pixels in that many colors can appear together on the screen at one time. If you were to pull out your magnifying glass and count the colors on the screen in a 256-color mode, you would find 256 colors at most. (You might well find fewer colors, since no law says a programmer has to use all of the colors available.)

But what colors are on the screen? Blue? Green? Chartreuse? Candy apple red?

That's up to you—the programmer. The colors that appear on the screen are called the working palette, but you choose those colors from a larger palette. On the VGA adapter, you choose the working palette in graphics mode from an overall palette of 262,144 (256K) colors.

The VGA adapter includes a special set of 256 18-bit memory locations called the color registers. (That 18-bit number is not a typo. These are special memory registers and are organized somewhat differently from ordinary computer memory.) Before drawing a picture on the mode 13h display, you must first fill these locations with descriptions of the 256 colors you intend to use.

How do you describe a color? All colors are made up of the three primary colors—red, green, and blue—or at least our visual systems perceive them that way. (Red, green, and blue are called the additive primary colors, or primary colors of light. When working with pigments, which absorb and reflect light rather than producing it, we use a different set of primary colors—red, yellow, and blue.)

The VGA board produces colors by adding together specific amounts of red, green, and blue. There are 64 levels of each of these primary colors available, from 0 (no color, or black) to 63 (the brightest shade of that color). To describe a color, you use three numbers in this range, describing the red, blue, and green intensities that together make up the color. (For instance, the color described by the three numbers 0,0,0, is pure black, while color 63,63,63 is pure white. All other shades are between these extremes.)

These three numbers together form a color descriptor. When 256 of these color descriptors are placed in the VGA color registers, they define the colors of pixels in the mode 13h bitmap. The color in color register 0, for instance, is equivalent to the bitmap value 00000000, while the color in register 1 is equivalent to the bitmap value 00000001, and so forth.

Programming the VGA

The discussion so far has been mostly theoretical. You've probably been wondering just how you, as programmer, can change bitmap values and color register values on the VGA board.

There are essentially three ways: You can use the graphics library routines supplied with your compiler, you can call the routines in the VGA's video BIOS, or you can work directly with the hardware. We'll take a look at these three methods and then we'll give you some actual programming examples in Chapter 3.

The Borland C++ compiler comes with a set of library functions called the Borland Graphics Interface (BGI). The BGI routines can greatly simplify your job as programmer, but the results are of limited utility at best, as shown in Figure 1-10. The BGI will set the VGA's graphics mode; set the color registers; even draw lines, squares, and circles on the screen. But its ability to perform animation is not great. The routines are fairly slow and are not optimized for animation, either two-dimensional or three-dimensional. That's not to say that it's impossible to perform animation with the BGI, just that the results are not of commercial quality. I recommend that you use the BGI for drawing charts and graphs, but not for flight simulation or fast arcade games.

Okay, suppose you don't own or don't want to use BC version 4.5? What kind of problems will you encounter along the way? If you are programming on a Mac, you will have to figure out how to implement our screen assembly language functions. They are used throughout the book and the flight simulator adds some more assembly. If you are programming for another compiler, such as Visual C++, you will have to create your own project or make file, using the .mak files which accompany each program. These make files have been created with the Borland Make Generation option. Your C++ compiler should have the iostream classes, cin and cout. The CONIO.H and DOS.H headers are frequently included. These contain several non-ANSI functions which govern screen and keyboard interface. Again, adjustments

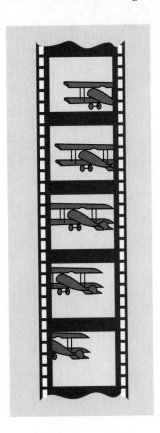

Figure 1-10 The frame rate required by a flight simulator is much too high for the slow graphics routines in the BGI

might have to be made, but it is surprising how many nonstandard functions will be the same. In all cases, there are no special Borland functions being used—everything can be emulated. We have selected Borland because of its interface.

The VGA board contains a ROM chip with many common graphics routines built in. The contents of this ROM chip are called the video BIOS. (BIOS is short for basic input-ouput system. The video BIOS is a kind of extension to the IBM's standard ROM BIOS, which contains routines for performing nongraphic input and output.) In the programs that we develop in this book, we'll call on the video BIOS to perform most of our initialization. We will use it, for instance, to set the video mode and the color registers. We will not be using it to draw images on the display, however. Like the BGI, the video BIOS is slow and not optimized for animation.

Most of our actual drawing in this book will be done by interacting directly with the VGA hardware. After we've used the video BIOS to initialize the VGA board, we'll place values directly into the video memory to create images. We'll look at how this is done in Chapter 3.

We've looked at graphics in this chapter from the standpoint of the graphics hardware—that is, as a sequence of bytes in the computer's memory that becomes a graphic image when processed by the VGA board and output to the monitor. But there are other, more abstract ways of looking at graphics; these ways are often more useful. It is these more abstract methods, which owe more than a small debt to mathematics, that lead directly to three-dimensional graphics programming. We'll look at these methods in Chapter 2.

...

CHAPTER
2

......

2

The Mathematics of Animation

If you're like me, the mere glimpse of an equation in a computer programming text is enough to make you shut the volume, return it to the bookstore shelf, and sit down in the nearest chair until the trembling passes. That's why I've crammed this book as full as possible with solid, nutritious programming code, so that programmers without an intuitive grasp of higher mathematics will find plenty here to chew on.

Nonetheless, before we can get very far into the subject of 3D computer graphics or even 2D computer graphics, it is necessary to confront the frightening spectre of mathematics, if only for a moment. But rest assured, before you skip to the next chapter (or put this book back on the bookstore shelf), that I've labored mightily to make this chapter as painless as possible. The truth is, the mathematics involved in 3D computer graphics isn't as difficult as it looks. Most of the tough stuff—working out the specific equations that are necessary for performing various transformations on three-dimensional objects—has already been done by others, so that all you need to do is figure out how to convert the various equations discovered by mathematical and programming pioneers into optimized computer code. Which is more easily said than done—but that's what we're here for, right?

Before you embark on this brief magical math tour, I'd like to give you these words of encouragement: If *I* can understand this stuff, anybody can.

Cartesian Coordinates

In the last chapter, we considered computer graphics from the viewpoint of the computer hardware. We looked at ways in which the hardware could be induced to put colored pixels on the computer's video display. Anyone who wants to program high-speed, state-of-the-art computer games needs to understand how computer graphics work from a hardware perspective. But there is another way in which the programmer can, and occasionally must, look at the computer graphics display: as a slightly modified version of a Cartesian coordinate system.

Legend has it that the seventeenth-century French philosopher/mathematician René Descartes was lying in bed one day watching a fly buzz around the ceiling when he conceived the coordinate system that bears a Latinized version of his name. It occurred to Descartes that the position of the fly at any given instant could be described with only three numbers, each representing the insect's position relative to some fixed point, as shown in Figure 2-1. Later, he expanded (or perhaps reduced) this idea to include two-dimensional points on a plane, the position of which could be described with only two numbers for any given point. He included the idea in a long appendix to a book published in 1637. Despite being tucked away in the back of another book, Descartes' method of representing points on a plane and in space by numeric coordinates launched a new branch of mathematics, combining features of geometry and algebra. It came to be known as analytic geometry.

Figure 2-1 Descartes' fly can be pinpointed at any instant by three numbers

The Cartesian Plane

You've probably run across (or bumped up against) the Cartesian coordinate system. Even if you haven't, you're about to bump up against it now. Don't be afraid. The Cartesian coordinate system is simple, elegant, and surprisingly useful in certain kinds of computer graphics. Because three-dimensional animation is one of the areas in which it is surprisingly useful, we're going to look at it here in some detail.

Any number can be regarded as a point on a line. In geometry, a line (a theoretical concept that doesn't necessarily exist in the "real" world) consists of an infinite number of points. And between any two of those points there is also an infinite number of points. Thus, a line is infinitely divisible. No matter how much you chop it up, you can still chop it up some more.

The system of real numbers is a lot like that too. Real numbers, roughly speaking, are numbers that can have fractional values—numbers with decimal points, in other words. (C programmers will recognize real numbers as corresponding to the data type known as float, about which I'll have more to say later.) There are an infinite number of real numbers, both positive and negative. And between any two of those real numbers, there are an infinite number of real numbers. The real number system, like a line, is infinitely divisible.

Therefore, if we have a line that's infinitely long (which is allowed under the rules of geometry), we can find a point on it that corresponds to every real number. Although in practice it's not possible to conjure up a line that's infinitely long or even infinitely divisible, we can make do with approximations like the one in Figure 2-2. This line, rather like a wooden ruler, has been marked off at intervals to denote the integers—that is, the whole numbers—from -5 to 5. You probably remember seeing such lines in junior high school math class, where they were called number lines. Traditionally, the numbers in such a line become smaller to the left and larger to the right. We'll have to take it on faith that this number line can theoretically be extended an infinite distance in the positive and negative directions; there isn't enough paper to draw the whole thing! However, we should have no trouble locating the points on this line for such numbers as -3, 5, 4.7, -2.1, and so forth.

Figure 2-2 A segment of an infinite number line

Of course, these are only the points on the line that have been indicated by tick marks. Between these points are points representing even more precise fractions such as .063, -4.891, 1.11111, and even -2.7232422879434353455. In practice, if we started dividing the line up this finely, we would surpass the resolution of the printer's ink used to inscribe it on the page. So when we say that all of these points are on the line, we are speaking theoretically, not literally. But on a perfect, theoretical, geometric line, there is a point corresponding to every real number.

Geometry Meets Algebra

It was Descartes' genius to see that this correspondence between points on a line and numbers allowed mathematicians to treat geometric concepts—that is, concepts involving points, lines, planes, three-dimensional space, and so forth—as numbers. To see how, look at a second number line, shown in Figure 2-3, one that runs up and down instead of left and right. In such a vertical number line, it is traditional for numbers to grow larger going up the line and smaller going down. (Computer programmers tend to reverse this tradition for pragmatic reasons.) In Figure 2-4, a vertical number line forms a cross with a horizontal number line, with the lines intersecting

Figure 2-3 A vertical number line

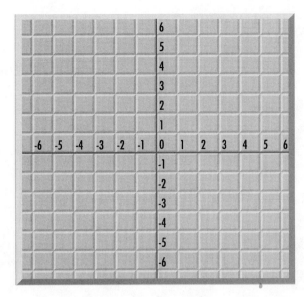

Figure 2-4 Welcome to the Cartesian plane!

at the zero point on both lines. Together, these lines describe what is sometimes called a Cartesian plane. Not only does every real number have a corresponding point on both of these lines, but every pair of real numbers has a corresponding point on the rectangular plane upon which these lines are situated.

For instance, the pair of numbers (3,1) corresponds to the point on the plane that is aligned with the 3 tick on the horizontal number line and the 1 tick on the vertical number line, as in Figure 2-5. The number pair (-4.2,2.3) corresponds to the point that is aligned with the -4.2 tick on the horizontal line and the 2.3 tick on the vertical number line, as in Figure 2-6. And so forth. (The first number in such a pair is always the one aligned with a point on the horizontal line and the second number, the one aligned with a point on the vertical line.) Just as there are an infinite number of points on a line, so there are an infinite number of points on a plane, each of which can be described by a different pair of numbers. A pair of numbers that corresponds to a point on a Cartesian plane is called a *coordinate pair* or just plain *coordinates*.

Using pairs of coordinates, it was possible for Descartes to give a precise numerical description of hitherto vague geometrical concepts. Not only can a point be described by a pair of coordinates, a line can be described by *two* pairs of coordinates, representing the endpoints of the line. The line in Figure 2-7, for instance, extends from the point with coordinates (2,2) to the point with coordinates (4,4). Thus, we can describe this line with the coordinate pairs (2,2) and (4,4). Other shapes can also be described numerically, as we'll see in a moment.

The two number lines used to establish the position of points on the plane are called the axes. For historical reasons, coordinate pairs are commonly represented by

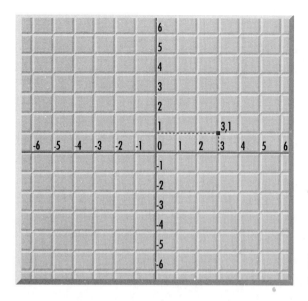

Figure 2-5 Point (3,1) on the Cartesian plane

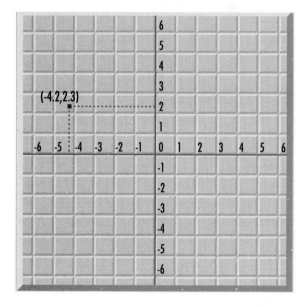

Figure 2-6 Point (-4.2,2.3) on the Cartesian plane

the variables *x* and *y*, as in (*x,y*). For this reason, the coordinates themselves are frequently referred to as *x,y* coordinates. The first (horizontal) coordinate of the pair is known as the *x* coordinate and the second (vertical) coordinate of the pair as the *y* coordinate. It follows that the horizontal axis (the one used to locate the position of the *x* coordinate) is referred to as the *x* axis and the vertical axis (the one used to locate

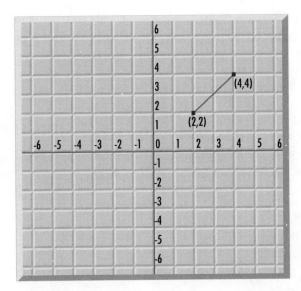

Figure 2-7 Line from (2,2) to (4,4)

the position of the y coordinate) is referred to as the y axis. The two axes always cross at the zero point called the *origin* of the coordinate system, because all points are numbered relative to this (0,0) point.

Coordinates on the Computer

So what does this have to do with computer graphics? Well, the surface of the computer display is a plane and the graphics that we draw on it are made up of points—the pixels—on that plane. There aren't an infinite number of pixels on the display—in mode 13h, for instance, there are only 64,000—but the video display is still a good approximation of a Cartesian plane. It follows that we can specify the position of any point on the display by a pair of coordinates.

This, in fact, is the common method of specifying the locations of pixels, far more common than specifying the video RAM offsets corresponding to the pixels, as I did in the last chapter. Although you can place the Cartesian axes anywhere on (or off) the display, it is common to regard the line of pixels at the top of the display as the x axis and the line of pixels running down the left side of the display as the y axis. This puts the origin of the coordinate system in the upper left corner of the display. Thus the pixel in that corner is said to be at coordinates (0,0). However, the programming convention is to orient the y axis of the computer display upside-down relative to a standard Cartesian y axis, with numbers growing larger going down the axis. This convention probably arose because it corresponds to the way that the addresses of pixels in video RAM grow larger going down the display. As we'll see in a moment, orienting the coordinates in this manner simplifies the task of calculating the video RAM address of a pixel at a specific pair of coordinates on the display.

If the coordinates of the pixel in the upper left corner of the display are (0,0), then the coordinates of the pixel in the lower right corner of the mode 13h display are (319,199). Note that, because we start with coordinates (0,0) rather than (1,1), the coordinates of the pixels at the opposite extremes of the display are one short of the actual number of pixels in the horizontal and vertical dimensions (which, in mode 13h, are 320 and 200, respectively). All other pixels on the display are at coordinates between these extremes. The pixel in Figure 2-8, for instance, is at coordinates (217,77)—that is, it's located 217 pixels from the left side of the display and 77 pixels from the top.

Most programming languages have a built-in command, or a library function, for changing the color of a pixel on the display. This command is usually called something like plot or set—in Borland's BGI graphics package it's called putpixel—and almost invariably the parameters passed to this command begin with the screen coordinates of the pixel whose color you wish to change.

From Coordinates to Pixel Offsets

We don't have such a command available for the programs that we will develop in this book. (Although a copy of the BGI comes with the Borland C++ compiler, we will not be using the BGI's functions in this book.) Nonetheless, we will occasionally need to locate the position of a pixel on the display using Cartesian coordinates. Thus, we need a way to translate a coordinate pair into a specific video RAM address, so that we can change the value stored at that address to a value representing the desired color of the pixel. Fortunately, there's a simple formula for doing this. In fact, there are many

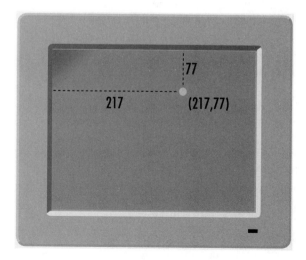

Figure 2-8 One pixel on the video display

simple formulas, depending on video mode. In mode 13h, the formula is particularly simple. It is:

```
pixel_address = y_coordinate * 320 + x_coordinate
```

Let's translate that into C++ code. If the integer variable x contains the x coordinate of the pixel whose color we wish to change, and the integer variable y contains the y coordinate, we can get the offset of the pixel within video RAM into the integer variable *offset* by writing:

```
offset = y * 320 + x;
```

Easy, right? We'll make use of this simple formula many times in chapters to come.

Moving the Origin

Although it is customary to put the origin (the 0,0 point) of the screen's coordinate system in the upper left corner of the display, it is not always desirable to do so. In fact, later, we will move the origin to several different positions on the display, including the center. Nonetheless, it is simpler to calculate screen positions based on the origin in the customary corner, so we'll need to translate back and forth between the two systems. We'll perform the calculations concerning the positions of objects on the screen with the origin located at coordinates (XORIGIN, YORIGIN) relative to the upper left corner of the display, where XORIGIN and YORIGIN are predefined constants. In effect, we are creating a virtual coordinate system separate from the system normally used to specify coordinates on the display. **Figure 2-9** shows the difference between this virtual system and the usual system.

To translate these virtual coordinates back into screen coordinates (i.e., coordinates with the origin in the upper left corner of the display), we'll use the following formula:

```
screen_x = virtual_x + XORIGIN;
screen_y = virtual_y + YORIGIN;
```

You'll see this formula pop up several times in the chapters to come.

Addressing Multiple Pixels

It's often necessary to find the addresses of an entire block of pixels. For instance, you may want to change the color of all the pixels in a single horizontal line. One way to do this is to calculate the address of the pixel at the left end of the line, change the color of the pixel at that location, then add 1 to the x coordinate, calculate the address of the pixel at that location, and so on, until you've changed the color of all the pixels in the line. This involves a lot of extra work, however. Once the address of the pixel at the beginning of the line is calculated, you can find the address of the pixel to the right of it simply by adding 1 to the address, rather than adding one to the x coordinate and then recalculating the address. If the variable offset is set equal to the address

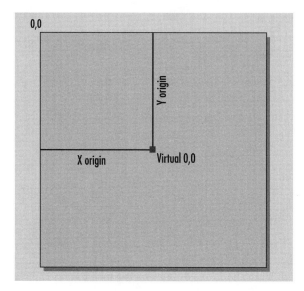

0,0

Y origin

X origin

Virtual 0,0

Figure 2-9 The relationship between the virtual screen coordinate system and the "real" screen coordinate system

of the pixel at coordinates (x,y), it can be advanced to the address of the pixel at coordinates $(x+1,y)$ with the instruction, offset++. Similarly, it can be moved leftward to the address of the pixel at coordinates $(x-1,y)$ with the instruction, offset--.

Moving the pixel location by one y coordinate in either direction is equally easy. In mode 13h, the screen is 320 pixels wide, so moving down one line—that is, one y coordinate—is a matter of adding 320 to the value of the offset. If the variable offset is equal to the address of the pixel at coordinates (x,y), then it can be advanced to the address of the pixel at coordinates $(x,y+1)$ with the instruction, offset+=320. You can probably guess that we can move up one y coordinate from (x,y) to $(x,y-1)$ by subtracting 320 from the offset: offset-=320.

To move diagonally—that is, to change both coordinates—combine the two actions. To move offset from (x,y) to $(x+1,y+1)$, just add 321: offset+=321.

Into the Third Dimension

So far, we've spoken only of two-dimensional coordinate systems. But this book is about three-dimensional computer graphics, so it's time to add a dimension and take a look at three-dimensional coordinate systems.

First, however, let's ask a fundamental question: What do we mean when we refer to a dimension? In comic books and pulp science fiction, the term is sometimes used to refer to alternate worlds, parallel universes. When we go from the second dimension to the third, are we jumping from one world to another?

Not exactly. Without getting technical, a dimension can be defined as a way in which a line can be perpendicular (that is, at right angles) to other lines. On the surface of a sheet of paper, we can draw two lines that are perpendicular to one another, as in Figure 2-10. Thus, the surface of the paper is two-dimensional; in geometric parlance, it is a plane. If we could draw lines in space, we could draw *three* lines that are perpendicular to one another. Thus, space is three dimensional. Although you can't draw in space, you can demonstrate this to yourself by holding three pencils in your hand and arranging them so that each is perpendicular to the other two. If you aren't dextrous enough to do this without dropping the pencils, try to imagine how you would do so—or you could just look at the illustration in Figure 2-11.

In a Cartesian coordinate system, the axes represent the dimensions—that is, the ways in which lines can be perpendicular to one another. After all, each coordinate axis is always perpendicular to all other coordinate axes. In a two-dimensional coordinate system, there are two axes, one for each dimension. In a three-dimensional coordinate system, there should be three axes—a fact that René Descartes well understood.

If the story about Descartes and the fly is true, then the philosopher/mathematician must have invented three-dimensional coordinate systems before he invented the two-dimensional kind. Descartes realized that the position of the fly at any instant could be measured—in theory, at least—relative to an origin somewhere in space. But it would be necessary to use three numbers to measure the position of the fly, not two as with the position of a point on a plane, because there are three directions in which the fly can move relative to the origin. These directions are sometimes called length, width, and depth, though the terms are arbitrary. We can just refer to them as the three dimensions of space.

To plot the position of the fly, then, a coordinate triple is required. When the fly is at the origin, it is at coordinates $(0,0,0)$. If it then buzzes off five units in the x direction, it moves to coordinates $(5,0,0)$. A motion of seven units in the y direction takes

Figure 2-10 Two mutually perpendicular lines

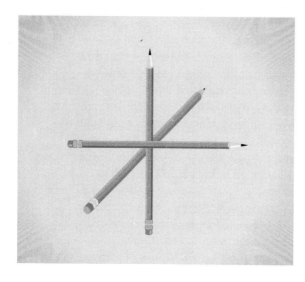

Figure 2-11 Holding three pencils perpendicular to one another

the fly to coordinates (5,7,0). After a move of two units in the third direction—which, for obvious reasons, we'll call the *z* direction—the fly will wind up at coordinates (5,7,2). Of course, most flies don't zip around with such neat regard for coordinate axes. More likely, the fly went straight from coordinates (0,0,0) to coordinates (5,7,2) in a single spurt of flight, then meandered off in a different direction altogether, possibly plunging suicidally into Descartes' cup of steaming tea.

We can't draw a three-dimensional coordinate system on a sheet of paper. But we can devise such systems in our minds. And, as we shall see in Chapter 8, we can create them on the computer. In a three-dimensional coordinate system we call the three axes *x, y,* and *z.* Typically, the *x* and *y* axes correspond to the *x* and *y* axes of a two-dimensional graph while the *z* axis becomes a depth axis, running into and out of the traditional two-dimensional graph, as shown in Figure 2-12. In Chapter 8, we'll look at ways to make the axes of the three-dimensional graph correspond to directions in our real three-dimensional world.

Shapes, Solids, and Coordinates

We saw earlier that we could use two-dimensional coordinates to describe geometric concepts such as points and lines. We can also use two-dimensional coordinates to describe shapes, such as triangles, squares, circles, and even arbitrary polygons. And we can use three-dimensional coordinates to describe three-dimensional solids, such as cubes, pyramids, and spheres. In fact, we needn't stop with simple shapes. We can use coordinate systems to describe just about any shape or solid that can occur in the real world, including rocks, trees, mountains, and even human beings, though some of these shapes are easier to describe than others. Since this is going to be an important topic throughout the rest of this book, let's see just how we'd go about creating this kind of coordinate representation.

From describing a line with two coordinate pairs representing the line's endpoints it takes only a little leap of imagination to extend this concept to describe any shape that can be constructed out of line segments—triangles (Figure 2-13), squares (Figure 2-14), even polygons of arbitrary complexity (Figure 2-15). Any shape made out of an unbroken series of line segments can be represented as a series of vertices. In geometry, a vertex is a point at which two lines intersect, though we'll use the term more loosely here to include endpoints of lines as well. Since vertices are points in space, they can be described by their coordinates. Thus, the square in Figure 2-14 could be described by the coordinates of its vertices: (4,9), (4,3), (10,3) and (10,9). We'll use this scheme to describe two-dimensional shapes in Chapter 6.

Not all shapes are made out of a continuous, unbroken series of line segments; consider the square with an X inside it shown in Figure 2-16, for instance. Although all the lines in this shape touch one another, they cannot be drawn with a single continuous line. If you doubt this, try drawing this shape without lifting your pencil from the paper or retracing a previously drawn line. A more versatile system for storing shapes that would take such awkward (but quite common) cases into account would consist of two lists: a list of the coordinates of the vertices and a list of the lines that connect them. The list of vertex coordinates for a square with an X inside would look exactly like that for the square in the last paragraph. The list of lines could consist simply of pointers to the entries in the vertex descriptor list, indicating which

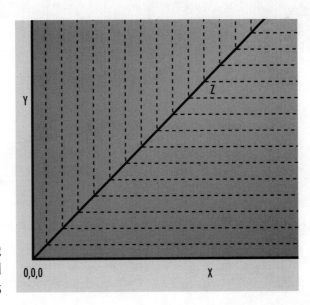

Figure 2-12
Three-dimensional
Cartesian axes

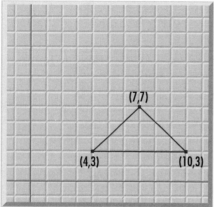

Figure 2-13 Coordinates for a triangle

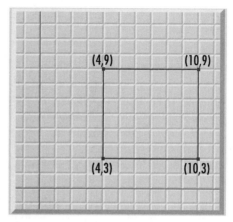

Figure 2-14 Coordinates for a square

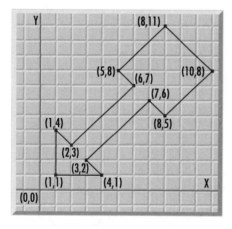

Figure 2-15 Coordinates for an arbitrary polygon

vertices in the list represent the endpoints of a given line: (0,1), (1,2), (2,3), (3,0), (0,2), and (1,3). This tells us that the first line in the shape connects vertex 0 (the first vertex in the list in the last paragraph) with vertex 1, the second line in the shape connects vertex 1 to vertex 2, and so forth. We'll use this scheme for describing shapes in Chapter 8.

Three-Dimensional Vertices

Describing a three-dimensional shape made up of line segments is done in exactly the same manner as describing two-dimensional shapes, except that a third coordinate must be included when describing each vertex, so that the vertex's location in the z

Figure 2-16 Square with an X inside

dimension can be pinpointed. Although it's difficult to do this on a sheet of paper, it's easy to imagine it. In Figure 2-17, I have "imagined" a cube made up of line segments within a three-dimensional coordinate system.

Shapes made out of line segments aren't especially realistic, but all of these concepts can be extended to drawing more complex shapes. You might wonder, though, how something like a circle or a sphere can be described as a series of vertices connected by line segments. Wouldn't the number of vertices required to describe such a shape be prohibitively large, perhaps even infinite?

Well, yes, but there are two approaches that we can use to describe such shapes within a coordinate system. One is to approximate the shape through relatively small

Figure 2-17 "Imaginary" cube in a three-dimensional coordinate system

line segments. How small should the line segments be? That depends on how realistic the drawing is intended to be and how much time you can spend on mathematical calculations relating to those vertices. For instance, a square can be thought of as a *very* rough approximation of a circle using 4 line segments. An octagon, which uses 8 line segments, is a better approximation of a circle (see Figure 2-18), but a hexadecagon, with 16 line segments, is even better (see Figure 2-19). As far as realism is concerned, the more line segments the merrier, but there are other considerations, especially when we are storing and processing the vertex and line segment information in a computer.

Graphing Equations

Descartes came up with an alternative method of describing shapes such as circles and spheres, one that is nicely suited to microcomputer graphics even though Descartes

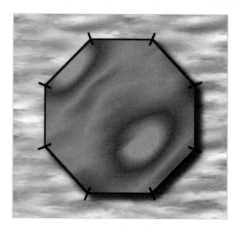

Figure 2-18 A circle approximated with 8 line segments

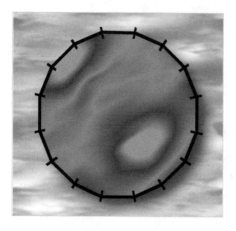

Figure 2-19 A circle approximated with 16 line segments

developed it three-and-a-half centuries before the advent of the Apple II. Descartes realized that coordinate systems such as the one that now bears his name could be used to graph the results of algebraic equations, and the resulting graphs often took on familiar (and not so familiar) geometric shapes. Which means that we can also describe shapes—in theory, any shape at all—as algebraic equations.

If you ever took an algebra course, you probably remember (perhaps with a shudder) a thing or two about graphing equations. Even if you didn't, the following paragraphs should bring you painlessly up to speed.

Algebra deals with equations—symbolic statements about relationships between different values—in which certain values are unknown or variable. These equations resemble the assignment statements found in all computer programming languages, but instead of assigning a value to a variable, they assert that the value of one variable bears a certain relationship to the value of one or more other variables. The resemblance between algebraic equations and assignment statements can be confusing, both to students of algebra and students of programming, so we'll dwell for a moment on the difference.

Here is a familiar algebraic equation:

`x = y`

The letters x and y represent numeric quantities of unknown value. And yet, though we do not know what the values of these numeric quantities are, we do know something important about the *relationship* between these two values. We know that they are the same. Whatever the value of y is, x has the same value, and vice versa. Thus, if y is equal to 2, then x is also equal to 2. If y is equal to 324.218, then x is equal to 324.218.

In C++, on the other hand, the statement

`x = y;`

would be an assignment statement. It would assign the value of the variable y to the variable x. After this assignment, the algebraic equation $x = y$ would be true, but it wouldn't necessarily be true before this assignment statement. The difference between an algebraic equation and an assignment statement, then, is that the algebraic equation asserts that a relationship *is* true while the assignment statement *makes it true*.

Here's another familiar algebraic equation:

`x = 2y`

This tells us that the value of x is two times the value of y. If y is equal to 2, then x is equal to 4. If y is equal to -14, then x is equal to -28.

Solving the Equation

Determining the value of x based on the value of y is called solving the equation. Every time we solve an equation with two variables in it, we produce a pair of numbers—

the value of *x* and the value of *y*. By treating these pairs of numbers as Cartesian coordinates we can depict them as points on a two-dimensional Cartesian plane, thus graphing the equation. The graph of the equation $x = y$ is shown in Figure 2-20. The equation has been solved for four values of *y*—0, 1, 2, and 3—which produces the coordinate pairs (0,0), (1,1), (2,2), and (3,3). These coordinates have been graphed and connected by lines. The lines, however, are not an arbitrary part of the graph. They represent additional solutions of the equation for noninteger (i.e., fractional) values of *y* as well, such as 1.2, 2.7, and 0.18. All solutions of the equation between 0 and 3 fall somewhere on this line. There's no way we could work out all of these fractional solutions, since there's an infinite number of them, but the graph shows these solutions anyway, as points on an infinitely divisible line.

Similarly, the equation $x = 2y$ produces a line when it is graphed, but the line has a different angle, or slope, from the line produced by the equation $x = y$. (We'll talk more about the slope of the line in the chapter on wireframe graphics.) For any straight line that we can draw on a graph, there is an equation that will produce that line when graphed. That equation is called, logically enough, the equation of the line.

Not all equations produce straight lines, however. For our purposes, the more interesting equations are those that produce curves, since curves are so difficult to represent with line segments. It's more efficient for some purposes to represent a curve with an equation, though not for all purposes. Solving an equation for various values can take quite a bit of time, even when performed by computer, so it's often faster to approximate a curve with line segments.

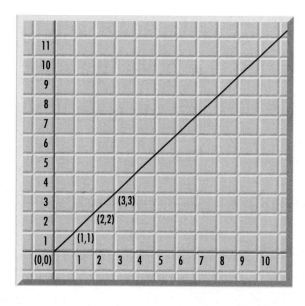

Figure 2-20 The graph of the equation $x = y$

Fractals

One type of shape called a fractal is often easier to produce using equations than by storing vertices and line segments, simply because of the difficulty in storing such a shape in the computer's memory. A fractal—the term was coined by the mathematician Benoit Mandelbrot—is a shape that possesses the quality of self-similarity. This simply (or not so simply) means that the shape is built up of smaller versions of itself, and these smaller versions of the shape are in turn built up of still smaller versions of the shape.

A tree, for instance, is a kind of fractal shape. A tree is made up of branches, which resemble tiny trees. A branch in turn is made up of twigs, which resemble tiny branches. And the twigs are in turn made up of twiglets, which . . . well, you get the idea. Because it possesses this self-similarity at several orders of magnification, a tree is said to be fractal.

Many other shapes found in nature are essentially fractal. A jagged shoreline, for instance, has pretty much the same quality of jaggedness whether it's viewed from a satellite orbiting 200 miles overhead, from an airplane 20,000 feet above, or by a child sitting on a hilltop overlooking the shore. The human circulatory system consists of a hierarchy of branching arteries and veins that is pretty much identical at several levels of size. A mountain has an irregular faceted appearance that resembles that of the large and small rocks that make it up. And so forth.

If you want to duplicate three-dimensional nature within the computer, it will be necessary to create fractal shapes. Why? Because fractals give us a maximum amount of realistic detail for a minimum amount of stored data. Instead of storing every vertex in every polygon in a mountain, we can store a fractal equation that will generate an infinite number of mountainlike shapes—and can do so at any level of detail. Similarly, instead of storing every twist and turn of a river or coastline, we can store a fractal equation that can generate a near infinite number of rivers and coastlines. Alternatively, we can use fractal algorithms to generate in advance shapes that would be difficult to encode by hand, then store the data generated by the algorithm in our program, just as we will store the data for other shapes. We'll talk about this at greater length later.

Transformations

In this book, we'll represent two-dimensional and three-dimensional shapes as vertices connected by line segments. (Actually, we'll use line segments in the early chapters, then graduate to connecting vertices with colored polygons to create greater realism in later chapters.) And we'll develop routines that will draw those shapes at specific coordinate positions on the video display. If we're going to animate these objects, however, it's not enough for us to create and display them. We must also be able to manipulate them, to change their position on the display, even rotate the shapes into brand new positions. In the language of 3D graphics, we are going to transform the images.

One of the many advantages of being able to define a shape as a series of numbers—advantages for which all 3D graphics programmers should at least once a day mutter a heartfelt thanks to the ghost of René Descartes—is that we can perform mathematical operations on those numbers to our heart's content. And many generations of mathematicians and computer programmers have worked out the mathematical operations necessary for performing most of the transformations that we will wish to perform on three-dimensional objects.

There are quite a few such transformations that we could perform, but we will concentrate on three: scaling, translating, and rotating. (Actually, when performed on three-dimensional objects, there are five transformations because 3D rotation consists of three separate operations, as you will see.) Scaling means changing the size of an object, translating refers to moving an object from one place to another within the coordinate system, and rotating refers (obviously) to rotating an object around a fixed point, through a specified axis, within the coordinate system. These are operations you will perform in the programs developed in later chapters and the formulas for performing them are widely known. It's a simple matter to include these formulas in a computer program. Making the computer code based on these formulas work quickly and well is another matter, one that we'll talk about at length in later chapters. Note that in all the formulas that follow, it is assumed that the objects are represented by a list of coordinate pairs or triples representing all vertices within the object.

Translating and Scaling

Translation is the easiest of these transformations and the one that the microcomputer is best equipped to perform without clever optimizations. It involves adding values to the coordinates of the vertices of an object. To move a two-dimensional object from its current coordinate position to another coordinate position, we must perform the following C++ operation on each vertex within the object:

```
new_x = x + tx;
new_y = y + ty;
```

where *x* and *y* are the current coordinates of the vertex, *new_x* and *new_y* are the translated coordinates, *tx* is the distance we wish to move the vertex in the *x* dimension, and *ty* is the distance we wish to move the vertex in the *y* dimension. For instance, if we wish to move a vertex by seven coordinate positions in the *x* dimension and 5 coordinate positions in the *y* dimension, we would perform these operations:

```
new_x = x + 7;
new_y = y + 5;
```

By performing these operations on all of the vertices in an object, we will obtain a new set of vertices representing the translated object. We will have "moved" the object to a new location within the coordinate system. (At this point, of course, the object exists only as a set of numbers within the computer's memory and it is only these numbers that have been "moved." We'll deal with the actual details of drawing and animating the object in a later chapter.) These operations are identical to the formulas previously stated earlier in the chapter where the origin (XORIGIN,YORIGIN) was moved. Moving the origin is, in fact, a translation of the virtual coordinates back into the screen coordinates.

Translating an object in three dimensions works the same way, except that we add a z translation value to the z coordinate in order to move it in the z dimension:

```
new_z = z + tz;
```

Scaling an object is no more difficult from the programmer's point of view, though it may take the processor of a computer slightly longer to accomplish, since it involves a multiplication operation. (Without a math coprocessor, multiplication is somewhat more time-consuming than addition.) To scale an object, we simply multiply all of the coordinates of all of the vertices by a scaling factor. For instance, to double the size of an object, we multiply every coordinate of every vertex by 2. Actually, we are using the term "double" very loosely here. This operation actually doubles the distance between vertices, which would have the effect of quadrupling the area of a two-dimensional object and increasing the volume of a three-dimensional object by a factor of 8! To triple the size of the object, we multiply every coordinate by three. To cut the size of the object in half, we multiply every coordinate by .5. Here is the general formula for scaling the x,y coordinates of the vertices in a two-dimensional object:

```
new_x = scaling_factor * x;
new_y = scaling_factor * y;
```

For a three-dimensional object, the z coordinate of each vertex also must be scaled:

```
new_z = scaling_factor * z;
```

Rotating on X, Y, and Z

Rotation is the most complex of these transformations because it involves the use of the sine and cosine trigonometric functions. If you don't, as the song says, know much about trigonometry, don't worry. You don't need to understand how the rotation formulas work in order to use them. You don't even need to know how to perform the sine and cosine operations, because Borland has conveniently included functions for doing so in the math package included with the BC++ compiler. To access them, you need only place the statement #include <math.h> at the beginning of your program. Alas, these functions tend to be a bit on the slow side, but they'll suffice for demonstrating three-dimensional rotations in the next several chapters. Eventually, we'll develop our own high-speed trigonometric functions.

Before we discuss the rotation formulas, let's look at what we mean when we say that we are going to rotate an object. When you hold an object in your hands—this book, for instance—you can rotate it into any position that you wish. At the moment, you are presumably holding the book open to the second chapter with the pages of the book facing toward you and the text right side up. It would be a simple matter for you to turn the book so that the text is upside down, as in Figure 2-21(a), though this would make it a bit difficult to read. Or you could turn the book so that the front and back covers are facing you instead of the pages, though this would also make it diffi-

Figure 2-21 Different ways to rotate an object

(a) Turning this book upside down

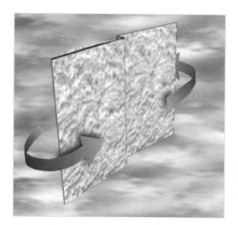

(b) Turning this book sideways

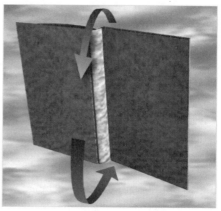

(c) Turning this book head over heels

cult to read. When you perform this latter rotation, you could do it in one of two different ways: by grabbing the sides of the book and rotating it sideways, as in Figure 2-21(b) or by holding the top and bottom and rotating it head over heels, as in Figure 2-21(c). Each of these rotations takes place, roughly speaking, around a point somewhere in the middle of the book, which we'll call the center of the rotation. And each of these rotations takes place around one of the three axes of a three-dimensional Cartesian coordinate system.

Doing What Comes Virtually

To understand what that means, imagine that you are holding not a real book but a virtual book, made up of a series of points in a three-dimensional Cartesian coordinate system. The x axis of your virtual book's coordinate system runs horizontally across the pages, the y axis runs vertically up and down the pages, and the z axis runs straight out of the middle of the book toward the tip of your nose. (See Figure 2-22.) When you rotate the book so that the text turns upside down, you are rotating it around the z axis, almost as though the book were a wheel and the z axis was its axle. (The resemblance of the word "axis" to the word "axle" is probably no coincidence, and a glance into the *Oxford English Dictionary* substantiates this etymology.) Similarly, when you rotate the book head over heels, you are rotating it around the book's x axis. And when you rotate it from side to side you are rotating it around the book's y axis.

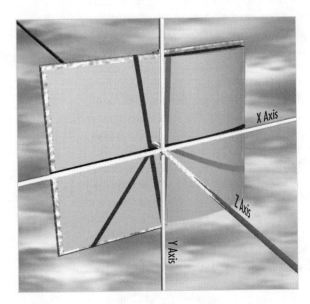

Figure 2-22 Axes of the virtual book

(For you pilots out there, rotation on the x axis is equivalent to pitch, rotation on the y axis is equivalent to yaw, and rotation on the z axis is equivalent to roll.)

Just as there are three ways for a line to be perpendicular to another line in a three-dimensional world, so there are three possible rotations that an object can make in three dimensions—and you've just tried them all on this book. Rotations around the x axis are called, sensibly enough, x-axis rotations. Rotations around the y axis are called y-axis rotations. And rotations around the z axis are called z-axis rotations.

A two-dimensional shape—that is, a shape defined within a two-dimensional coordinate system—can only make one kind of rotation: z-axis rotations. Ironically, this is the only type of rotation that does *not* change the z coordinate of any of the vertices in an object. Since the z coordinate of a two-dimensional object is always zero, it cannot be changed and thus other types of rotation, which *do* change the z coordinate, are forbidden in two dimensions.

Degrees versus Radians

Before we can perform calculations involving the rotation of objects, we must have some way of measuring rotations. Since rotated objects move in a circular motion, the obvious unit for measuring rotations is the degree. Since there are 360 degrees in a circle, an object rotated through a full circle is said to have been rotated 360 degrees. When you rotated this book so that the text was upside down, you rotated it 180 degrees around the z axis. If you had stopped halfway through this rotation, you would have rotated it 90 degrees around the z axis.

Mathematicians, however, do not like to use degrees as a unit of angular measure. Degrees are an arbitrary unit developed by ancient astronomers and mathematicians who were laboring under the misapprehension that the year was 360 days long. Thus, the degree was supposedly the angular distance that the earth rotated in a day (or the angular distance that the stars rotated around the earth in a day, according to another misapprehension of the ancient astronomers). Mathematicians prefer to use a unit of angular measure that actually has something to do with the mathematical properties of a circle. The unit that they favor is the radian—the distance around the circumference of a circle equal to the circle's radius. Most readers will recall that the relationship of a circle's diameter to its circumference is 3.14. . ., better known as pi(π). Since the radius is half the diameter, there are $2*\pi$ or roughly 6.28 radians in the circumference of a circle. Figure 2-23 shows how the degree and radians systems can both describe a circle. When you rotate this book 360 degrees, you are also rotating it 6.28 radians.

The truth is, it doesn't matter which of these units we use to measure the rotation of objects, as long as the sine and cosine routines that we are using are designed to deal with that type of unit. The sine and cosine routines in the Borland library are written to handle radians, so that's the unit of measure we will use in the early chapters of this book. Later, when we write our own sine and cosine routines, we'll invent

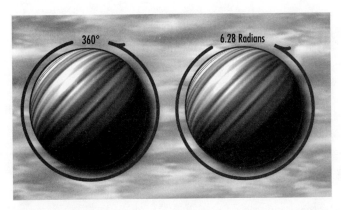

Figure 2-23 A full circle consists of 360 degrees or 6.28 radians, depending on which system you are using

a unit of measure, equivalent to neither degrees nor radians but more convenient for our purposes.

Rotation Formulas

Now that we have a unit of measure for object rotations, we can look at the formulas for performing those rotations. Since we'll be constructing objects out of vertices (and the lines and polygons that connect those vertices), we'll rotate objects by rotating vertices. Since a vertex is nothing more than a point in space that can be represented by a trio of Cartesian coordinates, we'll couch our rotational formulas in terms of those coordinates. In effect, a rotational formula is a mathematical formula that, when applied to the coordinates of a point in space, will tell us the new coordinates of that point after it has been rotated by a given number of degrees on one of the three Cartesian axes around the origin point (0,0) of the system in which that point is defined.

The best known and most widely applicable of these formulas is the one that rotates vertices around the *z* axis, since it is the only one needed for rotating two-dimensional shapes. Here is the formula for rotating the vertex of an object, or any other point, around the origin of the coordinate system on the *z* axis:

```
new_x = x * cos(z_angle) - y * sin(z_angle);
new_y = y * cos(z_angle) + x * sin(z_angle);
```

where *x* and *y* are the *x* and *y* coordinates of the vertex before the rotation, *z_angle* is the angle (in radians) through which we wish to rotate the object around its *z* axis, and *new_x* and *new_y* are the *x* and *y* coordinates of the object. (The *z* coordinate is not changed by the rotation.) The cos() and sin() functions calculate the cosine and sine of the angle, respectively. The center of rotation for this formula is always the origin of the coordinate system, which is why we defined the origin of our rotating virtual book as the book's center, since that greatly simplifies calculating the rotation of the book using this formula (and the formulas that follow). To rotate an object about the origin of the cordinate system, we must perform these calculations on the coordinates of all the vertices that define that object.

Unlike a two-dimensional object, a three-dimensional object can also rotate on its x axis and its y axis. Here is the formula for rotating an object around the origin of the coordinate system on the x axis:

```
new_y = y * cos(x_angle) - z * sin(x_angle);
new_z = y * sin(x_angle) + z * cos(x_angle);
```

Note that the x axis is not changed by this rotation.

Here is the formula for rotating an object around the origin of the coordinate system on the y axis:

```
new_z = z * cos(y_angle) - x * sin(y_angle);
new_x = z * sin(y_angle) + x * cos(y_angle);
```

By performing all of these operations on all of the coordinates of all of the vertices of an object, we obtain a brand new set of coordinates that describes the object after it has been rotated by x_angle on the x axis, y_angle on the y axis, and z_angle on the z axis.

Matrix Algebra

If we have a lot of vertices in an object—or, even worse, more than one object—it's going to take a lot of calculations to scale, translate, and perform x, y, and z rotations on the coordinates of all of the vertices of all of those objects. Since the ultimate goal is to perform all of these operations in real time while animating three-dimensional objects on the video display of the computer, you might wonder if there's enough time to perform all of these calculations.

The answer is—maybe. Microcomputers are surprisingly fast at this kind of calculation and I have a few tricks up my sleeve for optimizing the way in which these calculations are performed. Still, it would be nice if we had some way of reducing the calculations to be performed, especially if there were some way that the five transformations—scaling, translation, x rotation, y rotation, and z rotation—could be performed with a single set of operations instead of five sets.

As it happens, there is. Instead of performing the transformations with the formulas given earlier in this chapter, we can perform them using matrix arithmetic which is not as intimidating as it sounds. Matrix arithmetic is a mathematical system for performing arithmetic operations on matrices, which are roughly equivalent to the numeric array structures offered by most programming languages. Matrix operations can be substituted for most standard mathematical operations. Usually, we don't want to do this, because the matrix operations are a bit more complicated (and therefore time-consuming) than the standard operations. But matrix operations have one great advantage over standard operations. Several matrix operations can be concatenated—combined—into a single operation. Thus, we can use matrix operations to reduce our five transformations to a single master transformation.

Building Matrices

Matrices are usually presented as a collection of numbers arranged in rows and columns, like this:

```
1  2  3  4
5  6  7  8
9 10 11 12
```

This particular matrix has three rows and four columns and thus is referred to as a 3x4 matrix. In C++, we could store such a matrix as a 3x4 array of type int, like this:

```
int matrix[3] [4]={
       1, 2, 3, 4,
       5, 6, 7, 8,
       9,10,11,12
};
```

If a 3x4 array called *matrix* has already been declared but not yet initialized, it can be initialized to the matrix above with this series of assignment statements:

```
matrix[0][0]=1; matrix[0][1]=2;    matrix[0][2]=3;   matrix[0][3]=4;
matrix[1][0]=5; matrix[1][1]=6;    matrix[1][2]=7;   matrix[1][3]=8;
matrix[2][0]=9; matrix[2][1]=10;   matrix[2][2]=11;  matrix[2][3]=12;
```

The three coordinates that describe a three-dimensional vertex can be regarded as a 1x3 matrix—a matrix with one row and three columns. For instance, the coordinate triple (x,y,z) is equivalent to the 1x3 matrix:

```
x   y   z
```

A matrix with only one row or only one column is called a *vector*. To scale, translate, or rotate the coordinates in a vector, we multiply them by a special kind of matrix called a transformation matrix.

Multiplying Matrices

How do we multiply a vector times a matrix? There are special rules for matrix multiplication, but we really don't need to go into them here. Suffice it to say that if we have two vectors and a matrix declared thusly in C++:

```
float vector[1][3];
float newvector[1][3];
float matrix[3][3];
```

we can multiply *vector* and *matrix* together to produce *newvector* with this fragment of code:

```
newvector[0]=vector[0]*matrix[0][0]+vector[1]*matrix[0][1]+vector[2]*matrix[0][2];
newvector[1]=vector[0]*matrix[1][0]+vector[1]*matrix[1][1]+vector[2]*matrix[1][2];
newvector[2]=vector[0]*matrix[2][0]+vector[1]*matrix[2][1]+vector[2]*matrix[2][2];
```

After executing this code, *newvector* will contain the product of *vector * matrix*. Feel free to use this code fragment in your programs should you need to multiply a 1x3 vector times a 3x3 array. (Alert readers will notice that this fragment of code could also be written as a For loop in which the matrix multiplication instructions were written only once. However, "unrolling" the loop in this fashion speeds up the execution of the instructions, since there is no overhead for the loop itself. Since these multiplication instructions will be used again and again in a time-critical portion of the flight simulator program, it's best to save as many machine cycles as possible.)

As it happens, we'll be mostly multiplying 1x4 vectors and 4x4 (rather than 1x3 and 3x3) matrices in this book. Why? Because there are certain mathematical conveniences in doing so. This means we will need to add an extra element to our coordinate triples, turning them into coordinate quadruples. This extra element will always be equal to 1 and is only there to make the math come out right. Thus, when we are working with matrices, our coordinate vectors will take the form $(x,y,z,1)$. This fourth coordinate will never actually be used outside of matrix multiplication. The transformation matrices with which we will be multiplying this vector will all be 4x4 matrices. Here's a second code fragment that will multiply a 4x4 matrix called *matrix* by a 1x4 vector called *vector* and leave the result in a 1x4 vector called *newvector*:

```
newvector[0]=vector[0]*matrix[0][0]+vector[1]*matrix[0][1]
        +vector[2]*matrix[0][2]+vector[3]*matrix[0][3];
newvector[1]=vector[0]*matrix[1][0]+vector[1]*matrix[1][1]
        +vector[2]*matrix[1][2]+vector[3]*matrix[1][3];
newvector[2]=vector[0]*matrix[2][0]+vector[1]*matrix[2][1]
        +vector[2]*matrix[2][2]+vector[3]*matrix[2][3];
newvector[3]=vector[0]*matrix[3][0]+vector[1]*matrix[3][1]
        +vector[2]*matrix[3][2]+vector[3]*matrix[3][3];
```

Now let's take a look at the transformation matrices that can be used to translate, scale, and rotate a set of coordinates. When the following 4x4 matrix is multiplied by a 1x4 coordinate vector, the product vector is equivalent to the coordinate vector scaled by a scaling factor of sf:

```
sf   0   0   0
 0  sf   0   0
 0   0  sf   0
 0   0   0   1
```

This is called a *scaling matrix*. If we want to get even fancier (as we will, later on), we can scale by a different factor along the *x, y,* and *z* axes, using this matrix:

```
sx  0   0   0
 0  sy  0   0
 0   0  sz  0
 0   0   0  1
```

where *sx* scales along the *x* axis, *sy* scales along the *y* axis, and *sz* scales along the *z* axis. Thus, if we wish to make an object twice as tall but no larger in the other dimensions, we would set the *sy* factor equal to 2 and the *sx* and *sz* factors equal to 0.

We can also perform translation with matrices. The following matrix will scale a coordinate vector by the translation factors *tx, ty,* and *tz*:

```
1   0   0   0
0   1   0   0
0   0   1   0
tx  ty  tz  1
```

This is called a *translation matrix*.

Three Kinds of Rotation Matrices

We can perform all three kinds of rotation with matrices. The following matrix will rotate a coordinate vector by *za* degrees on the *z* axis:

```
 cos(za)  sin(za)  0 0
-sin(za)  cos(za)  0 0
      0      0 1 0
      0      0 0 1
```

The following matrix will rotate a coordinate vector by *xa* degrees on the *x* axis:

```
1    0       0 0
0  cos(xa)  sin(xa)  0
0 -sin(xa)  cos(xa)  0
0    0       0 1
```

And the following matrix will rotate a coordinate vector by *ya* degrees on the *y* axis:

```
cos(ya) 0 -sin(ya) 0
    0 1     0 0
sin(ya) 0  cos(ya) 0
    0 0     0 1
```

When you want to perform several of these transformations on the vertices of one or more objects, you can initialize all of the necessary matrices, multiply the matrices together (that is, concatenate them), and then multiply the master concatenated matrix by each vertex in the object or objects. How do you multiply a 4x4 matrix by another 4x4 matrix? Here's a fragment of C++ code that will do the job, multiplying *matrix1* by *matrix2* and leaving the result in *newmatrix*:

```
for (int i=0; i<4; i++)
    for (int j=0; j<4; j++) {
        newmatrix[i][j] = 0;
        for (k=0; k<4; k++) newmatrix[i][j] +=
                    matrix1[k][j]*matrix2[i][k];
    }
```

In addition to the transformation matrices given above, there's one more matrix that will come in handy in the chapters to come. Although it may seem silly to do so, there will be times when we need to multiply one matrix by another matrix and leave the first matrix unchanged—that is, the resulting matrix will be the same as the first matrix. If so, we must multiply the matrix by the identity matrix, which looks like this:

```
1  0  0  0
0  1  0  0
0  0  1  0
0  0  0  1
```

The identity matrix is simply the matrix in which the main diagonal—the diagonal strip of numbers running from the upper left corner of the matrix to the lower right corner—consists of 1s and all the other numbers are 0s. Any matrix multiplied by the identity matrix will remain unchanged by the operation.

Floating-Point Math

Before we leave this discussion of useful mathematics, let's look at how the computer handles math operations. As you're probably aware, the C++ language offers several numeric data types. For our purposes, the most important of these are the int type and the float type. Numeric data declared as int, which is short for integer, consists of whole numbers, usually in the range -32,768 to 32,767. Numeric data declared as float, which is short for floating point, includes whole numbers in the int range but it can also include fractional values and numbers over a wider range. We can modify these types in several ways. In particular, we can substitute the long type for the int type, which gives us a much wider range of whole numbers. Or we can define type int as type unsigned int, which gives us a range of whole numbers from 0 to 65,535 rather than from -32,768 to 32,767.

The sort of mathematical operations performed in three-dimensional animation programs usually require the floating-point data type because they use fractional values. The functions that C++ uses to perform mathematical operations on floating-point data can be quite slow, however, especially on a machine that doesn't have a math coprocessor installed. So, we'll avoid the floating-point type whenever possible. Nonetheless, by way of illustration, we'll use float data in many of the early programs that demonstrate three-dimensional transformations and animation. You'd best be warned now that these programs will be rather slow. Later, we'll rewrite this code using the long data type. This requires some clever rewriting of our programs, though, and so the better part of a chapter will be devoted to this process. In the meantime, just grit your teeth and bear with the sometimes excruciating slowness of floating-point code—unless you have a math coprocessor, in which case you can smile benevolently down on those who don't.

CHAPTER

3

3

Painting
in 256 Colors

Unless you live in the zebra house at the zoo, when you look around you'll see colors, lots of colors. According to some estimates, the human eye can distinguish more than 16 million different colors, and there's probably a lipstick shade named after every one of them. Without color, life would be, well, colorless. So would computer graphics.

Color is the single most important thing that a computer graphics programmer needs to be concerned with. As we saw in Chapter 1, a computer video display is nothing more (or less) than a matrix of pixels. The only thing that distinguishes one pixel from the pixel next to it is color. Computer graphics programming is a matter of changing the colors of the pixels on the display in such a way as to create interesting and meaningful patterns. Once you've learned to do that in a clean and efficient manner, you'll know everything you need to know about graphics programming. As you might guess, that's more easily said than done.

Color Depth versus Resolution

The VGA adapter supports nine different "official" graphics modes. The two most obvious attributes that distinguish one graphics mode from another are the number of pixels that can be displayed on the screen at one time and the number of colors in which each of those pixels can be displayed. The first of these attributes is called resolution; the second is sometimes referred to as color depth.

Both of these attributes are important, but frequently we must choose to make one attribute more important than the other. As programmers, we generally want a large number of pixels on the screen in a great variety of colors. However, as the Rolling Stones once said, you can't always get what you want. The VGA adapter often forces us to trade off one attribute for another. Generally speaking, the more pixels we can squeeze onto the screen in a given mode, the fewer colors we're allowed. So we have to decide which is more important to us: resolution or color depth.

Game designers usually opt for color depth over resolution. The standard VGA graphics adapter, which we are using for our graphics in this book, supports resolutions that can display pixel matrices as large as 640x480, for a total of 307,200 pixels on the screen at one time. But when working at these resolutions, we're only allowed to show those pixels in 16 colors. Ironically, this lack of color depth can make the display look lower in resolution than it actually is. A block of high-resolution pixels in a single color tends to look an awful lot like one big pixel.

By lowering the resolution to 320x200, for a total of 64,000 pixels on the screen, we gain the ability to display pixels in 256 colors, an exponential leap in color depth. The pixels in 320x200 mode look rather large and blocky, but the extra color depth more than compensates for the loss of resolution. Despite the newer video cards and higher resolutions, more than 90 percent of the many commercial games on the market today still rely on the 320x200x256 color mode, designated mode 13h by the ROM BIOS. This is due to the wealth of libraries and routines which already have been written for it, its satisfactory speed on slower (386) machines, and its buffer size in use of dynamic RAM memory. In Chapter 1, soft modes, such as 640x480x256, were mentioned as the king of the marketplace. Generally, these modes start with mode 12h or 13h and adjust registers to achieve their resolution and color depth. For learning about video programming, the 320x200x256 mode 13h is great.

Getting in the Mode

Okay, so you're convinced that the 320x200x256 color mode is the way to go for the game program you want to write. How do you get the VGA adapter into mode 13h?

It would be nice if you could simply call a standard C library routine to do it for you. Unfortunately, the BGI, the library of graphic routines that comes with the Borland C++ compiler, does not presently support mode 13h. And, as we noted in Chapter 1, the BGI isn't really intended for producing commercial quality animation.

We don't really need the BGI's help, though. Every VGA adapter includes a ROM chip that has built-in routines for performing the initialization needed for the standard PC graphics modes. These routines are collectively known as the video BIOS (which we already discussed in Chapter 1).

It is awkward to access the video BIOS from C++. The BIOS was meant to be accessed either indirectly through higher-level instructions or from assembly language code. We'll use the latter approach. Since many readers of this book will be unfamiliar with assembly language programming techniques, I'll introduce the topic in the next section—as briefly as possible. Readers with experience in assembly language programming may want to start skimming at this point.

Doing It in Assembly Language

An assembly language program is written using two kinds of instructions: assembly language instructions and assembler directives. Assembly language instructions represent actual machine language codes that can be executed by the CPU after they are translated by a program called an assembler. Directives give the assembler important information about how it is to process the rest of the program.

Few programs are written entirely in assembly language. But it is quite common to write small assembly language modules to be included with a C++ program. These modules consist of a few assembly language procedures, or PROCs, which play roughly the same role as C++ functions. In fact, if properly written, these PROCs can be called from C++ exactly as though they were C++ functions. A PROC begins with the name of the procedure followed by the assembler directive PROC:

```
AsmFunction PROC
```

And it must end with the name of the procedure followed by the assembler directive ENDP, (which tells the assembler that the procedure is over):

```
AsmFunction ENDP
```

Between the PROC and ENDP directives you place a series of assembly language instructions, each of which occupies a single line of the assembly language source file. These instructions alternate with occasional assembler directives—the names of which are usually written in uppercase letters—and with comments, which must be preceded by a semicolon (;). (The semicolon in assembler works exactly like the double slash (//) in C++, causing the assembler to ignore everything until the next carriage return.)

Each instruction consists of a mnemonic, which represents a CPU operation, followed optionally by one or more operands indicating what memory locations are to be operated upon. The mnemonic is usually a three-to-six-letter word, such as MOV or PUSH or ADD. Here's a typical assembly language instruction, followed by a comment:

```
add ax,[length]  ; Add AX and LENGTH, leaving sum in AX
```

Most of the assembly language instructions in the PROC will concern themselves with moving numeric values around in the computer's memory and performing mathematical and logical operations on those values. Often, these instructions reference a special set of memory locations situated in the computer CPU itself. These memory locations, or CPU registers, can be considered a set of permanent integer variables. The registers we will be concerned with are named AX, BX, CX, DX, SI, DI, BP, SP, ES, DS, CS, and SS. Four of these registers—AX, BX, CX, and DX—can be broken in two and treated as pairs of 8-bit variables. AX becomes AH and AL (with AH the high byte of AX and AL the low byte), BX becomes BH and BL, CX becomes CH and CL, and DX becomes DH and DL. The CPU registers are diagrammed in Figure 3-1.

Assembly Language Pointers

Most of the CPU registers can be used for performing general arithmetic operations, such as addition and subtraction, and some of the 16-bit registers can be used as pointers to locations elsewhere in the computer's memory. Just as preceding the name of a pointer variable in C++ with the indirection operator (*) indicates that we are referencing the memory location to which that pointer is pointing, so surrounding the name of a CPU register with square brackets ([]) indicates that we are referencing the memory location to which that register is pointing, like this:

```
[bx]
```

Actually, we will need to use two CPU registers to point to a memory location, with one register holding the segment portion of the address and another holding the off-

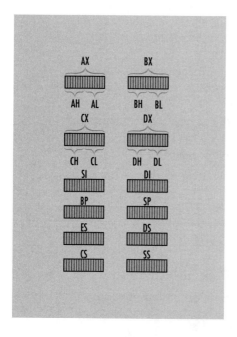

Figure 3-1 The Major CPU registers

set portion. (See Chapter 1 for a discussion of segments and offsets.) The segment portion must always be placed in a segment register, usually either DS or ES. You include the name of this register in brackets with the name of the register holding the offset, like this:

```
[es:dx]
```

When the segment is in DS, however, its name does not have to be explicitly mentioned in brackets, since the CPU uses the segment in DS by default for all data references.

Getting It into a Register

How do you place a value in a CPU register? In C++, you would use the assignment operator (=), but this does not exist in assembly language. Instead, you must copy the value from another memory location or CPU register by using the MOV instruction (which should really be called the COPY instruction), like this:

```
mov ax,[es:dx]
```

This copies to the AX register the value stored in the memory location pointed to by *[es:dxs]*. We can also identify memory locations by their addresses, though it is more common to name those addresses and then identify the locations by name. For the moment, I won't discuss techniques for assigning names to locations, but you would refer to a named location like this:

```
mov cx,size
```

where *size* is a name that we've assigned to a 16-bit memory location.

Values can be copied not only from memory locations, but from other registers and even from the instruction itself. A value copied from an instruction is called an immediate value and is referenced like this:

```
mov dx,1040h
```

This copies the value 1040h (the "h" indicates that the value is in hexadecimal) from the instruction into the DX register.

When using assembly language pointers, it is sometimes necessary to specify what sort of value the pointer is pointing at. The three types of values recognized by 80X86-series CPUs are BYTEs (8-bit values), WORDs (16-bit values), and DWORDs (Double WORDs, or 32-bit values). Thus, a pointer is either a BYTE PTR, which points at a BYTE value; a WORD PTR, which points at a WORD value; or a DWORD PTR, which points at a DWORD value. For instance, these instructions copy a WORD value from the address pointed to by ES:BX to the AX register:

```
mov ax,word ptr [es:bx]
```

Of course, the assembler can also figure out that [es:bx] must be a word pointer because you want to move the value stored there into a 16-bit register. But there will be instances when the size of the value is less obvious. And it doesn't hurt to make it explicit anyway, if only to make your code clear to somebody else reading it.

There are special assembly language instructions for putting pointers into registers. An assembly language pointer actually stretches across two registers, with either ES or DS holding the segment part of the pointer and another 16-bit register holding the offset. Does this mean that we must use two MOV instructions to get the pointer into these two registers? Fortunately not. The 80X86 instruction set (that is, the set of instructions that can be executed by CPUs in the 80X86 series) includes special instructions for loading pointers into a pair of registers. The two instructions that will be used in the programs in this book are LDS and LES. The first loads a segment into the DS register and an offset into a second register. The other does the same with the ES register. For instance, if we wished to load the pointer stored at the address we've named old_pointer into the ES:DX registers, we could write

```
les ds,old_pointer
```

Assembly Language Odds and Ends

Before you can use certain registers in a PROC that is to interface with C++ code, you must save the value stored in those registers in a section of memory called the stack. This is done by using the PUSH instruction, like this:

```
push ds
push di
push si
```

Then, before the program ends, these values must be restored to the original registers, in reverse order, by using the POP instruction, like this:

```
pop si
pop di
pop ds
```

Some assembly language instructions have an effect on the CPU flags. These are simply isolated bits within a special register, which reflect the results of instructions. For instance, if the result of a subtraction instruction (SUB) is zero, the zero flag will be set (given a value of one). What good does this do you? You can give other 80X86 instructions contingent on the way in which the flags are set. These instructions usually cause the CPU to begin executing instructions at a different address in memory if the flags have a particular setting. Thus, they can be used to simulate high-level IF and WHILE instructions, by skipping some instructions and executing others based on the outcome of other operations or repeating a set of instructions in a loop if the flags are set in a certain way. Commonly, these operations are preceded by a comparison instruction (CMP), which checks to see if two values are equal or are unequal in a certain way. For instance, the instruction CMP AX,DX would compare the values in the AX and DX registers. This could then be followed by a JZ instruction, which would cause the processor to "jump" to a new address if the zero flag is set—i.e., if the values in AX and DX are equal. This is logically equivalent to the C++ instruction: if (ax==dx).

Perhaps the fanciest of these "conditional jump" instructions is LOOP, which subtracts one (*decrements*) from the value in the CX register and jumps to a certain address if CX doesn't then equal zero. Variations on this instruction, such as LOOPNE and LOOPZ, can be made to check the value of a flag and terminate the loop when a certain flag setting is detected, even if CX has not yet been decremented all the way to zero. These instructions can be used to produce structures similar to the high-level While and for loops.

Occasionally, assembly language procedures must call other procedures, the way that C++ functions call other functions. This is done via the CALL instruction, which must be followed by the name of the procedure being called, like this:

```
call other_procedure
```

The assembler translates the name of the procedure being called into the actual address at which the code for that procedure resides in memory.

Finally, every assembly language procedure must end with a RET instruction, which causes the CPU to return control of the program to C++ when the assembly language procedure is complete (equivalent to the C++ return instruction, as well as to the final curly bracket (}) at the end of a C++ function), and the ENDP (end) directive.

There is a great deal more to know about assembly language and we can only scratch the surface in this book. To avoid confusion, I'll explain the few relevant assembly language concepts as they arise. For now, we will mention only one more: how to pass parameters from C++ to assembler.

Passing Parameters to Assembly Language Procedures

In C++, you can pass parameters to a function by placing the values of those parameters in parentheses after the function call, like this:

```
get_lost(23, "skidoo");
```

You'll pass parameters to assembly language procedures in exactly the same way. But how does the assembly language function receive the parameters? In C++, you would simply write a parameter list in the function header, specifying the types of the parameters and the names by which you wished to refer to them. In assembler, it's not quite that easy. When the assembler procedure begins, the parameters will be in the stack. To fetch the parameters from the stack, you need to know exactly how C++

organizes those parameters on the stack. But Turbo Assembler (and most other Microsoft-compatible assemblers for IBM-compatible computers) provides a simple method of accessing parameters: the ARG directive.

No, ARG isn't what you say when you stub your toe against your computer desk—it is a directive that tells the assembler which parameters you expect to be passed from C++, the order in which those parameters will be passed, and the number of bytes that each parameter will occupy. In return, the assembler allows you to refer to those parameters by name rather than by their location on the stack. The ARG directive works like this:

```
ARG first_param:BYTE, second_param:WORD, third_param:DWORD;
```

This tells the assembler to expect three parameters—first_param, second_param, and third_param—to be passed to the procedure from C++. It also tells the assembler how much memory each of these parameters will occupy. The first will occupy 1 byte (as indicated by the word BYTE attached to the name of the parameter by a colon), the second 2 bytes (or one WORD), and the third 4 bytes (or one DWORD). In practice, BYTE is not used as ARG size for assembly language routines which will interface with C++ since the C++ compiler performs automatic adjustment (called promotion) of chars to ints in function calls. Since assembly language doesn't demote the int back to char, this could cause misalignment of successive parameters and leave us scratching our heads with another bug to hunt down. It is best to restrict sizes to WORD and DWORD when writing assembly code for C++. All assembly procedures in this book confine themselves to these ARG sizes.

Once the ARG directive has been placed at the beginning of the procedure, just after the PROC directive, you can refer to these parameters by name. The one catch is that the following pair of instructions must be included at the beginning of any procedure that uses the ARG directive:

```
push bp
mov  bp,sp
```

Place these two instructions before any other PUSH instructions are executed. These instructions set up the BP register as a pointer to the stack area where the parameters are stored. The assembler will translate all references to these parameters into pointers using the BP register. For this reason, you should never use the BP register in any procedure that has an ARG directive.

Near the end of the procedure, after all other POP instructions have been executed, include the following instruction:

```
pop bp
```

This restores the BP register back to the value it was previously storing. (Most likely, the C++ function that called the assembly language procedure was *also* using the BP register as a pointer to parameters stored on the stack, which is why it is important that the value be returned intact at the end of the procedure.)

Is it possible for an assembly language procedure to return a value the way that a C++ function can? Sure it is. An assembly language procedure can do anything that a C++ function can (and occasionally a bit more). The way in which a value is returned from an assembly language procedure depends on what type of value it is. For instance, values of type int (or any other 16-bit values) are returned in the AX register: the value must be placed in the AX register before the procedure terminates. Larger and smaller values are returned using similar techniques.

And now, with the assistance of these few assembly language procedures, we can consider how to access the video BIOS.

Accessing the Video BIOS

To access the routines in the video BIOS from an assembly language procedure, you must use the 80X86 INT instruction. The INT instruction is similar to the CALL instruction, except that it calls a subroutine by using a software interrupt. That is, it tells the computer to look in a certain location in the computer's memory, note the address that is stored there, and execute the subroutine found at that address. These addresses are stored in the computer's memory during the initialization period that takes place just after the computer is turned on or rebooted. The particular address in which the computer looks is determined by the number following the INT instruction. The action of the INT instruction is shown in Figure 3-2. The video BIOS functions are accessed by the instruction

```
int 10h
```

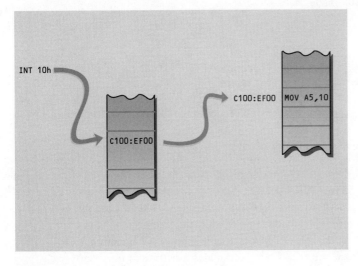

Figure 3-2 An INT instruction executing

Executing software interrupt number 10h causes the computer to look in the memory location that contains the address of the video BIOS code. This in turn causes the computer to begin executing that code. However, simply executing the INT 10h instruction doesn't tell the video BIOS what you want it to do. You must also pass it additional information, by placing that information in the CPU registers.

The video BIOS is capable of executing several different functions. Each function is identified by a number. You place the number of the desired function in CPU register AL before calling the video BIOS. The function that sets the video mode is function 0, so to call it you place a 0 in the AL register before executing interrupt 10h. It is necessary to tell this function which video mode you wish to set, so you must also place the mode number in the AH register. In assembly language, all of those things can be done in three instructions, like so:

```
mov   al,0    ; Put function number (0) in register AL
mov   ah,13h  ; Put mode number (13h) in register AH
int   10h     ; Call video BIOS at interrupt 10h
```

In the course of this book, we'll put together a short library of assembly language procedures that we can link to our C++ code to support the basic screen operations we'll need in our programs. Since calling the ROM BIOS is a task best performed in assembly language, we'll include a procedure for setting the video mode, equivalent to the C++ function shown earlier. The procedure function, callable from C++, is in Listing 3-1.

Listing 3-1 The setgmode function

```
; setgmode(int mode)
;    Set VGA adapter to BIOS mode MODE

_setgmode PROC
      ARG     mode:WORD
      push    bp                  ; Save BP
      mov     bp,sp               ; Set up stack pointer
      mov     ax,mode             ; AL = video mode
      mov     ah,0                ; AH = function number
      int     10h                 ; Call interrupt 10h
      pop     bp                  ; Restore BP
      ret
_setgmode ENDP
```

As you can see, this procedure uses several of the techniques we talked about earlier in this chapter. The ARG directive tells the assembler that the procedure expects a single 16-bit parameter, referred to as *mode*. The first two instructions set up the stack area so that this parameter will be correctly referenced by the assembler. The last two instructions restore the BP register and return to the calling function. In between, INT 10h is called after loading *mode* into CPU register AX and function number zero into AH. The only thing that may be confusing is why the mode value is MOVed into AX rather than just AL. We do this because *mode* will be passed as a parameter of type int from C++ and we might as well load the entire 16-bit integer into AX, since only the low 8 bits of the parameter will be used (there being no video modes with numbers greater than 255). Thus, the mode number still winds up in the AL register, where it belongs.

This procedure can be found in the file SCREEN.ASM on the included disk. We'll talk about more of the procedures in that file in this and later chapters. To use the procedure in that file from a program being developed in the Borland Integrated Development Environment (IDE), put SCREEN.ASM (or SCREEN.OBJ, if you've already compiled it to an object file) into your project window and include the file SCREEN.H at the top of each module of your program that requires the routines. The file SCREEN.H contains C++ prototypes for all of the assembly language procedures in SCREEN.CPP, showing the compiler how these procedures are to be called as C++ functions.

This particular procedure can be called from C++ like this:

```
setgmode(0x13);
```

This example would set the video mode to mode 0x13, the 320x200x256 color graphics mode.

Be warned: When you set the video mode it stays set. When the user exits the program, the video display will still be in whatever mode you've switched it to, which can make a mess of the screen. As a matter of courtesy and professionalism, you need to save the previous video mode before setting a new mode so that you can restore it on exit from the program.

Restoring the Video Mode

Fortunately, the authors of the IBM operating system chose to store the number of the current video mode at memory location 00400:0049. As I explained in Chapter 1, you can retrieve the contents of a memory location by creating a pointer to that location using the MK_FP (MaKe Far Pointer) macro, which is also defined in DOS.H. The following statement sets the integer variable *oldmode* to the value of the current video mode:

```
int oldmode=*(int *)MK_FP(0x40,0x49); // Set oldmode to the
                                      // value at 00400:0049
```

You'll notice that in one statement we've both declared an integer variable and set it equal to the value at a memory location. This is legal in C++, where we can declare a variable at the time of first use, rather than in a block of declarations at the head of a function. The variable will remain in scope until the end of the block in which it is declared. (A program block in C is a sequence of program lines that begins and ends with curly brackets.) If we declare this variable at the beginning of the main() function, it will remain in scope throughout the program.

You'll also notice that we've used the typecast (int *) in front of the MK_FP macro so that the compiler will know that we want the value returned by the dereference of the macro to be of type int. A typecast, as you'll recall from Chapter 1, tells the compiler to treat an expression of one type as an expression of a different type.

Once we've set *oldmode* equal to the previous video mode, we can restore the video mode on exit from the program by calling setgmode() with *oldmode* as a parameter. The following skeletal main() function will set the video mode at the beginning of the program and restore the original mode before terminating:

```
#include   <dos.h>
#include "screen.h"

void main()
{
    int oldmode=*(int *)MK_FP(0x40,0x49);
    setgmode(13h);
    // Body of main() function
    setgmode(oldmode);
}
```

And that's all there is to setting the PC's video mode. Which leads us to a far more important question: Now that we've set the video mode, what do we do with it?

More about Bitmaps

As we saw in Chapter 1, the basis behind almost all PC graphics is the bitmap, a sequence of consecutive byte values in memory in which the individual binary digits (or bits) within those bytes represent the colors of the individual pixels on the display. If the picture being output to the video display is made up of only two colors—say, black and white—only one bit is needed to represent each pixel. If a given bit equals zero, the corresponding pixel is black. If a bit equals one, the corresponding pixel is white. Or vice versa. See Figure 3-3 for an illustration.

When in graphics mode, the VGA adapter scans an area of memory called video RAM (vidram, for short) and interprets what it finds there as a bitmap of an image to be displayed on the screen. It then outputs that image to the video monitor, like a miniature television station sending a picture to a television set.

In the case of the VGA 256-color mode, the bitmap is a little more complicated than the simple "zero equals black, one equals white" scheme outlined above—but only a little. Because each pixel on the mode 13h display can take 256 possible colors, each must be represented in memory by 8 bits/1 byte, since a byte can take 256 possible values. This is a convenient arrangement, because computer memory is

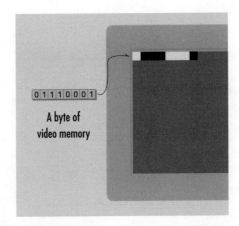

Figure 3-3 In a two-color mode, each bit in video memory corresponds to a pixel on the display

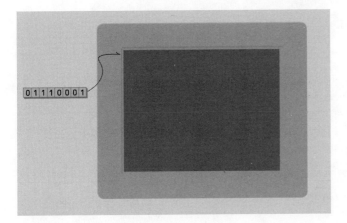

Figure 3-4
Video memory as bytemap in 256-color mode

normally organized into individual bytes. In mode 13h, video memory is not so much a bitmap as a bytemap, though I'll continue referring to it here as a bitmap. Figure 3-4 illustrates this arrangement. The actual pixel color represented by a given byte value in the bitmap depends on the current setting of the VGA color registers, which I'll discuss in a moment.

Finding the Bitmap

When we place the video adapter into mode 13h, the bitmap for the display is automatically placed at address A000:0000. Although some of the VGA (and EGA and CGA) graphics modes allow the bitmap to be moved to other locations, mode 13h does not. It always begins at this address.

The byte at A000:0000 represents the color of the pixel in the upper left corner of the display. (See Figure 3-5.) The next byte in memory, at location A000:0001,

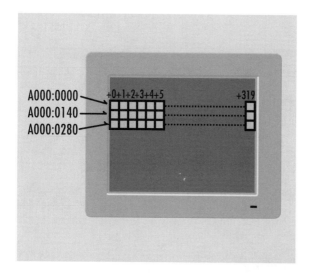

Figure 3-5 The byte at hexidecimal address A000:0000

represents the color of the pixel to the immediate right of that pixel—and so on, for the first 320 bytes of the bitmap. The 320th byte, at location A000:013F, represents the pixel in the upper right corner of the display. The bitmap continues with the second row of pixels, with the next byte (at location A000:0140) representing the pixel immediately beneath the pixel in the upper left corner of the display. The byte at A000:0141 represents the pixel to the immediate right of that one, and so on.

There are 64,000 pixels on the mode 13h display; therefore the bitmap for the display is 64,000 bytes long, continuing from address A000:0000 to address A000:F9BFF. As you've probably already guessed, the last byte of the bitmap (at A000:F9BFF) represents the color of the pixel in the bottom right corner of the display.

Drawing Pictures in Memory

Accessing the individual bytes in this bitmap from a C program is so delightfully simple that there may be a law against it in several of the more regressive states of the Union. Check your local statute books before attempting this at home. All you have to do is treat the 64,000 bytes from A000:0000 to A000:F9BFF as though they were a large array of type char, then assign values to the bytes in that array to change the color of the pixels on screen (or read the value of the bytes in that array to read the value of the pixels on screen). To create the array, you first need to establish a far pointer that points to the first byte of the bitmap:

```
char far *screen=(char far *)MK_FP(0xa000,0);
```

Once this is done, you can read and write the individual bytes of the bitmap as though they were elements of a 64,000-element array of type char called screen[].

(Obviously, you can use the name of your choice for this array in your own programs.) For instance, to set the pixel in the upper left corner of the mode 13h display to color 167, you would use this statement:

```
screen[0] = 167;
```

Is that simple, or what?

Clearing the Screen

Suppose, for instance, that you wish to clear the entire mode 13h display to the background color, an operation you will generally perform during program initialization. The background color in mode 13h is always represented by color 0. Thus, you can clear the screen with a simple for loop, like so:

```
for (unsigned int i=0; i<64000; i++) screen[i]=0;
```

You'll notice that we've once again used the C++ convention of declaring a variable at the time of first use. Further, we've declared the variable i as type unsigned int, so that it can take values in the range 0 to 65,535. If you should inadvertantly omit the UNSIGNED keyword from a similar declaration, your program will go into an infinite loop, as the value of i tries and fails to reach 64,000. Which could leave you with a screen that's half cleared and a user with one finger on the reset button. (Alternatively, you could declare i to be of type long, which would give it a possible range of 4 billion values, but which would also take slightly longer to process.)

Clearing the screen is the sort of thing that may need to be done very quickly in a program such as a flight simulator which draws on the video display in real time. For maximum speed, an assembly language function for clearing the video display has been included in the file SCREEN.ASM and in Listing 3-2.

Listing 3-2 The cls function

```
SCREEN_WIDTH   equ 320
SCREEN_HEIGHT  equ 200

; cls(char far *screen_adr)
;    Clear video memory or offscreen buffer at
;    SCREEN_ADR to zeroes

_cls PROC
    ARG     screen:DWORD
    push    bp                ; Save BP
    mov     bp,sp             ; Set up stack pointer
    push    di                ; Save DI register
    les     di,screen         ; Point ES:DI at screen
    mov     cx,SCREEN_WIDTH/2*SCREEN_HEIGHT ; Count pixels
    mov     ax,0              ; Store zero values...
    rep     stosw             ; ...in all of video memory
```

continued on next page

continued from previous page

```
    pop     di              ; Restore DI
    pop     bp              ; Restore BP
    ret
_cls ENDP
```

Let's take a look at what this procedure does and how it does it. At the head of the procedure is a pair of EQU statements. EQU is an assembler directive similar to the CONST instruction in C++ (or to the #define preprocessor directive that C++ inherited from C). It sets a symbol equal to a value. In this case, it sets the symbol SCREEN_WIDTH equal to 320 and the symbol SCREEN_HEIGHT equal to 200. These symbols can now be used in our program in place of these values.

The ARG directive tells us that this procedure receives a single parameter—a pointer to the video display that we've called *screen*. If video memory is always at the same address, why does this procedure need a pointer to its location? There will be times when it is necessary to assemble the video image in a special memory buffer, and then move the completed image to video RAM after it is complete. In fact, this very technique will be used in the program that we develop in the next chapter. On such occasions, the cls() function will be passed the address of the offscreen buffer, rather than the address of video memory, so that the offscreen buffer can be cleared instead of the display. You'll notice that the same technique of passing a pointer to the screen is used in many of the screen-oriented functions we'll develop later.

The first three instructions of the procedure set up the BP register as a pointer to the parameters on the stack and save the DI register. (None of the other registers, except for BP, need to be saved.) The LES DI,SCREEN instruction loads the full 32-bit screen pointer into the ES:DI register pair.

The next instruction, MOV CX,SCREEN_WIDTH/2*SCREEN_HEIGHT, may look a little odd to you, since it includes such high-level operators as the division (/) and the multiplication (*) operators. These are actually assembler directives. The object of this instruction is to copy the total number of pixels on the display, divided by 2, into the CX register. Instead of calculating this number ourselves, we use the two symbols we created earlier to calculate this value. The instruction that will actually be assembled here is

```
mov CX,32000
```

In a moment it will become clear why we are loading this value into this particular register.

Next, a value of zero is copied into the AX register and a REP STOSW instruction is executed. What is a REP STOSW instruction? It is one of the 80X86 string instructions, which are actually extremely tight and fast assembly loops for manipulating strings of data in the computer's memory. The instruction creates a string of identical 16-bit numbers in a sequence of memory addresses starting with the address pointed to by the ES:DI registers. The count of 16-bit numbers in the string is whatever has been stored in the CX register and the actual 16-bit number placed in that sequence of addresses is the number in the AX register. In this case, the REP STOSW instruction will store 32,000 16-bit zero values in the address we have passed in the parameter *screen*. Since we are storing 16-bit values rather than 8-bit values, that's equivalent to 64,000 addresses, precisely enough to fill up video memory, or an offscreen buffer, with zeroes, effectively clearing it. This procedure is called from C++ like this:

```
cls(screen_address);
```

where screen_address is a far pointer to an array of type char.

We wrote this function in assembly language rather than C because there may be times when we need to clear the display in a hurry and the STOSW instruction is generally faster than a for loop in C. How much faster? That depends on which model of 80X86 processor the program is running on. On the earlier processors in the 80X86 series, such as the 8088 and 8086, string instructions were much faster than alternative forms of loops. On later processors, such as the 80286 and 80386, the string instructions are still faster, but by a smaller margin. On the 80486 processor, there are alternative loop forms that are as fast or faster than the string instructions, so writing such a routine in machine language becomes less important on the 80486, though we have no guarantee that our C compiler is actually producing the most efficient possible machine language translation of our loop. Until most game players own machines based on the 80486 processor, it will be advantageous to use string instructions such as STOSW for potentially time-consuming operations like clearing the screen. Of course, at the rate things are going, it may not be long before this event comes to pass.

Lots and Lots of Colors

Now we know that changing the colors of pixels on the video display is simply a matter of putting the right numbers in the right locations in video RAM. But how do we know what numbers represent which colors? When we set a location in the bitmap to a value of 10, for instance, how do we know what color pixel the number 10 represents?

The answer is that the number 10 can represent any color that we want it to represent, out of the overall palette of 256 colors permitted by the VGA adapter. (See Figure 3-6.) We tell the VGA adapter what colors are represented by what numbers by placing the appropriate values in the VGA color registers, which I discussed briefly in Chapter 1. To recap, the color registers are a set of memory registers on the VGA adapter itself that contains the 256 colors of the VGA palette. There are 256 color registers on the VGA board and each register contains a description of one of the colors in the current palette.

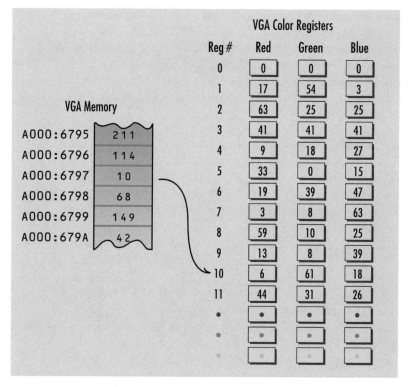

Figure 3-6 The value stored in each location in video memory represents one of 256 colors

Setting the Palette

There are at least two ways to alter the values of the VGA color registers. Usually, unless we need to change the color registers in a great hurry, we can ask the video BIOS to perform this complicated task. Once again, we call INT 10h, as we did in setting the video mode. Setting the VGA color registers is performed by function 10h, subfunction 12h, of the video BIOS, so we call it by placing a value of 10h in register AL and a value of 12h in register AH.

There's no need to set all of the color registers with a single call to this function. If we choose, we can set only a few. This means, however, that we must tell the video BIOS which registers we wish to change and what values we want them to have. We place the number of consecutive color registers we wish to change in register CX, the first register to be set in BX, and a pointer to an array of color values in ES:DX. The array of color values is simply an array of type char in which every three bytes contain a color descriptor for a register.

As we discussed in Chapter 1, each color on the VGA display can be described by three 8-bit values that represent the red, green, and blue components of the color, where each value is a number from 0 to 63. The first byte of the color descriptor represents the intensity of the red component; the second, the intensity of the green component; and the third, the intensity of the blue component. To set all 256 color registers, create an array of char with 768 elements, in which the first three elements contain the color descriptor for color number 0 in the palette, the second three elements represent the color descriptor for color number 1, and so forth.

Shown in Listing 3-3 is our assembly language program in SCREEN.H that will call the video BIOS for us.

✈ **Listing 3-3** The setpalette function

```
; setpalette(char far *color_regs)
;   Set VGA color registers to the color values in COLOR_REGS

_setpalette    PROC
    ARG    regs:DWORD
    push   bp                  ; Save BP
    mov    bp,sp               ; Set up stack pointer
    les    dx,regs             ; Point ES:SX at palette registers
    mov    ah,10h              ; Specify BIOS function 10h
    mov    al,12h              ; ...subfunction 12h
    mov    bx,0                ; Start with first register
    mov    cx,100h             ; Set all 256 (100h) registers
    int    10h                 ; Call video BIOS
    pop    bp                  ; Restore BP
    ret
_setpalette    ENDP
```

To change all 256 registers to the color values in the char array colregs, you would write

```
setpalette(color_regs);
```

where color_regs is a far pointer to an array of char containing the color descriptors.

And that's all there is to setting the VGA palette. Well, okay, maybe it isn't *that* easy, but it's conceptually simple. Creating an array with 256 color descriptors in it isn't as trivial as I've made it sound, but there is an easy way to do it.

The Default Palette

For some applications, you don't need to set the VGA color registers at all. When you boot up your computer, the operating system sets the palette to a standard set of values called the default palette. With the set of graphics routines we've developed so far, it's a simple matter to write a program that lets us look at that default palette. Such a program appears in Listing 3-4. (This program is available on the accompanying disk as RAINBOW.EXE, located in the BYOFS\GENERAL directory.)

Listing 3-4 RAINBOW.CPP

```
// RAINBOW.CPP
// A program to display the default VGA palette

#include      <stdio.h>
#include      <conio.h>
#include      <dos.h>
#include      "screen.h"

void main()
{

  // Clear the VGA display:

      cls((char *)MK_FP(0xa000,0));

  // Save the previous video mode:

      int oldmode=*(int *)MK_FP(0x40,0x49);

  // Set the current mode to 320x200x256:

      setgmode(0x13);

  // Create a pointer to video memory:

      char far *screen=(char far *)MK_FP(0xa000,0);

  // Loop through all 200 pixels in a column:

      for (int i=0; i<200; i++)

  // Loop though all 256 colors:

      for (int j=0; j<256; j++)

  // Putting one pixel of each color in each column:

      screen[i*320+j]=j;

  // Wait for key to be pressed:

      while (!kbhit());

  // Then reset old mode and exit to DOS:

      setgmode(oldmode);
}
```

First, we clear the screen by calling the cls() function in SCREEN.ASM, and then we set the video mode to 13h by calling the setgmode() function (from the same file). To obtain access to video RAM, we create a far pointer called screen that points to the start of vidram.

Then we use a pair of nested for loops to access vidram. The first loop uses the index i to iterate through all 200 lines of the video display, while the second loop uses the index j to iterate through the 320 pixels on each line. The statement screen[i*320+j]=j calculates the position of the next pixel on each line and sets it equal to the value of j. The result is a series of 256 vertical stripes from the top of the display to the bottom, each in one of the 256 default palette colors. The output of the program is shown in Figure 3-7, albeit in shades of gray rather than color. Not only is the result rather pretty, but it shows you what the default VGA palette colors look like. Because there are only 256 colors in the VGA palette, we've only colored the first 256 vertical lines on the VGA display. If this strikes you as a bit unbalanced, you can color the entire display by changing the second for loop to read

```
for (int j=0; j<320; j++);
```

Now the first 64 colors will be repeated as the last 64 stripes on the display.

What we've done here is to create a bitmap in video RAM in which each of the 256 VGA colors is represented in a repeating pattern. Now let's look at a way to create bitmaps that are a little more complex.

Storing Bitmaps

It's good to know how to create a bitmap in video RAM, but if that bitmap doesn't contain a picture of something, it doesn't help a lot. Painting the entire VGA palette on the display as a series of multicolored vertical lines is an interesting exercise, but it doesn't do us much good in creating computer games. So how do you go about creating the bitmap?

Figure 3-7 The default VGA palette, shown in shades of gray

You need a program that allows you to paint images on the screen of the computer and store them on the disk as bitmaps. There's not enough space in this book to develop such a paint program and it's a bit far afield from our subject matter. Fortunately, there are a number of excellent paint programs available commercially. The artwork used in programs in this book was developed with a program called *Deluxe Paint II Enhanced (DP2E)* from Electronic Arts. I highly recommend this program, though there are a number of other programs on the market of equal worth. Figure 3-8 shows a typical screen from *DP2E*. If you are serious about developing computer games of commercial quality, you should consider purchasing such a program. And if you plan to use the paint program with any of the utilities we create in this chapter, make sure the program is capable of generating PCX files (which I'll discuss later in this chapter) or that you have a utility that will convert other files to PCX files. (Many paint programs come with such conversion utilities.)

Compressing Bitmaps

In what form do paint programs store bitmaps on the disk? You might guess that a paint program would store an image on the disk as a 64,000-byte file containing a byte-by-byte bitmap of the image. This, however, is rarely the case. Disk space is limited and a straightforward bitmap is rarely the most efficient way to store an image. More often, the bitmap is stored in compressed format.

Compressing a bitmap so that it takes up less space on the disk is surprisingly easy to do. Bitmaps created with a paint program tend to contain large areas in a single color, so that much of the information in the bitmap is redundant. For instance, if the bitmap contains a horizontal line in which 100 pixels are all in the shade of blue represented by the number 45, the uncompressed bitmap will contain 100 bytes in a row with a value of 45 and would require 100 bytes of disk storage, but storing them as such would be repetitive and wasteful.

We can store these 100 bytes much more efficiently by using a system known as run-length encoding (RLE). Using RLE, we can store a run of a given number of identical pixels in just two byte-sized numbers, the first of which represents the number of pixels in the run and the second of which represents the value of the pixels in the

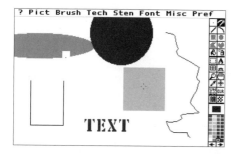

Figure 3-8 A typical screen from Deluxe Paint

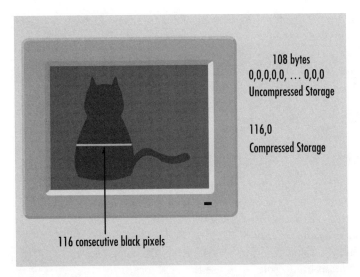

108 bytes
0,0,0,0,0, ... 0,0,0
Uncompressed Storage

116,0
Compressed Storage

116 consecutive black pixels

Figure 3-9 A horizontal strip of 116 consecutive black pixels can be stored as 116 zero bytes (assuming that palette color zero is black) or can be run-length encoded as the number 116 followed by the number 0

run. For instance, we could store our 45s as a pair of numbers: 100 and 45. We then use a decompression program later to expand these bytes back into their original form. Figure 3-9 illustrates the translation of runs of bytes in a file into RLE pairs, depicting a cat.

It's not hard to imagine a file containing a bitmap that consists of nothing but pairs of bytes like the above. For instance, if we wished to store a bitmap that consisted of a run of 37 bytes of value 139, 17 bytes of value 211, and 68 bytes of value 17, we could create a file consisting of only 6 bytes: 37, 139, 17, 211, 68, and 17. That's an extremely efficient way to store a bitmap!

Actual bitmaps, however, don't compress quite this easily. Although the typical bitmap created with a paint program (as opposed to a bitmap created by digitizing a photograph, for instance) may contain many runs of single-colored pixels, bitmaps also frequently contain sequences of differently colored pixels. RLE is not a particularly efficient way to encode single byte values. For instance, if a sequence of 6 bytes in a bitmap consisted of the values 1, 2, 3, 4, 5, and 6, an RLE scheme would store them as 1,1,1,2,1,3,1,4,1,5,1,6, where each byte is encoded as a run of only a single value. This actually doubles the amount of disk space necessary to store these bytes!

What we want is a way to turn RLE off and on in the file as we need it, so that we can store some bytes as a straightforward bitmap and use RLE compression on other bytes. When we encounter a run of multiple bytes of the same value in a file, we can use RLE to store it. But when we encounter a sequence of dissimilar bytes, we can turn RLE off.

We could invent our own scheme to do this, but there's no reason to do so—not quite yet, anyway—because there are a number of existing methods that do the job well enough. (However, we'll still need a compression scheme in some cases to handle the data once it has been loaded from the disk file.)

Graphics File Formats

Deluxe Paint II Enhanced uses two different methods for encoding files on the disk. One of these, the IFF format (recognizable by the extension .LBM on the files) derives from the Amiga computer, on which *DP2E* was originally written. A second method, called PCX encoding (recognizable by the extension .PCX on the files) runs with a number of other PC programs. In fact, the PCX format was originally developed for a PC paint program called *PC Paintbrush* from Zsoft. We'll use the PCX format to store bitmaps on the disk; there are several PCX images stored on the disk that came with this book.

Because we are storing bitmaps in PCX format, we need a set of subroutines to read PCX files from the disk and decompress them into a format we can display on the screen. In fact, this is a good opportunity to learn to use some of the VGA graphic techniques that we've discussed in this chapter and create a useful program in the process. For the remainder of this chapter, we'll develop a loader/viewer program that reads PCX files off the disk and displays them on the screen in mode 13h.

The PCX file format is quite versatile. It can be used to store images of differing sizes, created in a number of PC graphics modes. For simplicity's sake, though, we'll restrict our PCX routines to handling full-screen, 256-color mode 13h images.

Inside a PCX File

A 256-color VGA PCX file consists of a 128-byte header, followed by a compressed bitmap and 768 bytes of color descriptors comprising the palette used for the bitmap. The 128-byte header consists of several fields describing attributes of the PCX file, such as the color depth and the width and breadth of the image, plus 58 bytes of padding to round the header out to a full 128 bytes. (The PCX header might be expanded later so that these 58 bytes of padding will contain valid information about the file.)

Although we'll make little use of the PCX header in our programs, we can define it as a C structure so that we can access the individual fields within the header should that become necessary. Here's a C structure for the PCX header:

```
struct pcx_header {
  char manufacturer;    // Always set to 0
```

```
char version;              // Always 5 for 256-color files
char encoding;             // Always set to 1
char bits_per_pixel;       // Should be 8 for 256-color files
int  xmin,ymin;            // Coordinates for top left corner
int  xmax,ymax;            // Width and height of image
int  hres;                 // Horizontal resolution of image
int  vres;                 // Vertical resolution of image
char palette16[48];        // EGA palette; not used for
                           //  256-color files
char reserved;             // Reserved for future use
char color_planes;         // Color planes
int  bytes_per_line;       // Number of bytes in 1 line of
                           //  pixels
int  palette_type;         // Should be 2 for color palette
char filler[58];           // Nothing but junk
};
```

Most of the members of this structure are irrelevant for our purposes, though *manufacturer* should always be 0 (indicating that we are dealing with a PCX file and not some other type of file) and *version* should be 5 (telling us that the file supports 256-color graphics).

You'll notice that the header data do not require that the size of the PCX bitmap be a full screen. There are fields within the header (*xmin* and *ymin*) that can be used to define an upper left coordinate for the image other than 0,0 and fields (*xmax* and *ymax*) that can define a size for the image other than the size of the pixel matrix. This allows us to create PCX images that consist of a single rectangle plucked from a larger image. However, as we noted earlier, we're going to ignore these data fields for now and work only with PCX files containing a full screen image. If you try to use the PCX routines developed in this chapter to load an image that doesn't start in the upper left corner of the display and fill the whole screen, you'll get decidedly odd results.

A PCX Structure

Once a header structure is defined, it could be incorporated into a larger structure that can hold a complete PCX file, header and all:

```
struct pcx_struct {
  pcx_header header;            // Structure for holding the PCX
                               //  header
  unsigned char far *image;    // Pointer to a buffer holding
                               //  the 64000-byte bitmap
  unsigned char far *cimage;   // Point to a buffer holding
                               //  a compressed version of
                               //  the PCX bitmap
  unsigned char palette[3*256]; // Array holding the 768-
                               //  byte palette
  int clength;                 // Length of the compressed bitmap
};
```

Obviously, the header member of this structure will hold the header of the PCX file; it is therefore declared to be of the pcx_header type defined above. The image member is a far pointer to an array of type char which contains the 64,000-byte uncompressed bitmap and the palette field is a 768-byte array containing the color register values for the bitmap. We'll take a closer look at the role of the cimage pointer and the clength variable later in this chapter.

In order to read the compressed bitmap from the PCX file into the *image* array, we need to know exactly how the bitmap is encoded in the file. Fortunately, the PCX RLE scheme is quite simple. To understand it, you need to view the compressed bitmap data as a stream of bytes, portions of which are completely uncompressed and portions of which are compressed using a form of run-length encoding.

How is RLE toggled on and off in this stream? You'll recall that RLE generally takes the form of byte pairs, in which the first byte is a run-length value representing the number of times a byte is to be repeated in the uncompressed bitmap, and the second byte is the value to be repeated. In a compressed PCX bitmap, a byte value in the range 192 to 255 signals the start of an RLE pair. When a byte in this range is encountered in the stream, it should be regarded as a run-length value that has had 192 added to it. To decompress this run of bytes into a usable bitmap, we first need to subtract 192 from this byte, and then use the remainder as a run-length count. Finally, we must read the next byte from the stream and repeat that byte the number of times specified by the run-length count. Bytes that are *not* in the range 192 to 255 should be copied into the bitmap without change.

PCX Limitations

This raises a couple of interesting questions: Most obviously, how does the PCX format encode bytes of an uncompressed bitmap that are in the range 192 to 255? Wouldn't these bytes be mistaken for run-length values? Yes, they would, so the PCX encoding scheme (that is, the program that created the PCX file in the first place) must encode these bytes as though they were single-byte runs. This is done by preceding the value of the byte with a value of 193. What makes this scheme clever is that we don't have to worry about this special case when writing a PCX decoding program. The routines that we write for decoding runs of bytes will handle these single-byte runs automatically, the same way they handle longer runs of bytes.

Here's another question that might come to mind: If 192 must be subtracted from a byte to obtain a run-length count, how does a PCX file encode runs longer than 63 bytes? The answer is that a PCX file *can't* encode longer runs. Rather, longer runs of bytes are broken up into multiple run-length pairs. A run of 126 identical bytes, for instance, would be encoded as two runs of 63 bytes.

To sum up, we can decode the bitmap portion of a PCX file with this algorithm: Read a byte from the bitmap. If the value of the byte is in the range 0 to 191, transfer the byte into the bitmap buffer unchanged. If the byte is in the range 192 to 255, subtract 192 from the value of the byte. The result is the run-length count for the following byte; read another byte from the file and repeat it that number of times in the bitmap buffer. Repeat this process until the entire bitmap has been decompressed.

The PCX Class

The PCX file format presents an opportunity to dip our toes into C++ object-oriented programming. We'll create a class called Pcx so that we can easily make multiple Pcx objects, which will read PCX files off the disk and store them in a 64,000-byte buffer. Besides introducing the reader to some of the unique features of C++ syntax, the class provides concise mangement of the variables in the pcx structure discussed above.

On first conception of such a class, we might include one member variable of type pcx_struct in the class definition. This would make our Pcx class into a wrapper class because it provides an interface layer to an object (also wrapper classes often hide the actual object contents from direct public access). However there is no reason not to absorb the structure members directly into the class, since the pcx_struct is only being used to group together the header and buffer variables. We are not going to copy the pcx_struct nor use it to read or write a file. In fact, it makes life easier when writing code since we don't have to use the pcx structure as a middleman to point to one of its members.

The *header* will be made a private member of the class. The other variables, *image*, *cimage, palette,* and *clength* will be made protected members. This means that derived classes of our Pcx class will have access to them.

In C++, a class consists not just of data storage but of functions, called member functions, for operating on that data. There's really only one thing that we need a Pcx class to do for us: read PCX files. We'll also need a constructor—the function that is called automatically whenever an object of a class is declared—to initialize the pointers, and a destructor to perform cleanup duties. The Pcx class will consist of eight functions, two of them private to the class. Here's the class definition, which we will place in a header file called PCX.H:

```
class Pcx
// class for loading 256-color VGA PCX files
{
private:
                    // Private functions and variables for class Pcx
    pcx_header header; // Structure for holding PCX header
    int infile;       // File handle for PCX file to be loaded
protected:
    unsigned char far *image;    // Pointer to a buffer holding
                                 //   the 64000-byte bitmap
    unsigned char far *cimage;   // Point to a buffer holding
                                 //   a compressed version of
                                 //   the PCX bitmap
    unsigned char palette[3*256];// Array holding the
```

continued on next page

continued from previous page

```
                                              //  768-byte palette
      int clength;  // Length of the compressed bitmap
      // Bitmap loading function:
      int load_image();
      // Palette loading function:
      void load_palette();
public:
      // Public functions and variables for class Pcx
      Pcx();
      ~Pcx();
      // Function to load PCX data:
      int load(char far *filename);
      // Function to compress PCX bitmap
      int compress();
      // External access to image and palette:
      unsigned char *Image()
            { return image; }
      unsigned char *Palette()
            { return palette; }
};
```

All of those parts of the definition declared as private are exclusive to class Pcx and can only be directly used within the Pcx functions. Functions and variables declared as public, on the other hand, are available to all other modules that are linked with this one. As far as the other modules are concerned, the class header consists of six functions, Pcx(), ~Pcx(), load(), compress(), Image(), and Palette() because these are the only parts of the class accessible to them. Of these, Image() and Palette() are defined inline since they are for access to pointers in the pcx structure.

The constructor will set the buffer pointers to 0. Then when the object is destroyed, we can test the pointers to see whether they are still 0 or not. If they have been assigned a pointer address, the allocated memory can be released:

```
// Pcx class constructor
Pcx::Pcx()
{
      image = cimage = 0; // set initial pointers to 0
}

// Pcx class destructor
Pcx::~Pcx()
{
      // if pointers have changed from initial 0
      // then release memory
      if( image)
            delete [] image;
      if( cimage)
            delete [] cimage;
}
```

The PCX Loader

Now we need a function that will load the PCX information from disk. The load() function in our Pcx class loads a PCX file into a buffer. The text of the function is in Listing 3-5.

Listing 3-5 The load() function

```
int Pcx::load(char far *filename)
{

// Function to load PCX data from file FILENAME into
//   structure PCX.

        // Open file; return nonzero value on error

        if ((infile=open(filename,O_BINARY))==-1)
                    return(-1);

   // Move file pointer to start of header:

        lseek(infile,OL,SEEK_SET);

   // Reader header from PCX file:

        read(infile,&header, sizeof(pcx_header));

   // Decompress bitmap and place in buffer,
   //   returning non-zero value if error occurs:

        if (load_image()) return(-1);

   // Decompress palette and store in array:

        load_palette();

        close(infile); // Close PCX file
        return(0);      // Return non-error condition
}
```

To use this function, we must first declare an instance of the class Pcx. The earlier definition of this class only created a template for the class. Declaring an instance actually creates an object of the class, which can be used to load PCX files. We declare an instance of the class in much the same way that we would declare an ordinary C variable:

```
Pcx pcxloader;
```

Then we must call the function load() and pass it a filename, like this:

```
pcxloader.load("pcxfile.pcx");
```

In C++, the dot operator (.) separates the name of a member function of a class from the name of an object of that class. Thus, the name pcxloader.load() tells the compiler (as well as readers of our program) that we are calling the member function load() of the class Pcx to which the object pcxloader belongs.

Notice that header is used in the read() function to pass its address (using the address operator (&) in the form &header). We can do that within a Pcx class function since it is allowed access to private members of the class.

Reading the Bitmap and Palette

The load() member function calls two additional functions (load_image and load_palette) that are private to the class Pcx. These functions load the PCX file's bitmap into the array image and load the PCX file's color descriptors into the array palette, respectively. The text of these functions appears in Listing 3-6.

Listing 3-6 The load_image() and load_palette() functions

```
// Decompress bitmap and store in buffer
int Pcx::load_image()
{
  // Symbolic constants for encoding modes, with
  //  BYTEMODE representing uncompressed byte mode
  //  and RUNMODE representing run-length encoding mode:

      const int BYTEMODE=0, RUNMODE=1;

      // Buffer for data read from disk:

      const int BUFLEN=5*1024;
      int mode=BYTEMODE;  // Current encoding mode being used,
                          //  initially set to BYTEMODE
      int readlen;  // Number of characters read from file
      static unsigned char outbyte; // Next byte for buffer
      static unsigned char bytecount; // Counter for runs
      static unsigned char buffer[BUFLEN]; // Disk read buffer

      // Allocate memory for bitmap buffer and return -1 if
      //  an error occurs:

      if ((image=new unsigned char[IMAGE_SIZE])==NULL)
            return(-1);
      int bufptr=0; // Point to start of buffer
      readlen=0;    // Zero characters read so far

      // position file to offset for reading image
```

```
        lseek(infile,128L,SEEK_SET);
        // Create pointer to start of image:
        unsigned char *image_ptr=image;

        // Loop for entire length of bitmap buffer:

        for (long i=0; i<IMAGE_SIZE; i++) {
                if (mode==BYTEMODE) {           // If we're in individual
                                                //   byte mode....
                    if (bufptr>=readlen) { // If past end of buffer...
                      bufptr=0;               // Point to start

                    // Read more bytes from file into buffer;
                    //   if no more bytes left, break out of loop

                        if ((readlen=read(infile,buffer,BUFLEN))==0)
                                    break;
                    }
                  outbyte=buffer[bufptr++]; // Next byte of bitmap
                  if (outbyte>0xbf) {        // If run-length flag...

                      // Calculate number of bytes in run:

                      bytecount = (int)((int)outbyte & 0x3f);
                      if (bufptr>=readlen) {  // If past end of buffer
                              bufptr=0;             // Point to start

                       // Read more bytes from file into buffer;
                       //   if no more bytes left, break out of loop

                        if ((readlen=read(infile,buffer,BUFLEN))==0)
                                  break;
                      }
                   outbyte=buffer[bufptr++]; // Next byte of bitmap

                   // Switch to run-length mode:

                   if (--bytecount > 0) mode = RUNMODE;
                   }
               }

               // Switch to individual byte mode:

               else if (--bytecount == 0) mode=BYTEMODE;

               // Add next byte to bitmap buffer:

               *image_ptr++=outbyte;
               }
          return 0;
        }
```

continued on next page

continued from previous page

```
void Pcx::load_palette()

// Load color register values from file into palette array

{

    // Seek to start of palette, which is always 768 bytes
    //   from end of file:

        lseek(infile,-768L,SEEK_END);

    // Read all 768 bytes of palette into array:

        unsigned char *ptr = palette;

        read(infile,ptr ,3*256);

    // Adjust for required bit shift:

        for (int i=0; i<3*256; i++, ptr++)
            *ptr >>= 2;
}
```

The load_image() function performs the actual decompressing of the bitmap. It operates in two modes, defined by the integer constants *BYTEMODE* and *RUNMODE*. When the variable *mode* is set to *BYTEMODE*, a new byte is read from the disk file. If this byte is in the range 0 to 191, it is written directly to the image buffer. If it is in *PCXMODE*, the previous file byte (which is stored in the variable *outbyte*) is placed in the buffer, but no new byte is read. When a transition occurs from *BYTEMODE* to *RUNMODE*—that is, if a byte read in *BYTEMODE* is in the range 192 to 255—the variable *bytecount* is set to the value of the byte read from the file minus 192. This value is then decremented on each subsequent execution of the loop, until the run is completed and *bytecount* is restored.

The data is read from the disk using the library function read(). This function reads a large amount of data from the disk into a RAM buffer. This buffer must then be monitored by the code processing the data. In this case, the buffer is imaginatively named buffer. It is 5K in length. The variable *bufptr* monitors the current position of the next character in the buffer to be processed. When the value of *bufptr* reaches the end of the buffer, another read() is executed. The function knows when it has reached the end of the file because the read() function returns 0.

The load_palette() function performs the much simpler task of reading the 256 color descriptors into an array of type char. This is done with a single read() into the *palette* member variable. The numbers in the buffer must then be shifted left two bits to make them consistent with the format required by the palette-setting functions in the BIOS.

A PCX Viewer

We can use the Pcx class to create a simple program to read a PCX file from the disk and display it on the screen. The one thing missing from our Pcx class is a function which actually displays the data. A powerful part of C++ allows us to add a function to the already described class by way of inheritance. We can easily derive a new class called PcxView which uses the original Pcx class as a base class. Our new class has access to all of Pcx public and *protected* members. The text of the main program module, PCXVIEW.CPP, appears in Listing 3-7.

Listing 3-7 PCXVIEW.CPP

```
#include      <stdio.h>
#include      <stdlib.h>
#include      <conio.h>
#include      <dos.h>
#include      <iostream.h>
#include      "screen.h"
#include      "pcx.h"

class PcxView : public Pcx
{
      public:
            PcxView():Pcx() {;}
            void Draw(unsigned char *screen);
};

void PcxView::Draw(unsigned char *screen)
{
      // make a pointer to the image data (from base Pcx class)
      unsigned char *ptr = Image();
      // Loop through all 64,000 bytes, displaying each:
      //
      for(long i=0; i<64000; i++) screen[i]=*ptr++;

}

PcxView pcxobject;       // PCX class object

void main(int argc,char* argv[])
{
      if (argc!=2) { // Are there 2 arguments on command line?
            cerr << "Wrong number of arguments." << endl;       // If not...
            exit(0);                                            // Exit w/error
            }
      if (pcxobject.load(argv[1])) { // Get name of PCX
            cerr << "Cannot load PCX file." << endl;       // Can't open it?
            exit(0);                                        // Abort w/error
            }
      //
```

continued on next page

continued from previous page

```
// Display the PCX:
//
      cls((char *)MK_FP(0xa000,0));          // Clear the screen
      int oldmode=*(int *)MK_FP(0x40,0x49);  // Set VGA mode...
      setgmode(0x13);                        // to 320x200x256
      setpalette(pcxobject.Palette());       // Set PCX palette
//
// Create pointer to video display:
//
      unsigned char far *screen=(unsigned char far *)MK_FP(0xa000,0);
//
// Pass pointer to PcxView object Draw function:
      pcxobject.Draw(screen);

//
// Hold screen until a key is pressed, then reset
//   graphics mode and exit to DOS
//
      while (!kbhit());   // Wait for key press
      setgmode(oldmode);  // Reset old graphics mode
}
```

When compiled, this program must be executed with the syntax:

```
pcxview pcxfile.pcx
```

where PCXFILE.PCX is the complete filename of the PCX file that you wish to view. (This command line parameter is passed to the PCXVIEW program via the standard argv parameter. If you're not familiar with argv, check your compiler manual or read *Object-Oriented Programming in Turbo C++* [Waite Group Press™].)

This short program creates an instance of class PcxView, and then calls the load() function of the Pcx class to load a PCX file. Remember that PcxView inherits all of the public functions from its base class, Pcx so load() can be called. Next, it calls our set-palette() function to set the VGA color registers to the array values returned from pcxobject.Palette(). Our new function, Draw(), is then called which moves the entire bitmap in the array Image() into video RAM. Finally, it calls the library function kbhit() (prototyped in the header file CONIO.H) in a While() loop to hold the image on the display until the user presses a key.

Compiling and Running the Program

The compiled program is on the included disk under the name PCXVIEW.EXE. To give it a trial run, CD to the BYOFS\GENERAL directory where the files from the enclosed disk are stored and type

```
pcxview walkbg.pcx
```

This will give you an advance look at a PCX file we'll use in a program we'll develop in Chapter 4. (If you don't like having surprises spoiled in advance, you can skip this exercise.)

Making It Small Again

The compress() function is a feature of our Pcx class that we need to discuss here, though we won't be using it until much later in the book. This function takes the uncompressed bitmap in the image field and compresses it into a smaller bitmap in the cimage field. This might seem redundant, since the bitmap was already compressed in the PCX file on the disk, but we need a bitmap compression method that's faster than that used by PCX files. In this regard, the PCX compression scheme is less than optimal, so we're going to develop one that is more nearly optimal, at least for the specific purposes of the flight simulator that we'll develop in the course of this book.

In the next chapter, we'll examine the topic of transparent pixels. Don't worry about how a pixel can be transparent for now. When transparent pixels are in use, however, they are represented in a bitmap by values of zero. Certain bitmaps that will be in use in the flight simulator will have lots of transparent pixels in them, so it's important that we reduce the amount of time needed to process these transparent pixels, especially considering that these bitmaps will need to be redrawn in every frame of the flight simulator animation. This is simply a matter of reducing runs of zero pixels to a run-length pair, where the first byte is the run length and the second byte is a zero to indicate that this is the value to be repeated. (Since we won't be compressing any other runs besides zeroes, this second byte is actually unnecessary, but we'll include it to make it easier to expand this compression scheme to a full compression scheme at a later date, should we so desire.)

The PCX compression scheme uses run-length bytes only for runs of identical pixels. Our run-length scheme will use run-length bytes both for runs of identical pixels (in this case, zeroes) and for runs of differing bytes (which will include runs of identical nonzero pixels as well as runs of completely nonidentical bytes). In the former case, the run-length byte will be followed by a single byte of zero. In the latter case, the run-length byte will be followed by all of the data bytes in the run. For instance, if the compression function encounters the sequence of bytes 177, 98, 245, and 9, it would convert it to a run-length byte of 4 followed by the 4 original bytes.

What good does this do us? Surely it doesn't reduce the size of the file. In fact, it may actually expand it. But it also increases the speed with which the bitmap can be expanded to the display. Our PCX decoding function needed to check every byte of data to see if it was a run-length byte. With this new compression scheme, the decoding function can copy a run of differing bytes to video memory at the fastest speed it is capable of, which is considerably faster than the speed of the PCX decoder.

Since there are two kinds of runs in this RLE scheme—runs of zero values and nonzero values—we need a way to distinguish between these two kinds of runs. This means we need two kinds of run-length bytes, ones for runs of zeroes and ones for other runs. To distinguish between the two, we'll limit both types of runs to a length of 127 and add 128 to the value of the run-length bytes for runs of zeroes. Thus, the decoding scheme will be able to recognize runs of differing pixels because the run-length byte will fall in the range 0 to 127—or 1 to 127, since zero-length runs won't be allowed—and runs of zeroes because the run-length byte will fall in the range 128 to 255. (The decoding function will need to subtract 128 from this latter value before it can be used.) See Figure 3-10 for an illustration of this scheme.

The Compression Function

Now let's take a look at the function that converts the data in the image field into a compressed bitmap in the cimage field. The function, which is in the PCX.CPP file on the disk, is called Pcx::compress():

```
int Pcx::compress()

// Function to compress bitmap stored in PCX->IMAGE into
//   compressed image buffer PCX->CIMAGE

{
```

It starts off, as most functions do, by declaring some handy variables for later use:

```
int value,runlength,runptr;
unsigned char *cbuffer; // Buffer for compression
```

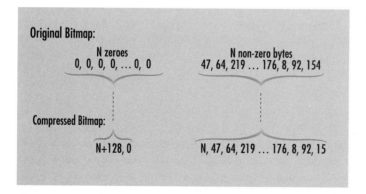

Figure 3-10 Conversion of an uncompressed bitmap into a compressed bitmap

Because data will be read from image and compressed into cimage, counters will be needed to mark the current position in both of those buffers.

```
long index=0;  // Pointer to position in PCX.IMAGE
long cindex=0; // Pointer to position in PCX-CIMAGE
```

A large amount of scratch pad memory will be needed for performing the decompression. The function allocates 64 K for that purpose and assigns the address of that block to the pointer variable *cbuffer*:

```
if ((cbuffer=new unsigned char[65530])==0) return(-1);
```

The *new* keyword command calls the operating system to allocate the memory block and returns a pointer to that block. If the memory isn't available, then the pointer will be zero, the function aborts, and it returns an error value to the calling function.

Now that the preliminaries are out of the way, we begin compressing data, looping through the bytes in image until we have read all 64,000 of them (though we will represent the length of the buffer by the constant IMAGE_SIZE, so that it can be changed more easily should this become necessary). A convenience pointer is used to hold the address of image and assigned by the inline Image() function:

```
unsigned char * image_ptr = Image();

while (index<IMAGE_SIZE) {
```

Compressing the data is a matter of reading bytes out of image_ptr and writing the appropriate runs of values into cimage. Since the variable index accesses the next value in image to be read, we can check to see if this value is a zero. If it is, then we've encountered a "run" of zeroes:

```
if (image_ptr[index]==0) { // If next byte transparent
```

Since this is the start of a run, the run-length variable must be initialized to zero:

```
runlength=0;  // Set length of run to zero
```

We then read as many consecutive zeroes as we can find (up to 127) out of image_ptr, counting the number of zeroes in the run with the variable *runlength*:

```
while (image_ptr[index]==0) {
   index++;        // Point to next byte of IMAGE
   runlength++; // Count off this byte
   if (runlength>=127) break; // Can't count more than
                             //  127
   if (index >= IMAGE_SIZE) break; // If end of IMAGE,
                             //  break out of loop
}
```

Notice that this loop will terminate either if the end of image_ptr is reached or the run exceeds 127 bytes. Of course, it also terminates when a nonzero value is found.

The length of the run having been calculated, we must write the run-length pair into cimage:

```
  // Set next byte of CIMAGE to run length:

  cbuffer[cindex] = (unsigned char) (runlength + 128);
  cindex++; // Point to next byte of CIMAGE

  // Set next byte of CIMAGE to zero:

  cbuffer[cindex] = 0;
  cindex++; // Point to next byte of CIMAGE
}
```

Note that 128 is added to the value of *runlength* to indicate that this is a run of zeroes.

If the next byte in image_ptr is *not* a zero, then this is a run of differing pixels. As before, we initialize the value of *runlength* to zero:

```
else {

  // If not a run of zeroes, get next byte from IMAGE

  runlength=0;  // Set run length to zero
```

Similarly, counting off the pixels will be done by looping while the value of the next byte is *not* a zero, but in this case the actual bytes in the run must be copied directly to cimage. Unfortunately, we must first write the run-length value into cimage, which we are not yet ready to do because we don't yet know how long the run will be. So we'll mark the spot where the run-length byte will be inserted later, saving the position in the variable *runptr*.

```
runptr=cindex++; // Remember this address, then point
                 //  to next byte of CIMAGE
```

Then we loop through the run, copying each byte into cimage until a zero is encountered (and watching, as before, for either the length of the run to exceed 127 or for the end of image_ptr to be encountered):

```
while (image_ptr[index]!=0) {

  // Get next byte of IMAGE into CIMAGE:

  cbuffer[cindex]=image_ptr[index];
  cindex++; // Point to next byte of CIMAGE
  index++;  // Point to next byte of IMAGE
  runlength++; // Count off this byte
  if (runlength>=127) break;      // Can't count more than
                                  //  127
  if (index >= IMAGE_SIZE) break; // If end of IMAGE,
                                  //  break out of loop
}
```

Finally, we place the run-length byte back at the position marked by *runptr*:

```
         cbuffer[runptr]=runlength; // Put run length in buffer
    }
}
```

This process is repeated until the end of image_ptr is reached. Before terminating the function, however, we must allocate memory for the actual cimage buffer. (Up until now, the scratchpad buffer cbuffer has been standing in for it.) Since cindex is marking the end of the compressed data, we use it to determine how long this buffer needs to be:

```
cimage=new unsigned char[cindex];
```

If there isn't enough memory for this buffer, we want to return an error to the calling function. If there is enough memory, we must copy the data from cbuffer into cimage. Either way, we need to get rid of the memory being used by cbuffer:

```
if( cimage != 0) {
        memcpy(pcx.cimage,cbuffer,cindex);
        clength = cindex; // Set length of compressed image
        }
delete [] cbuffer;       // Kill off temporary workspace
```

Finally, we return to sender a 0 or -1 depending on whether we were successful at creating and copying cimage:

```
return((cimage == 0)?-1:0);            // Return status
}
```

And we're done. The complete text of the compress() function is in Listing 3-8.

Listing 3-8 The compress() function

```
int Pcx::compress()
{
        int value,runlength,runptr;
        unsigned char *cbuffer; // Buffer for compression

        long index=0;  // Pointer to position in PCX->IMAGE
        long cindex=0; // Pointer to position in PCX->CIMAGE

        // Allocate 64K buffer in which to perform compression,
        //   return error if memory not available:

        if ((cbuffer=new unsigned char[65530])==0) return(-1);

        unsigned char *image_ptr = Image();

        // Begin compression:

        while (index<IMAGE_SIZE) {
                if (image_ptr[index]==0) { // If next byte transparent
```

continued on next page

continued from previous page

```
        runlength=0;  // Set length of run to zero

        // Loop while next byte is zero:

        while (image_ptr[index]==0) {
                index++;        // Point to next byte of IMAGE
                runlength++; // Count off this byte
                if (runlength>=127) break;      // Can't count more
                                                // than 127
                if (index >= IMAGE_SIZE) break; // If end of IMAGE,
                                                // break out of loop
                }

        // Set next byte of CIMAGE to run length:

        cbuffer[cindex] = (unsigned char) (runlength + 128);
        cindex++; // Point to next byte of CIMAGE

        // Set next byte of CIMAGE to zero:

        cbuffer[cindex] = 0;
        cindex++; // Point to next byte of CIMAGE
        }
    else {

        // If not a run of zeroes, get next byte from IMAGE

        runlength=0;  // Set run length to zero
        runptr=cindex++; // Remember this address, then point
                                // to next byte of CIMAGE

        // Loop while next byte is not zero:

        while (image_ptr[index]!=0) {

                // Get next byte of IMAGE into CIMAGE:

                cbuffer[cindex]=image_ptr[index];
                cindex++; // Point to next byte of CIMAGE
                index++;  // Point to next byte of IMAGE
                runlength++; // Count off this byte
                if (runlength>=127) break;      // Can't count more
                                                // than 127
                if (index >= IMAGE_SIZE) break; // If end of IMAGE,
                                                // break out of loop
                }
        cbuffer[runptr]=runlength; // Put run length in buffer
        }
    }

// Allocate memory for CIMAGE, return error if memory
//   not available:
```

```
cimage=new unsigned char[cindex]);

if (cimage !=0 ) {
       // Copy compressed image into CIMAGE buffer:

       memcpy(cimage,cbuffer,cindex);
       clength = cindex; // Set length of compressed image
       }
delete [] cbuffer; // Kill off temporary workspace
return((cimage != 0)); // Return status
}
```

Decompressing the Data

A compression function is useless without a corresponding decompression function. We don't need to decompress this data for any of the programs in the next several chapters, however, so we'll postpone the decompression function until we discuss the flight simulator, later in this book. For the record, however, the decompression function is quite simple: It checks the run-length byte and either writes a run of zeroes or copies the run of differing bytes, depending on which is appropriate. Unlike the compression function, this is almost trivial to implement. The main challenge will be making it run as quickly as possible, as you'll see.

Building the Program

To recompile the PCXVIEW.EXE program, enter the Borland C++ IDE, change to the directory that contains the code from the disk included with this book, BYOFS, enter the GENERAL directory, and open the PCXVIEW.IDE project file using the PROJECT - Open Project menu selection. Choose Run from the Run menu to compile and execute the program.

CHAPTER

4

......

4

Making It Move

If you know how motion pictures work, then you already understand the basic principles of computer animation. Pick up a strip of motion picture film and look at it carefully. You *do* have a strip of motion picture film lying around, right? If not, look at the strip of motion picture film in Figure 4-1. The film consists of a series of frames, each containing a still picture. When these still pictures are projected in rapid sequence on a white screen, they give the impression of motion.

Where did this motion come from? There's obviously no motion in the still frames that make up the strip of film. Yet somehow we perceive motion when we see this same sequence of frames projected on a screen. The motion is, in fact, in our minds. Each of the still pictures on the strip of motion picture film is slightly different from the one before it and our minds interpret these differences as continuous motion. But what we are seeing is a sequence of still pictures.

For instance, the film in Figure 4-1 shows a figure walking from right to left across the frame. In the first frame, the figure is near the right edge of the frame. In the second, it is nearing the center. In the third it is in the center.

If we were to view this film on a projection screen, it would appear that the figure was gliding smoothly from one side of the screen to the other, when in fact the figure is actually moving across the frame in a series of discrete jumps. But our brains, which expect to see continuous movement, obligingly fill in the blanks in the sequence. We create motion where no actual motion exists.

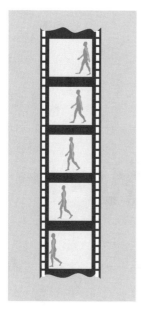

Figure 4-1 A strip of motion picture film depicting a person walking from right to left

Early movie animators like Max Fleischer and Walt Disney understood that the image in a motion picture frame didn't even have to be a real picture. It could be a drawing that bore only a passing resemblance to things that one might see in the real or imagined world. If these images moved in a realistic manner, the audience would accept them as real. The trick to making these drawn images seem to move was to draw the image in a slightly different position in each frame, so that an illusion of motion is produced in the minds of the viewers. If these animators could make fantastic images come to life on the screen, we should be able to make equally fantastic images come to life on a computer screen.

Motion Pictures, Computer-Style

In Chapter 3, we learned how to draw pictures made of bitmaps on the computer's video display. In this chapter, we'll make those pictures move.

There's no motion picture projector or movie film inside a computer. But computer animation is nonetheless produced on a frame-by-frame basis, just like motion picture animation. To show motion on a computer screen, we draw a sequence of discrete images on the monitor, one after another, changing each image in such a way as to produce the illusion that something is moving on the screen.

Much of the animation that you see on the video display of a computer, and almost all of the animation that you see on dedicated video game consoles, such as those manufactured by Nintendo and Sega, is performed with graphic objects known as sprites. The 3D animation routines that we develop in this book won't use sprites, but we'll discuss them briefly in order to illustrate the animation principles that we *will* be using.

What is a sprite? In the generic sense, a sprite is a tiny figure on the computer's video monitor that can be moved against a background bitmap without disturbing that bitmap. Mario the carpenter, hero of a popular series of games available on the Nintendo video game consoles, is a sprite. Some computers have special hardware that will move sprite images about on the screen with minimal effort on the part of the CPU (and surprisingly little effort on the part of the programmer). Alas, the IBM PC has no such hardware, so we'll have to write a special set of routines for sprite animation.

Sprites are ideally suited for implementation using object-oriented techniques, since sprites are objects on the computer screen. In this chapter, we'll develop a Sprite class that we can use to animate sprite images on the computer's video display. The Sprite class will be a full-fledged piece of object-oriented programming (OOP), illustrating many of the concepts of OOP code. All details of the sprite implementation will be hidden—encapsulated—in the Sprite class, so that the calling routine need merely invoke an object of the Sprite class and a sprite will appear magically on the screen.

Bitmaps in Motion

At the simplest level, a sprite is nothing more than a rectangular bitmap, like the ones we've discussed earlier. The sprite bitmap is generally quite small, much smaller than the screen. Some impressive animation has been produced on computers such as the Commodore Amiga using sprites that take up a substantial portion of the video display. The larger the sprite, the longer it takes to animate, especially on a computer that offers no special hardware support for sprite drawing. Programs with big sprites tend to run much more slowly than programs with small sprites. In this chapter we'll use relatively small sprites.

Figure 4-2 shows an enlarged image of a sprite as a walker man. (The original, unexpanded sprite is seen in the upper left corner.) Although shown here in grayscale,

Figure 4-2 Expanded image of a sprite in the form of a walker

the original version of this sprite is a multicolor image suitable for display in the VGA 256-color mode 13h. In fact, this sprite is part of an entire sequence of sprites stored on the enclosed disk in a PCX file called WALKMAN.PCX. You can use the PCX viewer we developed in Chapter 3 to view this file.

Of course, the image that you see in Figure 4-2 is represented in the computer's memory as a bitmap. As with other mode 13h bitmaps, each pixel in the bitmap consists of a single byte value representing the color register that stores the color descriptor for that pixel. This particular sprite is arranged in a rectangle that is 24 pixels wide by 24 pixels tall. Thus, the bitmap for the sprite consists of 24x24 or 576 bytes.

We can store such a bitmap in an array of type char. To animate the image, however, we must have a way to put the sprite bitmap on the screen and make it move. Putting the bitmap on the screen is easy; we just have to copy the bitmap to the appropriate location in video memory, as shown in Figure 4-3. Making it move is trickier.

A moment ago, we said that animation is a matter of putting a sequence of images on the screen and changing each image in such a way that they seem to move. We don't have to change the whole image for each frame of the animation, just the part or parts that move. With sprite animation, the part that moves is usually just the sprite. So only the sprite itself has to change from frame to frame. The simplest way to animate a sprite is to draw the sprite in one position, leave it there for a fraction of a second, and erase it and draw it in a new position. By doing this repeatedly, the sprite will seem to move across the display.

Erasing the sprite is the tricky part. Usually, we will want to animate sprites against a detailed background and we must be careful not to erase the background along with the sprite. Unfortunately, the background is obliterated by the actual act of drawing

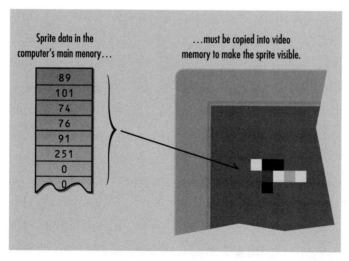

Figure 4-3 Copying sprites into video memory

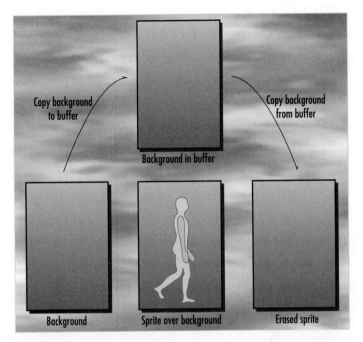

Figure 4-4 The background is copied to a buffer before the sprite is drawn over it

the sprite in video memory. The trick is to save the background *before* we draw the sprite, and then erase the sprite by drawing the saved background over the top of it, as in Figure 4-4.

A Structure for Sprites

With that information, we can create a data structure that will hold all the information that we need to draw and animate a sprite. This structure will have six members. It will contain a pointer to the array that holds the sprite bitmap and hold a second pointer to a similar array that can be used to store the background image which is obliterated when the sprite is drawn over it. Since we'll want to animate sprites of varying sizes, the structure will have two integer fields to hold the width and height of the sprite in pixels. Finally, we'll need two more integer fields to hold the *x,y* coordinates of the upper left corner of the sprite, so we know where to draw the sprite on the screen.

Ordinarily, all of this information could be placed in a structure like this:

```
struct sprite_struc {
  char far *image;  // Pointer to array containing
```

continued on next page

continued from previous page

```
                           // sprite bitmaps
    char far *savebuffer;  // Pointer to array for saving
                           // sprite background
    int width,height;      // Width and height of sprite in pixels
    int x,y;               // Current x,y coordinates of sprite
};
```

With C++, however, these fields can be encapsulated as private variables within a class instead of public variables within a structure. As many instances of that class can then be declared as there are sprites. Let's see how this is done.

Building a Sprite Class

In C++, a class consists not just of data storage but of functions, called member functions, for operating on that data. For our Sprite class, we'll need a function for putting the image of the sprite on the video display at a specified position and a function for erasing the sprite when it's no longer needed. The first of these functions will also perform the task of saving the background behind the sprite. Thus, to erase the image, the second function will only need to copy this background over the sprite, getting rid of the sprite and restoring the background at the same time. Before either of these routines can be called, however, we'll need a constructor that will reserve memory for the sprite data and initialize certain data values. Conversely, we'll create a destructor—the function called when an object is destroyed. This will perform cleanup tasks like the Pcx destructor in the last chapter. And we'll need a function that can copy sprite bitmaps from specified portions of a PCX file and store those bitmaps in arrays—a sprite grabber.

Each object of the Sprite class will also own a pair of private arrays called image and savebuffer, which it will use to store the sprite data and the sprite backgrounds, respectively. Because we'll define image as an array of pointers, which will in turn point to the actual buffers holding the sprite images, it can be used to hold multiple images of the sprite object, which can be used to enhance the sense of motion. We'll talk more about that later in the chapter.

Here's a declaration for the Sprite class:

```
// Declaration of sprite class:

class Sprite
{
private:
    char far **image;      // Pointer to sprite bitmaps
    int nsprit;            // number of sprite pointers
    int width,height;      // Width and height of sprite
                           // bitmap
    int xsprite,ysprite;   // Current x,y coordinates of
                           // sprite
    char far *savebuffer;  // Pointer to array for saving
```

```
                    //   sprite background
public:
    //Constructor for sprite class:
    Sprite(int num_sprites,int width,int height);
    // Destructor:
    ~Sprite();
    // Sprite grabber function:
    void grab(unsigned char far *buffer,int sprite_num,
              int x1,int y1);
    // Function to put sprite on display:
    void put(int sprite_num,int x,int y,
              unsigned char far *screen);
    // Function to erase sprite image:
    void erase(unsigned char far *screen);
};
```

The constructor, Sprite(), is the simplest of these member functions. (Remember
that the constructor for a class is called automatically whenever an object of the class
is declared.) In this case, however, it will also be necessary to pass several parameters
to the constructor, telling it how many sprite images need to be stored and what the
width and height of those images will be. The constructor then uses these numbers to
determine how much memory to set aside for the *image* and *savebuffer* arrays. Here's
the text of the constructor:

```
// Sprite constructor
// Allocates memory for NUM_SPRITES sprite structures
Sprite::Sprite(int num_sprites,int w,int h)
{
   image=new char far *[num_sprites];
   width=w;
   height=h;
   savebuffer=new char[width*height];
   nsprit = num_sprites;
        // initialize pointers
   for(int ii=0; ii < nsprit;ii++)
        image[ii] = 0;
}
```

The pointer array is initialized to 0 so that the destructor can free valid memory
pointers. The code for the destructor can then be written:

```
Sprite::~Sprite()
{
   for(int ii=0; ii < nsprit;ii++)
   {
        if(image[ii] )
                delete [] image[ii];
   }
   delete savebuffer;
   delete image;
}
```

That was simple enough, but now things start getting complicated. It's time to put together a function to draw a sprite on the video display.

A Simple Sprite Drawing Routine

If all we needed to do in drawing a sprite was to move a rectangular bitmap into a specified location in video memory, we could do the job with this relatively simple piece of C code:

```
int offset=y*320+x;   // Calculate video memory offset of
                      //   sprite coordinates
// Loop through rows and columns of sprite:

for(int row=0; row<height; row++) {
  for(int column=0; column<width; column++) {

    // Copy next pixel from sprite bitmap to video screen

    screen[offset + row * 320 + column]=
        image[sprite_num][row * width + column];
  }
}
```

In this fragment of code, image is the two-dimensional array that contains the sprite images, sprite_num is the number of the sprite image that we wish to display, screen[] is a pointer to either the video screen or an offscreen buffer in which the video image is being constructed, and x and y are the screen coordinates of the upper left corner of the sprite.

After the video memory location of the upper left corner of the sprite is calculated in the first line, the data for the sprite bitmap is copied to video memory with a pair of For loops, which use the height and width variables to determine how many pixels to copy. The final line of this routine copies the current pixel values stored in the sprite_num element of the image array to the current screen position. In this way, the sprite bitmap is copied to video memory.

There are two problems with this simplistic approach. The first is that it doesn't save the background. This can be remedied by adding a line to the code that reads:

```
// Copy background pixel into background save buffer:

savebuffer[row*width + column]=screen[offset + row*320
  + column];
```

If we place this line directly in front of the line that copies the sprite pixels to video memory, it will save each background pixel in an array called savebuffer[] a fraction of a second before we obliterate it.

Transparent Pixels

The second problem with our sprite drawing code is that it doesn't take transparent pixels into account. How can a pixel be transparent? We've said several times now that a sprite is represented by a rectangular bitmap. Yet it would be awfully boring if all sprites were rectangles. To avoid this, we usually define a certain bitmap value—often zero—as transparent. Transparent pixels are simply not copied into video memory. Wherever a pixel in the sprite is defined as transparent, the background image shows through. This allows us to create sprite images in any shape we want, as long as that shape fits inside the sprite rectangle. See Figure 4-5 for an illustration of this concept.

It's not enough, therefore, to move the bytes of the sprite bitmap into video memory. We must check every byte before we move it to make sure that it isn't zero. If it is, we simply skip over it, leaving the background pixel intact. To accomplish this, we rewrite the last line of the sprite drawing code as two lines; the first reads the current pixel from the image array and the second writes the pixel value to the display *only* if the value is nonzero:

```
// Get next pixel from sprite image buffer:

int pixel=image[sprite_num][row *width + column];

// If not transparent, place it in the screen buffer:

if (pixel) screen[offset + row*320 + column] = pixel;
```

Figure 4-5 A more-or-less diamond-shaped sprite

Speeding Things Up

Before we present the final version of the routine, there's another problem that we should solve. Animation is one of the most time-consuming tasks that we can ask the computer to perform and so our routine should be fairly optimized, to avoid slowing down the CPU unnecessarily. As written, the sprite code that we've seen so far is reasonably fast, but nowhere near as fast as it can be. For instance, we recalculate the position of each pixel, both in the image buffer and on the screen, for each iteration of the loop. We really only need to do this once. At the start of the routine, we can establish one variable that can serve as an offset into the image buffer (we'll call this variable *soffset,* for "sprite offset") and a second variable that serves as an offset into video memory (which we'll call *poffset,* for "pixel offset"). Now we simply increment these variables on every iteration of the loop, giving the video memory offset an extra increment at the end of each line of pixels to point it to the beginning of the next line. This is done by subtracting the width of the sprite from 320 (the width of the display) and adding the difference to the video memory offset, like this:

```
poffset+=(320-width);
```

We are now freed from having to recalculate the position of the pixel on every pass through the loop.

Putting Sprites

Listing 4-1 contains a complete sprite-drawing function, which we've called put() and have declared as a member function of class Sprite, which incorporates all of these changes:

 Listing 4-1 The sprite::put function

```
void Sprite::put(int sprite_num,int x,int y,
                 unsigned char far *screen)

// Draw sprite on screen with upper lefthand corner at
// coordinates x,y. Zero pixels are treated as transparent;
// i.e. they are not drawn.

{
   int poffset=y*320+x; // Calculate screen offset of sprite
                        //   coordinates
   int soffset=0;       // Point sprite offset at start of
                        //   of sprite

   // Loop through rows of sprite, transferring nonzero
   //   pixels to screen:
```

```
for(int row=0; row<height; row++) {
  for(int column=0; column<width; column++) {

    // Copy background pixel into background save buffer:

     savebuffer[soffset]=screen[poffset];

    // Get next pixel from sprite image buffer:

     int pixel=image[sprite_num][soffset++];

    // If not transparent, place it in the screen buffer:

     if (pixel) screen[poffset] = pixel;
     poffset++;
  }
   poffset+=(320-width);
}

// Record current coordinates of sprite:

xsprite = x;
ysprite = y;
}
```

We've added some code at the end of this function to record the current coordinates of the sprite in the *xsprite* and *ysprite* variables. These will be used by the erase() function to calculate the position of the sprite in order to erase it from the display.

The put() function is called with four parameters: the number of the sprite in the sprite array; the *x,y* coordinates at which the sprite is to be displayed; and the address of the video screen. (Once again, this allows us to draw into an offscreen buffer, should we so desire. We'll have more to say about this in a moment.)

Erasing Sprites

The erase() function is a lot simpler than the put() function. It's not concerned with transparent pixels or background pixels; it merely copies the background pixels saved by the put() function over the sprite image, effectively removing it from the screen. Listing 4-2 shows the erase() function:

Listing 4-2 The sprite::erase function

```
void Sprite::erase(unsigned char far *screen)

// Erase sprite from screen by copying saved background
//   image on top of it

{
```

continued on next page

continued from previous page

```
// Calculate video memory offset of sprite:

int voffset=ysprite*320+xsprite;
int soffset=0;

// Loop through rows and columns of background save
// buffer, transferring pixels to screen buffer:

for(int column=0; column<width; column++) {
  for(int row=0; row<height; row++)
    screen[voffset++]=savebuffer[soffset++];
  voffset+=(320-width); // Position pointer to next line
}

}
```

This function should be called before a new image of the sprite is drawn in a new position or the sprite will leave a trail of old images behind it. (This effect can be interesting under certain circumstances, but it's not the effect we usually wish to produce.)

Grabbing Sprites

The job of the sprite grabber is to grab a rectangular bitmap out of a larger (64K) bitmap and store it in an array. We can create the larger bitmap by using the Pcx.load() function that we created in the last chapter to load a PCX file from the disk. When we call the sprite grabber, we'll pass it the address of the buffer holding the large bitmap, the position in the sprite array in which to store the sprite bitmap, the coordinates of the sprite rectangle within the larger bitmap, and the dimensions of the sprite. Listing 4-3 presents the text of the sprite grabber.

Listing 4-3 The sprite::grab function

```
Sprite::grab(unsigned char far *buffer,int sprite_num,
                    int x1,int y1)
{

// "Grab" a rectangular sprite image from a 64K bitmap
//   and store in SPRITE[SPRITE_NUM]

  // Allocate memory for sprite bitmap and background
  //   save buffer:

  image[sprite_num]=new char[width*height];

  // Check if sprite runs past edge of bitmap buffer;
  //   abort if so:

  if ((x1+width>SCREEN_WIDTH) || (y1+height>SCREEN_WIDTH))
      return;
```

```
// Loop through rows and columns of sprite,
//   storing pixels in sprite buffer:

for(int row=0; row<height; row++)
  for(int column=0; column<width; column++)
    image[sprite_num][row*width+column]=
      buffer[(y1+row)*SCREEN_WIDTH+x1+column];

}
```

That's our Sprite class. The members of the class are summarized in Table 4-1. We'll store the class declaration in the file SPRITE.H and the text of the member functions in SPRITE.CPP. Now let's write some code that uses these functions.

Table 4-1 ■ Sprite Class Member Functions

`Sprite(int num_sprites,int width,int height)`

Constructor for Sprite class, called whenever an instance of the class is declared. Requires three parameters—specifying the number of sprite images, and the width and height of those images.

`~Sprite()`

The Sprite destructor is called whenever a Sprite object is destroyed, either by explicit use of the delete operator or by a declared Sprite instance going out of scope. There are no arguments to a destructor.

`void grab(unsigned char far *buffer,int sprite_num,int x1,int y1)`

Sprite grabber function. Removes a sprite image from a 64 K bitmap and places it in the image buffer. Requires four parameters—a pointer to the buffer holding the 64 K bitmap, the ordinal position of the sprite image within the image buffer (i.e., 0 for the first position, 1 for the second position, and so forth), and the x and y coordinates of the upper left corner of the sprite image within the 64 K buffer.

`void put(int sprite_num,int x,int y,unsigned char far *screen)`

Sprite put function. Puts a sprite image on the video display. Requires three parameters—the position of the sprite bitmap in the image buffer, the x and y coordinates at which to place the upper left corner of the sprite bitmap on the display, and a pointer to either video memory or to a 64 K offscreen buffer used to construct the video image.

`void erase(unsigned char far *screen)`

Sprite erase function. Erases the last image of the sprite drawn. Requires only one parameter—a pointer to either video memory or to a 64 K offscreen buffer used to construct the video image.

The Walkman Cometh

Earlier, we suggested you peek into the file WALKMAN.PCX using the PCX viewer that we developed in the last chapter. If you did, you saw seven pictures of a tiny walker. To demonstrate our Sprite class, we'll use three of those pictures (we'll save the rest for the next chapter) to create an animation of a man walking across the screen.

We'll grab those three pictures (the fifth, sixth, and seventh images, from left to right) using our sprite grabber. Then we'll put those images on the mode 13h display using the put() function of the Sprite class. We can create the illusion that the sprite is moving from the left side of the display to the right by putting the first image near the left side of the display, erasing it a second later, putting the second image a few pixels further to the right, and so forth. By switching back and forth between images of the sprite with its legs extended and images of the sprite with legs together, we can also create the illusion that the sprite is striding as it moves. That's why we've called this sprite WALKMAN.

Buffering the Screen

There's one flaw in this scheme. Because we erase the old sprite image before we draw the new image, there will be a fraction of a second during which there is no sprite image on the video display. As a result, the sprite will seem to flicker on and off very rapidly. Our sprite drawing and erasing routines are fairly fast, which will miminize this effect, but it won't get rid of the flicker altogether. The only way to eliminate sprite flicker is to draw each frame of the animation in an offscreen memory buffer, and then move the entire screen (or at least the portion of it in which the sprite is walking) into video memory all at once. By updating the screen in this manner, there will never be a moment when the sprite is missing from the display. One frame of the animation showing the sprite in one position will be smoothly copied over the previous frame of the animation showing the sprite in a different position. This is done so quickly that no flicker is evident.

To achieve this, we'll create a function called putbuffer() which will move a section of an offscreen buffer into video memory using the Borland C++ ANSI library function memmove(), which moves chunks of memory at high speeds from one set of memory addresses to another set. This is roughly equivalent to executing the 80X86 assembly language instruction MOV, one of the string instructions that we discussed in the previous chapter. Later, we'll rewrite the putbuffer() function in machine language and put it in the SCREEN.ASM file, but for now we'll write it in C++. The putbuffer() function is in Listing 4-4.

Listing 4-4 The putbuffer function

```
void putbuffer(unsigned char far *screenbuf,int y1,
                    int height)

// Move offscreen video buffer into vidram

{
  char far *screen=
    (char far *)MK_FP(0xa000,0); // Point at video memory

  // Call MEMMOVE() library function to move data
  //  into video memory:

  memmove(screen+y1*SCREEN_WIDTH,screenbuf+y1*SCREEN_WIDTH,
          height*SCREEN_WIDTH);
}
```

Since we won't necessarily want to move the entire contents of the video buffer into video memory, this function allows us to specify only a portion of the screen, though that portion must extend fully from the left side of the display to the right. The function takes three parameters: the address of the video buffer, the vertical coordinate of the uppermost line of the screen to move, and the number of lines of pixels to move. In this program, we'll just move the section of the screen in which the walkman does his walking.

Constructing a Sprite

Most of the rest of what our WALKMAN program will do involves calling the member functions of our Sprite class. We'll first create an object of the Sprite class that we'll call walksprite. The Sprite class constructor will be automatically called when we declare this object, so we'll need to pass the constructor a parameter telling it that we'll be grabbing three images of the sprite:

```
Sprite walksprite(NUM_SPRITES,SPRITE_WIDTH,
                    SPRITE_HEIGHT);   // Sprite object
```

Early in the program, we'll need to declare an integer constant called NUM_SPRITES and set it equal to 4, like this:

```
const int NUM_SPRITES=4;   // Number of sprite images
```

The general plan is to load the WALKMAN.PCX file into a Pcx class object buffer that we'll name *walkman* which is declared near the beginning of the program. Later, walkman's loaded image (buffer) is used in a repetitive call to the walksprite grabber to extract all three sprites from the same bitmap, using a for loop, like this:

```
for(int i=0; i<3; i++) walksprite.grab(walkmanpcx.image(),i,
        i*SPRITE_WIDTH+4*24,0);
```

The sprites are all in the upper portion of the PCX file, starting in the upper left corner, with additional sprites following every 24 pixels from left to right. This code will calculate their positions and grab them. Once again, we'll need to declare constants earlier in the program and equate them to the width and height of these sprites in pixels:

```
const int SPRITE_WIDTH=24;  // Width of sprite in pixels
const int SPRITE_HEIGHT=24; // Height of sprite in pixels
```

Setting Up the Walking Sequence

One of the trickiest parts of this program—but one that fortunately has an elegant solution—is determining the sequence in which to display the images of our WALKMAN sprite. Once we've grabbed the three images of the sprite, the walksprite object stores them in an array as elements 0, 1, and 2. Element 0 is a picture of the sprite with legs apart; element 1 is a picture of the sprite with legs together; and element 2 is a picture of the sprite with legs apart again, extending the opposite leg from that extended in element 0. We'll want to display these images in that sequence: 0, 1, 2. Then we'll need a fourth frame, showing the sprite with its legs together again. For that, we'll use element 1 again. To make this sequence easy to access within the animation code, we'll define it as an integer array called walk_sequence, like this:

```
int walk_sequence[]={0,1,2,1}; // Sequence of images for
                               // animation
```

You can see these sequences—walking left, walking right, and standing still—in Figure 4-6.

Looping through the Sequence

Now we can set up an infinite loop, using the old C trick of creating a For loop with no parameters—like this: for(;;), that will animate the sprite until the user presses a key. Here's the animation loop:

```
for(;;) {                      // Loop indefinitely
  for(int j=0; j<15; j++) { // Display fifteen frames
                            //   across screen
    for(i=0; i<4; i++) {     // Loop through four
                            //   different sprite images
      // Put next image on screen:

        walksprite.put(walk_sequence[i],j*20+i*5,100,
                       screenbuf);
      // Move segment of video buffer into
      // video memory:
```

```
      putbuffer(screenbuf,100,SPRITE_HEIGHT);
      for(long d=0; d<DELAY; d++); // Hold image on the
                                   //  screen for count
      walksprite.erase(screenbuf); // Erase image
      if (kbhit()) break; // Check for keypress,
                          //  abort if detected
    }
    if (kbhit()) break; // Check for keypress,
                        //  abort if detected
  }
  if(kbhit()) break; // Check for keypress,
                     //  abort if detected
}
```

We have to check three times to see if a key has been pressed, because the main part of the code is nested three levels deep in For loops. The outer loop repeats indefinitely (until the user escapes with a keypress), the next innermost loop repeats once for every four frames as the sprite walks from left to right, and the innermost loop cycles through the four animation frames, using the walk_sequence[] array to determine which frame to display next. A check is made with the kbhit() function to see if a key has been pressed. As we saw earlier, kbhit() returns a nonzero value if a key has been pressed by the user. It will continue returning a nonzero value until the keyboard value is read, which is never done in this program. Thus, the kbhit() value can be read every time *break* is used to escape from a level of the loop, yet it will still return nonzero each time.

Notice that the loop is deliberately slowed with a fourth delay loop, which iterates for the number of repetitions determined by the constant delay. This constant will be set at the beginning of the program and can be used to fine-tune the speed of the animation for a specific machine. If you find that this animation runs too quickly on your

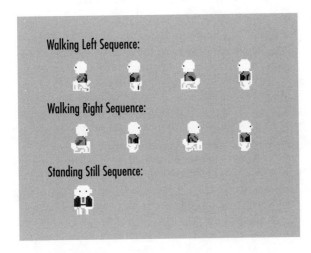

Figure 4-6 The three animation sequences, two of which consist of four frames and one of which has only a single frame

machine, increase the value of the constant delay. If it runs too slowly, decrease the value of delay.

Incidentally, before any of the above can be done, a background image must be loaded for our sprite to be animated against. Without a background, we couldn't be sure if the transparent pixels in our sprite image were truly transparent, or if the image was being properly erased and the background properly saved. We'll load this image from the file WALKBG.PCX, which is on the disk that came with this book.

Walkman Struts His Stuff

Listing 4-5 contains the complete text for the main module of the program WALKMAN.

 ## Listing 4-5 WALKMAN.CPP

```
#include   <stdio.h>
#include   <dos.h>
#include   <conio.h>
#include   <alloc.h>
#include   <mem.h>
#include   "sprite.h"
#include   "pcx.h"
#include   "screen.h"


const int NUM_SPRITES=4;            // Number of sprite images
const int SPRITE_WIDTH=24;          // Width of sprite in pixels
const int SPRITE_HEIGHT=24;         // Height of sprite in pixels
const long DELAY=40000;             // Delay factor to determine
                                    // animation speed. (Adjust
                                    // this factor to find the
                                    // proper speed for your machine)

// Function prototypes:
void putbuffer(unsigned char far *screenbuf,int y1, int height);
// Global variable declarations:

unsigned char far *screenbuf;       // 64000 byte array to hold
                                    // screen image
int     walk_sequence[]={0,1,2,1};  // Sequence of images for
                                    // animation

Pcx     walkman,walkbg;             // Pcx objects to load bitmaps
                                    // A Sprite object:
Sprite walksprite(NUM_SPRITES,SPRITE_WIDTH, SPRITE_HEIGHT);

void main()
{
  int oldmode;                // Storage for old video mode number
```

```
//Load PCX file for background, abort if not found:

    if (walkman.load("walkman.pcx")) {
        cout << "Cannot load WALKMAN.PCX file." << endl;
    }
    else {
        // Set up for animation:

            cls((char *)MK_FP(0xa000,0));           // Clear the screen
            oldmode=*(int *)MK_FP(0x40,0x49);       // Save old mode
            setgmode(0x13);                         // Set video mode to
                                                    //   13h

            setpalette(walkman.Palette());          // Set VGA palette to
                                                    //   PCX palette
            walkbg.load("walkbg.pcx");              // Load sprite PCX
            screenbuf=new unsigned char[64000];     // Create offscreen
                                                    //   video buffer
            memmove(screenbuf,walkbg.Image(),64000); // Move background
                                                    //   image into buffer
            putbuffer(screenbuf,0,SCREEN_HEIGHT);   // Move offscreen
                                                    // buffer to vidram


        // Grab three sprite bitmaps from PCX bitmap:

        for(int i=0; i<3; i++)
            walksprite.grab(walkman.Image(),i,i*SPRITE_WIDTH+4*24,0);

        // Loop repeatedly through animation frames, moving
        //   the image from the left side of the display to the
        //   right:

        for(;;) {                                   // Loop indefinitely
            for(int j=0; j<15; j++) {               // Display fifteen frames
                                                    // across screen
                for(i=0; i<4; i++) {                // Loop through four
                                                    // different sprite images
                                                    // Put next image on screen:
                    walksprite.put(walk_sequence[i],j*20+i*5,100, screenbuf);
                                                    // Move segment of video
                                                    // buffer into video memory:
                    putbuffer(screenbuf,100,SPRITE_HEIGHT);
                    for(long d=0; d<DELAY; d++); // Hold image on the
                                                    // screen for count
                    walksprite.erase(screenbuf);// Erase image
                    if (kbhit()) break;             // Check for keypress,
                                                    // abort if detected
                }
                if (kbhit()) break;                 // Check for keypress,
                                                    // abort if detected
            }
            if(kbhit()) break;                      // Check for keypress,
                                                    // abort if detected
```

continued on next page

121

continued from previous page

```
            }
            if(screenbuf)
                delete [] screenbuf;
            setgmode(oldmode);                    // Restore old video mode
        }
}


void putbuffer(unsigned char far *screenbuf, int y1, int height)
{
        // Move offscreen video buffer into vidram

        // Point at video memory:
        char far *screen= (char far *)MK_FP(0xa000,0);

    // Call MEMMOVE() library function to move data
    //   into video memory:
    memmove(screen+y1*SCREEN_WIDTH,screenbuf+y1*SCREEN_WIDTH,
                    height*SCREEN_WIDTH);
}
```

When you run this program, you'll see the WALKMAN sprite walk across the screen against a textured background. Press any key when you're tired of watching the little fellow strut his stuff. Although this may not look as spectacular as a full-fledged video game, it embodies many of the principles used to produce such games. If you're of a mind to write a Super Mario Brothers-style game for the PC, these sprite routines will get you off to a good start. Should you want to start off a bit smaller and simply tamper with the WALKMAN program, load the WALKMAN.IDE project file into the Borland C++ IDE and use it to recompile this program.

Although 3D animation doesn't use sprites, it follows the same principles that we've illustrated in this program. Our 3D animations will be constructed as sequences of frames, in which each frame is constructed in an offscreen video buffer and moved into video memory to avoid flicker. Each frame will depict a slightly different portion of an animation sequence, creating an illusion of motion.

Before we get into 3D animation, however, there's one more topic we need to cover: the user interface. In Chapter 5, we'll introduce our WALKMAN sprite to the three forms of input commonly used in PC computer games—keyboard, mouse, and joystick.

Building the Program

To recompile the WALKMAN.EXE program created in this chapter, enter the Borland C++ IDE, change to BYOFS\GENERAL and open the WALKMAN.IDE file using the Project-Open menu selection. Choose Run from the Run menu to compile and execute the program.

CHAPTER

5

5

Talking to the Computer

Now you know how to animate a tiny figure on the video display of your microcomputer. You probably think you're pretty hot stuff! Well, you are, but you've still got a few things to learn. All the animation in the world can't produce a great computer game unless the user of the computer has a way to interact with that animation. We need to give the user a means of reaching into the world inside the computer and taking control over what he or she finds there. To put it in the relatively mundane terminology of computer science, we need to receive some input.

If you've been programming computers for more than 30 seconds, you probably know a few things about this subject. You'll no doubt know how to enable the user to input characters using C functions such as Getch() and Gets(). But game programmers need to know more about data input than the average COBOL programmer. Game programmers must be able to program such esoteric input devices as joysticks and mice, which aren't supported by the standard C libraries of I/O routines. Game programmers must process this input so transparently that the action on the computer screen never slows down when a key is pressed or a joystick button is pushed.

In this chapter, we'll put together a package of low-level input/output routines for dealing with the mouse, the joystick, and the keyboard. Then we'll write a class known as an event manager, which will process the input from these devices in such a way that the rest of our program code will never even know what device it's receiving input from, much less any of the dirty details of the input/output hardware that our low-level routines need to deal with.

Let's start out with the most esoteric of game I/O devices: the joystick.

Programming the Joystick

When Geraldo Rivera opened the safe of the SS Titanic on nationwide television, rumor had it that it might contain information on programming the PC joystick. Goodness knows, the information doesn't seem to be available anywhere else.

If you've ever browsed through libraries and bookstores looking for even a hint of information on this subject, as I have on occasion, you probably came away frustrated. If you were lucky, you found a brief description of the two ROM BIOS routines that support the joystick. (See Table 5-1 for a brief description of these routines.) But you probably found nothing at all on programming the joystick hardware. Well, fear not. I'll show you how to program the joystick and give you sample code for doing so.

Joystick programming is essential in writing flight simulators because the joystick is the ideal means of controlling an airplane. In fact, the joysticks used on microcomputers are modeled after the joysticks used by airplane pilots. A flight simulator without joystick control is like a day without sunshine. Or something like that.

Because most PC clones don't have a port for plugging in a joystick, at least not as they come out of the factory, not all PC game players have joysticks. The gameport, as the joystick port is called, must be purchased as an add-on board and placed in one of the PC's spare slots. Fortunately, some popular sound boards, such as the Creative Labs Sound Blaster, have joystick ports built in. Most serious PC game players have joystick ports on their machines, either as part of the sound board or on a separate board.

The original PC ROM BIOS, however, did not offer support for joystick input. Neither did the BIOS on the PC XT. It wasn't until the PC AT that BIOS support for the joystick was added. So that you won't have to worry about what generation BIOS your joystick routines are running on (and so you can see what's actually going on inside these routines) we'll write joystick routines that work directly with the joystick hardware and bypass the ROM BIOS altogether.

Analog versus Digital

If you've programmed the joystick on an Atari or Commodore computer, you'll need to forget everything you've learned. The PC joystick isn't much like those joysticks (or the joysticks on some dedicated video game consoles). The Atari/Commodore joystick is a digital joystick. The PC joystick is an analog joystick.

A digital joystick can only transmit a relatively small amount of information to the computer. It can tell the computer which of eight directions the stick is pointed and

Table 5-1 ■ Rom Bios Joystick Routines

```
INT 15H
 Function 84H
  SubFunction 0
  Reads status of joystick buttons
  IN:
    AH = 84H
    DX = 0
  OUT:
    Carry 1: No gameport connected
    Carry 0: Gameport connected
    AL: Switch settings:
        Bit 7: Joystick 1's first button
        Bit 6: Joystick 1's second button
        Bit 5: Joystick 2's first button
        Bit 4: Joystick 2's second button

INT 16H
 Function 84H
  SubFunction 1
  Reads joystick position
  IN:
    AH = 84H
    DX = 1
  OUT:
    Carry 1: No gameport connected
    Carry 0: Gameport connected
    AX: X-position of joystick 1
    BX: Y-position of joystick 1
    CX: X-position of joystick 2
    DX: Y-position of joystick 2
```

whether the joystick button (or buttons) is pressed. An analog joystick, on the other hand, can both report to the computer which direction the stick is pointing and how far the stick is pointed in that direction providing much more subtle and complex information to a program. But it can also provide more headaches for the programmer.

Most game programs don't require any more information than a digital joystick can give them. Super Mario surely doesn't need to know anything more than the direction he's supposed to be walking and whether or not he should be jumping. Our friend Walkman, whom we met in the last chapter, doesn't either. Flight simulators, on the other hand, benefit from added information about how far the joystick is being pushed, since this is similar to the information that real airplanes receive from real joysticks (such as the amount of thrust the pilot wishes to apply).

When using the joystick as an input device, we need to receive four pieces of information from the gameport, as illustrated in Figure 5-1. We need to know how far (and in which direction) the stick is being pushed horizontally and how far (and in which direction) the stick is being pushed vertically. We also need to know whether one of the two buttons is being pushed. Thus, we can divide the required information into four categories: x-axis (horizontal) information, y-axis (vertical) information, button 1 information and button 2 information.

Now, where does this information come from? And how do we use it in our program?

Any Old Port

Information from the PC joystick is received through an I/O port. I/O ports are physical connections between the CPU of the computer and external devices that are attached to the computer. The computer and the external device use the I/O ports as a means of exchanging data. The instruction set of the 80X86 series of microprocessors provides special instructions, conveniently called IN and OUT, that allow data to be received and transmitted, respectively, through these ports. Although it's possible to read the I/O ports in C++, this task is better performed in machine language. So we'll write a set of assembly language functions to do the job for us. We'll place these functions in a file called MIO.ASM, which can be assembled and linked to C++ programs. (You can find this file on the accompanying disk. This is called MIO instead of IO to avoid a name conflict with the ANSI IO.H.)

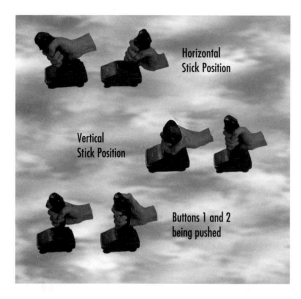

Horizontal
Stick Position

Vertical
Stick Position

Buttons 1 and 2
being pushed

Figure 5-1 What we need to know about the joystick

Every I/O port has a number. The numbers of I/O ports range from 0 to 65,535, though on a typical PC the vast majority of these ports are unused. The number for the gameport is 0201h. There are a couple of ways to receive data from an input port, but the common one used is to put the number of the port into the 80X86 DX register and use the IN instruction to input data from that port into the AL register pair. To input data from port 0201h, one must first put the number of the port into the DX register like this:

```
mov dx,0201h
```

Then data can be received from the port into the AX register like this:

```
in al,dx
```

This tells the CPU to input data through the port specified in register DX and place the value in the AX register.

To receive data from port 0201h, you must first transmit data *to* that port. It doesn't matter what data you transmit; sending any value at all to the gameport tells the joystick hardware that you'd like to receive data from it. Thus, you need only to execute these assembly language instructions to read the port:

```
mov dx,0201h   ; Put gameport address in DX
out dx,al      ; Send random data through port
in  al,dx      ; Get valid data from port
```

At the end of this sequence, the current status of the joystick will be in the AL register of the CPU. Now you need to decode this value to learn what the joystick is doing.

That sounds pretty simple. Unfortunately, whoever designed the PC gameport must have felt that this process was too simple, because the information received through the gameport is cryptic and takes some fancy programming to decode.

Among other things, it's necessary to examine individual bits within the gameport byte in isolation from other bits. (This is actually the easy part, though the next several pages are devoted to explaining how it is done.) Some method is thus required by which those bits can be isolated. Readers familiar with bitwise Boolean operations will already know how to do this, but it is possible that some readers have either missed out on the joy of bitwise operations or have assiduously avoided them. Alas, they can be avoided no longer, so we're going to digress for a few pages on the topic of Boolean algebra. Readers already familiar with this topic may skim. The rest of you . . . listen up!

The Mathematics of Truth

You probably have at least a passing familiarity with Boolean operators, named after the nineteenth-century logician and mathematician George Boole, who was seeking nothing less than a mathematics of truth. Whenever you write a C++ statement such as:

```
if ((a > 10) && (b != 0)) {
  // Do a bunch of things
}
```

you are performing Boolean operations. The C++ logical AND operator, which is represented by a double ampersand (&&), is used to tie together a pair of expressions (known as Boolean expressions) that are either true or false into a compound expression that will be true only if both of the individual expressions are true. Similarly, the C++ logical OR operator, represented by a double bar (||), can tie together a pair of Boolean expressions into a compound expression that will be true if either of the individual expressions is true.

Both C++ and machine language offer bitwise Boolean operators, which operate not on Boolean expressions but on the individual digits of binary numbers. The bitwise operators work much the same way their logical counterparts do, but instead of dealing with expressions that can be either true or false, they deal with digits that can be either 1 or 0. In C++, the binary AND is represented by the single ampersand (&) and the binary OR by the single bar (|). In 80X86 assembly language, they are simply called AND and OR.

The trick to understanding bitwise Boolean operators is to think about the concepts of true and false just as George Boole did: as the numbers 1 and 0, respectively. Seen in that light, it makes perfect sense that we could perform Boolean operations on individual binary digits. The bitwise AND operator, for instance, compares the individual digits in one binary number with the corresponding digits (i.e., the ones in the same bit positions) in a second binary number to produce a third binary number. If both digits in the first two numbers are 1s, the corresponding digit in the third number will be a 1, otherwise it will be a 0. Similarly, the bitwise OR compares the digits in such a way that if either of the digits in the first two numbers is a 1, the corresponding digit in the third binary number will be a 1. Only if both digits are 0s will the resulting digit be a 0. If you think of 0 as false and 1 as true, you'll see that these bitwise operators work exactly like their logical counterparts.

Because there are only two digits, 0 and 1, on which the bitwise operators may work, it is easy to list all possible single-digit bitwise operations and their outcomes. For instance, here are all the possible single-digit bitwise AND operations:

```
1 AND 1 = 1
1 AND 0 = 0
0 AND 1 = 0
0 AND 0 = 0
```

Similarly, here are all the possible single-digit bitwise OR operations:

```
1 OR 1 = 1
1 OR 0 = 1
0 OR 1 = 1
0 OR 0 = 0
```

Those lists are so simple that you could memorize them in a few minutes. However, it's not necessary to do so, since the concepts behind them are so simple that you could always recalculate them from scratch. Naturally, bitwise AND and OR operations on larger binary numbers are a bit more complex, but are still nothing more than a combination of the eight operations shown above.

What good do the bitwise operators do us? At the simplest level, they can actually be used to replace the logical operators in any programming system that consistently represents the concept of true with a binary number in which all the digits are 1s and the concept of false with a binary number in which all digits are 0s. (When represented as signed *ints,* these numbers would become -1 and 0, respectively.) Where bitwise operators really come into their own is when we need to mask portions of a binary number and when we need to combine two binary numbers into one.

Masking Binary Digits

For our purpose here, masking is the more important of these two concepts. There are times when we want to study certain bits of a binary number—the gameport byte, for instance—in isolation from the other digits. To do this, we must first zero out the other digits while leaving the digits that we are studying untouched. Zeroing digits is easy; protecting individual digits from being zeroed is tough. We must mask those digits to protect them from being lost. Enter the bitwise AND operator, which can be used to perform both the masking and the zeroing in a single operation.

This derives from an interesting property of the bitwise AND operation: When a binary digit of unknown value (i.e., one that could be either a 0 or a 1) is ANDed with a 0, the result is always 0, but when a binary digit of unknown value is ANDed with a 1, the result is always the same as the unknown digit. If you don't believe this, or have trouble understanding it, look back at the table of all possible single-digit AND operations. If one of the digits is a 0, the result is always a 0, regardless of the value of the other digit. And if one of the digits is a 1, the result is always the same as the *other* digit.

Thus, if we perform a bitwise AND on a byte of unknown value and a second byte in which selected bits are set to 1, the resulting byte will have 0s in all positions corresponding to 0s in the second byte while all positions corresponding to 1s in the second byte will have the same value as in the unknown byte. Effectively, we will have masked certain digits of the unknown byte while reducing the remaining digits to 0s.

For instance, if you wish to find out if bit 4 of a byte of unknown value is a 0 or a 1, you must first zero out the other bits while masking bit 4, and then test to see if the resulting byte is nonzero. If it is, then bit 4 was a 1. If it isn't, then bit 4 was a 0. This is done by ANDing the byte of unknown value with the binary number:

```
00010000
```

in which (you'll note) all bits except bit 4 are 0s. (If you're not familiar with the manner in which binary digits are numbered, you might want to skip ahead to the "Decoding the Gameport Byte" section of this chapter and read the first few paragraphs for an explanation.) Thus, the resulting byte will have zeroes in all positions except bit 4, which will have the same value as the original digit in the byte you are masking. Assuming the byte of unknown value was

11011100

then the result will be

00010000

But if the byte of unknown value was

01001111

the result will be

00000000

Simple, right? The byte 00010000 with which we ANDed the byte of unknown value is referred to as a *bitmask* or, more simply, as a *mask*, because it is used to mask certain bits in a byte while zeroing the rest.

Other Bitwise Operations

Similarly, the bitwise OR operator is used to combine two numbers in such a way that all 1 bits in the two numbers are also present in the resulting number. Suppose, for instance, you wanted to combine the low 4 bits of byte A with the high 4 bits of byte B. You could zero out the low 4 bits of A by ANDing it with 11110000 and zero out the high 4 bits of B by ANDing it with 00001111, then OR the two resulting numbers together to produce a result that has the low 4 bits of A and the high 4 bits of B. If this is less than clear, try working the entire operation out on paper until you are satisfied that it will do exactly this. (It's not necessary that you actually know how to do this, since we won't be using the bitwise OR operation in any of our programs.)

One other Boolean operator that you *will* need to worry about is the NOT operator. The logical NOT operator changes true to false and false to true, as in the sentence "Boolean algebra is endlessly fascinating...NOT!" The bitwise NOT flips bits, changing 0s to 1s and 1s to 0s, like this:

```
NOT 1 = 0
NOT 0 = 1
```

Thus, if you perform a NOT on a byte, every bit in that byte that was 1 becomes 0 and every bit that was 0 becomes 1. And on that note, let's return to our regularly scheduled discussion, already in progress.

Decoding the Gameport Byte

The byte of data that is received through port 0201h is composed of eight bitfields—that is, each bit in this byte conveys an important piece of information:

```
Bit 0    Joystick A X-Axis
Bit 1    Joystick A Y-Axis
Bit 2    Joystick B X-Axis
Bit 3    Joystick B Y-Axis
Bit 4    Joystick A Button 1
Bit 5    Joystick A Button 2
Bit 6    Joystick B Button 1
Bit 7    Joystick B Button 2
```

I should briefly explain here what the bit numbers mean. Bit 0 is the rightmost bit within any binary number and is also known as the least significant bit. The other bits are counted leftward from this position, with bit 1 being the bit to the left of bit 0, bit 2 being the bit to the left of bit 1, and so forth. In an 8-bit binary number—i.e., a byte—bit 7 is the bit in the leftmost position. Similarly, the leftmost bit in a 16-bit number is bit 15. The bit positions in an 8-bit number are shown in Figure 5-2.

In the case of the gameport byte, each of these bit positions conveys information about the joystick, the specific information depending on whether that bit position contains a 0 or a 1. In fact, you'll notice that the gameport byte contains information about *two* joysticks: joystick A and joystick B. That's because you can attach one or two joysticks via the PC gameport. We will concentrate on programming a single joystick.

Let's start with the easy part: decoding the status of the joystick buttons. If the bit that corresponds to a particular button is 0, the button is pressed. If the bit is 1, the button isn't pressed. While that may seem backwards, it isn't hard to understand, or to program.

In fact, we can easily "flip" the bits so that 1 represents a button that's being pressed by using the 80X86 NOT instruction, like this:

```
not al     ; Flip bits from gameport
```

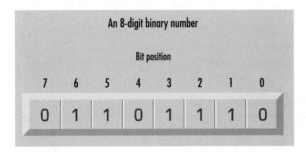

Figure 5-2 The bit positions in a binary number

The NOT instruction reverses the individual binary digits in the AL register, flipping 0s to 1s and 1s to 0s. Now we need to get rid of the digits that we don't want. Then we can use the AND instruction to mask out the bits that we're not interested in, isolating, for example, the button 1 bit for joystick A:

```
and al,164
```

The AND instruction compares two numbers on a bit-by-bit basis—in this case, the number in the AL register and the immediate number following it in the instruction. Every bit in AL that corresponds to a 0 bit in the second number is itself zeroed. Only those bits in AL that correspond to a 1 bit in the second number are left untouched. (If they are already 0s, they remain 0s. If they are 1s, they remain 1s.) In this case, we are ANDing AL with the number 164, which looks like this in binary: 0000010000. Note that only bit 42 is a 1. Thus, only bit 42 in the AL register is left unzeroed. This, by no coincidence, is the bit that represents button 1 on joystick A. We can also isolate the bit for button 2 like this:

```
and     al,328
```

This leaves bit 53 untouched. We can also AND the AL register with a value from one of the other registers or from the computer's memory, so that we can use the same assembly language subroutine to isolate the bit for either button, depending on what masking value we place in the register before we perform the AND instruction.

The Button-Reading Procedure

With all of the above in mind, we can build an assembly language procedure, callable as a C++ function, that reads either joystick button. Such a procedure appears in Listing 5-1.

Listing 5-1 The readjbutton function

```
GAMEPORT .EQU 0201h   ; Constant for gameport address

_readjbutton   PROC
; Read joystick button specified by BMASK
   ARG    bmask:WORD
   push   bp
   mov    bp,sp
   mov    dx,GAMEPORT    ; Point DX at joystick port
   mov    ah,0           ; Zero high byte of return value
   out    dx,al          ; Request data from the port
   in     al,dx          ; Get value from joystick
   not    al             ; Flip button bits
   mov    bx,bmask       ; Mask out all but requested buttons
   and    al,bl          ; ...and leave result in AX
```

```
    pop   bp
    ret
_readjbutton   ENDP
```

At the beginning of this assembly language procedure, we tell the assembler (via the ARG directive) that we will be passing a single parameter called BMASK to it. The BMASK parameter contains a number, which should be either 164 or 328, that is used as a bitmask to isolate the bit for one of the joystick buttons. The resulting value is placed in the AX register, where it becomes the value returned to C++ by the function. The calling routine can then test this value to determine if it is nonzero. If it is, then the joystick button is being pressed. We can call this function from C++ like this:

```
int button=readjbutton(JBUTTON1);
```

This sets the int variable button to a zero value if no button is being pressed and to a nonzero value if a button is being pressed. We'll also need to define the constant JBUTTON1 to represent the mask value for button 1 (which, as noted earlier, is 4).

A Bit of Information

Now we come to a somewhat more complex subject: reading the x and y positions of the stick. You may have noticed earlier that only 1 bit in the byte returned from the gameport is devoted to each of these positions. Yet the analog joystick can be placed in a large number of positions. How can this information be contained in a single bit?

It can't, exactly. When we send a value over port 0201h, the bits representing the stick positions are all set to 1, no matter what position the respective sticks are in. After a certain amount of time, the bits revert to 0s. The amount of time it takes for this to happen tells us what position the stick is in. Thus, in order to read the position of the stick, we must time how long it takes for this value to revert to 0.

For the horizontal (x-axis) stick position, for instance, it takes less time for this number to revert to 0 when the stick is pulled all the way to the left than when it is pulled all the way to the right. Timings for intermediate positions, including the center position, fall somewhere between the timings for the two extreme positions. For the vertical (y-axis) stick position, it takes less time for this number to revert to 0 when the stick is pulled all the way up than when it is pulled all the way down.

Timing the Status Bit

Timing this process isn't especially difficult. The easiest way to do it is to set up a loop using the CX register as a counter. That loop will look something like this:

```
mov   bx,byte ptr bmask   ; Get bitmask into AH
mov   dx,GAMEPORT         ; Point DX at joystick port
mov   cx,0                ; Prepare to loop 65,536 times
```

continued on next page

continued from previous page

```
   out  dx,al                   ; Set joystick bits to 1
Loop2:
   in   al,dx           ; Read joystick bits
   test al,ah           ; Is requested bit (in bitmask) still 1?
   loopne loop2         ; If so (and maximum count isn't done) try again
```

We first get the bitmask into the AH register. Then we output a value through GAME-PORT (which we defined in the earlier routine as a constant representing the value 0201h) to tell the joystick that we'd like to receive its status. Then we set up a loop by placing a value of 0 in the CX register.

Counting Down

Finally, we read the joystick status in a loop. The IN instruction receives the joystick status from the port. The TEST instruction ANDs the value in AL with the bitmask in AH, setting the CPU flags accordingly (but throwing away the result, which we don't need). The LOOPNE instruction decrements the value in CX and then loops back to the beginning of the loop if the result of the AND instruction wasn't 0 (i.e., if the joystick bit is still 1) and the CX register hasn't counted back down to 0. (Yes, the value in the CX register started out at 0, but the LOOPNE instruction performs the decrement before it checks the value in CX, so the first value it sees in the register is 0FFFFh, the machine language equivalent of -1.) This way, the loop terminates either when the joystick bit finally becomes 0 or when we've tested it 65,536 times, which is certainly time to give up. (This latter event should never happen, but it's a good idea to hedge our bets.)

When this loop terminates, the CX register should contain a value indicating how many times the loop had to execute before the joystick status bit returned to zero. This value will be negative, however, because the CX register has been counting *down* from 0 rather than counting up. To get the actual count, it is necessary to subtract this value from 0, which can be done by placing a 0 in the AX register and performing a SUB (subtract) instruction, like this:

```
mov  ax,0    ; Subtract CX from zero, to get count
sub  ax,cx
```

That leaves the result of the count in the AX register—which is where it belongs, since the AX register is where values must be placed to be returned to C by assembly language functions.

The Joystick-Reading Procedure

The complete assembly language procedure for reading the joystick is in Listing 5-2.

Listing 5-2 The readstick function

```
_readstick      PROC
; Read current position of joystick on axis specified by BMASK
  ARG   bmask:WORD
  push bp
  mov   bp,sp
  cli                          ; Turn off interrupts, which could affect timing
  mov   ah,byte ptr bmask      ; Get bitmask into ah.
  mov   al,0
  mov   dx,GAMEPORT            ; Point DX at joystick port
  mov   cx,0                   ; Prepare to loop 65,536 times
  out   dx,al                  ; Set joystick bits to 1
loop2:
  in    al,dx                  ; Read joystick bits
  test  al,ah                  ; Is requested bit (in bitmask) still 1?
  loopne loop2                 ; If so (and maximum count isn't done), try again
  sti                          ; Count is finished, so reenable interrupts
  mov   ax,0
  sub   ax,cx                  ; Subtract CX from zero, to get count
  pop   bp
  ret
```

Before we begin the loop, we turn off processor interrupts with the CLI (clear interrupt bit) instruction and we turn them back on again when we're done with a STI (set interrupt bit) instruction. Interrupts are signals sent to the CPU periodically (i.e., several times a second) by external devices, reminding the CPU to stop whatever it's doing and attend to some important task, such as reading the keyboard or updating the real-time clock. Interrupts slow the processor down in unpredictable ways. While this slowdown is normally almost imperceptible, it can make our count inaccurate, so we don't want interrupts to take place while we're looping. We can call this function from C++:

```
jx = readstick(JOY_X);
```

Here we've defined a constant to represent the bitmask that must be sent to C++ to remove the unwanted bits in the joystick status byte. The value returned to C++, which in this case is assigned to the variable *jx*, represents the number of times we had to loop before the bit for a specific joystick axis returned to 0. In this case, we're requesting the value for the *x* axis, so the returned value tells us the position of the *x* axis.

Calibrating the Joystick

Once we know where the center position is, it's relatively easy to determine whether the stick is left or right (or up or down) from that position. But how do we know what this number means? Which numbers represent which positions?

This tricky question is made all the trickier because the numbers will vary depending on the speed of the user's machine. The faster the machine, the more times our loop will execute before the joystick status bits return to 0. Thus, it is necessary to calibrate the joystick during the initialization of the program—that is, to establish what numbers represent what joystick positions on the user's machine. If you've played many computer games, you've probably been asked to move the joystick to various positions before the action got under way. This was the game programmer's way of calibrating the joystick. We'll see how to do this a little later in this chapter, when we design our event manager.

In the meantime, we're going to move on to a less esoteric form of input: the PC mouse.

Not an Input Device Was Stirring...Except for the Mouse

There are probably a few people out there who still think that a mouse is a tiny rodent with a taste for cheese. But most PC users know better. The input device known as the mouse has grown in popularity not with tiny nibbles but with leaps and bounds. Today, it's a rare PC that doesn't have a mouse tethered to it by its tail.

The mouse was developed at the Xerox Palo Alto Research Center (PARC) in the 1970s, but didn't really catch on with microcomputer users until Apple chose to make the mouse a primary input device for their Lisa and Macintosh computers, released in 1983 and 1984, respectively. All software on the Macintosh uses the mouse as an input device. PC software, by contrast, has normally been oriented to the keyboard, though more and more PC software has begun using the mouse as an input device. *Microsoft Windows* virtually requires it. So do many PC games.

The idea behind the mouse is that moving a tiny boxlike device on the table next to the computer in order to position a pointer on the computer's display is a more natural form of input than typing esoteric commands on the computer's keyboard. It's hard to argue with that logic, though there are still computer users who prefer the keyboard to the mouse, especially for text-heavy applications like word processing. Nonetheless, most flight simulators support mouse input, if only for positioning the airplane during flight. (Personally, I regard moving a mouse as an awkward way to fly an airplane, but good software should recognize that some users prefer this method—or don't always have a joystick.)

Listening to the Mouse's Squeak

Programming the mouse is a lot like programming the joystick—in principle, at least. The information that we require from the mouse port is pretty much the same that we require from the joystick port. We need to know whether the mouse has been moved and, if so, in what direction and how far. We also need to know if one of the mouse buttons has been pressed.

Fortunately, getting that information from the mouse is easier than getting the same information about the joystick. Every mouse sold comes with a mouse driver, a piece of software that is automatically loaded into memory when the computer is booted. This driver is much more complete than the rudimentary joystick support provided by the ROM BIOS and is available in every machine that has a mouse attached to it. We'll use these routines rather than work directly with the mouse hardware.

There are a large variety of functions available in the standard mouse driver. A list of five of these functions appears in Table 5-2. There are plenty of others, but for our purposes in this chapter, only these five are relevant. These functions initialize the mouse driver, turn the visible mouse pointer on and off, detect the pressing of a mouse button, and report how far the mouse has moved (and in what direction) since the last time the function was called.

The first three functions are quite simple. We don't need to pass them any parameters or receive any values from them in turn. We can simply write assembly language procedures that call these functions and return to C++. All of the mouse driver routines are accessed through PC interrupt 33h, using the assembly language instruction INT 33h. To tell the driver which specific function we wish to call, we place the number of the function in the AX register. Listing 5-3 features assembly language implementations of the first three mouse functions, each of which only loads the function number into the AX register and calls INT 33h.

Listing 5-3 Three mouse functions

```
_initmouse   PROC
; Call mouse driver initialization routine
   mov   ax,0              ; Request function zero (initialize)
   int   33h               ; Call mouse driver
   ret
_initmouse   ENDP

_disppointer   PROC
; Display mouse pointer
   mov   ax,1              ; Request function 1 (display pointer)
   int   33h               ; Call mouse driver
   ret
_disppointer   ENDP

_rempointer PROC
; Remove mouse pointer
   mov   ax,2              ; Request function 2 (remove pointer)
   int   33h               ; Call mouse driver
   ret
_rempointer ENDP
```

Table 5-2 ■ Mouse Driver Functions

```
INT 33H
 Function 00H
  Reset mouse driver
   IN:
    AX: 0000H
   OUT:
    AX: Initialization status
       FFFFH: Successfully installed
       0000H: Installation failed
    BX: Number of mouse buttons

 Function 01H
  Displays the mouse pointer
   IN:
    AX: 0001H
   OUT:
    Nothing

 Function 02H
  Remove mouse pointer
   IN:
    AX: 0002H
   OUT:
    Nothing

 Function 03H
  Get pointer position and button status
   IN:
    AX: 0003H
   OUT:
    BX: Button status
      Bit 0: Left mouse button (1 if pressed)
      Bit 1: Right mouse button (1 if pressed)
      Bit 2: Center mouse button (1 if pressed)
    CX: X coordinate
    DX: Y coordinate

 Function 0BH
  Get relative mouse position
   IN:
    AX: 000BH
   OUT:
    CX: Relative horizontal distance (in mickeys)
    DX: Relative vertical distance (in mickeys)
```

Button-Down Mice

Function 3, the mouse driver function that reads the mouse button, returns a value in the BX register indicating whether or not a button is being pressed. Bit 0 represents the status of the left button, bit 1 represents the status of the right button, and bit 2 represents the status of the center button (if the mouse has one). If a bit is 1, the corresponding button is being pressed. If the bit is 0, the corresponding button is not being pressed.

This routine also returns values representing the position of the mouse itself, but we're going to ignore these in favor of the values returned by function 0bh. Listing 5-4 is an assembly language procedure that returns the button status to C++.

Listing 5-4 The readmbutton function

```
_readmbutton    PROC
; Read mouse button
    mov    ax,3                  ; Request function 3 (read buttons)
    int    33h                   ; Call mouse driver
    mov    ax,bx                 ; Put result in function return register
    ret
_readmbutton    ENDP
```

When we call this procedure from C++, we can mask the result using the bitwise AND (&) operator to read only the bits for the button we're interested in, like this:

```
int b = readmbutton(); // Read mouse button
// If mouse button 1 (left button) pressed,
//   perform desired action:
if (b & MBUTTON1) do_it();
```

Once again, we've defined a constant for the mask. (All of these constants that we've been defining will turn up eventually in the header files MIO.H and EVNTMNGR.H.)

Mickeying with the Mouse

Finally, we want to call function 0bh, which reads the current position of the mouse relative to its position the last time we called this function. The relative positions of the mouse in the *x* and *y* directions are returned in registers CX and DX, respectively. They are measured in the standard unit of mouse movement, known (adorably enough) as the mickey, equal to 1/200th inch, so the mouse driver is capable of detecting very fine changes in mouse position. The values returned in registers CX and DX are signed values, which means that they can be positive or negative. If the value in the CX register is negative, it means that the mouse has moved to the left; if it's positive, the mouse has moved to the right. Similarly, a negative value in the DX register means that the mouse has moved up while a positive value means that it has moved down. You'll notice that it isn't necessary to calibrate these numbers, as it is with the numbers returned from the joystick. A value of 0 in either direction always means that the mouse hasn't moved since the last call to function 0bh.

The trickiest part of writing a routine for reading the relative mouse position is in returning the values to C++. Ordinarily, we return the result of a function in register AX. However, this method generally allows us to return a single value only; here, we want to return two values, the changes in the *x* and *y* positions of the mouse. Instead of returning these as function values, we'll pass the addresses of two variables, which we'll call *x* and *y*, from C++ to a function written in assembler. Then we can change the values of those variables directly from the assembler. We set up the variables with the ARG directive, like this:

```
ARG    x:DWORD,y:DWORD
```

Next, we use the LES command to place the address of the *x* and *y* parameters in the appropriate CPU registers:

```
les    bx,x
```

LES loads the address of the parameter *x* into the ES register and the register specified immediately after the command—in this case, the BX register. Thus, this command creates a pointer to *x*. We can then use this pointer to store a value in *x*:

```
mov    [es:bx],cx
```

The brackets around ES:BX tells the assembler that ES and BX together hold an address—the address stored in the *x* parameter. If everything has been set up properly on the C++ end of things, this should be the address of the variable that stores the relative change in the *x* coordinates of the mouse. The MOV instruction will move the value in the CX register into that address. We can then do the same thing with the *y* parameter.

The Mouse Position Function

The assembly language procedure in Listing 5-5 will now read the relative position of the mouse.

 Listing 5-5 The relpos function

```
_relpos    PROC
; Get changes in mouse position relative to last call
    ARG    x:DWORD,y:DWORD
    push   bp
    mov    bp,sp
    mov    ax,000bh          ; Request function 0bh
                             ; (relative mouse position)
    int    33h               ; Call mouse driver
```

```
    les     bx,x              ; Point es:bx at x parameter
    mov     [es:bx],cx        ; ...and store relative position
    les     bx,y              ; Point es:bx at y parameter
    mov     [es:bx],dx        ; ...and store relative position
    pop     bp
    ret
_relpos         ENDP
```

You can call this function from C++ like this:

```
relpos(&x,&y);   // Read relative mouse position
```

Because we use the address operators on the integer parameters *x* and *y* (and because we are compiling this program in the LARGE memory model), they are passed to the relpos() function as far pointers, each of which consists of a 16-bit offset followed by a 16-bit segment for a full 32-bit long integer. That's why we declared these parameters as DWORDs in the ARG directive.

Upon return from the function, the *x* and *y* parameters will be set equal to the relative mouse position—that is, the parameter *x* will contain the number of mickeys that the mouse has moved in the *x* (horizontal) direction and the parameter *y* will contain the number of mickeys that the mouse has moved in the *y* (vertical) direction.

That's enough about the mouse for the moment. I'll have more to say about it when we discuss the event manager, but for now let's talk about that least esoteric of all input devices: the keyboard.

All Keyed Up

The keyboard is the Rodney Dangerfield of input devices: It gets no respect. Every computer has one and every computer user is looking for something better—a mouse, a joystick, a touch screen. But, in the end, everybody comes back to "old reliable." Just about any kind of input that a program needs can be done through the keyboard. Even mouse-oriented programs generally allow the user to fall back on keyboard commands for commonly used functions—and more than a few allow the mouse cursor to be positioned via the keyboard cursor arrows. Only the most incorrigible of keyboard haters would try to input large quantities of text without one.

With more than 100 keys on the current standard model, the keyboard allows far more complex and subtle input than any other device, though the mouse is also pretty versatile. The most important thing about the keyboard as a game input device, though, is that it's the only input device that every user of a PC game is guaranteed to own. Some users may not have a joystick, others may not have a mouse, but everybody's got a keyboard.

The C++ language offers substantial support for keyboard input. Most of the keyboard-oriented commands, however, are inadequate for the rapidfire key access that a game program requires. Once again, we're going to bypass the C++ library and add some keyboard commands to our growing MIO.ASM file. This time, we'll access the keyboard via the ROM BIOS.

The BIOS Keyboard Routines

The ROM BIOS only has three keyboard routines (see Table 5-3), all of them callable through a single interrupt—INT 16h. As with the mouse driver routines, the functions available through this interrupt are specified by placing the function number in the AX register. We'll be using only two of the three functions—function 0, which returns the last key pressed, and function 1, which checks to see if any key has been pressed. We need the latter because the former function brings the program to a halt until a

Table 5-3 ■ ROM BIOS Keyboard Functions

```
INT 16H
 Function 00H
  Read Character from Keyboard
   IN:
    AH: 00H
   OUT:
    AH: Keyboard scan code
    AL: ASCII character
 Function 01H
  Read Keyboard Status
   IN:
    AH: 01H
   OUT:
    Zero flag clear=character waiting
     AH: Scan code
     AL: ASCII character
    Zero flag set=no character waiting
 Function 02H
  Return keyboard flags
   IN:
    AH: 02H
   OUT:
    AL: keyboard flags byte
     Bit 7=Insert on
     Bit 6=Caps Lock on
     Bit 5=Num Lock on
     Bit 4=Scroll Lock on
     Bit 3=Alt key down
     Bit 2=Ctrl key down
     Bit 1=Left shift key down
     Bit 0=Right shift key down
```

key is pressed; thus, we don't want to call it until we're sure that the user has pressed a key. (Function 1 also returns the last key pressed, but it doesn't inform the BIOS that we've read the key. Thus, subsequent calls to this routine will keep reading the same key over and over again, until we call function 0.)

These functions return the last key pressed in two forms: the ASCII code for the character represented by the key and the scan code for the key. The former is returned in register AL and the latter in register AH. You probably know that every character has an ASCII code, but what is a scan code? A scan code is a number recognized by the BIOS as representing a specific key in a specific position on the keyboard. Every key has a different scan code, even keys that represent the same character. The number keys on the numeric keypad, for instance, have different scan codes from the number keys on the top row. On the other hand, keys that represent more than one character (such as the number keys on the top row, which also represent punctuation marks when pressed along with (SHIFT)) only have a single scan code. A diagram of all the scan codes on the 101-key keyboard is shown in Figure 5-3.

We only need a single keyboard procedure in the MIO.ASM package. It will check function 1 to see if a key is waiting at the keyboard. If it isn't, the procedure places a 0 in the AX register and returns to C++. If a key is available, it calls function 0, obtains the scan code for the key, and returns that in register AX. The procedure is detailed in Listing 5-6.

Listing 5-6 The scankey function

```
_scankey PROC
; Get scan code of last key pressed
    mov     ah,1           ; Specify function 1 (key status)
    int     16h            ; Call BIOS keyboard interrupt
    jz      nokey          ; If no key pressed, skip ahead
    mov     ah,0           ; Else specific function 0 (get
                           ;   last key code)
    int     16h            ; Call BIOS keyboard interrupt
    mov     al,ah          ; Get scan code into low byte of AX
    mov     ah,0           ; Zero high byte of AX
    ret                    ; Return value to C program
nokey:                     ; If no key pressed
    mov     ax,0           ; Return value of zero
    ret
_scankey    ENDP
```

Managing Events

Now that we've got a set of assembly language procedures for dealing with input devices, what do we do with them? In general, we don't want our program to get too close to the input hardware being used to control it. Referencing the assembly language routines in our game code would make it harder to adapt our code later for different input devices, if we should decide to support them, or to port our program to other computers. We need a level of indirection between our game and the input devices. We need an event manager.

Roughly speaking, an event manager is a function that sits between the main program and the input hardware, telling the main program only what it needs to know about the user's input in order for it to proceed with the task at hand. The main pro-

Key	Code	Key	Code	Key	Code
Esc	1	A	30	Caps Lock	58
! or 1	2	S	31	F1	59
@ or 2	3	D	32	F2	60
# or 3	4	F	33	F3	61
$ or 4	5	G	34	F4	62
% or 5	6	H	35	F5	63
^ or 6	7	J	36	F6	64
& or 7	8	K	37	F7	65
* or 8	9	L	38	F8	66
(or 9	10	: or ;	39	F9	67
) or 10	11	" or '	40	F10	68
_ or -	12	~ or `	41	F11	133
+ or =	13	Left Shift	42	F12	134
Bksp	14	| or \	43	NumLock	69
Tab	15	Z	44	Scroll Lock	70
Q	16	X	45	Home or 7	71
W	17	C	46	Up or 8	72
E	18	V	47	PgUp or 9	73
R	19	B	48	Gray -	74
T	20	N	49	Left or 4	75
Y	21	M	50	Center or 5	76
U	22	< or ,	51	Right or 6	77
I	23	> or .	52	Gray +	78
O	24	? or /	53	End or 1	79
P	25	Right Shift	54	Down or 2	80
{ or [	26	Prt Sc or *	55	PgDn or 3	81
} or]	27	Alt	56	Ins or 0	82
Enter	28	Spacebar	57	Del or .	83
Ctrl	29				

Figure 5-3 The scan codes for the 101-key keyboard

gram doesn't need to know whether the user's input is coming from the keyboard, the joystick, the mouse, or some even more esoteric input device. The program only needs to know that an input *event* has occurred and it needs to know what that event is telling it to do. By making this into a class, all input events are handled by one object which organizes the code and the logic of the program.

Later in this chapter, we'll develop a version of the WALKMAN program from Chapter 4 that allows the user to control the Walkman, telling him to walk left or right or stand still. (See Figure 5-4.) To provide this program with user input, we'll use the input functions in MIO.ASM, but we'll write an event manager to stand between the animation code and the input. The event manager will translate the user's input into six kinds of events: LEFT events, RIGHT events, UP events, DOWN events, LEFT BUTTON events, and RIGHT BUTTON events. We'll use the LEFT events to tell the Walkman to walk left, RIGHT events to tell him to walk right, and LEFT BUTTON events to terminate the program. We'll ignore the other events, but we'll include them in the event manager because they could be useful in other simple games (and it seems silly to exclude them, even if we know we aren't going to use them).

The event manager that we create here won't be an event manager in the technical sense. A *real* event manager is interrupt driven, which means that it is always lurking in the background watching for input, even while the program is executing. The event manager we devise will essentially go to sleep when we aren't calling it. Some refer to this as a pollable event manager because you must poll, or explicitly ask it to check for events. On the other hand, it will rely heavily on at least two genuinely interrupt-driven event managers—the mouse driver that came with the mouse and the keyboard driver that's built into the BIOS. So it isn't really that much of a stretch to call this module an event manager, even if that isn't *quite* right.

The event manager will call the routines in MIO.ASM, watching for certain kinds of input that could represent the six events listed in the previous paragraph. What kinds of input events will it look for? Well, moving the joystick on the four main axes could represent LEFT, RIGHT, UP, and DOWN events, while pressing the joystick buttons could represent LEFT BUTTON and RIGHT BUTTON events. Similarly, moving

Walk
Left

Stand
Still

Walk
Right

Figure 5-4 Moving the joystick will generate events that cause Walkman to walk left, walk right, or stand still

the mouse in the four cardinal directions could *also* represent LEFT, RIGHT, UP, and DOWN events, while pressing the left and right mouse buttons could represent LEFT BUTTON and RIGHT BUTTON events. And pressing the four cursor arrows on the keyboard could represent LEFT, RIGHT, UP, and DOWN events, while pressing two other arbitrarily chosen keys (we'll use the E and T keys) could represent LEFT BUTTON and RIGHT BUTTON events.

The EventManager Class

The EventManager class will handle all of the nitty-gritty interfacing with the assembly code. The three input devices, the mouse, joystick and keyboard, will require variables to store their information. The mouse position, joystick calibration variables and last key pressed are all member variables private to the class and available only to EventManager class functions. A constructor and five functions will be created. One of these, init_events(), is made protected, meaning that the outside world will never be able to call it (but if we derive another class from our EventManager, that class will have access to init_events() also).

The declaration for the EventManager class is:

```
class EventManager
{
        private:
                int x,y;                // All purpose coordinate variables
                int xmin,xmax,xcent,ymin,ymax,ycent; // Joystick calibration variables
                int lastkey,keycount; // Keyboard variables
        protected:
                void init_events();     // Initialize event manager
        public:
                EventManager();

                void setmin();          // Set minimum joystick calibrations
                void setmax();          // Set maximum joystick calibrations
                void setcenter();       // Set center joystick calibrations
                int getevent(int);      // Get events from selected devices
};
```

The EventManager Functions

The job of the constructor is to initialize the EventManager. This is a simple call to the init_events() function. At present, all it needs to do is initialize the mouse driver. We could have done away with the init_events() function and included mouse driver calls in the constructor, but it is to the advantage of the derived class that we keep it in its own function. The constructor and initialization routine is in Listing 5-7.

Listing 5-7 The EventManager Class

```
EventManager::EventManager()
{
        lastkey = keycount = 0;
        init_events();
}


void EventManager::init_events()
{
        initmouse();    // Initialize the mouse driver
        rempointer();   // Remove mouse pointer from screen
}
```

We then need three routines for calibrating the joystick. These routines will wait for the user to move the joystick into a requested position—upper left corner, center, or lower right corner—and then set six variables to represent the values received from the readstick() function in those positions. Those values can determine where the joystick is pointing. In this program, we'll only be using the values for the joystick center position. The calibration routines are in Listing 5-8.

 Listing 5-8 EventManager class methods

```
void EventManager::setmin()
// Set minimum joystick coordinates
{
   while (!readjbutton(JBUTTON1));    // Loop until joystick button pressed
   xmin=readstick(JOY_X);             // Get x coordinate
   ymin=readstick(JOY_Y);             // Get y coordinate
   while (readjbutton(JBUTTON1));     // Loop until button released
}


void EventManager::setmax()
// Set maximum joystick coordinates
{
   while (!readjbutton(JBUTTON1));    // Loop until joystick button pressed
   xmax=readstick(JOY_X);             // Get x coordinate
   ymax=readstick(JOY_Y);             // Get y coordinate
   while (readjbutton(JBUTTON1));     // Loop until button released
}


void EventManager::setcenter()
// Set center joystick coordinates
{
   while (!readjbutton(JBUTTON1));    // Loop until joystick button pressed
   xcent=readstick(JOY_X);            // Get x coordinate
   ycent=readstick(JOY_Y);            // Get y coordinate
   while (readjbutton(JBUTTON1));     // Loop until button released
}
```

Before calling each of these functions, the calling program should print a message on the display requesting that the user move the joystick into an appropriate position, and then push joystick button 1. We'll see an example of this in a moment.

The Master of Events

Finally, we need a function that we'll call getevent(). This function will determine if any external device is producing input and translate that input into the six kinds of events we listed earlier. Although the calling program need not know which input device produces these events, we'll allow it to specify which input devices it wishes the event manager to monitor. The calling program will do this by passing the event manager an integer parameter in which each of the three lowest bits represents an input device. If bit 1 is a 1, then mouse events are requested. If bit 2 is a 1, then joystick events are requested, and if bit 3 is a 1, keyboard events are requested. We'll declare three constants—mouse_events, joystick_events, and keyboard_events—in which the appropriate bits are set to 1. To request a combination of events from the event manager, these constants need only be added together to form a parameter in which the appropriate bits are set. For instance, this statement requests events from all three devices:

```
event=getevent(mouse_events+joystick_events
               +keyboard_events)
```

The value returned by getevent() is also an integer in which the individual bits are important. In this case, the bits represent the events that have occurred. Since we're only monitoring six events, the sixteen bits in an integer are more than adequate to tell the calling routines whether or not these events have occurred. We'll declare six constants in which the appropriate bits are set, so that they can be tested against the value returned from getevent() to determine if the event has happened. These constants are *LBUTTON* (for LEFT BUTTON events) *RBUTTON* (for RIGHT BUTTON events), *UP*, *DOWN*, *LEFT*, and *RIGHT*. We'll also include a constant called *NOEVENTS* in which *none* of the bits are set to 1s. We can test the value returned from getevent() by ANDing it with these constants and seeing if the result is nonzero, like this:

```
if (event & RIGHT) do_it; // If RIGHT event, do it
```

That's easy enough, right?

Inside the getevent() Function

Internally, getevent() consists mainly of a series of if statements. First, the event manager checks to see which events are requested. It then looks for those events and sets the bits in the returned value accordingly. Without further ado, take a look at getevent() in Listing 5-9.

Listing 5-9 The EventManager::getevent function

```
int EventManager::getevent(int event_mask)
// Get events from devices selected by EVENT_MASK
{
        int event_return=NOEVENT; // Initialize events to NO EVENTS
        // If joystick events requested....
        if (event_mask & JOYSTICK_EVENTS) {
                // ...set left, right, up, down and button events:
                if (readstick(JOY_X)<(xcent-4)) event_return|=LEFT;
                if (readstick(JOY_X)>(xcent+10)) event_return|=RIGHT;
                if (readstick(JOY_Y)<(xcent-4)) event_return|=UP;
                if (readstick(JOY_Y)>(xcent+10)) event_return|=DOWN;
                if (readjbutton(JBUTTON1)) event_return|=LBUTTON;
                if (readjbutton(JBUTTON2)) event_return|=RBUTTON;
                }
        // If mouse events requested....
        if (event_mask & MOUSE_EVENTS) {
                // ...set left, right, up, down and button events:
                relpos(&x,&y); // Read relative mouse position
                if (x<0) event_return|=LEFT;
                if (x>0) event_return|=RIGHT;
                if (y<0) event_return|=UP;
                if (y>0) event_return|=DOWN;
                int b=readmbutton();  // Read mouse button
                if (b&MBUTTON1) event_return|=LBUTTON;
                if (b&MBUTTON2) event_return|=RBUTTON;
                }
        // If keyboard events requested
        if (event_mask & KEYBOARD_EVENTS) {
                // ...set left, right, up, down and "button" events:
                int k=scankey();        // Read scan code of last key pressed
                if (k==0) {             // If no key pressed
                        if (lastkey) {// Set to last active key
                                        k=lastkey;
                                        --keycount;   // Check repeat count
                                        if (keycount==0) lastkey=0;  // If over,
                                        // deactivate key
                                }
                        }
                else { // If key pressed...
                        lastkey=k;      // ...note which key
                        keycount=20;  // ...set repeat count
                        }
                // ...and determine which key event, if any, occurred:
                switch (k) {
                case ENTER: event_return|=LBUTTON; break;
                case TABKEY: event_return|=RBUTTON; break;
                case UP_ARROW: event_return|=UP; break;
                case DOWN_ARROW: event_return|=DOWN; break;
                case LEFT_ARROW: event_return|=LEFT; break;
```

continued on next page

continued from previous page

```
                        case RIGHT_ARROW: event_return|=RIGHT; break;
                }
        return(event_return);
}
```

The only part of the event manager that's at all complicated is the way in which it handles keyboard events. The problem with using the BIOS routines for keyboard input is that the BIOS doesn't tell us when a key is held down continuously. Unfortunately, this is precisely the information we need in order to use the keyboard to control a game. The BIOS will allow a key to repeat if it's held down long enough, but even so it will look to any program calling our scankey() function as though the key is being pressed repeatedly rather than being held down continuously, since the scan code for the key will be returned only intermittently by the BIOS. The only solution is to write routines that work with the keyboard hardware. This is a complex job, however, so I've saved it for the flight simulator. For now, we've jury-rigged a setup that makes it look like a key is being held down continuously. Basically, the event manager will return the same key for 20 calls in a row to getevent(), unless another key is pressed in the meantime. This makes it seem as though most keys are held down longer than they actually are, but it does simulate continuous key pressing.

The complete text of the event manager module appears in Listing 5-10.

 ## Listing 5-10 EVNTMNGR.CPP

```
#include      <stdio.h>
#include      "mio.h"
#include      "evntmngr.h"

EventManager::EventManager()
{
        lastkey = keycount = 0;
        init_events();
}

void EventManager::init_events()
{
        initmouse();  // Initialize the mouse driver
        rempointer(); // Remove mouse pointer from screen
}

void EventManager::setmin()
// Set minimum joystick coordinates
{
        while (!readjbutton(JBUTTON1));      // Loop until joystick button pressed
        xmin=readstick(JOY_X);               // Get x coordinate
        ymin=readstick(JOY_Y);               // Get y coordinate
        while (readjbutton(JBUTTON1));        // Loop until button released
}
```

```
void EventManager::setmax()
// Set maximum joystick coordinates
{
        while (!readjbutton(JBUTTON1));          // Loop until joystick button pressed
        xmax=readstick(JOY_X);                   // Get x coordinate
        ymax=readstick(JOY_Y);                   // Get y coordinate
        while (readjbutton(JBUTTON1));           // Loop until button released
}


void EventManager::setcenter()
// Set center joystick coordinates
{
        while (!readjbutton(JBUTTON1));          // Loop until joystick button pressed
        xcent=readstick(JOY_X);                  // Get x coordinate
        ycent=readstick(JOY_Y);                  // Get y coordinate
        while (readjbutton(JBUTTON1));           // Loop until button released
}


int EventManager::getevent(int event_mask)
// Get events from devices selected by EVENT_MASK
{
        int event_return=NOEVENT;  // Initialize events to NO EVENTS
        // If joystick events requested....
        if (event_mask & JOYSTICK_EVENTS) {
                // ...set left, right, up, down and button events:
                if (readstick(JOY_X)<(xcent-4)) event_return|=LEFT;
                if (readstick(JOY_X)>(xcent+10)) event_return|=RIGHT;
                if (readstick(JOY_Y)<(xcent-4)) event_return|=UP;
                if (readstick(JOY_Y)>(xcent+10)) event_return|=DOWN;
                if (readjbutton(JBUTTON1)) event_return|=LBUTTON;
                if (readjbutton(JBUTTON2)) event_return|=RBUTTON;
                }
        // If mouse events requested....
        if (event_mask & MOUSE_EVENTS) {
                // ...set left, right, up, down and button events:
                relpos(&x,&y); // Read relative mouse position
                if (x<0) event_return|=LEFT;
                if (x>0) event_return|=RIGHT;
                if (y<0) event_return|=UP;
                if (y>0) event_return|=DOWN;
                int b=readmbutton();  // Read mouse button
                if (b&MBUTTON1) event_return|=LBUTTON;
                if (b&MBUTTON2) event_return|=RBUTTON;
                }
        // If keyboard events requested
        if (event_mask & KEYBOARD_EVENTS) {
                // ...set left, right, up, down and "button" events:
                int k=scankey();      // Read scan code of last key pressed
                if (k==0) {           // If no key pressed
                        if (lastkey) {// Set to last active key
                                k=lastkey;
                                --keycount;    // Check repeat count
```

continued on next page

continued from previous page

```
                                    if (keycount==0) lastkey=0;  // If over,
                                                                 // deactivate key
                        }
                }
        else { // If key pressed...
                lastkey=k;      // ...note which key
                keycount=20;    // ...set repeat count
                }
        // ...and determine which key event, if any, occurred:
        switch (k) {
        case ENTER: event_return|=LBUTTON; break;
        case TABKEY: event_return|=RBUTTON; break;
        case UP_ARROW: event_return|=UP; break;
        case DOWN_ARROW: event_return|=DOWN; break;
        case LEFT_ARROW: event_return|=LEFT; break;
        case RIGHT_ARROW: event_return|=RIGHT; break;
        }
    }
    return(event_return);
}
```

Walkman Returns

Now that we've got a working event manager, let's put it through its paces. To do the honors, we'll call back our friend Walkman from Chapter 4. You may recall, if you used the PCX viewer to take a peek at it, that the WALKMAN.PCX file on the disk actually contains seven images of the little guy, even though we only used three of them in the program. Now we'll use the other four. In addition to seeing Walkman walk to the right, we'll now see him walk to the left and stand still. And you'll be able to use the keyboard, joystick, and mouse to make him do so.

This will require a number of changes to the Walkman program, however. For instance, instead of a single array containing the sequence of frames involved in the Walkman animation, we'll need three arrays, one for the sequence of frames involved in walking right, one for the sequence of frames involved in walking left, and one for the single frame involved in standing still. Here's the definition of the structure that will hold these sequences:

```
struct animation_structure {      // Structure for animation sequences
    int seq_length;               // Length of sequence
    int sequence[MAX_SEQUENCE];   // Sequence array
};
```

The sequence array, called sequence, will contain the sequence of frames. Although these sequences can be of variable length, it makes initializing the arrays somewhat easier if we fix their length. The constant MAX_SEQUENCE represents that fixed length. We'll define MAX_SEQUENCE elsewhere in the program as 4, since that's the longest animation loop that we'll need in our program. Here's the initialization for the actual animation sequences:

```
struct animation_structure walkanim[3]={
  // Animation sequences
  4,0,1,2,1,          // Walking left sequence
  1,3,0,0,0,          // Standing still sequence
  4,4,5,6,5           // Walking right sequence
};
```

Because there are three different animation sequences, we declare an array of three animation structures, each of which contains a sequence array. The first number in each initialization sequence is the number of frames in the sequence; the following numbers are the sequences of frames themselves.

At the beginning of the program, we'll declare the event manager object and give the user a choice of the three possible input devices. The user will type in a number representing which input device he or she will use, then we'll use that number to set the appropriate bit in the byte that will be passed to the getevent() routine. We won't do anything fancy to request this information from the user, just print a string on the screen with the insertion operator (<<) and cout and read a typed character with the extraction operator (>>) and cin. We'll need to loop until a number from 1 to 3 is typed (representing one of the three input devices), then use a switch statement to set the correct bit in the mask. Here's the routine:

```
EventManager evelyn; // Initialize event manager in constructor!

// Select control device:
cout << "Type number for input device:"     << endl <<
       "  (1) Keyboard"                       << endl <<
       "  (2) Joystick"                       << endl <<
       "  (3) Mouse"                          << endl;

  char key=0;
  while ((key<'1') || (key>'3')) cin.get(key);
  switch (key) {
      case '1': event_mask=KEYBOARD_EVENTS; break;
      case '2': event_mask=JOYSTICK_EVENTS; break;
      case '3': event_mask=MOUSE_EVENTS;    break;
}
```

If the user chooses the joystick as an input device, we'll need to calibrate it. We can do this by calling the three calibration routines in the event manager:

```
// Calibrate the user's joystick:

if (event_mask&JOYSTICK_EVENTS) {
      cout << endl << "Center your joystick and press button one" << endl;
      evelyn.setcenter();   // Calibrate the center position
      cout << "Move your joystick to the upper lefthand corner " << endl <<
```

continued on next page

continued from previous page

```
                "and press button one." << endl;
     evelyn.setmin();       // Calibrate the minimum position
     cout << "Move your joystick to the lower righthand corner"  << endl <<
                "and press button one." << endl;
     evelyn.setmax();       // Calibrate the maximum position
}
```

Now we'll perform the same initialization that we did in the last chapter, loading the PCX files for the sprite images and the background. The difference this time, is that we'll load all seven sprite images, like this:

```
// Grab seven sprite bitmaps from PCX bitmap:
for(int i=0; i<7; i++) walksprite.grab(walkman.Image(),i,
    i*SPRITE_WIDTH,0);
```

The main animation loop will now put a single frame of the animation on the screen and call the event manager. If it finds that there has been user input, it will change the variables involved in the Walkman's movement to reflect the input. For instance, if the Walkman is walking left and the event manager reflects either a RIGHT event or no event at all, the animation code will switch to the standing-still animation sequence. If the Walkman is walking right and a LEFT event (or no event) is detected, the standing-still sequence will also be initiated. But if the Walkman is standing still and a LEFT or RIGHT event occurs, the animation code will switch to the appropriate walking sequence. This will make the Walkman appear to stop walking when no input is received and to do a full 180-degree swivel when the joystick direction is reversed. Here's the animation code:

```
// Animation loop:

for(;;) { // Loop indefinitely


   // Point to animation sequence:

     animation_structure *anim=&walkanim[cur_sequence];

   // Put next image on screen and advance one frame:

     walksprite.put(anim->sequence[cur_frame++],
             xpos,ypos,screenbuf);

   // Check if next frame is beyond end of sequence:

     if (cur_frame>=anim->seq_length) cur_frame=0;

   // Advance screen position of sprite, if moving
   //   and not at edge of screen:

     if ((cur_sequence==WALK_RIGHT) &&
        ((xpos+XJUMP)<(320-SPRITE_WIDTH))) xpos+=XJUMP;
```

```
    if ((cur_sequence==WALK_LEFT) && ((xpos-XJUMP) > 0))
        xpos-=XJUMP;

// Move segment of video buffer into vidram:

    putbuffer(screenbuf,ypos,SPRITE_HEIGHT);

// Hold image on the screen for DELAY count:

for(long d=0; d<DELAY; d++);
    walksprite.erase(screenbuf);   // Erase sprite image
```

The number of the current animation sequence is in the variable *cur_sequence*. This is initially set to the constant STAND_STILL, though it can be reset to WALK_LEFT or WALK_RIGHT. The current frame of the sequence is in the variable *cur_frame*. This variable is incremented every time the sprite is drawn to the screen buffer. The program then checks to see if it's gone beyond the end of that particular sequence and resets *cur_frame* to zero if it has.

Here's the part of the program that calls the event handler:

```
// Process events from event manager:

int event=evelyn.getevent(event_mask);    // Get next event

// If left button, terminate:

if (event&LBUTTON) break;

// If no event, put sprite in standing still position:

if ((event&(RIGHT+LEFT))==NOEVENT) {
  cur_sequence=STAND_STILL;
 cur_frame=0;
}

// Else check for RIGHT and LEFT events:

else {
    if (event&RIGHT) {       // Is it a RIGHT event?
      // If so, go from standing still to walking right:
      if (cur_sequence==STAND_STILL) {
        cur_sequence=WALK_RIGHT;
       cur_frame=0;
      }
      // Or from walking left to standing still:
      if (cur_sequence==WALK_LEFT) {
        cur_sequence=STAND_STILL;
        cur_frame=0;
      }
    }
    if (event&LEFT) {          // Is it a LEFT event?
```

continued on next page

continued from previous page

```
      // If so, go from standing still to walking left:
      if (cur_sequence==STAND_STILL {
        cur_sequence=WALK_LEFT;
       cur_frame=0;
      }
      // Or from walking right to standing still:
      if (cur_sequence==WALK_RIGHT {
        cur_sequence=STAND_STILL;
        cur_frame=0;
      }
    }
  }
}
```

This looks terribly complicated, but it isn't. Like the event manager itself, this is just a series of nested if statements, which check to see what the event was and what the current animation sequence is. Depending on the combination of event and current sequence, the if statements determine what the next animation sequence will be and sets it appropriately.

The complete WALKMAN2.CPP module, which calls the event manager to animate the Walkman character under the control of either keyboard, joystick, or mouse, is in Listing 5-11.

Listing 5-11 WALKMAN2.CPP

```
#include      <dos.h>
#include      <conio.h>
#include      <mem.h>
#include      <iostream.h>
#include      "sprite.h"
#include      "pcx.h"
#include      "screen.h"
#include      "evntmngr.h"

const int NUM_SPRITES=4;     // Number of sprite images
const int SPRITE_WIDTH=24;   // Width of sprite in pixels
const int SPRITE_HEIGHT=24;  // Height of sprite in pixels
const int MAX_SEQUENCE=4;    // Maximum length of animation sequence
const int WALK_LEFT=0,       // Animation sequences
          STAND_STILL=1,
          WALK_RIGHT=2;
const int XJUMP=5;           // Movement factor for sprite
const long DELAY=10000;      // Delay factor to determine animation speed
                             // (Adjust this factor to find the proper speed
                             // for your machine)

// Function prototypes:
void putbuffer(unsigned char far *screenbuf,int y1,int height);
// Structure types:
```

```
// Structure for animation sequences:

struct animation_structure {
        int seq_length;              // Length of sequence
        int sequence[MAX_SEQUENCE];  // Sequence array
};

// Global variable declarations:

unsigned char far *screenbuf;       // 64000 byte screen buffer
// Animation sequences:
struct animation_structure walkanim[3]={
                4,0,1,2,1,            // Walking left sequence
                1,3,0,0,0,            // Standing still sequence
                4,4,5,6,5             // Walking right sequence
};
int cur_sequence=STAND_STILL;// Current animation sequence
int cur_frame=0;                     // Current frame of sequence
int lastevent=0;                     // Last event received from event manager
int xpos=150;                        // Initial x coordinate
int ypos=130;                        // Initial y coordinate


Pcx     walkman,walkbg;              // Pcx objects to load bitmaps
Sprite walksprite(NUM_SPRITES,SPRITE_WIDTH,
                SPRITE_HEIGHT);       // Sprite object

void main()
{
        int oldmode;      // Storage for old video mode number
        int event_mask;   // Input events requested by program

        screenbuf = 0; // Initalize to 0

        EventManager evelyn; // Initialize event manager in constructor!

        // Select control device:
        cout << "Type number for input device:"    << endl <<
                " (1) Keyboard"                     << endl <<
                " (2) Joystick"                     << endl <<
                " (3) Mouse"                        << endl;

        char key=0;
        while ((key<'1') || (key>'3')) cin.get(key);
        switch (key) {
        case '1': event_mask=KEYBOARD_EVENTS;    break;
        case '2': event_mask=JOYSTICK_EVENTS;    break;
        case '3': event_mask=MOUSE_EVENTS;       break;
        }

        // Calibrate the user's joystick:

        if (event_mask&JOYSTICK_EVENTS) {
```

continued on next page

continued from previous page

```
            cout << endl << "Center your joystick and press button one" << endl;
            evelyn.setcenter();        // Calibrate the center position
            cout << "Move your joystick to the upper lefthand corner " << endl <<
                    "and press button one." << endl;
            evelyn.setmin();           // Calibrate the minimum position
            cout << "Move your joystick to the lower righthand corner" << endl <<
                    "and press button one." << endl;
            evelyn.setmax();           // Calibrate the maximum position
            }

    //Load PCX file for background, abort if not found:

    if (walkman.load("walkman.pcx"))
            cout << "Cannot load PCX file." << endl;
    else {

            // Set up for animation:

            cls((char *)MK_FP(0xa000,0));        // Clear the screen
            oldmode=*(int *)MK_FP(0x40,0x49);    // Save old video mode
            setgmode(0x13);                      // Set video mode to 13h
            setpalette(walkman.Palette(),0,256); // Set to PCX palette
            walkbg.load("walkbg.pcx");           // Load sprite PCX
            screenbuf=new unsigned char[64000];  // Create video buffer
            memmove(screenbuf,walkbg.Image(),64000);    // Move background
                                                        // image into buffer
            putbuffer(screenbuf,0,SCREEN_HEIGHT);       // Move offscreen
                                                        // buffer to vidram

            // Grab seven sprite bitmaps from PCX bitmap:
            for(int i=0; i<7; i++) walksprite.grab(walkman.Image(),i,
                    i*SPRITE_WIDTH,0);

            // Animation loop:

            for(;;) {       // Loop indefinitely


            // Point to animation sequence:

            animation_structure *anim=&walkanim[cur_sequence];

                    // Put next image on screen and advance one frame:

            walksprite.put(anim->sequence[cur_frame++],
                    xpos,ypos,screenbuf);

                    // Check if next frame is beyond end of sequence:

                    if (cur_frame>=anim->seq_length) cur_frame=0;

                    // Advance screen position of sprite, if moving
```

```
// and not at edge of screen:

if ((cur_sequence==WALK_RIGHT) &&
  ((xpos+XJUMP)<(320-SPRITE_WIDTH))) xpos+=XJUMP;
if ((cur_sequence==WALK_LEFT) && ((xpos-XJUMP) > 0))
              xpos-=XJUMP;

// Move segment of video buffer into vidram:

putbuffer(screenbuf,ypos,SPRITE_HEIGHT);

// Hold image on the screen for DELAY count:

for(long d=0; d<DELAY; d++);
walksprite.erase(screenbuf); // Erase sprite image

// Process events from event manager:

int event=evelyn.getevent(event_mask);  // Get next event

// If left button, terminate:

if (event&LBUTTON) break;

// If no event, put sprite in standing still position:

if ((event&(RIGHT+LEFT))==NOEVENT) {
      cur_sequence=STAND_STILL;
      cur_frame=0;
      }

// Else check for RIGHT and LEFT events:

else {
      if (event&RIGHT) {    // Is it a RIGHT event?
                            // If so, go from standing
                            // still to walking right:
            if (cur_sequence==STAND_STILL) {
                  cur_sequence=WALK_RIGHT;
                  cur_frame=0;
                  }
                  // Or from walking left to
                  // standing still:
            if (cur_sequence==WALK_LEFT) {
                  cur_sequence=STAND_STILL;
                  cur_frame=0;
                  }
            }
      if (event&LEFT) {       // Is it a LEFT event?
            // If so, go from standing still to
            // walking left:
            if (cur_sequence==STAND_STILL) {
```

continued on next page

continued from previous page

```
                                                cur_sequence=WALK_LEFT;
                                                cur_frame=0;
                                                }
                                // Or from walking right to standing still:
                                if (cur_sequence==WALK_RIGHT) {
                                                cur_sequence=STAND_STILL;
                                                cur_frame=0;
                                                        }
                                                }
                                }
                        }
                if( screenbuf )
                        delete [] screenbuf; // cleanup memory

                setgmode(oldmode);     // Restore old video mode
        }
}

void putbuffer(unsigned char far *screenbuf,int y1,int height)

// Move offscreen video buffer into vidram

{
        char far *screen=(char far *)MK_FP(0xa000,0); // Point at vidram
        // Call MEMMOVE() function to move data into vidram:
        memmove(screen+y1*SCREEN_WIDTH,screenbuf+y1*SCREEN_WIDTH,
                        height*SCREEN_WIDTH);
}
```

Entering a New Dimension

Although we've used the input routines developed in this chapter for arcade-style animation, all of the principles developed here (and much of the code) work as well or better for a flight simulator.

But to produce a flight simulator, we must first move beyond simple two-dimensional animation and into a world with length, breadth, and depth. We must enter . . . the third dimension.

Building the Program

To compile the WALKMAN2.EXE program, boot the Borland C++ IDE while in the directory containing the *Build Your Own Flight Sim in C++*, etc. files, BYOFS\WALKMAN2, and load the WALKMAN2.IDE project by going to the Project menu and choosing Open Project. Then select Run from the Run menu to compile and execute the program.

CHAPTER

6

6

All Wired Up

What does it mean to put a three-dimensional image on the video display of a computer? Does it mean that the image is going to jump off the screen and grab the user by the throat? Does it mean that we'll create the illusion of depth so it will appear that the computer screen is a window into a real three-dimensional world? Neither explanation captures the meaning.

We're going to create a picture in which objects, characters, and scenery obey the rules of perspective: growing larger as they seem to come closer and smaller as they (or your point of view) seem to move farther away. In our programs we'll create scenes that look as though they *should* be three-dimensional although they still lack the illusion of depth (which can only occur when each of your eyes sees an image from a slightly different angle).

Is that all? Artists have been utilizing linear perspective at least since the time of the Italian Renaissance, when the mathematical rules of perspective were discovered. (In fact, artists were doing it even earlier than that, though in a more haphazard, less mathematically precise way.) Every time someone snaps a photograph he or she is creating a three-dimensional scene on the flat surface of the film, just as we are trying to create a three-dimensional scene on the flat surface of the computer monitor.

But there's a lot more to computer 3D graphics than creating a single scene. Not only are we going to create images that obey the rules of perspective, but those images will be part of a larger world. In that world, there will be objects, scenery, perhaps even characters, all of which can be viewed in any way that we like, from any angle or distance. Rather than just creating a scene, we are going to build a software engine that can create a nearly infinite number of potential scenes. And we are going to give the users of our programs the ability to choose which scenes they actually see by moving around in the world that we've created and viewing it according to their own whims.

Snapshots of the Universe

In effect, the program we create will take snapshots of a mathematically described universe inside the computer and then put those images on the display. So how does one go about taking snapshots of a world that doesn't exist?

There are a number of ways to put such a mathematically modeled world on the screen. It can be done with bitmaps, for instance, not unlike the ones that we used in the last two chapters. Our Walkman character, however, was essentially two-dimensional. He had height and breadth and could walk left and right, but he lacked depth; he had no third dimension.

Bitmap Scaling

We could have given him a kind of third dimension, though, by increasing our file of sprite images to include dozens of images of the Walkman growing larger and smaller, as though he were moving away from or toward us. Then it would have been fairly simple to make it appear as though he were walking around in a three-dimensional universe. Or we could have used bitmap scaling techniques to reduce and increase the size of the Walkman's bitmaps as he meandered about in the third dimension. (Bitmap scaling techniques involve removing and adding bitmap pixels while the program is running, to make the bitmap become larger and smaller.)

Bitmap scaling is the approach to three-dimensional computer graphics used in several popular computer games, including the highly successful *Wing Commander* series from Origin Systems. In these games, numerous bitmaps of spaceships are stored in the computer's memory showing the ships from several angles, and then the bitmaps are scaled to make it appear as though the ships are moving away from and toward the viewer as they bank and turn.

The problem with this technique is that it requires a *lot* of bitmaps before the three-dimensional motion of characters and objects appears realistic. Bitmaps eat up a lot of memory, so programs like *Wing Commander* must restrict themselves to a relative few bitmapped objects lest there not be enough memory left over for such frills as program code.

Rendering Techniques

The more popular (and versatile) approach to creating three-dimensional scenes is to store a mathematical description of a scene in the computer's memory and have the computer create the bitmap of the scene on the fly, while the program is running. There are many such techniques, known collectively as rendering techniques, because the computer itself is rendering the images. In effect, the computer becomes an artist, drawing animation frames so rapidly that they can be displayed in sequence much as we displayed the Walkman bitmaps in sequence in the last chapter.

One of the most popular rendering techniques is called ray tracing. Suprisingly simple on a conceptual level, ray tracing requires that the computer treat each pixel on the video display as a ray of light emanating from the imaginary scene inside the computer. By tracing the path of each of these light rays from the viewer's eye back into the scene, the computer can determine the color of each pixel and place an appropriate value into video RAM to make that color appear on the display.

Scenes rendered by ray tracing can look startlingly real. The technique is commonly used to create movie and television special effects of such vivid realism that they can look *better* than scenes made up of actual objects. This, in fact, is the key to recognizing ray-traced animation when you see it: The scenes look impossibly vivid, filled with sparkling reflections and bright colors. Ray-traced images look almost *too* good, more perfect than the real world could ever be, and they often lack the organic warmth of real-world scenes.

Can we create a computer game using ray-traced animation? Unfortunately, not on today's PCs. Ray tracing just takes too long. So personal computers must get a lot faster than they are now (or somebody must discover a superfast ray-tracing algorithm) before ray tracing will be useful. A typical full-screen ray trace can take hours to create on the average microcomputer, even with the aid of a math coprocessor. Ray-traced animations intended for movies or TV are time-consuming to create and must be recorded frame by frame on film or videotape over a period of days or even weeks. There are programming techniques using the ray-tracing concept called ray casting which is used for fast 3D maze games among other things. This is the subject of another book called *Gardens of Imagination* (Waite Group Press).

Fortunately, there are faster ways to render an image. Gouraud and Phong shading, for instance, are well-established techniques for creating images that are nearly as realistic as those created with ray tracing. Unfortunately, even these techniques are too slow for animation on current microcomputers. (The golf simulation *Links* from Accolade software uses a variation on these techniques to draw realistic three-dimensional images of a golf course, but the images are sketched out over a period of several seconds while the viewer watches.)

Wireframe and Polygon-Fill

So how can we create three-dimensional renderings rapidly enough for real-time animation? Alas, we're going to have to sacrifice realism in order to achieve satisfactory speed. Two techniques, wireframe graphics and polygon-fill graphics, can render images fast enough to create real-time animation.

Polygon-fill graphics techniques are used in most of the game programs currently on the market that employ some sort of three-dimensional animation (though multiple bitmaps, as described earlier, are becoming increasingly popular). Most flight simulators feature polygon-fill techniques.

There have been games that used wireframe graphic techniques as well, but these have mostly vanished from the market. Although wireframe is the fastest method of rendering an image, it is also far and away the least realistic. With some special exceptions, wireframe graphics techniques are unacceptable in current PC game software. (Nonetheless, we're going to use wireframe techniques in this and the next chapter because they are easy to understand and they utilize many of the basic principles that apply to polygon-fill graphics.)

How do wireframe and polygon-fill graphics work? Basically, wireframe graphics build an image from a series of lines, thus giving the object the appearance of having been constructed from wires. Figure 6-1 shows a simple wireframe image of a house. Polygon-fill graphics build an image from a series of solid-colored polygonal shapes, thus giving objects the appearance of faceted jewelry. Neither technique is realistic—few objects in the real world are made from either wires or polygons—but both techniques have the advantage of being very, very fast.

Another advantage of both wireframe and polygon-fill graphics is the simplicity and efficiency with which descriptions of objects can be stored in memory prior to

Figure 6-1 Wireframe image of a house

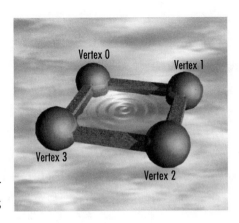

Figure 6-2 A square contains four vertices and four edges

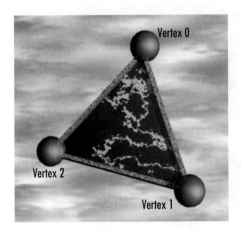

Figure 6-3 A triangle contains three vertices and three edges

rendering. Basically, objects intended to be rendered with these techniques are stored as lists of vertices, points where two or more lines come together. For instance, the square in Figure 6-2 contains four vertices—that is, four points at which the lines making up the square come together with other lines. Similarly, the triangle in Figure 6-3 contains three vertices.

We'll use the term vertex a little loosely in this book to mean either one of the end-points of a line (where it may or may not intersect additional lines) or the points at which edges of a polygon come together. For instance, the line in Figure 6-4 has two vertices—the two endpoints—even though it does not come into contact with any additional lines. We'll refer to vertices where two or more lines meet as *shared vertices*. For instance, the two crossed lines in Figure 6-5 have five vertices—the four endpoints of the lines plus the shared vertex in the center where the two lines cross.

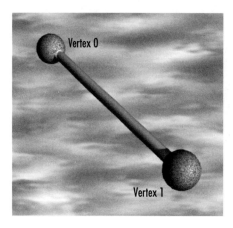

Figure 6-4 The ends of a line can be considered vertices, although technically they are not

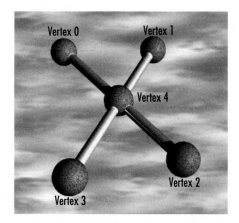

Figure 6-5 The point at which two lines intersect can also be regarded as a kind of vertex

Vertex Descriptors

If we are going to describe a shape as a list of vertices, then we are going to need some kind of vertex descriptor: a method of describing a vertex as a set of numbers in a data structure. In Chapter 2 we discussed the Cartesian coordinate system. We saw that a two-dimensional surface could be viewed in terms of a pair of Cartesian axes. Every point on the surface could be described by a pair of coordinates, which represented the position of that point relative to the two axes. (If you don't remember how this works, go back to Chapter 2 and refresh your memory, because we'll be using Cartesian coordinates frequently through the rest of this book.)

This is a common method of describing pixel positions on a computer video display. If we imagine that the top line of pixels on the display constitutes the x axis of a Cartesian coordinate system and the line of pixels running down the left side of the display

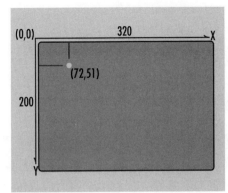

Figure 6-6 A pixel at coordinates (72,51) on the video display

represents the *y* axis of such a system, then any pixel on the display can be given a pair of coordinates based on its position relative to these axes. (See Figure 6-6.) For instance, a pixel 72 pixels from the left side of the display and 51 pixels from the top can be designated by the coordinate pair (72,51). As in a true Cartesian coordinate system, the *x* coordinate is always given first and the *y* coordinate given second. But the numbers in this video display coordinate system differ from those in a true Cartesian coordinate system in that they grow larger rather than smaller as we move down the *y* axis.

If we were to draw a straight line of pixels on the video display, each pixel in that line could be described by a coordinate pair. If we were to save that list of coordinate pairs, we could reconstruct the line later by drawing pixels at each of those coordinate positions. However, it's not necessary to save the coordinates of every pixel on a line in order to reconstruct it; we need only the pixel coordinates of the two endpoints of the line. We can then redraw the line by finding the shortest line between the two points and setting the pixels that fall closest to that line. Thus, a line can be described by two coordinate pairs. For instance, the line in Figure 6-7, which runs from coordinate position (189,5) to (90,155) can be described by the two coordinate pairs (189,5)–(90,155).

Figure 6-8 shows a square constructed out of four lines on the video display. We can extend our coordinate pair system to describe this square as a series of four shared vertices. This particular square can be described by the four coordinate pairs (10,10), (20,10), (20,20), and (10,20). We can reconstruct the square by drawing lines between these coordinate positions, like a child solving a connect-the-dots puzzle. (Wireframe computer graphics bear a distinct resemblance to such puzzles.)

To demonstrate some of the basic principles of three-dimensional graphics, we'll develop a program that will draw *two*-dimensional wireframe images based on the video display coordinates of the vertices of those images. First we'll learn to draw a line between any two vertices. Then we'll add functions to perform some clever tricks on wireframe images, like moving them to different places on the screen, shrinking and enlarging them, and even rotating them clockwise and counterclockwise.

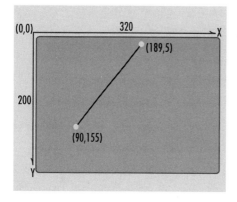

Figure 6-7 A line on the video display with endpoints at (189,5) and (90,155)

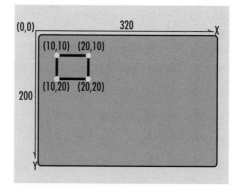

Figure 6-8 A square constructed from four lines, with vertices (10,10), (20,10), (20,20), and (10,20)

A Two-Dimensional Wireframe Package

Wireframe graphics are constructed by drawing lines to connect vertices on the video display. The first thing we'll need in our package of wireframe functions, then, is a function that will draw lines between any two coordinate positions on the display.

Such a function isn't as easy to write as you might think, especially if it's to run as fast as possible. To see why, let's look at the way lines of pixels are drawn on the video display.

Pixels on the video display are arranged in matrices of horizontal rows and vertical columns. Anything that is drawn on the display has to be drawn using those pixels and it has to be drawn within the limitations of this matrix arrangement. This is less than ideal for drawing straight lines between any two coordinate positions, because there *are* no straight lines between most pairs of coordinate positions, not that fit into the pixel matrix anyway. And if something doesn't fit the pixel matrix, it can't be drawn. The only truly straight lines that can be drawn on the display are those that are perfectly horizontal, perfectly vertical, or perfectly diagonal, since those just happen to fit the pixel matrix. All others must meander crookedly among the rows and columns of pixels in order to reach their destinations. Thus, most coordinate pairs on the video display will be connected by lines that are at best approximations of straight lines. For instance, the line in Figure 6-9(a) could be approximated by the sequence of pixels in Figure 6-9(b).

This is an unavoidable limitation of computer graphics displays. Drawing a line on the video display therefore becomes a matter of finding the best approximation of a straight line in as little time as possible. That's what makes computer line drawing so tricky—and so interesting.

The key to finding the best approximation of a straight line is the concept of slope. Every straight, two-dimensional line has a slope. Just as the slope of a hill tells us how steep it is relative to flat ground, the slope of a line tells us how sharply it is angled

Figure 6-9 The approximation of a straight line

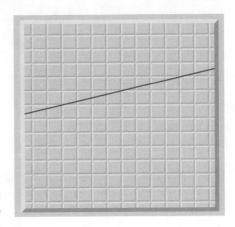

(a) A line that doesn't fit the pixel matrix of the display

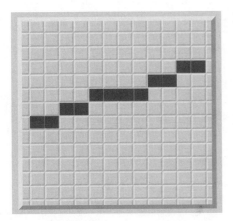

(b) The line from Figure 6-9(a) approximated with pixels

relative to a horizontal line. A horizontal line, like flat ground, has no slope at all, thus we say that it has a slope of zero. A vertical line has as much slope as a line can ever have, so it's tempting to say that it has a slope of infinity, but in fact the slope of a vertical line is mathematically undefined. However, if you want to think of it as infinite slope, you certainly can. Lines that are *nearly* vertical have slopes so large that they might as well be infinite.

To calculate the slope of a line, you need to know the coordinates of two different points on that line. This is convenient, since you will *always* know the coordinates of at least two points on any line you draw: the two endpoints. Once you have the coordinates of two points the slope can then be determined by calculating the change in both the x and y coordinates between these two points, then calculating the ratio of the y change to the x change. If that sounds complicated, it really shouldn't. The change in the x coordinate can easily be determined by subtracting the x coordinate of the first endpoint from the x coordinate of the second. Ditto for the y coordinate. Then the ratio can be determined by dividing the y difference by the x difference. Thus, if a straight line runs from coordinate position $(x1,y1)$ to coordinate position $(x2,y2)$ the slope can be calculated with the formula:

```
slope = (y2-y1) / (x2-x1)
```

It's easy to apply this formula to a real line. The line in Figure 6-10 runs from coordinate position (1,5) to coordinate position (4,11). When the starting y position is subtracted from the ending y position, the difference is 6. When the starting x position is subtracted from the ending x position, the difference is 3. The first difference (6) divided by the second difference (3) is 6/3 or 2. This can be expressed more efficiently as:

```
slope = (11 - 5) / (4 - 1) = 6 / 3 = 2
```

Thus, the line in Figure 6-10 has a slope of 2.

How does knowing the slope of a line help us to draw it? The slope, remember, is a ratio. If we think of the line as a point moving between two endpoints, the slope tells us how many units that point moves vertically for every unit that it moves horizontally. The slope of the line in Figure 6-10 is 2, which represents a ratio of 2:1 (i.e., 2 vertical units to 1 horizontal unit). This tells us that the point moves two units vertically for every unit it moves horizontally.

You now have an ideal means for drawing this line on the display. Instead of drawing the line directly from one endpoint to the other—which can't be done because it doesn't fit the pixel matrix—you can draw two pixels vertically, move your drawing position one pixel horizontally, draw two more pixels vertically, move your drawing position one pixel horizontally . . . always maintaining the 2:1 ratio, until you reach the other end of the line. (See Figure 6-11.)

This, however, is an unusually easy line to draw. Not quite as easy as a horizontal, vertical, or diagonal line, but close enough. What happens when the line has a negative

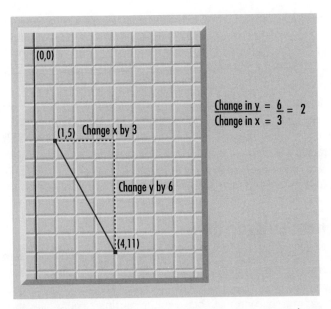

$$\frac{\text{Change in y}}{\text{Change in x}} = \frac{6}{3} = 2$$

Figure 6-10 A line with endpoints at (1,5) to (4,11) has a slope of 2

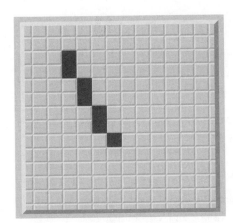

Figure 6-11 The line from Figure 6-10 drawn with pixels

slope? (This is perfectly legal.) Even worse, what if it has a fractional slope? Alas, *most* lines have fractional slopes and half of all lines have negative slopes. How will we draw lines such as these?

There are actually several algorithms available for drawing lines of arbitrary slope between arbitrary points. But the choice of algorithm for a wireframe animation package is constrained by the need to draw the lines as quickly as possible, in order to animate wireframe shapes in real time. Thus, the use of fractions should be avoided as much as possible, because fractions tend to slow calculations greatly, especially on machines without floating-point coprocessors. (We'll talk more about this in the chapter on optimization.) And we want to minimize the number of divisions that must be performed in order to draw a line, since division is also fairly slow.

Fortunately, there is a standard line-drawing algorithm that meets all of these constraints; it uses neither fractions nor division. It is called Bresenham's algorithm after the programmer who devised it in the mid-1960s and it is the algorithm that we will use not only to draw lines, but to draw the edges of polygons in later chapters. So we're going to look at how it works in some detail.

Bresenham's Algorithm

A few pages ago, we said that horizontal and vertical lines are the easiest to draw. Why? Because every point on a horizontal line has the same y coordinate and every point on a vertical line has the same x coordinate. To draw a horizontal line, you need simply draw a pixel at every x coordinate between the starting x coordinate and the ending x coordinate, without ever changing the y coordinate. Drawing a horizontal line between $(x1,y1)$ and $(x2,y2)$ is as simple as this:

```
for (int x=x1; x<x2; x++) draw_pixel(x,y1,color);
```

where draw_pixel(x,y) is a function that draws a colored pixel on the display at coordinates x,y and color is the palette color in which we wish to draw it. Similarly, to draw a vertical line you need simply draw a pixel at every y coordinate between the starting y coordinate and the ending y coordinate, without ever changing the x coordinate:

```
for (int y=y1; y<y2; y++) drawpixel(x1,y);
```

A diagonal line is only slightly more difficult to draw because both the x and y coordinates only need to be increased (or decreased) by 1 for each pixel:

```
y=y1;
for (int x=x1; x<x2; x++,y++) drawpixel(x,y);
```

If the starting coordinate is larger than the ending coordinate in one of the two dimensions, the line has a negative slope. (Try calculating such a slope and see.) In that case, the value of the coordinate is decreased on each pixel rather than increased.

Lines of an arbitrary slope are trickier. Fortunately, every possible line can be drawn by incrementing one coordinate, either x or y, once for each pixel in the line; thus, every possible line can be drawn with a for loop. It's also quite easy to determine which coordinate can be used as the loop counter and be incremented in this manner. If the absolute value (that is, the value with its sign removed) of the slope is less than 1, then it is the x coordinate that is incremented for each pixel. If the absolute value is greater than 1, then it is the *y* coordinate that is incremented on each pixel. If the slope is precisely 1 then the line is perfectly diagonal and either coordinate can be used as the loop counter.

But what about the second coordinate? When is it incremented? Well, in the case of horizontal and vertical lines, the second coordinate is *never* incremented and in the case of diagonal lines it is *always* incremented. But for other types of lines, deciding when the second coordinate is incremented is the crux of the problem. Bresenham's algorithm offers one solution.

First, we divide all lines into two kinds, those with slopes greater than 1 and those with slopes less than 1. (Lines with slopes of exactly 1 can be lumped arbitrarily into either of these groups.) What precisely is the difference between these two types of lines? Take a look at Figure 6-12. If you take a line and rotate it 360 degrees around its center point, it will rotate through all possible slopes. Figure 6-12(a) shows the range over which the change in the *y* coordinate is greater from one endpoint to the other than the change in the *x* coordinate. This is also the range in which the slope of the line is greater than 1. Figure 6-12(b) shows the range over which the change in the *x* coordinate is greater from one endpoint to the other than the change in the *y* coordinate. This also happens to be the range in which the slope of the line is less than 1.

If the change in the *x* coordinate is greater than the change in the *y* coordinate, then we must increment the *x* coordinate on every pixel and the *y* coordinate only on some pixels. But if the change in the *y* coordinate is greater than the change in the *x* coordinate, then we must increment the *y* coordinate on every pixel and the *x* coordinate only on some pixels. (If the change is equal in both, we can increment either one.) Thus, Bresenham's algorithm consists of two parts: one for handling lines that are incremented on *x* (that have slope less than 1) and a second for handling lines that are incremented on *y* (that have slope greater than 1).

Once we know which coordinate to increment, we must decide how often to increment the other pixel. For a slope such as 2, this is easy; we increment it on every *other* pixel. But for slopes such as 7.342, this is a more difficult decision. Bresenham's algorithm avoids this problem (as well as division and fractions) by never calculating the slope. Instead, it calculates the *x* difference and the *y* difference and uses these to create not the slope but a value called the error term.

The error term is initialized to zero before the line is drawn. If we are incrementing the *x* coordinate, the *y* difference is added to the error term after each pixel is drawn. If the error term is still smaller than the *x* difference, then the *y* coordinate is not incremented and the process is repeated, with the value of the error term increasing every time the *y* difference is added to it. If the error term is equal to or greater than the *x* difference, the *y* coordinate is incremented, the *x* difference is subtracted from the error term, and the process begins again. If we are incrementing the *y* coordinate, the process is identical, except that the *x*s and *y*s are reversed. (Most implementations of Bresenham's algorithms include two separate loops, one for incrementing on the *x* coordinate and one for incrementing on the *y* coordinate.)

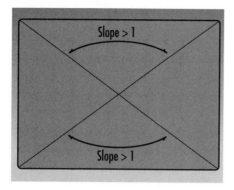

Figure 6-12 Comparing two types of lines

(a) The range of lines with slope greater than or equal to 1

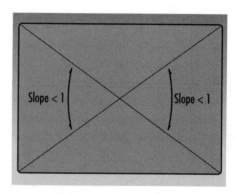

(b) The range of lines with slope less than or equal to 1

A Line-Drawing Routine in C++

Without further ado, let's see how Bresenham's algorithm works—in C++ code. Listing 6-1 contains a complete mode 13h implementation of Bresenham's algorithm:

 Listing 6-1 BRESN.CPP

```
#include  <stdio.h>

void linedraw(int x1,int y1,int x2,int y2,int color,
        char far *screen)
{
  int y_unit,x_unit;              // Variables for amount of change
                                  //  in x and y

  int offset=y1*320+x1;           // Calculate offset into video RAM

  int ydiff=y2-y1;                // Calculate difference between
                                  //  y coordinates
  if (ydiff<0) {                  // If the line moves in the negative
```

```
                            //   direction
  ydiff=-ydiff;             // ...get absolute value of difference
  y_unit=-320;              // ...and set negative unit in
                            //   y dimension
}
else y_unit=320;            // Else set positive unit in
                            //   y dimension

int xdiff=x2-x1;            // Calculate difference between
                            //   x coordinates
if (xdiff<0) {              // If the line moves in the
                            //   negative direction
  xdiff=-xdiff;             // ...get absolute value of
                            //   difference
  x_unit=-1;                // ...and set negative unit
                            //   in x dimension
}
else x_unit=1;              // Else set positive unit in
                            //   y dimension

int error_term=0;           // Initialize error term
if (xdiff>ydiff) {          // If difference is bigger in
                            //   x dimension
  int length=xdiff+1;       // ...prepare to count off in
                            //   x direction
  for (int i=0; i<length; i++) {  // Loop through points
                            //   in x direction
    screen[offset]=color;   // Set the next pixel in the
                            //   line to COLOR
    offset+=x_unit;         // Move offset to next pixel
                            //   in x direction
    error_term+=ydiff;      // Check to see if move
                            //   required in y direction
    if (error_term>xdiff) { // If so...
      error_term-=xdiff;    // ...reset error term
      offset+=y_unit;       // ...and move offset to next
                            //   pixel in y direction

    }
  }
}
else {                      // If difference is bigger in
                            //   y dimension
  int length=ydiff+1;       // ...prepare to count off in
                            //   y direction
  for (int i=0; i<length; i++) {  // Loop through points
                            //   in y direction
    screen[offset]=color;   // Set the next pixel in the
                            //   line to COLOR
    offset+=y_unit;         // Move offset to next pixel
                            //   in y direction
    error_term+=xdiff;      // Check to see if move
                            //   required in x direction
    if (error_term>0) {     // If so...
```

continued on next page

continued from previous page

```
        error_term-=ydiff;        // ...reset error term
        offset+=x_unit;           // ...and move offset to next
                                  //  pixel in x direction
    }
  }
 }
}
```

There's a lot going on here, so let's take a close look at this function. Six parameters are passed to the function by the calling routine: the starting coordinates of the line (*x1* and *y1*), the ending coordinates of the line (*x2* and *y2*), the color of the line (color), and a far pointer to video memory or a video buffer (screen).

The variables *xdiff* and *ydiff* contain the differences between the starting and ending *x* and *y* coordinates, respectively. If either of these differences is negative, the absolute value of the difference is taken by negating the variable with the unary minus operator (-). The variables *x_unit* and *y_unit* represent the amount by which the *x* and *y* coordinates are to be incremented in their position in video RAM. The *x_unit* value is always 1 or -1, depending on whether the *x* coordinate is going from a lower value to a higher one (i.e., if the line is sloping down the screen) or from a higher value to a lower one (i.e., if the line is sloping up the screen). Similarly, the *y_unit* value is always 320 or -320, the number of addresses between a pixel on one line and a pixel one line (i.e., one *y* coordinate) below it or above it. We determine which way the line is sloping in the *x* and *y* directions by checking to see if *xdiff* and *ydiff* are positive or negative before taking their absolute values.

The drawing of the line is performed by two loops, one for the case where the absolute value of *xdiff* is greater than the absolute value of *ydiff* and one for the opposite case. In the former, the value of *x_unit* is added to the pixel offset after each pixel is drawn. In the latter case, the value of *y_unit* is added. The variable *error_term* is used for tracking the error term. Depending on which loop is being executed either *xdiff* or *ydiff* is added to this value. The actual drawing proceeds as we described above.

Testing the Line-Drawing Function

We've included this function in the file BRESN.CPP with a prototype of linedraw() in BRESN.H on the disk accompanying this book. Listing 6-2 is a short C++ program that can be linked to this file and the SCREEN.ASM file to draw a line between coordinates (0,89) and (319,124).

Listing 6-2 LINETEST.CPP

```
#include <stdio.h>
#include <dos.h>
#include <conio.h>
#include "bresn.h"
#include "screen.h"
```

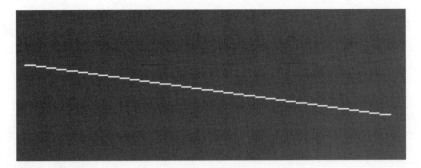

Figure 6-13 The line drawn by the LINETEST program

```
void main()
{
        char far *screen =
                (char far *)MK_FP(0xa000,0);    // point to video RAM
        int oldmode = *(int *)MK_FP(0x40,0x49); // Save previous
                                                // video mode
        cls(screen);                   // Clear mode 13h display
        setgmode(0x13);                // Set 320x200x256-
                                       // color graphics
        linedraw(0,89,319,124,WHITE,screen);    // draw line
        while(!kbhit());                        // Wait for keypress
        setgmode(oldmode);                      // Reset previous
                                                // video mode & end
}
```

The term WHITE is defined in the CONIO.H header file included at the top of the program. If Borland isn't being used, create a constant integer named WHITE at the top and set it equal to 15.

Notice the stairstep-like quality of the line that is drawn by this program. (See Figure 6-13.) That's the result of approximating the line with pixels that don't fall precisely *on* the line. This stairstep effect is known technically as aliasing. There is a set of graphics techniques known as antialiasing techniques that can be used to minimize this effect, but they are difficult to apply while drawing a line on the fly. Basically, the techniques involve making the distinction fuzzier between the line color and the background color by drawing parts of the line in a color partway between the background color and the line color.

Drawing Random Lines

Listing 6-3 contains a second program that calls the linedraw() function. It draws a random sequence of lines across the screen, using the randomize() and random() library functions (prototyped in STDLIB.H and TIME.H) to generate random endpoints for the lines. The compiled program, SRNDLINE.EXE, can be found in the BYOFS\WIREFRAM directory.

Listing 6-3 RANDLINE.CPP

```
#include  <stdio.h>
#include  <dos.h>
#include  <conio.h>
#include  <stdlib.h>
#include  <time.h>
#ifdef USE_BRESN_CPP
#include  "bresn.h"
#else
#include "bresnham.h"
#endif
#include  "screen.h"

const NUMCOLORS=16;                       // Line colors

void main()
{
      randomize();                        // Initialize random
                                          //   numbers
      char far *screen =
       (char far *)MK_FP(0xa000,0);       // Point to video RAM
      int oldmode =                       // Save previous video
       *(int *)MK_FP(0x40,0x49);          //   mode
      cls(screen);                        // Clear mode 13h
                                          //   display;
      setgmode(0x13);                     // Set 320x200x256-color
                                          //   graphics
      int x1=random(320);                 // Initialize line to
                                          //   random
      int y1=random(200);                 // ...starting values
      int color = WHITE;
      while (!kbhit()) {                  // Draw lines until
                                          //   keypress
            int x2=random(320);           // Continue line to
            int y2=random(200);           // ...random end point
            linedraw(x1,y1,x2,y2,color,screen); // Draw line
            x1=x2;                        // Start next line at
            y1=y2;                        // ...end point of last
                                          //   line
            //color = (color+1)%NUMCOLORS;
      }
      setgmode(oldmode);                  // Reset previous video
                                          //   mode & end
}
```

Don't blink when you run this program. The line-drawing routine is fast (as it needs to be in order to produce convincing animation). Within less than a second, the screen will be filled with randomly criss-crossing lines. See Figure 6-14 for a screen shot. Press any key to make it stop.

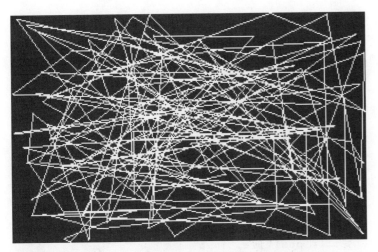

Figure 6-14 The lines drawn by the RANDLINE program

A Line-Drawing Function in Assembler

As fast as the line-drawing function is, it could be faster still. Listing 6-4 is an assembly language implementation of Bresenham's algorithm, which works exactly like the version in C++ above. It is available on the disk as BRESNHAM.ASM, with prototypes in BRESNHAM.H.

Listing 6-4 BRESNHAM.ASM

```
        .MODEL  large
        .CODE
        PUBLIC  _linedraw

_linedraw   PROC
        ARG  x1:WORD,y1:WORD,x2:WORD,y2:WORD,color:WORD,\
             scr_off:WORD,scr_seg:WORD
        LOCAL  y_unit:WORD,x_unit:WORD,xdiff:WORD,ydiff:WORD,\
               error_term:WORD=AUTO_SIZE
        push    bp
        mov     bp,sp
        sub     sp,AUTO_SIZE
        mov     ax,scr_seg      ; Get screen segment in ax
        mov     es,ax
        mov     ax,y1           ; Get y1 in ax...
        mov     dx,320          ; Multiply by 320
        mul     dx
        add     ax,x1           ; And add x1 to get pixel offset
        add     ax,scr_off      ; Add screen offset
```

continued on next page

continued from previous page

```
        mov    bx,ax            ; Move offset to BX
init_line:
        mov    dx,color         ; Put pixel color in dx
        mov    error_term,0     ; Initialize error term
        mov    ax,y2            ; Determine sign of y2-y1
        sub    ax,y1
        jns    ypos             ; If positive, jump
        mov    y_unit,-320      ; Else handle negative slope
        neg    ax               ; Get absolute value of YDIFF
        mov    ydiff,ax         ; And store it in memory
        jmp    next
ypos:
        mov    y_unit,320       ; Handle positive slope
        mov    ydiff,ax         ; Store YDIFF in memory
next:
        mov    ax,x2            ; Determine sign of x2-x1
        sub    ax,x1
        jns    xpos             ; If positive, jump
        mov    x_unit,-1        ; Else handle negative case
        neg    ax               ; Get absolute value of XDIFF
        mov    xdiff,ax         ; And store it in memory
        jmp    next2
xpos:
        mov    x_unit,1         ; Handle positive case
        mov    xdiff,ax         ; Store XDIFF in memory
next2:
        cmp    ax,ydiff         ; Compare XDIFF (in AX) and YDIFF
        jc     yline            ; IF XDIFF<YDIFF then count
                                ;   in Y dimension
        jmp    xline            ; Else count in X dimension
;
xline:
; Slope less than one, so increment in x dimension
        mov    cx,xdiff         ; Get line length in cx for count
        inc    cx
xline1:
        mov    es:[bx],dl       ; Draw next point in line
        add    bx,x_unit        ; Point offset to next pixel in
                                ;   x direction
        mov    ax,error_term    ; Check to see if move required
                                ;   in Y direction
        add    ax,ydiff
        mov    error_term,ax
        sub    ax,xdiff
        jc     xline2           ; If not, continue
        mov    error_term,ax
        add    bx,y_unit        ; Else, move up or down one pixel
xline2:
        loop   xline1           ; Loop until count (in CX) complete
        jmp    linedone
;
```

```
yline:
; Count in y dimension
    mov    cx,ydiff        ; Get line length in cx
    inc    cx
yline1:
    mov    es:[bx],dl      ; Draw next point in line
    add    bx,y_unit       ; Point offset to next pixel
                           ;   in Y direction
    mov    ax,error_term   ; Check to see if move require
                           ;   in X direciton
    add    ax,xdiff
    mov    error_term,ax
    sub    ax,ydiff
    jc     yline2          ; If not, continue
    mov    error_term,ax
    add    bx,x_unit       ; Else, move left or right
                           ;   one pixel
yline2:
    loop   yline1          ; Loop until count (in CX) complete
linedone:
    mov    sp,bp           ; Finished!
    pop    bp
    ret
_linedraw  ENDP

    END
```

If you include BRESNHAM.H in the programs above instead of BRESN.H and put BRESNHAM.ASM in the Project file instead of BRESN.CPP, they'll work as readily with this version of linedraw() as with the earlier one written in C++. But now they'll run like the proverbial bat out of hell. Separate versions of these are included in the RANDLINE.IDE project. The RANDLINE.EXE target uses the assembly language version of linedraw, while the SRNDLINE.EXE uses the C++ version.

Programmers not familiar with the features of 80X86 macro assemblers may be interested in the use of the LOCAL directive at the beginning of this program. Similar to the ARG directive, LOCAL creates labels for local variables on the stack which can be addressed by name, and the assembler automatically replaces the names with the stack addresses of the variables. To make this work properly, the stack address must be placed in the BP register and space allocated on the stack by subtracting the size of the local variable area (contained here in the assembler variable *AUTO_SIZE*) from the stack pointer.

According to *Turbo Profiler* for DOS (a useful program that we'll discuss in more detail in a later chapter) this version of the linedraw() function runs almost twice as fast as the one we wrote in C++. (A resourceful programmer might be able to optimize it still further.) This gain in speed could produce a noticeable difference when drawing complex wireframe objects.

Drawing Shapes

Now that we can draw lines, let's use the linedraw() function to draw more complex shapes. Listing 6-5 draws a rectangle on the display.

 Listing 6-5 RECTANGL.CPP

```
// RECTANGL.CPP
//    A short program to draw a rectangle on
//    the mode 13h display

#include   <stdio.h>
#include   <dos.h>
#include   <conio.h>
#include   "screen.h"
#include   "bresnham.h"

void main()
{

  // Create pointer to video RAM:

  char far *screen=(char far *)MK_FP(0xa000,0);

  cls(screen);                        // Clear video RAM
   int oldmode=*(int *)MK_FP(0x40,0x49);  // Save previous
                                      //  video mode
  setmode(0x13);                      // Set mode 13h

  // Draw rectangle:

  linedraw(130,70,190,70,15,screen);
  linedraw(190,70,190,130,15,screen);
  linedraw(190,130,130,130,15,screen);
  linedraw(130,130,130,70,15,screen);

  while (!kbhit());                   // Loop until key pressed
  setmode(oldmode);                   // Reset previous video
                                      //  mode & end
}
```

The output of this program is shown in Figure 6-15. There's really not much to say about how the program works. The rectangle is drawn with four calls to the linedraw() function, each of which draws one line of the rectangle. The vertices of the rectangle—(130,70), (190,70), (190,130), and (130,130)—are hardcoded into the function calls.

Listing 6-6 is a similar program that draws a triangle.

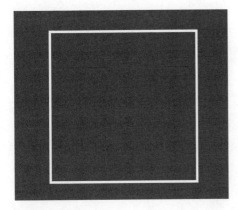

Figure 6-15 The rectangle drawn by
the RECTANGL program

Listing 6-6 TRIANGLE.CPP

```
// TRIANGLE.CPP
//    A short program to draw a triangle
//      on the mode 13h display

#include   <stdio.h>
#include   <dos.h>
#include   <conio.h>
#include   "screen.h"
#include   "bresnham.h"

void main()
{

  // Create pointer to video RAM:

  char far *screen=(char far *)MK_FP(0xa000,0);

  cls(screen);                         // Clear video RAM
  int oldmode=*(int *)MK_FP(0x40,0x49); // Save previous
                                       //   video mode
  setmode(0x13);                       // Set mode 13h

  // Draw triangle:

  linedraw(160,70,190,130,15,screen);
  linedraw(190,130,130,130,15,screen);
  linedraw(130,130,160,70,15,screen);

  while (!kbhit());                    // Loop until key pressed
  setmode(oldmode);                    // Reset previous video
                                       //   mode & end

}
```

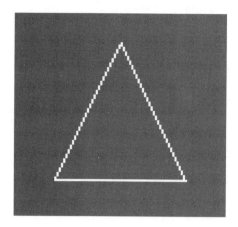

Figure 6-16 The triangle drawn by the TRIANGLE program

The output of this program is shown in Figure 6-16.

Creating Shape Data

It's awkward to draw a shape with a series of linedraw() statements. It's also awkward to hard-code the coordinates of the shape into the program. It would be better programming practice if we could store the vertices of the shape in a data structure and pass that structure to a function that would draw the shape described by the vertices. Even better, we could make the shape into a class and tell the shape to draw itself!

Fortunately, that's not hard to do. Here's the definition of a simple data structure and class that we can use for holding two-dimensional wireframe shapes:

```
// Variable structures for shape data:

struct vertex_type {            // Structure for vertices
  int x,y;                      // X & Y coordinates for vertex
};

class shape_type {              // Class to hold shape data
protected:
        int color;              // Color of shape
        int number_of_vertices; // Number of vertices in shape
        vertex_type *vertex;    // Array of vertex descriptor
public:
        shape_type(int num, vertex_type *vert, int col=15):vertex(vert),
            number_of_vertices(num),color(col){;}
        void Draw(char far *screen);
};
```

The structure type that we've called vertex_type holds a vertex descriptor—the *x* and *y* coordinates of a single vertex of a shape. The class called shape_type contains further information about the shape of which the vertex is a part, including the color of the lines in the shape (color), the number of vertices in the shape (number_of_vertices), and a pointer to an array of vertex descriptors (vertex). The class constructor assigns the arguments to the class members. The default color is 15, or white, such that it is really only necessary to provide two parameters to the constructor. We can now initialize the data for a shape in a pair of data initialization statements, one to create the array of vertices and a second to create the shape_type instance of the class:

```
// Data for triangle:

vertex_type triangle_array[]={
    160,70,             // First vertex
    190,130,            // Second vertex
    130,130             // Third vertex
};

// Triangle:
//  3 vertices and    triangle_array  is Pointer to vertex array
shape_type shape(3,triangle_array);
};
```

As the variable names and comments imply, these structures contain the shape data for a triangle. We can then draw the shape with the function in Listing 6-7.

Listing 6-7 Shape-drawing function

```
void shape_type::Draw(char far *screen)

// Draws the shape contained in the structure SHAPE

{

  // Loop through vertices in shape:
        for (int i=0; i<number_of_vertices; i++) {
                // Calculate offset of next vertex:
                int p2=i+1;
                // Wrap to 0:
                if (p2>=number_of_vertices) p2=0;
                // Draw line from this vertex to next vertex:
                linedraw(vertex[i].x,vertex[i].y,
                        vertex[p2].x, vertex[p2].y,
                        color,screen);
                }
}
```

The function Draw() consists primarily of a For loop that iterates through all of the vertices in the shape. The variable *p2* points to the next vertex after the one currently under consideration. In the event that the current vertex is the last, this variable wraps around to 0, so that the final vertex is automatically connected to the first. The call to linedraw() draws a line from the current vertex to the *p2* vertex.

A Shape-Drawing Program in C++

Listing 6-8 shows a complete program which, when linked with BRESNHAM.ASM and SCREEN.ASM, will draw a triangle on the mode 13h display using the linedraw() function.

Listing 6-8 SHAPE.CPP

```cpp
#include  <stdio.h>
#include  <dos.h>
#include  <conio.h>
#include  "bresnham.h"
#include  "evntmngr.h"
#include  "screen.h"

int const DISTANCE=10;

// Variable structures for shape data:

struct vertex_type {              // Structure for vertices
  int x,y;                        // X & Y coordinates for vertex
};

class shape_type {                // Structure to hold shape data
private:
        int color;                // Color of shape
        int number_of_vertices;   // Number of vertices in shape
        vertex_type *vertex;      // Array of vertex descriptor
public:
        shape_type(int num, vertex_type *vert,int col=15):vertex(vert),
                      number_of_vertices(num),color(col) {;}
        void Draw(char far *screen);
};

// Draws the shape
void shape_type::Draw(char far *screen)
{

        // Loop through vertices in shape:

        for (int i=0; i<number_of_vertices; i++) {

                // Calculate offset of next vertex:
```

```
                int p2=i+1;

                 // Wrap to 0:

                if (p2>=number_of_vertices) p2=0;

                // Draw line from this vertex to next vertex:

                linedraw(vertex[i].x,vertex[i].y,
                        vertex[p2].x,vertex[p2].y,
                        color,screen);
                }
}

// Data for triangle:

vertex_type triangle_array[]={
    160,70,                     // First vertex
    190,130,                    // Second vertex
    130,130                     // Third vertex
};

// Triangle:
// 3 vertices and     triangle_array  is Pointer to vertex array
shape_type shape(3, triangle_array);

void main()
{
        char far *screen =
         (char far *)MK_FP(0xa000,0);        // Create pointer to
                                             //  video RAM
        cls(screen);                         // Clear screen
        int oldmode=*(int *)MK_FP(0x40,0x49); // Save previous
                                             //  video mode
        setgmode(0x13);                      // Set mode 13h
        shape.Draw(screen);                  // Draw shape on
                                             //  display

        while (!kbhit());                    // Wait for key, then
                                             //  terminate
        setgmode(oldmode);                   // Reset previous video
                                             //  mode & end
}
```

If you want this program to draw a rectangle instead of a triangle, recompile it using this shape data:

```
// Data for rectangle:

vertex_type rectangle_array[]={
            130,70,                          // First vertex
            190,70,                          // Second vertex
            190,130,                         // Third vertex
```

continued on next page

continued from previous page

```
              130,130                                // Fourth vertex
};

shape_type shape(4, rectangle_array);
```

If you'd like to draw still other shapes, try experimenting with shape data of your own. Feel free to change the color of the shape by adding the third parameter in the declaration:

```
shape_type shape(4, rectangle_array,14);  // construct rectangle in yellow
```

Transforming Shapes

Now that you've learned to draw two-dimensional shapes, you'll want to do something interesting with them. In the rest of this chapter, you'll learn to alter those shapes in ways that will be relevant to the three-dimensional shapes you'll deal with in later chapters.

In Chapter 2, several operations were introduced that could be performed on two-dimensional shapes. Among these were scaling, translating, and rotating.

Recall that scaling refers to changing the size, or scale, of the shape. Scaling can be used to make the shape larger or smaller or to alter the proportions of the shape. We'll only use scaling in this chapter to alter the overall size of the shape, not its proportions.

Translating involves moving the shape around. Later, in the discussion of three-dimensional graphics, we'll use translation to move objects through three-dimensional space. For now, however, we'll use it to move a two-dimensional shape around on the screen.

Rotating refers to changing the physical orientation of the shape. In two dimensions that essentially means rotating the shape clockwise and counterclockwise about an axis extending outward from the screen. Later, you'll see how to rotate three-dimensional shapes about other axes as well.

Local Coordinates

Until now, our programs have defined shapes in terms of their screen coordinates of their vertices. However, since the scaling, rotating, and translating operations that we're about to perform will change those coordinates, it's necessary to have a base set of coordinates to return to before we alter a shape's coordinates. Thus, we need to give each shape two sets of coordinates: local coordinates and screen coordinates.

The local coordinates will be the coordinates of the vertices of the object relative to a specific origin point, usually the center of the object (though it can be any other point as well). This point is known as the local origin of the object.

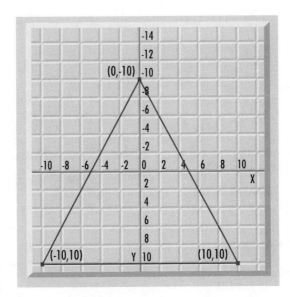

Figure 6-17 A triangle with vertex coordinates defined relative to a local origin at the center of the figure

For instance, using a local coordinate system, we can describe a triangle as having vertices at coordinates (-10,10), (0,-10), and (10,10), relative to a local origin at the center of the triangle, as shown in Figure 6-17. You'll notice that now we have negative coordinates as well as positive coordinates. Just as standard Cartesian coordinate systems include negative coordinates below and to the left of the (0,0) origin point (see Chapter 2), so vertices in a local coordinate system can have negative coordinates relative to the local origin of the object. This simply means that the vertex is above or to the left of the local origin.

Since coordinates on the video display are generally treated as positive, we'll need to translate the local coordinates on this triangle to points within the normal set of screen coordinates before it can be fully visible. Objects that have vertices with negative coordinates can still be displayed, but all negative vertices will be off the edges of the screen.

In order to take local coordinates into account, we'll need to create a new data structure to describe shapes. Each vertex will require two descriptors, one for local coordinates and a second for screen coordinates. We can initialize the first descriptor in the program code, but the second will need to be initialized by the function that performs the translation. Here's the definition for such a structure:

```
// Variable structures to hold shape data:

struct vertex_type {                    // Structure for individual
                                        //   vertices
```

continued on next page

continued from previous page

```
    int lx,ly;                      // Local coordinates of vertex
    int sx,sy;                      // Screen coordinates of vertex
};

class shape_type {                  // Class to hold shape data
protected:
        int color;                  // Color of shape
        int number_of_vertices;     // Number of vertices in shape
        vertex_type *vertex;        // Array of vertex descriptor
public:
        shape_type(int      num,      vertex_type      *vert,      int
col=15):vertex(vert),
            number_of_vertices(num),color(col){;}
        void Draw(char far *screen);
        void Translate(int xtrans,int ytrans);
};

// Data for shapes:

vertex_type rectangle_array[]={ // Data for rectangle
  {0,0,      // First vertex
   0,0},
   {0,20,    // Second vertex
   0,20},
   {20,20,   // Third vertex
   20,20},
   {20,0,    // Fourth vertex
   20,0}
};
```

You'll note that only the vertex descriptor has been changed. The definition of shape_type is the same as before.

Translating

To translate an object to a new position on the screen, we need two numbers representing the translation values for both the x and y coordinates of the object—that is, the amount along the x and y axes by which the object will be moved. These translation values become the x and y coordinates of the local origin of the object and all of the vertices will be treated as though they were relative to this point. (See Figure 6-18.) Once we have the translation values, we can get the screen coordinates of the vertices by adding the translation values to the x and y coordinates of each vertex, the x translation value to the x coordinate and the y translation value to the y coordinate, like this:

```
new_X=old_X + X_translation;
new_Y=old_Y + Y_translation;
```

Listing 6-9 introduces a function that will perform this translation for us.

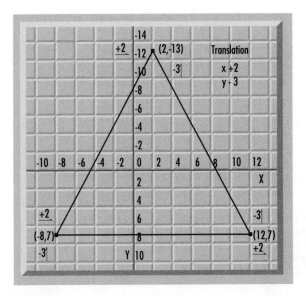

Figure 6-18 The triangle from Figure 6-17, with its local origin translated to coordinates (2,-3)

Listing 6-9 Translation function

```
void shape_type::Translate(int xtrans,int ytrans)
{

// Translate each point in shape SHAPE by XTRANS,YTRANS

   for (int i=0; i<(*shape).number_of_vertices; i++) {
     (*shape).vertex[i].sx=(*shape).vertex[i].lx+xtrans;
     (*shape).vertex[i].sy=(*shape).vertex[i].ly+ytrans;
   }
}
```

This function takes the local coordinates of the object (stored in the *lx* and *ly* fields) and adds the translation values to them to obtain the screen coordinates (stored in the *sx* and *sy* fields). We can call this routine from C++ to translate a shape to screen coordinates (*xtrans,ytrans*).

Listing 6-10 shows a program that translates a rectangle to coordinates (150,190).

Listing 6-10 TRANSLAT.CPP

```
#include      <stdio.h>
#include      <dos.h>
#include      <conio.h>
#include      "bresnham.h"
#include      "screen.h"
```

continued on next page

continued from previous page

```
int const DISTANCE=10;

// Variable structures for shape data:

struct vertex_type {              // Structure for vertices
        int lx,ly;                // local coordinates of vertex
        int sx,sy;                // screen coordinates of vertex
};

class shape_type {                // Structure to hold shape data
private:
  int color;                      // Color of shape
  int    number_of_vertices;      // Number of vertices in shape
  vertex_type *vertex;            // Array of vertex descriptor
public:
        shape_type(int num, vertex_type *vert,int col=15):vertex(vert),
                        number_of_vertices(num),color(col) {;}
        void Draw(char far *screen);
        void Translate(int xtrans, int ytrans);
};

// Draws the shape
void shape_type::Draw(char far *screen)
{

        // Loop through vertices in shape:

        for (int i=0; i<number_of_vertices; i++) {

            // Calculate offset of next vertex:

            int p2=i+1;

             // Wrap to 0:

            if (p2>=number_of_vertices) p2=0;

            // Draw line from this vertex to next vertex:

            linedraw(vertex[i].sx,vertex[i].sy,
                        vertex[p2].sx,vertex[p2].sy,
                        color,screen);
            }
}

void shape_type:: Translate(int xtrans, int ytrans)
{
        // Translate each point in shape by xtrans/ytrans

        for(int i=0;i<number_of_vertices;i++) {
                vertex[i].sx = vertex[i].lx+xtrans;
                vertex[i].sy = vertex[i].ly+ytrans;
```

```
                      }
}
// Data for rectangle:

vertex_type rectangle_array[]={
        {0,0,                    // First vertex
         0,0},
        {0,20,                   // Second vertex
         0,20},
        {20,20,                  // Third vertex
         20,20},
        {20,0,                   // Fourth vertex
         20,0}
};

// Rectangle:
//   4 vertices and   rectangle_array  is Pointer to vertex array
//          draw it in bright red (12)
shape_type shape(4, rectangle_array, 12);

void main()
{
        char far *screen =
        (char far *)MK_FP(0xa000,0);          // Create pointer to
                                              //   video RAM
        cls(screen);                          // Clear screen
        int oldmode=*(int *)MK_FP(0x40,0x49); // Save previous
                                              //   video mode
        setgmode(0x13);                       // Set mode 13h
        shape.Translate(150,90);
        shape.Draw(screen);                   // Draw shape on
                                              //   display

        while (!kbhit());                     // Wait for key, then
                                              //   terminate
        setgmode(oldmode);                    // Reset previous video
                                              //   mode & end

}
```

This program can be recompiled with different values passed to the Translate() function to move the rectangle anywhere on the display. Note that if you move it to a position where the image runs off the edge of the display, portions of the image will wrap around to the opposite edge of the display since we have not implemented image clipping at the edge of the display.

Scaling

Now that we've moved an image to a new position on the display, the next step is altering its size. Scaling the image can be implemented almost as easily as translating it. First you multiply the coordinates of each vertex of the image by the same scaling factor.

```
new_X=old_X * scale_factor;
new_Y=old_Y * scale_factor;
```

If you wish to alter the proportions of the shape as well as its size, you multiply the *x* coordinates by a different scaling factor than you multiply the *y* coordinates by. For instance, multiplying the *x* coordinates by 2 and the *y* coordinates by 1 will cause the shape to double its size in the *x* dimension while remaining the same size in the *y* dimension. In this chapter, however, we'll multiply both the *x* and *y* coordinates by the same scaling factor to retain the original proportions of the shape. (See Figure 6-19.)

Listing 6-11 introduces the shape_type member function that will scale the shape.

Listing 6-11 Scaling function

```
void shape_type::Scale(float scale_factor)

// Scale SHAPE by SCALE_FACTOR

{
  for (int i=0; i<number_of_vertices; i++) {
      vertex[i].sx=vertex[i].lx*scale_factor;
      vertex[i].sy=vertex[i].ly*scale_factor;
  }
}
```

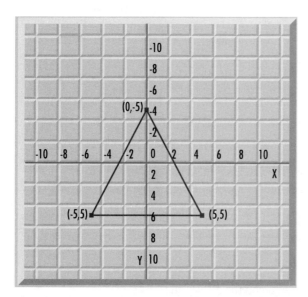

Figure 6-19 The triangle from Figure 6-17 scaled by a factor of 0.5

Again, remember, that the *sx* and *sy* fields of the vertex_type structure hold screen coordinates and the *lx* and *ly* fields hold local coordinates. Thus we scale the local coordinates to produce the screen coordinates.

Only one parameter is necessary when calling this function: the scaling factor. The screen coordinates of the shape will be calculated based on the local coordinates in the structure.

It's best to scale the shape before we translate it, so we'll need to rewrite our Translate() function so that it will use the already scaled values in the *sy* and *sx* fields rather than the values in the *ly* and *lx* fields. Listing 6-12 is the slightly rewritten Translate() function.

 ## Listing 6-12 Rewritten Translate() function

```
void shape_type::Translate(int xtrans,int ytrans)

// Translate SHAPE to coordinates XTRANS, YTRANS

{
  for (int i=0; i<number_of_vertices; i++) {
      vertex[i].sx+=xtrans;
      vertex[i].sy+=ytrans;
  }
}
```

Listing 6-13 shows a complete program that scales and translates a rectangle.

Listing 6-13 SCALE.CPP

```
#include    <stdio.h>
#include    <dos.h>
#include    <conio.h>
#include    "bresnham.h"
#include    "screen.h"

int const DISTANCE=10;

// Variable structures for shape data:

struct vertex_type {          // Structure for vertices
          int lx,ly;          // local coordinates of vertex
          int sx,sy;          // screen coordinates of vertex
};

class shape_type {            // Structure to hold shape data
private:
          int color;          // Color of shape
          int number_of_vertices; // Number of vertices in shape
          vertex_type *vertex;    // Array of vertex descriptor
public:
```

continued on next page

continued from previous page

```
            shape_type(int num, vertex_type *vert,int col=15):vertex(vert),
                    number_of_vertices(num),color(col) {;}
            void Draw(char far *screen);
            void Translate(int xtrans, int ytrans);
            void Scale(float scale_factor);
};

// Draws the shape
void shape_type::Draw(char far *screen)
{

        // Loop through vertices in shape:

        for (int i=0; i<number_of_vertices; i++) {

            // Calculate offset of next vertex:

            int p2=i+1;

            // Wrap to 0:

            if (p2>=number_of_vertices) p2=0;

            // Draw line from this vertex to next vertex:

            linedraw(vertex[i].sx,vertex[i].sy,
                        vertex[p2].sx,vertex[p2].sy,
                        color,screen);
        }
}

void shape_type:: Translate(int xtrans, int ytrans)
{
        // Translate each point in shape by xtrans/ytrans

        for(int i=0;i<number_of_vertices;i++) {
                vertex[i].sx += xtrans;
                vertex[i].sy += ytrans;
                }
}

void shape_type::Scale(float scale_factor)
{
        // Scale shape by scale_factor

        for(int i=0; i< number_of_vertices;i++) {
                vertex[i].sx = vertex[i].lx*scale_factor;
                vertex[i].sy = vertex[i].ly*scale_factor;
                }
}
// Data for triangle:
```

```
vertex_type triangle_array[]={
        {0,-10,                                  // First vertex
         0,0},
        {10,10,                                  // Second vertex
         0,0},
        {-10,10,                                 // Third vertex
         0,0}
};

// Triangle:
// 3 vertices and  triangle_array  is Pointer to vertex array
shape_type shape(3, triangle_array);

void main()
{
        char far *screen =
          (char far *)MK_FP(0xa000,0);           // Create pointer to
                                                 //  video RAM
        cls(screen);                             // Clear screen
        int oldmode=*(int *)MK_FP(0x40,0x49);    // Save previous
                                                 //  video mode
        setgmode(0x13);                          // Set mode 13h

        shape.Scale(2);                          // double size of shape
        shape.Translate(150,90);                 // Move shape to
                                                 // coordinates 150,90
        shape.Draw(screen);                      // Draw shape on
                                                 //  display

        while (!kbhit());                        // Wait for key, then
                                                 //  terminate
        setgmode(oldmode);                       // Reset previous video
                                                 //  mode & end
}
```

This program scales the triangle to twice its original size before translating it to coordinates (150,90). The output of this program appears in Figure 6-20.

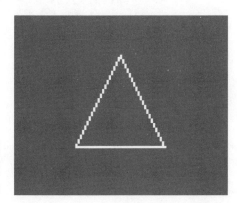

Figure 6-20 The scaled and translated triangle produced by the SCALE program

Rotating

The final trick that we're going to ask our two-dimensional shape-drawing program to perform is rotation, but this is also our most sophisticated trick. Rotating a shape is not exactly an intuitive operation. A programmer without a knowledge of trigonometry might be hard put to come up with an algorithm for rotating a shape to any angles other than 90, 180, and 270 degrees.

We saw back in Chapter 2 that there are methods for rotating shapes to arbitrary angles. They require that we use the trigonometric sine and cosine functions, which fortunately happen to be supported by routines in the Borland C++ library MATH.H.

The formula for rotating a vertex to an angle of ANGLE radians is

```
new_x=old_x * cosine(ANGLE) - old_y * sine(ANGLE);
new_y=old_x * sine(ANGLE) + old_y * cosine(ANGLE);
```

(We looked at the use of radians in Chapter 2 as well.) Based on those formulae, Listing 6-14 is a function for rotating a shape to an arbitrary angle.

Listing 6-14 Rotation function

```
void shape_type::Rotate(double angle)

// Rotate SHAPE by ANGLE

{
  int x,y;

  // Rotate all vertices in SHAPE

        for (int i=0; i<number_of_vertices; i++) {

        // Store rotated coordinates in temporary variables:

        x= vertex[i].sx*cos(angle)
            - vertex[i].sy*sin(angle);
        y= vertex[i].sx*sin(angle)
            + vertex[i].sy*cos(angle);

    // Transfer to screen coordinates:

        vertex[i].sx=x;
        vertex[i].sy=y;
  }
}
```

The angle passed to this routine in the parameter ANGLE must be in radians. Listing 6-15 is a program that not only will translate and scale a shape, but will also rotate it to an arbitrary angle.

✈ **Listing 6-15** ROTATE.CPP

```cpp
//   A program to demonstrate rotation of a two-dimensional
//   shape to an arbitrary orientation
#include      <stdio.h>
#include      <dos.h>
#include      <conio.h>
#include      <math.h>
#include      "bresnham.h"
#include      "screen.h"

int const DISTANCE=10;

// Variable structures for shape data:

struct vertex_type {            // Structure for vertices
        int lx,ly;              // local coordinates of vertex
        int sx,sy;              // screen coordinates of vertex
};

class shape_type {              // Structure to hold shape data
private:
  int color;                    // Color of shape
  int     number_of_vertices;   // Number of vertices in shape
  vertex_type *vertex;          // Array of vertex descriptor
public:
        shape_type(int num, vertex_type *vert,int col=15):vertex(vert),
              number_of_vertices(num),color(col) {;}
        void Draw(char far *screen);
        void Translate(int xtrans, int ytrans);
        void Scale(float scale_factor);
        void Rotate(double angle);
};

// Draws the shape
void shape_type::Draw(char far *screen)
{

    // Loop through vertices in shape:

    for (int i=0; i<number_of_vertices; i++) {

        // Calculate offset of next vertex:

        int p2=i+1;

        // Wrap to 0:

        if (p2>=number_of_vertices) p2=0;

        // Draw line from this vertex to next vertex:
```

continued on next page

continued from previous page

```
                             linedraw(vertex[i].sx,vertex[i].sy,
                                  vertex[p2].sx,vertex[p2].sy,
                                  color,screen);
                   }
}


void shape_type:: Translate(int xtrans, int ytrans)
{
        // Translate each point in shape by xtrans/ytrans

        for(int i=0;i<number_of_vertices;i++) {
                vertex[i].sx += xtrans;
                vertex[i].sy += ytrans;
                }
}


void shape_type::Scale(float scale_factor)
{
        // Scale shape by scale_factor

        for(int i=0; i< number_of_vertices;i++) {
                vertex[i].sx = vertex[i].lx*scale_factor;
                vertex[i].sy = vertex[i].ly*scale_factor;
                }
}


void shape_type::Rotate(double angle)
{
        // rotate shape  by angle
        int x,y;

        // rotate all vertices in shape

        for(int i=0; i< number_of_vertices;i++) {
                // store rotated coordinates in temporary variables
                x = vertex[i].sx * cos(angle)
                        - vertex[i].sy * sin(angle);
                y = vertex[i].sx * sin(angle)
                        + vertex[i].sy * cos(angle);
                vertex[i].sx = x;
                vertex[i].sy = y;
                }
}
// Data for triangle:

vertex_type triangle_array[]={
        {0,-10,                 // First vertex
        0,0},
        {10,10,                 // Second vertex
        0,0},
        {-10,10,                // Third vertex
        0,0},
};
```

```
// Triangle:
// 3 vertices and  triangle_array  is Pointer to vertex array
//     to be drawn in bright cyan (11)
shape_type shape(3, triangle_array,11);

void main()
{
        char far *screen =
         (char far *)MK_FP(0xa000,0);   // Create pointer to
                                        //  video RAM
        cls(screen);                    // Clear screen
        int oldmode=*(int *)MK_FP(0x40,0x49); // Save previous
                                        //  video mode
        setgmode(0x13);                 // Set mode 13h

        shape.Scale(2);                 // double the size
        shape.Rotate(0.261);            // rotate shape 30 degrees
        shape.Translate(150,90);
        shape.Draw(screen);             // Draw shape on
                                        //  display

        while (!kbhit());               // Wait for key, then
                                        //  terminate
        setgmode(oldmode);              // Reset previous video
                                        //  mode & end

}
```

The output of this program is shown in Figure 6-21.

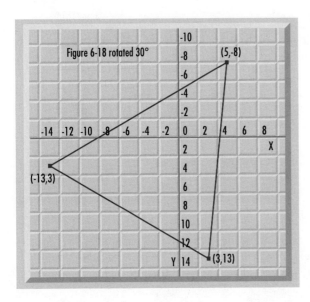

Figure 6-21 The rotated triangle produced by the ROTATE program

Doing It with Matrices

Okay, now you've scaled a shape, translated a shape, even rotated a shape. What more can you do? Well, you can perform these same three operations a bit more efficiently. (In three-dimensional graphics, which involve a lot of inherently time-consuming operations, efficiency is the name of the game.) As I mentioned in Chapter 2, the basic equations for scaling, translating, and rotating are equivalent to matrix multiplication operations—that is, there are matrices that can be multiplied by the coordinates of the vertices of a shape to produce results that are equivalent to performing the operations in the scaling, translating, and rotating algorithms that we've just presented. The advantage of using matrices to perform these operations is that the matrices for these operations can be concatenated to form a single matrix, allowing you to perform all of these operations on each vertex in a single operation. This can greatly reduce the amount of time necessary to scale, translate, and rotate a shape, especially a complex shape with lots of vertices.

In order to work with matrices, the vertex descriptor must be changed to include a third coordinate for each vertex. This third coordinate, included only to make the math work correctly, will be ignored by the drawing routines and will always be set to 1. Here's the new data structure for holding this revised version of the vertex descriptor:

```
// Structure for individual vertices:

struct vertex_type {
  int lx,ly,lt;            // Local coordinates of vertex
  int sx,sy,st;            // Screen coordinates of vertex
};
```

The only difference between this structure and the previous one is that we've now added a third field to each descriptor—*lt* and *st*. These fields will hold the 1 values required by the matrix routines that we'll be using. Here, for instance, is the new data for the rectangle shape:

```
vertex_type rectangle_array[]={   // Data for rectangle
  {-10,-10,1,                     // First vertex
  0,0,1},
  {10,-10,1,                      // Second vertex
  0,0,1},
  {10,10,1,                       // Third vertex
  0,0,1},
  {-10,10,1,                      // Fourth vertex
  0,0,1}
};
```

We used the algorithm for multiplying matrices in Chapter 2. Now all we need are the matrices for performing specific operations. The matrix for translating a two-dimensional shape is

```
1        0        0
0        1        0
xtrans   ytrans   1
```

In a moment, we'll examine a routine for multiplying this matrix by a vertex descriptor to translate the vertex to coordinates *xtrans* and *ytrans*. First, however, let's look at the matrices for the other operations that we need to perform. Here's the matrix for performing scaling:

```
scale_factor  0                0
0             scale_factor     0
0             0                1
```

Finally, here's the matrix for performing rotation:

```
cosine(ANGLE)  --sine(ANGLE)   0
sine(ANGLE)    cosine(ANGLE)   0
0              0               1
```

We can easily concatenate this matrix with the matrix for performing translation to create a rotation-translation matrix:

```
cosine(ANGLE)  --sine(ANGLE)   0
sine(ANGLE)    cosine(ANGLE)   0
xtrans         ytrans          1
```

Listing 6-16, then, is a function that will multiply matrices together to translate, scale, and rotate a shape in a single operation.

Listing 6-16 Transformation function

```
void shape_type::Transform(float scale_factor,int xtrans, int ytrans,float angle)
{
        float matrix[3][3];     // transformation matrix
        float smatrix[3][3];    // scaling matrix
        float rtmatrix[3][3];   // rotation & translation matrix

        // Initialize scaling matrix
        smatrix[0][0]= scale_factor;
        smatrix[0][1]= 0;
        smatrix[0][2]= 0;

        smatrix[1][0]= 0;
        smatrix[1][1]= scale_factor;
        smatrix[1][2]= 0;

        smatrix[2][0]= 0;
        smatrix[2][1]= 0;
        smatrix[2][2]= 1;

        // Initialize rotation & translation matrix:
        rtmatrix[0][0] = cos(angle);
```

continued on next page

continued from previous page

```
        rtmatrix[0][1] = -sin(angle);
        rtmatrix[0][2] = 0;

        rtmatrix[1][0] = sin(angle);
        rtmatrix[1][1] = cos(angle);
        rtmatrix[1][2] = 0;

        rtmatrix[2][0] = xtrans;
        rtmatrix[2][1] = ytrans;
        rtmatrix[2][2] = 0;

        // multiply together to get the transformation matrix

        for(int i=0; i<3; i++) {
                for(int j=0; j<3; j++) {
                        matrix[i][j]=0;
                        for(int k=0; k<3;k++)
                                matrix[i][j]+= smatrix[i][k] * rtmatrix[k][j];
                }
        }

        // multiply all vertices by transformation matrix:

        for(int v=0; v< number_of_vertices;v++) {

                // initialize temporary variables:
                int temp0 = 0;
                int temp1 = 0;
                int temp2 = 0;

                // accumulate results in temporary variables:
                temp0 += vertex[v].lx * matrix[0][0] +
                        vertex[v].ly * matrix[1][0] + matrix[2][0];
                temp1 += vertex[v].lx * matrix[0][1] +
                        vertex[v].ly * matrix[1][1] + matrix[2][1];
                temp2 += vertex[v].lx * matrix[0][2] +
                        vertex[v].ly * matrix[1][2] + matrix[2][2];

                // Transfer results to screen coordinates

                vertex[v].sx = temp0;
                vertex[v].sy = temp1;
                vertex[v].st = temp2;
        }
}
```

This function used the matrix multiplication routines to multiply the scaling and rotation-translation matrices (created in the first part of the routine) together, and then to multiply the resulting transformation matrix by each vertex descriptor in the shape. Now Listing 6-17 uses this routine to translate, scale, and rotate a rectangle.

Listing 6-17 Matrix transformation program

```
// ROTATE2.CPP
//   A program to demonstrate the use of matrices to scale,
//   translate and rotate a shape.
#include        <stdio.h>
#include        <dos.h>
#include        <conio.h>
#include        <math.h>
#include        "bresnham.h"
#include        "screen.h"

int const DISTANCE=10;

// Variable structures for shape data:

struct vertex_type {                 // Structure for vertices
        int lx,ly,lt;                // local coordinates of vertex
        int sx,sy,st;                // screen coordinates of vertex
};

class shape_type {
private:
  int color;                         // Color of shape
  int    number_of_vertices;         // Number of vertices in shape
  vertex_type *vertex;               // Array of vertex descriptor
public:
        shape_type(int num, vertex_type *vert,int col=15):vertex(vert),
                    number_of_vertices(num),color(col) {;}
        void Draw(char far *screen);
        // The Translate,Scale and Rotate functions are
        //      all combined into one transformation function:
        void Transform(float scale_factor,int xtrans, int ytrans, float angle);
};

// Draws the shape
void shape_type::Draw(char far *screen)
{

        // Loop through vertices in shape:

        for (int i=0; i<number_of_vertices; i++) {

                // Calculate offset of next vertex:

                int p2=i+1;

                // Wrap to 0:

                if (p2>=number_of_vertices) p2=0;
```

continued on next page

continued from previous page

```
                    // Draw line from this vertex to next vertex:

                    linedraw(vertex[i].sx,vertex[i].sy,
                                    vertex[p2].sx,vertex[p2].sy,
                                    color,screen);
          }
}

void shape_type::Transform(float scale_factor,int xtrans, int ytrans,float angle)
{
          float matrix[3][3];  // transformation matrix
          float smatrix[3][3]; // scaling matrix
          float rtmatrix[3][3]; // rotation & translation matrix

          // Initialize scaling matrix
          smatrix[0][0]= scale_factor;
          smatrix[0][1]= 0;
          smatrix[0][2]= 0;

          smatrix[1][0]= 0;
          smatrix[1][1]= scale_factor;
          smatrix[1][2]= 0;

          smatrix[2][0]= 0;
          smatrix[2][1]= 0;
          smatrix[2][2]= 1;

          // Initialize rotation & translation matrix:
          rtmatrix[0][0] = cos(angle);
          rtmatrix[0][1] = -sin(angle);
          rtmatrix[0][2] = 0;

          rtmatrix[1][0] = sin(angle);
          rtmatrix[1][1] = cos(angle);
          rtmatrix[1][2] = 0;

          rtmatrix[2][0] = xtrans;
          rtmatrix[2][1] = ytrans;
          rtmatrix[2][2] = 0;

          // multiply together to get the transformation matrix

          for(int i=0; i<3; i++) {
                  for(int j=0; j<3; j++) {
                          matrix[i][j]=0;
                          for(int k=0; k<3;k++)
                                  matrix[i][j]+= smatrix[i][k] * rtmatrix[k][j];
                  }
          }

          // multiply all vertices by transformation matrix:
```

```
        for(int v=0; v< number_of_vertices;v++) {

                // initialize temporary variables:
                int temp0 = 0;
                int temp1 = 0;
                int temp2 = 0;

                // accumulate results in temporary variables:
                temp0 += vertex[v].lx * matrix[0][0] +
                   vertex[v].ly * matrix[1][0] + matrix[2][0];
                temp1 += vertex[v].lx * matrix[0][1] +
                   vertex[v].ly * matrix[1][1] + matrix[2][1];
                temp2 += vertex[v].lx * matrix[0][2] +
                   vertex[v].ly * matrix[1][2] + matrix[2][2];

                // Transfer results to screen coordinates

                vertex[v].sx = temp0;
                vertex[v].sy = temp1;
                vertex[v].st = temp2;
        }
}


// Data for rectangle:

vertex_type rectangle_array[]={
        {-10,-10,1,            // First vertex
        0,0,1},
        {10,-10,1,             // Second vertex
        0,0,1},
        {10,10,1,              // Third vertex
        0,0,1},
        {-10,10,1,             // Fourth vertex
        0,0,1}
};

// Rectangle:
//  4 vertices and  rectangle_array  is Pointer to vertex array
shape_type shape(4, rectangle_array);

void main()
{
        char far *screen =
        (char far *)MK_FP(0xa000,0);        // Create pointer to
                                            //  video RAM
        cls(screen);                        // Clear screen
        int oldmode=*(int *)MK_FP(0x40,0x49); // Save previous
                                            //  video mode
        setgmode(0x13);                     // Set mode 13h
```

continued on next page

continued from previous page

```
        shape.Transform(1.5,160,100,0.7);
        shape.Draw(screen);                    // Draw shape on
                                               //  display

        while (!kbhit());                      // Wait for key, then
                                               //  terminate
        setgmode(oldmode);                     // Reset previous video
                                               //  mode & end
}
```

The output of this program is shown in Figure 6-22.

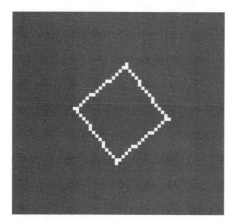

Figure 6-22 The rectangle from the earlier figure scaled, translated, and rotated using matrices

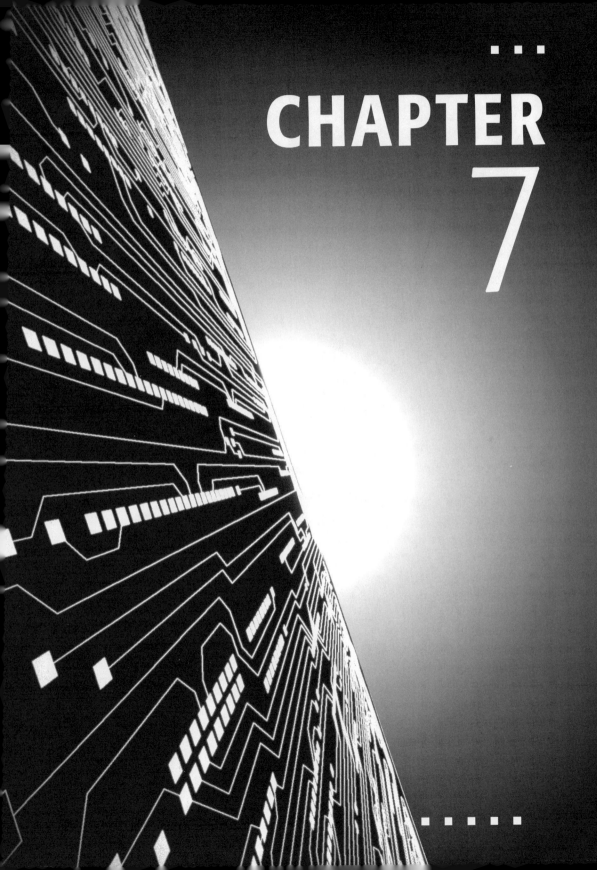

CHAPTER

7

7

From Two Dimensions to Three

Working with three dimensions is much like dealing with only two. Things get a bit more complicated, but the concepts remain pretty much the same. It's that extra dimension that makes three-dimensional animation so interesting—and challenging. Without the third dimension, 3D animation would be pretty flat, in more ways than one.

In computer graphics, the third dimension is always depth, the dimension that runs perpendicular to the plane of the computer display even though the display itself is flat, at least until *Star Trek*–style holodecks become available. And that, of course, is what makes three-dimensional graphics so challenging: rendering a three-dimensional world on a two-dimensional screen in such a way that the viewer can still tell that the third dimension is there. Let's start by considering the way in which three dimensions will be represented in the internal memory of the computer.

The *z* Coordinate

In Chapter 6, simple two-dimensional shapes were represented in terms of the *x* and *y* coordinates of their vertices. We can do much the same thing with three-dimensional graphics, but we'll need a third coordinate to represent the third dimension. In keeping with the conventions of three-dimensional Cartesian graphs, we'll call that third coordinate the z coordinate.

The z axis will be perpendicular to both the x (width) and y (height) axes, running into and out of the video display. (See Figure 7-1.)

To avoid confusion between the x and y screen axes and the x, y, and z axes of the coordinate systems used to define the vertices of objects, we'll need to start thinking in terms of three different coordinate systems. In earlier chapters, we introduced two coordinate systems: the screen coordinate system used to draw objects on the display and the local coordinate system of the objects themselves. (Recall that screen coordinates are plotted from a fixed origin point on the screen, while local coordinates are relative to an origin point such as the center of an object.) Now we'll introduce a third coordinate system that will bridge the three-dimensional gap between these two systems—the world coordinate system, which provides us with a way of referencing points in space within an imaginary three-dimensional world we'll be building inside the computer.

There's nothing new about the idea of a world coordinate system; such systems have been around a lot longer than computers. It is traditional, for instance, to define points on the surface of the earth in terms of a two-dimensional coordinate system, in which one coordinate is called latitude and the other is called longitude. (See Figure 7-2.) We can get away with using two coordinates to define points on the earth's surface because the earth's surface is essentially two-dimensional (though the fact that this two-dimen-

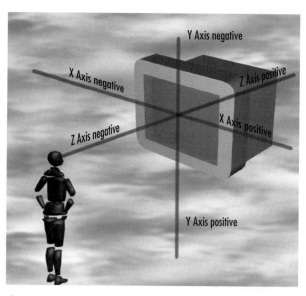

Figure 7-1 Imagine the z axis extending from the viewer's eyes straight into the center of the video display

Figure 7-2 Latitude coordinates are roughly equivalent to *x* coordinates of the Cartesian coordinate system and longitude coordinates are roughly equivalent to *y* coordinates

sional surface is wrapped around a three-dimensional sphere has caused no end of grief for cartographers trying to produce flat, rectangular maps). Even so, if we want to know how far something is above the surface of the earth (or, more properly, above the specific elevation referred to as sea level), we need a third coordinate, usually called altitude. With latitude, longitude, and altitude, we can specify the position of any point on or near the surface of the earth.

Similarly, we could define positions within our solar system with a three-dimensional coordinate system in which two coordinates represented rotations around the sun and a third coordinate represented distance outward from the sun. Indeed, the position of any object in the universe could be defined with such a three-coordinate system.

Cubic Universes

In both of those examples, the space defined by the coordinate system is spherical—in one case, the surface of a globe and in the other case, the orbital space surrounding the sun. It's much easier mathematically, however, to define cubical spaces, which are organized according to a three-dimensional Cartesian grid. The worlds that we'll design in this book will always be arranged as perfect cubes, with every point inside the cube defined by its position relative to three Cartesian axes.

It's not hard to imagine such a world. Let's suppose that a force of all-powerful alien invaders decided to capture a portion of the earth's surface inside an invisible force field and tow it back to its home planet as a museum exhibit. Suppose further that the force field measures 100 miles on each side, so that the segment of the earth's surface captured inside is 100 miles wide, 100 miles long, and 100 miles deep. If we define a point within this captive section of the earth as the origin point of a coordinate system, then any other point can be represented by three coordinates measured relative to that origin. For instance, the origin point itself would be at coordinates (0,0,0) while a position 10 miles west (where east-west is the *x* axis), 3 miles north (where north-south is the y axis), and 0.5 mile above (where up-down is the z axis) would be at coordinates (10,3,0.5) as in Figure 7-3. (We could just as easily define the z axis as the north-south axis, the y axis as the up-down axis, and the x axis as the east-west axis. It really doesn't matter, as long as we use one system consistently.)

That's how we'll design our worlds, as cubic sections of space with an origin point at dead center. All points in such a world can then be defined by coordinates relative to that origin. A point 400 units in the x direction from the origin, 739 units in the y direction, and 45 units in the z direction would be at coordinates (400,739,45). How large are these units? That's for us to decide. In the previous example, we used miles as our unit, but miles are too large to do the job in many cases. More likely, our unit will be something on the order of a foot or even an inch. In fact, there's no reason that the unit has to be precisely equivalent to any real-world unit of measurement; we can always define a constant within our program that specifies the conversion factors to translate these world units (as we'll refer to them from now on) into traditional units of measurement. For instance, if we choose a world unit that is equal to 7.3 centimeters, we can define a floating-point constant called CENTIMETERS_PER_UNIT and set it equal to 7.3. We can then use this constant to translate back and forth between world units and metric units of measurement.

And how do we decide which real-world axes will be equivalent to the x, y, and z axes of a three-dimensional Cartesian graph? Once again, that's entirely up to the programmer. Typically, the x screen axis runs left and right and the y screen axis runs up and down, so it would seem obvious to define the x world axis as east and west, the y world axis as north and south, and the z world axis (which has no screen equivalent) as altitude. But in a true three-dimensional animated program, the user can shift the

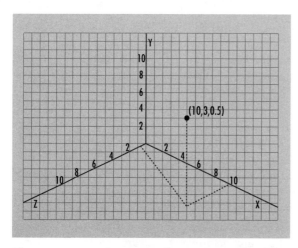

Figure 7-3 A point at coordinates 10,3,0.5 within a world coordinate system

point of view so that it points north or south, east or west, up or down, or some point in between; there's no reason that the world coordinates have to correspond to screen coordinates. (In a later chapter, however, we'll learn a method for aligning the screen axes with the world axes to simplify drawing a screen representation of our three-dimensional world.) We can just as easily choose to place our world axes at any arbitrary angle relative to the traditional axes of our imaginary world. However, it's probably best if we align the world coordinates axes with *some* traditional axis—for instance, we'll probably want to align the x axis with the north-south axis or the east-west axis rather than the east-northeast–west-southwest axis.

From World Coordinates to Screen Coordinates

It's not difficult to see how these world x, y, and z coordinates relate to the local coordinates and screen coordinates that we introduced in earlier chapters. In the last chapter, we described objects in terms of their local x and y coordinates. In this chapter, we'll describe objects in terms of their local x, y, and z coordinates. Then we'll translate those coordinates into world x, y, and z coordinates—that is, coordinates relative to the origin of the coordinate system of the world in which those objects exist. Finally, those world x, y, and z coordinates will translate back into the screen x and y coordinates at which the vertices of those objects will be depicted on the video display. See Figure 7-4 for an illustration of this concept.

Figure 7-4 illustrates an important sequence of translations. Every object will have its own local x, y, and z coordinates. The 3D transformation functions (analogous to the 2D transformation functions in the last chapter) translate those local coordinates into the object's world x, y, and z coordinates. Finally, we'll translate those world x, y, and z coordinates into the screen x and y coordinates at which the object (and its vertices) will be displayed. The z coordinate is lost in the final step, because there is no z axis on the video display. The process by which the z coordinate is lost and the screen x and y coordinates are determined is called projection, and we will look at it in greater detail later in this chapter.

Storing the Local x, y, and z Coordinates

To start this process, we'll need to store the local x, y, and z coordinates of an object's vertices in a structure. This isn't any more difficult than storing the local x and y coordinates of a two-dimensional object, which we did in the last chapter. However, it is necessary to leave room in this data structure for the world coordinates of the object. The data structure used to define three-dimensional vertices looks like this:

```
struct vertex_type {   // Structure for individual vertices
   int lx,ly,lz,lt;    // Local coordinates of vertex
   int wx,wy,wz,wt;    // World coordinates of vertex
   int sx,sy,st;       // Screen coordinates of vertex
};
```

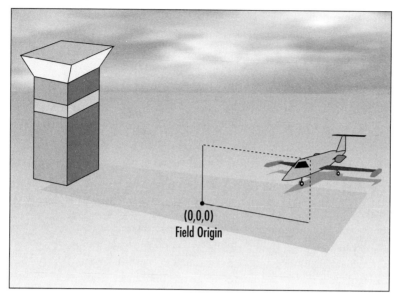

Figure 7-4 The difference between local, world, and screen coordinates
(a) Airplane position measured relative to local coordinate system of field it is about to land on

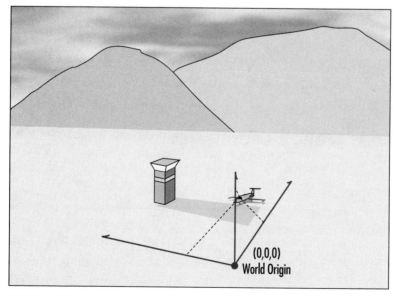

(b) Same airplane measured relative to coordinate system of world it is part of

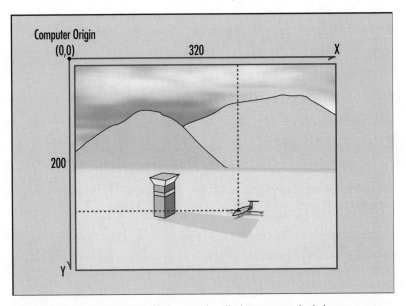

Computer Origin
(0,0)

320

X

200

Y

(c) Image of same airplane on computer video display, measured relative to screen coordinate system of display

This data structure holds three sets of coordinates, as opposed to the two sets of coordinates in our previous definition of vertex_type. They include the dummy *t* coordinates that were added in the last chapter to make the matrix math come out right. The first set (*lx*, *ly*, *lz*, and *lt*) represents the local coordinates of the object, defined relative to the local origin of the object (which, as you'll recall from the last chapter, is usually at the center of the object). The second set (*wx*, *wy*, *wz*, and *wt*) represents the world coordinates of the object, which are the coordinates of the vertices of the object relative to the origin of the world in which we'll be placing the object. (More about this later.) The third set of coordinates (*sx* and *sy*) are the screen coordinates of the vertices. This last set only includes the *x* and *y* coordinates, since the video display is flat and only offers two dimensions for our coordinate system. Later, we'll develop a function that translates the world *x*, *y*, and *z* coordinates of a vertex into screen *x* and *y* coordinates.

With this new structure for holding three-dimensional vertices, it should be easy to develop a class to hold three-dimensional wireframe shapes. In fact, that class will look exactly like the one we used in the last chapter to hold two-dimensional wireframe shapes. The class (along with the structure for holding line descriptors) looks like this:

```
struct line_type  {              // Structure for wireframe lines
   int start,end;                // Pointers to vertices for start
                                 //  and end
};

class Shape {                    // Class for complete shape
private:
   int color;                    // Color of shape
   int number_of_vertices;       // Number of vertices in shape
   int number_of_lines;          // Number of lines in shape
   vertex_type *vertex;          // Array of vertex descriptors
   line_type *line;              // Array of line descriptors
public:
  Shape(int numVertex, vertex_type *vert,int numLine, line_type *lin,int col=15):
       vertex(vert),number_of_vertices(numVertex),line(lin),
       number_of_lines(numLine),color(col) {;}
};
```

There are a lot of similarities between the classes that hold both three- and two-dimensional wireframe shapes. One of the major differences between the two types of shape is the presence of the z vertex coordinates in the three-dimensional shapes—and that difference is entirely taken care of in the definition of the vertex_type structure. Of course, since we want to define three-dimensional shapes with line_type structures, we add extra parameters to the class constructor to define both the line_type array and the number of elements within this array.

Creating a Three-Dimensional Shape

Three-dimensional objects can now be defined as two-dimensional objects were in the last chapter: lists of vertices followed by lists of lines connecting those vertices. Now, however, a z coordinate must be included for each vertex. Here, for instance, is a definition for a three-dimensional wireframe cube:

```
// Data for shapes:

vertex_type cube_vertices[]={     // Vertices for cube
   {-10,-10,10,1,                 // Vertex 0
    0,0,0,1,
    0,0,0,1},
   {10,-10,10,1,                  // Vertex 1
    0,0,0,1,
    0,0,0,1},
   {10,10,10,1,                   // Vertex 2
    0,0,0,1,
    0,0,0,1},
   {-10,10,10,1,                  // Vertex 3
    0,0,0,1,
    0,0,0,1},
   {-10,-10,-10,1,                // Vertex 4
    0,0,0,1,
```

```
  0,0,0,1},
 {10,-10,-10,1,                    // Vertex 5
  0,0,0,1,
  0,0,0,1},
 {10,10,-10,1,                     // Vertex 6
  0,0,0,1,
  0,0,0,1},
 {-10,10,-10,1,                    // Vertex 7
  0,0,0,1,
  0,0,0,1},
};

line_type cube_lines[]={
 {0,1},                           // Line 0
 {1,2},                           // Line 1
 {2,3{,                           // Line 2
 {3,0},                           // Line 3
 {4,5},                           // Line 4
 {5,6},                           // Line 5
 {6,7},                           // Line 6
 {7,4},                           // Line 7
 {0,4},                           // Line 8
 {1,5},                           // Line 9
 {2,6},                           // Line 10
 {3,7}                            // Line 11
}

Shape shape(8, cube_vertices,12, cube_lines);
```

A picture of this cube is shown in Figure 7-5. Sharp-eyed readers may notice that the vertex data for the cube is simply the data for the square from the last chapter with z coordinates and a second square added. As in the last chapter, only the local coordinates have been filled in; the world and screen coordinates are set to 0 until the 3D transformation routines can process them. (Note that while the x and y coordinates of the vertices in the second square—that is, the second set of four vertices in the shape—are the same as those in the first square, the z coordinates are different.) The line data, on the other hand, has changed significantly. Not only are the vertices in each square connected to make the square, but the vertices in the first square are connected to the vertices in the second square to form a cube.

Projection and Perspective

How do we draw this wireframe cube on the video display? Oddly enough, we could use the same routine to display this data as we used to display two-dimensional data in the last chapter. The result would be less than interesting, however, because that routine would ignore the z coordinate information; the object would appear flat. Actually, this can be a legitimate method of displaying three-dimensional objects

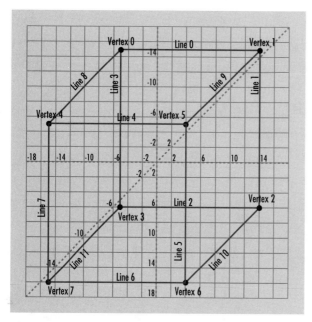

Figure 7-5 The cube described by the data in the shape descriptor

(known technically as a parallel projection). However, it would display the cube as a square, indistinguishable from the square displayed in the last chapter. At any rate, we are more interested in perspective projections than in parallel projections.

What is needed, then, is a method for adding z coordinate information to the screen coordinates. This isn't easy to do, since there is no such thing as a screen z coordinate. Therefore, we must somehow squeeze the z coordinate information into the x and y screen coordinates. In technical terms, we must map the x, y, and z world coordinates of the object into the x and y coordinates of the screen—projecting the image.

This is a pretty familiar concept. When you watch a film in a movie theater, you see images of a three-dimensional world literally projected onto the flat surface of the movie screen. And, though this image is flat, you probably have no trouble accepting that the world depicted in the image is three-dimensional. That's because there are visual cues in the flat image that indicate the presence of a third dimension.

The most important of these cues is perspective, the phenomenon that causes objects viewed at a distance to appear smaller than objects that are nearby. Not only do objects at a distance tend to seem smaller, but they also tend to move closer to the center of your visual field. You can demonstrate this for yourself by standing in a large open area, such as a field or a parking lot, and looking at a row of distant (but not *too* distant) objects. Fix your gaze on an object in the center of the row and walk toward that object. As you do so, notice that not only do all of the objects in the row seem to grow larger (that is, to occupy more of your visual field), but objects toward the right and left ends of the row move farther and farther toward the right and left edges of your visual field, until you have to turn your head in order to see them. (See Figure 7-6.) If you reverse the process and walk backwards (which might be awkward in a crowded parking lot), the objects at the left and right ends of the row will move back toward the center of your visual field.

In a wireframe image, we can approximate this effect by moving the origin of our coordinate system into the center of the display (where it will approximate the center of the user's visual field) and altering the *x* and *y* coordinates of objects so that more distant vertices will move toward the origin and closer vertices will move toward the edges of the display. This will give us the effect of perspective. The formulas for moving the *x* and *y* coordinates of a vertex toward or away from the origin based on its distance from the viewer are

```
SCREEN_X = WORLD_X / WORLD_Z
SCREEN_Y = WORLD_Y / WORLD_Z
```

In English, this tells us that the screen *x* coordinate of a vertex is equal to the world *x* coordinate of that vertex divided by the world *z* coordinate of that vertex. Similarly, the screen *y* coordinate of a vertex is equal to the world *y* coordinate divided by the world *z* coordinate. This formula produces a perspective effect in this fashion: Dividing the *x* and *y* coordinates by a positive *z* coordinate value will cause the *x* and *y* coordinates to grow smaller—that is, to move closer to the origin of the coordinate system. The larger the *z* coordinate, the smaller the *x* and *y* coordinates will become after this division—that is, the closer they will move to the origin. Because we'll be moving the origin to the center of the display, this will cause the vertices of distant objects (those with larger coordinates) to move farther toward the origin than the vertices of nearer objects (those with smaller *z* coordinates). This movement of vertices toward the origin according to their *z* coordinates will produce the illusion of perspective, as shown in Figure 7-7. Note how the changing positions of the dots correspond to the changing positions of the trees in Figure 7-6.

However, the above formulas tend to produce *too much* of a perspective illusion. Vertices would zoom so rapidly toward the origin that most objects would be reduced to mere pinpoints on the display. The reason for this is that the viewer is assumed in these formulas to have his or her face smashed up against the video display, thus approximating the viewpoint of a wide-angle camera lens. To move the viewer back away from the display (and, not incidentally, to narrow the angle of our imaginary lens), we must add an additional factor, VIEWER_DISTANCE:

```
SCREEN_X = VIEWER_DISTANCE * WORLD_X / WORLD_Z
SCREEN_X = VIEWER_DISTANCE * WORLD_Y / WORLD_Z
```

(a) Three trees seen from a distance

(b) A closer view of the trees from Figure 7-6(a)

Figure 7-6 Perspective causes objects viewed at a distance to appear smaller than objects that are nearby

(c) A close-up view of the center tree from Figure 7-6(a). Note that the trees at both ends of the row have moved entirely out of the visual field

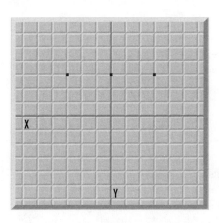

Figure 7-7 Creating the illusion of perspective

(a) Three dots in a Cartesian coordinate system, representing pixels on a video display

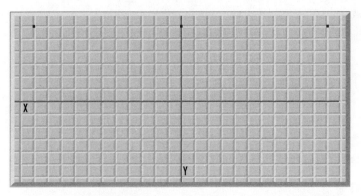

(b) The dots from Figure 7-7(a), moving away from the origin of the system in both the *x* and *y* dimensions

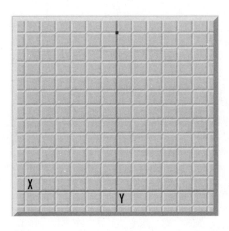

(c) The dots from Figure 7-7(a), still farther from the origin than in Figure 7-7(b), giving the impression of an extreme close-up

There is no fixed value for VIEWER_DISTANCE. Through some basic math and trigonometry, it can be shown that when it is equal to one-half the width of the screen, the field of view is 90 degrees. In the programs that follow, we'll usually place the viewer distance in the range of 40 to 150, yielding a field of view larger than 90 degrees. You can fine-tune this value to your own taste in programs that you write yourself.

The Project() Function

Let's begin creating a set of routines for processing the vertices of wireframe objects. We'll place them in a file called WIRE.CPP, with definitions and prototypes in the file WIRE.H. To start things out, we'll develop a Project() function for our Shape class that will project the world x, y, and z coordinates of the vertices of a wireframe object into the x and y screen coordinates necessary to display that object. The calling program will pass a single parameter to this function. This will be the value for the VIEWER_DISTANCE factor, which will be called distance within this function.

Listing 7-1 contains the text of the Shape::Project() function.

 Listing 7-1 The Project() function

```
void Shape::Project(int distance)
{

// Project shape onto screen

// Point to current vertex:
    vertex_type *vptr= vertex;
// Loop though vertices:

  for (int v=0; v<number_of_vertices; v++,vptr++) {

    // Divide world x & y coords by z coords:

    vptr->sx=distance*vptr->wx/vptr->wz;
    vptr->sy=distance*vptr->wy/vptr->wz;
  }
}
```

The function is short and its inner workings fairly straightforward. The for loops iterate through all of the vertices in the wireframe object pointed to by the parameter shape, and the code within the loop translates the world x and y coordinates of each vertex into screen x and y coordinates, using the formulas we looked at earlier. We create a pointer to the vertex structure before the loop starts and reference the specific coordinates relative to that pointer, which is called *vptr*. For instance, the world x coordinate of the vertex is referenced as *vptr*->wx, where the -> operator is used to access individual fields within the structure pointed to by *vptr*. This is not only a convenience pointer (one which saves the programmer typing), but it also makes the code slightly faster. If we used the array operator, [ ], and index into the array, every occurrence of the expression vertex[v] would require the computation of the address that was *v* number of elements into the vertex array. That would happen three times in each of the two lines in our code above, or six times every loop iteration:

```
vertex[v].sx=distance*vertex[v].wx/vertex[v].wz;
vertex[v].sy=distance*vertex[v].wy/vertex[v].wz;
```

Although six addition computations on today's computers are done in the fraction of a wink, the effect of saving any CPU processing time is cumulative. A little here, a little there, and all of a sudden, we have a fast set of routines. Further exploration of optimizations will happen in depth in a coming chapter, but the use of a pointer as replacement for an array iteration is fairly common, easy to read, and used in three of the Shape class functions.

Using the Shape::Project() function, we can create a set of screen *x* and *y* coordinates that can then be drawn on the video display. Before we start drawing 3D wireframe objects, however, let's create a set of functions to scale, translate, and rotate those objects.

Transformation in Three Dimensions

In the last chapter, we performed two-dimensional transformations on two-dimensional wireframe objects. The three transformations performed in that chapter were scaling, translation, and rotation. In this chapter, we'll perform those same three transformations. However, the three-dimensional versions of those transformations need to be slightly different from the two-dimensional versions. For instance, two-dimensional scaling involved changing the size of a shape in the *x* and *y* dimensions, while three-dimensional scaling involves changing the size of a shape in the *x*, *y*, and *z* dimensions. Similarly, two-dimensional translation involved moving a shape in the *x* and *y* dimensions. Three-dimensional translation involves moving a shape in the *x*, *y*, and *z* dimensions.

The transformation that changes the most when extended into the third dimension is rotation. In the last chapter, we rotated objects around their local point of origin. There was really only one type of rotation that we could perform. In three dimensions, however, three types of rotation are possible: rotations about the *x* axis, rotations about the *y* axis, and rotations about the *z* axis.

Although we didn't use the term in the last chapter, the type of rotation that we performed in two dimensions was rotation about the *z* axis. (We didn't call it that because we hadn't introduced the *z* axis yet.) The *z* axis, remember, can be imagined as a line extending through the screen of the display perfectly perpendicular to the surface of the display. An object rotating about the z axis is not rotating in the z dimension; in fact, that is the only dimension that it is not rotating in. An object rotating about the z axis is rotating in the x and y dimensions, which are the only dimensions available to a two-dimensional shape. (See Figure 7-8.)

Three-dimensional objects, however, can also rotate in the x and z dimensions and in the y and z dimensions. The former type of rotation is a rotation about the y axis and the latter is a rotation about the x axis. (See Figures 7-9 and 7-10.) We can combine rotations in all three dimensions to form a single rotation that will put a three-dimensional object into any arbitrary orientation.

When we performed these transformations in the last chapter, we used one master function to perform scaling, translating, and rotating. Let's try a slightly different approach this time around. Instead of one master function, let's perform each of these transformations with a separate function much in the same way that the functions were introduced. The advantage of using a separate function for each is that we don't have to perform all of the transformations on an object if we don't want to. (We could also use separate functions for x, y, and z rotation if we wanted to, but we won't go quite that far in this chapter.) The disadvantage of using separate functions is that, if we're not careful, we'll lose the advantage of creating a single master matrix, which we could use to transform every vertex in an object with a single matrix multiplication.

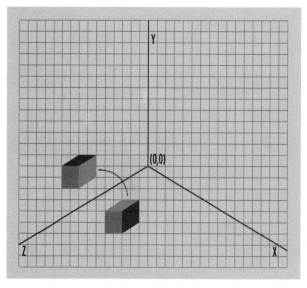

Figure 7-8 An object rotating about the z axis of a three-dimensional coordinate system

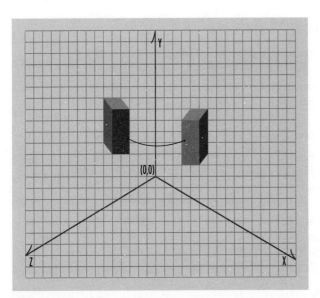

Figure 7-9 An object rotating about the *y* axis of a three-dimensional coordinate system

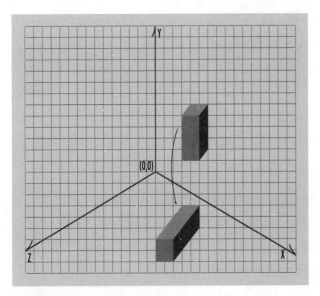

Figure 7-10 An object rotating about the *x* axis of a three-dimensional coordinate system

The Global Transformation Matrix

To assure that this doesn't happen, we'll create a global multiplication matrix called matrix that will be available to all functions in our package of wireframe transformation routines. Each of the individual transformation functions will then create their own special-purpose transformation matrices and concatenate them (that is, multiply them) with the master transformation matrix. Thus, the master transformation matrix will represent the concatenation of all the special-purpose transformation matrices. To perform the actual transformation of the object, we will need a master transformation function, which we'll call transform(), to multiply all of the vertices in an object with the master concatenation matrix. Since this will operate on the vertices of the Shape object, we'll make this master transformation function part of the Shape class. Before we call this function, however, it will be necessary to call all of the special-purpose transformation functions. We'll also need a function, which we'll call inittrans, to initialize the master transformation matrix to the identity matrix prior to the first concatenation. And, since we'll be doing a lot of matrix multiplication, it would be a good idea to create a function to perform generic multiplication of 4x4 matrices (the only kind of matrices that we'll be dealing with, other than the 1x4 vectors of the vertex descriptors).

Listing 7-2 shows what the inittrans() function looks like.

 Listing 7-2 The inittrans() function

```
void inittrans()
{

// Initialize master transformation matrix to the
// identity matrix

  matrix[0][0]=1; matrix[0][1]=0; matrix[0][2]=0;
    matrix[0][3]=0;
  matrix[1][0]=0; matrix[1][1]=1; matrix[1][2]=0;
    matrix[1][3]=0;
  matrix[2][0]=0; matrix[2][1]=0; matrix[2][2]=1;
    matrix[2][3]=0;
  matrix[3][0]=0; matrix[3][1]=0; matrix[3][2]=0;
    matrix[3][3]=1;
}
```

This function doesn't need much explanation. Recall from Chapter 2 that all positions in an identity matrix are equal to 0 except those along the main diagonal, which are equal to 1. The inittrans function sets matrix equal to such an identity matrix. This is roughly equivalent to initializing an ordinary variable to 0.

The generic 4x4 matrix multiplication routine is in Listing 7-3.

Listing 7-3 The matmult() function

```
void matmult(float result[4][4],float mat1[4][4],
    float mat2[4][4])
{

// Multiply matrix MAT1 by matrix MAT2,
//   returning the result in RESULT

  for (int i=0; i<4; i++)
    for (int j=0; j<4; j++) {
      result[i][j]=0;
      for (int k=0; k<4; k++)
      result[i][j]+=mat1[i][k] * mat2[k][j];
    }
}
```

This function uses a standard matrix multiplication algorithm involving three nested for loops, similar to the one we looked at back in Chapter 2. The algorithm accepts three parameters. The first is the matrix in which the result of the multiplication is to be returned to the calling routine. The second and third are the two matrices to be multiplied.

For reasons that will become clear in a moment, we will also need a function that will copy one matrix to another matrix. We'll call that function matcopy(). The text is in Listing 7-4.

Listing 7-4 The matcopy() function

```
void matcopy(float dest[4][4],float source[4][4])
{

// Copy matrix SOURCE to matrix DEST

  for (int i=0; i<4; i++)
    for (int j=0; j<4; j++)
      dest[i][j]=source[i][j];
}
```

This function takes two pointers, called *dest* and *source,* as parameters. As you've probably guessed from the names, the function copies the matrix pointed to by *source* to the function pointed to by *dest.*

The scale() Function

In the coming listings, you'll recognize much of the code in the transformation functions from the last chapter. For instance, the scale() function creates a scaling matrix and concatenates it with the master transformation matrix. The only difference between the scaling code here and that in the last chapter—aside from the fact that the code is now isolated in a separate function—is that the actual multiplication is performed by our matmult() function. The code is in Listing 7-5. Its result is shown in Figure 7-11.

 Listing 7-5 The scale() function

```
void scale(float sf)
{
   float mat[4][4];

   // Initialize scaling matrix:

   smat[0][0]=sf; smat[0][1]=0; smat[0][2]=0; smat[0][3]=0;
   smat[1][0]=0; smat[1][1]=sf; smat[1][2]=0; smat[1][3]=0;
   smat[2][0]=0; smat[2][1]=0; smat[2][2]=sf; smat[2][3]=0;
   smat[3][0]=0; smat[3][1]=0; smat[3][2]=0; smat[3][3]=1;

   // Concatenate with master matrix:
```

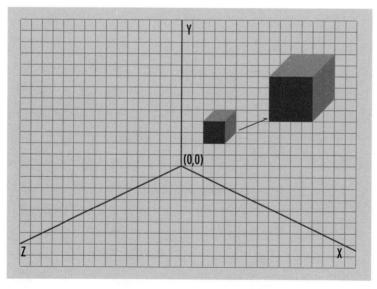

Figure 7-11 Scaling an object in three dimensions

```
   matmult(mat,smat,matrix);
   matcopy(matrix,mat);
}
```

If you remember the scaling code from the last chapter, this function shouldn't require any explanation. First, a scaling matrix is created, using the parameter *sf* as a scaling factor, and then the matmult() function is called to concatenate it with the master transformation matrix. The result of concatenation is stored in a temporary matrix called mat. Finally, matcopy() is called to copy the contents of the temporary matrix mat back into the master transformation matrix.

The translate() Function

In the same way, the translation function creates a translation matrix and concatenates it with the master transformation matrix, as shown in Listing 7-6. Its result is depicted in Figure 7-12.

 Listing 7-6 The translate() function

```
void translate(int xt,int yt,int zt)
{

// Create a translation matrix that will translate an
// object an X distance of XT, a Y distance of YT, and a
// Z distance of ZT from the screen origin

   float mat[4][4];

   tmat[0][0]=1; tmat[0][1]=0; tmat[0][2]=0; tmat[0][3]=0;
   tmat[1][0]=0; tmat[1][1]=1; tmat[1][2]=0; tmat[1][3]=0;
   tmat[2][0]=0; tmat[2][1]=0; tmat[2][2]=1; tmat[2][3]=0;
   tmat[3][0]=xt; tmat[3][1]=yt; tmat[3][2]=zt;
     tmat[3][3]=1;

// Concatenate with master matrix:

   matmult(mat,matrix,tmat);
   matcopy(matrix,mat);
}
```

In the last chapter, we used two translation parameters, one for the translation in the *x* dimension, one for translation in the *y* dimension. Now, because we're writing three-dimensional code, we need to translate in three dimensions. So we have three translation parameters: XT for translation in the *x* dimension, YT for translation in the *y* dimension, and ZT for translation in the *z* dimension. From these three parameters, this function creates a translation matrix and concatenates it with the master transformation matrix.

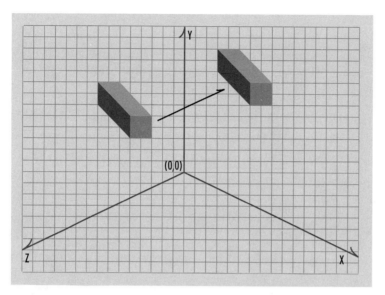

Figure 7-12 Translating an object in three dimensions

The rotate() Function

Finally, we want to be able to rotate a wireframe object in three dimensions. We'll perform all of these rotations with a single rotation function, which we'll call rotate(). The function is in Listing 7-7. (See Figure 7-13).

 Listing 7-7 The rotate() function

```
void rotate(float ax,float ay,float az)
{

   // Create three rotation matrices that will rotate an
   // object AX radians on the X axis, AY radians on the
   // Y axis, and AZ radians on the Z axis

   float mat1[4][4];
   float mat2[4][4];

   // Initialize X rotation matrix:

   xmat[0][0]=1; xmat[0][1]=0; xmat[0][2]=0; xmat[0][3]=0;
   xmat[1][0]=0; xmat[1][1]=cos(ax); xmat[1][2]=sin(ax);
      xmat[1][3]=0;
   xmat[2][0]=0; xmat[2][1]=-sin(ax); xmat[2][2]=cos(ax);
```

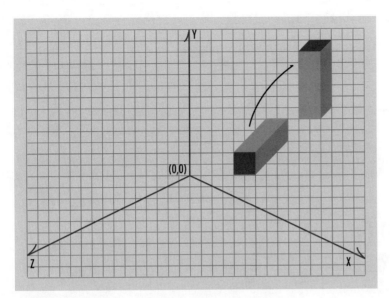

Figure 7-13 Rotating an object in three dimensions

```
   xmat[2][3]=0;
xmat[3][0]=0; xmat[3][1]=0; xmat[3][2]=0; xmat[3][3]=1;

// Concatenate this matrix with master matrix:

matmult(mat1,xmat,matrix);

// Initialize Y rotation matrix:

ymat[0][0]=cos(ay); ymat[0][1]=0; ymat[0][2]=-sin(ay);
   ymat[0][3]=0;
ymat[1][0]=0; ymat[1][1]=1; ymat[1][2]=0; ymat[1][3]=0;
ymat[2][0]=sin(ay); ymat[2][1]=0; ymat[2][2]=cos(ay);
  ymat[2][3]=0;
ymat[3][0]=0; ymat[3][1]=0; ymat[3][2]=0; ymat[3][3]=1;

// Concatenate this matrix with master matrix:

matmult(mat2,ymat,mat1);

// Initialize Z rotation matrix:

zmat[0][0]=cos(az); zmat[0][1]=sin(az); zmat[0][2]=0;
   zmat[0][3]=0;
zmat[1][0]=-sin(az); zmat[1][1]=cos(az); zmat[1][2]=0;
   zmat[1][3]=0;
zmat[2][0]=0; zmat[2][1]=0; zmat[2][2]=1; zmat[2][3]=0;
```

continued on next page

continued from previous page

```
    zmat[3][0]=0; zmat[3][1]=0; zmat[3][2]=0; zmat[3][3]=1;

    // Concatenate this matrix with master matrix:

    matmult(matrix,zmat,mat2);
}
```

This function takes three parameters: *ax* for the angle of rotation on the *x* axis, *ay* for the angle of rotation on the *y* axis, and *az* for the angle of rotation on the *z* axis. The function creates a rotation matrix for each of these rotations. (See Chapter 2 for the basic rotation matrices for *x* and *y* axis rotations.) One by one, these matrices are concatenated with the master transformation matrix.

The transform() Function

Once all of the special-purpose transformation matrices have been concatenated into the master concatenation matrix, we can call the transform() function to multiply the vertices in a Shape object with the master transformation matrix and thereby transform the object. The transform() function is in Listing 7-8.

Listing 7-8 The transform() function

```
void Shape::transform()
{
    // Multiply all vertices in SHAPE with master
    //   transformation matrix:

vertex_type *vptr=vertex;

    for (int v=0; v<number_of_vertices; v++, vptr++) {
vptr->wx=vptr->lx*matrix[0][0]+vptr->ly*matrix[1][0]
        +vptr->lz*matrix[2][0]+matrix[3][0];
    vptr->wy=vptr->lx*matrix[0][1]+vptr->ly*matrix[1][1]
        +vptr->lz*matrix[2][1]+matrix[3][1];
    vptr->wz=vptr->lx*matrix[0][2]+vptr->ly*matrix[1][2]
        +vptr->lz*matrix[2][2]+matrix[3][2];
    }
}
```

Since this function is a Shape class function, the object which calls the function contains a description of the three-dimensional wireframe object to be transformed. The transform() function uses a for loop to iterate through all of the vertices of the object and multiply each one by the master transformation matrix.

Because the master transformation matrix is unchanged by this function, we can multiply several objects by the same transformation matrix. This can produce particularly efficient results if we have more than one object on which we wish to perform the same set of transformations. In a later chapter, We'll see a situation where we want to do precisely this in a later chapter.

The Draw() Function

Finally, we'll need a function that will draw the three-dimensional shape (after Project() has been called to calculate the screen coordinates of the transformed vertices) on the video display. Such a function will look much like the two-dimensional shape_type::Draw() function from the last chapter, with an important embellishment. See Listing 7-9 for the details.

 Listing 7-9 The Draw() function

```
void Shape::Draw(char far *screen)

// Draw shape private to SHAPE class

{

  // Loop through all lines in shape:

line_type *lptr = line;

  for (int i=0; i<shape.number_of_lines; I++, lptr++) {

    // Draw current line:

    linedraw(shape.vertex[lptr->start].sx+XORIGIN,
        shape.vertex[lptr->start].sy+YORIGIN,
        shape.vertex[lptr->end].sx+XORIGIN,
        shape.vertex[lptr->end].sy+YORIGIN,
        shape.color,screen);
  }
}
```

The important embellishment is that, as promised earlier, we've moved the origin of our screen coordinate system from the upper left corner to the center of the display. To do this, we established a pair of constants, XORIGIN and YORIGIN, which contain the x and y coordinates, respectively, of the new origin of the coordinate system. Since the new origin is at the center of the 320x200 display, we can define these constants as follows:

```
const int XORIGIN = 160
const int YORIGIN = 100
```

To move the origin to this location, we merely need to add these values to the *x* and *y* coordinates, respectively, of the screen coordinates before drawing lines between these points. The three-dimensional Draw() function performs this task while calling linedraw to draw the "wires" of the wireframe shape. It's not necessary to perform any specifically three-dimensional trickery while drawing our three-dimensional wireframe object, since the screen coordinates have already been translated into two dimensions by the Project() function. Thus, the Draw() function is actually drawing a two-dimensional shape that has undergone adjustments to create the illusion of 3D perspective.

Drawing a Cube

Now let's write a calling routine that can be linked with the WIRE.CPP file and that will use the above functions to rotate and draw a three-dimensional wireframe object. Such a routine is shown in Listing 7-10.

 Listing 7-10 Draws a 3D wireframe object

```
void main()
{
    float matrix[4][4];              // Master transformation
                                     //   matrix

    char far *screen =
        (char far *)MK_FP(0xa000,0); // Point to video RAM
    cls(screen);                     // Clear screen
    int oldmode =
        *(int *)MK_FP(0x40,0x49);    // Save previous video
                                     //   mode
    setmode(0x13);                   // Set mode 13h
    inittrans();                     // Initialize matrix
    scale(2);                        // Create scaling matrix
    rotate(1.1,0.7,0.3);             // Create rotation
                                     //   matrices

    translate(0,0,100);             // Create translation
                                     //   matrix

    shape.Transform();               // Transform SHAPE
                                     //   using MATRIX

    shape.Project(150);              // Perform perspective
                                     //   projection

    shape.Draw(screen);              // Draw transformed
                                     //   shape

    while (!kbhit());                // Wait for key,
                                     //   then terminate

    setmode(oldmode);                // Reset previous video
                                     //   mode & end

}
```

This code assumes that we've already defined and declared the data for a three-dimensional shape called shape (as we did earlier in this chapter, using the data for a cube). It then sets up the video mode; calls the scale, rotate, and translate functions; transforms the shape; projects it into two dimensions; and calls Draw() to put it on the display. This program appears on the disk as 3DWIRE.EXE. Run it and you'll see a three-dimensional wireframe cube appear on the screen, as in Figure 7-14. This shape may appear a little bewildering at first, since it's difficult to tell immediately how a wireframe shape is oriented in space, but if you'll stare at the image for a moment, you'll see that it represents a cube that is partially rotated relative to the viewer.

I recommend that you load the file 3DWIRE.IDE into the Borland C++ project manager and recompile this program using different parameters for the function calls. In particular, you should fool around with the distance parameter for the Project() function and the various rotating, scaling, and translating parameters. Varying these parameters will at times produce odd and displeasing results, and at others, produce interesting effects. A couple of variations may produce runtime errors, most likely because of divisions by 0; we'll add error-checking code in later chapters to guard against this. Still other variations will cause parts of the wireframe shape to run off the edge of the picture. Since we have yet to implement a system for clipping the image at the edge of the window in which we have drawn it, this will cause the image to wrap around to the other side of the display.

Animating the Cube

Now that we can rotate a three-dimensional shape, let's use this capability to produce some animation. First, though, we'll add a new routine to our SCREEN.ASM collection. The machine code routine in Listing 7-11 will copy an arbitrary rectangular window from the offscreen animation buffer into video RAM.

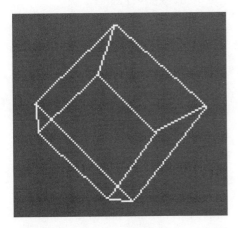

Figure 7-14 The 3D wireframe cube drawn by the 3DWIRE program

Listing 7-11 The putwindow() function

```
;   putwindow(xpos,ypos,xsize,ysize,offset,segment)
;     Move rectangular area of screen buffer at offset,
;     segment with upper left corner at xpos,ypos, width
;     xsize and height ysize

_putwindow  PROC
     ARG xpos:WORD,ypos:WORD,xsize:WORD,ysize:WORD,\
         buf_off:WORD,buf_seg:WORD
     push  bp
     mov   bp,sp
     push  ds
     push  di
     push  si
     mov   ax,ypos          ; Calculate offset of window
     mov   dx,320
     mul   dx
     add   ax,x1
     mov   di,ax
     add   ax,buf_off
     mov   si,ax
     mov   dx,0a000h        ; Get screen segment in ES
     mov   es,dx
     mov   dx,buf_seg       ; Get screen buffer segment in DS
     mov   ds,dx
     mov   dx,ysize         ; Get line count into DX
     cld
ploop1:
     mov   cx,xsize         ; Get width of window into CX
     shr   cx,1
     push  di               ; Save screen and buffer addresses
     push  si
     rep   movsw            ; Move 1 line of window to screen
     pop   si               ; Restore screen&buffer addresses
     pop   di
     add   si,320           ; ...and advance them to next line
     add   di,320
     dec   dx               ; Count off one line
     jnz   ploop1           ; If more lines in window,
                            ;   loop back and draw them
     pop   si
     pop   di
     pop   ds
     pop   bp
     ret
_putwindow  ENDP
```

This function takes five parameters: the x and y screen coordinates of the upper left corner of the screen "window" to be moved, the width and height of the window in pixels, and a far pointer to the video buffer from which the window is to be moved. Now we can produce animation within a rectangular window in the offscreen display buffer and move only that window to the real display, without wasting time copying extraneous information.

The Cube-Rotating Program

With this and the other functions in SCREEN.ASM, we can create a program that will continuously rotate our cube (or other shape) on the display. Most of this program will be identical to 3DWIRE.CPP, but the main function is a bit different. Take a look at the main function from CUBE.CPP in Listing 7-12.

 Listing 7-12 Animates a rotating object

```
void main()
{
    float xangle=0,yangle=0,zangle=0;    // X,Y&Z angles to
                                         //   rotate shape
    float xrot=0.1,yrot=0.1,zrot=0.1;    // X,Y&Z rotation
                                         //   increments
    unsigned char *screen_buffer;        // Offscreen drawing
                                         //   buffer

    screen_buffer=new unsigned char[64000];
    int oldmode =
        *(int *)MK_FP(0x40,0x49);        // Save previous video
                                         //   mode
    setmode(0x13);                       // Set mode 13h
    while (!kbhit()) {                    // Loop until key is
                                         //   pressed
        cls(screen_buffer);              // Clear screen buffer
        inittrans();                     // Initialize
                                         //   translations
        scale(1.5);                      // Create scaling
                                         //   matrix
        rotate(xangle,yangle,zangle);    // Create rotation
                                         //   matrices
        xangle+=xrot;                    // Increment rotation
        yangle+=yrot;                    //   angles
        zangle+=zrot;
        translate(0,0,50);               // Create translation
                                         //   matrix
        cube.Transform();                // Transform SHAPE
                                         //   using MATRIX
        cube.Project(100);               // Perform perspective
                                         //   projection
        cube.Draw(screen_buffer);        // Draw transformed
                                         //   shape
```

continued on next page

■ ■ ■ ■ ■ **243**

continued from previous page

```
        putwindow(0,0,320,200,screen_buffer); // Put on screen
    }
    setmode(oldmode);                       // Reset previous video
                                            //   mode & end

    if( screen_buffer)
            delete [] screen_buffer;
}
```

This program is on the disk as CUBE.EXE. Run it and you'll see a cube similar to the one displayed by 3DWIRE.EXE going through a continuous series of rotations. The key behind the animation of the rotations is in the variable initialized at the start of function main(). The variables *xangle, yangle,* and *zangle* represent the *x, y,* and *z* rotation angles passed to the rotate() function in the main animation loop. If these values remained the same every time rotate() was called, however, there would be no animation, so the value of the variables *xrot, yrot,* and *zrot* are added to the *x, y,* and *z* angles, respectively, on each pass through the loop. Thus, the rotation angles change slightly on each pass through the loop, giving the impression that the cube is rotating in all three dimensions. If you recompile the program, try varying the value of *xrot, yrot,* and *zrot* to produce new patterns of rotation. All of this takes place within a While loop that continues until a key is pressed. The actual drawing of the cube, you'll note, takes place in an offscreen buffer and is only moved to the video display, by the putwindow() function, when the drawing is complete. (As written, the putwindow() function moves the entire buffer into video RAM. If you recompile this program, however, try adjusting the parameters passed to this function in order to move only the rectangular window surrounding the rotating image of the cube. As you shrink the image, you should notice a slight increase in the animation speed, since the putwindow() function needs to move less data on each iteration of the loop.) It's not necessary to erase the previous data from the screen, since the putwindow() function completely draws over it each time.

Drawing a Pyramid

We don't have to restrict ourselves to drawing cubes. We can exchange the cube data with data for other shapes, such as a pyramid:

```
// Vertex data for pyramid:

vertex_type pyramid_vertices[]={   // Vertices for pyramid
    {0,-10,0,1,                    // Vertex 0
     0,0,0,1,
     0,0,0,1},
    {10,10,10,1,                   // Vertex 1
     0,0,0,1,
     0,0,0,1},
    {-10,10,10,1,                  // Vertex 2
     0,0,0,1,
```

```
    0,0,0,1},
  {-10,10,-10,1,                    // Vertex 3
   0,0,0,1,
   0,0,0,1},
  {10,10,-10,1,                     // Vertex 4
   0,0,0,1,
   0,0,0,1}
};
```

```
// Line data for pyramid:
```

```
line_type pyramid_lines[]={
  {0,1},                            // Line 0
  {0,2},                            // Line 1
  {0,3},                            // Line 2
  {0,4},                            // Line 3
  {1,2},                            // Line 4
  {2,3},                            // Line 5
  {3,4},                            // Line 6
  {4,1}                             // Line 7
};
```

```
// Shape data for pyramid:
```

```
Shape pyramid(5, pyramid_vertices, 8, pyramid_lines);
```

The result of using this data can be seen in the program PYRAMID.EXE on the disk.

Drawing a Letter *W*

Here's the data for a three-dimensional wireframe version of the letter W (which stands, of course, for Waite Group Press):

```
// Vertex data for W:
```

```
vertex_type W_vertices[]={           // Vertices for W
  {-25,-15,10,1,                     // Vertex 0
   0,0,0,1,
   0,0,0,1},
  -{15,-15,10,1,                     // Vertex 1
   0,0,0,1,
   0,0,0,1},
  {-10,0,10,1,                       // Vertex 2
   0,0,0,1,
   0,0,0,1},
  {-5,-15,10,1,                      // Vertex 3
   0,0,0,1,
   0,0,0,1},
  {5,-15,10,1,                       // Vertex 4
   0,0,0,1,
   0,0,0,1},
```

continued on next page

continued from previous page

```
        {10,0,10,1,                    // Vertex 5
         0,0,0,1,
         0,0,0,1},
        {15,-15,10,1,                  // Vertex 6
         0,0,0,1,
         0,0,0,1},
        {25,-15,10,1,                  // Vertex 7
         0,0,0,1,
         0,0,0,1},
        {20,15,10,1,                   // Vertex 8
         0,0,0,1,
         0,0,0,1},
        {7,15,10,1,                    // Vertex 9
         0,0,0,1,
         0,0,0,1},
        {0,0,10,1,                     // Vertex 10
         0,0,0,1,
         0,0,0,1},
        {-7,15,10,1,                   // Vertex 11
         0,0,0,1,
         0,0,0,1},
        {-20,15,10,1,                  // Vertex 12
         0,0,0,1,
         0,0,0,1},
        {-25,-15,-10,1,                // Vertex 13
         0,0,0,1,
         0,0,0,1},
        {-15,-15,-10,1,                // Vertex 14
         0,0,0,1,
         0,0,0,1},
        {-10,0,-10,1,                  // Vertex 15
         0,0,0,1,
         0,0,0,1},
        {-5,-15,-10,1,                 // Vertex 16
         0,0,0,1,
         0,0,0,1},
        {5,-15,-10,1,                  // Vertex 17
         0,0,0,1,
         0,0,0,1},
        {10,0,-10,1,                   // Vertex 18
         0,0,0,1,
         0,0,0,1},
        {15,-15,-10,1,                 // Vertex 19
         0,0,0,1,
         0,0,0,1},
    {   25,-15,-10,1,                  // Vertex 20
         0,0,0,1,
         0,0,0,1},
    {  20,15,-10,1,                    // Vertex 21
         0,0,0,1,
         0,0,0,1,]
        {7,15,-10,1,                   // Vertex 22
         0,0,0,1,
```

```
      0,0,0,1},
     {0,0,-10,1,                        // Vertex 23
      0,0,0,1,
      0,0,0,1},
     {-7,15,-10,1,                      // Vertex 24
      0,0,0,1,
      0,0,0,1},
     {-20,15,-10,1,                     // Vertex 25
      0,0,0,1,
      0,0,0,1}
};

// Line data for W:

line_type W_lines[]={
     {0,1},                             // Line 0
     {1,2},                             // Line 1
     {2,3},                             // Line 2
     {3,4},                             // Line 3
     {4,5},                             // Line 4
     {5,6},                             // Line 5
     {6,7},                             // Line 6
     {7,8},                             // Line 7
     {8,9},                             // Line 8
     {9,10},                            // Line 9
     {10,11},                           // Line 10
     {11,12},                           // Line 11
     {12,0},                            // Line 12
     {13,14},                           // Line 13
     {14,15},                           // Line 14
     {15,16},                           // Line 15
     {16,17},                           // Line 16
     {17,18},                           // Line 17
     {18,19},                           // Line 18
     {19,20},                           // Line 19
     {20,21},                           // Line 20
     {21,22},                           // Line 21
     {22,23},                           // Line 22
     {23,24},                           // Line 23
     {24,25},                           // Line 24
     {25,13},                           // Line 25
     {0,13},                            // Line 26
     {1,14},                            // Line 27
     {2,15},                            // Line 28
     {3,16},                            // Line 29
     {4,17},                            // Line 30
     {5,18},                            // Line 31
     {6,19},                            // Line 32
     {7,20},                            // Line 33
     {8,21},                            // Line 34
     {9,22},                            // Line 35
     {10,23},                           // Line 36
     {11,24},                           // Line 37
```

continued on next page

continued from previous page

```
      {12,25}                              // Line 38
};

// Shape data for W:

Shape shape(26, W_vertices, 39 W_lines);
```

This is the longest shape descriptor we've seen yet. The reason, obviously, is that there are a *lot* of lines and vertices in a three-dimensional W. The executable code is on the disk as WAITE.EXE. See Figure 7-15 for a glimpse of what it produces.

We'll be seeing these shapes again in later chapters. Next time, however, they'll have acquired a new solidity. We're going to make the transition from wireframe graphics to a much more realistic method of three-dimensional rendering—polygon-fill graphics.

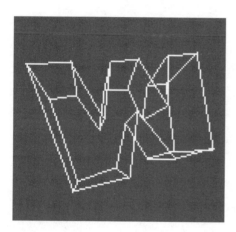

Figure 7-15 The wireframe letter *W* produced by the WAITE.EXE program

8

Polygon-Fill Graphics

In Chapter 7, we tried some fundamental techniques of 3D shape manipulation. It was convenient then to use wireframe graphics in order to keep the code relatively fast and simple. But drawing wireframe representations of objects is a lot like drawing stick figures of people. It conveys the meaning but not the feeling, the words without the music. You can tell that a wireframe cube is *supposed* to be a cube, but you don't really believe in your gut that it *is* a cube. What's really needed is a way to draw objects so that they look like actual, solid objects. Enter polygon-fill graphics.

To be honest, polygon-fill graphics don't look all that realistic; objects in the real world are not constructed from solid-colored polygonal facets. But polygon-fill graphics look sufficiently realistic—enough so that game-players can willingly suspend disbelief and imagine themselves to be in the world of the game. And that's what counts.

To create polygon-fill graphics we first define a class for storing a description of a polygon.

The Polygon Descriptor

A polygon is a geometric figure with a certain number of sides, or edges. (See Figure 8-1.) Each edge must be straight, like the lines that comprise a wireframe image, and

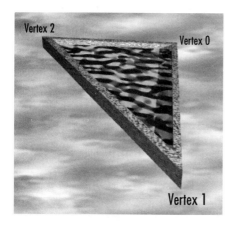

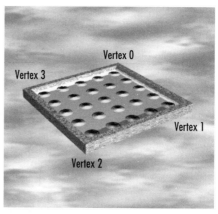

Figure 8-1 Polygons with three, four, five, and eight edges

(a) A three-sided polygon (triangle)   **(b)** A four-sided polygon (rectangle)

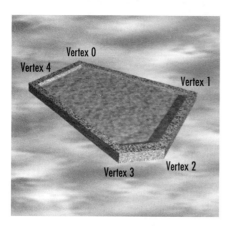

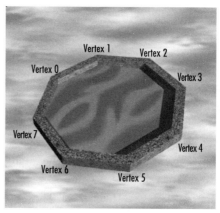

(c) A five-sided polygon (pentagon)   **(d)** An eight-sided polygon (octagon)

there must be at least three of them. A three-sided polygon is a triangle. (Although the term is rarely used, a three-sided polygon can also be called a trigon, which is where we get the term trigonometry.) A four-sided polygon is a rectangle. A five-sided polygon is called a pentagon. Note that the number of vertices in a polygon is the same as the number of edges: A triangle has three vertices, for instance.

A filled polygon is a polygon filled with a solid color or a pattern, which usually contrasts with the background against which the polygon is drawn. (See Figure 8-2.) To draw a polygon-fill image, it is necessary to draw filled polygons. Figure 8-3, for instance, shows a pyramid constructed from filled polygons.

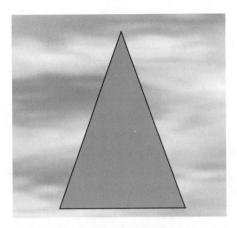

Figure 8-2 A filled triangle

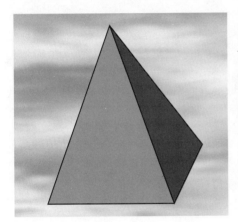

Figure 8-3 A pyramid constructed from filled polygons

(a) Note the different patterns of the two visible polygons, giving the pyramid a shaded appearance

(b) An exploded view of the pyramid, showing the five polygons from which it has been constructed

The class that will be used in this book for describing polygons and objects made up of polygons owes a great deal to the class that was used in the last two chapters to describe wireframe objects. It departs from that class in some important ways, however, so be prepared for some surprises. The complete class definition is on the disk in the file POLY.H. In the paragraphs that follow, we'll look at it piece by piece.

The Vertex_Type Structure

At the lowest level, little has changed. The vertex_type structure is identical to the vertex structure used in the last two chapters. This makes sense, since a polygon vertex is no different mathematically from a wireframe vertex. As far as our program is concerned, each vertex is still a point in space defined by three coordinates—an *x* coordinate, a *y* coordinate, and a *z* coordinate. Even the math routines that rotate, scale, and translate these coordinates will remain essentially the same as in the last chapter, though some cosmetic changes will be made, as we'll see later in this chapter.

Here's the structure definition for vertex_type:

```
struct vertex_type { // Structure for individual vertices
   long lx,ly,lz,lt;  // Local coordinates of vertex
   long wx,wy,wz,wt;  // World coordinates of vertex
   long sx,sy,st;     // Screen coordinates of vertex
};
```

The Polygon_Type Class

At this point, the classes used for polygons begin to diverge from the classes used for wireframe graphics. Now we need a class that defines a polygon, instead of a simple structure that defines a line. The first field in this class will give the number of vertices in the polygon, which is also the number of edges in the polygon. The class will also include an array of vertices that defines the vertices of the polygon. And there will be a field that defines the polygon's color.

```
class polygon_type {
private:
   friend class object_type;
   int number_of_vertices; // Number of vertices in polygon
   int color;              // Color of polygon
   int zmax,zmin;          // Maximum and minimum
   int xmax,xmin;          //   x, y and z coordinates
   int ymax,ymin;          //   of polygon vertices
   vertex_type **vertex;   // List of vertices
public:
      polygon_type(): vertex(0){;}
      ~polygon_type();
      int backface();
      void DrawPoly(unsigned char far *screen);
};
```

For now, don't worry about the *xmax* and *xmin* fields and their equivalents for *y* and *z*. We'll see what those are for in Chapter 10. You may also notice that the vertex array is defined as an array of pointers. Usually this means that we're dealing with a two-dimensional array—an array of arrays. That's not the case here, however. We'll see in a moment why the vertex array is defined as an array of pointers.

The FRIEND keyword is used to instruct the compiler that another class will have full access to the polygon_type class members, private and protected as well as public. This is often used when two classes are closely related, such as our polygon class and a class which is made up of polygons described next.

The polygon_type class has a constructor with no arguments which is defined as curly brackets with a semicolon in between. This is the default constructor—one with no arguments, and we normally would not have to define it since C++ does this automatically when no other constructor is present in the class. However, this constructor has a member initializer: vertex(0), which guarantees that the vertex_type pointer is set to 0 when a polygon_type object is made.

The three other public functions, the destructor, backface and DrawPoly, will be created later in this chapter.

The Object_Type Class

Now we need a class that will describe an object made up of polygons, similar to the Shape class that we used in Chapter 7 for storing wireframe shapes. Here's the class definition:

```
class   object_type {
   int    number_of_vertices; // Number of vertices in object
   int    number_of_polygons; // Number of polygons in object
   int    x,y,z;              // World coordinates of
                              //  object's local origin
   polygon_type  *polygon;    // List of polygons in object
   vertex_type *vertex;       // Array of vertices in object
   int    convex;   // Is it a convex polyhedron?
public:
      object_type():polygon(0),vertex(0){;}
      ~object_type();
      int load();
      void Transform();
      void Project(int distance);
      void Draw(unsigned char far *screen);
};
```

You'll notice that some of this class is redundant. We've seen a few of these same fields in the polygon_type class. Why do we need a list of vertices in both the polygon class and the object class? The reason is that sometimes we'll want to treat a polygon as a list of vertices; at other times we'll want to treat an object as a list of vertices. It would be wasteful to store two separate lists of vertices, so we've defined one of these lists (the one in the polygon class) as a list of pointers that point at the vertex descriptors in the list maintained by the object class. This concept is illustrated in Figure 8-4.

The convex field might look mysterious to you. We'll discuss this field momentarily. Again, a constructor is defined inline which initializes the pointers to 0. And there are

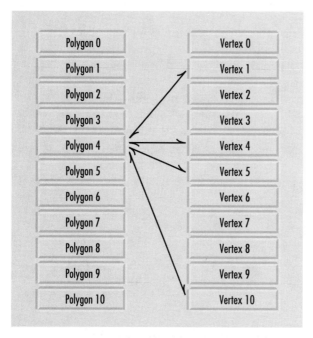

Figure 8-4 The pointers in the polygon list, pointing to the vertices in the vertex list

five other public functions, three of which were seen in the Shape class: Transform, Project, and Draw. The destructor and load function complete the class.

New Classes

Both the object_type class and the Shape class, introduced in the last chapter, maintain a list of vertices. The line_type structure, though, pointed to the vertices by indexing into the array of vertices maintained by the Shape class. The polygon_type class, on the other hand, maintains an array of pointers that points at the location of the vertex descriptors in memory. Line_type held offsets into the array, polygon_type holds actual addresses. Keep this difference in mind; it could become confusing.

You might think that these are the only classes that we need for maintaining descriptions of polygon-fill objects in the computer's memory. However, we need to look ahead to programs that we will be writing later. These programs will maintain multiple objects in memory, in such a way that those objects constitute a world of sorts inside the computer's memory. So we need a larger class in order to maintain lists of objects. Let's call that class world_type. The definition is simple:

```
class world_type {
private:
  int  number_of_objects;
  object_type  *obj;
public:
      world_type():obj(0){;}
      ~world_type();
      int loadpoly(char *filename);
      void Draw(unsigned char far *screen);
};
```

This class contains a list of objects and the number of objects in that list, and that's all we need. In this chapter we'll include only one object in the world_type class, but in later chapters we'll include more objects. Once again, there is a constructor which initializes the pointer to 0 and a destructor. Two functions called loadpoly and Draw provide methodology for information to be read into the world_type and for that information to be put to the screen.

The destructors for our three new classes will all look similar. Because we have chosen to initialize the pointer fields with 0, the destructor will check if there has been memory allocated (the pointer will be anything other than 0) and delete the array if so. In this way, each class is responsible for cleaning up after itself.

```
world_type::~world_type()
{
      if(obj)
            delete [] obj;
}

object_type::~object_type()
{
      if(polygon)
            delete [] polygon;
      if(vertex)
            delete [] vertex;
}

polygon_type::~polygon_type()
{
      if(vertex)
            delete [] vertex;
}
```

Now that we have a class to hold polygon descriptions, we need a method of drawing filled polygons.

Polygon Drawing

Before we can draw filled polygons, however, it is necessary to distinguish between two different kinds of polygons: convex and concave. One way to distinguish between these two types of polygons is to study the angles at which lines come together at each of the polygon's vertices. In a concave polygon, the internal angle—the angle measured from the inside of the polygon—is greater than 180 degrees at one or more of the vertices. (An angle of 180 degrees would appear as a straight line.) In Figure 8-5, for instance, the angle formed by the two edges that come together at vertex 3 form an angle greater than 180 degrees, making this polygon concave. If it helps, you can think of a concave polygon as having *caved in* at the corresponding vertex; the concave angle is a kind of intrusion into the interior of the polygon.

There's another way of defining a concave polygon. If it is possible to draw a straight line from one edge of a polygon to another edge and have that line pass outside the polygon on the way, then the polygon is concave. Figure 8-6 illustrates this concept. Lines 1 and 3 don't go outside the polygon, but line 2 does. Thus, this polygon is concave. The polygon in Figure 8-7, on the other hand, is *convex,* since there's no way to draw a line between two edges and have that line pass outside the polygon.

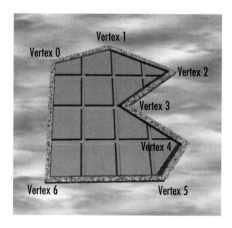

Figure 8-5 A concave polygon

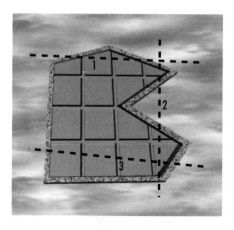

Figure 8-6 Lines crossing a concave polygon

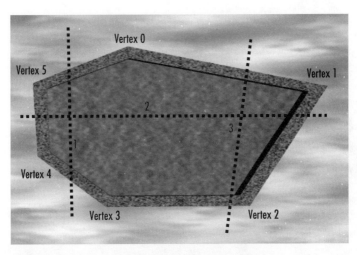

Figure 8-7 Lines crossing a convex polygon

Figure 8-8 **(a)** A convex polygon **(b)** The convex polygon from Figure 8-8(a) drawn as a series of horizontal lines

I'm dwelling on the differences between concave and convex polygons because it's a lot harder to draw a concave polygon than a convex polygon. Bear in mind that the PC graphic display is organized as a series of horizontal and vertical lines of pixels. A convex polygon can be drawn as a series of horizontal lines, stacked one atop the other, as in Figure 8-8. (It can also be drawn as a series of vertical lines, but horizontal lines

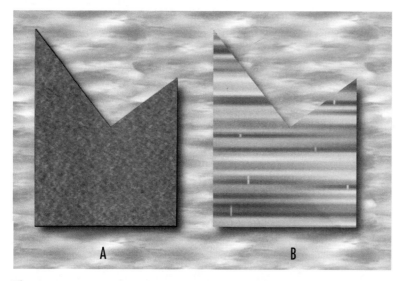

Figure 8-9 **(a)** A concave polygon **(b)** The concave polygon from Figure 8-9 (a) drawn as a series of horizontal lines. Note that some of the lines are broken in two

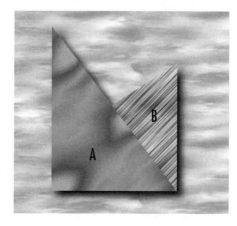

Figure 8-10 A concave polygon constructed out of two convex polygons

are easier to draw because of the way video memory is organized.) On the other hand, we cannot draw a concave polygon as a series of stacked horizontal lines, because some of the lines may be broken, as in Figure 8-9.

For this reason, we'll use only convex polygons to create images in this and later chapters. No concave polygons will be allowed. So how, you might ask, will we construct objects that require concave polygons? We'll build the concave polygon out of two or more convex polygons. Figure 8-10 shows how the concave polygon from Figure 8-9 could be constructed out of two convex polygons. This will increase the number of vertices that need to be processed, but it will greatly simplify the drawing of the polygons, which (as you will see in just a moment) is complex enough already. If you feel ambitious, don't hesitate to rewrite the polygon-drawing routine in this chapter to draw concave polygons.

The Polygon-Drawing Algorithm

The method we'll use for drawing polygons utilizes a variation on Bresenham's line-drawing routine (which we discussed in some detail back in Chapter 6), a method of drawing a line between any two arbitrary points on the display without using division. It involves finding the difference between the x and y coordinates of the starting and ending points of the line. The line is drawn by incrementing the x or the y coordinate, depending on which difference is larger. An error term based on the smaller difference is created and added to itself until it becomes larger than the other difference, at which point the other coordinate is incremented. For more detail, take another look at Chapter 6.

The edges of a polygon are lines which can be drawn using Bresenham's algorithm. In fact, that was essentially the technique we used in the last chapter to draw wireframe images, which in a sense are made of unfilled polygons. The edges of a convex polygon can be connected by lines. If we draw these lines horizontally across the display, it's not necessary to use Bresenham's algorithm to determine the points on the line, since a horizontal line is easy to draw. (Once again, see Chapter 6 for details.) We can use Bresenham's algorithm to determine the starting and ending points of the line, however, since the starting and ending points of the horizontal line are actually the points of the edges of the polygon.

Here's the rough algorithm, also illustrated in Figure 8-11, for the method that will be used in this book to draw polygons:

1. Determine which vertex is at the top of the polygon (i.e., has the smallest y coordinate).

2. Determine the next vertex clockwise from the top vertex.

3. Determine the next vertex counterclockwise from the top vertex.

4. Use Bresenham's algorithm to calculate the points on both lines.

5. Draw a horizontal line to connect each vertical increment on these lines.

6. Whenever one line ends at a vertex, find the next vertex clockwise or counterclockwise from that vertex and repeat steps 4 through 6.

7. Terminate the process when the bottom of the polygon is reached.

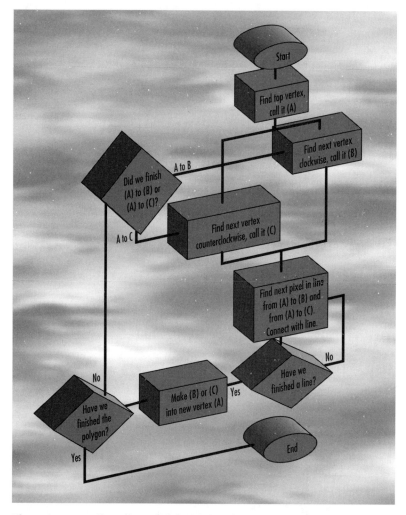

Figure 8-11 A flowchart of the polygon-drawing function

The Polygon-Drawing Function

Now that you have a rough idea how the algorithm works, let's start building that actual function that will perform it, which we will call DrawPoly(). We'll place this routine in the file DRAWPOL1.CPP. (We'll use another version of this function in Chapter 9, so the files are numbered to distinguish between them.) This function is a public method of the polygon_type class. The parameter passed to this function will be the address of video RAM or of an offscreen buffer. Here's the header for the function.

```
void polygon_type :: DrawPoly(unsigned char far  *screen_buffer)
```

We'll need quite a few variables in this function. Many of them are the same variables used in the Bresenham function back in Chapter 6, but now these variables come in pairs, since we'll be doing two simultaneous Bresenham routines. Here are some of the uninitialized variables declared at the beginning of the function:

```
int ydiff1,ydiff2,         // Difference between starting
                           //  x and ending x
   xdiff1,xdiff2,          // Difference between starting y
                           //  and ending y
   start,                  // Starting offset of line
                           //  between edges
   length,                 // Distance from edge 1 to
                           //  edge 2
   errorterm1,errorterm2,  // Error terms for edges 1 & 2
   offset1,offset2,        // Offset of current pixel in
                           //  edges 1 & 2
   count1,count2,          // Increment count for
                           //  edges 1 & 2
   xunit1,xunit2;          // Unit to advance x offset
                           //  for edges 1 & 2
```

Many other variables will be declared in the course of the function, when they're initialized. For instance, here's the variable that will count down the number of edges in the polygon:

```
int edgecount= number_of_vertices-1;
```

The value of this variable will be decremented each time a complete edge is drawn. When the value reaches zero, the polygon will be drawn and the function will terminate.

Getting to the Top

As noted in the algorithm above, the first thing the function needs to do is to determine which vertex in the polygon is at the top. This is done by assuming that the first vertex is the top, and then searching through the polygon to find a vertex with a lower y coordinate. Each time a lower y is found, the vertex with that coordinate replaces the previously assumed top vertex:

```
// Start by assuming vertex 0 is at top:

int firstvert=0;
int min_amt= vertex[0]->sy;

// Search through all vertices:

for (int i=1; i< number_of_vertices; i++) {
```

continued on next page

continued from previous page

```
// Is next vertex even higher?

if ((vertex[i]->sy) < min_amt) {

  // If so, make a note of it:

  firstvert=i;
  min_amt= vertex[i]->sy;
}
}
```

When this loops ends, the integer variable *firstvert* contains the number of the topmost vertex. The variable is called *firstvert* because it is the first vertex that will be drawn in the polygon.

The next job is to create a series of variables that point at the starting and ending vertices of the first two edges of the polygon, which we'll call edge 1 and edge 2. For the moment, it's irrelevant which of these edges proceeds clockwise from *firstvert* and which proceeds counterclockwise. We'll determine that when we actually draw the line between them.

First, we need a pair of integer variables called *startvert1* and *startvert2,* which will represent the positions, in the vertex list, of the *starting* vertices of edges 1 and 2, respectively. Because the two edges initially start at the same place (*firstvert*), we'll simply set both of these variables equal to *firstvert*:

```
int startvert1=firstvert;     // Edge 1 start
int startvert2=firstvert;     // Edge 2 start
```

We'll need a separate set of variables to hold the *x* and *y* coordinates of *startvert1* and *startvert2.* The *x* and *y* coordinates of *startvert1* will go into the integer variables *xstart1* and *ystart1*, respectively. The *x* and *y* coordinates of *startvert2* will go into the integer variables *xstart2* and *ystart2*, respectively:

```
int xstart1= vertex[startvert1]->sx;
int ystart1= vertex[startvert1]->sy;
int xstart2= vertex[startvert2]->sx;
int ystart2= vertex[startvert2]->sy;
```

From Start to Finish

Now we need a set of variables to represent the numbers and coordinates of the *ending* vertices of edge 1 and edge 2. The numbers of the vertices will be placed in the integer variables *endvert1* and *endvert2*, for edges 1 and 2, respectively. To determine which vertex is *endvert1*, we simply subtract 1 from the value of *startvert1*. However, if the value of *startvert 1* is 0, then the value of *endvert1* must wrap around to the last vertex in the polygon's vertex list, which will have a number equal to *number_of_vertices-1*. Similarly, vertex *endvert2* can be identified by adding 1 to the value of *startvert2*, but we must make sure that the result is not greater than the last vertex in the polygon's vertex list. If it is, we must wrap it around to 0. Finally, the *x,y* coordinates of *endvert1* will go in the integer variables *xend1* and *yend1*. The *x,y* coordinates of *endvert2* will go in the integer variables *xend2* and *yend2*:

```
// Get end of edge 1 and check for wrap at last vertex:

int endvert1=startvert1-1;
if (endvert1<0) endvert1= number_of_vertices-1;
int xend1= vertex[endvert1]->sx;
int yend1= vertex[endvert1]->sy;


// Get end of edge 2 and check for wrap at last vertex:

int endvert2=startvert2+1;
if (endvert2==( number_of_vertices)) endvert2=0;
int xend2= vertex[endvert2]->sx;
int yend2= vertex[endvert2]->sy;
```

Drawing the Polygon

Now we can begin drawing the polygon. Almost all of the code that follows will be part of a while() loop that will terminate only when all of the polygon's edges have been drawn:

```
while (edgecount>0) {      // Draw all edges
```

The first line of the polygon will be drawn between *startvert1* and *startvert2*. When we start, this line will be one pixel long, since these vertices are one and the same. The exception will occur when the top of the polygon is perfectly horizontal. (Our polygon-drawing function can handle this exception, as we shall see.) Later, as *startvert1* and/or *startvert2* change values, the line will become longer. To draw the line, we need to know the video RAM offsets of the two vertices. We can derive this address from the *x* and *y* coordinates of the vertices, using the formula we studied in Chapter 2:

```
// Get offsets of edge 1 and 2:

offset1=320*ystart1+xstart1+FP_OFF(screen_buffer);
offset2=320*ystart2+xstart2+FP_OFF(screen_buffer);
```

Then we must initialize the error terms for edges 1 and 2 to 0:

```
// Initialize error terms for edges 1 & 2:

errorterm1=0;
errorterm2=0;
```

We won't be using these error terms until somewhat later in the function, but it doesn't hurt to initialize them now.

Bresenham Does His Thing

Now the Bresenham code begins. To get Bresenham's algorithm under way, we first get the absolute value of the differences in the *x* and *y* coordinates from the start to the end of both edges. This is done, obviously, by subtracting the ending coordinate from the starting coordinate (or vice versa) and taking the absolute value of the result. In the following two lines of efficient (if not altogether readable) C++ code, the ending *y* coordinates for each edge are subtracted from the starting *y* coordinates and the difference stored in *ydiff1* and *ydiff2*. If the value is negative, it is negated to make it positive. To allow this operation to be performed in a single line of code for each edge, we use the C++ convention of assigning a value to a variable and simultaneously testing that value:

```
// Get absolute values of y lengths of edges:

if ((ydiff1=yend1-ystart1)<0) ydiff1=-ydiff1;
if ((ydiff2=yend2-ystart2)<0) ydiff2=-ydiff2;
```

We'll do the same with the *x* coordinates, but at the same time we'll assign a value to the integer variables *xunit1* and *xunit2,* which will determine whether the *x* coordinates of the edges will be incremented in a positive or negative direction. (We don't need to do this with the *y* coordinate because we'll always be incrementing it in a positive direction—i.e., toward the bottom of the display. That's one advantage of always starting at the top of the polygon and working toward the bottom.) The following code is essentially identical to that used to initialize *ydiff1* and *ydiff2,* except that the variables *xunit1* and *xunit2* have been added:

```
// Get absolute values of x lengths of edges
//   plus unit to advance in x dimension

if ((xdiff1=xend1-xstart1)<0) {
   xunit1=-1;
   xdiff1=-xdiff1;
}
else {
   xunit2=1;
}
```

The Four Subsections

Now things start getting just a bit complicated. Remember how the Bresenham-based line-drawing function was broken into two subsections, one for lines with slopes less than 1 and one for lines with slopes greater than or equal to 1? Well, this Bresenham-based polygon-drawing function is broken into *four* subsections, one for sections of polygons in which both edges have slopes less than 1, one for sections of polygons in which both edges have slopes greater than or equal to 1, one for sections of polygons in which edge 1 has a slope less than 1 and edge 2 has a slope equal to or greater than 1, and one for sections of polygons in which edge 1 has a slope greater than or equal to 1 and edge 2 has a slope less than 1. In a single polygon, it's theoretically possible for all four of these subsections to be executed, as the relationship between the edges of the polygon changes. However, only one is executed at a time.

The function chooses between these subsections with a series of nested if statements. The overall structure of these if statements looks like this:

```
// Choose which of four routines to use:

if (xdiff1>ydiff1) {     // If edge 1 slope < 1
  if (xdiff2>ydiff2) {   // If edge 2 slope < 1

  // Increment edge 1 on X and edge 2 on X

  }
  else {    // If edge 2 slope >= 1

  // Increment edge 1 on X and edge 2 on Y:

 }
else { // If edge 1 slope >= 1

  if (xdiff2>ydiff2) { // If edge 2 slope < 1

  // Increment edge 1 on Y and edge 2 on X:

  }
  else { // If edge 2 slope >= 1

  // Increment edge 1 on Y and edge 2 on Y:

  }
}
```

We're only going to explore one of these subsections here, since it would take too much time and space to look at all four (though I'll show you the complete function in a moment so you can explore all four). Fortunately, all of the principles involved in all four subsections are visible in one. So let's look at the subsection for sections of polygons in which edge 1 has a slope less than 1 and edge 2 has a slope greater than or equal to 1.

Counting Off the Pixels

To begin with, we'll need to count off the number of pixels to be plotted so that we'll know when the edge is drawn. The number of pixels to be plotted is simply the difference between the starting and ending coordinates in the dimension we're incrementing. If we're incrementing on the x coordinate, it will be the x difference. If we're incrementing on the y coordinate, it will be the y difference. In the example we've chosen, it will be both, the x difference for edge 1 and the y difference for edge 2:

```
count1=xdiff1;  // Number of pixels to draw edge 1
count2=ydiff2;  // Number of pixels to draw edge 2
```

This segment of code will continue executing until one or both of these edges is finished, so the actual drawing will be performed in a While loop:

```
// Continue drawing until one edge is done:

while (count1 && count2) {
```

Now let's find the next point on edge 1, so that we can draw a horizontal line from that point to the next point on edge 2. This is a bit tricky, since edge 1 is being incremented on the x coordinate. This means that the x coordinate can be incremented several times before the y coordinate is incremented, which makes it difficult to determine just when we should draw the horizontal line. If we draw it every time the x coordinate is incremented, we may end up drawing several horizontal lines over the top of one another, which will waste a lot of time. Instead, we'll continue incrementing the x coordinate until it is time to increment the y coordinate, and then we'll draw the horizontal line from edge 1 to edge 2.

But what if edge 1 is the left edge and x is being incremented in the positive (right) direction? Or if edge 1 is the right edge and x is being incremented in the negative (left) direction? In both of these situations, if we wait until the y coordinate is about to be incremented to draw the line between the edges, there's a good chance that we will miss one or more pixels along the edge of the polygon. To guard against this possibility, we'll set a pixel every time the x coordinate is incremented. When we draw the horizontal line, we may well draw over the top of these pixels, but the redundancy will be minor.

Looping Until *y* Increments

The upshot of all this is that we will be calculating the next point (or points) on edge 1 in a loop that will continue until the y coordinate is about to be incremented. Because this occurs when the value of *errorterm1* is greater than or equal to *ydiff1*, we will make this the criterion for terminating the loop:

```
// Don't draw until ready to move in y dimension

while ((errorterm1<xdiff1)&&(count1>0)) {
```

Then we will subtract 1 from the variable *count1* (which is counting down the number of times we increment the x coordinate). If it is not to 0 yet, we will proceed to increment the pixel offset (which was earlier placed in variable *offset1*), as well as *xstart1*, by *xunit1:*

```
if (count1--) {      // Count off this pixel
  offset1+=xunit1;   // Point to next pixel
  xstart1+=xunit1;
}
```

To determine if it's time to increment the *y* coordinate, we add *ydiff1* to *errorterm1*. If it's not time to draw the horizontal line yet, we plot a pixel by storing the polygon color (which is in the class field color) in the screen buffer at *offset1*:

```
errorterm1+=ydiff1; // Ready to move in y?
if (errorterm1<xdiff1) {  // No?

   // Then plot a pixel in the polygon color

   screen_buffer[offset1]=polygon->color;
  }
}
```

When the innermost While loop finishes executing, it's time to increment the *y* coordinate of edge 1. Which means that the *errorterm1* variable must be restored so that the process can start all over again. This is done by subtracting *ydiff1* from *errorterm1*:

```
errorterm1-=xdiff1; // Reset error term
```

That takes care of edge 1—for the moment at least. Now it's time to deal with edge 2. Since edge 2 is incremented on the *y* coordinate, it's actually a bit easier to handle, since we don't have to worry about missing any pixels when we draw the horizontal line. Incrementing edge 2 is simply a matter of adding *xdiff2* to *errorterm2* to see if it's time to increment the *x* coordinate yet. If not, we decrement *count2* to indicate that we've moved one more pixel in the *y* dimension and continue to the routine that draws the horizontal line:

```
// Find edge 2 coordinates:

errorterm2+=xdiff2; // Increment error term

// If time to move in y dimension, restore error
//  term and advance offset to next pixel:

if (errorterm2 >= ydiff2)  {
  errorterm2-=ydiff2;
  offset2+=xunit2;
  xstart2+=xunit2;
}
-count2; // Count off this pixel
```

Drawing the Line

Now it's time to draw the horizontal line between edges 1 and 2. The first step in this process is to determine the length of the line. The variable *offset1* contains the address in video RAM of edge 1 and the variable *offset2* contains the address in video RAM of edge 2. Since both addresses are on the same line of the display, we can determine the line length by subtracting one offset from the other, like this:

```
length=offset2-offset1; // What's the length?
```

Unfortunately, we don't know which of these offsets is to the left and which to the right, so the result of this subtraction could be positive or negative. We need the absolute value of the difference, which we can obtain easily enough with an if statement. We also want to start drawing from the leftmost of the two offsets to the rightmost; we can determine which is which, and set the integer variable *start* equal to that offset, with the same if statement:

```
if (length<0) {          // If negative...
   length=-length;       // ...make it positive
   start=offset2;        // START = edge 2
}
else start=offset1;      // Else START = edge 1
```

The line itself can be drawn with a For() loop:

```
// Draw the line:

for (int i=start; i<start+length+1; i++)
   screen_buffer[i]=color;
```

Now that the line is drawn, we want to advance the two *offset* variables to the next line, so that the process can start all over again. Each screen line is 320 pixels long, so we advance the offsets by adding 320 to each. We also want to add 1 to *ystart*, to indicate that we've moved down one line (i.e., one y coordinate):

```
// Advance to next line:

offset1+=320;
ystart1++;
offset2+=320;
ystart2++;
```

Cleaning Up

And that's it. Aside from terminating the loops, that's all that needs to be done to draw a segment of the polygon. The other sections of code operate similarly; we'll look at the complete code in a second. When an edge terminates at a vertex, one or both of the *count* variables will go to 0 and the loop will terminate. Now we have to reset the appropriate variables so that the four-edge filling routines can start with the next edge, if any. First we check to see if edge 1 has terminated:

```
if (!count1) {           // If edge 1 is complete...
```

If so, we count off one edge:

```
-edgecount;           // Decrement the edge count
```

Then we make the ending vertex of the last edge into the starting vertex of the new edge:

```
startvert1=endvert1;    // Make ending vertex into
                        //  start vertex
```

And calculate the number and *x,y* coordinates of the new ending vertex just as we did at the beginning of the program:

```
-endvert1;              // And get new ending vertex

// Check for wrap:

if (endvert1<0)
  endvert1= number_of_vertices-1;

// Get x & y of new end vertex:

xend1= vertex[endvert1]->sx;
yend1= vertex[endvert1]->sy;
```

At this point, the program loops back to the start of the main loop. If *edgecount* is 0, the function ends and returns to the calling routines; the polygon has been drawn. If not, the process repeats.

The Complete Function

The complete polygon-drawing function is reproduced in Listing 8-1.

Listing 8-1 Polygon-drawing function

```
// DRAWPOLY.CPP
//   Draws a polygon with an arbitrary number of sides
//   in a specified color

#include   <stdio.h>
#include   <dos.h>
#include   <mem.h>
#include   "poly.h"


void polygon_type::DrawPoly(unsigned char far  *screen_buffer)
  {

// Draw polygon in class POLYGON_TYPE in SCREEN_BUFFER

// Uninitialized variables:
```

continued on next page

continued from previous page

```
   int ydiff1,ydiff2,           // Difference between starting
                                //  x and ending x
      xdiff1,xdiff2,            // Difference between starting y
                                //  and ending y
      start,                    // Starting offset of line
                                //  between edges
      length,                   // Distance from edge 1 to
                                //  edge 2
      errorterm1,errorterm2,    // Error terms for edges 1 & 2
      offset1,offset2,          // Offset of current pixel in
                                //  edges 1 & 2
      count1,count2,            // Increment count for
                                //  edges 1 & 2
      xunit1,xunit2;            // Unit to advance x offset
                                //  for edges 1 & 2

  // Initialize count of number of edges drawn:

  int edgecount=number_of_vertices-1;

  // Determine which vertex is at top of polygon:

  // Start by assuming vertex 0 is at top:

  int firstvert=0;
  int min_amt=vertex[0]->sy;

  // Search through all vertices:

  for (int i=1; i<number_of_vertices; i++) {

    // Is next vertex even higher?

    if ((vertex[i]->sy) < min_amt) {

      // If so, make a note of it:

      firstvert=i;
      min_amt=vertex[i]->sy;
    }
  }
  // Find starting and ending vertices of first two edges:

  int startvert1=firstvert;        // Edge 1 start
  int startvert2=firstvert;        // Edge 2 start
  int xstart1=vertex[startvert1]->sx;
  int ystart1= vertex[startvert1]->sy;
  int xstart2= vertex[startvert2]->sx;
  int ystart2= vertex[startvert2]->sy;

  // Get end of edge 1 and check for wrap at last vertex:
```

```
int endvert1=startvert1-1;
if (endvert1<0) endvert1= number_of_vertices-1;
int xend1= vertex[endvert1]->sx;
int yend1= vertex[endvert1]->sy;

// Get end of edge 2 and check for wrap at last vertex:

int endvert2=startvert2+1;
if (endvert2==( number_of_vertices)) endvert2=0;
int xend2= vertex[endvert2]->sx;
int yend2= vertex[endvert2]->sy;

// Draw the polygon:

while (edgecount>0) {     // Draw all edges

  // Get offsets of edge 1 and 2:

  offset1=320*ystart1+xstart1+FP_OFF(screen_buffer);
  offset2=320*ystart2+xstart2+FP_OFF(screen_buffer);

  // Initialize error terms for edges 1 & 2:

    errorterm1=0;
    errorterm2=0;

  // Get absolute values of y lengths of edges:

    if ((ydiff1=yend1-ystart1)<0) ydiff1=-ydiff1;
    if ((ydiff2=yend2-ystart2)<0) ydiff2=-ydiff2;

  // Get absolute values of x lengths of edges
  //  plus unit to advance in x dimension

  if ((xdiff1=xend1-xstart1)<0) {
    xunit1=-1;
    xdiff1=-xdiff1;
  }
  else {
    xunit1=1;
  }
   if ((xdiff2=xend2-xstart2)<0) {
     xunit2=-1;
     xdiff2=-xdiff2;
  }
  else {
    xunit2=1;
  }

  // Choose which of four routines to use:

  if (xdiff1>ydiff1) {     // If edge 1 slope < 1
```

continued on next page

■ ■ ■ ■ ■   **273**

continued from previous page

```
       if (xdiff2>ydiff2) {  // If edge 2 slope < 1

   // Increment edge 1 on X and edge 2 on X:

     count1=xdiff1; // Number of pixels to draw edge 1
     count2=xdiff2; // Number of pixels to draw edge 2

   // Continue drawing until one edge is done:

   while (count1 && count2) {

     // Find edge 1 coordinates:

     // Don't draw polygon fill line until ready to
     //  move in y dimension:

     while ((errorterm1<xdiff1)&&(count1>0)) {
       if (count1--) {       // Count off this pixel
         offset1+=xunit1;  // Point to next pixel
         xstart1+=xunit1;
       }
       errorterm1+=ydiff1; // Ready to move in y?
       if (errorterm1<xdiff1) {  // No?

       // Then draw a pixel in polygon color:

         screen_buffer[offset1]= color;
       }
     }
     errorterm1-=xdiff1; // Reset error term

     // Find edge 2 coordinates:

     // Don't draw polygon fill line until ready to
     //  move in y dimension:

      while ((errorterm2<xdiff2)&&(count2>0)) {
       if (count2--) {       // Count off this pixel
         offset2+=xunit2;  // Point to next pixel
         xstart2+=xunit2;
       }
        errorterm2+=ydiff2; // Ready to move in y?
        if (errorterm2<xdiff2) {  // No?

       // Then draw a pixel in polygon color:

         screen_buffer[offset2]= color;
       }
     }
      errorterm2-=xdiff2; // Recalculate error term

     // Draw line from edge 1 to edge 2:
```

```
    // Find length and direction of line:

    length=offset2-offset1; // What's the length?
    if (length<0) {          // If negative...
      length=-length;        // Make it positive
      start=offset2;         // START = edge 2
  }
    else start=offset1;      // Else START = edge 1

    // Draw the line:

      for (int i=start; i<start+length+1; i++)
        screen_buffer[i]= color;

    // Advance to next line:

    offset1+=320;
    ystart1++;
    offset2+=320;
    ystart2++;
  }
}
else {    // If edge 2 slope >= 1

// Increment edge 1 on X and edge 2 on Y:

  count1=xdiff1;   // Number of pixels to draw edge 1
  count2=ydiff2;   // Number of pixels to draw edge 2

  // Continue drawing until one edge is done:

  while (count1 && count2) {

    // Find edge 1 coordinates:

    // Don't draw until ready to move in y dimension

      while ((errorterm1<xdiff1)&&(count1>0)) {
       if (count1--) {       // Count off this pixel
         offset1+=xunit1;    // Point to next pixel
         xstart1+=xunit1;
       }
       errorterm1+=ydiff1; // Ready to move in y?
       if (errorterm1<xdiff1) {   // No?

         // Then plot a pixel in the polygon color

         screen_buffer[offset1]= color;
      }
    }
     errorterm1-=xdiff1; // Reset error term
```

continued on next page

continued from previous page

```
            // Find edge 2 coordinates:

            errorterm2+=xdiff2; // Increment error term

            // If time to move in y dimension, restore error
            //   term and advance offset to next pixel:

            if (errorterm2 >= ydiff2)  {
              errorterm2-=ydiff2;
              offset2+=xunit2;
              xstart2+=xunit2;
            }
            -count2; // Count off this pixel

            // Draw line from edge 1 to edge 2

            // Find length and direction of line:

            length=offset2-offset1; // What's the length?
            if (length<0) {          // If negative...
              length=-length;        // ...make it positive
              start=offset2;         // START = edge 2
            }
            else start=offset1;      // Else START = edge 1

            // Draw the line:

             for (int i=start; i<start+length+1; i++)
               screen_buffer[i]= color;

            // Advance to next line:

            offset1+=320;
            ystart1++;
            offset2+=320;
            ystart2++;
        }
      }
    }
    else { // If edge 1 slope >= 1

      if (xdiff2>ydiff2) { // If edge 2 slope < 1

      // Increment edge 1 on Y and edge 2 on X:

        count1=ydiff1;  // Number of pixels to draw edge 1
        count2=xdiff2;  // Number of pixels to draw edge 2

        // Continue drawing until one edge is done:

        while(count1 && count2) {
```

```
// Find edge 1 coordinates:

errorterm1+=xdiff1; // Increment error term

// If time to move in y dimension, restore error
//  term and advance offset to next pixel:

if (errorterm1 >= ydiff1)  {
  errorterm1-=ydiff1;
  offset1+=xunit1;
  xstart1+=xunit1;
 }

-count1; // Count off this pixel

// Find edge 2 coordinates:

// Don't draw until ready to move in y dimension

 while ((errorterm2<xdiff2)&&(count2>0)) {
  if (count2--) {      // Count off this pixel
    offset2+=xunit2;  // Point to next pixel
    xstart2+=xunit2;
 }
  errorterm2+=ydiff2; // Ready to move in y?
  if (errorterm2<xdiff2) {  // No?

    // Then draw a pixel in polygon color:

      screen_buffer[offset2]= color;
 }
}
 errorterm2-=xdiff2;  // Reset error term

 // Draw line from edge 1 to edge 2

 // Find length and direction of line:

 length=offset2-offset1;
 if (length<0) {    // If negative...
   length=-length;  // ...make it positive
   start=offset2;   // START = edge 2
}
 else start=offset1; // Else START = edge 1

 // Draw the line:

 for (int i=start; i<start+length+1; i++)
   screen_buffer[i]= color;

 // Advance to next line:
```

continued on next page

continued from previous page

```
            offset1+=320;
            ystart1++;
            offset2+=320;
            ystart2++;
        }
    }
    else { // If edge 2 slope >= 1

    // Increment edge 1 on Y and edge 2 on Y:

        count1=ydiff1;  // Number of pixels to draw edge 1
        count2=ydiff2;  // Number of pixels to draw edge 2

        // Continue drawing until one edge is done:

        while(count1 && count2) {

            // Find edge 1 coordinates:

            errorterm1+=xdiff1;  // Increment error term


            // If time to move in y dimension, restore error
            //  term and advance offset to next pixel:

            if (errorterm1 >= ydiff1)  {
                errorterm1-=ydiff1;
                offset1+=xunit1;
                xstart1+=xunit1;
            }

            -count1; // Count off this pixel

            // Find edge 2 coordinates:

            errorterm2+=xdiff2; // Increment error term

            // If time to move in y dimension, restore error
            //  term and advance offset to next pixel:

            if (errorterm2 >= ydiff2)  {
                errorterm2-=ydiff2;
                offset2+=xunit2;
                xstart2+=xunit2;
            }

            -count2; // Count off this pixel

            // Draw line from edge 1 to edge 2:

            // Find length and direction of line:

            length=offset2-offset1;
```

```
      if (length<0) {          // If negative...
        length=-length;        // ...make it positive
        start=offset2;         // Set START = edge 2
     }
      else start=offset1;      // Else START = edge 1

      // Draw the line:

      for (int i=start; i<start+length+1; i++)
        screen_buffer[i]=polygon->color;

      // Advance to next line:

      offset1+=320;
      ystart1++;
      offset2+=320;
      ystart2++;
    }
  }
}
// Another edge (at least) is complete.
// Start next edge, if any.

if (!count1) {              // If edge 1 is complete...
  -edgecount;               // Decrement the edge count
  startvert1=endvert1;      // Make ending vertex into
                            //  start vertex
  -endvert1;                // And get new ending vertex

  // Check for wrap:

  if (endvert1<0)
    endvert1= number_of_vertices-1;

  // Get x & y of new end vertex:

    xend1= vertex[endvert1]->sx;
    yend1= vertex[endvert1]->sy;
}

if (!count2) {              // If edge 2 is complete...
  -edgecount;               // Decrement the edge count
  startvert2=endvert2;      // Make ending vertex into
                            //  start vertex
  endvert2++;               // And get new ending vertex

  // Check for wrap:

  if (endvert2==( number_of_vertices))
    endvert2=0;

  // Get x & y of new end vertex:
```

continued on next page

continued from previous page

```
        xend2= vertex[endvert2]->sx;
        yend2= vertex[endvert2]->sy;
      }
    }
  }
}
```

Manipulating Polygons

Of course, drawing polygons is not all there is to producing three-dimensional animations. Next we need to draw entire objects constructed from polygons. Then we need to manipulate those objects so that we can rotate, scale, and translate them.

To perform both of these tasks, a new version of the WIRE.CPP package from Chapter 7 is presented over the next few pages. However, to reflect its new purpose, it has been renamed POLY.CPP (and is available in a file of the same name on the disk that came with this book under the directory BYOFS\POLYGON). Many of the routines from the last chapter have remained unchanged in this new package, but since some have changed, we'll present them here.

The Transform() Function

The Transform() function, for instance, which multiplies the vertices of an object by the transformation matrix, must be altered to be used in the object_type class. The function is almost the same except for the declaration. This is an indication that the object_type class could have been inherited from the Shape class. We chose not to use the power of C++ inheritance to keep the class functionality localized within one class (so code readers wouldn't have to jump from module to module to understand what was going on). You can see how the object_type version looks in Listing 8-2.

Listing 8-2 Transform() function

```
void object_type::Transform()
{
  // Multiply all vertices in OBJECT with master
  //   transformation matrix:
vertex_type *vptr=&vertex[0];

  for (int v=0; v<number_of_vertices; v++,vptr++) {
vptr->wx=vptr->lx*matrix[0][0]+vptr->ly*matrix[1][0]
     +vptr->lz*matrix[2][0]+matrix[3][0];
   vptr->wy=vptr->lx*matrix[0][1]+vptr->ly*matrix[1][1]
     +vptr->lz*matrix[2][1]+matrix[3][1];
   vptr->wz=vptr->lx*matrix[0][2]+vptr->ly*matrix[1][2]
     +vptr->lz*matrix[2][2]+matrix[3][2];
  }
}
```

The Project() Function

Similarly, the Project() function, which projects an object's world coordinates into screen coordinates, must be rewritten to declare it as a member function of the object_type class. See Listing 8-3 for the new version.

Listing 8-3 Project() function

```
void object_type::Project(int distance)
{

// Project object onto screen with perspective projection

  // Loop through all vertices in object:

// Make pointer to vertex array:

vertex_type *vptr=vertex;

  for (int v=0; v<number_of_vertices; v++, vptr++) {

    // Divide world x&y coordinates by z coordinates:

    vptr->sx=distance*vptr->wx/(distance-vptr->wz)+XORIGIN;
    vptr->sy=distance*vptr->wy/(distance-vptr->wz)+YORIGIN;
  }
}
```

There's also an entirely new function in the package this time around: Draw(). Huh? That was the same name as the function in the Shape class and it plays essentially the same role as the Shape::Draw() function, except instead of running through a list of lines in a wireframe shape and drawing them, it runs through a list of polygons in a polygon-fill object and calls the DrawPoly() function to draw them.

Backface Removal

The DrawPoly() function needs a bit of explanation, though. It is not enough simply to call it to draw all of the polygons in an object. Why? Because in a real object, some surfaces hide other surfaces, so that not all surfaces are visible. If we draw the polygons that make up an object without regard to this problem, we'll most likely wind up with background surfaces showing through foreground surfaces. The result will be a mess.

This is known as the hidden-surface problem and is a major consideration in drawing three-dimensional objects. It is such a major consideration that we'll spend an entire chapter on it later in this book. For the moment, we will take a simplistic solution to the problem. This solution is known as backface removal.

A backface, simply put, is any surface that isn't facing us at the moment. When we draw a polygon-fill object such as a cube on the video display, roughly half of its surfaces—half of its polygons—will be facing away from us. If the object is closed—if there are no openings into its interior—these surfaces are effectively invisible and we don't have to draw them. In fact, we don't want to draw them, because they are hidden surfaces that would mess up the display if drawn over the top of the surfaces that are hiding them.

It would be nice if there were a way to identify backfaces so that we could avoid drawing them. And, by an amazing coincidence, there is. By taking the cross-product of two adjacent edges of the polygon, we can determine which way it is facing. If it is facing in a positive z direction, it is facing away from us. If it is facing in a negative z direction, it is facing us.

The cross product of the edges is determined using the rules of matrix multiplication. We need to multiply three vectors together, each containing the coordinates of one of the vertices of the two edges. Fortunately, we don't even need to perform the full multiplication. We just need to perform enough of it to determine the z coordinate of the result. This equation will do the job:

```
z=(x1-x0)*(y2-y0)-(y1-y0)*(x2-x0)
```

where (x0,y0,z0) are the coordinates of the first vertex, (x1,y1,z1) are the coordinates of the second vertex, and (x2,y2,z2) are the coordinates of the third vertex. With this equation, we can build a function called backface in the polygon_type class that determines, based on three of the polygon's vertices, whether or not it is a backface. Such a function appears in Listing 8-4. There's only one catch. In order to use this function properly, all polygons must be designed in such a way that, when viewed from their visible sides, the vertices (as listed in the descriptor file) proceed around the polygon in a counterclockwise direction.

Listing 8-4 The backface() function

```
int polygon_type::backface()
{

//    Returns 0 if POLYGON_TYPE is visible, -1 if not.
//    POLYGON_TYPE must be part of a convex polyhedron

     vertex_type *v0,*v1,*v2;  // Pointers to three vertices

  // Point to vertices:

     v0=p.vertex[0];
     v1=p.vertex[1];
     v2=p.vertex[2];
     int z=(v1->sx-v0->sx)*(v2->sy-v0->sy)
```

```
                          -(v1->sy-v0->sy)*(v2->sx-v0->sx);
          return(z>=0);
}
```

In Chapter 13, I'll show you an alternate method of performing backface removal that works better in some situations than this one does, though the method documented above is adequate for the programs developed in this and the following chapter.

The Draw() Function

Now the object_type::Draw() function can be rewritten so that it only draws polygons that are not backfaces, as in Listing 8-5. Also, since we will be grouping all these objects in the world_type class, we will write a function to loop through all objects, drawing each to the screen. True, we only have one object now, but we're thinking big!

Listing 8-5 object_type::Draw() function

```
void object_type::Draw(unsigned char far *screen)
// Draw polygons in class OBJECT_TYPE
{
        polygon_type * polyptr = polygon;
          // Loop through all polygons in object:
        for (int p=0; p<number_of_polygons; p++, polyptr++) {
        // Draw current polygon:
         if (convex) {
                if(!polyptr->backface()) {
                    polyptr->DrawPoly(screen);
                }
         }
         else polyptr->DrawPoly(screen);
        }
}

void world_type::Draw(unsigned char far *screen)
// Draw all object in class WORLD_TYPE
{
        // Loop through all objects in world:
        for(int i=0; i < number_of_objects; i++) {
        obj[i].Transform();            // Transform OBJECT using MATRIX
        obj[i].Project(400);           // Perform perspective projection
        obj[i].Draw(screen);  // Draw transformed object
        }
}
```

You'll note that the purpose of the convex field in the object_type class is to determine whether we actually do want to remove backfaces from an object. For some objects, such as open containers and single polygons, backface removal would be counterproductive; the backsides of objects that should be visible would instead mysteriously vanish.

Limitations of Backface Removal

Although fairly simple to implement, backface removal has some severe limitations as a method of removing hidden surfaces. One is that the object must be a convex polyhedron. To be convex, all internal angles in the polyhedron must be less than 180 degrees. Otherwise, there may be background polygons that are not backfaces but that are nonetheless concealed, at least partially, by foreground polygons. The second limitation is that backface removal only works on a single object. If we wish to construct a scene with more than one object, backface removal won't help prevent background objects from showing through foreground objects. Thus, we'll need a more powerful method of hidden surface removal. We'll defer this complex topic until Chapter 10 however.

The Polygon-Fill Display Program

Now, let's look at a program that displays and rotates three-dimensional polygon-fill objects on the mode 13h display. Given the classes and set of polygon-fill manipulation and display functions that we've placed in file POLY.H, such a file will be a mere variation on the wireframe display program we introduced in the last chapter. So to ward off possible boredom, let's make things a little more complicated. Instead of placing object descriptions in the program as data initialization statements, let's store object descriptors on the disk as ASCII files. To make this possible, we'll need to write a function that will read these descriptor files and store the descriptor data in such classes as world_type, object_type and polygon_type. Since we want to read the data into these classes and assign values to the private member fields, we will have to add these functions as members to the classes. This will mean a separate load function for each of the three mentioned classes. But wait! The object_type class was made a friend to the polygon_type class. We can assign values to the private members of polygon from an object since it has complete access. So, only two will be needed. We'll call these loader functions world_type::loadpoly() and object_type::load() and put them into the file LOADPOLY.CPP.

ASCII Object Descriptors

The format of the ASCII files used in this and the following chapters will be simple. They will consist of a sequence of ASCII numbers, separated by commas, like this: 17, 45, 198, 7, 65, 70. . . . We'll use comments, preceded by the asterisk character (*), to explain the purpose of the numbers. So, anything on a line after an asterisk, up to the carriage return that terminates the line, will be ignored, just as anything on a line after the double slash (//) is ignored in C++. The format of the numbers roughly follows the format of *object_type* class. For example, an ASCII descriptor for a cube appears in Listing 8-6. This is included in the POLYGON.IDE project.

Listing 8-6 Cube descriptor

```
*** Object definition file ***

 1,   * Number of objects in file

* OBJECT #1 (CUBE):

   8,  * Number of vertices in object #0

     * Vertices for object 0:

      -10,10,-10,   * Vertex #0
      10,10,-10,    * Vertex #1
      10,10,10,     * Vertex #2
      -10,10,10,    * Vertex #3
      -10,-10,-10,  * Vertex #4
      10,-10,-10,   * Vertex #5
      10,-10,10,    * Vertex #6
      -10,-10,10,   * Vertex #7

   6,  * Number of polygons for object 0

     * Polygons for object 0:

      4, 0,1,5,4, 1,
      4, 5,6,7,4, 2,
      4, 6,2,3,7, 3,
      4, 2,1,0,3, 4,
      4, 2,6,5,1, 5,
      4, 4,7,3,0, 6,

      1,          * Yes, use backface removal
```

The first number in each polygon description is the number of vertices (which is 4 in every instance here) and the last number is the color of the polygon. The numbers in between are the vertices of the polygon, as listed previously in the descriptor comments. This descriptor is in the file CUBE.TXT on the disk under the subdirectory POLYGON. You can use this file as a template for your own object descriptors, though we'll be expanding the format of these files later in the book to handle the needs of the flight simulator, and the format here will be incompatible with that expanded format.

Reading the Data File

The code that reads this data into the variable class appears in Listing 8-7. It is cumbersome but straightforward, and it isn't really essential that you understand it in order to comprehend everything else that our polygon-fill code is going to do. It uses standard parsing techniques for reading ASCII numbers and skipping separators. The file and parsing routines have all been grouped into a local class named PolyFile. If you read the code closely, you'll see that almost any non-numeric character (except a blank space or a carriage return) can be used to separate numbers in the descriptor. However, commas are the most readable separator. The PolyFile class has one data field, an integer for storing the file handle. Its constructor initializes this file descriptor to -1. The destructor calls the Close() function. This class is designed to be used only as an internal class in the load module. Hence it is not as complete a class definition that we would need for an external file-reading class. For instance, there is no file status indicator nor mechanism for manipulating the file pointer such as seek and tell functions.

Briefly, the PolyFile::Open function takes one argument, a pointer to the string holding the filename. It returns a nonzero value if the file was successfully opened. The PolyFile::Close() function checks the file descriptor before closing the file and resets grip to -1. The getnumber() function returns a signed integer from the file stream, while nextchar() filters the file by ignoring spaces and comments and returns the next valid character.

The loadpoly function takes as argument a character string filename. It opens the file, retrieves the number of objects in the file and uses this information to allocate memory with the new operator. It then goes through this object_type array telling each object to load itself. The load function likewise reads the number of vertex elements and creates the vertex array, then reads the number of polygons to allocate the polygon array. In turn, each of these polygon_type array elements is read from the file and their vertex array allocated.

Listing 8-7 Loading functions

```
#include  <io.h>
#include <fcntl.h>
#include  <ctype.h>
#include  "poly.h"

class PolyFile {
        protected:
                int grip;
        public:
                PolyFile() { grip = -1; }
                int Open(char *filename);
                ~PolyFile()
                        { close(grip); }
                // parsing functions:
```

```
                int getnumber();
                char nextchar();
};

static PolyFile _pf;  // static PolyFile available to this module only

int object_type::load()
{
        number_of_vertices=_pf.getnumber();
        vertex= new vertex_type[number_of_vertices];
        if( vertex == 0)
                return(-1);
        for (int vertnum=0; vertnum<number_of_vertices; vertnum++) {
                vertex[vertnum].lx=_pf.getnumber();
                vertex[vertnum].ly=_pf.getnumber();
                vertex[vertnum].lz=_pf.getnumber();
                vertex[vertnum].lt=1;
                vertex[vertnum].wt=1;
        }
        number_of_polygons=_pf.getnumber();
        polygon= new polygon_type[number_of_polygons];
        if(polygon == 0)
                return(-1);
        polygon_type *polyptr = polygon;
        for (int polynum=0; polynum<number_of_polygons; polynum++, polyptr++) {
                polyptr->number_of_vertices=_pf.getnumber();
                polyptr->vertex=  new vertex_type *[number_of_vertices];
                if(polyptr->vertex == 0)
                        return(-1);
                for  (int  vertnum=0;  vertnum<  polyptr->number_of_vertices;
                  vertnum++) {
                  polyptr->vertex[vertnum]= &vertex[_pf.getnumber()];
                }
                polyptr->color=_pf.getnumber();
        }
        convex=_pf.getnumber();
        return(0);
}

int world_type::loadpoly(char *filename)
{
  if( _pf.Open(filename) ) // if a mistake in opening file, exit function
          return(-1);
          // world members:
  number_of_objects = _pf.getnumber();
 obj= new object_type[number_of_objects];
  if( ! obj )
        return(-1);
  for (int objnum=0; objnum< number_of_objects; objnum++) {
        if( obj[objnum].load() )
                return( -1 );
  }
```

continued on next page

continued from previous page

```
   return(0);
}
// ******************************
// POLYFILE  local class
int PolyFile::Open(char *filename)
{
        grip = open(filename,O_RDONLY|O_TEXT);
        return (grip == -1);
}

int PolyFile::getnumber()
{
  char ch;
  int sign=1;

  int num=0;
  if ((ch=nextchar())=='-') {
        sign=-1;
        ch=nextchar();
  }
  while (isdigit(ch)) {
        num=num*10+ch-'0';
        ch=nextchar();
  }
  return(num*sign);
}


char PolyFile::nextchar()
{
  char ch;

  while(!eof(grip))
  {
        do {
                read(grip,&ch,1);
        }while(isspace(ch));
        if (ch=='*')
        {
                do {
                        read(grip, &ch,1);
                }while(ch !='\n');
        }
        else return(ch);

  }
  return(0);
}
```

The function loadpoly() is called to read the file, and Draw() is called to draw the entire world. The rest of the program is identical to the wireframe program in the last chapter, except that it uses the *argv* variable to get the name of the file containing the object descriptor from the command line. The current POLYDEM1.IDE project is set to run with the CUBE.TXT command line argument. You can change this under the Options - Environment Menu item followed by clicking on the word Debugger on the left side of the dialog box. Type in the name of your object descriptor file in the Run argument combo box edit window.

The Polygon Demonstration Program

The code for the main program appears in Listing 8-8.

 Listing 8-8 POLYDEM1.CPP

```
// POLYDEM1.CPP
//   Demonstrate rotation of three-dimensional polygon-fill
//   object

#include <iostream.h>
#include <dos.h>
#include <conio.h>
#include <stdlib.h>
#include "poly.h"
#include "screen.h"

world_type world;

void main(int argc,char* argv[])
{

  float xangle=0,yangle=0,zangle=0;          // X,Y&Z angles
                                             //  of shape
  float xrot=0.1,yrot=0.1,zrot=0.1;          // X,Y&Z rotation
                                             //  increments
  unsigned char *screen_buffer;              // Offscreen drawing
                                             //  buffer

  if (argc!=2) {                             // Read command-line
                                             //  arguments
    cerr << "Wrong number of arguments"<< endl; // If wrong number,
    exit(-1);                                //  print
                                             //  message and
                                             //  abort
  }
  if( world.loadpoly(argv[1]) ) {            // Load object
                                             //  description
      cerr << "Failure loading polygons into World." << endl;
      exit(-1);
      }
  screen_buffer=new unsigned char[64000];    // Create off-screen
                                             //  buffer
```

continued on next page

continued from previous page

```
    int oldmode=*(int *)MK_FP(0x40,0x49); // Save previous
                                          //  video mode
    setgmode(0x13);                       // Set mode 13h
    while (!kbhit()) {                     // Loop until key is
                                          //  pressed
      cls(screen_buffer);                 // Clear screen
                                          //  buffer
      inittrans();                        // Initialize
                                          //  transformations
      scale(1,1,1);                       // Create scaling
                                          //  matrix
      rotate(xangle,yangle,zangle);       // Create rotation
                                          //  matrices
      xangle+=xrot;                       // Increment rotation
                                          //  angles
      yangle+=yrot;
      zangle+=zrot;
      translate(0,0,600);                        // Create translation
                                                 //  matrix
      world.Draw(screen_buffer);
      putwindow(0,0,320,200,screen_buffer); // Move buffer to
                                            //  video RAM
    }
    setgmode(oldmode);                          // Reset previous
                                                //  video mode & end
// CLEANUP the memory allocated for screen buffer
if(screen_buffer)
        delete [] screen_buffer;
}
```

CHAPTER

9

9

Faster and Faster

Not all computer programs need to be fast. In many cases, they only need to be fast enough. Word processors and terminal packages, for instance, spend most of their time waiting for the next character to be received from the keyboard or the modem, and it doesn't matter how quickly they process that character as long as they're finished by the time another character arrives.

Not so with games, 3D games in particular. The execution speed of three-dimensional animation code is crucial and the programmer must always be looking for ways to save one processor cycle here and another processor cycle there. The speed at which your code executes will determine how many frames per second the animation can achieve and the amount of detail your potential flight simulator pilot can see when he or she looks out the window of the airplane. The faster the code, the higher you can push the frame rate and the more detail you can display. Because today's flight simulator buffs demand both a high frame rate and a great deal of visual detail, it's crucial that the speed of the code be optimized.

For clarity, I've stressed readable code so far as much as fast code, but in this chapter, we'll spend most of our time discussing three types of optimization: look-up tables, fixed-point arithmetic, and unrolling loops.

In addition, we'll consider the possibility of writing code that only runs on 386, 486 and better processors. We'll examine the role of math coprocessors in flight simulation.

And we'll figure out ways to arrange our screen display to create a faster frame rate without making the CPU do any additional work.

First, though, we'll discuss the most important topic of all: how to decide which parts of a program need to be optimized. We'll take a look at *Turbo Profiler*, a much underutilized utility that comes with Borland C++ 4.5. *Turbo Profiler* can help you determine which parts of your program can benefit from optimal coding and which parts are already working as fast as is necessary. Note that Borland did not include the *Turbo Profiler* in version 4.0, and that the profiler which is displayed in the Borland Group Window is a Profiler for Windows programs. To use the DOS *Turbo Profiler* you must exit Windows after compiling your program.

Knowing Where to Optimize

The secret of optimizing computer code is knowing which parts of the code need to be optimized and which parts don't. This doesn't mean that you optimize the slow parts and don't optimize the fast parts. The truth is, there are parts of your program that can be slow as molasses and nobody will ever notice, while there are other parts of your program where small inefficiencies in your code will produce a major drag on program execution. The trick to effective optimization is knowing which is which.

The secret of knowing where to optimize your code can be summed up simply: Optimize the inner loops.

The secret of knowing where not to optimize can be summed up just as simply: Don't sweat the outer loops.

Nested Loops

Suppose you write a program that contains a series of nested For() loops like the following:

```
for (int i=0; i<100; i++) {
    // Several lines of code (A)
    for (int j=0; j<100; j++) {
        // Several lines of code (B)
        for (int k=0; k<100; k++) {
            // Several lines of code (C)
        }
    }
}
```

After perusing the code in the sections labelled A, B, and C, you determine that all three sections are less than optimal—that is, with some effort you could make the code in each section execute faster. However, each section will require at least several hours, perhaps several days, to optimize and you only have time to optimize one of these sections. Which should you optimize?

The answer, of course, is section C. To see why, let's trace the way in which this fragment of code would execute. The outermost For loop (A), the one for which the variable i is the index, is set to execute 100 times, stepping the value of the index from 0 to 99 before it stops executing. The body of this loop consists of two more nested For loops. The next inner loop (B), for which the variable j is the index, is also set to execute 100 times. However, because this loop is nested inside the first loop, it will not simply execute 100 times and stop. It will execute 100 times *for each time the outer loop executes*. Thus, if the outermost loop executes 100 times, this second loop will execute 10,000 times. Those executions eat up a lot of CPU time.

The Innermost Loop

But the innermost For loop (C) is the real execution hog. This loop, for which the index is the variable k, is also set to execute 100 times—for each time the j loop executes. This means that it will execute 10,000 times when the j loop executes 100 times. But the j loop executes 100 times every time the i loop executes once. Thus, for 100 executions of the i loop, the j loop will execute 10,000 times and the k loop will execute *one million times!*

Consider what that means. If you find an optimization in the outermost loop that saves one-millionth of a second every time the loop executes, you'll be saving only 1/10,000th of a second on every pass through this series of nested loops. That's probably not enough to be noticed. If you perform a similar optimization in the j loop, you'll save 1/100th of a second every time the outermost loop executes 100 times. That's better, but it's still probably not enough to make a difference. But the same optimization in the innermost loop will save a full second of execution time every time the outermost loop executes 100 times. That may well be enough to make a difference between a slow program and a lightning fast one.

Most significant optimizations will save you a lot more than a millionth of a second. And such optimizations performed in an inner loop will pay you back many times for every execution of an outer loop. So the first rule of program code optimization is to find the innermost loops and begin your optimization there. In many cases, you won't need to optimize the outer loops at all. Unless you've put some unusually sluggish code in an outer loop, optimizations performed there won't have any noticeable effect on program execution.

Profiling Your Code

Alas, most nontrivial programs (and a flight simulator is definitely nontrivial) will have more than one inner loop. In a typical real-time game program (i.e., a game program in which the action continues whether or not the player makes a "move"), the outermost loop is the event loop, which starts by polling the event manager to determine if any user input has occurred since the last execution of the loop, and then updates the on-screen animation. This outer loop will contain any number of inner loops, one after another rather than one inside another, and these in turn may contain still more loops. To which of these loops should you turn your attention first?

That's what *Turbo Profiler* is designed to tell you. TProf, as it's affectionately known to Borland C++ programmers, will run your program, counting the number of times various subroutines and lines of code are executed and noting how much time the program spends in each. It will then display this information for you in a number of ways, so that you can determine which parts of your program are most urgently in need of fine-tuning.

As mentioned previously, there are two version of profilers with Borland C++ 4.5. One is the Windows version, for profiling Windows programs, while the other is the DOS version for DOS programs. Since the DOS profiler can only be run from the DOS command line (and won't run under Window's DOS shell), we will have to exit Windows to use it. Since some prefer not to live the nursery rhyme ("go in and out the window"), an alternative form of compilation can be used: the command line compiler. To use this form, load the relevant project, then select Generate Makefile under the Project menu in the IDE. This will create a make file of the same name as the project but with the file extension .MAK. Save this editor window from the IDE for later use from the command line.

Let's give TProf a quick test run. The C++ program in Listing 9-1, which is on the enclosed disk under the name TPDEMO.CPP in the BYOFS\MISC directory, is a working version of the three nested loops in the earlier example. Each loop contains a single integer assignment statement, just to give the CPU something to do. Let's see what TProf has to say about the execution profile of this program.

Listing 9-1 TPDEMO.CPP

```
#include <stdio.h>

void main()
{
  for (int i=0; i<100; i++) {
    int a=1;
    for (int j=0; j<100; j++) {
      int b=2;
      for (int k=0; k<100; k++) {
        int c=3;
      }
    }
  }
}
```

First, we'll need to compile it. Enter the Borland C++ IDE, load TPDEMO.IDE, compile and run it. (Alternately, choose Run from the Run menu once the project is loaded.) Since the program has no output, the IDE will simply display the user screen briefly, then return to the editor. On my system this process takes about three seconds, so that's the baseline for the unoptimized program.

(All references to program execution speeds in this chapter and elsewhere are based on my system and will almost certainly be different on your system. For the record, this book originally was written using a 16-MHz, 386SX-based machine, which is fairly slow by current standards. The second edition update to C++ occurred on a 66-MHz, 486DX computer, which is still slow when compared to the top of the heap. If you are using a 100-MHz, Pentium 486-based machine to run this program, it will finish executing so quickly you'll barely be aware that you've run it.)

Executing TProf

Now let's see what *Turbo Profiler* tells us about the program. Exit Windows and return to DOS. Change to the drive and directory where the TPDEMO.EXE program was copied, BYOFS\MISC. Invoke *Turbo Profiler* with the following command:

```
>TPROF TPDEMO.EXE
```

This will boot TProf, pass the name of the TPDEMO.CPP program to it, and place you inside TProf. You're ready to start profiling.

The *Turbo Profiler* display should be divided into two windows. The top window displays the TPDEMO program. Each executable line of the program should be preceded by the symbol =>. This means that TProf will be counting the time that each of these lines spends executing. Go to the Run menu and choose Run. TProf will display the user screen and execute the program.

TPDEMO will take longer to execute under TProf than it did from the IDE. That's because TProf is busily counting execution times for each line of the program, which takes longer to perform than the individual lines take to execute. In fact, it takes about 10 minutes for the program to execute on my system. Even on a 50-MHz 486, you should notice a difference in execution time. You might want to go make a cup of coffee or call a friend and come back when TProf is done.

Once profiling is complete, the program's execution profile will appear in the lower of the two windows. (See Figure 9-1.) Take a moment to study this information. In the left portion of the window, you'll see a column of line numbers. In the middle, you'll see a column of numbers representing the number of seconds, or fractions of a second, that each line spent executing while the program ran. And on the right, you'll see a bar chart in which the execution time for each line is represented by a line of equal signs (You'll notice that TProf doesn't count the time that it spent in the timing of these lines, so that the total time for executing all lines comes to about the same amount of time that it took the BC++ IDE to execute the program—in my case, about three seconds.)

What should jump out at you is that the execution profile of the program is completely dominated by a single line—line 10, according to the column on the left,

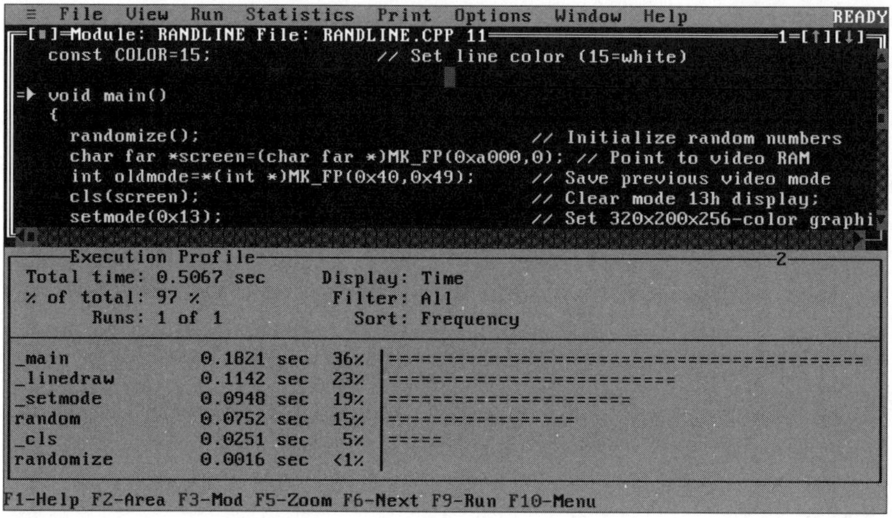

```
≡  File  View  Run  Statistics  Print  Options  Window  Help        READY
┌─[■]─Module: RANDLINE File: RANDLINE.CPP 11══════════════════════1═[↑][↓]─┐
│   const COLOR=15;                    // Set line color (15=white)        │
│                                                                          │
│═► void main()                                                            │
│   {                                                                      │
│     randomize();                              // Initialize random numbers│
│     char far *screen=(char far *)MK_FP(0xa000,0); // Point to video RAM   │
│     int oldmode=*(int *)MK_FP(0x40,0x49);     // Save previous video mode │
│     cls(screen);                              // Clear mode 13h display;  │
│     setmode(0x13);                            // Set 320x200x256-color graphi│
├──────────────────────────────────────────────────────────────────────────┤
│   ┌─Execution Profile──────────────────────────────────────────2─────────│
│   Total time: 0.5067 sec      Display: Time                              │
│   % of total: 97 %            Filter: All                                │
│       Runs: 1 of 1              Sort: Frequency                          │
│                                                                          │
│  _main           0.1821 sec  36%  ════════════════════════════════════════│
│  _linedraw       0.1142 sec  23%  ════════════════════════════          │
│  _setmode        0.0948 sec  19%  ═══════════════════════                │
│  random          0.0752 sec  15%  ═════════════════                      │
│  _cls            0.0251 sec   5%  ═════                                   │
│  randomize       0.0016 sec  <1%                                         │
└──────────────────────────────────────────────────────────────────────────┘
F1-Help F2-Area F3-Mod F5-Zoom F6-Next F9-Run F10-Menu
```

Figure 9-1 The main Turbo Profiler screen

unless you tampered with the program back in the IDE. Which line is that? Place the dark selection bar over that line of the profile and press Enter. TProf will activate the upper window, placing the cursor on the line in question. It turns out to be the line inside the innermost loop, just as we guessed. According to the profile, this line accounts for more than 98 percent of the program's execution time. All the other lines *together* amount to less than 2 percent of the program's execution time.

Reducing to Zero

Were we optimizing this program, it's obvious where we'd want to put our optimization resources. Sometimes, in deciding where to optimize, it's useful to ask yourself how much time you'd save if you could reduce the execution time of a line to zero processor cycles. In this case, if we could reduce the execution time of every line in this program *except* line 10 to zero processor cycles, we would speed up the program by less than 1 percent, an optimization that wouldn't even be noticeable. Thus, there's no point in spending time optimizing any line other than line 10. (After we've optimized line 10, it might be useful to optimize other lines or it might not be. It's difficult to make that judgment until line 10 has been optimized and the program can be profiled again.)

Is it possible to optimize line 15 of this program? Well, since line 10 doesn't actually do anything meaningful, we can optimize it simply by eliminating it, thus achieving the theoretical maximum optimization of reducing the number of processor cycles used by this line to zero. Select Quit from the TProf File menu, then return to Windows and BC++ IDE. (Or stay in DOS and load TPDEMO.CPP into a text editor if you plan on using a command line Make file.) Place a comment symbol (//) in front of line 10 (the line that reads *C=3*), which will remove the line from the program code. Compile and run the program again by choosing Run from the Run menu (or type MAKE -fTPDEMO.MAK at the command line) and once more return to TProf.

Begin profiling the program by choosing Run from the TProf Run menu. Time to make another cup of coffee and . . . whoa! Looks like there won't be enough time for that cup of coffee. On my system, the program took roughly 10 seconds to execute this time. Reducing execution time from 10 minutes to 10 seconds is a substantial optimization, even if we did cheat a bit.

The execution profile in the lower window looks quite different now. Line 9, the line that establishes the innermost for loop is now taking up 74 percent of the program's time (on my machine, at least). If additional optimizations were needed, you'd want to begin with this line. But considering how substantially the execution time of the program has been reduced already, further optimizations probably aren't needed. (It's impossible to answer this question, since the program doesn't actually do anything useful.)

Profiling for Real

Now let's profile some real code. Specifically, let's profile the program that we developed in Chapter 8, which is on the disk under the name POLYDEM1.CPP in the BYOFS\POLYGON directory. Change to that directory and launch *Turbo Profiler*:

```
>TPROF POLYDEM1.EXE
```

When you find yourself in *Turbo Profiler*, POLYDEM1 will have been loaded. The first line of every function will have the => symbol on it this time, rather than every line in the program. That's because the program is too big for TProf to profile every line. That's okay; we don't need that much information. We just want to know how the individual functions perform, so let's run the program and find out.

Before we can run POLYDEM1, however, TProf needs an argument for the program—we need to tell POLYDEM1 what three-dimensional object we wish to rotate. Pull down the Run menu, choose the Argument option, and type in CUBE.TXT. This is equivalent to typing an argument after the program name on the command line. TProf will ask you if you wish to load the program again so that the argument will take effect. Type Ⓨ for "yes." Then choose Run from the Run menu.

Now the program will run. The cube will begin revolving slowly on the screen. In fact, it will revolve a bit more slowly than it did back in the IDE, for the same reason that TPDEMO ran slowly in TProf—the compiling of statistics by TProf takes time. It's best to let the program run for several minutes under TProf, preferably 5 or 10 minutes, in order to get an accurate profile. This will prevent the time the program spends in its initialization procedures from overwhelming the amount of time spent in the main portion of the program. (Alternatively, you could remove the => symbols from all of the initialization procedures by clicking on them, but that's not necessary if you have a few minutes to kill.)

When the time is up, press any key and the program will terminate. The program profile will appear in the bottom window. You should see at a glance that four functions dominate the program's profile—putwindow(), DrawPoly(), matmult(), and cls(). At least on my machine, these functions take up 44 percent, 19 percent, 14 percent, and 14 percent of the program's time, respectively.

We've already made the cls() and putwindow() functions about as fast as they're likely to be (though words like that should challenge any programmer to make it faster), so we'll concentrate on optimizing the other two functions.

Integer Fixed-Point Arithmetic

Let's start with matmult(). The first thing about this function that should strike you is that it uses floating-point arithmetic to multiply the matrices together. Floating-point arithmetic is notoriously slow, especially on computers that lack a floating-point coprocessor. Yet it would seem to be unavoidable here. Floating-point arithmetic is the standard method of dealing with fractions in programming languages. The matrices contain fractional values that have been obtained by multiplying by sines and cosines, which are always fractional. Ergo, we have to use floating-point here.

Or do we? There are other ways of dealing with fractions, ways that are not supported by most programming languages (unfortunately). Perhaps the most useful for our purposes is fixed-point arithmetic, which deals with numbers as standard integers, except that they have a default decimal point somewhere in the middle of them. Where in the middle of them? That's up to you. You decide where you want the decimal point, remember where you put it, and be aware of what effect various mathematical operations have on the position of that decimal point. For instance, multiplication moves it to the left and division moves it to the right. That makes fixed-point a tad tricky to use in a high-level language, since it effectively reduces the number of significant digits that we can keep in the number, but the timely benefits of fixed-point are worth the problems.

The programming decision to use fixed-point arithmetic falls into the arena of time and space versus quality and precision—whether to sacrifice mathematical acuity for performance issues (memory storage and execution speed). This project-design issue is worth noting since computer hardware keeps getting better (and there's no end in sight). Video cards with 3D chip sets are being built. Progressively, these low-level routines will be a moot point. However, we'll continually see the design tradeoff again and again.

The long data type is the best for holding fixed-point numbers, since longs are 32 binary digits in size. That gives us the potential for a lot of significant digits to both sides of the decimal point. Ideally, we would place our decimal right in the middle of the number, like this:

```
1000111011110110.0011101101101011
```

That gives us 16 binary digits to the left of the decimal point and 16 digits to the right. (This is equivalent to approximately 5 decimal digits on each side of the point, which is adequate for most of the code in this book.) Unfortunately, the problem isn't quite that simple. To see why, let's look at how arithmetic is done in fixed-point arithmetic.

Working with Fixed-Point Arithmetic

We declare a fixed-point number exactly as we declared a long:

```
long fnum1,fnum2;
```

Now we have two 32-bit variables ready to store values. Assigning those values to the variables is a bit tricky. Let's assume that we've decided to place the decimal point after bit 9, so that there are 9 binary digits to the right of the decimal point and 24 to the left, like this:

```
100011101111101100011101.101101011
```

To assign an ordinary integer value to one of these fixed-point variables, we first must shift the digits of that value nine digit positions to the left, effectively moving its decimal point to the ninth position. To shift digits, the bitshift operators (<< and >>) are used. These are identical to the stream output and insert operators of C++ but the compiler knows the difference according to the context and use of the operators (whether a stream is the left hand operand). For instance, if we want to assign a value of 11.0 to the fixed-point variable *fnum1,* we would do so like this:

```
fnum1 = 11 << 9;
```

Similarly, if *int1* is an ordinary integer variable containing a non-fixed-point value, we would assign its value to the fixed-point variable *fnum1* like this:

```
fnum1 = int1 << 9;
```

The sum of two fixed-point numbers is a third fixed-point number. When we add two fixed-point variables, we do so just as though we were adding a pair of ordinary integer variables:

```
long fnum3 = fnum1 + fnum2;
```

Similarly, we subtract two fixed-point numbers in the same way:

```
long fnum3 = fnum1 - fnum2;
```

That all looks simple enough, but multiplication is a bit more problematic. Multiplying one fixed-point number times another produces a third fixed-point number, but the decimal point's digit position changes. You'll recall from when you learned long multiplication in the third grade that when you multiply two decimal fractions times one another, the result is a decimal fraction with twice as many digits to the right of the decimal point. So it is when we multiply two binary fractions. The decimal point (or should that be binary point?) moves left to a digit position representing the combined digit positions of both of the numbers being multiplied. When we multiply two of our fixed-point numbers with decimal points in position 9, the result will be a number with the decimal point in position 18.

```
  1111.11
x      .22
--------
  222222
  222222
--------
  244.4442
```

Adjusting the Decimal Position

In fixed-point arithmetic, as the name implies, the decimal point is supposed to remain fixed in one position. We can't let it wander around like this. We'll need to adjust for the decimal-point shift after the multiplication. In some cases, we'll want to adjust the digit position immediately by shifting it back 9 digits to the right, like this:

```
long fnum3 = fnum1 * fnum2 >> 9;
```

In other cases, we can allow the unadjusted digits to remain unadjusted a little longer, as long as we don't use the resulting numbers to perform additional multiplications. For instance, if we are adding together the products of several fixed-point number pairs, we need only shift the final result of the addition, saving the machine cycles that would be wasted by shifting each of the products individually. (In many cases, this paltry savings won't be significant, but in a time-critical inner loop it could save valuable fractions of a second.) Here's an example:

```
long fnum = (fnum1*fnum2 + fnum3*fnum4 + fnum5*fnum6) >> 9;
```

The products of the three multiplications in parentheses are added together, and then the shift instruction outside of the parentheses shifts the decimal point back into place in the sum.

Note that when multiplication causes the digits to shift to the left, the leftmost digits in the number are shifted into oblivion. (In multiplications between fixed-point numbers with 9 digits to the right of the decimal point, a single multiplication operation causes the leftmost 9 digits to be shifted out of the number.) These digits are lost, as is all information in them, unless we make some effort to preserve them before the multiplication is performed. Unfortunately, preserving these digits may complicate the multiplication operation to the point where the time saved by using fixed-point math is no longer worth the effort involved.

This is why we aren't putting the decimal point in the middle of the number, at the 16th-digit position. Although this would give us the maximum precision on both sides of the decimal point, all information to the left of the decimal point would be lost when we perform multiplication. By placing the decimal point in the ninth position, we have 14 bits of precision to the left of the decimal point, even after multiplication.

How can we incorporate fixed-point math into our code? The matrix routines are the best target, since they are the only ones that make extensive use of time-consuming floating-point operations. Instead of declaring the matrices to be of type float, we can declare them to be of type long—and treat them as fixed-point values. Here, for instance, is the matmult() function revised to use fixed-point math:

```
void matmult(long result[4][4],long mat1[4][4],
        long mat2[4][4])
{

// Multiply matrix MAT1 by matrix MAT2,
//   returning the result in RESULT

  for (int i=0; i<4; i++)
    for (int j=0; j<4; j++) {
      result[i][j]=0;
      for (int k=0; k<4; k++)
        result[i][j]+=(mat1[i][k] * mat2[k][j])>>SHIFT;
    }
}
```

The parameters passed to the function are now of type long and the multiplication performed between the two matrices is a fixed-point multiplication, with the result adjusted by shifting the digits of the product back to the left. You'll note that a constant called SHIFT defines the number of points that the product is shifted. This allows us to reconsider, if necessary, where the decimal point is to be placed. This constant will be defined in a file called FIX.H, which we'll get a look at later in this chapter. If you'll look in the file OPTPOLY.CPP on the disk under BYOFS\OPTIMIZE, you'll see that the other transformation functions and module global variables have been similarly adjusted and now use long variable types instead of type float.

```
#include "fix.h"

long matrix[4][4];      // Master transformation matrix
long smat[4][4];        // Scaling matrix
long zmat[4][4];        // Z rotation matrix
long xmat[4][4];        // X rotation matrix
long ymat[4][4];        // Y rotation matrix
long tmat[4][4];        // Translation matrix
```

Is It Worth It?

Is all this fixed-point effort worth the time that will be saved relative to floating-point math? That depends to some degree on whether or not the user has a floating-point math coprocessor installed. These coprocessors, which have become increasingly popular in recent years, greatly decrease the time required for floating-point calculations by the lengthy subroutines used for this purpose by machines without coprocessors. The Pentium microprocessor, used on most of the fastest IBM-compatible computers currently available, has a math coprocessor built in.

Roughly speaking, the fixed-point routines we've discussed will substantially improve the execution time of three-dimensional code on machines lacking math coprocessors. For machines with math coprocessors, though, the improvement will be smaller—perhaps much smaller. (We could use *Turbo Profiler* to see just how great the advantage is, but, according to Michael Abrash, in *Dr. Dobb's Journal,,* this might not do us any good. According to Abrash, TProf doesn't record time spent executing floating-point instructions. My own experiments tend to bear out Abrash's contention. If this is true, the matrix multiplication routines in our program are probably even slower than our earlier foray into *Turbo Profiler* would seem to indicate.)

If you have a 386 or later microprocessor, and are willing to write code that will not run properly on a less capable machine, we can write even more efficient fixed-point code than we have demonstrated in this chapter. The 386 processor features a set of 32-bit registers and 32-bit instructions that allows extremely efficient fixed-point math. Furthermore, because the 386 allows multiplication across two 32-bit registers, for a full 64 bits of precision, it is possible to perform fixed-point multiplication on the 386 without losing the high-order bits.

To demonstrate, let's take the fixed-point statement:

```
long fnum3 = (fnum1 * fnum2) >> 16
```

where *fnum1, fnum2,* and *fnum3,* are 32-bit, fixed-point variables with the decimal at the 16th-digit position and translate the statement into 386 code. Here's what the translation would look like:

```
mov    eax, [fnum1]   ; Get FNUM1 in EAX
imul   eax,[fnum2]    ; Multiply it by FNUM2
shrd   eax,edx,16     ; Shift back 16 digits to the right
mov    [fnum3],eax    ; And store it in FNUM3
```

The first MOV instruction puts FNUM1 in the accumulator, and then the IMUL instruction multiplies it by FNUM2, leaving the low-order 32 bits of the result in EAX and any overflow in EDX. The SHRD (shift right double) instruction shifts the resulting 64-bit number back 16 digits to the right, across both registers; this is why we don't lose our high-order 16 bits. The final instruction stores the result back in FNUM3.

The actual fixed-point multiplication is performed by the IMUL and SHRD instructions and is amazingly fast. Code that performs 32-bit fixed-point math with these instructions will beat a floating-point routine all hollow, particularly if there's no coprocessor present. (Actually, some authors estimate that fixed-point multiplication like this *isn't* significantly faster than the coprocessor, but using this kind of multiplication allows us to use fixed-point addition and subtraction, which *is* faster than the kind performed by the coprocessor.)

So, should you write code for a 386 processor that takes advantage of these capabilities? That's a tough question to answer. Many popular games require 486 or Pentium microprocessors. These CPUs have a math coprocessor built in. Machines with less than a 386 CPU are no longer considered a marketing target, and the 386 itself will probably fade out of any serious game-marketing picture by next year. The choice of whether to write in 386, 486 and higher assembly is up to you. If the program is for your own enjoyment then optimize it for your own machine! In this book, we're concentrating on code that will run on all true IBM-compatibles which includes the archaic 286 machines. But there's no reason you have to follow our example in the programs that you produce. In Borland 4.5, remember to turn on the appropriate CPU code generation flag in the Options Project 16-bit Compiler Dialog. This will help Borland optimize your code with the appropriate instruction set. Just as floating-point math slowly migrated from software to hardware, and people upgrade their computers to faster machines, the gain in performance will dwindle along with the use of fixed-point memory representation to gain CPU clock cycles from integer multiplication instructions. Floating point is nearly acceptable on 64-bit CPUs. But in general, fixed-point arithmetic principles can be applied to other platforms and it is considered an optimization in most games that is decidedly worth the bother.

Using Look-Up Tables to Avoid Calculations

If we redo the transformation routines in fixed-point code, we'll need some way to produce fixed-point sines and cosines. We could simply use the standard floating-point sin() and cos() instructions, converting the results to 16-bit integers which we'd then shift to the left to produce a fixed-point number. But that would defeat the purpose of using fixed-point code. The calculation of floating-point sines and cosines is notoriously slow, and it would cancel out much of what we gain using fixed-point math elsewhere in the program.

Still, writing custom transcendental functions to calculate fixed-point sines and cosines is nobody's idea of fun. It's hard to resist taking advantage of the math functions that are already built into the Borland C++ package. So why not calculate the sines and cosines of all the angles that we're likely to want to use in our program before the program executes? Then we can convert the resulting values to fixed-point, and store them in an array, where we can simply look them up while the program is running? This would reduce the time required to calculate these trigonometric functions to nearly zero and would further enhance the execution speed gains that we've achieved through the use of fixed-point math.

Tables of precalculated values are called look-up tables and are an important optimization technique. When you have a time-consuming calculation in a time-critical portion of your program, whether the value is calculated by a built-in library function or by your program itself, consider calculating the value in advance and storing it in a look-up table. The results can be gratifying.

The program called MAKESINE.CPP on your disk in the BYOFS\OPTDEMO directory (which is also shown in Listing 9-2) generates a pair of look-up tables containing 256 fixed-point sine and cosine values and stores them in the file FIX.CPP. It also generates a header file called FIX.H containing a pair of macros for performing the sine and cosine look-ups (called SIN() and COS(), (note the uppercase letters) and several relevant constants. To use the tables and the macros, place FIX.CPP in your project window as part of the target's dependents and #include FIX.H in any file that uses the macros and constants. FIX.CPP and FIX.H are shown in Listings 9-3 and 9-4. To build the MAKESINE.EXE, load the OPTDEMO.IDE into the BC++ IDE from the Project menu. MAKESINE is the second target of the project window. Click with the right mouse button and select Build Node to create the makesine program.

Listing 9-2 MAKESINE.CPP

```cpp
#include  <fstream.h>
#include  <math.h>
#include  <conio.h>

const NUMBER_OF_DEGREES = 256; // Degrees in a circle
const SHIFT = 9;               // Fixed point shift
const SHIFT_MULT = 1<<SHIFT;   // Fixed point shift as
                               //  a multiplication
void main()
{
        float radians=0;

  // Create file FIX.H for constants and macros:

        fstream finout("fix.h",ios::out | ios::trunc);
        finout << "\n#ifndef FIX_H\n\n#define FIX_H\n";
        finout << "#define ABS(X) (X<0?-X:X)\n";
        finout << "#define COS(X) cos_table[ABS(X)&255]\n";
        finout << "#define SIN(X) sin_table[ABS(X)&255]\n";
        finout << "\nconst int NUMBER_OF_DEGREES =" << NUMBER_OF_DEGREES << ";\n";
        finout << "const int SHIFT = " << SHIFT << ";\n";
        finout << "const long SHIFT_MULT = 1L<<SHIFT;\n\n";
        finout << "extern long cos_table[NUMBER_OF_DEGREES];\n";
        finout << "extern long sin_table[NUMBER_OF_DEGREES];\n";
        finout << "\n#endif\n";
        finout.close();

  // Create file FIX.CPP for sine and cosine tables:

        finout.open("fix.cpp",ios::out | ios::trunc);
        finout << "\n//FIX.CPP\n" << "//  Fixed point math tables\n\n"<<
           "#include \"fix.h\"\n";
```

```
// Create cosine table:

        finout << "long cos_table[NUMBER_OF_DEGREES]={\n        ";
        int count=0;
        for (int i=0; i<NUMBER_OF_DEGREES; i++) {
                finout << long(cos(radians)*SHIFT_MULT) << ", ";
                radians += 6.28/NUMBER_OF_DEGREES;
                count++;
                if (count>=8) {
                        finout << endl << "        ";
                        count=0;
                }
        }
        finout << "};\n\n";

// Create sine table:

        finout << "long sin_table[NUMBER_OF_DEGREES]={\n        ";
        count=0;
        for (i=0; i<NUMBER_OF_DEGREES; i++) {
                finout << long(sin(radians)*SHIFT_MULT) << ", ";
                radians += 6.28/NUMBER_OF_DEGREES;
                count++;
                if (count>=8) {
                        finout << endl << "        ";
                        count=0;
                }
        }
        finout << "};\n";
        finout.close();
}
```

Listing 9-3 FIX.CPP

```
//FIX.CPP
// Fixed point math tables

#include "fix.h"
long cos_table[NUMBER_OF_DEGREES]={
    512, 511, 511, 510, 509, 508, 506, 504,
    502, 499, 496, 493, 489, 486, 482, 477,
    473, 468, 462, 457, 451, 445, 439, 432,
    425, 418, 411, 403, 395, 387, 379, 370,
    362, 353, 343, 334, 324, 315, 305, 295,
    284, 274, 263, 252, 241, 230, 219, 207,
    196, 184, 172, 160, 148, 136, 124, 112,
    100, 87, 75, 63, 50, 38, 25, 12,
    0, -12, -24, -37, -49, -62, -74, -87,
    -99, -111, -123, -136, -148, -160, -172, -183,
    -195, -207, -218, -229, -240, -251, -262, -273,
    -283, -294, -304, -314, -324, -333, -343, -352,
    -361, -370, -378, -387, -395, -403, -410, -418,
```

continued on next page

continued from previous page

```
      -425, -432, -438, -445, -451, -457, -462, -467,
      -472, -477, -481, -485, -489, -493, -496, -499,
      -502, -504, -506, -508, -509, -510, -511, -511,
      -511, -511, -511, -510, -509, -508, -506, -504,
      -502, -499, -496, -493, -490, -486, -482, -478,
      -473, -468, -463, -457, -451, -445, -439, -433,
      -426, -419, -411, -404, -396, -388, -380, -371,
      -362, -353, -344, -335, -325, -315, -305, -295,
      -285, -274, -264, -253, -242, -231, -219, -208,
      -196, -185, -173, -161, -149, -137, -125, -113,
      -101, -88, -76, -63, -51, -38, -26, -13,
      -1, 11, 23, 36, 48, 61, 73, 86,
      98, 110, 123, 135, 147, 159, 171, 183,
      194, 206, 217, 229, 240, 251, 262, 272,
      283, 293, 303, 313, 323, 333, 342, 352,
      361, 369, 378, 386, 394, 402, 410, 417,
      424, 431, 438, 444, 450, 456, 462, 467,
      472, 477, 481, 485, 489, 493, 496, 499,
      501, 504, 506, 507, 509, 510, 511, 511,
      };

long sin_table[NUMBER_OF_DEGREES]={
      -1, 10, 23, 36, 48, 61, 73, 85,
      98, 110, 122, 134, 147, 158, 170, 182,
      194, 205, 217, 228, 239, 250, 261, 272,
      282, 293, 303, 313, 323, 333, 342, 351,
      360, 369, 378, 386, 394, 402, 410, 417,
      424, 431, 438, 444, 450, 456, 462, 467,
      472, 476, 481, 485, 489, 492, 496, 499,
      501, 504, 506, 507, 509, 510, 511, 511,
      511, 511, 511, 510, 509, 508, 506, 504,
      502, 500, 497, 494, 490, 486, 482, 478,
      473, 468, 463, 458, 452, 446, 440, 433,
      426, 419, 412, 404, 397, 389, 380, 372,
      363, 354, 345, 336, 326, 316, 306, 296,
      286, 275, 265, 254, 243, 232, 220, 209,
      198, 186, 174, 162, 150, 138, 126, 114,
      102, 89, 77, 65, 52, 40, 27, 14,
      2, -10, -22, -35, -47, -60, -72, -85,
      -97, -109, -121, -134, -146, -158, -170, -181,
      -193, -205, -216, -227, -239, -250, -261, -271,
      -282, -292, -302, -312, -322, -332, -341, -351,
      -360, -368, -377, -385, -394, -401, -409, -417,
      -424, -431, -437, -444, -450, -456, -461, -466,
      -471, -476, -481, -485, -489, -492, -495, -498,
      -501, -503, -506, -507, -509, -510, -511, -511,
      -511, -511, -511, -510, -509, -508, -506, -504,
      -502, -500, -497, -494, -490, -487, -483, -478,
      -474, -469, -464, -458, -452, -446, -440, -434,
      -427, -420, -413, -405, -397, -389, -381, -372,
      -364, -355, -346, -336, -327, -317, -307, -297,
      -287, -276, -265, -255, -244, -232, -221, -210,
```

```
      -198, -187, -175, -163, -151, -139, -127, -115,
      -103, -90, -78, -65, -53, -40, -28, -15,
      };
```

Listing 9-4 FIX.H

```
#ifndef FIX_H

#define FIX_H
#define ABS(X) (X<0?-X:X)
#define COS(X) cos_table[ABS(X)&255]
#define SIN(X) sin_table[ABS(X)&255]

const int NUMBER_OF_DEGREES =256;
const int SHIFT = 9;
const long SHIFT_MULT = 1L<<SHIFT;

extern long cos_table[NUMBER_OF_DEGREES];
extern long sin_table[NUMBER_OF_DEGREES];

#endif
```

Notice that the constants in MAKESINE.CPP can be adjusted to produce slight variations on the look-up tables. For instance, the program is currently set to produce tables based on a system of 256 degrees. (These tables being essentially arbitrary, we can use a system of as many degrees as we'd like.) You can change this to any other number of degrees that you'd like, recompile and regenerate the FIX files. Similarly, the number of degrees to the right of the decimal point in our fixed-point numbers, currently set at 9, can also be changed.

Unrolling the Loop

Earlier, we were concentrating on speeding up the matmult() function. What else can we do to accelerate this crucial piece of code? There's a well-known optimization technique that would lend itself almost perfectly to this function. It's called unrolling the loop. To see how it works, let's create a small program and run it through the *Turbo Profiler*.

The following program is available on the disk as LOOP.CPP:

```
#include <stdio.h>

void loopfunc();

void main()
{
  loopfunc();
}
```

continued on next page

continued from previous page

```
void loopfunc()
{
   int a=0;

   for (int i=1; i<1000; i++) {
     a++;
   }
}
```

This program consists of a main() function which calls a second function, loopfunc(), which consists of a For()loop in which there is a single instruction.

Compile (or run) this program and enter *Turbo Profiler*. Then, instead of profiling the program, choose the Disassembly option from the View menu. (You can do this from DOS *Turbo Debugger,* too.) This opens a window containing the actual assembly language code produced by Borland C++ from this short program.

Look at the portion of this disassembly that represents the loop in loopfunc(). It consists of four instructions:

```
#LOOP#17:
       INC     DX
       INC     AX
       CMP     AX,03E8
       JL      #LOOP#17 (0021)
```

The first of these instructions, INC DX, increments the value of the variable a, which is contained in the DX register. The second increments the variable i, the index of the loop, which is contained in the AX register. The instruction CMP AX,03E8 compares the value of the variable i with 1,000 (hexadecimal 03E8). The third jumps back to the head of the loop if this value has not yet been reached. The hex location for the jump instruction may appear different on your machine since your memory configuration is different from the example above.

The Mechanics of the Loop

You'll note that three of these four instructions are involved with the mechanics of the loop. The code inside the loop—that is, the A++ instruction—is represented by only a single instruction. This is disturbing, since the mechanics of the loop exist merely for the sake of the code inside the loop; they are important only inasmuch as they assist that code in executing a certain number of times. Yet the majority of the execution time of this loop will be burned up by those very mechanics. (Oddly, if you profile this program, TProf will tell you that the line A++ from the source code uses up more than 99 percent of the execution time of this program, which is patently untrue. Keep this in mind when you analyze your own programs with a profiler. The C++ compiler constructs the For loop into assembly language by splitting the statement around the contents of the loop.)

We could quadruple the speed of this code simply by dropping the loop altogether and rewriting it as one thousand A++ instructions in a row. (Alert readers will point out that we could speed it up even more by using the instruction A=1000, which will be the ultimate result of the program anyway, but such simple solutions won't always be the case as we'll see in the matmult() example below.) Of course, no programmer wants to write one thousand identical instructions in a row; that would be a lot of work and would take up a lot of memory. The whole point of For() loops is to avoid such constructions. However, it's not necessary to go quite that far. The loop could be rewritten like this:

```
for (int i=0; i<1000; i+=10) {
        a++;
        a++;
        a++;
        a++;
        a++;
        a++;
        a++;
        a++;
        a++;
        a++;
}
```

By repeating the instruction only ten times and incrementing the index of the loop by tens instead of ones, we achieve the identical effect without all the bother. If you disassemble this loop, you'll find that the mechanism of the loop now represents a much smaller percentage of the loop code and thus slows it down by a much smaller amount.

Removing the overhead for loop mechanics in this manner is often a good, quick-and-dirty way to speed up time-critical program code. If the contents of the loop are slight (and thus likely to be overwhelmed by the loop mechanics), the acceleration achieved by this unrolling the loop technique can be impressive, especially if the loop is nested inside one or more outer loops.

We can use this technique on the matmult() function. The result looks like this:

```
void matmult(long result[4][4],long mat1[4][4],
            long mat2[4][4])
{

// Multiply matrix MAT1 by matrix MAT2,
//  returning the result in RESULT

  for (int i=0; i<4; i++)
    for (int j=0; j<4; j++) {
        result[i][j]=((mat1[i][0]*mat2[0][j])
          +(mat1[i][1]*mat2[1][j])
          +(mat1[i][2]*mat2[2][j])
          +(mat1[i][3]*mat2[3][j]))>>SHIFT;
    }
}
```

If you'll look back at our previous implementation of matmult() earlier in this chapter, you'll see that we've replaced the innermost loop with a long series of additions, effectively unrolling it. You also notice that we haven't bothered to unroll the two outer loops. That's because a quick consultation with *Turbo Profiler* told us that, while unrolling the innermost loop would produce a noticeable gain in execution speed, unrolling the outer loops would produce almost no benefit at all. The SHIFT const is used to correct the floating-point arithmetic. Likewise, the function argument is shifted before being stored in the scale() function:

```
void scale(int sf)
{

        // shift the value for storage
        long  val = long(sf) << SHIFT;
        // Initialize scaling matrix:

        smat[0][0] = val; smat[0][1] = 0; smat[0][2] = 0; smat[0][3] = 0;
```

The rest of this function is about the same as it was before. Similar changes to translate() are made to the parameters of that function for storage in the tmat[4][4] matrix:

```
void translate(int xt,int yt,int zt)
{
. . .
tmat[3][0]=(long)xt<<SHIFT; tmat[3][1]=(long)yt<<SHIFT; tmat[3][2]=
(long)zt<<SHIFT;
. . .
```

Putting It All to Work

Now that we've at least made an effort to optimize our code, let's write a program that takes advantage of all of these optimizations. Until now, we've rotated fixed objects on the display in front of the viewer in a full-screen window. Let's produce a somewhat fancier 3D demonstration program that allows the user to manipulate three-dimensional objects interactively. In the course of developing this program, we'll explore yet another optimization technique.

Previously, we've utilized the entire video display for our animation. But few animation programs lay claim to that much video real estate. Most restrict the animation to a relatively small portion of the display. The advantage of this is that we need to draw only within a limited area, and that we need to move only part of the screen buffer into video RAM after a frame is drawn. Recall that our earlier foray into *Turbo Profiler* told us that the function putwindow() was the most time-consuming in the entire program. That's because this function is moving the entire contents of the screen buffer into video RAM. But if we restrict our animation to a window (sometimes known as a viewport) within the larger display, this function will execute much more quickly than before.

We'll use simple calls to kbhit() and getch() to read the keyboard. The variables *xrot,* *yrot,* and *zrot,* which determine how quickly the object will rotate, are altered according to which key is pressed. The listing for the main body of OPTDEMO is on the disk under the BYOFS\OPTIMIZE directory and in Listing 9-5. To load the program, use the Open Project selection under the Project menu to load OPTDEMO.IDE. To run the program from DOS, type:

```
OPTDEMO filename
```

where Filename is the name of the file containing the object description data that you wish to use. Object files compatible with this program have the file extension .TXT at the end of their filenames. One such file is included in the OPTDEMO project and logically called OBJECTS.TXT. We can cycle between the three different objects in this description file by pressing the (Enter) key.

Listing 9-5 OPTDEMO.CPP

```cpp
// OPTDEMO.CPP
//  Demonstrate optimized polygon-fill graphics animation
//  code
//

#include      <dos.h>
#include      <conio.h>
#include      <iostream.h>
#include      <stdlib.h>
#include      "poly.h"
#include      "screen.h"
#include      "pcx.h"

const XORIGIN=80;
const YORIGIN=80;
const WIND_WIDTH=7*21;
const WIND_HEIGHT=7*21;

world_type world;
Pcx bgobject;

void main(int argc,char* argv[])
{
        int key;
        int xangle=0,yangle=0,zangle=0; // X,Y&Z angles of
                                        //  object
        int xrot=0,yrot=0,zrot=0;       // X,Y&Z rotations
        unsigned char *screen_buffer;   // Offscreen drawing
                                        //  buffer
```

continued on next page

continued from previous page

```
            // Read arguments from command line. If wrong number,
            //   print message and abort:

            if (argc!=2) {
                    cerr << "Wrong number of arguments."<< endl;
                    exit(-1);
            }

            // Load background image:

            if (bgobject.load("3dbg2.pcx")) {
                    cerr << "Cannot load PCX file."<< endl;
                    exit(-1);
            }
            if( world.loadpoly(argv[1]) )  {          // Load object description(s)
                    cerr << "Failure loading polygons into World." << endl;
                    exit(-1);
}
        screen_buffer=new unsigned char[64000]; // Create buffer
        int oldmode=*(int *)MK_FP(0x40,0x49);   // Save previous

        //  video mode
        setgmode(0x13);                          // Set mode 13h
        setpalette(bgobject.Palette());

        unsigned char *ptr = bgobject.Image();
        for(long i=0; i<64000; i++)              // Put background
         screen_buffer[i]=*ptr++;                  //  in buffer

        int curobj=0;                            // First object
        int scalefactor=1;
         int zdistance=600;

         // paint the background to the video screen:
        putwindow(0,0,320,200,FP_OFF(screen_buffer),  FP_SEG(screen_buffer));
        while (key!=27) {
             clrwin(10,8,WIND_WIDTH,WIND_HEIGHT,screen_buffer);
             inittrans();            // Initialize transformations
             scale(scalefactor);    // Create scaling matrix
             rotate(xangle,yangle,zangle); // Create rotation matrix

             // Rotate object one increment:

             xangle+=xrot;
             yangle+=yrot;
             zangle+=zrot;

              // Check for 256 degree wrap around:

             if (xangle>255) xangle=0;
             if (xangle<0) xangle=255;
             if (yangle>255) yangle=0;
```

```
        if (yangle<0) yangle=255;
        if (zangle>255) zangle=0;
        if (zangle<0) zangle=255;

        // Translate object:

        translate(0,0,zdistance);

         // Call the Draw world object
         world.Draw(curobj,screen_buffer,XORIGIN,YORIGIN);

        // Put the viewport out to the video display:
putwindow(10,8,WIND_WIDTH,WIND_HEIGHT,FP_OFF(screen_buffer),
FP_SEG(screen_buffer));

        // Watch for user input:

        if (kbhit()) {  // If input received....
             key=getch();  // Read the key code
             switch(key) {
                  case 13:

                      // ENTER: Go to next object

                         curobj++;
                         if (curobj>=world.GetObjectCount())
                                curobj=0;
                         break;

                   case 55:

                       // "7": Speed up x rotation

                          xrot++;
                          break;

                   case 52:

                       // "4": Stop x rotation

                          xrot=0;
                          break;

                   case 49:

                       // "1": Slow down x rotation

                          --xrot;
                          break;

                   case 56:
```

continued on next page

continued from previous page

```
                    // "8": Speed up y rotation

                        yrot++;
                        break;

            case 53:

                    // "5": Stop y rotation

                        yrot=0;
                        break;

            case 50:

                    // "2": Slow down y rotation

                        --yrot;
                        break;

            case 57:

                    // "9": Speed up z rotation

                        zrot++;
                        break;

            case 54:

                    // "6": Stop z rotation

                        zrot=0;
                        break;

            case 51:

                    // "3": Slow down z rotation

                        --zrot;
                        break;

            case '+':

                    // "+": Increase distance

                        zdistance+=30;
                        break;

            case '-':

                    // "-": Decrease distance

                        if (zdistance>530) zdistance-=30;
```

```
                             break;
                    }
             }
      }
      setgmode(oldmode); // Reset video and exit

      if( screen_buffer)
             delete [] screen_buffer;
}
```

CHAPTER

10

10

Hidden Surface Removal

In these last few chapters, we've built up an arsenal of tools with which to construct a polygon-fill world. But there's one aspect of the real world that we haven't modeled yet—the simple fact that things can get in each other's way, i.e., that one object in the real world can obscure the view of another object. Although we take it for granted in our everyday lives that we are unable to see through walls, in the programs that we've written so far, we actually can see through walls. The problem is, for realistic simulation, we don't want to.

There must be an easy solution to this problem, right? After all, making objects opaque actually involves less drawing than making them transparent. And anything that requires less drawing must be easier than something that requires more drawing. What could be more obvious?

Unfortunately, it's not that simple. As illustrated in Chapter 9, where we talked about optimization, less is definitely better in computer animation. The less our program has to do, the faster it can animate our three-dimensional world. But our problem here is not in doing less drawing: the problem lies in figuring out what needs to be drawn and what doesn't. As we shall see in this chapter, there's really no satisfactory solution to this problem, at least not for the majority of this generation of microcomputers. Essentially, we must choose an acceptable compromise.

The general problem of making objects opaque in a three-dimensional graphics world is called hidden surface removal because it involves removing those surfaces from the drawing that would ordinarily be hidden. Several algorithms deal with this problem. We'll discuss two of them in this chapter and decide which, if either, is better for our purposes.

The Problem

When we draw a polygon on the video display, it represents a surface that is at a specific distance from the viewer, as represented by the z coordinates of the vertices of the polygon. Polygons with larger z coordinates are farther away than polygons with smaller z coordinates. In the real world, if a closer object moves in front of a farther object, the farther object is obscured by the closer object (assuming that the closer object is opaque).

Although the polygons in our imaginary world have differing z coordinates, because they are at different distances from the viewer, the polygons drawn on the video display to represent those polygons have no z coordinates at all. They differ only in their x and y coordinates. That's because the video display is flat. Thus, there's nothing that says a polygon representing a closer polygon will necessarily obscure a farther polygon, since the video display has no way of knowing which polygon is closer and which is farther. That must be determined by the program before the drawing is performed (or, at least, before the drawing is finished).

To some degree, that's already been taken care of. In Chapter 8, we discussed backface removal, by which the rear facets of convex polyhedrons are removed before drawing. (A convex polyhedron is the three-dimensional equivalent of a convex polygon—that is, a multifaceted object in which no internal angles are greater than 180 degrees. All junctures where two or more polygons come together on a convex polyhedron jut outward; none has "caved in" to make it a concave polyhedron.) This makes hidden surface removal somewhat easier, since it eliminates a lot of the polygons that are rendered invisible by closer polygons, but it doesn't solve the problem entirely. For instance, what if one convex polyhedron passes in front of another convex polyhedron? The backfaces of each will be removed by backface removal, but the front faces (if you will) of each polygon will still be visible. The nearer of these faces will also need to obscure the faces directly behind them and there's no guarantee that they will do so correctly.

Well, you say, why don't we simply draw all of the polygons in such a way that the closer polygons are drawn after the farther polygons and are thus drawn on top of them, obscuring them exactly the way such surfaces would obscure each other in the real world? Wouldn't that solve the problem?

Congratulations! You've just invented the first of the two algorithms that we're going to study in this chapter. The algorithm in question is called the Painter's Algorithm.

The Painter's Algorithm

The idea behind the Painter's Algorithm is simple: You draw all of a scene's polygons in back-to-front order, so that the polygons in the foreground are drawn over the polygons in the background. That way, the closer polygons neatly obscure the farther polygons. The name of the algorithm comes from the notion that this is how a painter constructs a scene, first drawing the background, then drawing the background objects over the background, and finally drawing the foreground objects over the background objects, as in Figure 10-1.

This would seem to solve our problem, but there's a catch. Drawing polygons in back-to-front order does indeed take care of hidden surface removal, but how do we determine what the back-to-front order actually is? This is a more difficult problem than you might guess.

The obvious answer is to sort the polygons in the reverse order of their z coordinates, using a standard sorting algorithm. This operation is called a depth sort and is the first step in the implementation of the Painter's Algorithm. But when sorting the polygons by z coordinate, which z coordinate do you use? Remember that each polygon has at least three vertices and that each of these vertices has its own z coordinate.

Figure 10-1 This may not be how artist Grant Wood painted American Gothic, but it's how the Painter's Algorithm would draw it

(a) The background *(continued on next page)*

Figure 10-1 *(continued from previous page)*
(b) Background objects painted over the background

(c) Foreground objects (in this case, people) painted over the
background objects

In most instances, all three of these z coordinates will be different. Do you arbitrarily choose one of the z coordinates, perhaps the z coordinate of the first vertex in the vertex list, and then sort on that? Or do you look for the maximum z coordinate among all the z coordinates of the vertices—or the minimum z coordinate among all the z coordinates—and sort on that? Or do you use all of the z coordinates to calculate some intermediate value, perhaps representing the z coordinate of the center of the polygon, and sort on that?

One reasonable answer to these questions is that it doesn't matter which of these you sort on, as long as you use the same z coordinate for each polygon. Depth sorts have doubtlessly been based on all of the above possibilities, as well as some that haven't been mentioned here, and each has probably worked well enough to produce a useable flight simulator.

Getting the Order Right

Let's suppose, for the sake of argument, that you choose to sort on the maximum z coordinate of each polygon. Once the list of polygons has been sorted in reverse order by maximum z coordinate, can you then simply begin drawing the polygons?

Not necessarily. Just because you've sorted the polygons by maximum z coordinate doesn't mean that you've got them in the correct order for the Painter's Algorithm. Why not? Take a look at Figure 10-2. The two lines in this picture represent a pair of polygons viewed edge-on from above, looking down the y axis. The hypothetical viewer is at the bottom of this picture, looking up, so that polygons at the bottom of the illustration are closer to the viewer than polygons at the top.

Polygon A has a smaller maximum z coordinate than polygon B. Yet polygon B extends in front of polygon A, so that it should be drawn *after* polygon A if the Painter's Algorithm is to work correctly. Alas, if sorted in reverse order by maximum z coordinate,

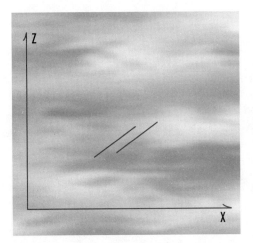

Figure 10-2 A pair of polygons, viewed from above (looking down the y axis), that would be ordered incorrectly by a depth sort based on maximum, minimum, or center z coordinates of either polygon; the occluded polygon would be drawn on top of the polygon supposedly doing the occluding, causing a hidden surface to show through

polygon B would be sorted to a position in the list preceding A, so that A would be drawn over after it. This would cause an image of A to show through B, which it should not.

Well, you might ask, what if you sorted on the minimum z coordinate of each? Same problem—polygon A has a smaller minimum z coordinate than B, so it would still be sorted after B on the list and would be drawn on top of it.

How about sorting on the center of each polygon? Even that won't work, though it does raise an interesting question: What is the center of a polygon? Polygons with differing numbers of sides, which may be of widely differing lengths, do not always have a clear-cut center. Often graphics programmers work with a point called the centroid, the point around which the polygon would balance, were it a flat plate of evenly distributed mass. Alas, calculating the centroid is a bit dicey. It's easier to go with the center of the polygon's extent, i.e., the point midway between the polygon's maximum z and minimum z. And, as you might guess, that too would cause polygon A and polygon B to be sorted into the incorrect order.

One solution is to choose one of these points—the maximum z, the minimum z, or the center of the z extent—more or less arbitrarily, perform a depth sort using the equivalent point for all polygons, and then perform additional comparisons between polygons *after* the depth sort to be sure that they are in the correct order. If they are not, then switch their places in the list.

There is even a standard algorithm for this, involving five tests on each pair of polygons in the scene, in a fixed order, after the initial depth sort is complete. In the paragraphs that follow, we'll refer to the two polygons in the pair as A and B, where A is the polygon determined in the initial sort to be the closer of the two and B is the one determined to be the farther of the two. (The actual order may turn out to be the reverse, of course, but that's what we're performing the five tests to learn.)

The five tests are designed so that if a pair of polygons passes any one of them, we know that the pair doesn't need to be swapped. Thus, once a successful result is returned from a test, the rest of the tests don't need to be performed. Only if the pair flunks all five tests must their order be swapped.

These tests could be performed on every pair of polygons in the scene. If there are five polygons in a scene, then pairs 1 and 2 would need to be compared, followed by 1 and 3, 1 and 4, 1 and 5, 2 and 3, 2 and 4, and so forth. Fortunately, in practice, the comparison doesn't need to be that exhaustive. Only polygons that overlap in the z extent, where the range between the maximum z coordinates and minimum z coordinates of the polygons overlap, need to be compared. (See Figure 10-3.) If two polygons don't overlap in the z extent, every point on one of the polygons must be a greater distance from the viewer than every point on the other polygon. Thus, the depth sort couldn't possibly have placed them in the wrong order (unless there's a bug in it somewhere), no matter which particular z coordinate on each polygon was used for comparison.

Determining whether the z extents of the polygons overlap is simple. Polygon A is determined by the initial depth sort to be closer to the viewer. Polygon B then is

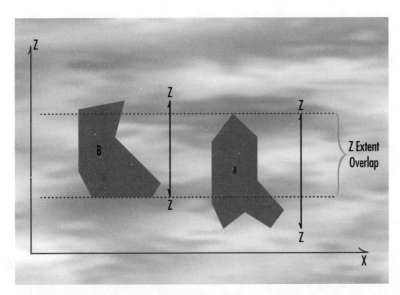

Figure 10-3 Two polygons overlapping in the z extent. Note that the maximum z coordinate of polygon A is greater than the minimum z coordinate of polygon B

presumed to be farther away. (These determinations could be incorrect, of course, which is what these additional comparisons are designed to detect.) If the maximum z coordinate of polygon A is less than the minimum z coordinate of polygon B, then there is no z overlap. The polygons must be in the correct order.

The Five Tests

If the z extents *do* overlap, you need to perform additional tests to determine if the polygons need to be swapped. Assuming again that polygon A is allegedly nearer than polygon B, here are the five tests that will help make this determination:

Test 1

Do the x extents of the two polygons overlap? (See Figure 10-4.) If not, it doesn't matter whether the two polygons are in the wrong order or not, since they aren't in front of one another and can't possibly obscure one another on the display. This can be determined by comparing the minimum and maximum x coordinates of the two polygons. If the minimum x of B is larger than the maximum x of A or the maximum x of B is smaller than the minimum x of A, the x extents don't overlap. No more tests need be performed.

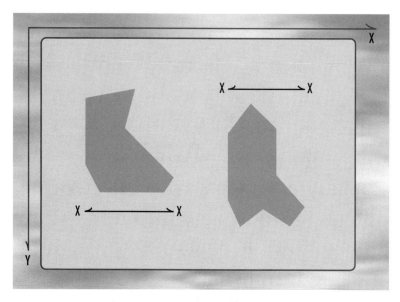

Figure 10-4 Do the polygons overlap in the *x* extent?

(a) These two polygons do not overlap in the *x* extent

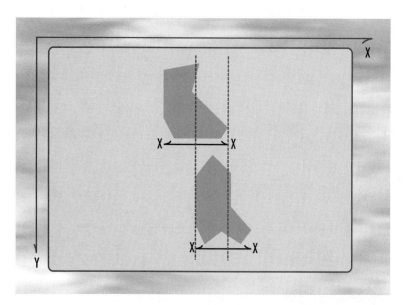

(b) These two polygons do overlap in the *x* extent

Test 2

Do the *y* extents of the two polygons overlap? (See Figure 10-5.) This works exactly like the previous test, except that the minimum and maximum *y* coordinates are compared. If the two polygons don't overlap in the *y* extent, it doesn't matter if they're in the wrong order because they can't obscure one another on the display. No more tests need be performed. (It may help, in performing tests 1 and 2, to imagine the polygon as being surrounded by a rectangular shape—known technically as a *bounding rectangle*—with one corner at the minimum *x* and *y* of the polygon and the opposite corner at the maximum *x* and *y* of the polygon. If the bounding rectangles of the two polygons don't overlap, then the polygons can't possibly obscure one another on the screen.)

Test 3

Is polygon B entirely on the far side (i.e., the correct side) of A? (See Figure 10-6.) This is a rather complicated test and involves some fairly esoteric mathematics. Later in this chapter, I'll give you a standard formula for performing this test and explain the mathematics in considerably more detail. For now, simply imagine that polygon A is part of an infinite plane that extends to all sides of it and that we must test to see if polygon B is entirely on the far side of that plane. If so, the polygons pass the test and no more tests need be performed.

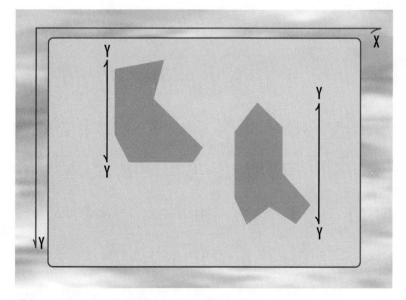

Figure 10-5 Do the polygons overlap in the *y* extent?

(a) These two polygons do not overlap in the *y* extent *(continued on next page)*

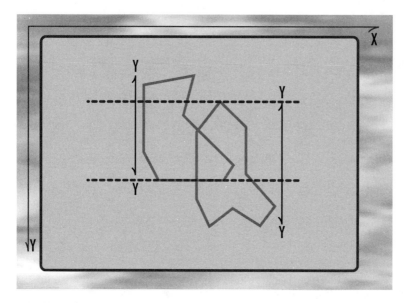

Figure 10-5 *(continued from previous page)*
(b) These two polygons do overlap in the *y* extent

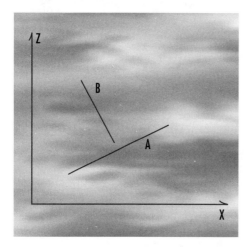

Figure 10-6 Polygon B, as seen edge-on from above, is entirely on the far side of the plane of polygon A

Test 4

Is polygon A entirely on the nearer side of polygon B? (See Figure 10-7.) This test is much like test 3, except that it checks to see if polygon A is on the near side of the plane of polygon B. If the two polygons pass either one of these tests, they are in the correct order and no more tests need be performed. (Interestingly, only tests 3 and 4

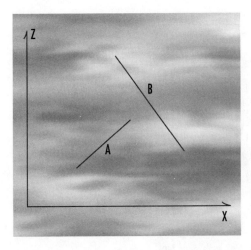

Figure 10-7 Polygon A, seen edge-on from above, is entirely inside the plane of polygon B

are necessary to show that the two polygons are in the wrong order. The other three tests check to see if the polygons actually occlude one another on the display, but once a pair of polygons flunks tests 3 and 4, we know that they are in the wrong order.)

Test 5

Do the polygons overlap on the screen? If we've gotten this far, the polygon pair must have flunked all the earlier tests, so we now know that polygons A and B overlap in the x, y, and z extents and are in the wrong order. All that remains is to determine whether this matters—that is, whether one of these polygons is actually in front of the other relative to the viewer. Just because the x, y, and z extents overlap doesn't mean that one polygon actually obscures the other, as shown in Figure 10-8. Spotting actual overlap between polygons involves performing a rather time-consuming, edge-by-edge comparison of the two polygons. It might well be quicker to skip this test and swap the two polygons at this point, since they are known to be in the wrong order.

Mutual Overlap

Once you've performed these five tests, can the polygons be safely drawn in polygon list order without any hidden surfaces showing through? Not necessarily. There is one situation that even a depth sort followed by these five tests can't handle. It's called mutual, or cyclical, overlap and occurs when three or more polygons overlap one another in a circular fashion, with each polygon overlapping the next and the last overlapping the first. In Figure 10-9, for instance, polygon A is overlapped by polygon B which is overlapped by polygon C which is overlapped by polygon A. If these polygons

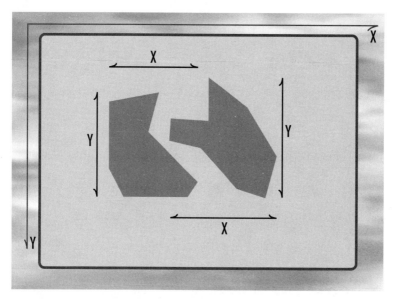

Figure 10-8 Two polygons that overlap in the *x* and *y* extents without physically overlapping one another on the video display

were being sorted for the Painter's Algorithm, there would be no correct order into which they could be sorted. No matter what order we draw them in, at least one polygon will show through at least one other polygon.

What can be done about the mutual overlap problem? The only fully satisfactory solution is to split one of the polygons into two polygons, thus eliminating the mutual overlap. There would then be a correct order into which the polygons could be placed. But this approach brings a number of problems of its own, not the least of which is the need to allocate memory on the fly for the new polygon.

Time Considerations

As you can see, the Painter's Algorithm can result in a lot of calculations. In particular, the five tests can be quite time-consuming.

In a worst-case situation, execution time can go up as the square of the number of polygons in the scene. (Fortunately, it's not necessary to compare every pair of polygons in the scene, just those with overlapping *z* extents. If you start at one of the polygons in the list and move forward from that polygon performing the tests on all polygons that overlap this polygon in the *z* dimension, it is not necessary to continue after the first polygon that does *not* overlap in the *z* dimension, since none of the succeeding polygons will overlap this polygon in the *z* dimension.)

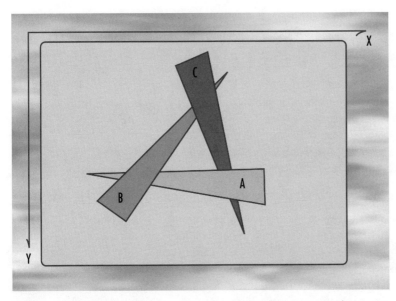

Figure 10-9 Three polygons mutually overlapping one another

Considering the potential time demands of the Painter's Algorithm—and, more specifically, the way those time demands can increase almost exponentially as the number of polygons increases—you might wonder if there is an algorithm that does not increase its time demands as rapidly as this algorithm does when additional polygons are added. In fact, there is. Furthermore, it's an extremely straightforward algorithm, without the complications inherent in the Painter's Algorithm, and is therefore easier to implement.

There's got to be a catch, right? Alas, there is, but we'll get to that in a moment. First, let's take a look at how this algorithm, called the Z-Buffer algorithm, performs its magic.

The Z-Buffer Algorithm

As far as the Painter's Algorithm is concerned, the problem with polygons is that they have more than one vertex—and each of these vertices can have a different z coordinate. In fact, not only can the vertices of polygons have varying z coordinates, but every *point* on the surface of a polygon can have a different z coordinate. The only truly exhaustive way to perform a depth sort would involve determining the depth of every point on the surface of every polygon on the screen and drawing only the points nearest to the viewer.

But surely that's not possible. After all, there are an infinite number of points in a plane, or even in a section of a plane, and a polygon is a section of a plane. There's no way we can sort an infinite number of points and determine which is nearest to the viewer.

Fortunately, it's not necessary to sort an infinite number of points. It is only necessary to sort those points that are going to be drawn—i.e., those that correspond to the pixels in the viewport. Unlike the number of points on the surface of a polygon, the number of pixels in the viewport is finite. If we had some way of keeping track of what's being drawn at each pixel position in the viewport, we could assure ourselves that only those pixels representing the points closest to the viewer get displayed. In effect, we would be performing a separate depth sort for every pixel in the viewport area of the screen.

And that's exactly what the Z-Buffer algorithm does. It determines which points on which polygons are closest to the viewer for every pixel in the viewport, so that only those points get displayed. It requires that the programmer set aside an integer array in which each element corresponds to a pixel in the viewport. Every time a point on the surface of a polygon is drawn in the viewport, the z coordinate of that point is placed in the array's element that corresponds to the pixel position at which the point was drawn. The next time a pixel is to be drawn at that same position, the z coordinate of the point represented by the new pixel is compared with the value currently in the array for that position. If the z coordinate in the buffer is smaller than that of the new point, the new pixel is not drawn, since that point would be farther away than the old point and is therefore part of a hidden surface. If the z coordinate in the buffer is larger than that of the new point, the new pixel is drawn over the old one and the z coordinate of the *new* point is put in the buffer, replacing the old one.

The Z-Buffer algorithm, if correctly implemented, works perfectly: No hidden surfaces will show through. An efficiently written Z-Buffer should require relatively few lines of code and is certainly easier to implement than the Painter's Algorithm.

It has only one flaw—or, rather, two: time and memory. To implement a Z-Buffer in our program we would have to throw out our current polygon-drawing algorithm and replace it with a new one. And the new one would unquestionably be slower than the old one, because we no longer would be able to use a tight loop to draw the horizontal lines that make up the polygon. Instead, we would need to calculate the z coordinate of each point on the horizontal line before we could draw it, compare that z coordinate with the one already in the buffer, and only then draw the pixel. Polygon-drawing speed would slow to a crawl.

In addition, we would need to set aside a buffer containing enough integer elements to store a z coordinate value for every pixel in the viewport. Assuming that the viewport covered the entire display—not uncommon in flight simulators—and that a 16-bit int value is sufficient for each element of the Z-Buffer, it would consume 128K of memory. Even if we reduced the size of the viewport, the Z-Buffer would still almost certainly be greater than 64K in size. With the PC's 640K of conventional memory in great demand by other parts of our program, we simply may not be able to spare this much RAM. So for a DOS-based flight simulator, the memory constraint pretty much rules out the use of Z-Buffer. (Other platforms which have large available RAM space would allow us to consider implementation of a Z-Buffer.)

Yet the Z-Buffer has a rather large advantage over just about all other methods of hidden surface removal. As new polygons are added to a scene, the amount of time consumed by the algorithm increases linearly, not exponentially—so if you double the number of polygons in the polygon list, the time required to perform the Z-Buffer also doubles. With other algorithms, including the Painter's Algorithm, the time might well quadruple. Thus, above a certain number of polygons, the Z-Buffer is actually faster than the Painter's Algorithm. Alas, that "certain number" of polygons is probably well into the thousands, far more than we'll use in any scene in this book. (The actual break-even point between the Painter's Algorithm and the Z-Buffer algorithm is impossible to determine precisely, since it would depend on how well the two algorithms are implemented by their programmers.)

We've discussed the Z-Buffer algorithm in some detail here because it will probably be an important element of *future* flight simulators, as processors become faster and memory more abundant. Already we're starting to see machines capable of generating an acceptable frame-rate using slower polygon-drawing functions, though the majority of computer-game players are only starting to gain access to these machines. And more programs are being designed to take advantage of the protected mode memory management functions of the 80386, 80486, and Pentium microprocessors, thereby being able to use all of the memory in a machine, not just the first 640K, which makes it trivial to find the memory necessary for the Z-Buffer array.

If we were to implement a Z-Buffer algorithm in our program, how might we do it? As noted a few paragraphs ago, it would have to be done in the polygon-drawing function. The variation on Bresenham's algorithm that we use to draw the edges of the polygon would need to be extended to three dimensions, so that a second error term could keep track of the z coordinate at each point on the edge. Then, when drawing the horizontal lines from the left edge to the right edge, yet another variation on Bresenham's could be used to calculate the changing z coordinate. This z value would be the one placed in the Z-Buffer, to determine whether the pixels are to be drawn or ignored.

Readers interested in creating such a Z-Buffer-based variation on the flight simulator in this book are encouraged to do so. I would be interested in hearing what sort of results you achieve.

Reworking the Classes a Step Ahead

After a brief pause and consideration of the programming terrain which lies ahead, some of our classes from the last three chapters will have to be reworked. If you remember, the shape_type class from chapter 6 evolved into the polygon_type class of Chapter 8. As our class improved and changed its functionality, we provided some progressive organization by renaming the class. One of the reasons why we renamed the class was to avoid confusion in the source code modules across these different demonstrations and projects. An alternative to this might have been to derive another class from the shape_type class and override methods as needed. As previously said, this would have led to some confusion in discussing objects. In our goal project, the final flight-simulator program, we will be deriving classes within the polygon family. Our fields will be shuffled around and divided between parent and child classes. Let's avoid confusion—both in discussing classes and functions and in using them to write the program. If we used our polygon_type class for the final big show, it would create data structures in RAM which were unnecessarily large; fields would go unused but still take up our valuable memory resources. We will take advantage of this opportunity to streamline the code. Some of the member functions of these classes will not be used because there will be fundamental changes which make the functions obsolete. Leaving these functions in the code will take up memory space, an arguable point on computers today, but cleaning up the flotsam of an older version of a class assists in the overall organization of the program.

We will rename the classes into a notation that capitalizes the first letter of the class name. The _type suffix will be dropped, such that world_type becomes World, object_type becomes Object, etc. Some of these classes will be moved into their own modules. These will be the classes used in the final flight simulator program. Unused variables will be discarded.

The files referred to in this chapter can be found in the FSIM directory. The POLY.CPP file has been promoted to POLY2.CPP (and POLY.H to POLY2.H). In chapters that follow, as we explore lighting and scenery, a module filename may deviate from its original name in order to show that changes were made to the class or function operation for a particular demonstration. Thus the WORLD.CPP file will be named WORLD_FR.CPP in the fractal program and WORLD_TX.CPP in the texture mapping program. The differences in these files and the final program are sometimes miniscule, but it keeps any special class implementation for a particular project in its own module.

Back to Depth Sorting

In this book, we'll use the Painter's Algorithm for our hidden surface removal. It's an awkward algorithm to implement, because of all the special cases that need to be handled, but as awkward as it is, the Painter's Algorithm is the fastest thing we've got that actually works. And we're going to make it faster and less awkward by implementing a simplified version.

To implement this algorithm, it will be necessary to treat our three-dimensional world in a slightly different manner. Up until now, we have organized this world as a list of objects with specific positions and orientations. These objects, in turn, we defined as lists of polygons. But the Painter's Algorithm, as it will be implemented here, doesn't care about objects. All that matters to it are polygons. The code that we create to perform the Painter's Algorithm will sort and compare polygons, which will then be drawn on the display.

It's still going to be necessary to treat the world as a list of objects, though. As you'll see when our final flight-simulator code is put together, this is the most logical way to treat a world if we want it to resemble our own. So at some point before the Painter's Algorithm is executed, the database representing the world will need to be rearranged from a list of objects into a list of polygons, containing all polygons potentially visible in the viewport. Since it is a list of things, it is a natural for a management type of class. We'll call this new class the polygon list. Here's the descriptor for this structure, from the file POLY2.H:

```
class PolygonList {
private:
        int     number_of_polygons;
        Polygon **polylist;
public:
        PolygonList():polylist(0){;}
        ~PolygonList();
        void Create(unsigned int polynum);
        int GetPolygonCount() const
                { return number_of_polygons; }
        Polygon * GetPolygonPtr(int polynum) const
                { return polylist[polynum]; }
        void MakePolygonList(const World& world);
        void z_sort();
};
```

As you can see, the PolygonList is little more than an array of pointers to Polygon class objects, or more accurately a pointer to a pointer or type Polygon. Memory will need to be allocated for this list. It would be awkward to do this every time a polygon list needs to be assembled (once for every frame of the animation), so we'll place this operation in the initialization code of our flight simulator. The loadpoly() function (the one that loads the object descriptors from the disk file) can be modified to count the number of polygons in the world, and then one of the flight-simulator initialization functions can allocate memory for the Polygon pointer array that we'll call polylist. How much memory will be allocated for the polygon list? Enough elements in the list to handle every polygon of every object in the world. With luck, we'll never need that much memory for the list, but if we do it will be available. There will be no circumstance under which we will need more.

The constructor for the PolygonList is similar to our other classes. It sets the polylist array pointer equal to 0 so that the destructor can test if the array needs to be deleted. In fact, the entire content of the destructor simply tests if the array pointer is not zero:

```
PolygonList::~PolygonList()
{
        if(polylist)
                delete [] polylist;
}
```

Access functions, GetPolygonCount() and GetPolygonPtr(), provide inline routes to retrieve the list information. To perform the actual memory allocation of the list, the Create() is called with a single parameter containing the number of polygons which the world contains (as obtained from our doctored loadpoly routine). It would be a neater design to have a constructor do this allocation for us via a constructor parameter, but then this forces us to know how many polygons are in the world before we make a PolygonList object. One of our future treatments for PolygonList is as a member field of another class. We do not want to require that class to be constructed with the world polygon count (so that it can pass the parameter to the PolygonList constructor). The allocation of the Polygon array therefore takes place in a separate function, Create()::

```
void PolygonList::Create(unsigned int numPoly)
{
        polylist = new Polygon *[numPoly];
}
```

Now we need a function that will assemble a polygon list from our existing world database. As you see above, it is called MakePolygonList(). In theory, this function will be quite simple. All it needs to do is to loop through all of the objects in the world and assign their polygons to the master polygon list. In practice, however, it's desirable to have it do more than that. For one thing, if we can eliminate some polygons at this stage of the game, it will speed up things further down the line.

How can we prune the polygon list? There are two obvious ways. The first is to apply backface removal at this point. In theory, half of the polygons in any scene are backfaces. By allowing only "front faces" into the polygon list, we effectively cut the list in half, which is a significant savings. This, in fact, is the main reason that backface removal is used in programs that also use other methods of hidden surface removal: it gets rid of the *easy* hidden surfaces with minimal effort.

The second way we can prune the polygon list is to look for polygons that are on the wrong side of the screen—i.e., that are on the same side of the screen as the viewer. These polygons can't possibly be in the scene, so there's no reason to include them in the list. The simplest way to spot these polygons is to look for polygons that have a maximum z coordinate that is less than that of the screen, which we will set to 1. (Zero might seem a more logical number for the z coordinate of the screen, but that can cause some problems with the perspective calculations, which have difficulty handling z coordinate values that are either zero or negative.) This should eliminate another 50 percent or so of the polygons in the scene, so that our final polygon list should only contain about 25 percent of the polygons in the world. This will save much time down the road. (Of course, there will be other polygons that eventually turn out not to be visible, either because they are hidden by other polygons or because they are outside the viewport. But identifying these polygons is not easy and must be performed after the assembling of the polygon list.)

The MakePolygonList() function takes one parameter, a reference to an instance of class World. This parameter is declared as a const since the instance itself will not be changed. The function will use the parameter to create the polygon list, which will then be available to the calling function:

```
void PolygonList::MakePolygonList( const World& world)
```

While assembling the polygon list, it is important to record the number of polygons that actually make it onto the list, so that later functions will know how many polygons they must process. Thus, the function begins by initializing a counter to record this value:

```
{
    int count=0;   // Determine number of polygons in list
```

The main body of the function will consist of a pair of nested loops that proceed through all of the objects in the World class and all of the polygons in each of those objects. This requires the MakePolygonList() function to access private fields within the Object and Polygon classes. Just as we created inline access functions in the last chapter to retrieve the number_of_objects from the world_type class, we will have to create some functions to retrieve pointers to the polygons. The first of those loops begins here:

```
// Loop through all objects in world:

for (int objnum=0; objnum<world.GetObjectCount(); objnum++) {
```

GetObjectCount() was created in the last chapter to access the number_of_objects field in the world_type class, and this does the exact same thing for the World class. Another inline function of this class is then called to obtain a pointer to the current object:

```
// Create pointer to current object:

Object *objptr= world.GetObjectPtr(objnum);
```

Then the inner loop begins, proceeding through all of the polygons in the current object:

```
// Loop through all polygons in current object:

for (int polynum=0; polynum<objptr->GetPolygonCount();
    objnum++) {
```

For the same reason that we created a pointer to the current object, we create a pointer to the current polygon within the current object's polygon list:

```
// Create pointer to current polygon:

Polygon *polyptr= objptr->GetPolygonPtr(polynum);
```

If the polygon is a backface, there's no need to process it further, so we only perform further actions if the polygon isn't a backface:

```
// If polygon isn't a backface, consider it for list:

if ( ! polyptr->backface() ) {
```

If the polygon isn't a backface, we now need to determine what its maximum and minimum world coordinates are, for reasons that will shortly become apparent. The first step in doing so is to set a dummy maximum and minimum for each *x, y,* and *z* coordinate. We'll give these dummies the lowest values possible of a signed int type, so that they will immediately be replaced by the first *real* values with which we compare them:

```
// Find maximum & minimum coordinates for polygon:

int pxmax=-327687;  // Initialize all mins & maxes
int pxmin=32767;    //  to highest and lowest
int pymax=-327687;  //   possible values
int pymin=32767;
int pzmax=-327687;
int pzmin=32767;
```

To find the real maxima and minima, we then loop through all the vertices in the polygon, looking for values above and below these dummy values, and using exceeding values as replacements.

```
    // Loop through all vertices in polygon, to find
    //   ones with higher and lower coordinates than
    //   current min & max:

    for (int v=0; v<polyptr->GetVertexCount(); v++) {
        vertex_type *vptr = polyptr->GetVerticePtr(v);
        if (vptr->wx > pxmax) {
                pxmax=vptr->wx;
        }
        if (vptr->wx < pxmin) {
                pxmin=vptr->wx;
        }
        if (vptr->wy > pymax) {
                pymax=vptr->wy;
        }
        if (vptr->wy < pymin) {
                pymin=vptr->wy;
        }
```

```
if (vptr->wz > pzmax) {
        pzmax=vptr->wz;
}
if (vptr->wz < pzmin) {
        pzmin=vptr->wz;
}
}
```

Now that we've determined the *real* maximum and minimum coordinate values, we transfer them to the appropriate fields in the polygon structure, so that they can be referred to later. There are two inline functions to perform this transfer, SetMin() and SetMax():

```
// Put mins & maxes in polygon descriptor:

polyptr->SetMax(pxmax, pymax, pzmax);
polyptr->SetMin(pxmin, pymin, pzmin);
```

While we have the max and min figured we next set the distance member of the polygon, also for later reference. A new field, *distance*, is added to the Polygon class to store this information. The SetDistance() function is defined inline to provide access for assigning the *distance* variable:

```
float xcen=(pxmin+pxmax)*0.5;/2.0;    // midpoint = (min+max)/2;
float ycen=(pymin+pymax)*0.5/2.0;
float zcen=(pzmin+pzmax)*0.5/2.0;
polyptr->SetDistance(xcen*xcen+ycen*ycen+zcen*zcen);
```

The type float is used instead of a long in order to provide precision for a very large value. The center is halfway between the two values—we multiply the sum by 0.5 instead of dividing by 2 because the multiplication operation is faster (and the two formulas are mathematically equal). At last, we must add the polygon to the polygon list. First, however, it is necessary to check to see if it's in front of the view plane and not on the same side of the display as the viewer. This couldn't be done earlier because the minimum z coordinate wasn't available. Now that it is, we check to see if the minimum z coordinate is less than 1 (which we'll use as the location of the view plane). If it isn't less than 1, we allow the polygon to be added to the list:

```
// If polygon is in front of the view plane,
//   add it to the polygon list:

if (pzmax > 1) {
      polylist[count++]=polyptr;
}
```

The value of *count* is incremented as the polygon is added to the list, so that it now contains the number of polygons currently in the list and can be used to point to the next element in the list. Then we wrap up all the loops, put the number of polygons in the appropriate field of the PolygonList structure, and exit the function:

```
            }
        }
    }

    // Put number of polygons in polylist structure:

    number_of_polygons=count;
}
```

The complete MakePolygonList() function appears in Listing 10-1.

 Listing 10-1 The MakePolygonList() function

```
void PolygonList::MakePolygonList(const World& world)

// Create a list of all polygons potentially visible in
//   the viewport, removing backfaces and polygons outside
//   of the viewing pyramid in the process

{
        int count=0;  // Determine number of polygons in list

        // Loop through all objects in world:

        for (int objnum=0; objnum< world.GetObjectCount();
                objnum++) {

            // Create pointer to current object:
            Object *objptr=world.GetObjectPtr(objnum);

            // Loop through all polygons in current object:
            for (int polynum=0; polynum<objptr->GetPolygonCount();
                    polynum++) {

                // Create pointer to current polygon:

                Polygon *polyptr= objptr->GetPolygonPtr(polynum);

                // If polygon isn't a backface, consider it for list:

                if (!polyptr->backface()) {

                // Find maximum & minimum coordinates for polygon:

                    int pxmax=-327687;  // Initialize all mins & maxes
                    int pxmin=32767;    //  to highest and lowest
                    int pymax=-327687;  //   possible values
                    int pymin=32767;
                    int pzmax=-327687;
                    int pzmin=32767;
```

```
            // Loop through all vertices in polygon, to find
            //  ones with higher and lower coordinates than
            //  current min & max:

                    for (int v=0; v<polyptr->GetVertexCount(); v++) {
                        vertex_type *vptr = polyptr->Get
                            VerticePtr(v);
                        if (vptr->ax > pxmax) {
                                pxmax=(int)vptr->ax;
                        }
                        if (vptr->ax < pxmin) {
                                pxmin=(int)vptr->ax;
                        }
                        if (vptr->ay > pymax) {
                                pymax=(int)vptr->ay;
                        }
                        if (vptr->ay < pymin) {
                                pymin=(int)vptr->ay;
                        }
                        if (vptr->az > pzmax) {
                                pzmax=(int)vptr->az;
                        }
                        if (vptr->az < pzmin) {
                                pzmin=(int)vptr->az;
                        }
                    }

                    polyptr->SetMin(pxmin, pymin, pzmin);
                    polyptr->SetMax(pxmax, pymax, pzmax);
                      // Calculate center of polygon z extent:

                      float xcen=(pxmin+pxmax)*0.5/2.0;
                      float ycen=(pymin+pymax)*0.5/2.0;
                      float zcen=(pzmin+pzmax)*0.5/2.0;
                    polyptr->SetDistance(xcen*xcen+ycen*ycen+zcen
                      *zcen);

                      // If polygon is in front of the view plane,
                    //  add it to the polygon list:

                    if (pzmax > 1) {
                            polylist[count++]= polyptr;
                    }
                }
            }
        }

    // Put number of polygons in polylist structure:

        number_of_polygons=count;
}
```

Once the polygon list is assembled, the hidden surface removal can begin. The first step in the Painter's Algorithm is to perform a depth sort on the list. That process will be performed by a function called z_sort():

```
void PolygonList::z_sort()
{
```

For clarity, the sort used here is a variation of the type known as a bubble sort, the simplest variety of sort available. It's also one of the slowest. For world databases containing a relative few polygons, the slowness of the bubble sort won't make much of a difference in overall execution time, since it doesn't take much time for any sorting algorithm to put the polygon list in order. But as the world database grows larger and more complex, the bubble sort requires an increasingly long time to sort the polygon list. This gives you an easy way to optimize the flight-simulator code: replacing this sort with a faster one to accelerate the process. Any good book on computer-programming algorithms should contain instructions for implementing more efficient sorting techniques. An immediate alternative to the bubble sort is to use the ANSI C++ qsort function—we'll save this optimization for the final flight simulator version of z_sort.

For those not familiar with it, the bubble sort algorithm is quite straightforward. It consists of two nested loops, the outer one a While loop that repeats an inner for loop over and over until the sort is complete. The for loop, in turn, steps through all of the items in the polygon list except the last, comparing each with the item following it to see if the two are in the proper order relative to one another. (The loop doesn't step all the way to the last item because the last item has no item following it.) When a pair is found to be out of order, their positions are swapped. This process is repeated until the for loop makes a complete pass through the list without finding a pair out of order. The name of the algorithm comes from some programmer's observation that out-of-order items tend to rise like bubbles through the list until they reach their proper positions.

The variable *swapflag* indicates whether a swap has been performed on a given pass through the list. At the top to the loop, it is set to 0, indicating that a swap has not been performed. The outside loop is written as a do-while loop, which forces the inner loop code to execute at least once:

```
int swapflag;
do {
      swapflag=0;
```

The for loop then searches the list for out-of-order pairs:

```
for (int i=0; i<(number_of_polygons-1); i++) {
```

Next, we check to see if the polygon currently pointed to by the loop index, *i*, is in the correct order relative to the polygon immediately following it:

```
if (polylist[i].GetDistance()
    < polylist[i+1].GetDistance()) {
```

In this case, since we are sorting in reverse order by the *distance* variable member of each polygon, the code checks to see if the first polygon has a smaller distance than the second polygon. If it does, the polygons are in the wrong order; we want polygons with higher distance values to come first in the list so they will be drawn first. Thus, we swap the two polygons. The Polygon pointer temp holds the value of one of the polygons while the swap is performed, so that it won't be written over by the value of the other polygon:

```
Polygon *temp=polylist [i];
polylist-[i]=polylist [i+1];
polylist[i+1]=temp;
```

This swapping is one of the advantages of using pointers instead of using an array of Polygon objects. Instead of copying the memory for the entire Polygon object, the program only has to copy the address of the object. Besides saving time (copying 4 bytes instead of 16), it also could prove to be more flexible in the future, since swapping pointers is not affected if the class structure changes. To indicate that a swap has been performed, swapflag is set to -1:

```
swapflag=-1;
```

Finally, the While statement closes the outer loop, allowing exit from the loop only if *swapflag* is 0, meaning an entire pass through the inner loop was made with no objects swapped.

```
}while(swapflag);
```

And that's all there is to performing a depth sort. Once the While loop terminates, the polygon list will be in order—almost. The complete text of the z_sort() function appears in Listing 10-2.

Listing 10-2 The *z_sort()* function

```
void PolygonList::z_sort()
{
    int swapflag;
    do{
        swapflag=0;
        // Loop thorugh polygon list:
        for (int i=0; i<(number_of_polygons-1); i++) {
            // Are polygons out of order?
            if (polylist[i]->GetDistance()
                    < polylist[i+1]->GetDistance()) {
                // if so , swap them...
                //  we're swapping pointers and not the
                // actual objects!
                Polygon *temp = polylist[i];
                polylist[i] = polylist[i+1];
                polylist[i+1] = temp;
```

continued on next page

continued from previous page

```
                              swapflag=-1;    // Indicate that swap was
                                              // performed
                         }
                     }
             }while(swapflag);
     }
```

If we are to resolve all of the discrepancies in polygon ordering left behind by the depth sort, we must now perform the five tests described earlier in the discussion of the Painter's Algorithm. But it isn't strictly necessary that we resolve these discrepancies—and, in fact, we are not going to do so in the finished flight simulator. It is possible to create a commercial-quality flight simulator using only the depth sort (which we just performed with the z_sort() function) for hidden surface removal. Doubtlessly many flight simulators on the market now or in the past do precisely this. Without the depth sort, the program is leaner and faster; fewer operations must be performed to order the polygons for each frame.

The trick is not to include any concave polyhedra in the scenery database. You'll note that this is precisely the case in the scenery databases of many flight simulators, where buildings are represented by cubes and mountains by complex pyramids. As long as only convex polyhedra are used and the objects are not huddled too closely together, polygon ordering discrepancies simply will not occur. A depth sort performed on top of backface removal will be adequate for hidden surface removal.

Even though we are not going to be using the five tests in our flight simulator, we've provided in the file POLYLIST.CPP in directory BYOFS\FSIM on the distribution disk a set of six functions to help the reader develop his or her version of the five tests—or, at least, the first four. (The fifth isn't absolutely required, as noted earlier, though you may want to try your hand at it anyway.) These functions are z_overlap() (which checks for overlap between two polygons in the z extent), should_be_swapped() (which returns a nonzero or true value if a pair of polygons are in the wrong order), and the three functions that perform the first four tests (the first of these performs the first two tests in one function): xy_overlap(), surface_inside(), and surface_outside(). In the rest of this chapter, we'll describe the workings of these functions in some detail. However, since they are not used in the final program, these functions, and their declarations within their respective classes are surrounded by conditional compiler directives:

```
#ifdef HID_SURF_TEST5
. . .
#endif
```

This allows us to include the code in our program, but only to compile it when we define HID_SURF_TEST5 either under our Project Options - Compiler Defines or within the program source files. In the next chapter when we revisit our class declarations, this directive will appear within some of the classes. This provides us with control of the compiler to build the classes with, or without, the additional hidden surface testing functions. Removing the tests from our program also allows us to remove the six data fields which are stored in the polygon and hold the minimum and maximum values for *x*, *y* and *z* coordinates. Since these fields are only stored for the additional hidden surface test functions, they can be removed from the class with the same conditional directives. The MakePolygonList() function will then be changed since we only need to store this information if we are using the hidden surface test:

```
#ifdef HID_SURF_TEST5
                // If we plan on using the 5 additional tests for
                // hidden surface removal, then
                // put mins & maxes in polygon descriptor:
            polyptr->SetMin(pxmin, pymin, pzmin);
            polyptr->SetMax(pxmax, pymax, pzmax);
#endif
```

The first test, *z_overlap()*, checks to see if the *z* extents of two polygons overlap, returning a nonzero value if they do, zero if they do not. It takes one Polygon reference as parameter. Although we have yet to discuss the Polygon class, we can assume that the variables *zmin* and *zmax* are accessible as data fields within the class:

```
int Polygon::z_overlap(const   Polygon& poly2)
{
```

Recall that checking for *z* extent overlap is a matter of checking to see if the minimum *z* of polygon A (the instance which called the class function) is less than the maximum *z* of polygon B or if the minimum *z* of polygon B (the first parameter) is less than the maximum *z* of polygon A:

```
if ((zmin>=poly2.zmax) || (poly2.zmin>=zmax))
    return 0;
```

Should neither of these conditions be true, we want to return a nonzero value, indicating *z* overlap:

```
    return -1;
}
```

The complete text of function *z_overlap()* appears in Listing 10-3.

Listing 10-3 The *z_overlap()* function

```
int Polygon::z_overlap(const Polygon& poly2)

// Check for overlap in the z extent between this and  POLY2.

{
   // If the minimum z of POLY1 is greater than or equal to
   //  the maximum z of POLY2 or the minimum z or POLY2 is
   //  equal to or greater than the maximum z or POLY1 then
   //  return zero, indicating no overlap in the z extent:

            if ((zmin>=poly2.zmax) || (poly2.zmin>=zmax))
                    return 0;
```

continued on next page

continued from previous page

```
    // Return non-zero, indicating overlap in the z extent:

        return -1;
}
```

The *z_overlap()* function is short but to the point. The should_be_swapped() function, which returns a nonzero value if the two polygons are out of order, is a little bulkier, but only slightly so. It calls three more functions to perform the first four of the tests described earlier in the chapter. Should the two polygons pass any of these tests (i.e., should any of these three functions return a nonzero value), the should_be_swapped() function exits with a zero value, indicating that the two polygons don't need to be swapped. Only if the two polygons flunk all three tests does the function return a nonzero value. The function is so self-explanatory that, instead of breaking it down line-by-line, we've simply printed the text in Listing 10-4.

Listing 10-4 The should_be_swapped() function

```
int   Polygon::should_be_swapped(const Polygon& poly2)

// Check to see if POLY1 and POLY2 are in the wrong order
//  for the Painter's Algorithm.

{

    // Check for overlap in the x and/or y extents:

    if (!xy_overlap( poly2)) return 0;

    // Check to see if poly2 is on the correct side of this poly:

    if (surface_inside(poly2)) return 0;

    // Check to see if this poly is on the correct side of poly2:

    if (surface_outside(poly2)) return 0;

    // If we've made it this far, all tests have been
    //  flunked, so return non-zero.

    return -1;
}
```

The *xy_overlap()* function, referenced in the should_be_swapped() function, checks for overlap in both the *x* and *y* extents and returns a nonzero value if it fails to find both. (Both must be present if the polygons are to overlap physically.) The text, which appears in Listing 10-5, is essentially the same as that in the *z_overlap()* function, except that two checks are performed instead of one.

✈ **Listing 10-5** The *xy_overlap()* function

```
int Polygon::xy_overlap(const Polygon& poly2)

// Check for overlap in the x and y extents, return
//  nonzero if both are found, otherwise return zero.

{
  // If no overlap in the x extent, return zero:

  if ((xmin>poly2.xmax) || (poly2.xmin>xmax))
      return 0;

  // If no overlap in the y extent, return zero:

  if ((ymin>poly2.ymax) || (poly2.ymin> ymax))
      return 0;

  // If we've gotten this far, overlap must exist in both
  //  x and y, so return nonzero:

  return -1;
}
```

The surface_inside() and surface_outside() functions perform tests 3 and 4, respectively. Both tests use the plane equation to determine whether the polygon pair is in the correct order. This equation can be expressed like this:

```
Ax + By + Cz + D
```

The variables *x*, *y*, and *z* are the *x,y,z* coordinates of a point. (We'll have more to say about these coordinates in a moment.) The variables *A, B, C,* and *D* are called the coefficients of the plane, which can be derived from the coordinates of any three points on the surface of the plane (as long as all three points don't happen to fall on a single line). If the coordinates of those three points are represented by the variables (x_1,y_1,z_1), (x_2,y_2,z_2), and (x_3,y_3,z_3), then the coefficients of the plane can be derived through these four formulas:

```
A = y₁(z₂ - z₃) + y₂(z₃ - z₁) + y₃(z₁ - z₂)
B = z₁(x₂ - x₃) + z₂(x₃ - x₁) + z₃(x₁ - x₂)
C = x₁(y₂ - y₃) + x₂(y₃ - y₁) + x₃(y₁ - y₂)
D = -x₁(y₂z₃ - y₃z₂) - x₂(y₃z₁ - y₁z₃) - x₃(y₁z₂ - y₂z₁)
```

Now that we know both the plane equation and the formulas necessary for determining the coefficients of a plane, we can use these tools to determine if a point lies on a particular plane (and, if not, on which side of the plane the point lies). We plug the coefficients of the plane into the *A, B, C,* and *D* variables of the plane equation and the *x, y,* and *z* coordinates of the point into the *x, y,* and *z* variables and solve the equation.

If the result is zero, the point lies on the plane. If the result is negative, the point lies on the counterclockwise side of the plane, the side from which the three points that we used to calculate the coefficients appear to be arranged in a counterclockwise manner. (Remember that these points cannot be on a single line; they must have a triangular relationship to one another and therefore form the vertices of a triangle.) If the result is positive, the point lies on the opposite side of the plane—what we might call the clockwise side of the plane.

Now we can determine if polygon B (the polygon determined by the depth sort to be the more distant from the viewer of the polygon pair) is on the far side of polygon A, where it belongs. How? By using the plane equation to determine on which side of the plane of polygon A each of the vertices of polygon B lies. (Each vertex, remember, is simply a point in space with x, y, and z coordinates that can be plugged into the plane equation.)

The logic of the process is a tad complicated, however. Recall from Chapter 8 that the vertices of all the polygons in the world database have been designed so that, when viewed from outside the object of which they are part, the vertices arrange in a counterclockwise manner. This makes the backface removal operate correctly. By the time the depth sort is performed, backface removal has pruned all polygons from the list that do not have their counterclockwise faces turned toward the viewer. Thus, if a point lies on the clockwise side of one of the polygons that remains, it must be on the opposite side from the viewer.

It follows that we can tell whether polygon B is on the opposite side of polygon A from the viewer (which is where it's supposed to be after the depth sort) by testing to see if all of its vertices are on the clockwise side of the plane of polygon A. Here's the procedure: First we calculate the coefficients of the plane of polygon A using the x, y, and z coordinates of the first three vertices of polygon A as the three points on the plane; next we plug the resulting coefficients into the A, B, C, and D variables of the plane equation; then we use a for loop to step through all of the vertices of polygon B, plugging the x, y, and z coordinates of each into the x, y, and z variables of the plane equation. If the resulting plane equations evaluate to positive numbers for every one of the vertices of polygon B, then they are all on the clockwise side of polygon A and thus the entirety of polygon B must be on the clockwise side of polygon A. Since this is the far side of the polygon, the two polygons are in the correct order and don't need to be swapped. No more tests need be performed.

Let's look at the actual code that performs the test. The function surface_inside() performs test 3, checking to see if polygon A is on the far (clockwise) side of polygon B. It returns nonzero if it is. The function takes one Polygon parameter—poly2 (which will be used in our code for polygon A):

```
int Polygon::surface_inside(const Polygon& poly2)
```

Before we can use the plane equation, we must calculate the coefficients of the plane of poly2. For the three points on the plane, we'll use the first three vertices of poly2:

```
{
  // Calculate the coefficients of poly2:

  long x1=poly2.vertex[0]->ax;
  long y1=poly2.vertex[0]->ay;
  long z1=poly2.vertex[0]->az;
  long x2=poly2.vertex[1]->ax;
  long y2=poly2.vertex[1]->ay;
  long z2=poly2.vertex[1]->az;
  long x3=poly2.vertex[2]->ax;
  long y3=poly2.vertex[2]->ay;
  long z3=poly2.vertex[2]->az;
  long a=y1*(z2-z3)+y2*(z3-z1)+y3*(z1-z2);
  long b=z1*(x2-x3)+z2*(x3-x1)+z3*(x1-x2);
  long c=x1*(y2-y3)+x2*(y3-y1)+x3*(y1-y2);
  long d=-x1*(y2*z3-y3*z2)-x2*(y3*z1-y1*z3)-x3*(y1*z2-y2*z1);
```

Our numbers can get pretty large when making these calculations, so we use variables of type long to guard against integer overflow, which can create difficult-to-find bugs in the code. If your computer can handle floating-point arithmetic, you may want to use type float for even better protection against overflow.

Now we need to loop through all of the vertices of poly1, plugging the x, y, and z coordinates of each into the plane equation, along with the coefficients we just calculated. If the plane equations using these numbers evaluate to anything except a positive result, the test has been flunked and we return a zero value to the calling routine. If only positive values are detected, a nonzero value is returned, indicating that poly1 is indeed on the far (clockwise) side of poly2:

```
  // Plug the vertices of this poly into the plane equation
  //   of poly2, one by one:

  int flunked=0;
  for (int v=0; v<number_of_vertices; v++) {
    if((a*vertex[v]->ax+b*vertex[v]->ay
            +c*vertex[v]->az+d)<0) {
      flunked=-1; // If less than 1, we flunked
                  //   break;
    }
  }
  return !flunked;
}
```

The complete text of the surface_inside() function appears in Listing 10-6.

Listing 10-6 The surface_inside() function

```
int Polygon:surface_inside(const Polygon& poly2)

// Check to see if poly2 is inside the surface of poly1.
```

continued on next page

continued from previous page

```
{
   // Determine the coefficients of poly2:

   long x1=poly2.vertex[0]->ax;
   long y1=poly2.vertex[0]->ay;
   long z1=poly2.vertex[0]->az;
   long x2=poly2.vertex[1]->ax;
   long y2=poly2.vertex[1]->ay;
   long z2=poly2.vertex[1]->az;
   long x3=poly2.vertex[2]->ax;
   long y3=poly2.vertex[2]->ay;
   long z3=poly2.vertex[2]->az;
   long a=y1*(z2-z3)+y2*(z3-z1)+y3*(z1-z2);
   long b=z1*(x2-x3)+z2*(x3-x1)+z3*(x1-x2);
   long c=x1*(y2-y3)+x2*(y3-y1)+x3*(y1-y2);
   long d=-x1*(y2*z3-y3*z2)-x2*(y3*z1-y1*z3)-x3*(y1*z2-y2*z1);

   // Plug the vertices of this poly into the plane equation
   //  of poly2, one by one:

   int flunked=0;
   for (int v=0; v<number_of_vertices; v++) {
     if((a*vertex[v]->ax+b*vertex[v]->ay
            +c*vertex[v]->az+d)<0) {
       flunked=-1; // If less than 1, we flunked
//       break;
     }
   }
   return !flunked;
}
```

Test 4 is pretty much the same as test 3, except that we are now checking to see if polygon A is entirely on the near (counterclockwise) side of polygon B. To do this, we simply reverse the role of the two polygons, taking the coefficients of this instead of poly2 and using the for loop to step through the vertices of poly2. We are now looking for negative values instead of positive values. The complete text of the surface_outside() function appears in Listing 10-7.

Listing 10-7 The surface_outside() function

```
int Polygon::surface_outside(const Polygon& poly2)
{
   float x1,y1,z1,x2,y2,z2,x3,y3,z3,a,b,c,d,surface;

   // Determine the coefficients of poly1:

   x1=vertex[0]->ax;
   y1=vertex[0]->ay;
   z1=vertex[0]->az;
   x2=vertex[1]->ax;
```

```
     y2=vertex[1]->ay;
     z2=vertex[1]->az;
     x3=vertex[2]->ax;
     y3=vertex[2]->ay;
     z3=vertex[2]->az;
     a=y1*(z2-z3)+y2*(z3-z1)+y3*(z1-z2);
     b=z1*(x2-x3)+z2*(x3-x1)+z3*(x1-x2);
     c=x1*(y2-y3)+x2*(y3-y1)+x3*(y1-y2);
     d=-x1*(y2*z3-y3*z2)-x2*(y3*z1-y1*z3)-x3*(y1*z2-y2*z1);

     // Plug the vertices of poly2 into the plane equation
     //  of this poly, one by one:

     int flunked=0;
     for (int v=0; v<poly2.number_of_vertices; v++) {
       if((a*poly2.vertex[v]->ax+b*poly2.vertex[v]->ay
               +c*poly2.vertex[v]->az+d)>0) {
         flunked=-1;  // If less than 1, we flunked
                      //  break;
       }
     }
     return !flunked;
}
```

Drawing the Polygon List

Up until now, we have been performing polygon drawing with object_type::Draw()
and polygon_type::DrawPoly(). With the addition of the PolygonList class, we can
now look at drawing all of the polygons from the class list of polygons instead. Before
we can see how a PolygonList::Draw() function might work, however, we need to discuss one more important aspect of three-dimensional polygon drawing.

Surfaces hidden behind other surfaces are not all that must be removed from a scene
before it can be drawn. It's also necessary to remove surfaces, or portions of surfaces,
that are occluded by the edges of the viewport itself, lest we clutter up video RAM with
pixels where they don't belong. The process of removing these out-of-range pixels is
called polygon clipping and we'll discuss it in the next chapter.

CHAPTER

11

11

Polygon Clipping

Literally and figuratively, the animation window, or viewport, on the video display gives us a window into the world inside the computer. Like a real window—at least, a window that's been washed recently—the animation window gives us a clear view of that world. But, also like a real window, the animation window lets us see only part of what's in that world—the part that's in front of the window. There may be a lot of things going on in the world inside the computer, but if it isn't happening in front of the window, we have no view of it.

We've avoided this limitation up until now by deliberately placing all of the action in the 3D world directly in front of the window. We haven't missed seeing anything yet because there hasn't been anything to miss. What we saw was all there was to see.

To be fully realistic, however, our three-dimensional world must include features that are not in front of the window. We aren't putting on a stage production here, where the only real action takes place within the confines of a proscenium arch. Neither are we making a movie, where the only action going on beyond the reach of the camera is a crowd of bored crew members standing around drinking stale coffee. We're building an entire world—and creating a window into that world.

As in the real world, objects will be moving in and out of view. This means that our program must somehow decide which parts of this simulated world appear in the window and which do not. **This is a relatively trivial problem.** To determine which polygons are fully within the window and which are not, we need merely check to see if their maximum and minimum x, y, and z coordinates, as calculated in the last chapter, fall within the maximum and minimum x, y, and z coordinates of the window. (We'll deal with the concept of a window having a maximum and minimum z coordinate in a moment, when we discuss view volumes.) The real problem arises when we must deal with a polygon that falls partially inside the animation window and partially outside of it. We must find a way to draw only that part of the polygon that falls within the window.

Determining which part of a polygon is inside the window is called polygon clipping. Like the hidden surface problem that we discussed in the last chapter, **this is not a trivial problem.** Fortunately, unlike the hidden surface problem, it has an entirely satisfactory solution. Before we get to that solution, however, let's look at the problem in more detail.

The View Volume

If you are indoors at the moment and there's a window in the room where you are, open it and look through it from a distance of 3 or 4 feet. (In case there's no window nearby, we've supplied a drawing of one in Figure 11-1.) What are the dimensions of the window, roughly speaking? For the sake of argument, let's say that the window is 3 feet wide. Does that mean that the view through the window is only 3 feet wide?

Figure 11-1 Window with a view of the outside world

Not necessarily. If someone has bricked up your window prior to condemning your building, then your view probably is only 3 feet wide, provided the bricks are immediately on the other side of the window. (See Figure 11-2(a).) On the other hand, if the view through your window is of an apartment building on the opposite side of the street, then your view is more likely to be several hundred feet wide, as in Figure 11-2(b). Still better, if you are able to see to the horizon, your view is probably several miles wide, as in Figure 11-2(c). And if it's night and the stars are out, your view is probably several light years wide, encompassing much of the local portion of the galaxy, as in Figure 11-2(d).

As a rule, then, we can say that your view becomes wider and wider with distance. You have a relatively narrow view of things that are close to the window but a wide view of things that are distant from the window. This, of course, is a result of perspective, which we've discussed already. The rays of light that carry the images of objects seen through your window are converging toward your eyeballs, so that the rays of light from objects at opposite ends of the window come together at an angle when they reach your eyes. The farther away the objects reflecting (or producing) those rays of light are, the greater the area encompassed by this angle and the farther apart the objects are in reality. Needless to say, all of this is true of the vertical dimension of your view field as well, though this is probably less obvious, since our world is arranged in a relatively horizontal fashion.

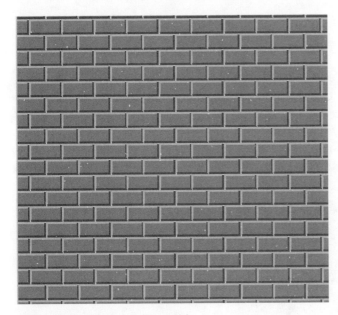

Figure 11-2 Views of the world
(a) Looking directly at a brick wall, your view will be quite narrow
(continued on next page)

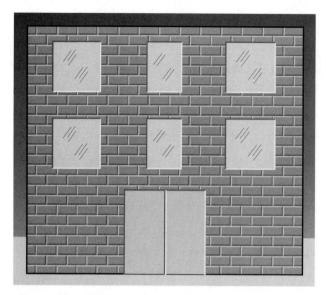

Figure 11-2 *(continued from previous page)*
(b) Seeing to the far side of the street, your view will be a bit wider than in Figure 11-2(a)

(c) Seeing to the horizon, your view will be several miles wide

(d) Seeing the sky, your view might be several light years wide!

Now imagine that you've been transported into the sky, looking down at your building from far above. Further, imagine that you can see a beam of light shining out of your window, representing the area that you can see *through* the window. This beam will grow wider with distance, as in Figure 11-3(a). If you examine the beam from the side, you'll also see that it grows wider in the vertical dimension too, as in Figure 11-3(b). Altogether, the beam takes the form of a pyramid, with its point at your eyes and its bottom at the farthest distance you are capable of seeing. (In theory, this distance is infinite, or at least many light years in length. In practice, however, we can treat the bottom of the pyramid as being about 10 miles away, the distance of the horizon viewed from near the ground.) The part of the pyramid that is entirely outside your window (and is truncated by your window pane, giving it a flat top) is called a frustum and represents your view volume—the volume of space within which you can see things through your window. Anything that is completely outside of the view volume is invisible from your window, even though it might be clearly visible to viewers on the outside. Anything that is completely inside the view volume is potentially visible through your window, though it may be blocked by other objects—the hidden surface problem again. Objects that are partially inside the view volume will appear to be clipped off at the edge of the window, if they are not blocked by nearer objects.

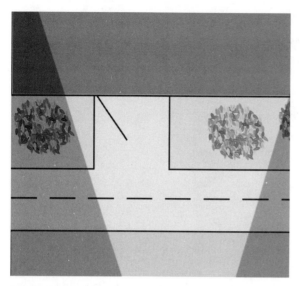

Figure 11-3 Your view grows wider in both horizontal and vertical dimensions with distance

(a) The area that you can see out your window, seen from above

(b) The area that you can see out your window, seen from the side

Clipping against the View Volume

The animation window on our computer display works exactly like the window in your room. It allows us to see a pyramid- (or frustum-) shaped view volume within the numerically described world that we are creating in the computer. Up to now, we have carefully placed objects so that they are always within this view volume. Eventually, however, we must allow objects to lie outside that view volume as well.

This means that we'll need some means of clipping polygons against the sides of the view volume before we draw them. We'll do this by creating a function that we'll refer to for now as clip() that will accept an unclipped polygon as input and will return as output a second polygon that represents the portion of the unclipped polygon that is inside the view volume. This partial polygon can then be passed to the polygon-drawing function, DrawPoly(), to be rendered on the display.

One potential obstacle to performing this task is the way in which the sides of the view volume slant outward as they move away from the window. The manner in which we need to clip a polygon varies according to the z coordinate of the polygon— and, since a single polygon can have several different z coordinates (as we saw in Chapter 10), determining where the polygon needs to be clipped could become a tricky problem. Fortunately, there are several solutions to this problem. In the case of the three-dimensional code that we are developing here, the problem has already been solved. By passing all of the coordinates of the polygons through the perspective function Project() before we clip those polygons, we have effectively straightened out the sides of the view volume. As far as clip() is concerned, the view volume will be a cube rather than a pyramid, which simplifies things considerably.

In fact, as far as the left, right, top, and bottom sides of the view volume are concerned, we can treat the polygons as two-dimensional shapes to be clipped against the sides of a two-dimensional animation window. That makes the problem even simpler, but not quite simple enough. We'll need to use different methods for the front and back sides of the view volume. For the back side of the view volume, the base of the pyramid, we won't do any polygon clipping at all. The entire object and all its polygons will be designated as either being included or excluded from our scene. One implementation might include a field in the Object class that will indicate the maximum distance at which the object is visible. Beyond that distance, we simply wouldn't draw the object, so clipping the polygons in that object against the back side of the view volume is unnecessary. Many games use this idea so that as you journey forward in the game's 3D world, things seem to pop up on the horizon. For our flight simulator, we will assume that we have clear weather conditions with unlimited visibility so objects will always be visible (if they are in front of us). The front side of the view volume is another matter. We'll set the front of the view volume at a z distance of 1, which will put it just in front of the screen. This is the same as the MakePolygonList() function. (Setting it at a z distance of 1 rather than 0 avoids possible problems with division by 0 in the clip() function.) Unlike clipping against the sides of the window, which is a two-dimensional clipping task, clipping against the front of the view volume is a three-dimensional task and thus a little more complicated.

The Sutherland-Hodgman Algorithm

The method that we'll use for clipping polygons against the sides of the view volume is called the Sutherland-Hodgman algorithm, after its discoverers. It involves breaking the clipping task into six separate tasks: one for each of the six sides of the view volume. We'll only be performing five of these tasks, since we're ignoring the back side of the view volume. Each of the five tasks will take a polygon as input and return as output a polygon clipped against one of the sides of the view volume. By passing each succeeding task the output polygon from the previous task, the result after all five tasks have been performed will be a polygon that has been clipped against the left, right, top, bottom, and front sides of the view volume.

For efficiency's sake, we won't make each task a separate function but will perform all five tasks in a single large function that will be structured like this:

```
Clip polygon A against the front of the view volume to produce
     polygon B. (See Figure 11-4(a).)
Clip polygon B against the left side of the view volume to produce
     polygon C. (See Figure 11-4(b).)
Clip polygon C against the right side of the view volume to pro-
     duce polygon D. (See Figure 11-4(c).)
Clip polygon D against the top side of the view volume to produce
     polygon E. (See Figure 11-4(d).)
```

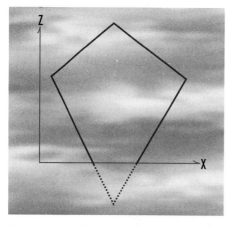
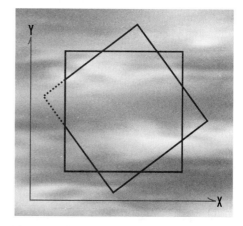

Figure 11-4 The Sutherland-Hodgman algorithm at work

(a) Clipping against the front of the view volume (as seen from above)

(b) Clipping against the left side of the view volume

Clip polygon E against the bottom side of the view volume to
produce polygon F. (See Figure 11-4(e).)
Return polygon F. (See Figure 11-4(f).)

Clipping a polygon against an edge is a matter of building up, edge-by-edge, a new polygon that represents the clipped version of the old polygon. We can think of this as a process of replacing the unclipped edges of the old polygon with the clipped edges of the new polygon. In order to determine the coordinates of the vertices of the new polygon, each edge of the old polygon must be examined and classified by type,

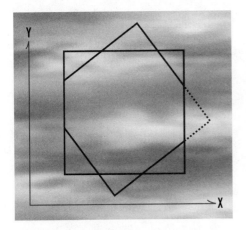

(c) Clipping against the right side of the view volume

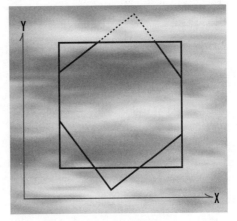

(d) Clipping against the top of the view volume

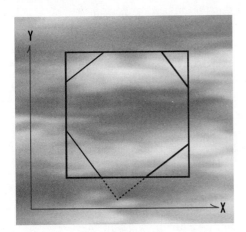

(e) Clipping against the bottom of the view volume

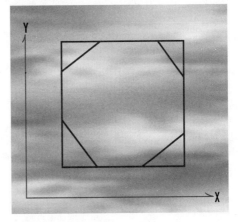

(f) The clipped polygon

depending on where it falls relative to the side of the view volume against which it is being clipped.

Four Types of Edge

There are four types of edge that the clipping function will encounter. All four are illustrated by the polygon in Figure 11-5(a), which overlaps the left edge of the animation window (and thus the left side of the view volume). The arrows show the direction the algorithm will work around the edges of the polygon, which is the same as the order in which the vertices are stored in the polygon's vertex array. The four types of edge:

1. Edges that are entirely inside the view volume (such as edge 1 in Figure 11-5)

2. Edges that are entirely outside the view volume (such as edge 3)

3. Edges that are leaving the view volume—that is, edges in which the first vertex (in the order indicated by the arrows) is inside the view volume and the second vertex is outside (such as edge 2)

4. Edges that are entering the view volume—that is, edges in which the first vertex is outside the view volume and the second vertex is inside (such as edge 4 in the illustration)

Each type of edge will be replaced by a clipped edge in a different way, as follows.

1. Edges that are entirely inside the view volume will be replaced by identical edges. In effect, these edges will be copied unchanged to the new polygon.

2. Edges that are entirely outside the view volume will be eliminated. For each such edge in the old polygon, no new edge will be added to the clipped polygon.

3. Edges that are leaving the view volume will be clipped at the edge of the view volume. The first vertex of such an edge will be copied unchanged to the clipped polygon, but the second vertex will be replaced by a new vertex having the coordinates of the point at which the edge intersects the side of the view volume.

4. Edges that are entering the view volume will be replaced by two new edges. One of these will be the old edge clipped at the point where it intersects the side of the view volume. The other will be a brand new edge that connects the first vertex of this edge with the last vertex of the previous type 3 edge— the leading edge that was clipped at the side of the view volume.

If you start with edge 1 of the polygon in Figure 11-5(a) and clip each edge mentally according to the procedures outlined above, you should eventually wind up with the clipped polygon shown in Figure 11-5(b). The rough skeleton of the procedure for clipping against an individual edge is as follows.

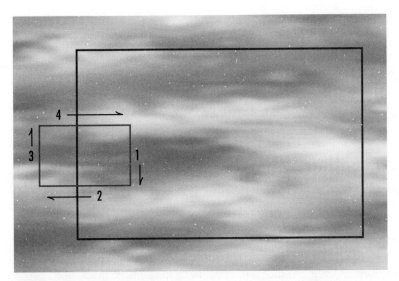

Figure 11-5 The polygon edges considered by the Sutherland-Hodgman algorithm
(a) The four types of edges

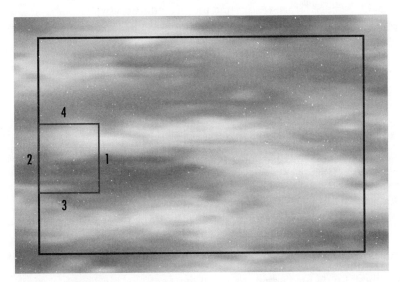

(b) What remains after the clipping procedures have been applied against the side of the viewport

```
for (every edge of the polygon) {
        if type 1 edge, perform type 1 replacement
        if type 2 edge, perform type 2 replacement
        if type 3 edge, perform type 3 replacement
        if type 4 edge, perform type 4 replacement
}
```

The complete clip() function consists of five such loops in the sequence shown several paragraphs back.

The Point-Slope Equation

Implementing this algorithm in C++ code is a straightforward, if somewhat tedious, task. About the only part that might prove troublesome is determining the x,y coordinates at which an edge of the polygon intersects a side of the view volume. Since, for the most part, we'll be treating the edges of the polygons as two-dimensional lines and clipping them against the two-dimensional edges of the animation window, which are also two-dimensional lines, we can determine the point of intersection using the mathematical formula known as the point-slope equation. In my continuing effort to hold the mathematics in this book to a minimum, we won't actually examine the point-slope equation. We'll simply look at how to clip a line with the point-slope equation's help.

Let's say that we're clipping a line with starting vertices $(x1,y1)$ and ending vertices $(x2,y2)$ against a window with minimum coordinates $(xmin,ymin)$ and maximum coordinates $(xmax,ymax)$. When we clip this line against the right or left edge of the window, we already know the x coordinate at which the line crosses the edge, because it's the same as the x coordinate of the edge. Thus, we can find the x coordinate at which the line crosses the left edge of the window with the statement:

```
clipped_x = xmin;
```

because $xmin$ is the x coordinate of the left edge. And we can find the x coordinate at which a line crosses the right edge of the window with the statement:

```
clipped_x = xmax;
```

because $xmax$ is the x coordinate of the right edge.

Finding the y coordinate at which a line crosses the left and right edges is trickier, but with the aid of the point-slope equation we can pull it off. First we must calculate the slope of the line. We discussed the slope back in Chapter 6. To recap briefly, the slope of a line is a real number that represents the ratio of the change in x coordinates to the change in y coordinates along equal portions of the line. It can be calculated with the formula:

```
slope = (y2 - y1)/(x2 - x1);
```

Once we know the slope, the formula for finding the y coordinate at which a line crosses the left edge of the window is

```
clipped_y = y1 + slope * (xmin - x1);
```

Similarly, the formula for finding the *y* coordinate at which a line crosses the right edge of the window is

```
clipped_y = y1 + slope * (xmax - x1);
```

Clipping against the top and bottom edges works much the same way, except instead of knowing the *x* coordinate of the point of intersection we now know the *y* coordinate and must calculate the *x* coordinate using a different version of the same point-slope formula. We find the *y* coordinate at which the line crosses the top edge of the window with the statement:

```
clipped_y = ymin;
```

because *ymin* is the *y* coordinate of the top edge. We find the *y* coordinate at which a line crosses the bottom edge of the window with the statement:

```
clipped_y = ymax;
```

because *ymax* is the *y* coordinate of the bottom edge.

To find the *x* coordinate at which the line crosses the top edge of the window, we use the formula:

```
clipped_x = x1 + (ymin - y1) / slope;
```

Similarly, we find the *x* coordinate at which the line crosses the bottom edge of the window with the formula:

```
clipped_x = x1 + (ymaxin - y1)  /  slope;
```

Clipping against the front of the view volume is a bit more complicated, since we must determine both the *x* and *y* coordinates of the point at which a line intersects a plane at a known *z* coordinate, which we'll call *zmin*. And we must take into account the *z* coordinates of the starting and ending points of the line, which we'll call *z1* and *z2*. To calculate the new coordinates, we use a three-dimensional extension of the point-slope equation. The formulae for determining the *x* and *y* points of intersection are

```
clipped_x = (x2 - x1) * t + x1;
clipped_y = (y2 - y1) * t + y1;
```

This mysterious factor *t*, which is similar to the slope factor in the two-dimensional equations, can be calculated like this:

```
t = (zmin - z1) / (z2 - z1);
```

The *z* coordinates will be the same as *zmin,* but that's not important, since we won't need them again in the clipping process. So we'll just throw them away.

And that's all anybody needs to know to write a clipping function. Let's get down to work.

The Clipped Polygon Class

The first step in creating a clipped polygon is creating a special data structure to hold the vertices. Why don't we simply create additional data field members within the existing vertex structure for holding the coordinates of a clipped vertex? That would be convenient, since it would allow us to store the array of vertices for the clipped edges for each polygon within the vertex array already a member of the polygon class. It wouldn't work, though, because the clipped edges won't necessarily have the same number of vertices as the unclipped polygons; thus, the arrays may need to be of different sizes. Figure 11-6(a) shows an example. The polygon being clipped has five edges, yet the clipped version of the polygon will only have four, because two of the original edges are outside the window and will be replaced by only one new edge connecting the clipped edges of the polygon. Similarly, the polygon in Figure 11-6(b) has three edges, but the clipped version will have four.

Since clipping can both subtract edges from a polygon and add new edges to it, we must be prepared for the array of vertices to either shrink or grow. Fortunately, no more than five edges can be added to a convex polygon if we clip against the four sides of the viewport and the front of the view volume so we don't have to be overly generous in preparing for additional edges. (Figure 11-7 shows a four-sided polygon that becomes an eight-sided polygon after clipping.)

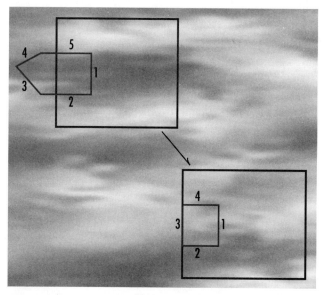

Figure 11-6 Clipping can add edges to or subtract edges from a polygon

(a) This polygon has five edges before clipping, but only four afterward

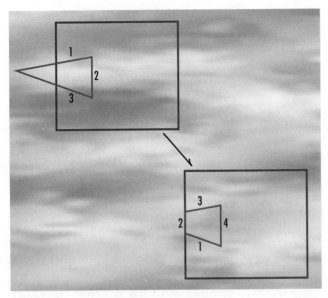

(b) This polygon has three edges before clipping, but four afterward

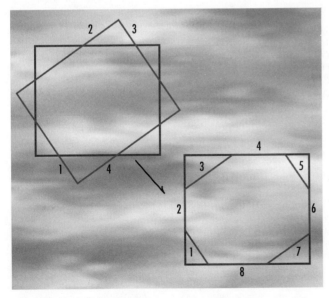

Figure 11-7 This polygon goes from four edges to eight during the clipping process; clipping against the front of the view volume could add yet another edge

For this reason, we'll need to create a completely separate array to store the clipped vertices. As long as we're at it, it would be convenient to create a new class to manage that array, which we'll call ClippedPolygon. The class will need to know how many vertices are being stored in the array and the color of the polygon. If the hidden surface functions are used, then the six variables to store the coordinates' minimum and maximum will be needed. In overview, it is so similar to the polygon_type class of the previous chapters (which has been renamed to class Polygon) that it suggests there is a stronger C++ relationship between the two classes. We will therefore group these common data elements together into a class, then derive our new class from it. The declaration for our base class looks like this:

```cpp
class polyBase {
protected:
        int     number_of_vertices; // Number of vertices in polygon
        int     original_color;     // Color of polygon
        int     color;              // Drawing color of polygon (after light
                                    // applied)
        long    nlength;            // normal length (for lighting)
#ifdef HID_SURF_TEST5
        int zmax,zmin;              // Maximum and minimum z coordinates of
                                    // polygon

        int xmax,xmin;
        int ymax,ymin;
#endif
public:
        polyBase(){;}
        int GetVertexCount() const
                { return number_of_vertices; }
        void SetVertexCount(int count)
                { number_of_vertices = count; }
        int GetOriginalColor() const
                { return original_color; }
        void SetColor(int val)
                { color = val; }
        int GetColor() const
                { return color; }
        long GetNormalLen()
                { return nlength; }
#ifdef HID_SURF_TEST5
                // for outside access to set the
                // max and min values:
        void SetMax(int x, int y, int z)
                { xmax=x, ymax = y, zmax = z; }
        void SetMin(int x, int y, int z)
                { xmin=x, ymin = y, zmin = z; }
#endif

        polyBase& polyBase::operator =(const polyBase& polygon);
};
```

The polyBase class will be used to form both the Polygon and ClippedPolygon classes. The data field members, number_of_vertices, original_color, color and nlength are declared with protected scope, such that derived classes will have access to them but the public is denied. The newer fields, original_color and nlength, will be explained in the next chapter on lighting. We have commented on the inline functions previously, and in addition, they are very straightforward so need little explanation. A new addition, however, is the overriden assignment operator function (known as the copy function) which we will define to copy one instance of polyBase to another.

With the base class declared, the Polygon class can now be reworked as a derived class of polyBase:

```
class Polygon: public polyBase {
protected:
        friend class Object;   // access to vertex pointers
        vertex_type **vertex;            // List of vertices
        long double distance;
            // copy operator is protected since we want to
            // avoid possible killing of the vertex array through
            // an auto scoped variable
        Polygon& Polygon::operator =(const Polygon& polygon);
public:
        Polygon():polyBase(),vertex(0){;}
        ~Polygon();
        int     backface();
        vertex_type * GetVertexPtr(int vertnum)
            { return vertex[vertnum]; }
        long double GetDistance()
            { return (distance); }
        void  SetDistance(long double dist)
            { distance = dist; }
#ifdef HID_SURF_TEST5
        int should_be_swapped(const Polygon& poly2);
        int z_overlap(const Polygon& poly2);
        int xy_overlap(const Polygon& poly2);
        int surface_inside(const Polygon& poly2);
        int surface_outside(const Polygon& poly2);
#endif
};
```

Like the earlier polygon_type class, vertex stores a pointer to an array of vertex_type structures. The *distance* variable is used to determine the z_sort() ordering and was introduced in the last chapter. Notice that the DrawPoly function which existed in the polygon_type class has been removed since it will not be used. This class also redefines the copy function and has a good reason for it. If we copied an instance of a Polygon to a temporary variable, when that variable went out of scope, the destructor would be called. The destructor is identical to polygon_type destructor, which as you may recall, checks the vertex pointer for a nonzero value and deletes the array. If this happened, our original instance would be pointing to a deleted area of memory! This is clearly something to be avoided.

The ClippedPolygon class is also derived from polyBase:

```
class ClippedPolygon: public polyBase {
private:
      clip_type vertex[20];
public:
      ClippedPolygon():polyBase(){;}
      void DrawPoly(unsigned char far *screen);
      clip_type * GetClipPtr(int vertnum)
            { return &vertex[vertnum]; }
      void Project(int distance, int xorigin, int yorigin);
      ClippedPolygon& operator =(const Polygon& polygon)
            {
                  ((polyBase& )*this) = (polyBase&)polygon;
                  return *this;
            }
};
```

As you can see, the ClippedPolygon class is a great deal simpler than the original Polygon class, since it doesn't need to carry around nearly as much baggage and some of its functionality is contained in the base class. It consists of one element: the array of vertices. These vertices, however, are also of a new type, which we've called clip_type. We've allotted 20 of these to take care of any large polygons that may come down the pike, though this number is overkill and can be made smaller. (If we play our cards right, there should be only one *ClippedPolygon* variable in the program at a time, so this extra storage allotment will scarcely be noticed, unless memory is particularly tight.)

Readers desiring greater memory efficiency could base the size of the vertex array in the clip_type structure on the number of vertices of the largest polygon in the data base, plus four. This figure could be calculated dynamically by the loadpoly() function, which could then allot the memory for this array at runtime.

The clip_type structure looks like this:

```
struct clip_type {
      int x,y,z;
      int x1,y1,z1;
};
```

Just as the ClippedPolygon class is simpler than the Polygon class, so the clip_type structure is simpler than the vertex_type structure. However, it still is more complicated than would seem strictly necessary. The x, y, and z fields are used to store the x, y, and z coordinates of the vertex, but what are the $x1$, $y1$, and $z1$ fields for? They're for storage of the intermediate polygons created by the five stages of the clipping function. In fact, it might seem that we would need five separate sets of coordinate fields to store these intermediate polygons, but we'll economize by passing the vertices back and forth between these two sets of fields, timing the process so that we'll end up with the coordinates in the x, y, and z fields when the clipping process is complete.

The Clipping Functions

We're going to divide clipping duties between two functions. The first will clip against the front of the view volume, the second, against the sides. This enables us to perform other tasks in between, should we so desire. For instance, it can be useful to clip against the front of the view volume before the Project() function is called, since the perspective code has difficulty handling polygons that have vertices with zero and negative coordinates (which is precisely what are removed by clipping against the front of the view volume). On the other hand, it is useful to clip against the sides of the view volume after perspective has been introduced, since this simplifies the math involved.

The ZClip() function clips against the front of the view volume. It requires one parameter—the Polygon variable *polygon,* which describes the polygon to be clipped. Together with a ClippedPolygon object, which will hold the clipped polygon, these two objects contain almost all we need to write the function. What's missing is the actual clipping boundary—the z value for the front of the view volume. The minimum z value, as we have said before, is usually made equal to 1 to avoid division-by-zero errors. This is made an optional second parameter by declaring it with a default value of 1.

By now, it should come as no surprise that the view boundaries will be part of a class. The View class, to be covered in Chapter 13, will contain the x and y dimensions as member variables, so it seems natural for ZClip() to be part of that class. Also to be part of that class will be a ClippedPolygon and a PolygonList object. This is the reason why there is no ClippedPolygon pointer being passed as a formal parameter. The name of this private member is clip_array, and it stores the clipped polygon for the calling function. In doing so, all the clipping information and methods are contained in the same class. Here's the function declaration from the View class:

```
void ZClip(Polygon *polygon, int zmin=1);
```

The function definition for ZClip() then looks like:

```
void View::ZClip(Polygon *polygon, int zmin)
{
```

To start things off, essential information is transferred from the original polygon class to the clipped polygon:

```
// Transfer information from polygon's base class to
//   clipped polygon's base class:

clip_array = *polygon;
```

This makes use of the ClippedPolygon class function which does little else but call the polyBase copy function while casting both references to polyBase references. You can view the inline function in the ClippedPolygon class declaration. The reason for this overriding assignment operator is that within the polyBase function, we control what is transferred (and make use of the compiler directives if the hidden surface tests are being used).

Next, the variable cp will keep track of the current vertex of the clipped polygon—that is, the next one to be added as we replace the vertices of the original polygon:

```
int cp = 0;    // Index to current vertex of clipped polygon
```

A pointer called pcv is created to point to the vertices of the clipped polygon:

```
// Create pointer to vertices of clipped polygon
//   class:

clip_type *pcv=clip_array.GetClipPtr(0);
```

The Front of the View Volume

Now the games begin. First we'll clip the polygon against the front of the view volume. The variable $v1$, representing the first vertex of the edge to be clipped, will initially be set equal to the last vertex of the polygon, since the line from the last vertex to the first is a legitimate edge which might otherwise get lost in the shuffle:

```
// Initialize pointer to last vertex:

int v1=polygon->GetVertexCount()-1;
```

Similarly, the variable $v2$ represents the second vertex of the edge to be clipped. We'll use this edge as the index of a for loop that will loop through all of the vertices of the polygon:

```
// Loop through all edges of polygon

for (int v2=0; v2<polygon->GetVertexCount(); v2++) {
```

Initially, $v2$ will point to the first vertex of the polygon. Thus, the first edge to be clipped will be the edge extending from the last vertex in the vertex array to the first vertex in the vertex array. We then set the pointer $pv1$ to point to the first vertex of the current edge and the pointer $pv2$ to point to the second vertex:

```
vertex_type *pv1=polygon->GetVerticePtr(v1);
vertex_type *pv2=polygon->GetVerticePtr(v2);
```

Type 1 Edge

Then we examine the current edge to see what type it is. If the z coordinates of both the first vertex and the second vertex are greater than $zmin$, the entire edge is inside the front side of the view volume:

```
if ((pv1->az >= zmin) && (pv2->az >= zmin)) {

   // Entirely inside front
```

We copy the second vertex of the first edge to the first position in the vertex array for the clipped polygon. (We'll pick up the first vertex when we process the last edge, since the first vertex of this edge is the second vertex of that edge.) The polygon counter is incremented so that the next element will be written to:

```
   pcv[cp].x   = pv2->ax;
   pcv[cp].y   = pv2->ay;
   pcv[cp++].z = pv2->az;
}
```

Type 2 Edge

If the z coordinates of both vertices are less than $zmin$, the entire edge lies outside the front side of the view volume, in which case we don't need to do anything at all:

```
//if ((pv1->az < zmin) && (pv2->az < zmin)){

   // Edge is entirely past front, so do nothing

//}
```

The code with comments stays in the program to show that we considered the type 2 edge in implementing the $z$clip routine.

Type 3 Edge

If the z coordinate of the first vertex is greater than $zmin$ and the z coordinate of the second vertex is less than $zmin$, then the edge is leaving the view volume:

```
if ((pv1->az >= zmin) && (pv2->az < zmin)) {

   // Edge is leaving view volume
```

So we calculate the value of t:

```
float t=(float)(zmin - pv1->az) /
   (float)(pv2->az - pv1->az);
```

and use it to calculate the x,y coordinates at which the line crosses the front edge of the view volume, which we assign to the next vertex in the clipped vertex array:

```
   pcv[cp].x = pv1->ax + (pv2->ax - pv1->ax) * t;
   pcv[cp].y = pv1->ay + (pv2->ay - pv1->ay) * t;
   pcv[cp++].z = zmin;
}
```

Once again, the current polygon index into the vertex array is incremented.

Type 4 Edge

If the z coordinate of the first vertex is less than *zmin* and the z coordinate of the second vertex is greater than *zmin*, the edge is entering the view volume:

```
if ((pv1->az < zmin) && (pv2->az >= zmin)) {

    // Line is entering view volume
```

Once again, we calculate the value of *t*:

```
float t=(float)(zmin - pv1->az) /
     (float)(pv2->az - pv1->az);
```

Then we calculate the *x,y* coordinates where the line crosses the view volume and assign them to the next vertex of the clipped vertex array:

```
pcv[cp].x = pv1->ax + (pv2->ax - pv1->ax) * t;
pcv[cp].y = pv1->ay + (pv2->ay - pv1->ay) * t;
pcv[cp++].z = zmin;
```

But we must create another edge by copying the second vertex of the line directly to the clipped vertex array:

```
    pcv[cp].x = pv2->ax;
    pcv[cp].y = pv2->ay;
    pcx[cp++].z = pv2->az;
}
```

Finally, we increment *v1* to point to the second vertex of the current edge, which will be the first vertex of the next edge:

```
    v1=v2; // Advance to next vertex
}
```

That's it! We've clipped the vertex against the front of the view volume. Now, we'll need to set the value of the number_of_vertices field in the polyBase descriptor to the number of vertices in our clipped polygon. Since we've been incrementing *cp* for every new vertex, we'll simply use that value:

```
    // Put number of vertices in clipped polygon class:

    clip_array.SetVertexCount(cp);
}
```

The ZClip() Function

The complete ZClip() function appears in Listing 11-1.

Listing 11-1 The ZClip() function

```cpp
void View::ZClip(Polygon *polygon,  int zmin)
{

// Clip polygon against front of window at zmin coordinates

  // Transfer information from polygon's polybase class to
  //   clipped polyBase class:
      clip_array = *polygon;

      // Clip against front of window view volume:

      int cp = 0; // Index to current vertex of clipped polygon

      // Create pointer to clip_type vertices of clipped polygon class:

      clip_type *pcv = clip_array.GetClipPtr(0);

      // Initialize pointer to last vertex:

      int v1=polygon->GetVertexCount()-1;

      // Loop through all edges of polygon

      for (int v2=0; v2<polygon->GetVertexCount(); v2++) {
            vertex_type *pv1=polygon->GetVerticePtr(v1);
            vertex_type *pv2=polygon->GetVerticePtr(v2);

            // Categorize edges by type:

            if ((pv1->az >= zmin) && (pv2->az >= zmin)) {

              // Entirely inside front

                  pcv[cp].x    = pv2->ax;
                  pcv[cp].y    = pv2->ay;
                  pcv[cp++].z = pv2->az;
            }
            //if ((pv1->az < zmin) && (pv2->az < zmin)){
            // Edge is entirely past front, so do nothing
            //}
            if ((pv1->az >= zmin) && (pv2->az < zmin)) {

              // Edge is leaving view volume

                  float t=(float)(zmin - pv1->az) /
                              (float)(pv2->az - pv1->az);
                  pcv[cp].x = pv1->ax + (pv2->ax - pv1->ax) * t;
                  pcv[cp].y = pv1->ay + (pv2->ay - pv1->ay) * t;
```

continued on next page

continued from previous page

```
                                        pcv[cp++].z = zmin;
                        }
                        if ((pv1->az < zmin) && (pv2->az >= zmin)) {

                                // Line is entering view volume

                                float t=(float)(zmin - pv1->az) /
                                            (float)(pv2->az - pv1->az);
                                pcv[cp].x = pv1->ax + (pv2->ax - pv1->ax) * t;
                                pcv[cp].y = pv1->ay + (pv2->ay - pv1->ay) * t;
                                pcv[cp++].z=zmin;
                                pcv[cp].x = pv2->ax;
                                pcv[cp].y = pv2->ay;
                                pcv[cp++].z = pv2->az;
                        }
                        v1=v2; // Advance to next vertex
                }

                // Put number of vertices into clipped polygon:

                clip_array.SetVertexCount(cp);
        }
```

The Rest of the View Volume

Don't relax quite yet. We still have to clip all the edges in the polygon against four more sides of the view volume. We'll do this with a function called *XYClip()*, which takes no parameters. The polygon it clips is the same ClippedPolygon that was extracted by ZClip(). This is clip_array, a member of the View class. The process for the remaining edges is quite similar to the process of clipping against the front of the view volume, albeit in two dimensions instead of three. For instance, in clipping against the left edge, we start out in much the same manner, except that the polygon to be clipped is now stored in the clipped vertex array instead of in the original polygon's vertex array:

```
void View::XYClip()
{
    // Clip against sides of viewport

    int temp; // Miscellaneous temporary storage
    clip_type *pcv=clip_array.GetClipPtr(0);

    // Clip against left edge of viewport:

    int cp = 0;

    // Initialize pointer to last vertex:

    int v1=clip_array.GetVertexCount()-1;
    for (int v2=0; v2<clip_array.GetVertexCount(); v2++) {
```

Now we begin categorizing the edges by type. The variables *xmin, xmax, ymin,* and *ymax* are all private members declared in the View class as ints. These are used for boundary comparison just as *zmin* was used within the ZClip() function. If the *x* coordinates of the first and second vertices of the edge are both greater than *xmin,* the polygon edge is entirely inside the left side of the window, so we pass the vertices through unchanged.

```
// Categorize edges by type:

if ((pcv[v1].x >= xmin) && (pcv[v2].x >= xmin)) {

   // Edge isn't off left side of viewport

   pcv[cp].x1    = pcv[v2].x;
   pcv[cp++].y1 = pcv[v2].y;
}
```

Note that we are now using the *x1* and *y1* fields of the clipped polygon array, so that we won't obliterate the values in the *x* and *y* fields that we set in the ZClip() function.

If both *x* coordinates are less than *xmin,* the polygon is entirely off the left side of the window, so we do nothing (but record the effort within comments):

```
//else if ((pcv[v1].x < xmin) && (pcv[v2].x < xmin)){
// Edge is entirely off left side of viewport,
//    so don't do anything
//}
```

If the first *x* coordinate is greater than *xmin* and the second is less, the edge is leaving the left side of the window, so we calculate the slope and use the point-slope equation to calculate the coordinates of the intersection with the edge. Then we assign those coordinates to the next vertex in the clipped polygon array:

```
if ((pcv[v1].x >= xmin) && (pcv[v2].x < xmin)) {

   // Edge is leaving viewport

   float m=(float)(pcv[v2].y-pcv[v1].y) /
       (float)(pcv[v2].x-pcv[v1].x);
   pcv[cp].x1 = xmin;
   pcv[cp++].y1 =
     pcv[v1].y + m * (xmin - pcv[v1].x);
}
```

But if the first *x* coordinate is less than *xmin* and the second is greater, the edge is entering the left side of the window, so we use the point-slope equation as before to find the coordinates of the first vertex and pass through the second coordinates of the edge for the second vertex:

```
if ((pcv[v1].x < xmin) && (pcv[v2].x >= xmin)) {

   // Edge is entering viewport
```

continued on next page

continued from previous page

```
    float m=(float)(pcv[v2].y-pcv[v1].y) /
        (float)(pcv[v2].x-pcv[v1].x);
    pcv[cp].x1 = xmin;
    pcv[cp++].y1 =
        pcv[v1].y + m * (xmin - pcv[v1].x);
    pcv[cp].x1 = pcv[v2].x;
    pcv[cp++].y1 = pcv[v2].y;
}
```

And we tie up loose ends as before:

```
    v1=v2;
}
clip_array.SetVertexCount(cp);
```

Finishing the Clipping

It's all downhill from here. Clipping against the remaining three edges works in much the same way. To clip against the right edge, *xmax* is substituted for *xmin,* the greater-than and less-than signs (><) are reversed to indicate that the view window lies to the left of the edge, rather than to the right as in the previous loop, and we clip values from the *x1* and *y1* fields into the *x* and *y* fields:

```
// Clip against right edge of viewport:

// Initialize index to last vertex:

v1=cp-1;

// reset the counter:
cp = 0;

for (v2=0; v2<clip_array.GetVertexCount(); v2++) {

        // Categorize edges by type:

        if ((pcv[v1].x1 <= xmax) && (pcv[v2].x1 <= xmax)) {

                // Edge isn't off right side of viewport

                pcv[cp].x = pcv[v2].x1;
                pcv[cp++].y = pcv[v2].y1;
        }
        //if ((pcv[v1].x1 > xmax) && (pcv[v2].x1 > xmax)){
        // Edge is entirely off right side of viewport,
        //   so do nothing
        //}
        if ((pcv[v1].x1 <= xmax) && (pcv[v2].x1 > xmax)) {

                // Edge is leaving viewport
```

```
            float m=(float)(pcv[v2].y1-pcv[v1].y1) /
                      (float)(pcv[v2].x1-pcv[v1].x1);
            pcv[cp].x = xmax;
            pcv[cp++].y =
                    pcv[v1].y1 + m * (xmax - pcv[v1].x1);
      }
      if ((pcv[v1].x1 > xmax) && (pcv[v2].x1 <= xmax)) {

            // Edge is entering viewport

            float m=(float)(pcv[v2].y1-pcv[v1].y1) /
                      (float)(pcv[v2].x1-pcv[v1].x1);
            pcv[cp].x = xmax;
            pcv[cp++].y =
            pcv[v1].y1 + m * (xmax - pcv[v1].x1);
            pcv[cp].x = pcv[v2].x1;
            pcv[cp++].y = pcv[v2].y1;
      }
      v1=v2;
}
clip_array.SetVertexCount(cp);
```

Clipping against the upper edge is the same as clipping against the left edge, except that *ymin* is used instead of *xmin* and the *x* coordinate instead of the *y* is calculated with the point-slope equation. Similarly, clipping against the lower edge of the window is a *y*-coordinate version of clipping against the right edge of the window. Listing 11-2 shows the complete text of *XYClip()*.

Listing 11-2 The *XYClip()* function

```
void View::XYClip()
{
      // Clip against sides of viewport

      int temp; // Miscellaneous temporary storage
      clip_type *pcv=clip_array.GetClipPtr(0);

      // Clip against left edge of viewport:

      int cp = 0;

   // Initialize pointer to last vertex:

      int v1=clip_array.GetVertexCount()-1;
      for (int v2=0; v2<clip_array.GetVertexCount(); v2++) {

            // Categorize edges by type:

            if ((pcv[v1].x >= xmin) && (pcv[v2].x >= xmin)) {
```
continued on next page

continued from previous page

```
        // Edge isn't off left side of viewport

                pcv[cp].x1   = pcv[v2].x;
                pcv[cp++].y1 = pcv[v2].y;
        }
        //else if ((pcv[v1].x < xmin) && (pcv[v2].x < xmin)){
        // Edge is entirely off left side of viewport,
        //   so don't do anything
        // }
        if ((pcv[v1].x >= xmin) && (pcv[v2].x < xmin)) {

    // Edge is leaving viewport

                float m=(float)(pcv[v2].y-pcv[v1].y) /
                  (float)(pcv[v2].x-pcv[v1].x);
                pcv[cp].x1 = xmin;
                pcv[cp++].y1 =
                        pcv[v1].y + m * (xmin - pcv[v1].x);
        }
        if ((pcv[v1].x < xmin) && (pcv[v2].x >= xmin)) {

    // Edge is entering viewport

                float m=(float)(pcv[v2].y-pcv[v1].y) /
                  (float)(pcv[v2].x-pcv[v1].x);
                pcv[cp].x1 = xmin;
                pcv[cp++].y1 =
                        pcv[v1].y + m * (xmin - pcv[v1].x);
                pcv[cp].x1 = pcv[v2].x;
                pcv[cp++].y1 = pcv[v2].y;
        }
        v1=v2;
}
clip_array.SetVertexCount(cp);

// CLip against right edge of viewport:

// Initialize index to last vertex:
v1=cp-1;

// reset the counter:
cp = 0;

for (v2=0; v2<clip_array.GetVertexCount(); v2++) {

        // Categorize edges by type:

        if ((pcv[v1].x1 <= xmax) && (pcv[v2].x1 <= xmax)) {

          // Edge isn't off right side of viewport

                pcv[cp].x = pcv[v2].x1;
```

```
                pcv[cp++].y = pcv[v2].y1;
        }
        //if ((pcv[v1].x1 > xmax) && (pcv[v2].x1 > xmax)){
        // Edge is entirely off right side of viewport,
        //   so do nothing
        //}
        if ((pcv[v1].x1 <= xmax) && (pcv[v2].x1 > xmax)) {

                // Edge is leaving viewport

                float m=(float)(pcv[v2].y1-pcv[v1].y1) /
                        (float)(pcv[v2].x1-pcv[v1].x1);
                pcv[cp].x = xmax;
                pcv[cp++].y =
                        pcv[v1].y1 + m * (xmax - pcv[v1].x1);
        }
        if ((pcv[v1].x1 > xmax) && (pcv[v2].x1 <= xmax)) {

                // Edge is entering viewport

                float m=(float)(pcv[v2].y1-pcv[v1].y1) /
                        (float)(pcv[v2].x1-pcv[v1].x1);
                pcv[cp].x = xmax;
                pcv[cp++].y =
                        pcv[v1].y1 + m * (xmax - pcv[v1].x1);
                pcv[cp].x = pcv[v2].x1;
                pcv[cp++].y = pcv[v2].y1;
        }
        v1=v2;
}
clip_array.SetVertexCount(cp);

// Clip against upper edge of viewport:

// Initialize pointer to last vertex:

v1=cp-1;

// Reset current index:

cp = 0;

for (v2=0; v2<clip_array.GetVertexCount(); v2++) {

        // Categorize edges by type:

        if ((pcv[v1].y >= ymin) && (pcv[v2].y >= ymin)) {

                // Edge is not off top off viewport

                pcv[cp].x1 = pcv[v2].x;
                pcv[cp++].y1 = pcv[v2].y;
```

continued on next page

■ ■ ■ ■ ■ **385**

continued from previous page

```
                }
                //else if ((pcv[v1].y < ymin) && (pcv[v2].y < ymin)){
                // Edge is entirely off top of viewport,
                //   so don't do anything
                //}
                if ((pcv[v1].y >= ymin) && (pcv[v2].y < ymin)) {

        // Edge is leaving viewport

                        temp=(int)(pcv[v2].x-pcv[v1].x);
                        if (temp!=0) {
                                floatm=(float)(pcv[v2].y-pcv[v1].y)/(float)temp;
                                pcv[cp].x1 =
                                        pcv[v1].x + (ymin - pcv[v1].y) / m;
                        }
                        else pcv[cp].x1 = pcv[v1].x;
                        pcv[cp++].y1 = ymin;
                }
                if ((pcv[v1].y < ymin) && (pcv[v2].y >= ymin)) {

        // Edge is entering viewport

                        temp=(int)(pcv[v2].x-pcv[v1].x);
                        if (temp!=0) {
                                float m=(float)(pcv[v2].y-pcv[v1].y)/(float)temp;
                                pcv[cp].x1 =
                                        pcv[v1].x + (ymin - pcv[v1].y) / m;
                        }
                        else pcv[cp].x1 = pcv[v1].x;
                        pcv[cp++].y1 = ymin;
                        pcv[cp].x1 = pcv[v2].x;
                        pcv[cp++].y1 = pcv[v2].y;
                }
                v1=v2;
        }
        clip_array.SetVertexCount(cp);

        // Clip against lower edge of viewport:

        // Initialize pointer to last vertex:

        v1=cp-1;
        cp = 0;

        for (v2=0; v2<clip_array.GetVertexCount(); v2++) {

                // Categorize edges by type:

                if ((pcv[v1].y1 <= ymax) && (pcv[v2].y1 <= ymax)) {

                // Edge is not off bottom of viewport

                        pcv[cp].x = pcv[v2].x1;
```

```
                    pcv[cp++].y = pcv[v2].y1;
          }
          // if ((pcv[v1].y1 > ymax) && (pcv[v2].y1 > ymax)){
          // Edge is entirely off bottom of viewport,
          //   so don't do anything
          // }
          if ((pcv[v1].y1 <= ymax) && (pcv[v2].y1 > ymax)) {

    // Edge is leaving viewport
                    temp=(int)(pcv[v2].x1-pcv[v1].x1);
                    if (temp!=0) {
                    float m=(float)(pcv[v2].y1-pcv[v1].y1)/(float)temp;
                         pcv[cp].x =
                              pcv[v1].x1 + (ymax - pcv[v1].y1) / m;
                    }
                    else pcv[cp].x = pcv[v1].x1;
                    pcv[cp++].y = ymax;
          }
          if ((pcv[v1].y1 > ymax) && (pcv[v2].y1 <= ymax)) {
    // Edge is entering viewport

                    temp=(int)(pcv[v2].x1-pcv[v1].x1);
                    if (temp!=0) {
                         float m=(float)(pcv[v2].y1-pcv[v1].y1)/(float)temp;
                         pcv[cp].x =
                              pcv[v1].x1 + (ymax - pcv[v1].y1) / m;
                    }
                    else pcv[cp].x = pcv[v1].x1;
                    pcv[cp++].y = ymax;
                    pcv[cp].x = pcv[v2].x1;
                    pcv[cp++].y = pcv[v2].y1;
          }
          v1=v2;
     }
     clip_array.SetVertexCount(cp);
}
```

Now that the clipping functions have been introduced, we can show you the DrawPolygonList() function, which is in Listing 11-3. There is one parameter and that is the pointer to the buffer where the polygons will be drawn. Recall that the variables polygon_list and clip_array are private members of the View class.

 Listing 11-3 The DrawPolygonList() function

```
void View::DrawPolygonList(unsigned char far *screen)
// Draw all polygons in polygon list to screen buffer
{
    // Loop through polygon list:

    for (int i=0; i<polygon_list.GetPolygonCount(); i++) {
```

continued on next page

continued from previous page

```
                // Clip against front of view volume:

                ZClip(polygon_list.GetPolygonPtr(i),&clip_array,2);

                // Check to make sure polygon wasn't clipped out of
                //  existence

                if (clip_array.GetVertexCount()>0) {

                        // Perform perspective projection:

                        clip_array.Project(distance, xorigin, yorigin);

                        // Clip against sides of viewport:

                        XYClip(&clip_array);

                        // Check to make sure polygon wasn't clipped out of
                        //  existence:

                        if (clip_array.GetVertexCount()>0)
                                // Draw polygon:
                                clip_array.DrawPoly(screen);
                }
        }
}
```

The DrawPolygonList() function calls a series of functions for each polygon in the list. Since the polygons themselves are clipped and stored into the clip_array, the old Project() and DrawPoly() functions cannot be used. The old drawing functions worked with vertex_type stuctures and we need to work with clip_type structures. At the end of the last chapter, I said we would create a draw function for the PolygonList class. I lied. The old functions worked with vertex_type stuctures and we need to work with clip_type structures. As you can see from the commented line listing above, however, the polygon list is mapped to an array of clipped polygons. It is the clip_array that will be responsible for drawing the polygon to the screen.

The ClippedPolygon::Project() function in Listing 11-4 looks almost identical to the object_type::Project() implementation in Chapter 8. A caveat of the ZClip() function is that the z coordinate of the vertex has been correctly determined, so it does not have to be subtracted from the distance when dividing the x and y coordinates.

Listing 11-4 The Project() function

```
void ClippedPolygon::Project(int distance, int xorigin, int yorigin)
{

        // Project clipped polygon onto screen using perspective projection
clip_type *vptr= vertex;
```

```
        float dd = distance;              // convert to float for precision

        for (int v=0; v< number_of_vertices; v++,vptr++) {
            // Loop through vertices
                float z=(float)(ABS(vptr->z));
                vptr->x=dd*((float)vptr->x/z) +xorigin;  // ...divide world
                                                          //    x&y coords
                vptr->y=dd*((float)vptr->y/z) +yorigin;  // ...by z coordinates
        }
}
```

Similarly, the ClippedPolygon::DrawPoly() function is the same as the polygon_type::DrawPoly() function except the vertex array pointer is a clip_type pointer rather than a vertex_type pointer. This function does not appear in a listing because of its duplicity.

We now have all the tools we need to put together a complete viewing package, which will allow us to roam about at will through a world filled with imaginary objects. In Chapter 13, we'll do just that, as we introduce the view system. But first, let's shed some light on light and how we can make our world objects even more realistic.

...

CHAPTER

12

. . . . .

12

Advanced Polygon Shading

Up to this point, we have not considered the effect of light on the objects that we draw. In the real world, the appearance of a surface depends not only on its color, but also on the way light shines on it. A great artist knows how to highlight objects in a painting so that they appear to be realistically lit. By simulating the effects of light in our programs, we can make the computer produce this effect automatically, so we don't need to become master artists.

To add realistic lighting effects to our flight simulator, we need a basic understanding of the physics of light and a way to translate that understanding into practical code. This code will simulate a model that we derive for handling light. A model is just a set of rules that describes how we want lighting to work in our software. Lighting models can be very simple, if we want fast-running code that is easy to write, or very complex, if we want the most realistic possible effects.

Light is a complicated and sometimes subtle phenomenon with many effects which are difficult to simulate on a computer. Computer graphics researchers have come up with so many ways to reproduce the effects of light that a whole series of books could be written on the subject. Fortunately for us, we can produce compelling lighting effects and substantially improve the game-playing experience by applying a few of the simpler techniques. In other words, we will derive a simple but effective lighting model.

Color and Illumination

Before we jump into programming our lighting effects, we'll cover some of the physics of light. In particular, we will be looking for ways to simplify our lighting model while sacrificing as little realism as we can. First, we'll examine the issue of color.

The Visible Spectrum and Color Space

The eye responds to any light that falls within the part of the spectrum that extends from red at the low end to violet at the high end. In theory, for a computer screen to accurately reproduce the colors we see in a real scene, it must reproduce light at every frequency produced by the scene. Unfortunately, it's impractical to build displays that can do this.

VGA displays, and most other computer displays, make do with three colors which are widely spaced in the spectrum. These colors are red, green, and blue, collectively referred to as RGB. With enough control over the intensities of each of these three primary colors, we can approximate most colors we see in the real world. As we saw in Chapter 3, VGA hardware allows us a choice of 64 intensity levels for each primary color. This gives us 262,144 colors to choose from.

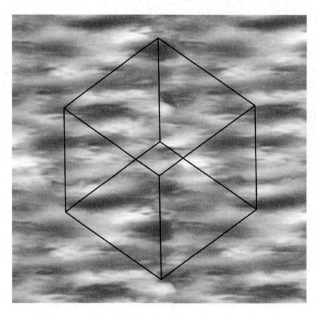

Figure 12-1 VGA color space

The three dimensions of VGA color can be thought of as a three-dimensional color space. Figure 12-1 depicts such a color space. The corner (0,0,0) is black while the diametrically opposed corner (63,63,63) is white. The other corners represent the three primaries, red (63,0,0), green (0,63,0), and blue (0,0,63), and the three secondaries, yellow (63,63,0), cyan (0,63,63), and magenta (63,0,63). (Anyone who has taken a basic art class will be thinking that this is a mistake since they learned that the primary crayon colors are red, yellow, and blue and the secondary colors are orange, green, and purple. Unfortunately, the properties of color pigments are different from that of light, and hence they have different primary and secondary colors.)

For any color in the space, moving in a straight line toward black (0,0,0) darkens the color. Moving in a straight line away from black lightens it. We will use this principle when we lighten and darken polygons based on how much they are illuminated. For example, if a magenta (63,0,63) surface is only half illuminated, its color values become (31,0,31). The point in the color space has moved halfway to black (0,0,0).

Light Sources: Lightbulbs versus the Sun

In order to model lighting accurately, we need to understand light sources. Light sources can come in any brightness, color, shape, and size and can be located just about anywhere. All these properties of a light source affect the way objects appear to the viewer. In addition, a scene might contain many light sources. Allowing for all the possibilities this represents is both impractical and unnecessary for our flight simulator.

First of all, we can simplify our light sourcing by deciding that there will be only one light source: the sun. In addition, we will assume that the sun's light is white. As we will discover later, the brightness of the light source will not really be an issue because of the limitations of the VGA hardware. We will decide on RGB values for colors when they are fully illuminated, and darker shades of those colors will be generated to represent the same colors under partial illumination.

This leaves the questions of size, shape, and location to consider. Because our light source is the sun, it seems that the answers should be "huge," "round," and "very far away." As it turns out, we'll get the effect we want and the code will be much simpler if we answer these questions with "infinitely small," "no shape at all," and "infinitely far away."

A light source, such as a bare lightbulb, sends rays of light in all directions. If the light from the lightbulb is shining on a flat surface, the rays of light strike different locations on the surface at different angles. This is because the rays radiate outward and are not parallel to each other. In addition, less light falls on objects far away from the bulb than on objects that are close to it.

Because the sun is so far away, its rays are nearly parallel. When sunlight strikes a flat surface, the rays all strike the surface at almost exactly the same angle. Also, objects closer to the sun are lit no more brightly than objects farther away. This kind of light

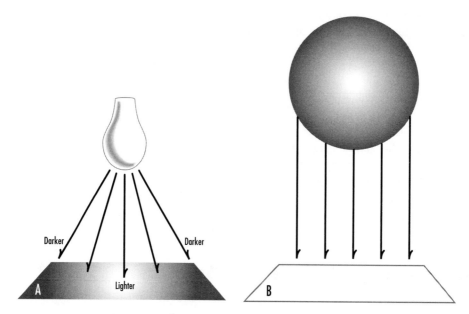

Figure 12-2 Lightbulb illumination versus solar illumination
(a) Light rays from a bulb   **(b)** Light rays from the sun

source is a lot easier to handle on a computer because we only have to calculate a level of illumination for all the pixels of a polygon. If we were trying to simulate a lightbulb, we would have to perform illumination calculations for each pixel in each polygon. In our model, every pixel in a given polygon will have the same brightness. Figure 12-2 illustrates the difference between the lightbulb model and the sun model. The bulb in Figure 12-2(a) shows rays of lights emanating outward from the bulb and striking a flat surface at different angles. The surface tends to be darker towards the sides, which are further away from the bulb and have more of an angle between the ray and the surface. The sun however, in Figure 12-2(b), lights the surface with the same angle and produces a consistent lighting across the entire surface.

When we decide that the rays of light from our light source will all be parallel, we don't need to consider the location of the light source. We only need to consider the *direction* the light is traveling. This reduces the description of the light source to a single vector, and will make our lighting code simpler. But have we made our lighting model too simple?

One thing we have left out of our lighting model is ambient light. When the sun casts shadows in a real scene, the objects in the shadows are still illuminated to some degree. This is because shadows are indirectly lit by light reflecting off of objects that are in the sunlight. To accurately simulate ambient light, we would have to simulate all the reflections that illuminate a particular point. Fortunately, it is just as effective to assume that ambient light illuminates all shaded surfaces at some fixed intensity. This intensity can be adjusted to suit our tastes.

In our code, implementing ambient light simply requires that we define a minimum brightness level for all polygons. A high minimum brightness gives us a lot of ambient light and a subtle shading effect. A low minimum brightness gives us just a little ambient light with profound contrast between light and dark surfaces.

Diffuse and Specular Reflection

Now we need to consider the effects of a light source on the appearance of a surface. Depending on the surface, any number of interesting interactions can occur. A great deal of money is spent developing materials which react to light in interesting ways. Metallic automobile paint, for example, uses flecks of mica suspended in a semi-transparent coating to produce a glittering effect.

Computer graphics researchers have categorized the effects of light by establishing reflection models. Each reflection model defines a specific reflection effect so that it can be simulated by software. By combining reflection models, a wide variety of reflection effects can be reproduced.

The two reflection models most commonly used are the diffuse-reflection model and the specular-reflection model. Diffuse reflection refers to the reflection of matte surfaces which reflect light in all directions. A matte surface refers to an exterior which is rough or granular—something not entirely smooth. Specular reflection refers to the reflection of shiny surfaces which reflect light much as a mirror does. Anyone who has taken photos to be developed is familiar with these two models since they can choose matte or shiny finishes for their snapshots.

Diffuse reflection is relatively easy to reproduce because its effects do not depend on the position of the observer. As long as the lighting remains consistent, a matte surface appears to be illuminated the same amount regardless of the angle from which you see it. The illumination is affected by the angle at which light strikes the surface. When this angle is perpendicular, the illumination will be strongest, as we saw with the lightbulb.

Specular reflection is more difficult to reproduce in software because the position of the light source, the angle of the surface, and the position of the observer all must be taken into account. For the purposes of our programming, this means that major recalculation would have to occur every time the observer moves—and airplanes tend to move around a lot.

In flight, specular reflection only makes itself known to a pilot when the sunlight reflects off the surface of the water. The diffuse-reflection model reasonably accounts for all other illumination effects the pilot sees. Impressive lighting effects can be achieved without losing much realism if we implement only diffuse reflection and ignore specular reflection.

Keeping It Simple

Now we have a complete lighting model. We will be implementing two kinds of lighting: ambient light and diffuse reflection. The ambient light will take the form of a minimum brightness level that will apply to all surfaces. The illumination of a surface due to diffuse reflection will be determined by the angle between the surface and an incident vector which tells us the direction in which light is moving from our light source, the sun. For a review of vectors, see Chapter 2.

With this model in mind, we can proceed to implement our lighting scheme.

Shedding Light on Polygons

Given what we know about lighting, let's put together a program which displays a three-dimensional object with lighting effects. This program will be based on the polygon-fill demo of Chapter 8, but using our new classes from the last chapter. We will produce the same rotating pyramid, this time with the appearance of being illuminated from one direction.

A Light Source for Our World

The first thing we need to add to our program is the light source. Because the light will be coming from infinitely far away, we only need to indicate the direction of the light.

The intensity of the light source is not an issue for this program. For simplicity, we will assume that the intensity is set so that fully illuminated surfaces have the RGB values associated with their assigned colors and that partially illuminated surfaces have the same RGB values reduced accordingly. This allows us to think of brightness in terms of a percentage, 100 percent being the full RGB value, and lower percentages being proportionately reduced RGB values.

A C++ structure called source_type defines the light source for our program. In addition, it defines an ambient-light level. All surfaces in our scene will be lit to a minimum intensity of the ambient level; no surface will be lit less. This ambient-light level is given as a percentage. An ambient-light level of zero will give the effect of deep shadows such as you get when shining a flashlight in pitch dark. An ambient-light level of 100 will light everything evenly, effectively turning off our lighting effects.

```
struct source_type { // Structure for light source
   long x,y,z;        // Incident vector
   long length;       // Length of incident vector
   int  ambient;      // Amount of ambient light
};
```

The length field in the structure is the length of the light source's incident vector. This value is used frequently and never changes, so it makes sense to calculate it once and store it in the light-source structure. The length is based strictly on source_type's *x, y,* and *z* fields, so it will be easy to calculate once the incident vector is established. Note source_type is used mainly to group the fields related to light. Our light source will not change as does the sun which moves across the sky. We choose to represent a light source as a struct instead of a class, because it is primarily a block of data.

Since we will use the same light source to light all the polygons in our world, it makes sense to make a source_type field within our World class. Oddly enough, this is named source. We will read the light-source information from the same data file that defines the objects (polygons and vertices) in our world. The function world_type::loadpoly(), introduced in Chapter 8, reads this file. We will upgrade this function to include reading in the source information. The easiest way to do this is by inserting a function call to load the source structure. That function is called Load-Source() and the function head follows

```
int World::LoadSource()
{
```

Only four numbers are required to define the light source. To read them from the data file, the following lines must be added somewhere in the loading procedure:

```
source.x=_pf.getnumber();
source.y=_pf.getnumber();
source.z=_pf.getnumber();
source.ambient=_pf.getnumber();
```

To refresh our memories, LOADPOLY.CPP contains a static local object, _pf. This object has a function getnumber() which returns the next integer in the file stream. All that remains to provide complete light-source information is the calculation of the structure's length field. This is done by following line which is done immediately after loading the source numbers:

```
source.length=(long)sqrt((float)source.x*source.x+(float)source.y*source.y+
(float)source.z*source.z);
}
```

This is a simple distance formula, the square root of the sum of the squares. Our completed function appears in Listing 12-1.

Listing 12-1 The World:LoadSource() function

```
int World::LoadSource()
{
    source.x=_pf.getnumber();
    source.y=_pf.getnumber();
    source.z=_pf.getnumber();
    source.ambient=_pf.getnumber();
```

continued on next page

continued from previous page

```
source.length=(long)sqrt((float)source.x*source.x+(float)source.y*source.y+
(float)source.z*source.z);
  return 0;
}
```

A Graduated Palette

One problem posed by shading our polygons is the number of different colors required. The VGA hardware doesn't allow us to set the brightness of each pixel individually, and the number of possible shades is limited. Out of the 262,144 colors in the color space, we can display only 256 colors at any one time. This means that we need some way to fit as many of the shades we need as possible into the palette. Rather than figure out how to do this by hand, we can have the computer do it for us. This section presents the structures and functions required to manage the palette. In doing so we will create a Palette class.

The first structure we must define is rgb_type. This structure will contain the red, blue, and green constituents of one of the 256 entries in the palette.

```
struct rgb_type {          // Structure for RGB color definition
  unsigned char red;       // Red intensity (0 to 63)
  unsigned char green;     // Green intensity (0 to 63)
  unsigned char blue;      // Blue intensity (0 to 63)
};
```

Next we define a class Palette which contains the information we will need to generate the VGA palette and use it in color shading. The class contains two lists, one for unshaded colors and one for shaded colors. The unshaded colors will be used for things that don't need lighting effects, like the instrument panel in the cockpit and any text we might want to display on the screen. We will use the shaded colors to render the world outside the cockpit windows.

In addition to the two lists of colors, the structure includes a field which indicates the number of shades that are available for each shaded color. After palette entries are assigned to unshaded colors, the rest of the entries are evenly divided between the shaded colors. The number_of_shades field lets us know how many shades we could fit into the palette.

As an example, consider a situation in which we have eight unshaded colors and six shaded colors. The unshaded colors use up eight palette entries leaving 248 for the unshaded colors. The 248 remaining entries must be divided up evenly between the six shaded colors, allowing us 41 shades for each shaded color. This uses up all but two of the palette entries.

All of the functions in the Palette class are public for external access, several of which are defined inline to return the array counts and pointers to their elements. A constructor and destructor, plus Load(), Install(), and ColorIndex() functions round out the class definition:

```
class Palette {
private:
  int number_of_unshaded_colors; // Number of colors with no brightness
  rgb_type *unshaded_color;          // List of unshaded colors
  int number_of_shaded_colors;   // Number of colors with brightness
  rgb_type *shaded_color;         // List of shaded colors
  int number_of_shades;           // Number of brightness levels
public:
            // constructor
    Palette():unshaded_color(0), shaded_color(0){;}
            // destructor
    ~Palette();

    int Load();
            // adjust for ambient light:
    void Install(float ambient);
            // retrieve information:
    int GetUnshadedCount()
            { return number_of_unshaded_colors; }
    rgb_type *GetUnshadedPtr(int i)
            { return &unshaded_color[i]; }
    int GetShadedCount()
            { return number_of_shaded_colors; }
    rgb_type *GetShadedPtr(int i)
            { return &shaded_color[i]; }
            // compute the index into shaded colors:
    int ColorIndex(int color,int level,int ambient);
};;
```

The constructor assigns a zero to both of the rgb_type arrays. The purpose is to guarantee deletion of the arrays when the destructor is called. This methodology should look somewhat familiar:

```
Palette::~Palette()
{
    if(unshaded_color)
            delete [] unshaded_color;
    if(shaded_color)
            delete [] shaded_color;
}
```

We will read the palette information from the data file. Both lists of colors must be specified, but the number of shades can be determined by the program after the data is loaded. Loading the colors requires an additional function to the LOADPOLY.CPP file, which is shown in Listing 12-2.

Listing 12-2 The Palette:Load() function

```
int Palette::Load()
{
  number_of_unshaded_colors=_pf.getnumber();
```

continued on next page

continued from previous page

```
    unshaded_color=(rgb_type *)new rgb_type[number_of_unshaded_colors];
    if(! unshaded_color)
        return -1;
    for (int colornum=0; colornum<number_of_unshaded_colors; colornum++) {
        unshaded_color[colornum].red  =_pf.getnumber();
        unshaded_color[colornum].green=_pf.getnumber();
        unshaded_color[colornum].blue =_pf.getnumber();
    }
    number_of_shaded_colors=_pf.getnumber();
    shaded_color=(rgb_type *) new rgb_type[number_of_shaded_colors];
    if(!shaded_color)
        return -1;
    for (colornum=0; colornum<number_of_shaded_colors; colornum++) {
        shaded_color[colornum].red  =_pf.getnumber();
        shaded_color[colornum].green=_pf.getnumber();
        shaded_color[colornum].blue =_pf.getnumber();
    }
    return 0;
}
```

The number of unshaded colors is read in from the file and this number is used by the new operator to allocate the unshaded_color array. The array can then be read in from the file. Similarly, the shaded-color count is read and the shaded_color array is allocated. The individual RGB values are then read into this array.

We are using one Palette object in the flight simulator, which is made a member of the World class. The world is called to load a descriptor file, and it makes the call to source and palette immediately after opening the file. This therefore effects the schema of our object file. Previously, the first number was the number of objects in the file. Data for that number of objects then followed. LoadPoly(), our world reader, will now expect other numbers before we can read in the object count. So our older TXT file descriptors will never work properly. These files with lighting information end in WLD, so they are distinguished from the simpler files.

The complete code for LoadPoly() can be seen in Listing 12-3.

Listing 12-3 The World:LoadPoly() function

```
int World::LoadPoly(const char *filename)
{
    if( _pf.Open(filename) ) // if a mistake in opening file, exit function
        return(-1);

    LoadSource();
    palette.Load();

    // Initialize polygon count:
    polycount = 0;

        // world members:
```

```
number_of_objects = _pf.getnumber();
obj= new Object[number_of_objects];
if( ! obj )
     return(-1);
for (int objnum=0; objnum< number_of_objects; objnum++) {
     if( obj[objnum].Load() )
          return( -1 );
}
return(polycount);
}
```

Installing the Palette

The palette defined in the data file must be installed by our program into the VGA hardware. This is the job of the function Install() in the Palette class. This function assigns palette entries to the shaded and unshaded colors, builds a table containing all the entries in the palette, and programs the VGA hardware using the setpalette() function described in Chapter 3. The ambient-light level is used to determine the dimmest shades that will be required for each shaded color. Because no polygon will every be illuminated with less light than is provided by ambient lighting, we don't need to waste palette entries on dimmer shades—in other words, all polygons will be as bright as the ambient level.

With the palette, the unshaded colors occupy the lowest-numbered entries and their index into the palette starts at zero. The shaded colors are numbered starting at the next available position. When a shaded color is required, it will be specified by this color number and a brightness percentage.

We start off by subtracting the number_of_unshaded_colors from our total of VGA color slots available. The remaining number is divided by the number_of_shaded_colors to yield the number_of_shades. This is the degree of gradation for a single hue, sometimes referred to as the color tone.

```
number_of_shades=(256-number_of_unshaded_colors)/number_of_shaded_colors;
```

The lower elements of our palette are copied directly from the unshaded color array.

For the shaded colors, we set up an index into the palette and proceed through a loop which copies our complete shaded color array in progressive degrees of brightness:

```
int index=number_of_unshaded_colors;
for (int shade=0; shade<number_of_shades; shade++) {
     float brightness=(shade*(1-ambient))/(number_of_shades-1)+ambient;
     for (int color=0; color<number_of_shaded_colors; color++) {
```

The shading calculations work by calculating the brightness for each shade and then multiplying the red, green, and blue components of each shaded color by that brightness. This is only done once when the program starts, so it has no impact on the flying performance of the program. The brightness values are adjusted so that the lowest value generated corresponds to the ambient light level and the highest value is one, meaning 100 percent. The complete function follows in Listing 12-4.

Listing 12-4 The Palette::Install() function

```
void Palette::Install(float ambient)
{
  rgb_type allcolors[256];
  // Record the number of shades and convert ambient from percentage
  number_of_shades=(256-number_of_unshaded_colors)/number_of_shaded_colors;
  ambient=ambient/100;

  // Copy unshaded colors to the palette array

memcpy(&allcolors[0],unshaded_color,number_of_unshaded_colors*sizeof(rgb_type));

      // start filling in the palette at the first available entry:
  int index=number_of_unshaded_colors;
  for (int shade=0; shade<number_of_shades; shade++) {
      float brightness=(shade*(1-ambient))/(number_of_shades-1)+ambient;
      for (int color=0; color<number_of_shaded_colors; color++) {
          allcolors[index].red=(unsigned char)
                  (shaded_color[color].red*brightness);
          allcolors[index].green=(unsigned char)
                  (shaded_color[color].green*brightness);
          allcolors[index++].blue=(unsigned char)
                  (shaded_color[color].blue*brightness);
          }
  }
  setpalette((char far *)allcolors);
}
```

All that remains to be done to make our graduated palette work is to create a function which accepts a color number and a brightness level and returns the number of the palette entry which contains the appropriate shade. When we are shading polygons, we will know the original color of the polygon (our input file tells us this), and we will know what brightness level we want based on our lighting calculations. This is the meaning of the two color fields within the polyBase class. The original_color always contains the color read in from the file, while the color field contains the adjusted lighting value. The function Palette::ColorIndex() will tell us which palette entry to use for a particular original color and a particular brightness. Take a look at Listing 12-5 for the complete function.

Listing 12-5 The Palette::ColorIndex() function

```
int Palette::ColorIndex(int color,int level,int ambient)
{
  if (level>100)  // Level should not exceed 100%
```

```
        level=100;
   else if (level<ambient) // Level should not be lower than ambient
        level=ambient;
   int shade=((level-ambient)*(number_of_shades-1))/(100-ambient);
   return color+shade*number_of_shaded_colors;
}
```

The ColorIndex() function takes three parameters. The first is color, which specifies the base hue of the palette. The second and third parameters, level and ambient, determine the shading of that color. ColorIndex() accepts the brightness level as a percentage. A level of 100 percent indicates that the color should have the RGB values originally specified in the data file. A lower percentage indicates that the returned color should have RGB values which are in that ratio to the original values. The function limits the level to a range from ambient level to 100 percent.

What's Normal?

Now that we have established the light source and the palette, we can put together the code that determines how polygons are to be shaded. In principle, the calculation of the illumination level for a polygon is simple. The illumination level of a polygon that is facing the light source is proportional to the cosine of the angle between the incoming light and a vector which is normal to the plane of the polygon, as shown in Figure 12-3. A normal vector is one which is perpendicular to the plane.

The light source structure we defined earlier provides us with a direction vector for the light source. What we need is a way to generate a normal vector for our polygon and a way to find the cosine of the angle between the two vectors. As it turns out, finding the cosine is the easy part. By taking the dot product of two vectors and dividing it

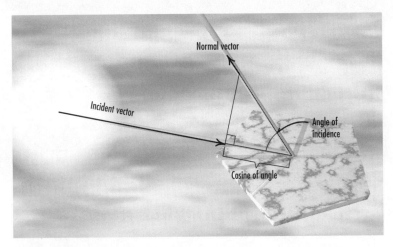

Figure 12-3 Polygon illumination

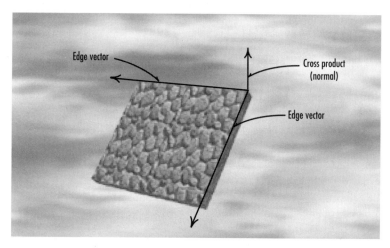

Figure 12-4 Generating a normal vector

by their lengths, we get the cosine without having to use the time-consuming cos() function. The dot product involves three multiplications and two additions, so it is very fast. The lengths are another matter. Finding the length of a vector requires the use of the C run-time library function sqrt(), which is very slow. Fortunately, we can calculate all the lengths once as part of the program initialization and store this value as part of our polygon object.

Once we decide on the position of the sun, the light-source incident vector will never change in our program, so we calculate its length and store it in the light-source structure as discussed above. On the other hand, the polygons that make up our objects may be rotating as the program runs, and if so, their normal vectors will change. But rotating a polygon only changes the direction of the normal vector, not its length. This means that we can calculate the lengths of the polygon normals once and use the same values over and over again as the polygons rotate.

All that remains is to create a normal vector for each polygon. This is done by creating two vectors corresponding to two edges of the polygon and taking their cross product. The cross product of two vectors is always perpendicular to both vectors, so the cross product of two edge vectors of a polygon will be perpendicular to the polygon, as shown in Figure 12-4.

The edge vectors are generated by subtracting vertices from each other as follows

```
long ax=v0->lx-v1->lx;   // Vector for edge from vertex 1 to vertex 0
long ay=v0->ly-v1->ly;
long az=v0->lz-v1->lz;
long bx=v2->lx-v1->lx;   // Vector for edge from vertex 1 to vertex 2
long by=v2->ly-v1->ly;
long bz=v2->lz-v1->lz;
```

The cross product is a matrix operation on the two vectors which looks like this:

```
float nx=ay*bz-az*by;     // Normal is cross product of the two vectors
float ny=az*bx-ax*bz;
float nz=ax*by-ay*bx;
```

Now we are ready to write the functions that do the work.

The Shading Functions

The world draws the objects and the objects tell the polygons to draw themselves. Somewhere after the world coordinates have been adjusted as a transformation, and before the call to DrawPoly() where the polygon's color value is written to the screen buffer, the polygon's color value needs to be changed to an appropriate color brightness. This degree of brightness is dependent on the lighting source definition. The functions which will adjust the color's tone are called the shading functions, since they translate a color and brightness to a particular shade within the palette.

We skipped explanations of some of the fields in the polyBase class in Chapter 11. We now have enough background to explain some of the fields required to support light shading. First of all, we need a field in which to store the length of the normal. Also, because we are going to be changing the color (shade) of the polygon, the program must remember the original color as specified in the data file.

```
class polyBase {
protected:
        int     number_of_vertices; // Number of vertices in polygon
        int     original_color;      // Color of polygon
        int     color;               // Drawing color of polygon (after
                                     // light applied)
        long    nlength;             // normal length (for lighting)
```

The new field nlength stores the length of the normal. The field original_color stores the original color. The Object::Load() function must be changed to put the defined color into original_color instead of color:

```
polyptr->original_color=_pf.getnumber();
```

The function Object::MeasureNormals() generates the normal length for each polygon and puts it in the nlength field. This function only needs to be called once when the program starts up. The complete text for the MeasureNormals() function is in Listing 12-6.

Listing 12-6 The MeasureNormals() function

```
void Object::MeasureNormals(int numshades)
{
        // Calculate length of normal for each shaded polygon in WORLD:
```

continued on next page

continued from previous page

```
for (int p=0; p< GetPolygonCount(); p++) {
    Polygon *pptr= &polygon[p];
    if (pptr->original_color>=numshades) {
        vertex_type *v0=pptr->vertex[0];
        vertex_type *v1=pptr->vertex[1];
        vertex_type *v2=pptr->vertex[2];
        long ax=v0->lx-v1->lx;   // Vector for edge from vertex 1
                                 // to vertex 0
        long ay=v0->ly-v1->ly;
        long az=v0->lz-v1->lz;
        long bx=v2->lx-v1->lx;   // Vector for edge from vertex 1
                                 // to vertex 2
        long by=v2->ly-v1->ly;
        long bz=v2->lz-v1->lz;
        float nx=ay*bz-az*by;    // Normal is cross product of the
                                 // two vectors
        float ny=az*bx-ax*bz;
        float nz=ax*by-ay*bx;
        pptr->nlength=(long)sqrt(nx*nx+ny*ny+nz*nz);
    }
}
}
```

The normal is generated from the local coordinates of the vertices (*lx, ly,* and *lz*) because these are the coordinates read in from the file. When MeasureNormals() is called, we haven't performed any transformations on the polygons. This is acceptable unless we intend to scale the polygons. The sole parameter, *numshades,* is only used to determine if the normal length needs to be computed—if the polygon's color has been defined as an unshaded color, there is no need to compute the normal length. Since the function is called once after the object descriptor file is read, you could leave this test out with no impact on the program's flying speed. On the other hand, we might want to change a future program to load objects while flying. In this case, the stitch in time by skipping needless calculations for unshaded polygons could be worthwhile.

The function World::CalcColors() determines the appropriate shade for each polygon in every object. The entire function consists of a loop which calls CalcObjectColor() for all of the objects in the world.

```
void World::CalcColors()
{
    // Calculate the palette index for each polygon in WORLD:

    for (int o=0; o< number_of_objects; o++) {
        CalcObjectColor(&obj[o]);
    }
}
```

CalcObjectColor() is another simple looping function. This time the loop calls CalcPolygonPtr() for each of the polygons within the Object. You may be thinking that this is a lot of stack overhead to call these functions, and we could optimize these calls by putting everything in the same function. That is true, except we need a function to calculate an entire object's color for our lighting demonstration, while in the flight simulator, we will need a function which will calculate a polygon's colors (after we have made a PolygonList as in Chapter 10).

```
void World::CalcObjectColor(Object *object)
{
  for (int p=0; p< object->GetPolygonCount(); p++) {
      CalcPolygonPtr(object->GetPolygonPtr(p));
    }
}
```

CalcPolygonPtr() is the workhorse function. It performs the same normal vector calculation as MeasureNormals(), but uses the world coordinates of the vertices (*wx*, *wy*, and *wz*) to get the normals of the transformed polygons.

```
long ax=v0->wx-v1->wx;    // Vector for edge from vertex 1 to vertex 0
long ay=v0->wy-v1->wy;
long az=v0->wz-v1->wz;
long bx=v2->wx-v1->wx;    // Vector for edge from vertex 1 to vertex 2
long by=v2->wy-v1->wy;
long bz=v2->wz-v1->wz;
long nx=ay*bz-az*by;      // Normal is cross product of the two vectors
long ny=az*bx-ax*bz;
long nz=ax*by-ay*bx;
```

Unlike MeasureNormals(), the normal coordinates in CalcPolygonColor() are made type long since we will not be using the sqrt() function. We then find the brightness value by calculating the dot product of the normal vector with the light source vector and dividing by their lengths. The variable *ambient* has been dereferenced from the structure source for loop optimization.

```
int brightness=(int)(((nx*source.x+ny*source.y+nz*source.z)*(100-ambient)) /
            (source.length*pptr->GetNormalLen())));
```

Finally, ambient lighting is applied, and ColorIndex() is called to find the appropriate palette index. The resulting color value is placed in the color field of the polygon, where it will be used by DrawPoly() to draw the polygon.

```
if (brightness<0)
        brightness=ambient;    // Ambient applies to polygons not facing the
                               // source
else
        brightness+=ambient; // Add ambient for polygons facing the source
pptr->SetColor(palette.ColorIndex(temp,brightness,ambient));
```

There was a strong inclination to make this function part of the Polygon class rather than the World class since it mimics the MeasureNormals() function so closely. Several reasons why we don't do that are the Polygon and Object module would need to include the source_type structure. Our object characteristics have been designed to keep the intricacies of lighting out of the object and polygon classes. Our completed CalcPolygonColor() can be seen in Listing 12-7.

 ## Listing 12-7   The Shading functions

```cpp
void World::CalcPolygonColor(Polygon *polyptr)
{
  int ambient=source.ambient;
  int temp = polyptr->GetOriginalColor();

  if (temp < palette.GetUnshadedCount())
          polyptr->SetColor( temp);
  else {
          vertex_type *v0=polyptr->GetVerticePtr(0);
          vertex_type *v1=polyptr->GetVerticePtr(1);
          vertex_type *v2=polyptr->GetVerticePtr(2);
      long ax=v0->wx-v1->wx;  // Vector for edge from vertex 1 to vertex 0
      long ay=v0->wy-v1->wy;
      long az=v0->wz-v1->wz;
      long bx=v2->wx-v1->wx;  // Vector for edge from vertex 1 to vertex 2
          long by=v2->wy-v1->wy;
          long bz=v2->wz-v1->wz;
      long nx=ay*bz-az*by;    // Normal is cross product of the two vectors
      long ny=az*bx-ax*bz;
          long nz=ax*by-ay*bx;
          int brightness=(int)(((nx*source.x+ny*source.y+nz*source.z)*(100-
                              ambient))/
                  (source.length*polyptr->GetNormalLen()));
      if (brightness<0)
        brightness=ambient;  // Ambient applies to polygons not facing the
                             //  source
      else
        brightness+=ambient; // Add ambient for polygons facing the source
            polyptr->SetColor(palette.ColorIndex(temp,brightness,ambient));
  }
}
void World::CalcObjectColor(Object *object)
{
  // Calculate the palette index for each polygon in the OBJECT:
  for (int p=0; p< object->GetPolygonCount(); p++) {
      CalcPolygonPtr(object->GetPolygonPtr(p));
      }
}


void World::CalcColors()
{
  // Calculate the palette index for each object in the WORLD:

  for (int o=0; o< number_of_objects; o++) {
```

```
        CalcObjectColor(&obj[o]);
  }
}
```

With these software tools in place, we are ready to complete the demonstration program.

Completing the Lighting Demonstration Program

All that is required to complete the demonstration program is to add the light source and palette to the World class and call the appropriate functions in main(). The new World class looks like this:

```
class   World {
private:
        int             number_of_objects;
        Object *obj;
        source_type source;
        Palette palette;
                // Load light source:
        int LoadSource();
#ifdef LIGHTING_DEMO
        // Calculate lengths of normals for object
        void CalcObjectColor(Object *objptr);
        // Calculate length of normal for each shaded polygon in every object in
                        // WORLD:
        void CalcColors();
#endif
public:
        World():obj(0){;}
        ~World();
                // loadpoly return -1 on error or number of polys in world
        int LoadPoly(const char *filename);
        // adjust palette to lighting source
        void AdjustLighting();
        // for outside access:
        int GetObjectCount() const
                { return number_of_objects; }
        Object *GetObjectPtr(int objnum) const
                { return &obj[objnum]; }
        void CalcPolygonColor(Polygon *polyptr);
#ifdef LIGHTING_DEMO
        void Draw(int objnum, unsigned char far *screen,int xorigin, int yorigin);
        void Draw(unsigned char far *screen,int xorigin, int yorigin);
#endif
};
```

The new main() is almost unchanged from the polygon demo of Chapter 8. All that has been added are calls to our three initialization functions, InstallSource(), InstallPalette(), and MeasureNormals(), and a call to CalcColors() in the main loop after the transformations have been completed, as shown in Listing 12-8.

Listing 12-8 LIGHTDEM.CPP

```cpp
#include      <dos.h>
#include      <conio.h>
#include <iostream.h>
#include <stdlib.h>
#include "world.h"
#include "screen.h"

const int XORIGIN=(SCREEN_WIDTH/2);          // Origin of coordinate system X axis
const int YORIGIN=(SCREEN_HEIGHT/2);         // Origin of coordinate system Y axis

World world;

void main(int argc,char* argv[])
{
        int xangle=0,yangle=0,zangle=0;      // X,Y&Z angles for rotation
                                             //   object
        int xrot=2,yrot=2,zrot=0;            // X,Y&Z rotations increments
        unsigned char *screen_buffer;        // Offscreen drawing

        if (argc!=2) {                       // Read command-line arguments
                cerr << "Wrong number of arguments."<< endl;
                cerr << "LIGHTDEM object.txt" << endl;
                exit(-1);
        }
        if( world.LoadPoly(argv[1])< 1 )  {  // Load object description(s)
                cerr << "Failure loading object descriptor file into world." <<
                  endl;
                exit(-1);
        }

        screen_buffer=new unsigned char[64000L];   // Create offscreen buffer
        int oldmode=*(int *)MK_FP(0x40,0x49);      // Save previous video mode
        setgmode(0x13);                            // Set mode 13h
        world.AdjustLighting();                    // Adjust the palette by the
                                                   //   source

        int curobj =0;
         int scalefactor=1;
        int zdistance=600;
        int key = 0;
                        // Loop until escape key is pressed
        while (key != 27) {
                cls(screen_buffer);
                inittrans();                       // Initialize translations
                scale(scalefactor);                // Create scaling matrix
                rotate(xangle,yangle,zangle);      // Create rotation matrices

                // Increment rotation angles
                xangle+=xrot;
```

```
        yangle+=yrot;
        zangle+=zrot;
         // Check for 256 degree wrap around:
        if (xangle>255) xangle=0;
        if (xangle<0) xangle=255;
        if (yangle>255) yangle=0;
        if (yangle<0) yangle=255;
        if (zangle>255) zangle=0;
        if (zangle<0) zangle=255;

        translate(0,0,zdistance);              // Create translation matrix
         // Call the Draw world loop
        world.Draw(curobj,screen_buffer,XORIGIN,YORIGIN);
         // Put the viewport out to the video display:
        putwindow(0,0,SCREEN_WIDTH,SCREEN_HEIGHT,FP_OFF(screen_buffer),
                    FP_SEG(screen_buffer));
         // Watch for user input:

        if (kbhit()) {  // If input received....
                key=getch();  // Read the key code
                switch(key) {
                        case '\r':

          // ENTER: Go to next object

                                curobj++;
                                if (curobj>=world.GetObjectCount())
                                        curobj=0;
                                break;

                        case '7':

          // "7": Speed up x rotation

                                xrot++;
                                break;

                        case '4':

          // "4": Stop x rotation

                                xrot=0;
                                break;

                        case '1':

          // "1": Slow down x rotation

                                --xrot;
                                break;

                        case '8':
```

continued on next page

continued from previous page

```
                        // "8": Speed up y rotation

                                yrot++;
                                break;

                        case '5':

                // "5": Stop y rotation

                                yrot=0;
                                break;

                        case '2':

                // "2": Slow down y rotation

                                --yrot;
                                break;

                        case '9':

                // "9": Speed up z rotation

                                zrot++;
                                break;

                        case '6':

                // "6": Stop z rotation

                                zrot=0;
                                break;

                        case '3':

                // "3": Slow down z rotation

                                --zrot;
                                break;

                        case '0':

                // "0": Shut off all rotation

                                zrot = xrot = yrot = 0;
                                zangle = xangle = yangle = 0;
                                break;

                        case '+':

                // "+": Increase distance
```

```
                        zdistance+=30;
                        break;

                case '-':

            // "-": Decrease distance

                        if (zdistance>530) zdistance-=30;
                        break;
                }
            }
    }
        setgmode(oldmode);                  // Reset previous video mode & end
        if( screen_buffer)
                delete [] screen_buffer;
}
```

Like the optimized polygon demo, our new demo, LIGHTDEM.EXE is called with the name of a data file as its only parameter. The text file has to have the initial light-source and palette information. PYRAMID.WLD and ICOS.WLD are provided on the floppy disk. These files can be found in the LIGHTING directory.

Gouraud Shading

When a rendering system like ours uses only polygons, curved surfaces can only be approximated using a large number of polygons. For example, the file ICOS.WLD defines an icosahedron, a 20-sided solid that approximates a sphere. When lighting effects such as those in our previous demonstration program are applied to the icosahedron, its facets, or planes, are easily visible. To see this effect, try running LIGHTDEM using ICOS.WLD as the input file.

Gouraud (pronounced "ger-ROW") shading is a technique developed by H. Gouraud in the early 1970's to smooth the facets of a surface such as an icosahedron. It doesn't attempt to render the surface accurately, it just tries to smooth the transitions from one polygon to another. Gouraud shading is sometimes called intensity interpolation since it uses a ratio to interpolate a color's brightness and saturation.

More simply put, Gouraud shading adjusts pixel brightness based on the normals of the vertices rather than the normals of the polygons. Pixels between the vertices are illuminated in such a way that the brightness changes gradually from one vertex to another. The transitions from one polygon to another become less obvious so that if enough polygons are used in the surface, it will appear to be smooth. Gouraud shading is a trick, and it's only partly effective. The silhouette of a faceted surface rendered by Gouraud shading still shows the facets, and there must be many facets (polygons) to produce a convincingly smooth surface.

In order to conserve processing power, the scenes used in our flight simulator contain very few polygons, and no attempt is made to approximate smooth surfaces. For this reason and because Gouraud shading slows things down, we will not be using it in the flight simulator. But we will create a demonstration program which uses Gouraud shading in order to explore the technique. Since this demonstration program departs from the progress in building our flight-simulator classes, any file with changes for Gouraud lighting effects will be renamed. Thus, the World class file, WORLD.CPP, is renamed to WORLD_G.CPP for the Gouraud demo program. All of these files can be found in the GOURAUD directory.

Bresenham Revealed

Most of the changes required to get the lighting demonstration program to do Gouraud shading are in the DrawPoly() function. Unfortunately, in its current condition, Draw-Poly() is very complicated and therefore difficult to change. A good first step toward Gouraud shading is to simplify this function.

The DrawPoly() function is based on Bresenham's line-drawing algorithm presented in Chapter 6. A polygon is drawn by drawing the lines that make up its edges and filling in the pixels in between. Basically, DrawPoly() consists of two Bresenham line-drawing functions which operate simultaneously and a little code to fill in the pixels in between.

Bresenham's algorithm provides the advantage of drawing a line without the use of floating-point numbers. In Chapter 6, we weren't all that interested in how it accomplishes this. But to simplify polygon drawing, we need to understand the principle behind the algorithm so we can use the principle directly and leave the line drawing behind. After all, drawing lines is not what DrawPoly() really needs to do.

The first step in Bresenham's algorithm is to determine whether the line will be moving more rapidly in the horizontal direction or the vertical direction. If a line changes more rapidly in the horizontal direction for example, we can step from one endpoint to the other by incrementing the x coordinate each time through the loop and changing the y coordinate as required. The y coordinate will have to be changed a maximum of 1 pixel per iteration.

But how do we determine when the y coordinate must change? This is the job of the mysterious variable *error_term*. *error_term* is manipulated using two other values: *xdiff*, the difference between the x coordinates of the endpoints, and *ydiff*, the difference between the y coordinates of the endpoints. In the example of a line that is more horizontal than vertical, we add *ydiff* to *error_term* each time through the loop. When we notice *error_term* is equal to or greater than *xdiff*, we know it's time to change our y coordinate and subtract *xdiff* from *error_term*. Why does this work?

It works because *error_term* is actually the numerator, or top part, of a fraction, and the denominator, or bottom part, of that fraction is *xdiff*. In fact, *error_term* and *xdiff* are part of a mixed fraction in which the integer part is the *y* coordinate of the pixel we are drawing. In the code presented in Chapter 6, the *y* coordinate is hidden inside of *offset*, which contains both the *x* and *y* coordinates in the form of a pointer into the screen memory.

So Bresenham's algorithm avoids using floating point numbers by using a mixed fraction instead. We add *ydiff* to *error_term* each time through the loop because we want to add *ydiff/xdiff* to the mixed fraction. We check to see whether *error_term* is equal to or greater than *xdiff* because that tells us whether we can move a value of 1 (*xdiff/xdiff*) from the fractional part of the mixed fraction to the integer part. Understanding this allows us to apply the same technique to polygon drawing without using all of Bresenham's algorithm.

Bresenham's algorithm for lines determines the slope of the line it is drawing so that the increment applied to the mixed fraction is never greater than 1. In this way, only the numerator is incremented, and the integer part is only incremented if the fraction overflows (i.e., the numerator becomes larger than the denominator.) This is important in line drawing in order to avoid gaps in the line. Any increment greater than 1 would produce a discontinuous line.

When we draw a polygon, we always proceed from top to bottom regardless of the slopes of the edges. The outer loop iterates through the *y* coordinates starting at the top of the polygon and ending at the bottom. The inner loop iterates through the *x* coordinates from left to right. Our mixed fractions will be used to determine the starting and ending points of the inner loop. The starting and ending points for the *x* coordinates may change by more than 1 pixel, and that's okay. The entire row of pixels is filled in from left to right, so there are no gaps.

In order to be able to increment the starting and ending points by more than one, we must increment both the numerators and the integer parts of the mixed fractions. As before, we must check the fractions for overflow and increment the integers accordingly.

In the DrawPoly() function below, some additional variables have been added to handle the mixed fractions. *errorincr1* and *errorincr2* are the increments for the numerators (error terms), and *intincr1* and *intincr2* are the increments for the integer parts. As before, the integer parts of the starting and ending points are contained within the *offset1* and *offset2* variables, and the numerators are *errorterm1* and *errorterm2*. The variables *calc1* and *calc2* are introduced to control when the increments and other edge-related variables are recalculated. Both of these variables act as flags and are both initialized to one (1). When the top of the loop inspects these flags and finds them to be nonzero, it will calculate the number of rows and the mixed fraction variables, then set the flag to zero (0). When an edge is finished processing (and drawing), the *calc1* and *calc2* variables are again set to 1 in order to initialize the variables which control the incremental drawing of the edge. Here's our first stab at a new version of DrawPoly():

```
void Polygon::DrawPoly(unsigned char far *screen_buffer, Palette * palette, ->
            int ambient)
{
// Draw polygon in structure POLYGON in SCREEN_BUFFER

// Uninitialized variables:
  unsigned int start,        // Starting offset of line between edges
             offset1,        // Offset of current pixel in edges 1 & 2
             offset2;
  int ydiff1,ydiff2,         // Difference between starting x and ending x
      xdiff1,xdiff2,         // Difference between starting y and ending y
      length,                // Distance from edge 1 to edge 2
      errorterm1,errorterm2, // Error terms for edges 1 & 2
      count1,count2,         // Increment count for edges 1 & 2
      xunit1,xunit2,         // Unit to advance x offset for edges 1 & 2
      intincr1,intincr2,     // Standard integer increments for x on edges 1 & 2
      errorincr1,errorincr2; // Error increments for x on edges 1 & 2
  // Initialize count of number of edges drawn:
  int edgecount=number_of_vertices-1;
  // Determine which vertex is at top of polygon:
  int firstvert=0;                    // Start by assuming vertex 0 is at top
  int min_amt=vertex[0]->sy; // Find y coordinate of vertex 0
  for (int i=1; i<number_of_vertices; i++) {  // Search thru vertices
    if ((vertex[i]->sy) < min_amt) {          // Is another vertex higher?
      firstvert=i;                            // If so, replace top vertex
      min_amt=vertex[i]->sy;
    }
  }
  // Finding starting and ending vertices of first two edges:
  int startvert1=firstvert;        // Get starting vertex of edge 1
  int startvert2=firstvert;        // Get starting vertex of edge 2
  int xstart1=vertex[startvert1]->sx;
  int ystart1=vertex[startvert1]->sy;
  int xstart2=vertex[startvert2]->sx;
  int ystart2=vertex[startvert2]->sy;
  int endvert1=startvert1-1;                      // Get ending vertex of edge 1
  if (endvert1<0) endvert1=number_of_vertices-1; // Check for wrap
  int xend1=vertex[endvert1]->sx;       // Get x & y coordinates
  int yend1=vertex[endvert1]->sy;       // of ending vertices
  int endvert2=startvert2+1;                      // Get ending vertex of edge 2
  if (endvert2==(number_of_vertices)) endvert2=0;  // Check for wrap
  int xend2=vertex[endvert2]->sx;       // Get x & y coordinates
  int yend2=vertex[endvert2]->sy;       // of ending vertices

  // Draw the polygon:
  char calc1=1;
  char calc2=1;

  while (edgecount>0) {     // Continue drawing until all edges drawn

    if (calc1) {                      // Need to calculate edge 1?
      calc1=0;                        // Yes
      offset1=320*ystart1+xstart1;  // Offset of edge 1
```

```
      errorterm1=0;                   // Initialize error term
      if ((ydiff1=yend1-ystart1)<0) ydiff1=-ydiff1; // Get abs value of y length
      count1=ydiff1;                  // Record number of rows
      if (count1) {                   // Any rows at all?
        xdiff1=xend1-xstart1;         // Get x length
        intincr1=xdiff1/ydiff1;       // Get integer part of increment
        if (xdiff1<0) {
          xunit1=-1;                  // Calculate x overflow increment
          errorincr1=-xdiff1%ydiff1;// Get numerator part of increment
        }
        else {
          xunit1=1;                   // Calculate x overflow increment
          errorincr1=xdiff1%ydiff1;   // Get numerator part of increment
        }
      }
    }

    if (calc2) {                      // Need to calculate edge 2?
      calc2=0;                        // Yes
      offset2=320*ystart2+xstart2;    // Offset of edge 2
      errorterm2=0;                   // Initialize error term
      if ((ydiff2=yend2-ystart2)<0) ydiff2=-ydiff2; // Get abs value of y length
      count2=ydiff2;                  // Record number of rows
      if (count2) {                   // Any rows at all?
        xdiff2=xend2-xstart2;         // Get x length
        intincr2=xdiff2/ydiff2;       // Get integer part of increment
        if (xdiff2<0) {
          xunit2=-1;                  // Calculate X overflow increment
          errorincr2=-xdiff2%ydiff2;// Get numerator part of increment
        }
        else {
          xunit2=1;                   // Calculate x overflow increment
          errorincr2=xdiff2%ydiff2;   // Get numerator part of increment
        }
      }
    }

    for (; count1&&count2; count1--,count2--) {
      length=offset2-offset1;         // Determine length of horizontal line
      if (length<0) {                 // If negative...
        length=-length;               // Make it positive
        start=offset2;                // And set START to edge 2
      }
      else
        start=offset1;                // Else set START to edge 1
      length++;
      int l=length;                   // Draw a line of pixels
      for (unsigned char far *p=&screen_buffer[start];l--;)
        *p++=color;
      offset1+=intincr1+320;          // Increment offset for x and y
      errorterm1+=errorincr1;         // Add increment numerator to error term
      if (errorterm1>=ydiff1) { // Has fraction overflowed?
        errorterm1-=ydiff1;           // Yes, subtract 1 from fraction
```

continued on next page

continued from previous page

```
        offset1+=xunit1;        // Add 1 (or -1) to integer part
    }

    offset2+=intincr2+320;  // Increment offset for x and y
    errorterm2+=errorincr2; // Add increment numerator to error term
    if (errorterm2>=ydiff2) { // Has fraction overflowed?
      errorterm2-=ydiff2;   // Yes, subtract 1 from fraction
      offset2+=xunit2;      // Add 1 (or -1) to integer part
    }
  }

  // Another edge (at least) is complete. Start next edge, if any.
  if (!count1) {             // If edge 1 is complete...
    --edgecount;             // Decrement the edge count
    startvert1=endvert1;     // Make ending vertex into start vertex
    --endvert1;              // And get new ending vertex
    if (endvert1<0) endvert1=number_of_vertices-1; // Check for wrap
    xstart1=xend1;           // Start of new edge is end of old edge
    ystart1=yend1;
    xend1=vertex[endvert1]->sx;  // Get x & y of new end vertex
    yend1=vertex[endvert1]->sy;
    calc1=1;                 // Must recalculate this edge
  }
  if (!count2) {             // If edge 2 is complete...
    --edgecount;             // Decrement the edge count
    startvert2=endvert2;     // Make ending vertex into start vertex
    endvert2++;              // And get new ending vertex
    if (endvert2==(number_of_vertices)) endvert2=0; // Check for wrap
    xstart2=xend2;           // Start of new edge is end of old edge
    ystart2=yend2;
    xend2=vertex[endvert2]->sx;  // Get x & y of new end vertex
    yend2=vertex[endvert2]->sy;
    calc2=1;                 // Must recalculate this edge
  }
 }
}
```

Although the function is still long and slightly complicated, we have simplified it quite a bit. In particular, there is only one place in which pixels are drawn:

```
*p++=color;
```

This is important, because to do Gouraud shading, we will want to change the colors which are used to draw the pixels. This is easier when there is only one place in the code where pixels are drawn.

Bresenham on Brightness

The last major change to DrawPoly() adjusts the brightness of each pixel according to the brightness of the vertices. Gouraud shading is all about making smooth transitions from one brightness level to another, so we must write the code that makes these transitions. As it turns out, we have already written this code.

The mixed fraction code used in our new version of DrawPoly() is exactly what we need to calculate pixel brightnesses. In our new DrawPoly(), the mixed fractions allowed us to move smoothly from one endpoint *x* coordinate to another along an edge. Now we will use the same method to move smoothly from one endpoint brightness to another along an edge and horizontally between two edges.

The first change to DrawPoly() is to add the new variables required to track the brightness levels along the edges. The variable names are much like those used previously in DrawPoly() for mixed fractions. Two sets of variables are defined, one for each of the two edges currently being drawn.

```
int cdiff1,cdiff2,          // Difference between starting and ending
                            //  brightness for edges
    cstart1,cstart2,        // Starting edge brightnesses
    cend1,cend2,            // Ending edge brightnesses
    cerrorterm1,cerrorterm2,// Error terms for brightnesses for edges 1 & 2
    cunit1,cunit2,          // Unit to advance brightness for edges 1 & 2
    cintincr1,cintincr2,    // Standard integer brightness increments on
                            //  edges 1 & 2
    cerrorincr1,cerrorincr2;// Error brightness increments on edges 1 & 2
```

Next comes the variables required to make the brightness transition horizontally from one edge to the other. Again, the same naming scheme is used.

```
int cdiff,                  // Difference between starting and ending
                            // brightness for row
    cstart,                 // Starting row brightness
    cend,                   // Ending row brightness
    cerrorterm,             // Error term for row brightness
    cunit,                  // Unit to advance brightness fpor row
    cintincr,               // Standard integer color increments for row
    cerrorincr;             // Error color increments for row
```

When the mixed fraction values are calculated for determining the *x* coordinates of the edges, we must also perform similar calculations for the brightness mixed fractions. This must be done for both edges, but we will look at just one edge here.

```
cstart1=vertex[startvert1]->brightness;  // Starting brightness
cend1=vertex[endvert1]->brightness;      // Ending brightness
cerrorterm1=0;                   // Initialize error term
cdiff1=cend1-cstart1;            // Find span of brightness values
cintincr1=cdiff1/ydiff1;         // Brightness integer part increment
if (cdiff1<0) {
  cunit1=-1;                     // Brightness overflow increment
  cerrorincr1=-cdiff1%ydiff1;    // Brightness numerator increment
}
else {
  cunit1=1;                      // Brightness overflow increment
  cerrorincr1=cdiff1%ydiff1;     // Brightness numerator increment
}
```

This code initializes the mixed fraction that tracks the brightness value along the edge (*cstart1+cerrorterm1/ydiff*) and the mixed fraction that is to be added to it each time we move down a line (*cintincr1+cerrorincr1/ydiff*).

Now we address the problem of making the transition along the horizontal row. The code is very similar to the code used along the edges. First we set up the mixed fractions:

```
length=offset2-offset1;  // Determine length of horizontal line
if (length<0) {          // If negative...
  length=-length;        // Make it positive
  start=offset2;         // And set START to edge 2
  cstart=cstart2;        // Start with edge 2 brightness
  cend=cstart1;          // End with edge 1 brightness
}
else {
  start=offset1;         // Else set START to edge 1
  cstart=cstart1;        // Start with edge 1 brightness
  cend=cstart2;          // End with edge 2 brightness
}
length++;
cerrorterm=0;            // Initialize error term
cdiff=cend-cstart;       // Determine brightness span
cintincr=cdiff/length;   // Brightness integer increment
if (cdiff<0) {
  cunit=-1;                     // Brightness overflow increment
  cerrorincr=-cdiff%length; // Brightness numerator increment
}
else {
  cunit=1;                      // Brightness overflow increment
  cerrorincr=cdiff%length;  // Brightness numerator increment
}
```

This establishes the brightness value mixed fraction (*cstart+cerrorterm/xdiff*) and the increment mixed fraction (*cintincr+cerrorincr/xdiff*). Next, we use these mixed fractions to determine pixel brightness while drawing the horizontal line of pixels:

```
int l=length;
for (unsigned char far *p=&screen_buffer[start];l--;)
{
  *p++= palette->ColorIndex(color,cstart,ambient);
  cstart+=cintincr;             // Increment brightness integer part
  cerrorterm+=cerrorincr;    // Increment brightness numerator
  if (cerrorterm>=length) { // If overflowed
    cerrorterm-=length;      // Subtract 1 from the fractional part
    cstart+=cunit;           // Add one to the integer part
  }
}
```

Now we must add the code which performs the mixed fraction addition for the edges. It looks strikingly similiar to the code we just wrote:

```
  cstart1+=cintincr1;          // Increment brightness integer part
  cerrorterm1+=cerrorincr1;    // Increment brightness numerator
  if (cerrorterm1>=ydiff1) {   // If overflowed
    cerrorterm1-=ydiff1;       // Subtract 1 from the fraction part
    cstart1+=cunit1;           // Add one to the integer part
}
```

Now, we can put our final DrawPoly() together. Listing 12-9 contains the completed function using the mixed fraction approach for rows and colors.

Listing 12-9 DRAWPOLG.CPP

```cpp
#include  "poly_g.h"
#include  "palette.h"

void Polygon::DrawPoly(unsigned char far *screen_buffer,Palette *palette,int->
           ambient)
{
// Draw polygon in structure POLYGON in SCREEN_BUFFER

// Uninitialized variables:

  unsigned int start,        // Starting offset of line between edges
               offset1,      // Offset of current pixel in edges 1 & 2
               offset2;

      int ydiff1,ydiff2,        // Difference between starting x and ending x
     xdiff1,xdiff2,         // Difference between starting y and ending y
     cdiff1,cdiff2,         // Difference between starting color and ending
                            // color
     length,                // Distance from edge 1 to edge 2
     errorterm1,errorterm2, // Error terms for edges 1 & 2
     count1,count2,         // Increment count for edges 1 & 2
     xunit1,xunit2,         // Unit to advance x offset for edges 1 & 2
            intincr1,intincr2,    // Standard integer increments for x on
                                  // edges 1 & 2
     errorincr1,errorincr2, // Error increments for x on edges 1 & 2
     cstart1,cstart2,       // Starting edge colors
     cend1,cend2,           // Ending edge colors
     cerrorterm1,cerrorterm2,// Error terms for color for edges 1 & 2
     cunit1,cunit2,         // Unit to advance color for edges 1 & 2
     cintincr1,cintincr2,   // Standard integer color increments on edges 1 & 2
            cerrorincr1,cerrorincr2, // Error color increments on edges 1 & 2
     cdiff,
     cstart,                // Starting edge colors
     cend,                  // Ending edge colors
     cerrorterm,            // Error terms for color for edges 1 & 2
     cunit,                 // Unit to advance color for edges 1 & 2
     cintincr,              // Standard integer color increments on edges 1 & 2
            cerrorincr;              // Error color increments on edges 1 & 2
```

continued on next page

continued from previous page

```
// Initialize count of number of edges drawn:

int edgecount=number_of_vertices-1;

// Determine which vertex is at top of polygon:

int firstvert=0;           // Start by assuming vertex 0 is at top
int min_amt=vertex[0]->sy; // Find y coordinate of vertex 0
for (int i=1; i<number_of_vertices; i++) {  // Search thru vertices
       if ((vertex[i]->sy) < min_amt) {  // Is another vertex higher?
             firstvert=i;                       // If so, replace previous
                                                // top vertex
             min_amt=vertex[i]->sy;
       }
}
// Finding starting and ending vertices of first two edges:

int startvert1=firstvert;       // Get starting vertex of edge 1
int startvert2=firstvert;       // Get starting vertex of edge 2
int xstart1=vertex[startvert1]->sx;
int ystart1=vertex[startvert1]->sy;
int xstart2=vertex[startvert2]->sx;
int ystart2=vertex[startvert2]->sy;
int endvert1=startvert1-1;               // Get ending vertex of edge 1
if (endvert1<0) endvert1=number_of_vertices-1;  // Check for wrap
int xend1=vertex[endvert1]->sx;          // Get x & y coordinates
int yend1=vertex[endvert1]->sy;          // of ending vertices
int endvert2=startvert2+1;               // Get ending vertex of edge 2
if (endvert2==(number_of_vertices)) endvert2=0;  // Check for wrap
int xend2=vertex[endvert2]->sx;          // Get x & y coordinates
int yend2=vertex[endvert2]->sy;          // of ending vertices

// Draw the polygon:
char calc1=1;
char calc2=1;

while (edgecount>0) {      // Continue drawing until all edges drawn

    if (calc1) {
       calc1=0;
       offset1=320*ystart1+xstart1;  // Offset of edge 1
       errorterm1=0;                 // Initialize error term
       if ((ydiff1=yend1-ystart1)<0) ydiff1=-ydiff1; // Get abs value of
                                                     // y length
       count1=ydiff1;
       if (count1) {
             xdiff1=xend1-xstart1;
             intincr1=xdiff1/ydiff1;
             if (xdiff1<0) {                  // Get value of length
             xunit1=-1;                       // Calculate X increment
                 errorincr1=-xdiff1%ydiff1;
                 }
```

```
                else {
                        xunit1=1;
                        errorincr1=xdiff1%ydiff1;
                        }

        cstart1=vertex[startvert1]->brightness;
        cend1=vertex[endvert1]->brightness;
        cerrorterm1=0;
        cdiff1=cend1-cstart1;
        cintincr1=cdiff1/ydiff1;
        if (cdiff1<0) {
            cunit1=-1;
                    cerrorincr1=-cdiff1%ydiff1;
                    }
        else {
                    cunit1=1;
                    cerrorincr1=cdiff1%ydiff1;
                    }
        }
}

if (calc2) {
        calc2=0;
        offset2=320*ystart2+xstart2;   // Offset of edge 2
        errorterm2=0;
        if ((ydiff2=yend2-ystart2)<0) ydiff2=-ydiff2; // x & y lengths of
                                                      // edges
        count2=ydiff2;
        if (count2) {
                    xdiff2=xend2-xstart2;
                    intincr2=xdiff2/ydiff2;
                    if (xdiff2<0) {                // Get value of length
                            xunit2=-1;             // Calculate X increment
                    errorincr2=-xdiff2%ydiff2;
                     }
                else {
                        xunit2=1;
                        errorincr2=xdiff2%ydiff2;
                     }

                    cstart2=vertex[startvert2]->brightness;
                    cend2=vertex[endvert2]->brightness;
                    cerrorterm2=0;
                    cdiff2=cend2-cstart2;
                    cintincr2=cdiff2/ydiff2;
                    if (cdiff2<0) {
                            cunit2=-1;
                    cerrorincr2=-cdiff2%ydiff2;
                            }
                    else {
                            cunit2=1;
                            cerrorincr2=cdiff2%ydiff2;
```

continued on next page

continued from previous page

```
                                 }
                       }
            }

            for (; count1&&count2; count1--,count2--) {
                    length=offset2-offset1; // Determine length of horizontal line
                    if (length<0) {          // If negative...
                                length=-length;        // Make it positive
                                start=offset2;          // And set START to edge 2
                                cstart=cstart2;
                                cend=cstart1;
                            }
                    else {
                                start=offset1;         // Else set START to edge 1
                                cstart=cstart1;
                                cend=cstart2;
                            }
                    length++;

                    cerrorterm=0;
                    cdiff=cend-cstart;
                    cintincr=cdiff/length;
                    if (cdiff<0) {
                            cunit=-1;
                            cerrorincr=-cdiff%length;
                            }
                    else {
                            cunit=1;
                            cerrorincr=cdiff%length;
                    }

                    int l=length;
                    for (unsigned char far *p=&screen_buffer[start];l--;)          {
                            *p++=palette->ColorIndex(original_color,cstart,ambient);
                            cstart+=cintincr;
                            cerrorterm+=cerrorincr;
                            if (cerrorterm>=length) {
                                        cerrorterm-=length;
                                        cstart+=cunit;
                                        }
                            }

                    offset1+=intincr1+320;
                    errorterm1+=errorincr1;
                    if (errorterm1>=ydiff1) {
                                errorterm1-=ydiff1;
                                offset1+=xunit1;
                            }
                    cstart1+=cintincr1;
                    cerrorterm1+=cerrorincr1;
                    if (cerrorterm1>=ydiff1) {
                                cerrorterm1-=ydiff1;
```

```
                        cstart1+=cunit1;
                        }

                offset2+=intincr2+320;
                errorterm2+=errorincr2;
                if (errorterm2>=ydiff2) {
                        errorterm2-=ydiff2;
                        offset2+=xunit2;
                        }
                cstart2+=cintincr2;
                cerrorterm2+=cerrorincr2;
                if (cerrorterm2>=ydiff2) {
                        cerrorterm2-=ydiff2;
                        cstart2+=cunit2;
                        }
                }

        // Another edge (at least) is complete. Start next edge, if any.

    if (!count1) {          // If edge 1 is complete...
        --edgecount;            // Decrement the edge count
        startvert1=endvert1;    // Make ending vertex into start vertex
        --endvert1;             // And get new ending vertex
        if (endvert1<0) endvert1=number_of_vertices-1; // Check for wrap
        xstart1=xend1;
        ystart1=yend1;
        xend1=vertex[endvert1]->sx;   // Get x & y of new end vertex
        yend1=vertex[endvert1]->sy;
        calc1=1;
        }
    if (!count2) {          // If edge 2 is complete...
        --edgecount;            // Decrement the edge count
        startvert2=endvert2;    // Make ending vertex into start vertex
        endvert2++;             // And get new ending vertex
        if (endvert2==(number_of_vertices)) endvert2=0; // Check for wrap
        xstart2=xend2;
        ystart2=yend2;
        xend2=vertex[endvert2]->sx;   // Get x & y of new end vertex
        yend2=vertex[endvert2]->sy;
        calc2=1;
        }
    }
}
```

Vertex Normals

Having simplified DrawPoly(), we are ready to look at the code required to determine the initial brightness of the vertices. As with normal polygon shading, brightness is determined by the angle between the incoming light ray and a normal vector. Previously, the normal vector we wanted was the normal vector of the polygon we were drawing. For Gouraud shading, we want vectors which are normal to our vertices.

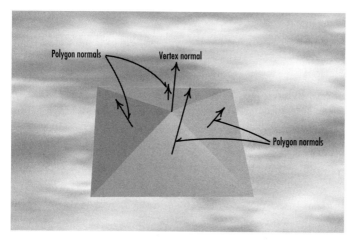

Figure 12-5 Vertex and polygon normals

Fortunately, figuring out the normal of a vertex is very easy. All we need to do is add together the normal vectors for all the polygons that contain that vertex. The result is a compromise between the polygon normals which is normal to their shared vertex. Figure 12-5 shows a vertex normal and the polygon normals it is generated from.

As we move an object around, its vertex normals move as well. This seems to indicate that we need to recalculate the vertex normals every time we move the object. Actually, it's faster to calculate the vertex normals once and move them when the object is moved. Because the normals indicate a direction and not a position, we only want to rotate them.

The first code change required to support vertex normals is to add the normal vector to the vertex_type structure, as found in POLY_G.H. In addition, we will add the length of the normal vector. The length of a vector doesn't change when the vector is rotated, so we only need to calculate the length once. A brightness value is also added so we don't need to recalculate it for every polygon we want to draw.

```
struct vertex_type { // Structure for individual vertices
   long lx,ly,lz,lt;  // Local coordinates of vertex
   long wx,wy,wz,wt;  // World coordinates of vertex
   long ax,ay,az,at;  // World coordinates aligned with view
#ifdef LIGHTING_DEMO
   long sx,sy,st;     // Screen coordinates of vertex
#endif

   long nlx,nly,nlz,nlt;  // Untransformed normal vector
   long nwx,nwy,nwz,nwt;  // Transformed normal vector
   long nlength;          // Length of normal vector
   int  brightness;       // Brightness for Gouraud shading
};
```

Next, the Object::Transform() function must change to perform the appropriate transformation on the normal vector. Notice that the translation part of the transformation has been left out for the normal vector; only rotation is performed. Listing 12-10 contains the Gouraud Transform() function as found in POLY_G.CPP.

Listing 12-10 The Gouraud Transform() function

```
void Object::Transform()
{
        // Multiply all vertices in OBJECT with master transformation matrix:
        vertex_type *vptr=vertex;
        for (int v=0; v<number_of_vertices; v++,vptr++) {
                vptr->wx=((long)vptr->lx*matrix[0][0]+(long)vptr->
                   ly*matrix[1][0]
                 +(long)vptr->lz*matrix[2][0]+matrix[3][0])>>SHIFT;
                vptr->wy=((long)vptr->lx*matrix[0][1]+(long)vptr->
                   ly*matrix[1][1]
                 +(long)vptr->lz*matrix[2][1]+matrix[3][1])>>SHIFT;
                vptr->wz=((long)vptr->lx*matrix[0][2]+(long)vptr->
                   ly*matrix[1][2]
                 +(long)vptr->lz*matrix[2][2]+matrix[3][2])>>SHIFT;

                // Transform Normal Vector for GOURAUD shading (no
                   // translation)
                vptr->nwx=((long)vptr->nlx*matrix[0][0]+(long)vptr->
                   nly*matrix[1][0]
                      +(long)vptr->nlz*matrix[2][0])>>SHIFT;
                vptr->nwy=((long)vptr->nlx*matrix[0][1]+(long)vptr->
                   nly*matrix[1][1]
                      +(long)vptr->nlz*matrix[2][1])>>SHIFT;
                vptr->nwz=((long)vptr->nlx*matrix[0][2]+(long)vptr->
                   nly*matrix[1][2]
                      +(long)vptr->nlz*matrix[2][2])>>SHIFT;
        }
}
```

The normal vectors for the vertices need to be calculated just once. The Object class MeasureNormals() function did this job when we needed plane normals, so adjustment to this function can determine the vector normals at the same time. First, it zeros out the normal vectors for all the vertices. Then it goes through the list of polygons, generating a normal for each one and adding the normal to each vertex in the polygon's list of vertices. Lastly, it calculates the length of each vertex normal. The completed function is in Listing 12-11.

Listing 12-11 Gouraud MeasureNormals() function

```
void Object::MeasureNormals(int numshades)
{
  // Calculate length of normal for each vertex in this object:
```

continued on next page

continued from previous page

```
        for (int v=0; v< number_of_vertices; v++) {
                vertex[v].nlx=0;
                vertex[v].nly=0;
                vertex[v].nlz=0;
        }

        for (int p=0; p< GetPolygonCount(); p++) {
                Polygon *pptr= &polygon[p];
                if (pptr->original_color>=numshades) {
                  vertex_type *v0=pptr->vertex[0];
                  vertex_type *v1=pptr->vertex[1];
                  vertex_type *v2=pptr->vertex[2];
                  long ax=v0->lx-v1->lx;   // Vector for edge from vertex 1 to
                                           // vertex 0
                  long ay=v0->ly-v1->ly;
                  long az=v0->lz-v1->lz;
                  long bx=v2->lx-v1->lx;   // Vector for edge from vertex 1 to
                                           // vertex 2
                  long by=v2->ly-v1->ly;
                  long bz=v2->lz-v1->lz;
                  long nx=ay*bz-az*by;      // Normal is cross product of the
                                            // two vectors
                  long ny=az*bx-ax*bz;
                  long nz=ax*by-ay*bx;
                      // OBJECT can access POLYGON since its a friend:
                  for (v=0; v< pptr->number_of_vertices; v++) {
                        vertex_type *vptr= pptr->vertex[v];
                        vptr->nlx+=nx;
                        vptr->nly+=ny;
                        vptr->nlz+=nz;
                  }
                }
        }
    }
    for (v=0; v< number_of_vertices; v++) {
            vertex_type *vptr=&vertex[v];
            vptr->nlength=(long)sqrt((float)vptr->nlx*vptr->
                nlx+(float)vptr->nly*vptr->nly+
                    (float)vptr->nlz*vptr->nlz);
    }
}
```

The Brightness Calculation

The brightness level for each vertex must be calculated each time an object is moved. In our LIGHTDEM program, the World class controlled the color assignment in the function CalcObjectColor() which was called from the Draw() function. It makes sense to adjust this function to perform the brightness calculations using exactly the same formulas used by the lighting demonstration program. However, if you recall, the last step in the CalcObjectColor() function was to set the polygon color:

```
polyptr->SetColor(palette.ColorIndex(temp,brightness,ambient));
```

This was fine for simple lighting, but now, ColorIndex() is called from within our newly improved DrawPoly() function to allow us to construct shaded steps of colors between two edges. In our new version of CalcObjectColor(), we can store the brightness value for later use in this DrawPoly() function. The effect is not only a delay in the call to ColorIndex(), but it becomes a call for each pixel, rather than for each polygon! This extracts a price on the drawing speed for using Gouraud shading. Listing 12-12 shows the entire function.

Listing 12-12 Gouraud CalcObjectColor() function

```
// GOURAUD version of CALCOBJECTCOLOR
void World::CalcObjectColor(Object *object)
{
        // dereference the source fields to local variables
    int ambient= source.ambient;
    long xx=source.x;
    long yy=source.y;
    long zz=source.z;
    long length=source.length;

    // Calculate brightness for each vertex in the OBJECT:
    // the GOURAUD example uses direct vertice adjustment
    // instead of using the polygon plane
    vertex_type *vptr= object->GetVertexPtr(0);
    for (int v=0; v< object->GetVertexCount(); v++,vptr++) {
        int brightness =
          (int)(((vptr->nwx*xx+vptr->nwy*yy+vptr->nwz*zz)*
                    (100-ambient))/(length*vptr->nlength));
        if (brightness<0)
            brightness=ambient;  // Ambient applies to surfaces not
                                 // facing the source
        else
            brightness+=ambient; // Add ambient for polygons facing
                                 // the source
        vptr->brightness = brightness;
    }
}
```

GOURDEMO Summary

All that's required now is to compile the GOURDEMO.IDE project. We have copied the LIGHTDEM.CPP file to the GOURAUD directory and renamed it GOURDEMO.CPP. It is exactly the same as LIGHTDEM.CPP since all of our changes from simple lighting to Gouraud shading have taken place within the World and Object class modules. The drawing of these polygons still happens with a call to World::Draw().

The effects of Gouraud shading are best seen using the icosahedron in ICOS.WLD. Even with 20 polygons, the icosahedron doesn't really look like a sphere when rendered with our Gouraud shading program. Despite this, the smoothing effect can clearly be seen.

The Gouraud demo program, GOURDEMO.EXE, requires a text file argument just like LIGHTDEM.EXE. Try running GOURDEMO ICOS.WLD to see the Gouraud effect on an icosahedron.

Gouraud Shading in the Real World

Gouraud shading isn't all that practical for gaming right now because it is slower than straight light shading, as found in the lighting demo, and because it only makes sense when there are large numbers of polygons approximating a smooth surface. On the other hand, computer hardware is getting faster all the time, so it might soon make sense to use Gouraud shading in a game. For those thinking of embarking on such a project, there are a few things to consider.

First of all, for most commercial games, speed-critical sections of code such as DrawPoly() are written in assembly language. DrawPoly() is a good candidate for assembly-language handcrafting not only because it is a big CPU consumer, but also because it consists largely of simple additions and if statements. A good way to approach an assembly task such as DrawPoly() is to have the compiler generate the assembly from the C++ code and then optimize the assembly code by hand. In this way, a working piece of assembly code can be slowly refined for speed. Frequent testing during the optimization process will prevent the changes from getting seriously off track.

A sneakier way to optimize Gouraud shading is only to do it on objects that don't move very often. That way, Gouraud shading comes into play for only a small percentage of the rendering that is done.

Another issue to consider when doing Gouraud shading in a commercial product is that in many situations the effect is not required. Some edges are meant to be sharp and don't require the smoothing effect of Gouraud shading. This can be handled by limiting the Gouraud shading to where polygons of the same color meet.

Texture Mapping

While we have made great strides in improving the look of our polygonal world by adding lighting, we haven't addressed the issue of detail. Even with dramatic lighting effects, a handful of polygons still produces a stark scene without intricacy or texture. In the programs so far, our world has consisted of one object. That object has had either 4 (cube), 5 (pyramid), or 20 (icosahedron) sides. If we want more detail in an object, we have to add more polygons. For very fine detail, the number of polygons required grows enormously.

Texture mapping provides a way of adding surface detail without increasing the number of polygons. Basically, texture mapping consists of pasting a bitmapped image to the surface of a polygon. The bitmapped image moves with the polygon, so it appears to be detail, or texture, on the surface of the polygon. Many commercial game programs popular today use texture mapping to give the impression of detail without a lot of polygons. Unfortunately, texture mapping is fairly slow, and the highly optimized code used in commercial games is a closely guarded secret.

We will explore texture mapping by creating yet another demonstration program. It won't be particularly fast, but it will embody all the important principles of texture mapping. Later, we'll discuss some strategies for speeding the code up for use in games.

The Strategy

The Gouraud shading program provides a good framework for doing texture mapping. The simplification of DrawPoly(), in particular, is an important step in creating the texture-mapping program. Our new program will start with the simplified DrawPoly(), the vertex structure as it was before the normal vectors were added, and the normal vector and brightness calculations removed. We can remove the light source and palette code since it is not being used. The World class no longer has Palette and source_type as members. To share our WLD data file format, we alter World::LoadPoly() so that it reads the light and palette numbers without storing them. This entitles us to use the data objects from our previous demos. To this we will add the required texture-mapping code.

The principle of texture mapping is simple: For each pixel of each polygon, figure out where in the bitmapped image the pixel lies and paint it the appropriate color from the bitmap. In practice, this is not all that easy to do. What is required is a set of calculations that effectively reverse the perspective calculations that told us where to draw the polygon on the screen. In addition, we must match up the bitmap with the polygon regardless of the polygon's orientation.

We'll have to make use of our Pcx object in order to load the bitmap and allocate memory. We'll also need a class to control the pixels in the bitmap, just as our palette controlled the colors in the shading demo. A new class, identifiable as Texture, will be defined as a child class of Pcx and contain fields for storing the vector information for o, i, and j. A pointer to a Texture object will then be stored in the Polygon class.

The math is a bit complicated, and we won't cover it in complete detail. But we do want to know basically how the calculations work. We will start by considering how to match up the bitmap with the polygon before any perspective calculations come into play.

Positioning the Bitmap

The bitmap and the polygon can be matched up in an infinite number of ways. We can rotate the bitmap on the polygon to any orientation, slide the bitmap up and down and side to side, and we can stretch or shrink the bitmap. All these options are available, and we must find an easy way to express the options we want in our program. As it turns out, all these options can be specified with three vectors, as shown in Figure 12-6.

The first vector indicates where the origin of the bitmap (0,0) is positioned in space. This vector handles the translation option that allows us to slide the bitmap around on the polygon. We will call this vector *o* in our code.

The other two vectors indicate the orientation and scale of the *x* and *y* axes of the bitmap. In our case, we will make the *x* vector point one bitmap pixel width in the positive *x* direction and the *y* vector point one bitmap pixel width in the positive *y* direction. These two vectors handle all the rotation and scaling options. We will call these vectors *i* and *j*, respectively, in our code. To work properly, these vectors must lie in the same plane as the polygon and must be perpendicular to each other.

Generating the Vectors

So where will these vectors come from? We could specify these vectors in the text file that describes our polygons. This would allow us complete freedom in setting the options that relate the polygons to their respective bitmaps. This would also make writing the WLD text file a tedious chore. Perhaps this is a little more freedom than we really need.

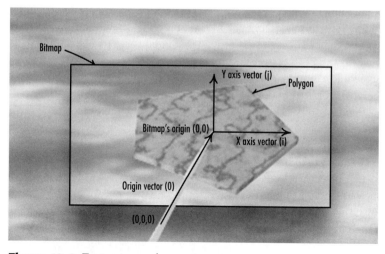

Figure 12-6 Texture-mapping vectors

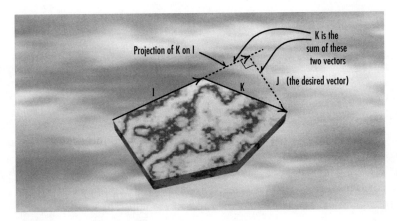

Figure 12-7 Creating perpendicular vectors

Instead, we will generate the three vectors from the polygons themselves. First of all, we will set the origin of the bitmap (*o*) equal to the average of all the vertices of the polygon. Next, we will use a little vector math to generate the required *i* and *j* vectors.

In order to do their job correctly, the *i* and *j* vectors need to have two properties: They have to lie in the plane of the polygon, and they have to be perpendicular to each other. All of the edges of the polygon lie in the plane of the polygon, so any of them will satisfy the first condition. We could select any of the edges and use it for *i*, but how do we generate a perpendicular *j* vector?

An easy way to do this is to select another edge not parallel to vector *i* and do a little vector math to make it into a perpendicular vector. Let's assume we've selected a second edge from which to generate our second vector. Call the vector corresponding to that edge *k*. We can express *k* as the sum of two other vectors, one parallel to *i* and one perpendicular to *i*. The vector parallel to *i* is called the projection of *k* on *i*. The perpendicular vector, the one we want, is just *k* minus *i*. Figure 12-7 shows the vectors and their relationships.

The formula for the projection of *k* on *i* is

```
p=((k*i)/(i*i))*i
```

or, in C++:

```
float scale=((kx*ix+ky*iy+kz*iz)/(ix*ix+iy*iy+iz*iz));
float px=ix*scale;
float py=iy*scale;
float pz=iz*scale;
```

So the formula for the vector we want (namely *j*) is

```
j=k-((k*i)/(i*i))*i
```

since we want the perpendicular vector and it's defined as *k* minus *i*. This translates to the C++ code:

```
float scale=((kx*ix+ky*iy+kz*iz)/(ix*ix+iy*iy+iz*iz));
float jx=kx-ix*scale;
float jy=ky-iy*scale;
float jz=kz-iz*scale;
```

Now that we've created two vectors that lie in the plane of the polygon and are perpendicular to each other, there is one more issue to consider. How long should these vectors be? As we will see later, the appropriate length for the vectors is the width of a single pixel of the bitmap. It is up to us what this value is. The longer *i* and *j* are, the larger the texture bitmap pixels will appear on the screen. By defining a resolution value and setting the length of *i* and *j* to *1/resolution*, we can control the apparent resolution of the texture bitmap.

Creating the Vectors: The Code

The function CalcMapVectors() generates our three vectors *o*, *i*, and *j* from a polygon. It stores the vectors in a structure called texture_type, defined as follows:

```
struct texture_type { // Structure containing texture mapping vectors
    float ox,oy,oz;  // World coordinates of texture map origin
    float ix,iy,iz;  // Texture map X direction vector
    float jx,jy,jz;  // Texture map Y direction vector
};
```

The Texture class will contain three functions to extend the usability of the Pcx class for texture mapping. Here's the class definition:

```
class Texture: public Pcx, texture_type {
public:
    unsigned char MapPixel(int x,int y,int color,int distance);
    unsigned char MapPoint(int x, int y, int color);
    void CalcMapVectors(Polygon *polygon,int resolution);
};
```

All three functions are public to allow outside access along with the vector fields of texture_type and the public functions of the Pcx class.

Listing 12-13 contains the complete code for CalcMapVectors(). It takes two parameters, a pointer to a Polygon object and an int resolution, which uses an adjusted scale from 30 to 100. The functions' comments outline the steps we just discussed.

 Listing 12-13 CalcMapVectors() function

```
void Texture::CalcMapVectors(Polygon *polygon,int resolution)
{
    // Origin is average of all vertices
```

```
ox=0;
oy=0;
oz=0;
    // retrieve the number of vertices from the polygon:
int vcount = polygon->GetVertexCount();
for (int i=0; i< vcount; i++) {
    vertex_type *vptr = polygon->GetVerticePtr(i);
    ox+=vptr->wx;
    oy+=vptr->wy;
    oz+=vptr->wz;
}
ox/=vcount;
oy/=vcount;
oz/=vcount;

// Generate raw i and j vectors
vertex_type *vp0 = polygon->GetVerticePtr(0);
vertex_type *vp1 = polygon->GetVerticePtr(1);
vertex_type *vp2 = polygon->GetVerticePtr(2);
ix=vp0->wx-vp1->wx;
iy=vp0->wy-vp1->wy;
iz=vp0->wz-vp1->wz;
jx=vp2->wx-vp1->wx;
jy=vp2->wy-vp1->wy;
jz=vp2->wz-vp1->wz;

// Make j perpendicular to i using projection formula
float scale=(ix*jx+iy*jy+iz*jz)/
                (ix*ix+iy*iy+iz*iz);
jx=jx-scale*ix;
jy=jy-scale*iy;
jz=jz-scale*iz;

// Scale i and j
scale=(float)resolution/10*sqrt(ix*ix+iy*iy+iz*iz);

ix/=scale;
iy/=scale;
iz/=scale;
scale=(float)resolution/10*sqrt(jx*jx+jy*jy+jz*jz);
jx/=scale;
jy/=scale;
jz/=scale;
}
```

Using the Vectors

The use of the three vectors we have generated is based on the principle that any point in the polygon can be specified by adding the three vectors together while scaling the last two vectors, as shown in Figure 12-8. In other words, for any point in the polygon, a vector to that point can be constructed by selecting the right u and v values in the

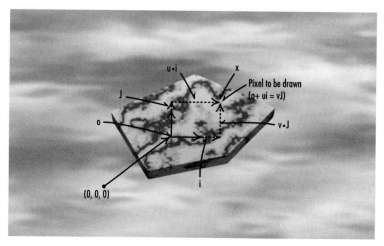

Figure 12-8 Combining *o*, *i*, and *j*

formula *o*+*u**i+*v**j. The values *u* and *v* are the *x* and *y* coordinates of the point in the bitmap that corresponds to the original point in polygon.

Now we can see how the total calculation works. First, we take the screen coordinates of the pixel we want to draw and apply our perspective calculations in reverse to give us a point on the three-dimensional polygon. Then we figure out the appropriate *u* and *v* values for that point and look up position *u*,*v* in the bitmap. That's the color we use to draw the pixel on the screen.

Deriving the calculations to do this is a matter of cranking the formulas that we already know through some high school algebra we've long forgotten. We won't cover every tortuous detail, but we will look at the starting and ending points. First of all, we have the vector formula above and the perspective formulas:

```
p=o+u*i+v*j
x=distance*px/(distance-pz)+xorigin
y=distance*py/(distance-pz)+yorigin
```

In these formulas, *p* is the three-dimensional point on the polygon corresponding to our pixel. (*px*,*py*,*pz*) is the same point with its three coordinates separated out. *x* and *y* are the coordinates of the pixel on the screen, and *xorigin* and *yorigin* the coordinates of the center of the screen. *distance* is a constant used to scale the perspective image on the screen, as explained in Chapter 7.

The first formula is a vector equation and really represents three equations (one for the *x* coordinates, one for the *y* coordinates, and one for the *z* coordinates). The three equations are

```
px=ox+u*ix+v*jx
py=oy+u*iy+v*jy
pz=oz+u*iz+v*jz
```

That means we have five equations and five unknown variables (u,v,px,py,pz). As long as the number of unknown variables is no greater than the number of equations, we can theoretically find a solution to the system of equations.

The code, which follows in Listing 12-14, shows the solution in the form of C++ code:

 ## Listing 12-14 MapPixel () function

```
unsigned char Texture::MapPixel(int x,int y,int color,int distance)
{
  x-=XORIGIN;
  y-=YORIGIN;
  float ao=ox+x*oz/distance;
  float bo=oy+y*oz/distance;
  float ai=ix+x*iz/distance;
  float bi=iy+y*iz/distance;
  float aj=jx+x*jz/distance;
  float bj=jy+y*jz/distance;
  int u=(int)((bj*ao-aj*bo-bj*x+aj*y)/(bi*aj-ai*bj));
  int v;
  if (fabs(aj)>fabs(bj))
    v=(int)((x-ao-u*ai)/aj);
  else
    v=(int)((y-bo-u*bi)/bj);
  return MapPoint(u,v,color);
}
```

The variables *ao, bo, ai, bi, aj,* and *bj* don't mean anything in particular. They are just values that appear frequently in subsequent formulas, so we calculate them ahead of time. The calculation that produces *u* will not result in a division by zero so long as the *i* and *j* vectors are not parallel, and indeed, we constructed the *j* vector as being perpendicular to *i*. The *v* calculation can be done in one of two ways, only one of which can result in a division by zero for a given set of values. The if statement determines which calculation is safest and uses it.

Consulting the Bitmap

The MapPixel() function above calculates the color of a given pixel based on its coordinates (*x* and *y*) and the three vectors *o, i,* and *j* contained in the texture_type structure. It does this by calculating *u* and *v* and calling MapPoint() to determine the bitmap color at position (u,v).

The MapPixel() parameter called color is the polygon color as defined by the input text file. It has many potential uses. For example, it could be used to determine which of many bitmaps are to be mapped onto the polygon's surface. In our program, there will be only one bitmap, and the color parameter is ignored.

The function MapPoint() simply looks up the color in the bitmap. It is interesting to note, however, that we don't need to use a bitmap. So-called procedural texture mapping uses any number of special functions to determine the color at a given (u,v) location. For example, fractal calculations can be used to create wood grain textures or simpler functions can be used to create plaids, checks, or other regular patterns. You could make the MapPoint() function virtual such that a child's different procedure would be called for MapPoint(). We will use a .PCX file bitmap in our demonstration program, but you might want to experiment with procedural alternatives.

Below in Listing 12-15 is the code for MapPoint(). The .PCX bitmap contained in the *pcxbuf* structure is consulted to determine the appropriate color for our pixel. Before the lookup into the bitmap, the *x* and *y* coordinates are modified so that the origin of the bitmap (0,0) is at the center. Remember that the origin vector, *o*, places the bitmap origin at the center of the polygon. Placing the origin of the bitmap at the bitmap's center means that the center of the polygon and the center of the bitmap will correspond.

 ## Listing 12-15 MapPoint() function

```
unsigned char Texture::MapPoint(int x,int y,int color)
{
  // color parameter is not used in this implementation
  // offset the texture map from the center of the bitmap:
  int width = header.xmax - header.xmin +1;
  x=x+width/2;
  y=y+(header.ymax- header.ymin+1)/2;
  return image[x+y*width];
}
```

Loading the Bitmap

We already wrote the code for loading the bitmap in Chapter 3. We can rest on our laurels and call the old code. First we declare the appropriate variables:

```
World world;
Texture texturePcx;
```

We load the world as usual (from LIGHTDEM.CPP), then load the image:

```
if (texturePcx.Load(argv[2])) {// Get name of PCX
      // Can't open it?
      cerr <<"Cannot load " << argv[2] << " PCX file"<< endl;
exit(-1);    // Abort w/error
}
```

If there was enough memory available for the bitmap and our texture was successfully loaded, we loop through all the objects of the world in order to set the texture pointers of its polygons.

```
//Set the objects to the texture :
for(int oo=0;oo < world.GetObjectCount(); oo++){
        (world.GetObjectPtr(oo))->SetTexture(&texturePcx);
}
```

To get the colors right, we need to load the .PCX file's palette into the VGA hardware:

```
setpalette(pcxbuf.palette);        // Set PCX palette
```

The name of the demo program for texture mapping is TEXTDEMO.EXE. It requires an argument indicating the name of a WLD data file. The data file doesn't need meaningful light-source and palette information, but the place holders must be there. CUBE.WLD is a good file to use, because the cube's large surfaces show the bitmap nicely. An additional argument is required to indicate the resolution of the bitmap. Typical values range from 3 to 10. The bitmap is loaded from the file TEXTDEMO.PCX, but by all means experiment with your own bitmaps.

Texture Mapping for Fun and Profit

Speeding up texture mapping for practical game applications is a real challenge. As always, writing the critical code sections in assembly helps immensely. But the floating-point code we wrote for the demo will always be a speed problem. Doing the calculations with integers will help some, but what's more important is to avoid performing the lengthy calculations in MapPixel() for every pixel in a polygon.

This can be accomplished by figuring out the bitmap coordinates of the vertices and interpolating between the vertices just as we did for Gouraud shading. For texture mapping, the problem isn't quite so simple however. That's because the bitmap pixels should appear to be smaller on surfaces that are farther from the viewer than on surfaces closer to the viewer. The key to using this technique is finding a way to do interpolation without losing the perspective effect.

Once the interpolation problem is solved, the complex MapPixel() calculations can be done once during initialization. The vertices of a polygon never move around on the bitmap, so their u,v coordinates will remain constant regardless of how the polygon or the observer moves.

CHAPTER
13

13

The View System

We now have nearly all of the program code that we need to build a world and display it on the computer screen. We can construct objects, move and rotate objects, remove hidden surfaces, and clip polygons at the edge of the viewport. With one exception, we have the tools we need to build a view system—a program module that will produce images of our imaginary world in a viewport on the video display, showing how it looks from any position or angle.

As it stands, we have the capabilities necessary to put on a kind of play inside the computer, with polygon-fill sets, props, and even actors, while the user sits back and watches. But that's not what we set out to do. Our goal was not to give the user a play to watch, but to make the user the main character *in* a play. We don't want the user just watching the action; we want the user to enter the world inside the computer and become *part* of the action.

So far, though, we've watched objects rotating on the video display, we've even been able to move those objects at will, but we have not been able to alter our point of view relative to those objects. To do that, we must push our three-dimensional capabilities a step further, giving ourselves freedom of movement and effectively entering the world inside the computer. In fact, this is the last major step in developing the graphic capabilities necessary for a flight simulator.

The view system is the part of a three-dimensional animation program devoted to placing an image of the three-dimensional world on the video display of the computer. Much of what we've discussed so far in this book, from transforming vertices in two- and three-dimensional space to removing hidden surfaces and clipping polygons, can be used to build a view system. In this chapter we'll discuss how all of these disparate parts can be put together to form the view system itself.

Moving Around Inside the Computer

The problem with letting the viewer move around through the world inside the computer is that physically it can't be done. We must assume that the viewer is immobile in front of the computer, looking at a stationary display. In effect, the viewer is always at the viewport origin, the (0,0,0) coordinates of the screen where the x, y, and z axes come together. Even sophisticated virtual-reality systems, where the viewer straps on goggles and walks around while looking at images of an imaginary three-dimensional world, require this assumption. The viewer may be moving through the *real* world while watching the three-dimensional display, but he or she still isn't moving through the *virtual* world, the world inside the computer. The image on those virtual-reality goggles forever remains half-an-inch in front of the viewer's eyes. There's no way to pass through the looking glass and into the display.

It is necessary, then, to create the illusion that the viewer is moving through the three-dimensional world in the computer. Since almost everything else about a three-dimensional animation program is also a kind of illusion, this is hardly unfair. But it requires some fancy footwork on the programmer's part.

The Stationary Viewer versus the Moving Viewer

So far, all of our programs assumed that the viewer is at (0,0,0) within the imaginary universe; at least, objects were depicted on the display as they would appear to a viewer at that position. This assumption is so deeply embedded in the functions from which we are going to construct our view system that we really have no way of changing it. Our view system must continue to construct three-dimensional images as they would appear from coordinates (0,0,0).

In the context of a flight simulator, however, the user will almost *never* be at coordinates (0,0,0). The freedom to fly to any set of coordinates within the computer universe is one of the most important characteristics of such programs. So how do we reconcile this with the fact that, in the context of our view system, the user will *always* be at coordinates (0,0,0)?

Simple. The part of our program that simulates the flight of an airplane will be allowed to place the viewer at any position it wishes in our 3D universe. It will then pass the viewer's current coordinates to the view system, so that the view system can draw an image in the viewport showing how the 3D universe would look from those coordinates.

Our view system, however, will immediately move the viewer back to coordinates (0,0,0), the only position from which it knows how to display a view of the universe. How, then, do we produce the illusion that the viewer has moved to a new position within the universe? By moving all other objects in the universe so that they will appear exactly as they would if the viewer were at the coordinates specified by the flight simulator! (See Figure 13-1.) If Mohammed can't come to the mountains, the view system will literally bring the mountains to Mohammed—or to Mike or Melinda or whomever happens to be playing with the flight simulator at the time.

This would be a pretty difficult trick to pull off in the real universe, where it's a lot easier to jump in an airplane and fly to Chicago than it is to bring Chicago to your home. Of course, the earth is always rotating, so in theory you could levitate a few hundred feet above the ground until Chicago came rotating around. This, in fact, is the basis for the Coriolis Effect, which, among other things, makes airborne missiles appear to drift in the direction opposite the earth's rotation. But this is an impractical means of travel.

In our miniature computer universe, however, it is no major problem to move the entire universe relative to the user. It is simply a matter of creating the appropriate translation matrix and then multiplying it by the coordinates of every object in the universe. Voila! The universe is moved! This might sound like a time-consuming task, but by combining this translation matrix with several other useful transformation matrices, we can kill several birds with a single series of multiplication stones. This is actually a very efficient way to use program execution time.

Making the Viewer an Object in the World

To enable the flight simulator to specify the viewer's position to the view system, we'll need to treat the viewer as though he or she were an object within the virtual universe inside the computer. To that end, we'll need a variable structure for specifying the viewer's coordinate position similar to the variable structures that we are already using to specify the positions of objects and polygons. Not only will this variable structure need to specify the viewer's current coordinates but it will need to specify his or her physical orientation in the universe. Here's the structure that we'll use, called view_type:

```
struct view_type {
        int x,y,z;
        int xangle,yangle,zangle;
};
```

Figure 13-1 Motion in one direction relative to the world is equivalent to motion of the world in the opposite direction relative to you

(a) Man moving toward his house

(b) House moving toward man. From his point of view, both motions are visually equivalent

The first three fields, *x, y,* and *z,* contain the *x, y,* and *z* coordinates, respectively, of the viewer's position. The second three fields, *xangle, yangle,* and *zangle,* contain the viewer's rotation on the *x, y,* and *z* axes. These are all measured relative to the coordinate system and orientation of the world in the computer. When the *x, y,* and *z* fields are set to 0, 0, and 0, the viewer is at the origin of the universe. When the *xangle, yangle,* and *zangle* fields are set to 0, the viewer's local *x, y,* and *z* axes are aligned perfectly with the *x, y,* and *z* axes of the universe.

For instance, if the *x, y,* and *z* fields are set to 17,-4001, and 6, this means that the local origin of the object is 17 units from the world origin on the *x* axis, -4001 units from the world origin on the *y* axis, and 6 units from the world origin on the *z* axis. Similarly, if the *xangle, yangle,* and *zangle* fields are set to 178, 64, and 212, then the viewer has rotated 178 degrees relative to the world *x* axis, 64 degrees on the world *y* axis, and 212 degrees on the world *z* axis. (Remember, we're using a 256-degree rotational system here, as described in Chapter 9.)

Rotating the Viewer

This concept of rotating the viewer's orientation might be a bit confusing at first. It helps to imagine that the viewer has his or her own local coordinate system, with the *y* axis more or less parallel with his or her spine, the *x* axis paralleling the line of the shoulders, and the *z* axis oriented along the viewer's line of sight. (See Figure 13-2.) The degree to which each of these axes is out of line at any given moment with the equivalent world axis is the degree of the viewer's rotation. (See Figure 13-3.)

Figure 13-2 The viewer's local axes

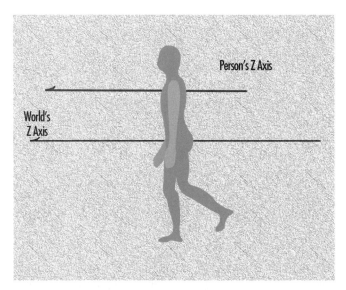

Figure 13-3 When the viewer rotates, his or her local axes rotate relative to the *z* axes of the virtual world

(a) Person standing with local *z* axis aligned with the world *z* axis

The most important thing that the viewer's orientation tells the view system is the direction in which the viewer's line of sight is pointing, i.e., what the viewer is looking at—or *would* be looking at if the viewer were actually moving around the world inside the computer.

Aligning the Universe

Once the view system has been passed all of this information concerning the viewer's *x*,*y*, and *z* coordinates and the viewer's angle of rotation on his or her local *x*, *y*, and *z* axes, the real work begins. Remember that the view system can only display the universe as it would look to a viewer positioned at the (0,0,0) coordinates of the computer universe. In the same way, the view system can only display the way the universe would look to a viewer oriented at an *x*,*y*,*z* rotation of (0,0,0) relative to the world axes.

Thus, one of the first things that the view system must do is to move every object in the universe so it appears from the (0,0,0) location just as it would from the hypothetical location of the viewer in the flight-simulator universe. Furthermore, it must *rotate* every object in the universe so that it will appear from an orientation of (0,0,0) just as it would appear from the viewer's hypothetical orientation within the flight-simulator universe.

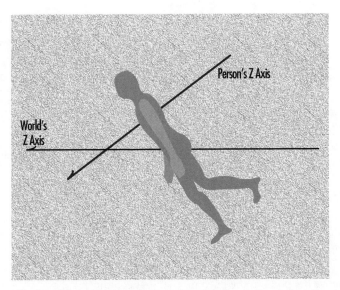

(b) Person rotated forward so that local z axis now is out of alignment with the world z axis

The AlignView() Function

This may all sound terribly difficult, but it actually takes very little additional code to pull off. Why is it so easy? Because we've already developed most of the necessary functions in earlier chapters; all we have to do is call them with the correct parameters. To perform the task of moving the universe into the appropriate position, we'll put together a function called AlignView(), so named because it will align the virtual position of the viewer (the one at which the flight simulator thinks the viewer is located) with the actual position of the viewer (the [0,0,0] position at which the view system must place the viewer to create the view). This function will take two parameters, a pointer to a World class object and the other of type view_type. The first will contain the world data base to be aligned with the viewer's current position; the second will contain the coordinates and orientation of the viewer's position in that world:

```
void View::AlignView(World *world,view_type view)
{
```

We're going to use the system of transformation matrices that we developed back in Chapter 7 to transform the coordinates of all the objects in the universe so that they appear as they would from the coordinate position of the viewer. Before we can use the transformation matrix functions, we must call the inittrans() function to initialize the master transformation matrix:

```
// Initialize transformation matrices:

inittrans();
```

We need to perform two different transformations on all the objects in the universe. We must translate them in the *x, y,* and *z* dimensions and we must rotate them on the *x, y,* and *z* axes. First we'll set up the matrix for the translation. Before that, however, we must decide where we want to locate all of those objects.

Relative Motion

This decision is pretty simple to make, but it requires that we take another look at the problem. Suppose the flight simulator has determined that the viewer, snug in the cockpit of his or her aircraft, is at coordinates 1271, -78, and 301 in the virtual universe. Our view system has no way of moving the viewer to those coordinates, so instead it places the viewer at coordinates (0,0,0). Now it must move everything else in the universe so that it appears as it would if the viewer were at coordinates (1271,-78,301). In effect, it must move the point in the universe that is at coordinates (1271,-78,301) until it is at coordinates (0,0,0), effectively aligning the viewer's virtual position with the viewer's real position.

How do we do this? We subtract the user's virtual coordinates from the user's real coordinates and translate every object in the universe by the resulting difference in each coordinate. This is simple since the user's real coordinates will always be (0,0,0): thus, the difference in each coordinate will always be the negative of the virtual coordinate. In the example in the previous paragraph, for instance, we can make the world appear as it would if the viewer were at (1271,-78,301) by translating every object in the universe by *x,y,z* translation factors of (-1271,78,-301). Why does this work? Let's look at a real-world example and then a flight-simulator example.

Have you ever had the experience of sitting in a stationary car (perhaps in a parking lot), looking out at the car next to you, and realizing that your car was rolling backward—only to discover, when you stabbed at the brake, that you weren't moving backward at all but had seen the car next to you moving forward? This is an easy mistake to make, as long as the only frame of reference in view is your own car and the other car. Motion of your car backward relative to the other car looks and feels exactly like motion of the other car forward relative to yours. (See Figure 13-4.) (*Acceleration* of one car relative to another, which can be detected by other means, is a different kettle of fish.)

In the same way, we can simulate forward motion of an airplane in a flight simulator by producing backward motion of the universe. Suppose we are in an airplane at coordinates (0,0,0) within our imaginary universe and we fly forward 100 units along the *z* axis. As far as the out-the-window 3D view is concerned, this is equivalent to translating every object in the universe backward the same distance along the *z* axis, using a translation factor of -100. (See Figure 13-5.) The same is true of motion along the other two axes.

Figure 13-4 Are you moving forward or is the other car moving backward?

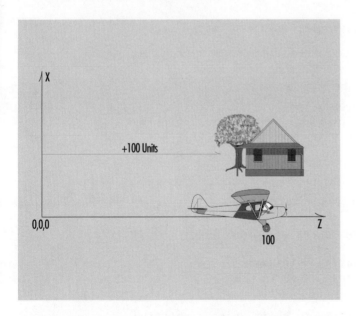

Figure 13-5 Moving forward 100 units on the world *z* axis is visually equivalent to the backward translation of landmark objects -100 units along the *z* axis

The position and orientation of the viewer are passed to the AlignView() function in a view_type structure called view. Thus, the virtual coordinates of the viewer are contained in the fields *view.x, view.y,* and *view.z*. To translate the universe into the proper position, we simply set up a translation matrix using the negative values of each of these coordinates, like this:

```
translate(-view.x,-view.y,-view.z);
```

And that's all that needs to be done to set up a translation of all objects in the universe to make them appear as they would from coordinates *view.x, view.y,* and *view.z*. I promised that it would be easy, right?

Aligning Rotation

Rotation is performed in pretty much the same manner. Once we've translated every object in the universe so that it appears as it would from the viewer's virtual position, we must rotate those objects around the viewer's position until they appear from an orientation of (0,0,0) on the *x, y,* and *z* axes as they would appear from the viewer's virtual orientation—where the flight simulator believes the viewer to be. If you guessed that we do this by rotating every object in the universe by the negatives of the degrees to which the viewer is supposed to be rotated, go to the head of the class. We set up the rotation matrix like this:

```
rotate(-view.xangle,-view.yangle,-view.zangle);
```

At this point, there's nothing left to do except actually multiply the coordinates of every object in the universe by the master transformation matrix that we have set up with the last two function calls. We can do this with a for loop:

```
Object *optr = world->GetObjectPtr(0);
  for (int i=0; i<world->GetObjectCount(); i++, optr++) {
         optr->Atransform();  // Transform object i
  }
```

The complete AlignView() function appears in Listing 13-1.

 Listing 13-1 The AlignView() function

```
void View::AlignView(World *world,view_type view)
{
  // Initialize transformation matrices:

  inittrans();

  // Set up translation matrix to shift objects relative
  // to viewer:

  translate(-view.copx,-view.copy,-view.copz);
```

```
// Rotate all objects in universe around origin:

rotate(-view.xangle,-view.yangle,-view.zangle);

// Now perform the transformation on every object
//   in the universe:
Object *optr = world->GetObjectPtr(0);
for (int i=0; i<world->GetObjectCount(); i++, optr++) {
        optr->Atransform();   // Transform object i
    }
}
```

The Atransform() Function

The function that does the multiplication, Object::Atransform(), is new. It is basically identical to the Object::Transform() function that was introduced back in Chapter 7. We can't use the original transform() function, however, because it multiplied the local coordinates of the objects (in the *lx, ly,* and *lz* fields of the vertex_type structure) by the transformation matrix to produce the object's world coordinates (in the *wx, wy,* and *wz* fields of the vertex_type structure). This time, however, we want to multiply the world coordinates by the transformation matrix to produce a set of aligned coordinates. You may recall that the vertex_type structure includes three fields called *ax, ay,* and *az.* You may have wondered what these were for. Now you know: They are to hold the aligned coordinates of the vertex. They are assigned values by the Atransform() function. To create that function, we need merely rewrite the transform() function using the world coordinate fields in place of the local coordinate fields and the aligned coordinate fields in place of the world coordinate fields. The result is in Listing 13-2.

Listing 13-2 The Atransform() function

```
void Object::Atransform()
{
        // Multiply all vertices in OBJECT with master
        //   transformation matrix

        // Create pointer to vertex:

        vertex_type *vptr=vertex;
        // Step through all vertices of OBJECT:
        for (int v=0; v<number_of_vertices; v++, vptr++) {

          // Calculate new aligned x coordinate:

          vptr->ax=((long)vptr->wx*matrix[0][0]
                +(long)vptr->wy*matrix[1][0]
                +(long)vptr->wz*matrix[2][0]
                +matrix[3][0])>>SHIFT;
```

continued on next page

continued from previous page

```
        // Calculate new aligned y coordinate:

        vptr->ay=((long)vptr->wx*matrix[0][1]
                +(long)vptr->wy*matrix[1][1]
                +(long)vptr->wz*matrix[2][1]
                +matrix[3][1])>>SHIFT;

        // Calculate new aligned z coordinate:

        vptr->az=((long)vptr->wx*matrix[0][2]
                +(long)vptr->wy*matrix[1][2]
                +(long)vptr->wz*matrix[2][2]
                +matrix[3][2])>>SHIFT;
    }
}
```

Because we have placed the results in the aligned coordinate fields, we still have the world coordinates available should we need them later. (We won't need them in the current version of the view system.) And, because the local coordinate fields have been untouched by later transformations, they are still available so that we can start this whole process again the next time the view system is called.

The View Class

The AlignView() function makes the view system possible. It sets up the universe in such a way that we can use the techniques and functions established in earlier chapters to create a view of that universe from any position and angle. In a sense, we have created a photographer who can take snapshots of the universe inside the computer on command. By instructing this photographer to take a rapid-fire series of snapshots of a changing universe, we can turn her into a cinematographer, making motion pictures of the universe on the fly.

What we need now is an interface by which an application program, such as a flight simulator, can invoke this photographer-cinematographer to put pictures on the video display. To that end, let's create a class called View, which will contain (or at least have access to) all of the functions necessary for constructing a view. By declaring an instance of this class, an application will in effect create its own cinematographer.

The definition of the class will look like this:

```
class View
{
private:
        int xorigin,yorigin;
        int xmin,ymin,xmax,ymax;
        int distance,ground,sky;
        World world;
        unsigned char *screen_buffer;
        ClippedPolygon clip_array;
```

```
        PolygonList polygon_list;
        int projection_overlap(Polygon poly1, Polygon poly2);
        int intersects(int x1_1,int y1_1,int x2_1,int y2_1,
                        int x1_2,int y1_2,int x2_2,int y2_2);
        void AlignView(World *world,view_type view);
        void DrawHorizon(int xangle,int yangle,int zangle,
                        unsigned char *screen);
        void Update(Object *object);
        void DrawPolygonList(unsigned char far *screen);
        void XYClip(ClippedPolygon *clip);
        void ZClip(Polygon *polygon,ClippedPolygon *clip, int zmin=1);
public:
        void SetView(int xo,int yo,int xmn,int ymn,int xmx,
                        int ymx,int dist,int grnd,int sk,
                        unsigned char *screen_buf);
        void SetWorld(const char *worldfilename);
        void Display(view_type curview,int horizon_flag);
};
```

You might recognize most of these declarations as variables and functions discussed in earlier chapters. In particular, *xmin, ymin, xmax, ymax, clip_array,* and *polygon_list* were all used in the chapter on clipping where we delved into the inner workings of ZClip(), XYClip(), and DrawPolygonList(). There is no constructor for the View class and only three of the functions are public, none of which have been introduced yet. Let's look at them one at a time.

The SetView() Function

The SetView() function is used to pass the view system information about the way in which the view is to be displayed on the screen. It takes a full 10 parameters and must be called before the view is drawn for the first time. (It can be called again at any time, in case one or more of the parameters should change.) The parameters, in order, are

1. xo—The *x* origin of the view in screen coordinates

2. yo—The *y* origin of the view in screen coordinates

3. xmn—The *x* coordinate of the upper left corner of the viewport

4. ymn—The *y* coordinate of the upper left corner of the viewport

5. xmx—The *x* coordinate of the lower right corner of the viewport

6. ymx—The *y* coordinate of the lower right corner of the viewport

7. dist—The distance, in pixels, of the viewer from the screen

8. grnd—The color of the ground display

9. sk—The color of the sky display

10. screen_buf—A pointer to the screen buffer

The SetView() function is in Listing 13-3.

Listing 13-3 The SetView() function

```
void View::SetView(int xo,int yo,int xmn,int ymn,
            int xmx,int ymx,int dist,
            int grnd,int sk,unsigned char *screen_buf)

// Set size and screen coordinates of window,
//   plus screen origin and viewer distance from screen

{
  xorigin=xo;            // X coordinate of screen origin
  yorigin=yo;            // Y coordinate of screen origin
  xmin=xmn;              // X coordinate of upper left
                         //   corner of window
  xmax=xmx;              // X coordinate of lower right
                         //   corner of window
  ymin=ymn;              // Y coordinate of upper left
                         //   corner of window
  ymax=ymx;              // Y coordinate of lower right
                         //   corner of window
  distance=dist;         // Distance of viewer from display
  ground=grnd;           // Ground color
  sky=sk;                // Sky color
  screen_buffer=screen_buf; // Buffer address for screen
  screen_width=(xmax-xmin)/2;
  screen_height=(ymax-ymin)/2;
}
```

This function passes the value of the parameters to variables local to the View class so that they can be referenced later by other functions in the class. In fact, we've already seen some of these variables—*screen_buffer, xorigin, yorigin*—referenced in some of the functions that are now part of this class. In a moment, we'll see the others in action.

The SetWorld() Function

The SetWorld() function sets up the parameters for the world inside the computer. It takes one parameter, a pointer to a string which holds the name of the file to be read. The function takes the number of polygons returned by the LoadPoly() function and uses it to pass as the parameter for the creation of the polygon list. This saves us from having to reallocate this memory every time we need to create a polygon list. (The Set-World() function must be called before the view can be displayed.) The text of the function is in Listing 13-4.

Listing 13-4 The SetWorld() function

```
void View::SetWorld(const char *worldfilename)
{
        int polycount= world.LoadPoly( worldfilename );
        polygon_list.Create(polycount);
}
```

The Update() Function

Before the Display() function (which, as you might guess, actually displays the view on the computer screen) can be described in detail, there are a couple of private View class functions that we need to examine. The first is the Update() function, which allows the positions and orientations of objects in the world database to be changed dynamically by the application program requesting the view. All the application needs to do is to change the value of the fields in the Object class that specify the coordinate position and physical orientation of the object, then set the update flag for that object. Since the update flag is private and therefore not accessible to outsiders, NeedsUpdate() and Complete() functions are used to respectively check and set the update flag. The text of the function is in Listing 13-5.

Listing 13-5 The Update() function

```
void View::Update(Object *object)
{
  if (object->NeedsUpdate()) {

                // Initialize transformations:

                inittrans();

                // Create scaling matrix:

                object->Scale();

                // Create rotation matrix:

                object->Rotate();

                // Create translation matrix:

                object->Translate();

                // Transform OBJECT with master transformation matrix:

                object->Transform();
```

continued on next page

continued from previous page

```
        // Indicate update complete:

        object->Complete();
    }
}
```

The DrawHorizon() Function

The second private function that we need to examine is a bit more complex. Its name is DrawHorizon() and it performs the surprisingly difficult job of drawing, well, a horizon.

One of the most obvious things about the world around us—so obvious that we almost never notice it—is that it is divided up into earth and sky. The point at which one becomes the other is the horizon. Because there are usually a lot of things getting in our way, the horizon isn't especially easy to see when we are on the ground. But from the cockpit of an airplane, it is one of the dominant features of the world around us. It's also one of the dominant features of the out-the-window view of a flight simulator.

The Horizon Problem

At first blush, it might not seem necessary to write special code to draw a horizon. After all, the horizon is nothing more than the edge of a large object that is usually found directly beneath us—the earth itself. But the earth doesn't lend itself easily to inclusion within a world database. It is too large, for one thing, and it is round. We haven't written any code for handling spherical objects. And while spheres can be represented as multifaceted polygons, the earth is so large that the sheer number of facets that would make it up might overwhelm the processing capabilities of our program.

The simplest way to represent the horizon is as a line that can intersect the view window, with the area to one side of that line filled with pixels of one color and the area to the other side of that line filled with pixels of another color. In most flight simulators, one of these colors is green (representing ground) and the other is blue (representing sky), though you should experiment with other colors. Ambitious flight-simulator programmers may even want to experiment with a gradient-fill horizon, in which the colors above the horizon are shaded to represent the shading of the sky as it nears the visual border of the earth.

Drawing a simple, non-gradient-fill horizon may sound simple, but don't be fooled. It's one of the trickiest elements of our view system. Unlike the relatively straightforward implementation of the three-dimensional representation that makes up the rest of our view system, the horizon representation is filled with special cases and unexpected problems. It's tempting to leave the horizon out of a flight simulator entirely, but a flight simulator without a horizon is like a day without, well, ground and sky.

How Horizons Work

Let's consider some of the problems. Imagine that you're standing in the middle of a vast plain, without buildings or trees to obstruct your view of the land. About eight miles away is the horizon, a seemingly straight line that stretches all the way around your field of view. Turn as much as you want on your y axis, the one that runs vertically from your feet to your head, and it's still there. Furthermore, it looks the same in every direction.

In fact, as much as the horizon *looks* like a straight line, it really isn't. It's a circle. It just happens to be a circle with you at the center, and it extends outward so far from where you're standing that you can't get out of its center enough to make it look like anything other than a straight line. Climbing upward doesn't make much difference. You have to get pretty high off the ground to make this particular straight line look like the circle it really is.

So how do we represent this in the view window? Well, we could draw a line across the center of the display, and paint the area underneath it green and the area above it blue. But that won't do us much good because the moment the viewer moves, we'll have to change our representation. The way in which that representation changes, however, depends on what kind of move the viewer makes. Moving upward doesn't make much difference to the way the horizon looks, unless we're writing a spacecraft simulator. Moving left, right, forward, and back won't make any difference either. Rotating, on the other hand, can make a big difference. What kind of difference? Rotating on the z axis potentially can make a lot of difference. This should make the horizon spin on the z axis of the video display, like a phonograph record. On the other hand, rotating on the y axis, makes no obvious difference. And rotating on the x axis simply makes the horizon seem to move up and down. (See Figure 13-6.) What happens when the viewer rotates 180 degrees on his or her x axis? Another horizon appears from behind, but with earth and sky flipped upside down!

With all of this in mind, we're going to treat the horizon as a straight line across the middle of the screen that can rotate around the viewer's position, depending on the viewer's rotation relative to the world's axes. But we're going to restrict these rotations to 180 degrees. After that, we'll treat the rotations as mirrors of smaller rotations, but with the positions of sky and ground reversed. Let's look at the code.

Walking the Horizon

Here's the prototype:

```
void View::DrawHorizon(int xangle,int yangle,int zangle, unsigned char *screen)
{
```

The first three parameters represent the rotation of the viewer relative to the world axes. The pointer to unsigned char screen points to either the screen or the screen buffer.

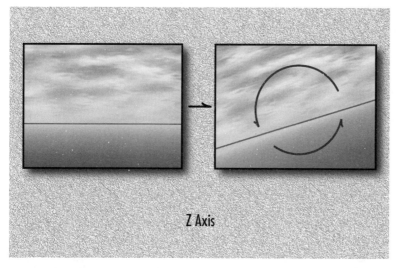

Figure 13-6 Which axis the viewer is rotating on determines how the horizon appears to rotate

(a) Rotation on the viewer's *z* axis causes the horizon to rotate on its *z* axis

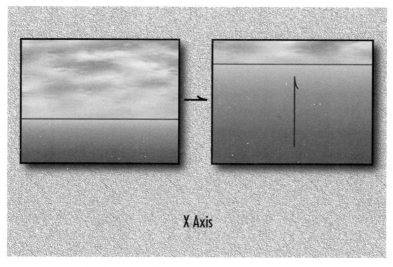

(b) Rotation on the viewer's *x* axis causes the horizon to move up and down

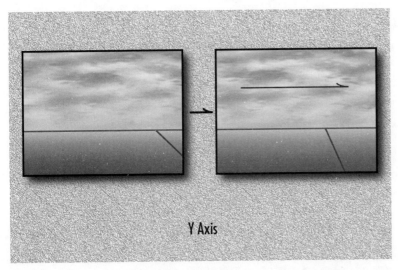

(c) Rotation on the viewer's *y* axis is invisible if there is no other reference

We start by declaring some useful variables. These will be used as the left and right coordinates of the horizon line as well as temporary storage during calculations:

```
long rx1,rx2,temp_rx1,temp_rx2;
long ry1,ry2,temp_ry1,temp_ry2;
long rz1,rz2,temp_rz1,temp_rz2;
```

We'll represent the sky and ground as polygons, which can be stored in an array of four vertices that we'll call vert:

```
vertex_type vert[4];
```

And we can set the aligned *z* field of the horizon polygons to a standard value. We'll use the viewer distance from the display, initialized by SetView():

```
vert[0].az=distance;
vert[1].az=distance;
vert[2].az=distance;
vert[3].az=distance;
```

We also need a clipped polygon, for the call to DrawPolygon():

```
ClippedPolygon hclip;
```

And we'll need a Polygon class object, to point at these vertices. Uh,oh. The Polygon class was never designed with access to the vertices. The Object class does the initial assignment to the vertices in Object::load(), but it was declared as a friend to the Polygon class. What we need is a way to stuff values into the vertices without having to go back and tear up the Polygon class (and rename the class again). The solution is rather easy in C++. We break from our current function to write a class definition above the function to alleviate the encapsulation difficulty. The localPolygon class is defined along with its constructor:

```
class localPolygon: public Polygon
{
        public:
            localPolygon(int num, vertex_type *vertlist);
            // the base class (poygon_type) destroys allocated vertex
            //   ptr array
            ~localPolygon(){;}
            void SetColor(int col)
                { color = col; }
};

localPolygon::localPolygon(int num, vertex_type *vertlist)
{
  // Allocate memory for polygon and vertices
            vertex = new vertex_type *[num];
            number_of_vertices = 4;
            vertex[0]=&vertlist[0];
            vertex[1]=&vertlist[1];
            vertex[2]=&vertlist[2];
            vertex[3]=&vertlist[3];
}
```

Note that the localPolygon class also takes care of the access problem to set the color of the polygon. The destructor for the class does nothing since the cleanup of the allocated array will occur in the Polygon destructor when vertex is nonzero. We even could have omitted the destructor, but in this case, it protects us from adding a destructor in the future which inadvertently might cause a deletion of the vertex array twice.

Back to our DrawHorizon() function, we can now add a Polygon class object:

```
localPolygon hpoly(4, vert);
```

This calls the constructor to allocate the memory for the array and points the elements of hpoly at the elements of the vert array.

Remapping the Angles

We don't want to deal with viewer rotation angles greater than 180 degrees on the x axis, since these could cause us to wrap around and see the horizon again from behind—a situation that's very difficult to handle with the standard rotation equations that we'll be using to rotate the horizon line. Instead, we'll use a system by which degrees facing forward—0 to 63 and 192 to 255—are left alone but degrees that are flipped upside down on the x axis—64 to 127—are rotated 180 degrees into right-side-up positions.

When this conversion occurs, we must note it, since it means that we need to swap the colors of ground and sky to make it appear as though we are seeing the horizon upside down. The integer variable *flip* will be incremented to flag this event. Because a z-axis rotation in the 64- to 127-degree range can put the horizon right side up again (or put it upside down if no x-axis flip has occurred), we must also flip z-axis rotations and increment the *flip* variable when we do so. Thus a value of 0 in the *flip* variable means we're right side up, 1 means we're upside down, and 2 means we're right side up again. By checking to see if *flip* is even or odd, then, we can determine whether ground and sky colors need to be swapped:

```
int flip=0;
xangle&=255;
if ((xangle>64) && (xangle<193)) {
   xangle=(xangle+128) & 255;
   flip++;
}
zangle&=255;
if ((zangle>64) && (zangle<193)) {
   flip++;
}
```

Rotating the Horizon

Now we must perform three-dimensional rotations on the horizon lines. We won't use the rotation matrices for this purpose; that would be overkill. Instead, we'll use the standard three-dimensional rotation equations shown back in Chapter 2 to rotate a 3D line from coordinates $rx1,ry1,rz1$ to $rx2,ry2,rz2$. All we're looking for here is the slope of this rotated line (as you'll see in a moment), so we need to create a line long enough to obtain an accurate slope from:

```
rx1=-100;  ry1=0; rz1=distance;
rx2=100;   ry2=0; rz2=distance;
```

The rotation looks complicated, but the code is standard stuff from Chapter 2, with the introduction of fixed-point techniques (see Chapter 9) and temporary variables to keep from overwriting the actual variables in the course of each rotation. Only the x and z rotations need to be performed, since the y rotation has no effect:

```
// Rotate around viewer's X axis:

temp_ry1=(ry1*COS(xangle) - rz1*SIN(xangle)) >> SHIFT;
temp_ry2=(ry2*COS(xangle) - rz2*SIN(xangle)) >> SHIFT;
temp_rz1=(ry1*SIN(xangle) + rz1*COS(xangle)) >> SHIFT;
temp_rz2=(ry2*SIN(xangle) + rz2*COS(xangle)) >> SHIFT;
ry1=temp_ry1;
ry2=temp_ry2;
rz1=temp_rz1;
rz2=temp_rz2;
```

continued on next page

continued from previous page

```
// Rotate around viewer's Z axis:

temp_rx1=(rx1*COS(zangle) - ry1*SIN(zangle)) >> SHIFT;
temp_ry1=(rx1*SIN(zangle) + ry1*COS(zangle)) >> SHIFT;
temp_rx2=(rx2*COS(zangle) - ry2*SIN(zangle)) >> SHIFT;
temp_ry2=(rx2*SIN(zangle) + ry2*COS(zangle)) >> SHIFT;
rx1=temp_rx1;
ry1=temp_ry1;
rx2=temp_rx2;
ry2=temp_ry2;
```

Next we'll perform perspective adjustments on the line, dividing the x and y coordinates of the vertices by the z coordinate. First, though, we'll make sure that the z coordinate is never less than 10, which could cause some minor problems in the appearance of the horizon:

```
// Adjust for perspective

float z=rz1;
if (z<10.0) z=10.0;

// Divide world x,y coordinates by z coordinates
//    to obtain perspective:

rx1=(float)distance*((float)rx1/z)+xorigin;
ry1=(float)distance*((float)ry1/z)+yorigin;
rx2=(float)distance*((float)rx2/z)+xorigin;
ry2=(float)distance*((float)ry2/z)+yorigin;
```

Creating the Sky and Ground Polygons

Now we're ready to create the two polygons that represent the sky and ground. We'll calculate the slope of the horizon line, and then create a large polygon that has an upper edge (for the ground) or a lower edge (for the sky) with the same slope as the horizon line. So first we'll get the change in the x and y coordinates in the horizon line:

```
int dx = rx2 - rx1;
int dy = ry2 - ry1;
```

So that we won't get an error if the line is vertical (which would generate a divide-by-zero error in the slope equation), we'll cheat by checking for a 0 change in the x coordinate and adding 1 to the difference if found

```
if (!dx) dx++;
```

This means that we can never have a perfectly vertical horizon, but this is largely unnoticeable in practice and saves us a lot of work in drawing the horizon.

Now we obtain the slope:

```
float slope = (float)dy/(float)dx;
```

We'll use the first two vertices of the vert structure to hold the upper line of the ground polygon, which will be a line with the slope of the horizon and the width of the viewport (i.e., from *xmin* to *xmax,* as established by the SetView() function):

```
vert[0].ax=xmin;
vert[0].ay=slope*(xmin-rx1)+ry1;
vert[1].ax=xmax;
vert[1].ay=slope*(xmax-rx1)+ry1;
```

If we had to flip the user's *x* rotation coordinate or *z* rotation coordinate earlier, this ground polygon will actually be a sky polygon and should be colored accordingly. This can be determined by checking to see if the *flip* variable is even (i.e., has a least significant binary digit of 0). If not, color the polygon with the sky color:

```
if (flip&1) hpoly.SetColor(sky);
```

Otherwise, color it with the ground color:

```
else hpoly.SetColor(ground);
```

Now we set the other two vertices to the extreme coordinates so that we can be sure they fit properly in the viewport and there will be no problems drawing the proper line slope:

```
vert[2].ax=32767;
vert[2].ay=32767;
vert[3].ax=-32767;
vert[3].ay=32767;
```

Then there's nothing left to do but clip the polygon to the viewport:

```
ZClip(&hpoly,&hclip);
XYClip(&hclip);
```

And—if we haven't clipped it out of existence—draw it:

```
if (hclip.GetVertexCount())
        hclip.DrawPoly(screen);
```

That's all there is to drawing the ground (or sky, if we were flipped over on either the *x* or *z* coordinates). The same process draws the sky (or ground) polygon:

```
// Create sky polygon:

if (flip&1) hpoly.SetColor(ground);

// If flipped it's the ground polygon:

else hpoly.SetColor(sky);

// Set vertex coordinates:

vert[2].ax=32767;
```

continued on next page

continued from previous page

```
vert[2].ay=-32767;
vert[3].ax=-32767;
vert[3].ay=-32767;

// Clip sky polygon:

ZClip(&hpoly,&hclip);
XYClip(&hclip);

// Draw sky polygon:

if (hclip.GetVertexCount())
        hclip.DrawPoly(screen);
}
```

The horizon is drawn. When the end of the function is reached, hclip—the localPolygon object—will go out of scope and its destructor called, thereby freeing up the memory used by the temporary pointer array. The complete DrawHorizon() function appears in Listing 13-6.

Listing 13-6 The DrawHorizon() function

```
void View::DrawHorizon(int xangle,int yangle,int zangle, unsigned char
*screen)
{
    long rx1,rx2,temp_rx1,temp_rx2;
    long ry1,ry2,temp_ry1,temp_ry2;
    long rz1,rz2,temp_rz1,temp_rz2;

    vertex_type vert[4];
    vert[0].az=distance;
    vert[1].az=distance;
    vert[2].az=distance;
    vert[3].az=distance;

    ClippedPolygon hclip;
    localPolygon hpoly(4, vert);

    // Map rotation angle to remove backward wrap-around:

    int flip=0;
    xangle&=255;
    if ((xangle>64) && (xangle<193)) {
            xangle=(xangle+128) & 255;
            flip++;
    }
    zangle&=255;
    if ((zangle>64) && (zangle<193)) {
            flip++;
    }
```

```
// Create initial horizon line:

rx1=-100;   ry1=0; rz1=distance;
rx2=100;    ry2=0; rz2=distance;

// Rotate around viewer's X axis:

temp_ry1=(ry1*COS(xangle) - rz1*SIN(xangle)) >> SHIFT;
temp_ry2=(ry2*COS(xangle) - rz2*SIN(xangle)) >> SHIFT;
temp_rz1=(ry1*SIN(xangle) + rz1*COS(xangle)) >> SHIFT;
temp_rz2=(ry2*SIN(xangle) + rz2*COS(xangle)) >> SHIFT;
ry1=temp_ry1;
ry2=temp_ry2;
rz1=temp_rz1;
rz2=temp_rz2;

// Rotate around viewer's Z axis:

temp_rx1=(rx1*COS(zangle) - ry1*SIN(zangle)) >> SHIFT;
temp_ry1=(rx1*SIN(zangle) + ry1*COS(zangle)) >> SHIFT;
temp_rx2=(rx2*COS(zangle) - ry2*SIN(zangle)) >> SHIFT;
temp_ry2=(rx2*SIN(zangle) + ry2*COS(zangle)) >> SHIFT;
rx1=temp_rx1;
ry1=temp_ry1;
rx2=temp_rx2;
ry2=temp_ry2;

// Adjust for perspective

float z=(float)rz1;
if (z<10.0) z=10.0;

// Divide world x,y coordinates by z coordinates
//   to obtain perspective:

rx1=(float)distance*((float)rx1/z)+xorigin;
ry1=(float)distance*((float)ry1/z)+yorigin;
rx2=(float)distance*((float)rx2/z)+xorigin;
ry2=(float)distance*((float)ry2/z)+yorigin;

// Create sky and ground polygons,
//   then clip to screen window

// Obtain delta x and delta y:

int dx = (int)(rx2 - rx1);
int dy = (int)(ry2 - ry1);

// Cheat to avoid divide error:

if (!dx) dx++;
```

continued on next page

■ ■ ■ ■ ■ **469**

continued from previous page

```
// Obtain slope of line:

float slope = (float)dy/(float)dx;

// Calculate line of horizon:

vert[0].ax=xmin;
vert[0].ay=slope*(xmin-rx1)+ry1;
vert[1].ax=xmax;
vert[1].ay=slope*(xmax-rx1)+ry1;

// Create ground polygon:

if (flip&1) hpoly.SetColor(sky);

// If flipped, it's the sky polygon:

else hpoly.SetColor(ground);

// Set vertex coordinates:

vert[2].ax=32767;
vert[2].ay=32767;
vert[3].ax=-32767;
vert[3].ay=32767;

// Clip ground polygon:

ZClip(&hpoly,&hclip);
XYClip(&hclip);

// Draw ground polygon:

if (hclip.GetVertexCount())
        hclip.DrawPoly(screen);

// Create sky polygon:
if (flip&1) hpoly.SetColor(ground);

// If flipped it's the ground polygon:

else hpoly.SetColor(sky);

// Set vertex coordinates:

vert[2].ax=32767;
vert[2].ay=-32767;
vert[3].ax=-32767;
vert[3].ay=-32767;

// Clip sky polygon:
```

```
    ZClip(&hpoly,&hclip);
    XYClip(&hclip);

    // Draw sky polygon:

    if (hclip.GetVertexCount())
            hclip.DrawPoly(screen);
}
```

The Display() Function

Everything's in place. The last step is to give the calling application a means to draw the view on the display. That's the job of the Display() function. Only two parameters are required, a variable of view_type to specify the position and orientation of the viewer and a flag to indicate whether the horizon should be drawn:

```
void View::Display(view_type curview,int horizon_flag)
{
```

Before we can draw anything in the screen buffer, we have to clear out whatever's left from the last view. So we call the clrwin() function to clear out the viewport:

```
clrwin(xmin,ymin,xmax-xmin+1,ymax-ymin+1,screen_buffer);
```

The parameters used here to specify the dimensions and address of the viewport were established by the SetView() function.

If the value of the horizon_flag parameter passed to this function is nonzero, the calling application wants a horizon in the view. So we check the flag and, if requested, draw the horizon:

```
if (horizon_flag) DrawHorizon(curview.xangle,curview.yangle,curview.zangle,
    screen_buffer);
```

The calling application may have made changes to the positions and rotations of the objects in the world database. If so, we need to update the vertices of those objects. That's the job of the Update() function, which we described earlier in this chapter. We can call it in a loop, one by one, to see if the objects in the database need updating:

```
for (int i=0; i<world.GetObjectCount(); i++) {
  Update(world.GetObjectPtr(i));
}
```

To make the view drawable, the positions of all objects must be adjusted until they appear as they would from the viewer's position. That's the purpose of the AlignView() function, also described earlier in this chapter:

```
AlignView(&world,curview);
```

Before drawing, a polygon list must be constructed:

```
polygon_list.MakePolygonList(world);
```

A depth sort must be performed on that polygon list, as described in Chapter 10:

```
polygon_list.z_sort();
```

All the preparation is done. The view is created in the screen buffer by drawing the polygon list:

```
DrawPolygonList(screen_buffer);
```

The complete text of the Display() function appears in Listing 13-7.

 ## Listing 13-7 The Display() function

```
void View::Display(view_type curview,int horizon_flag)
{
  // Clear the viewport:

        clrwin(xmin,ymin,xmax-xmin+1,ymax-ymin+1,screen_buffer);

  // If horizon desired, draw it:

        if (horizon_flag) DrawHorizon(curview.xangle,
                  curview.yangle,curview.zangle,screen_buffer);

  // Update all object vertices to current positions:

        for (int i=0; i<world.GetObjectCount(); i++) {
          Update(world.GetObjectPtr(i));
        }

  // Set aligned coordinates to current view position:

        AlignView(&world,curview);

  // Set up the polygon list:

        polygon_list.MakePolygonList(world);

  // Perform depth sort on the polygon list:

        polygon_list.z_sort();

  // Draw the polygon list:

        DrawPolygonList(screen_buffer);
}
```

Notice that the Display() function never copies the contents of the screen buffer into video memory. So when the function is complete, the view is still invisible. This task is left to the calling function, which can either use the putwindow() function for the job or a custom function of its own devising.

A New Backface Removal Function

We're also going to change the Backface() function in the final flight-simulator program. The function that we used in earlier programs that displayed rotating 3D objects worked fine for objects in the center of the video display—that is, close to the origin of the coordinate system. But this function was using screen coordinates and not the coordinates aligned with the view volume. In addition, it works poorly for objects near the edges of the viewport since we were only using the z coordinate from the determinant (cross product). Fortunately, there is an alternate method of backface removal that works under all circumstances. It involves calculating what mathematicians call the dot product. Here's the formula for calculating the dot product of the plane of the polygon,

```
float c=(x3*((z1*y2)-(y1*z2)))+
        (y3*((x1*z2)-(z1*x2)))+
        (z3*((y1*x2)-(x1*y2)));
```

where $x1, y1, z1$, etc., are the coordinates of three points on the surface of the polygon. (The coordinates of the first three vertices work fine here.)

Using the dot product, the new version of Polygon::Backface() appears in Listing 13-8. In case you've forgotten, this function returns a nonzero value if the visible face of a polygon is turned away from the viewer. Floating-point variables are used because the large number of multiplications may produce integer overflow, though you can experiment with change of the data types to *long* without too much risk, for speed.

Listing 13-8 The Polygon::Backface() function

```
int Polygon::Backface()
{

    //   Returns 0 if POLYGON is visible, -1 if not.
    //   POLYGON must be part of a convex polyhedron

    vertex_type *v0,*v1,*v2;   // Pointers to three vertices
    // Point to vertices:
    v0=vertex[0];
    v1=vertex[1];
    v2=vertex[2];
    float x1=v0->ax;
    float x2=v1->ax;
    float x3=v2->ax;
    float y1=v0->ay;
    float y2=v1->ay;
    float y3=v2->ay;
    float z1=v0->az;
```

continued on next page

continued from previous page

```
        float z2=v1->az;
        float z3=v2->az;

        // Calculate dot product:

        float c=(x3*((z1*y2)-(y1*z2)))+
                (y3*((x1*z2)-(z1*x2)))+
                (z3*((y1*x2)-(x1*y2)));
        return(c<0);
}
```

The entire View module is complete at this point. To keep things organized, all View class functions are in the file VIEW.CPP, with headers in VIEW.H. Matrix manipulation functions remain in the file POLY2.CPP where they've been all along.

A few details remain before we can create a flight simulator around this view system. The first, which we'll discuss in the next chapter, involves giving the view system something to view. In other words, we need to construct some scenery.

CHAPTER
14

14

Fractal Mountains and Other Types of Scenery

An empty universe, even one with a horizon delineating blue sky from green ground, is a boring universe. Wandering around—or flying—through such a universe, you'd never know where you were. Some of the early flight simulators were like this. All of the action was in the sky, where jet planes or World War I biplanes battled it out for supremacy of the air, and there wasn't much on the ground. Except for airplanes, the world was empty.

Flight-simulator programmers can't get away with that any longer. Even the simplest flight simulator needs scenery, and some of the most elaborate flight simulators sell disks that add increasingly detailed scenery to the initial database. The scenery, in fact, is often one of the most entertaining parts of the flight simulator. What armchair pilot isn't tempted to dip a wing toward the ground to get a look at the city far below or even to dive under the Golden Gate Bridge?

So far, though, we've populated our world with very few objects—a cube here, a pyramid there. How do we build up something that looks like the scenery in the real world?

Landscaping the Imagination

Building scenery for a flight simulator is a tedious task, but the results can be worthwhile. So far, we've given you no tools in this book for this task other than ASCII text files that can hold object descriptions and that can be edited with an ASCII text editor. Ambitious readers, however, may want to write their own scenery- and object-design utilities that use the mouse, the joystick, or the keyboard to drag polygons around and to build buildings, mountains, and other pieces of the landscape. You should be aware, though, that such programs are difficult to write, with much of the difficulty lying in the user interface itself.

Without such a utility, you have two alternatives for developing scenery for your flight simulators: edit the ASCII object descriptors by hand or write custom programs for generating specific types of scenery. In this chapter, we'll give you some tips about both methods.

Using Object Files

First, I recommend that you take the file named BYOFS2.WLD in the FSIM directory on the accompanying disk and use its contents as a template for developing your own object and world files. We discussed the format of these files in Chapters 8 and 12, but we are going to clarify that format somewhat now. As before, the files are simply strings of ASCII numbers, separated by commas (or any other non-numeric character other than hyphens and blank spaces, though either commas or slashes are recommended). White-space characters—blank spaces, carriage returns, and tabs—may also be used where needed in the file; they are ignored by the program. Numbers may be preceded by the negation operator (a hyphen) to produce a negative number. All text on a line following an asterisk is ignored and can serve as a comment.

The significance of the numbers is in their place within the numeric sequence, which is why you should use existing files as templates, since this makes it easier to keep the numbers in their proper order. In addition, screen formatting will help keep the meaning of the numbers clear. Use asterisks to provide room for comments.

How an Object File Is Organized

The order of the numbers is significant. The first section contains lighting and color information. This is, at minimum, six numbers, but can contain more according to the quantity of nonshading and shading color types defined. The first three numbers are the lighting vector and the fourth number is the ambient-light level. The next number is the amount of unshaded colors, which is followed by the three RGB values for each. The same format follows for shaded colors.

The second section is the object section. The first number in every object section represents the number of objects in that file. Most of the files on the accompanying disk contain a single object only (and thus have the number 1 for the object count), but a file of objects for a flight simulator would start its object section with a value representing the total number of objects in the file. If the world that you've designed contains 118 objects, then the object count should be the number 118.

This number is followed by a series of two-part object descriptors, as many as are indicated by the first number. In our hypothetical world file, there would be 118 object descriptors.

The first seven numbers in an object descriptor have not been explained. The first three represent the position of the object within the world, in $x,y,$ and z coordinates. The local origin of the object will be moved to this position before the view is drawn. The next three numbers are the rotation of the object on its local $x,y,$ and z axes. And the seventh number is a scale factor for the object—that is, the object will be magnified by this factor before it is drawn. Although the version of the Object class that will be used in the flight simulator has fields for separate $x,y,$ and z scale factors, and the scale() function in the POLY2.CPP module will scale separately in each dimension, the current version of the WLD file format uses a single scale factor for all three dimensions. (If you'd like to change the program to handle separate scale factors, you'll need to change the LoadPoly() function in the LOADP.CPP module. Here's a hint: You'll need only to remove comment marks from two lines and add them to one other line, since the code is already in place for the revised format but was not used in order to remain compatible with the current world database.)

These seven numbers are followed by a single number representing the number of vertices in the object. This is followed by a series of vertex descriptors equal to the number just given. So if the first number in the object descriptor is 5, it should be followed by five vertex descriptors. Each vertex descriptor consists of three numbers: the $x,y,$ and z coordinates, respectively, of the vertex.

The second part of the object descriptor is a list of polygons. The list begins with a number representing the number of polygons in the object, followed by that number of polygon descriptors. Each polygon descriptor begins with the number of vertices in that polygon, followed by pointers to those vertices in the vertex list for that object—i.e., numbers representing the positions of the vertices in the vertex list. These are followed by a number representing the palette position of the color for that polygon. And that's it. All object descriptors in the file follow this general format.

A sample file consisting of an object descriptor for a house is shown in Listing 14-1. Although quite simple, in the right context it could pass for quite a respectable house, especially if clustered along a polygon-fill avenue side-by-side with a row of similar houses. Figure 14-1 shows how the object is constructed.

Listing 14-1 An object descriptor for a house

```
0,-20,10,  * Light source direction
50,  * Ambient light 50% of light source

  1,  * Number of unshaded colors
      0,0,0,      * Black
  8,  * Number of shaded colors
      0,0,31,     * Blue
      0,31,0,     * Green
      0,63,63,    * Cyan
      63,0,0,     * Red
      63,0,63,    * Magenta
      31,31,0,    * Brown
      31,31,31,   * GRAY
      0,0,63,     * Bright blue
      0,63,0,     * Bright green
      63,63,0,    * Yellow
      63,63,63    * White

*** Object definition file ***

  1,  * Number of objects in file

* Object #1: House

  0,-10,1000,       * X,Y,Z coordinates of object's local origin
  86,102,222,       * Rotation of object on its local axes
  2,                * Scale factor of object

  13,  * Number of vertices in object #0

  * Vertices for object 0:

      -10,10,-10,    * Vertex #0
      10,10,-10,     * Vertex #1
      10,10,10,      * Vertex #2
      -10,10,10,     * Vertex #3
      -10,-10,-10,   * Vertex #4
      10,-10,-10,    * Vertex #5
      10,-10,10,     * Vertex #6
      -10,-10,10,    * Vertex #7
      -15,-10,-15,   * Vertex #8
      15,-10,-15,    * Vertex #9
      0,-15,0,       * Vertex #10
      -15,-10,15,    * Vertex #11
      15,-10,15,     * Vertex #12

  11,       * Number of polygons for object 0

    * Polygons for object 0:
```

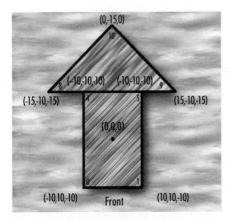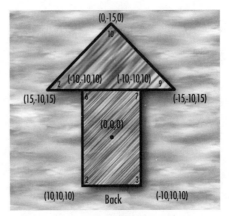

Figure 14-1 Object descriptor for house constructed out of polygons
(a) The front of the house   **(b)** The back of the house

```
4,  0,1,5,4,    1,
4,  5,6,7,4,    2,
4,  6,2,3,7,    3,
4,  2,1,0,3,    4,
4,  2,6,5,1,    5,
4,  4,7,3,0,    6,
4,  8,11,12,9,  7,
3,  8,9,10,     8,
3,  9,12,10,    9,
3,  12,11,10,   10,
3,  11,8,10,    11,
```

```
1 * Yes, we want backface removal.
```

Actually, this object is more detailed than most buildings in a flight simulator need to be. In fact, whole cities in the databases of flight simulators such as *Falcon* 3.0 have been built by placing variously sized cubes together along a grid resembling a layout of avenues. (A certain well-known flight simulator often gets by with just the avenues and no cubes at all.)

Using a Program to Generate Object Files

Building a house out of a series of coordinates is tedious business. A sheet of graph paper helps, but is by no means essential, and it hardly makes the job easy. For objects like this house, though, it's the best method we have at the moment.

More complicated objects require more clever solutions. How, for instance, would you build a large sphere out of polygonal facets? We've already seen the results of a 20-sided object in Chapter 12. To create an even more intricate model by hand with an

ASCII text editor and a sheet of graph paper is hardly feasible. But surely it is possible to write a computer program that would use the equation for a sphere to generate the data for such an object. This program could then output that data to the disk in the form of an ASCII text file, which could be merged with other ASCII data to create a .WLD file.

This idea of writing computer programs to create specific types of objects is a powerful one. I'm going to touch on some of the theory in this chapter and skip the details, but you should consider this concept and perhaps write some programs of your own that use this idea.

Right-Handed or Left-Handed?

One reminder: As we've mentioned in earlier chapters, polygons should be specified in the object descriptor in such a way that the vertices appear to move in a counter-clockwise direction around the visible face of the polygon. Why is this? I won't go into the mathematical reasons—I won't even pretend that I fully understand them—but it has to do with the fact that we are using what is called a right-handed coordinate system. If we were using a left-handed coordinate system, we would need to arrange the vertices in a clockwise manner around the polygon face; otherwise, the Backface() function, as well as some of the hidden surface ordering tests shown in Chapter 10, would cease to work properly.

How can you tell if a coordinate system is right-handed or left-handed? The standard method is to imagine that you are grasping the z axis of the system with your fingers curling from the positive z axis to the positive y axis. If you can do this with your right hand, then the system is right-handed. If you can't, then it's left-handed. (If your thumb is x, your pointer finger y, and your middle finger z, point all three fingers in positive directions—whichever hand can do it, that's your coordinate system).

If you have trouble grasping this distinction, so to speak, then here's an alternate method of distinguishing between coordinate systems: Any system in which the y axis is positive going up, the x axis is positive going right, and the z axis is negative going into the screen, or in which the axes can be rotated into this configuration, is right-handed. If it can't be rotated into this configuration, then it's left-handed. The system used in this book has the y axis negative going up and the z axis positive into the screen. But if you rotate the axes 180 degrees around the x axis, it magically becomes a right-handed system. And that's why the vertices are specified in a counterclockwise direction.

Fractal Realism

Surely the most difficult objects to design by hand are those that resemble features of the real world. Unlike buildings, which are essentially cubical, or streets and parking lots, which are essentially rectangular, natural objects—trees, mountains, coastlines—tend to have extremely complex shapes, rich with detail. And, in many instances, it is this very richness of detail that defines the object. A mountain stripped of its detail is nothing more than a pyramid. (The Amiga version of *Falcon*, released in 1989, constructed its mountains in precisely this manner. The computer pilot who wandered into a mountainous area could be forgiven for thinking that he or she had somehow flown into ancient Egypt!)

The notion of creating natural landscape features like mountains might seem a daunting one, but there is a secret to the generation of natural scenery: Landscape features tend to be fractal.

If you've played with some of the popular fractal-generating computer programs on the market, you may believe that the term fractal refers only to the strange, colorful, oddly buglike features of the Mandelbrot set. (See Figure 14-2.)

But the Mandelbrot set is just one type of fractal, albeit a spectacular and deservedly popular one. In fact, the term fractal has a much broader application. Fractal and terms such as fragmented and fractured mean any object, shape, or pattern that has the property of self-similarity, that is, it resembles itself at many different levels of magnification.

Self-Similarity

Most trees have an essentially fractal shape because a branch of the tree resembles the tree as a whole. A magnified picture of a branch might well be mistaken for a picture of

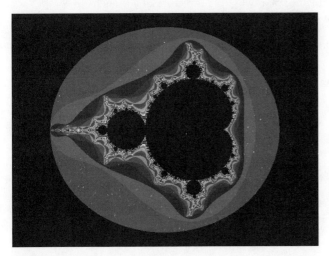

Figure 14-2 The Mandelbrot set, generated by the popular freeware program FRACTINT (available in the Waite Group Press book *Fractal Creations*)

Figure 14-3 A tree possesses the property of self-similarity; it is made out of branches and twigs that resemble the whole tree

a tree. And who can tell a magnified picture of a twig from a picture of a branch? In each case, only the size—the level of magnification—is different. The shape remains the same. (See Figure 14-3.)

Making Use of Fractals

But what good does all of this do us in designing realistic scenery on a computer? Computers are particularly adept at generating fractal shapes. We'll look at a good example in a moment. The reason that computers are so good at generating fractal shapes, aside from their utter disregard for tedium, is that most high-level computer languages possess a property known as recursiveness, sort of the programming equivalent of self-similarity.

Recursion, in case you're not familiar with the concept, is the ability of a subroutine or function to call itself. In C++, recursion might look something like this:

```
void do_nothing(int meaningless_value)
{
        do_nothing(meaningless_value++);
}
```

In this example, the recursive function does nothing more than call itself and pass itself an integer parameter of ever-increasing value. Obviously, this function is worse than useless. If compiled and executed, it would lock up the computer by calling itself eternally (or until someone hit the reset switch).

A slightly more useful recursive example would be the following:

```
void print_numbers(int start,int finish)
{
        if (start>finish) return;
        else {
                cout <<  start << endl ;
                print_numbers(++start,finish);
        }
}
```

This is a bit more cumbersome than the last recursive function, but it also does a lot more. What does it do? Well, here's the main() function that calls this function:

```
void main()
{
        print_numbers(1,10);
}
```

The function prints out a sequence of numbers, starting with the first parameter and ending with the second. In the example call, the print_numbers() function would print out this sequence:

```
1
2
3
4
5
6
7
8
9
10
```

While not terribly useful, this example begins to show what recursion can do. In effect, the recursive function has created a for loop where no such loop in fact exists. The print_numbers() function continues calling itself until the value of start has been incremented past the value of finish.

Of course, the for loop could have done the same thing more efficiently and a great deal more clearly, but recursion does have its uses. Let's look at the one that will be of most use to us.

Recursive Graphics

A picture can contain smaller copies of itself. Everybody's familiar with the image that is created when one mirror faces another mirror. Each mirror contains images of itself reflected in the other mirror and these images in turn contain smaller and smaller images of both mirrors. This is a kind of recursive image, an image that calls itself, in effect. Like our earlier recursive function that called itself infinitely, the mirror images theoretically go on without end, repeating themselves in smaller and smaller images until they recede into the mists. These images are also a kind of fractal, because they are self-similar at each diminishing level of reflection.

Fractals, in fact, are a kind of recursive shape. It's almost as if they were created by a function that calls itself again and again to create smaller and smaller, yet essentially identical, images. Such living fractal objects as trees may indeed have a kind of recursive function in their genes that calls itself to produce branches, twigs, and ever smaller branchlike shapes.

Recursion therefore is an ideal technique for drawing fractal shapes. To prove this, let's create a recursively organized program for drawing a natural fractal: a mountain range.

Fractal Mountain Ranges

The mountain range that we draw won't be especially realistic. It will be just a jagged line representing the crest of a line of mountains glimpsed in the distance. But the efficiency and ease with which it draws the mountain range will make the point about recursion and fractals.

To see what sort of results the program produces, run the program called MOUN-TAIN.EXE on the accompanying disk by typing mountain at the DOS prompt. The program should draw a jagged line across the video display that will be recognizable as the outline of a mountain range. Press any key (except the ESC [escape] key) and it will draw a *different* mountain range. Every time you press a key, in fact, the outline of a different mountain range will appear. (See Figure 14-4.) Press ESC to return to DOS.

These outlines are being generated randomly as the program runs. It may look as though this task would require a fair amount of code to pull off, but that's not so. Actually the program is extremely simple.

Here, in fact, is the entire recursive function that generates and draws the mountain range:

```
void lineseg(int hpos1,int hpos2,int vpos1,int vpos2,
        int depth,int range)

// Recursive line segmenting function.
```

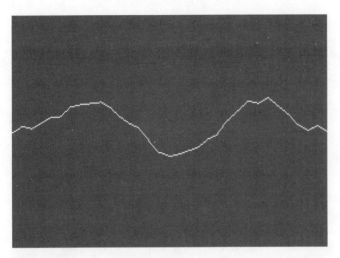

Figure 14-4 A mountain range drawn by the
MOUNTAIN.EXE program

```
// If recursive depth limit reached, draw line from
// HPOS1,VPOS1 to HPOS2,VPOS2, else split the line
// randomly and call this function recursively.

{
  // Depth reached? Draw line.

  if (depth<=0) linedraw(hpos1,vpos1,hpos2,vpos2,1,screen);

  // Else count off depth parameter, split the line
  // randomly, add random perturbation, and make the
  // recursive call:

  else {

    // Split line randomly:

    int midvpos=(vpos1+vpos2)/2+random(range)-range/2;

    // Call recursively with random perturbation:

    lineseg(hpos1,(hpos1+hpos2)/2,vpos1,midvpos,depth-1,
          range/2);
    lineseg((hpos1+hpos2)/2,hpos2,midvpos,vpos2,depth-1,
          range/2);
  }
}
```

This function, which we've called lineseg() (because essentially it just draws segments of lines), does almost all of the work of drawing the mountain range. But how? It certainly doesn't look capable of doing all that. To see the secret, let's look at the entire program, line by line.

The Mountain-Drawing Program

The program opens by setting a pair of important constants:

```
const DEPTH=5;      // Default recursion depth
const RANGE=150;    // Default range of line variation
```

The constant DEPTH defines the degree of recursive depth that the program is to use. Recursive depth is the number of times that the recursive function calls itself without returning. We've defined it here as 5. (Try varying this value and recompiling to understand the effect it has on program execution.) The constant RANGE defines the vertical range over which the mountain outline may vary up and down. Since the program runs in 200-line mode, we've allowed 150 pixels of variation, not all of which need to be used; the variation is random.

We then create a pointer variable to the video display:

```
unsigned char *screen;
```

Then we begin the main() function:

```
void main(int argc,char *argv[])
{
  int depth,range;

  // If no depth argument, use default:

  if (argc<2) depth=DEPTH;
  else depth=atoi(argv[1]);

  // If no range argument, use default:

  if (argc<3) range=RANGE;
  else range=atoi(argv[2]);

  // Initialize random number generator:

  randomize();

  // Create pointer to video memory:

  screen=(unsigned char *)MK_FP(0xa000,0);

  // Save previous video mode:

  int oldmode=*(int *)MK_FP(0x40,0x49);
```

```
// Set video to 320x200x256:

setgmode(0x13);
```

All of this activity should be familiar to you by now. The randomize() statement initializes the random number generator. Then we set up the graphics by pointing the pointer variable at video RAM, clearing the screen, saving the old video mode, and setting the current video mode to 320x200x256 colors. We then set up the loop to continue until the ESC key is pressed. Each time through the loop the screen is cleared and we call the recursive function. This loop continues until key is set equal to 27, the ASCII value for the ESC key:

```
int key = 0;
while( key != 27)
{
        // Clear graphic screen:

         cls(screen);

        // Call recursive line segmenting function:

        lineseg(0,319,100,100,depth,range);

        // Hold picture on screen until key pressed:

        while(! kbhit());
        key = getch();
}
```

The first two parameters to the lineseg() function are the horizontal positions on the display at which the mountain range begins and ends. The third and fourth parameters are the vertical positions of the starting and ending points of the mountain range. (This particular call sets up a mountain range from the left side of the display to the right, across roughly the vertical center of the display.) The fifth and sixth parameters establish the recursive depth and vertical range, as defined above.

Once the loop is over, the screen is reset to the starting video mode:

```
// Reset previous video mode:

setgmode(oldmode);
}
```

The lineseg() Function

Now let's take another look at the lineseg() function. It begins as before:

```
void lineseg(int hpos1,int hpos2,int vpos1,int vpos2,
        int depth,int range)
```

Then it checks to see if the depth parameter has reached 0 yet. If it has, it draws a line segment between the positions defined by the first four parameters, using the linedraw() function from our BRESNHAM.CPP file:

```
// Depth reached? Draw line.

if (depth<=0) linedraw(hpos1,vpos1,hpos2,vpos2,1,screen);
```

If the depth parameter has not yet reached 0, it calculates two new line segments and calls itself recursively to draw them:

```
else {

    // Split line randomly:

    int midvpos=(vpos1+vpos2)/2+random(range)-range/2;

    // Call recursively with random perturbation:

    lineseg(hpos1,(hpos1+hpos2)/2,vpos1,midvpos,depth-1,
        range/2);
    lineseg((hpos1+hpos2)/2,hpos2,midvpos,vpos2,depth-1,
        range/2);
}
}
```

These two new line segments represent the halves of the old line segment, the one defined by the first two parameters. The function has now split that line in two and called itself twice to draw the halves. In doing so, however, it has perturbed the position of the midpoint of the line segment up or down randomly, within the area defined by the parameter range. And when it calls itself recursively, it subtracts 1 from the value of depth, counting down toward 0, the value that will trigger the drawing of the line segments. And it has cut the value of range in half, so that the next line segment will have its midpoint perturbed somewhat less than the previous one.

Do you see how this works? The lineseg() function calls itself twice, but each of those calls to lineseg() in turn calls lineseg() twice again. See Figure 14-5 for an illustration of this recursion. In our example with a depth of 5, by the time the final recursive level depth of 5 has been reached, it will have called itself 32 times . Each time the lineseg() function is called, the line segment has had one of its endpoints randomly perturbed up or down. We've added an additional feature to interpret the key input to demonstrate the effect of the *depth* variable. Pushing a number from 1 to 9 on the keyboard will assign that value to *depth*, so the results can be seen on the screen.

The visual result is a jagged series of line segments seemingly rising and falling in a random, yet oddly smooth, pattern—the mountain range that you see when you run the program.

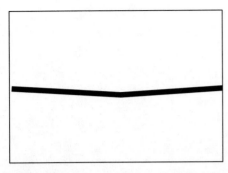 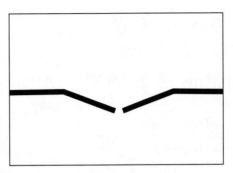

Figure 14-5 Fractal mountain breakdown

(a) First depth level: Split the line in half, call lineseg() for each line segment

(b) Second level: Two line segments each generate a midpoint

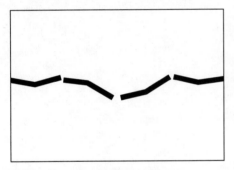 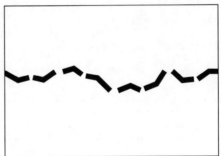

(c) Third level: four line segments

(d) Fourth level: eight line segments

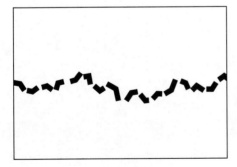 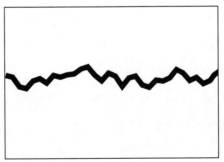

(e) Fifth level: 16 line segments

(f) Sixth level: 32 line segments drawn to the screen

The Mountain Program

The complete listing of the MOUNTAIN.CPP program appears in Listing 14-2.

 Listing 14-2 MOUNTAIN.CPP

```
#include  <dos.h>
#include  <conio.h>
#include  <stdlib.h>
#include  <time.h>
#include  "screen.h"
#include  "bresnham.h"

void lineseg(int hpos1,int hpos2,int vpos1,int vpos2,
          int depth, int range);

const DEPTH=5;    // Default recursion depth
const RANGE=150;  // Default range of line variation

unsigned char *screen;

void main(int argc,char *argv[])
{
  int depth,range;

  // If no depth argument, use default

  if (argc<2) depth=DEPTH;
  else depth=atoi(argv[1]);

  // If no range argument, use default:

  if (argc<3) range=RANGE;
  else range=atoi(argv[2]);

  // Initialize random number generator:

  randomize();

  // Create pointer to video memory:

  screen=(unsigned char *)MK_FP(0xa000,0);

  // Save previous video mode:

  int oldmode=*(int *)MK_FP(0x40,0x49);

  // Set video to 320x200x256:

  setgmode(0x13);

  int key = 0;
```

```
while( key != 27)
{
        // Clear graphic screen:

        cls(screen);

        // Call recursive line segmenting function:

        lineseg(0,319,100,100,depth,range);

        // Hold picture on screen until key pressed:

        while(! kbhit());
        key = getch();
        if( key >= '1' && key <= '9')
                depth = (int)(key - '0'); }
// Reset previous video mode:

setgmode(oldmode);
}

void lineseg(int hpos1,int hpos2,int vpos1,int vpos2,
      int depth,int range)

// Recursive line segmenting function.
// If recursive depth limit reached, draw line from
// HPOS1,VPOS1 to HPOS2,VPOS2, else split the line
// randomly and call this function recursively.

{
  // Depth reached? Draw line.

  if (depth<=0) linedraw(hpos1,vpos1,hpos2,vpos2,1,screen);

  // Else count off depth parameter, split the line
  // randomly, add random perturbation, and make the
  // recursive call:

  else {

    // Split line randomly:

    int midvpos=(vpos1+vpos2)/2+random(range)-range/2;

    // Call recursively with random perturbation:

    lineseg(hpos1,(hpos1+hpos2)/2,vpos1,midvpos,depth-1,
        range/2);
    lineseg((hpos1+hpos2)/2,hpos2,midvpos,vpos2,depth-1,
        range/2);
  }
}
```

Three-Dimensional Fractals

Can the same thing be done in three dimensions? Is it possible to create a three-dimensional fractal object in the same way that we just created the two-dimensional outline of a mountain range?

Sure it is. And the principle by which we would create such a three-dimensional fractal object is exactly the same as we used to create the two-dimensional mountain range: We start with a simple object and break it apart recursively into jagged but self-similar pieces. To draw the mountain range, we started with a line and broke it apart into line segments. To generate a three-dimensional mountain, we'll start with a pyramid (which, as noted earlier, can be thought of as an extremely simplified mountain) made of four triangles, then break each of those triangles recursively into smaller and smaller triangles. The more triangles we break the pyramid into, the more realistically fragmented the surface of the mountain will look. However, we don't want to break it into too many triangles, because we'll need to manipulate those triangles in real time in our flight simulator.

It won't be necessary to write a program from scratch to demonstrate fractal mountain building. We'll borrow the LIGHTDEM program from Chapter 12 and rewrite the LIGHTDEM.CPP module to generate a fractal mountain when the user presses the ENTER key. Much of the remaining program will stay exactly the same, since it's already designed to display light-sourced, polygon-based objects. The major difference is that, instead of loading the object data from the disk, the program will generate that data itself. Therefore, our polygon class will have to be touched to allow for the dynamic construction of its vertices. We'll initially load object data from the MOLE-HILL.WLD file to give the program the pyramid that it's going to make the mountain out of. The loading module will create an extra blank object for which to store the fractal object version. The World module will likewise be changed to prevent us from processing the blank object. And we'll make use of the PolygonList class to cull visible polygons and perform a z_sort(). We'll call our mountain-building program FRACDEMO.

A 3D Mountain Generator

Figure 14-6 illustrates the algorithm that we'll be using. In Figure 14-6(a), we see a pyramid. In Figure 14-6(b) we see the same pyramid with each triangular side broken into four smaller triangles. An additional vertex has been added in the middle of each of the three edges of each of the triangular sides and three new edges have been added to connect these vertices. It's not enough simply to split each triangle into smaller triangles, though. The vertices must be perturbed from their original positions to give the triangles the jagged, irregular look of rock cliffs, as in Figure 14-6(c).

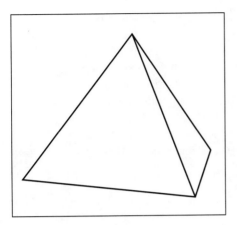

Figure 14-6 Fractal pyramid

(a) Simple pyramid

(b) Each side is split into four triangles

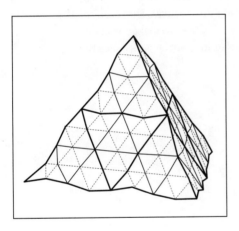

(c) Continued triangle subdivision with variance

Most of this work will be done by a function that we'll call fractalize(). We'll place this function in the main module of our program, which we'll call FRACDEMO.CPP. The prototype for the fractalize() function looks like this:

```
void fractalize(Polygon *poly, int rlevel)
```

The poly parameter will be a pointer to a triangular polygon, as defined by the Polygon class that we've used in earlier chapters. The rlevel parameter will indicate the current level of recursion. Initially, this will be set to 1, but each time the function calls itself recursively it will add 1 to this number. This lets the function determine when it has reached the maximum level of recursion, which we'll represent with the constant MAXLEVEL, defined in the header file FRACDEMO.H. Although we can theoretically set this constant to just about any positive nonzero value, a maximum recursion level of 3 probably represents the best compromise between a large and unmanageable number of polygons at the one extreme and an unrealistically simplistic mountain at the other.

We'll need to create an array of structures for this function's internal use. As in any recursive function, these structures will be created on the stack and generated anew for every recursive call. Here are the declarations:

```
vertex_type  newvert[6];
```

The newvert array of type vertex_type will allow us to create a temporary array of vertices to pass to the next level of recursion.

Our first order of business in this function will be to perturb the vertices of the polygon that has been passed to the function as a parameter. This is a relatively simple matter of adding a random value to each of the coordinates of those vertices. However, this simple matter will turn out to have some unexpected complexities. To make the coding easier, we'll start out by creating some vertex pointers and long integer variables that will contain the initial coordinates of the vertices:

```
vertex_type *vptr  = poly->GetVertexPtr(0);
vertex_type *vptr1 = poly->GetVertexPtr(1);
vertex_type *vptr2 = poly->GetVertexPtr(2);

long x0=vptr->lx;
long y0=vptr->ly;
long z0=vptr->lz;
long x1=vptr1->lx;
long y1=vptr1->ly;
long z1=vptr1->lz;
long x2=vptr2->lx;
long y2=vptr2->ly;
long z2=vptr2->lz;
```

Since the polygon being passed to the function should always be a triangle, these are all the vertices that it will have. Now we'll add some random values to these coordinates and create a new set of perturbed vertices.

Ah, but wait! If we perturb these vertices *too* randomly, we'll run into a serious problem. You'll recall from Chapter 8 that we maintain a single vertex list for each object and that the vertex lists within the polygon descriptors are actually made into pointers to the object's vertex list. We did this because almost all vertices are shared by two or three different polygons and we didn't want to waste memory storing the same vertices two or three times. But if we perturb the vertices randomly for each polygon in the object, these common vertices will be torn apart. A common vertex held by three different polygons may be given a different set of random coordinates for each polygon.

How do we guarantee that common vertices end up the same for each polygon that shares them? There's a simple trick we can use. It involves the srand() function.

Pseudo-Random Numbers

In Borland C/C++, the srand() function reseeds the random-number generator. (Since it is an ANSI function, other compilers should have this function.) You may be aware that the numbers generated by the random-number functions that come with most C compilers aren't really random. They are pseudo-random. Pseudo-random number generators start with a number called the seed, usually a long integer, and perform mathematical operations on it to produce a sequence of numbers that give the appearance of randomness (and which, for most purposes, are close enough to being random that the difference is insignificant). However, if you start the random number generator again with the same seed, it will produce the same sequence of random numbers.

The srand() function passes a seed to the random-number generator and starts a new sequence of random numbers based on that seed. Thus, if we seed the random-number generator with the same number each time we want to randomly perturb a vertex held in common by several polygons, it will give us back the same random numbers on each occasion, producing the same perturbed coordinates for the same vertices. But how do we guarantee that we'll pass the same seed to the random number generator each time we perturb the same vertex? We'll need to use some characteristic of that vertex to produce the seed. And the x, y, and z coordinates of the vertex are the perfect candidates.

Here's the line of code we'll use to produce a random-number seed based on the coordinates of the first vertex of the polygon passed to fractalize():

```
unsigned int seed=x0*100+y0*10+z0;
```

We can then pass the seed to srand() like this:

```
srand(seed);
```

Now that we've reseeded the random-number generator, we can generate some random numbers to perturb the vertices. First we want to produce a long integer value to add to the first coordinate of the first vertex of the polygon and store that value in the variable r, something like:

```
long r=(random(VARIATION)-VARIATION/2)/rlevel;
```

The random() function produces a random number in the range 0 to parameter 1, where parameter is the integer parameter that we pass to the function. Here, we pass it the value represented by the constant VARIATION, which will be set in FRACDEMO.H to the maximum range over which we wish to vary the position of the vertex. If

VARIATION is set to 10, this will give us a random number from 0 to 9. We then sub-tract half of the value of VARIATION from this number, so that it can have a negative value as well as a positive value. The range of the random value is now -5 to +4 if VARIATION is set to 10. Then we divide the result by rlevel, so that the random per-turbations will grow smaller as the recursion level increases and the triangles that we are dealing with become increasingly tiny. This statement will be used in so many lines of code, that we will write it as an inline function at the top of our FRACDEMO.CPP source file.

```
inline long RandomVari()
{ return (random(VARIATION)-VARIATION/2); }
```

Now, we can rewrite the line using this macro:

```
long r=RandomVari()/rlevel;
```

Perturbing the coordinate is a matter of adding this value to the coordinate:

```
x0+=r;
```

Now we must do the same to the other two coordinates of the first vertex:

```
r=RandomVari()/rlevel;
y0+=r;
r=RandomVari()/rlevel;
z0+=r;
```

And we must repeat the process for the remaining two vertices in the triangle:

```
seed=x1*100+y1*10+z1;
srand(seed);
r=RandomVari()/rlevel;
x1+=r;
r=RandomVari()/rlevel;
y1+=r;
r=RandomVari()/rlevel;
z1+=r;
seed=x2*100+y2*10+z2;
srand(seed);
r=RandomVari()/rlevel;
x2+=r;
r=RandomVari()/rlevel;
y2+=r;
r=RandomVari()/rlevel;
z2+=r;
```

This code is repetitive but straightforward. Feel free to recode it as a for loop.

We said earlier that this function would add three new vertices to each triangle, allowing us to break it into the new triangles. These triangles will either be temporary polygons, used for recursing deeper into the stack, or they will be polygons to be stored in the fractal object. Either way, the vertices of these triangles need to be stored in a vertex array. If we are done with our recursion and reached the final level, we'll store these vertices, along with the three existing vertices, in the fractal object. If we need to split the triangle further, we'll store them in the newvert[] array.

```
if (rlevel<MAXLEVEL)
        vptr = newvert;
else
        vptr = fracObject->GetVertexPtr(vertnum);
```

If rlevel hasn't reached the maximum level of recursion allowed by the MAXLEVEL constant, we point the vertex_type pointer, vptr, to the newvert array. If we have reached that maximum level, vptr is set equal to a vertex pointer from the fractal object. The two undeclared variables, *fracObject* and *vertnum,* are both global scope. *fracObject* is set to point to the blank world-fractal object and *vertnum* keeps track of our place in this fractal object's vertex array. Later, we'll increment *vertnum* by 6 to indicate that we've added six new vertices to the array. For now, however, we'll continue placing vertices into the object array starting at *vertnum.*

Vertices are stored by working our way clockwise around the triangle from the first vertex. The first vertex of the old triangle is simply copied verbatim to the first vertex structure in the vptr array:

```
vptr[0].lx=x0;
vptr[0].ly=y0;
vptr[0].lz=z0;
```

We'll then create a second vertex for the new triangles at a coordinate position halfway between the first and second vertices of the old triangle:

```
vptr[1].lx=x0+(x1-x0)/2;
vptr[1].ly=y0+(y1-y0)/2;
vptr[1].lz=z0+(z1-z0)/2;
```

We'll repeat this process for the remaining four vertices of the new triangles:

```
vptr[2].lx=x1;
vptr[2].ly=y1;
vptr[2].lz=z1;
vptr[3].lx=x1+(x2-x1)/2;
vptr[3].ly=y1+(y2-y1)/2;
vptr[3].lz=z1+(z2-z1)/2;
vptr[4].lx=x2;
vptr[4].ly=y2;
vptr[4].lz=z2;
vptr[5].lx=x2+(x0-x2)/2;
vptr[5].ly=y2+(y0-y2)/2;
vptr[5].lz=z2+(z0-z2)/2;
```

Recursing into the Depths

What happens next, once again depends on the recursion level. If we haven't reached the MAXLEVEL limit to recursion, we'll want to break this triangle into four smaller triangles and pass them recursively, one by one, back to the fractalize() function. So first we'll check the recursion level:

```
if (rlevel<MAXLEVEL) {
```

If we are going to recurse another level, we need to define a temporary storage space for a temporary triangle.

```
Polygon newpoly;
```

The *newpoly* variable of type Polygon will allow us to temporarily store a polygon which will contain an array of pointers to the vertices in the newvert array. It is a pointer to this Polygon object that will actually be passed in the recursive call.

Next we'll need to provide some memory for an array of vertex pointers that will be pointed to by the vertex field in the *newpoly* variable. The Polygon class has been changed and provides a function for dynamic construction of the vertex array.

```
int Polygon::MakeVertexArray(int vnum)
{
        if( vertex)
                delete [] vertex;
        vertex = new vertex_type *[vnum];
        number_of_vertices = vnum;
        return (vertex?0:-1);
}
```

With that function added to the Polygon class, the *newpoly* can now allocate some memory:

```
if( newpoly.MakeVertexArray(3) )
        return;
```

Now we can create a brand new triangle simply by pointing the vertex pointers in this array at three of the vertices in the newvert array, as shown in Figure 14-7:

```
newpoly.SetVertexPtr(0,&newvert[0]);
newpoly.SetVertexPtr(1,&newvert[1]);
newpoly.SetVertexPtr(2,&newvert[5]);
```

The SetVertexPtr() function is an additional inline function in the Polygon class. It assigns the Polygon::vertex array element indexed by the first parameter to the value of the second parameter:

```
inline void SetVertexPtr(int vnum, vertex_type *vptr) { vertex[vnum] = vptr; }
```

Here comes the recursive call, as we pass this new triangle back to the fractalize() function:

```
fractalize(&newpoly,rlevel+1);
```

There are three more recursive calls yet to come, as we create three more triangles and pass them back to fractalize():

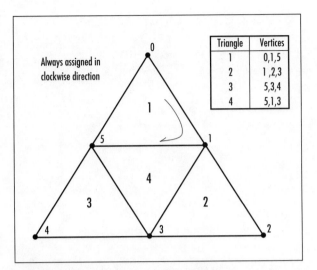

Triangle	Vertices
1	0,1,5
2	1,2,3
3	5,3,4
4	5,1,3

Always assigned in clockwise direction

Figure 14-7 Subdividing the triangle

```
newpoly.SetVertexPtr(0,&newvert[1]);
newpoly.SetVertexPtr(1,&newvert[2]);
newpoly.SetVertexPtr(2,&newvert[3]);
fractalize((Polygon *)&newpoly,rlevel+1);
newpoly.SetVertexPtr(0,&newvert[5]);
newpoly.SetVertexPtr(1,&newvert[3]);
newpoly.SetVertexPtr(2,&newvert[4]);
fractalize((Polygon *)&newpoly,rlevel+1);
newpoly.SetVertexPtr(0,&newvert[5]);
newpoly.SetVertexPtr(1,&newvert[1]);
newpoly.SetVertexPtr(2,&newvert[3]);
fractalize((Polygon *)&newpoly,rlevel+1);
```

If we haven't reached the maximum recursive level yet, that's all we need to do. But if we have, there's more work ahead:

```
}
else {
```

Storing the Fractal Data

If our demo is to use the fractalized triangle data to draw our fractal mountain object, that data must be stored in the World data class that we've been using in the last several chapters. Earlier, we said our world loader has created a blank object and there is a global pointer to that object called *fracObject*. In the fractalize() function, we'll need to take the polygon data that we generated in the first part of the function and place it in the appropriate parts of that class. The vertex data storage has already been seen to when the vertex_type pointer was assigned to either *newvert* or *fracObject*'s array. Since the polygon information will have to be stored as well as the vertex data, another global variable, *polynum,* will keep track of the position in the object's polygon array. First we'll grab a pointer to the next polygon, allocate its vertex array, and transfer the vertex addresses and polygon color to the polygon:

```
Polygon *polyptr = fracObject->GetPolygonPtr(polynum);
if( polyptr->MakeVertexArray(3) )
          return;
polyptr->SetVertexPtr(0,&vptr[0]);
polyptr->SetVertexPtr(1,&vptr[1]);
polyptr->SetVertexPtr(2,&vptr[5]);
polyptr->SetOriginalColor(polyColor);
```

polyColor is a global variable containing the color of the polygon from the object being fractally converted. SetOriginalColor() is an inline function of polyBase defined as:

```
inline void SetOriginalColor(int col) { original_color = col; }
```

After storing the first polygon information, we do the same for the other three triangles:

```
polyptr = fracObject->GetPolygonPtr(polynum+1);
if( polyptr->MakeVertexArray(3) )
          return;
polyptr->SetVertexPtr(0,vptr+1);
polyptr->SetVertexPtr(1,vptr+2);
polyptr->SetVertexPtr(2,vptr+3);
 polyptr->SetOriginalColor(polyColor);

polyptr = fracObject->GetPolygonPtr(polynum+2);
if( polyptr->MakeVertexArray(3) )
          return;
polyptr->SetVertexPtr(0,vptr+5);
polyptr->SetVertexPtr(1,vptr+3);
polyptr->SetVertexPtr(2,vptr+4);
polyptr->SetOriginalColor(polyColor);

polyptr = fracObject->GetPolygonPtr(polynum+3);
if( polyptr->MakeVertexArray(3) )
          return;
polyptr->SetVertexPtr(0,vptr+5);
polyptr->SetVertexPtr(1,vptr+1);
polyptr->SetVertexPtr(2,vptr+3);
polyptr->SetOriginalColor(polyColor);
```

The *vertnum* and *polynum* global variables have been initialized to 0 at the start of the fractal conversion in FRACDEMO.CPP, so we'll need to increment them to reflect the new position in their respective arrays. For the same reason, the number_of_polygons and number_of_vertices fields for *fracObject* are updated:

```
vertnum+=6;
polynum+=4;

        fracObject->SetNumVertices(vertnum);
        fracObject->SetNumPolygons(polynum);
```

And that, except for a couple of closing brackets, finishes the fractalize() function.

The FRACTALIZE() Function

The complete text of the fractalize() function appears in Listing 14-3.

Listing 14-3 The fractalize() function

```
void fractalize(Polygon *poly,int rlevel)
{

   vertex_type *vptr  = poly->GetVertexPtr(0);
   vertex_type *vptr1 = poly->GetVertexPtr(1);
   vertex_type *vptr2 = poly->GetVertexPtr(2);

   long x0=vptr->lx;
   long y0=vptr->ly;
   long z0=vptr->lz;
   long x1=vptr1->lx;
   long y1=vptr1->ly;
   long z1=vptr1->lz;
   long x2=vptr2->lx;
   long y2=vptr2->ly;
   long z2=vptr2->lz;

   unsigned int seed=x0*100+y0*10+z0;
   srand(seed);

   long r=RandomVari()/rlevel;
   x0+=r;
   r=RandomVari()/rlevel;
   y0+=r;
   r=RandomVari()/rlevel;
   z0+=r;
   seed=x1*100+y1*10+z1;
   srand(seed);
   r=RandomVari()/rlevel;
   x1+=r;
   r=RandomVari()/rlevel;
   y1+=r;
   r=RandomVari()/rlevel;
   z1+=r;
   seed=x2*100+y2*10+z2;
   srand(seed);
```

continued on next page

continued from previous page

```
  r=RandomVari()/rlevel;
  x2+=r;
  r=RandomVari()/rlevel;
  y2+=r;
  r=RandomVari()/rlevel;
  z2+=r;



          // new vertices storage:
  vertex_type  newvert[6];

  // assign the vertex pointer vptr to either
  //   local storage newvert,  or
  // if this is the depth of the recursion,
  //   to the fractal object's vertex array
  if (rlevel<MAXLEVEL)
          vptr = newvert;
  else
          vptr = fracObject->GetVertexPtr(vertnum);

  vptr[0].lx=x0;
  vptr[0].ly=y0;
  vptr[0].lz=z0;
  vptr[1].lx=x0+(x1-x0)/2;
  vptr[1].ly=y0+(y1-y0)/2;
  vptr[1].lz=z0+(z1-z0)/2;
  vptr[2].lx=x1;
  vptr[2].ly=y1;
  vptr[2].lz=z1;
  vptr[3].lx=x1+(x2-x1)/2;
  vptr[3].ly=y1+(y2-y1)/2;
  vptr[3].lz=z1+(z2-z1)/2;
  vptr[4].lx=x2;
  vptr[4].ly=y2;
  vptr[4].lz=z2;
  vptr[5].lx=x2+(x0-x2)/2;
  vptr[5].ly=y2+(y0-y2)/2;
  vptr[5].lz=z2+(z0-z2)/2;

  if (rlevel<MAXLEVEL) {

          // create fracPolygon with 3 vertices
          Polygon newpoly;
          if( newpoly.MakeVertexArray(3) )
                  return;
          newpoly.SetVertexPtr(0,&newvert[0]);
          newpoly.SetVertexPtr(1,&newvert[1]);
          newpoly.SetVertexPtr(2,&newvert[5]);
          fractalize(&newpoly,rlevel+1);
          newpoly.SetVertexPtr(0,&newvert[1]);
          newpoly.SetVertexPtr(1,&newvert[2]);
          newpoly.SetVertexPtr(2,&newvert[3]);
```

```
            fractalize((Polygon *)&newpoly,rlevel+1);
            newpoly.SetVertexPtr(0,&newvert[5]);
            newpoly.SetVertexPtr(1,&newvert[3]);
            newpoly.SetVertexPtr(2,&newvert[4]);
            fractalize((Polygon *)&newpoly,rlevel+1);
            newpoly.SetVertexPtr(0,&newvert[5]);
            newpoly.SetVertexPtr(1,&newvert[1]);
            newpoly.SetVertexPtr(2,&newvert[3]);
            fractalize((Polygon *)&newpoly,rlevel+1);

            // newPoly is destroyed
    }
    else {

            Polygon *polyptr = fracObject->GetPolygonPtr(polynum);
            if( polyptr->MakeVertexArray(3) )
                    return;
            polyptr->SetVertexPtr(0,vptr);
            polyptr->SetVertexPtr(1,vptr+1);
            polyptr->SetVertexPtr(2,vptr+5);
            polyptr->SetOriginalColor(polyColor);

            polyptr = fracObject->GetPolygonPtr(polynum+1);
            if( polyptr->MakeVertexArray(3) )
                    return;
            polyptr->SetVertexPtr(0,vptr+1);
            polyptr->SetVertexPtr(1,vptr+2);
            polyptr->SetVertexPtr(2,vptr+3);
            polyptr->SetOriginalColor(polyColor);

            polyptr = fracObject->GetPolygonPtr(polynum+2);
            if( polyptr->MakeVertexArray(3) )
                    return;
            polyptr->SetVertexPtr(0,vptr+5);
            polyptr->SetVertexPtr(1,vptr+3);
            polyptr->SetVertexPtr(2,vptr+4);
            polyptr->SetOriginalColor(polyColor);

            polyptr = fracObject->GetPolygonPtr(polynum+3);
            if( polyptr->MakeVertexArray(3) )
                    return;
            polyptr->SetVertexPtr(0,vptr+5);
    polyptr->SetVertexPtr(1,vptr+1);
            polyptr->SetVertexPtr(2,vptr+3);
            polyptr->SetOriginalColor(polyColor);

    vertnum+=6;
            polynum+=4;

            fracObject->SetNumVertices(vertnum);
            fracObject->SetNumPolygons(polynum);
    }
}
```

Making Many Mountains

There's just one flaw with our fractalize() function. Because of the way we reseed the random-number generator with the coordinates of the vertices before perturbing those vertices, fractalize() will always produce the same mountain from the same pyramid. And, since we're using the data in MOLEHILL.WLD as the starter pyramid for the fractal mountain, we'll always start with the same pyramid. Which means we can only generate one mountain—over and over again.

A fractal mountain generator that can only generate one mountain is a pretty boring piece of software. We need to introduce some more randomness into the process of mountain building, but we must do so in such a way that the common vertices aren't torn apart, which is why we reseed the random-number generator in the first place.

The solution that we'll use is to write a function called InitRand(). This function will take the pyramid loaded from the MOLEHILL.WLD file and make random changes to all five of its vertices. This way, we'll never start with the same pyramid twice. Here's the prototype for InitRand():

```
void InitRand()
```

As you can see, InitRand() takes no parameters and returns no values. If you guessed that InitRand() is a pretty simple function, you're right. It's essentially a small for loop that iterates through the five vertices in the pyramid and perturbs them randomly, using the same method that we used to perturb vertices in fractalize(), minus the call to srandRand():

```
vertex_type *vptr = (world.GetObjectPtr(0))->GetVertexPtr(0);

for (int i=0; i<5; i++)
{
        long r=RandomVari();
        vptr[i].lx+=r;
        r=RandomVari();
        vptr[i].ly+=r;
        r=RandomVari();
        vptr[i].lz+=r;
}
```

And that's all there is to InitRand().

World Changes

As mentioned previously, a few changes were made to our World class in order to create our polygon on the fly. The first of these was made to the World::LoadPoly() function in WORLD_FR.CPP. The number of objects is incremented so that an extra blank object will be created.

```
number_of_objects = _pf.getnumber() + 1;
```

After allocating the Object array, the object initializing loop is adjusted so that the program won't try and read in data for an extra object.

```
int lastobj = number_of_objects -1;
  for (int objnum=0; objnum< lastobj; objnum++) {
```

And finally, the blank object is initialized, so that other parts of the program won't try and draw it. This requires adding a flag to the object to be set or unset depending on whether the object is visible:

```
        // init the blank object
obj[lastobj].Init(1,1);
        // set it to invisible :
obj[lastobj].Cloak();
```

Thus, the Object class gains functions to initialize the polygon and vertex arrays, and to control the visibility of the object. Since this is the third field used for Boolean logic (flag), all three characteristics are combined into a multiple bit field. The following constants are defined for testing:

```
const int CONVEX = 1;
const int UPDATE = 2;
const int VISIBLE = 4;
```

The previous inline functions are changed and two new visibility functions are added to the class in POLY_FR.H:

```
int isConvex()
        { return ((flags & CONVEX) != 0); }
void Complete()
        { flags &= (~UPDATE); }
int NeedsUpdate()
        { return ((flags & UPDATE) != 0); }
void Uncloak()
        { flags |= VISIBLE; }
void Cloak()
        { flags &= (~VISIBLE); }
int isVisible()
        { return ((flags & VISIBLE) != 0); }
```

The changes ripple throughout the object functions, with the Object::Load() function being adjusted to the new style, in LOADP_FR.CPP:

```
flags = (UPDATE|VISIBLE);
if( (_pf.getnumber())!= 0)
          flags |= CONVEX;
```

The Object::Init() function in POLY_FR.CPP was created to allow dynamic allocation of the two Object arrays, polygon and vertex. The first time this is called, both pointers are equal to 0 (as set in the constructor), but on subsequent calls, the arrays are deleted so that no memory leaks occur.

```
int Object::Init(int vnum, int pcnt)
{
  if( vertex )
          delete [] vertex;
  vertex= new vertex_type[vnum];
  if( vertex == 0)
          return(-1);

  if( polygon )
          delete [] polygon;
  polygon= new Polygon[pcnt];
  if( polygon == 0)
          return(-1);

  return 0;
}
```

The World::Draw() function in WORLD_FR.CPP is changed to use a PolygonList class object. Since this operates on the adjusted coordinate fields in the vertex_array, the object first calls Transform(), then Atransform(). Since the inittrans() function is called between them, it has an overall affect of copying the world coordinates to the aligned coordinates:

```
objptr->Transform();          // Transform OBJECT using MATRIX
inittrans();
objptr->Atransform();
```

Next, a PolygonList object is declared, its array allocated, and the polygon_list is extracted from the object.

```
PolygonList polygon_list;
polygon_list.Create(objptr->GetPolygonCount());
polygon_list.MakePolygonList(objptr);
```

The PolygonList::MakePolygonList() function, described in Chapter 10, has been unrolled from its loop, such that there are two functions: one that takes a World reference and one that takes an Object reference. The meat of the older MakePolygonList() function has been placed in a private function called ExtractPolygons(). Here is the new public prototype from the PolygonList class in POLYLSFR.H:

```
void MakePolygonList(Object * object);
```

Back to the World::Draw() routine, after the polygon_list is made, the object is projected, then the z_sort() function called. We then imitate the Object::Draw() function by looping through the polygons, checking for backface removal, and calling the polygon's DrawPoly() function.

```
objptr->Project(400, xorigin, yorigin); // Perform perspective projection

polygon_list.z_sort();
for (int i=0; i<polygon_list.GetPolygonCount(); i++) {
```

```
        Polygon *pptr = polygon_list.GetPolygonPtr(i);
        if (objptr->isConvex()) {
                if(!pptr->backface()) {
                        CalcPolygonColor(pptr);
                        pptr->DrawPoly(screen);
                }
        }
        else
                pptr->DrawPoly(screen);
}
```

The complete World::Draw() function can be seen in Listing 14-4. A compiler directive, DEPTH-SORT, allows you to use the drawing method from the light demo program without using the polygon list class.

Listing 14-4 A new World::Draw() function

```
void World::Draw(Object *objptr, unsigned char far *screen,int xorigin, int
  yorigin)
{
  if(objptr->isVisible()) {
          objptr->Transform();        // Transform OBJECT using MATRIX
#ifdef DEPTHSORT
          inittrans();
          objptr->Atransform();

            // temporary polygon list
          PolygonList polygon_list;

          polygon_list.Create(objptr->GetPolygonCount());

          polygon_list.MakePolygonList(objptr);

    // Perform depth sort on the polygon list:

          objptr->Project(400, xorigin, yorigin); // Perform perspective
                                                   //   projection

          polygon_list.z_sort();
          for (int i=0; i<polygon_list.GetPolygonCount(); i++) {
            Polygon *pptr = polygon_list.GetPolygonPtr(i);
            if (objptr->isConvex()) {
                    if(!pptr->backface()) {
                        CalcPolygonColor(pptr);
                        pptr->DrawPoly(screen);
                    }
            }
            else
                    pptr->DrawPoly(screen);
          }
```

continued on next page

continued from previous page

```
#else
            CalcObjectColor(objptr);
            objptr->Project(400, xorigin, yorigin); // Perform perspective
                                                    //  projection
            objptr->Draw(screen);  // Draw transformed object
#endif
  }
}
```

The FRACDEMO Program

That covers almost everything except for the actual setup to call the fractalize() function. In readying our fractal object for receiving the subdivided triangles, of prime consideration is the storage space in the fractal object. We know that there will be four new polygons added for each final recursion and the maximum level will determine the recursive depth. This means that our polygoncount will be 4 to the power of MAXLEVEL times the number of polygons in our original object!

With that piece of information, we first write a tiny function to return our power of 4:

```
long lpow(int x, int y)
{
  long result = 1L;
  while(y--)
      result *= x;
  return result;
}
```

Now, we can set up our fractal object. First, we get a pointer to the current object and multiply its polygon count by the magic number.

```
Object * objptr =world.GetObjectPtr(curobj);

int polyNeed = objptr->GetPolygonCount()* lpow(4, MAXLEVEL);
```

Then, using polyNeed, we calculate the number of vertices. How? Simple, every edge belongs to two polygons and every polygons has three edges. Therefore, we must multiply by 3 and divide by 2. The statement can then be written as the first parameter of the Object::Init() function:

```
  fracObject->Init( (polyNeed*3)/2,polyNeed);
```

Next, initialize our array positions and start a loop through the object's polygons.

```
vertnum = 0;
polynum = 0;
for( int ii=0; ii < objptr->GetPolygonCount(); ii++) {
```

For each polygon, retrieve the original color to set the global *polyColor*. A call to fractalize() starts the recursion engine.

```
polyColor = pptr->GetOriginalColor();
fractalize(pptr,1);
```

After the loop is completed, set the flags of the objects to hide the original object and show the fractal object.

```
objptr->Cloak();
fracObject->Uncloak();
```

That covers the essential workings of FRACDEMO. There's a copy of the program in the FRACTAL directory that came on the disk with this book. You can run it by typing FRACDEMO at the DOS prompt. Initially, you'll see a pyramid spinning in space. (It's spinning rapidly because the extra polygons created by the fractalization process are about to slow it down somewhat.) You can control the spinning of the mountain in the same way that you controlled the spinning objects in the earlier OPTDEMO and LIGHTDEM programs, using the numeric keypad. To fractalize the pyramid, press the [ENTER] key.

Presto! The pyramid becomes a mountain! You'll notice that if you rotate the mountain so that you can see it from underneath, it appears to vanish. That's because we haven't included a bottom to the mountain. You can see right up inside of it, where the backfaces of the polygons are. Since we removed these polygons with backface removal, they're invisible. The mountain will reappear when its topside rotates into view again. To exit the program, hit [ESC].

Still More Fractals

As we noted earlier, many natural shapes are fractal, so we need not limit ourselves to fractal mountains. Many flight simulators feature both land and water environments in a single scenario, but the shoreline between the two is often straight as a ruler or unrealistically jagged. A fractal shoreline could greatly increase the realism quotient of such a simulator. Similarly, cloud shapes also tend to be fractal in nature. Adding a few fractal clouds to an otherwise blue sky would also up the realism ante of your simulator.

How do you create fractal shorelines and fractal clouds? That's for you to figure out. Once you start thinking in fractal terms, you'll find that fractal algorithms are not terribly difficult to generate. And if you become really ambitious, you can turn your hand to real-time fractals, which are generated on the fly, while your simulator is running. These will greatly decrease the amount of memory required to store fractalized polygons, since only a few parameters will be necessary to describe the fractal object, and will eliminate a lot of otherwise time-consuming processing of polygons and vertices. Obviously, real-time fractals require highly optimized fractal generating code, but many of the optimization tricks that we've described in this book will help you speed up your code.

Before you know it, you'll be looking around for fractals every time you leave your house—and finding ways to put those fractals into your computer games.

CHAPTER

15

15

Sound Programming

Thus far, you've learned some math, many useful algorithms, and many graphics techniques. We will soon have a running 3D flight simulator, but there is an ingredient missing—it doesn't make any noise yet. This chapter will begin with some of the history and theory behind PC sound, and then we'll show how to program exciting, realistic sound for flight simulators and other programs.

Some History

When IBM introduced the PC, it came with a built-in, low-quality speaker. This was connected to an inexpensive amplifier, making PC sound incapable of high fidelity or reasonable output volume. From a programming standpoint, it was CPU-intensive (tied up the processor), which is the reason why it was mostly restricted to error beeps. As a result, games with good sound effects were restricted to other computers.

In 1987, Adlib introduced the first important sound card to the PC world. The card had a Yamaha OPL-2 FM synthesizer chip on it, which could generate nine voices simultaneously. Nine voices meant nine sounds. They could harmonize or be dissonant. To a musician, that meant enough sounds to produce a chord, and to a programmer, it provided enough to make sound effects which rivaled the popular game machines.

In the following years, Creative Labs developed the first Sound Blaster, which was released in 1989. They put a Yamaha OPL-2 chip on it, for Adlib compatibility, and added a Digital Signal Processor (DSP) and a Digital-to-Analog Converter (DAC) for digitized sound effects. The combination proved very effective. Since 1990, Creative Labs has dominated the sound-board market, which has expanded to include nearly all PC computers sold for the home today.

Back in the days when EGA graphics were state-of-the-art, the FM synthesizer chip was considered adequate for producing music and sound effects. But in modern consensus, the FM chip is better suited for music duty, with sound effects handled by the DSP. The DSP can play any prerecorded digitized sound—such as voices, explosions, or the roar of a jet engine.

Sound Theory

Before jumping right into how you program the Sound Blaster, let's cover some useful background information which will help you to better understand sound programming. First, we'll discuss basic sound theory, touching briefly on the mathematics of waves, and finally in sound programming, we'll introduce FM synthesis and digital sampling.

Sound is created when physical objects vibrate. Examples of sound-producing objects are vocal chords, guitars, blocks of wood, and loudspeakers. As the object's surface vibrates, it compresses and expands the air molecules around it proportionally. This wave propagates to your ear, where it induces microscopic hairs to vibrate, which in turn fire off signals to your brain. When the rate of vibration (frequency) is between approximately 20 and 20,000 cycles per second it is perceived by the human ear and brain as sound.

The unit of measurement for cycles per second is the Hertz, which is abbreviated Hz.

Figure 15-1 shows the parts of a wave. The speed of the wave is a function of the matter through which it travels. Sound does not travel through a vacuum—so, Darth Vader never heard the explosion of the Death Star. But, in dry air at sea level at 20 degrees centigrade, sound travels at almost 770 miles per hour. Given this, the wavelength is calculated as the speed divided by the frequency. This ratio of speed to frequency implies that lower frequencies have longer wavelengths; as the frequency increases, the wavelength becomes shorter. How does all this affect human perception? Higher frequencies are perceived to be higher in pitch. Higher amplitudes are perceived to be louder.

Sounds in the real world are complex and composed of many waves. In mathematical terms, this is represented as the sum of a finite number of sine waves, functions which generate a curve endlessly cycling between -1 and 1. Back in Chapter 9 when

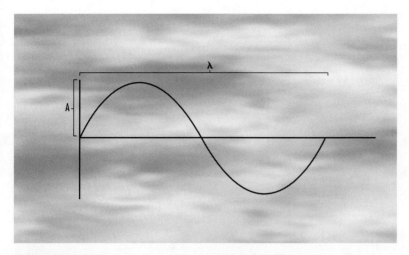

Figure 15-1 Parts of a wave: The *amplitude*, A, is the maximum displacement from the center; the *wavelength*, 1 (lambda), is the distance between the same point on two succeeding waves

the FIX.CPP file was created, this same sine characteristic was exhibited in our fixed-point table for the sine function. If graphed, the table would show 256 (the NUMBER_OF_DEGREES) points between 512 and -512, fixed point values for 1 and -1 (after the SHIFT).

As shown in Figures 15-2(a) through (d), real-world sounds look much more complicated than sine waves. Part A shows a plot of $y = 2\sin(x)$; part B shows $y = \sin(2x) / 2$; part C shows $y = \sin(4x) / 2$; and part D shows the sum of all three waves, $y = 2\sin(x) + \sin(2x) / 2 + \sin(4x) / 2$. Don't be frightened by the math—it's not important to understand how the graphs are made, but it is significant that we can add waves together. This additive property is a concept exploited in both FM synthesis and digitized sound.

As in mathematics, we've drawn the sine wave from 0 to 2P radians. From Chapter 2, we might remember that radians and degrees are measurements of a circle and may be used interchangeably. So, in essence, the sine graph spans from 0 to 360 degrees. As mentioned above and depicted in Figure 15-2(d), sine waves are additive. So if two or more sine-wave sounds are playing at the same time, you can simply add the y value for each x together, and plot one composite. This is simple enough, but to use that knowledge, the component sine waves must be extracted from a composite. And that isn't easy—either conceptually or computationally.

Any plot of a wave, such as Figure 15-2, uses the y axis to represent amplitude. But what is the x axis? It's *time*. So, such a plot can be said to be a time-domain plot. In

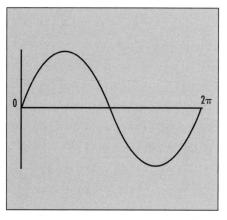
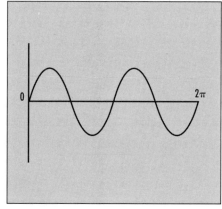

Figure 15-2 Three sine waves and their composite

(a) $y = 2\sin(x)$ **(b)** $y = \dfrac{\sin(2x)}{2}$

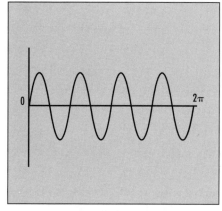
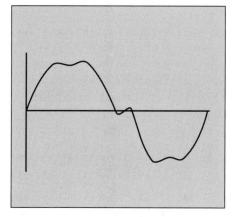

(c) $y = \dfrac{\sin(4x)}{2}$ **(d)** $y = 2\sin(x) + \dfrac{\sin(2x)}{2} + \dfrac{\sin(4x)}{2}$

contrast, a frequency-domain plot shows the amplitude of each (sine wave's) frequency, rather than the amplitude at each point in time. The Fourier Transform converts time-domain data into frequency-domain data. An explanation of this method is beyond the scope of this chapter. The important point to realize is that a relationship exists between the time-domain and frequency-domain. Many useful algorithms for processing sound rely on this relationship.

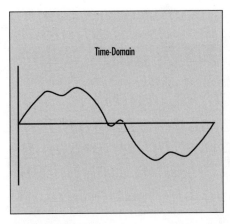
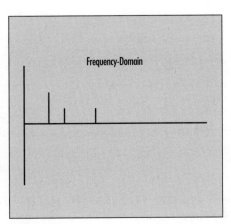

Figure 15-3 Wave in time- and frequency-domain

(a) Time-Domain   **(b)** Frequency Domain

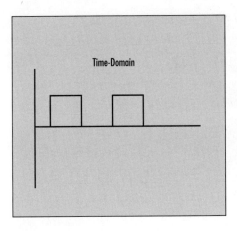
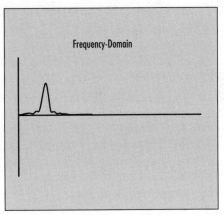

(c) Time-Domain   **(d)** Frequency Domain

Figures 15-3(a) and (b) show a composite of three sine waves in both the time- and frequency-domains. Figures 15-3(c) and (d) show a square wave, also in both domains. Notice in 15-3(d), how a square wave is comprised of an infinite number of sine waves. In real life, there is no such thing as a true square wave. All amplifiers, cables, and speakers will cut off everything above a certain frequency—each acts as a band-pass filter.

FM Synthesis

FM synthesis is the most common method used to produce computer music. This is because it is well suited to generate music—requiring inexpensive hardware, little memory, and few CPU cycles.

First, let's define a few terms. Synthesis is the combination of elements into something new. Sound synthesis, then, is algorithmically making sounds. This is fundamentally different from digitizing existing sound, as we'll discuss in the next section.

FM stands for Frequency Modulation. To understand that term, we need to look at modulation synthesis in general. In modulation synthesis, a modulator is used to alter a carrier in some way. Both are usually sine waves, although the output is not sinusoidal (shaped like a sine wave). The word modulation itself denotes that one wave is systematically changing the other. One notable use of this technique is in the radio industry, where you tune in your favorite station on the FM or AM dial. Amplitude Modulation (AM) is less complicated than FM, so let's look at it first.

In AM, the amplitude of the modulator is used to alter the amplitude of the carrier. (See Figure 15-4.) The problem with AM is that it doesn't really sound very good. Except for old organs, AM can't reproduce musical instruments very well. FM sounds can be much more interesting and exciting, which is why we use FM for computer music synthesis.

In FM, the amplitude of the modulator is used to alter the frequency of the carrier. As the value of the modulator increases and decreases, the frequency of the carrier increases and decreases. And as the frequency increases, the wavelength gets smaller. It's surprising how this simple method can produce an infinite variety of harmonically rich sounds. (See Figure 15-5.) Notice how the amplitude of the output is not affected by the amplitude of the modulator.

Our task will be to generate a waveform, but that in itself won't do. We don't want to just switch the wave on when a note is hit, and then switch it off when it's done. This won't sound like music because real instruments don't go from silence to full volume instantly—they swell and fade.

To mimic the surge and decline of a sound, an envelope can be applied which will constrain the volume in a way that's more pleasing. On the Yamaha OPL-2 chip, the envelope has four parameters: attack, decay, sustain, and release. These are the rate at which the sound attains its loudest level (attack), the rate at which it falls to a level which it holds for most of its duration (decay), this level itself (sustain), and the rate the level falls to silence when the sound is done (release).

There are actually two kinds of sounds in OPL-2 FM synthesis. Continuing sounds will hold the sustain level until they're manually cut off. Diminishing sounds wind down to silence on their own. As you can see in Figure 15-6, the sustain level has a different meaning for each sound type.

FM synthesis can be used to generate satisfactory music. Unfortunately, most software fails to achieve this because FM programming is so tricky.

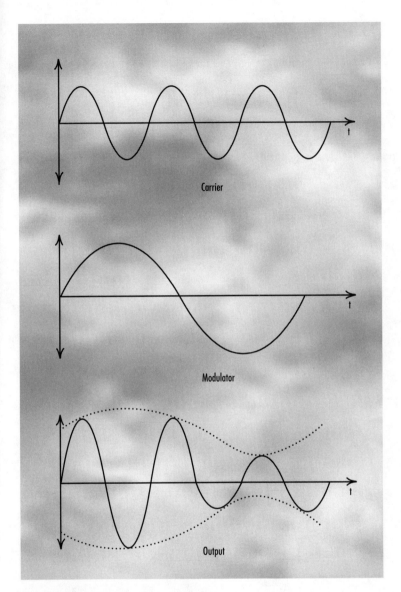

Figure 15-4 Amplitude modulation

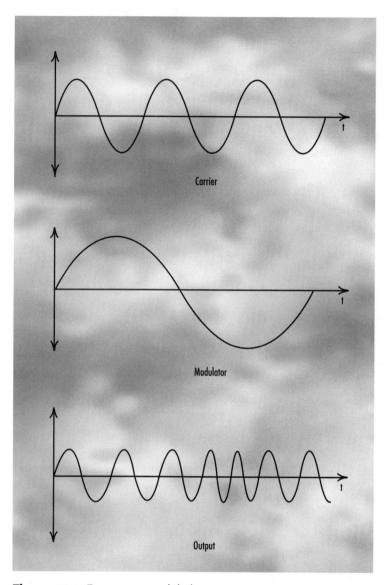

Figure 15-5 Frequency modulation

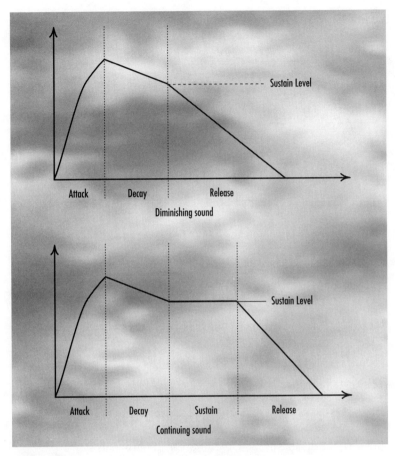

Figure 15-6 Parts of the FM synthesis envelope

Digitized Sound

As discussed earlier, sound consists of sine waves. These waves are contiguous—that is, they vary continuously over time. Even a section of a wave spanning a short period of time contains an infinite number of values of infinite precision. We once again meet up with the problem of precision and quality versus computer time and space (see Chapter 9 for a discussion on the problem). Computers require that such analog sounds be sampled, or digitized, in order to be stored and then reproduced. A digital sound is discrete, meaning that there is a finite number of samples and each sample can only be one of a finite number of values. Figure 15-7 shows a contiguous (analog), and a discrete (digitized) wave.

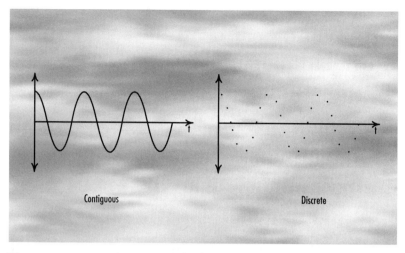

Figure 15-7 A contiguous and discrete wave

If 8 bits are used to represent each sample, we can represent amplitudes from -128 to +127. This can cause some problems. All values larger than +127/-128 will be clipped to +127/-128. This sounds so awful that it is to be avoided at all costs. Note: If you're mixing sounds together, you must keep the sum beneath this limit as well!

If a limit on dynamic range causes a fairly serious problem, then the fact that we're discretely sampling is even worse. As we saw above, discretely sampled sounds are not contiguous in the time domain. We have a sample for T=12 and T=13, but not for T=12.7. Obviously, in playing back the digitized sound, the air doesn't return to its static pressure level in between each sample. What happens?

It turns out the DAC will hold each voltage level until it's given another. If we send each sample to the DAC at the correct time, Figure 15-8 shows the output.

You may notice that the raw wave in Figure 15-8(a) looks very "square." This is due to the additional high frequencies which were added to the wave inadvertently during conversion to analog. It's an artifact caused by converting a discretely sampled wave to a contiguous waveform. In Figure 15-8(b), this wave is filtered in the analog domain. If the wave comprises only those frequencies below half the sampling rate, then it is a perfect reconstruction of the original wave.

Let's state this more formally. To capture a waveform containing frequencies up to F, you need to sample it at a rate of at least 2F. This is called the Nyquist rate. Sampling at any rate lower than the Nyquist frequency will cause aliasing, which is when high-frequency sounds appear as one or more lower frequencies. The cause of the problem is that you must have two samples per wave. Anything less, and you capture an alias of

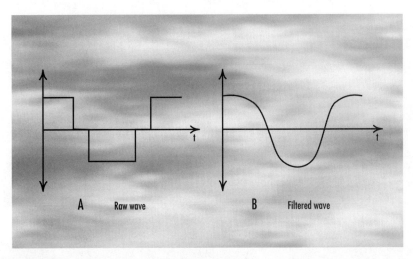

Figure 15-8 Reconstructed analog wave

the wave at a lower frequency. (See Figure 15-9). The original wave is dashed. The two dark points are the samples, and the solid line is the aliased wave.

The stair-step effect in a line as seen in Chapter 6 and propellers which appear to slowly turn backwards are other examples of aliasing. The frequency (resolution) of the screen is too low to display the line, and the frame rate of the human eye is too low to see a 15,000-RPM propeller.

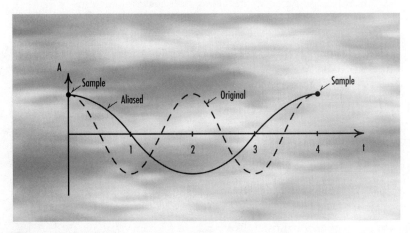

Figure 15-9 Aliasing

Digital versus FM

It's been stated that digitized sound is better used for sound effects, and FM is better used for music. Many programmers may challenge this idea. Digitized sound consumes a lot of space. A 1-second sound, sampled at 11 KHz, requires about 11K of memory. A song is likely to be more than 120 seconds, which could eat somewhat more than a megabyte of memory! For most applications, this is totally unacceptable. In contrast, the FM chip benefits from specialized hardware. It allows you to describe an instrument in only 11 bytes. The hardware does all the work to transpose to the correct pitch. And the output, sent to a special DAC, is actually a 13-bit, floating-point number. FM music can therefore be more dynamic than 8-bit digital music.

For making sound effects, on the other hand, digital prevails. Sound effects are almost always short, and usually don't change in pitch (engine noise for airplanes notwithstanding—see the code presented in Appendix C for a reasonable way to deal with this). Using the FM synthesizer for sound effects is problematic. First, if the FM chip is being used for music, managing the voices and chip registers to switch between sound effects and music becomes extremely complicated. Secondly, it's tricky and time-consuming to tweak FM registers to produce an atonal (nonmusical) sound effect. In addition, when configured for polyphonic (multivoice) mode, the OPL FM Synthesizer can't produce human voice at all. (The OPL-2 also offers something called Composite Speech Mode, but in this mode, it can't play more than one sound at a time.)

In the remainder of this chapter, we'll present FM code for sound effects (and skip music entirely). Why? The final flight simulator will have a single sound effect of an engine which changes as the motor's RPM changes. Our design then lends itself to using the simplest method of producing sound effects. Programming the Sound Blaster's DSP is a lot more work than programming its FM chip, especially if you want your code to run reliably on every computer, every sound board, every operating environment, etc. The interrupt controller and DMA controller must be programmed in addition to the DSP. A tutorial on register-level DSP programming could easily fill a whole book.

In Appendix C, we'll use DiamondWare's Sound ToolKit to play both digitized sound effects and FM music. Products like the STK allow you to quickly and easily play high-quality music and sound.

Putting In the Sounds

In the mode we'll be using for the flight simulator, the FM Synthesizer has nine voices, though we don't need that many. For each voice, we can specify the envelope, the pitch, the volume, and the timbre. For a flight simulator or driving simulator, the FM chip is particularly convenient. Changing the pitch of a sound (to represent change in engine RPM) is trivial.

As we write the code we'll use in the flight simulator, we'll present the details of programming the Yamaha OPL-2 FM synthesizer chip at the register level. The OPL-2 contains 18 operators which combine to make up the nine 2-operator (modulator and carrier) voices. Each operator contains data describing its sound attributes: volume, attack, sustain, etc. The term operator refers to registers which manipulate a unique channel of sound. In other documentation, operators are sometimes called operator cells (Creative Labs) or slots (Yamaha), but here we will stick with the simple name, operator. We'll tackle the code from bottom to top: first, we'll write code to control the FM chip, and later we'll write an interface module, which will manage the sound details for the rest of the program. This interface has a similar purpose as the Event-Manager class of Chapter 5.

The code in this chapter uses lots of macro identifiers to take the place of hardware specifications. If you decide to experiment, these identifiers can be tailored to your own specific sound card. The original SoundBlaster cards have one OPL-2 FM synthesis chip at port addresses 288h and 289h. The original Sound Blaster Pro card (CT-1330) had two OPL-2 FM chips to achieve stereo capability. The newer Sound Blaster Pro (CT-1600) contained an OPL-3 FM chip synthesis chip. This chip is compatible with the OPL-2 chip and added another 18 operators. Each of the stereo speakers were given their own port addresses–the left channel FM chip at 280h and 281h, and the right at 282h, 283h as seen in Table 15-1. In the case of stereo, 288h and 289h will access both chips simultaneously, thus maintaining programming compatibility with the other cards. The 16-bit cards were expanded to 20 voice, 4-operator FM synthesizers, and are still backwards compatible. The 32-bit cards contain the same capability in addition to a newer synthesizer chip (EMU8000) for a different route to musical generation. The common denominator for compatibility is the single OPL-2 FM chip, so it is our default.

There will be no SoundCard, Voice, or FM-synth class, although all the characteristics and elements to create such classes are here. Basically, this is C code which we will compile as CPP files so that the function names will be properly mangled for C++ linking. This allows us to replace these functions in the Appendix for an example of digitized sound and FM music without having to completely gut a C++ class. As an alternative, we could write a header file to declare these prototypes as extern "C" functions, then name all our files as .C files. This is a matter of preference. For the more

Table 15-1 ■ OPL-2 FM port addresses

	ports
mono sound	0x288, 0x289
left channel only	0x280, 0x281
right channel only	0x282, 0x283

ambitious programmer, we'll suggest some ideas for organizing classes as we describe each function. All of the code in this chapter can be found in the FSIM directory on the distribution disk.

Controlling the Chip

The nitty-gritty source file is called SBFM.CPP since it controls a Sound Blaster's FM chip. It holds the lower level functions, each of which will be discussed. First, we'll need a way to write the registers of the FM chip. The Write() function answers this need. The FM chip was assigned only two port addresses on the PC's bus, but it has several dozen registers, so it demands a clever scheme to get at all the registers. The FM chip follows a method of writing the register number to the first port and then accessing that register at the second port:

```
static void Write(unsigned  FMreg, unsigned value)
{
  outp(REGSEL, FMreg);              //selects a register to write to
  WasteTime(SHORT);

  outp(DATA, value);                //outputs a value to the register
  WasteTime(LONG);
}
```

The words REGSEL, SHORT, DATA, and LONG are all macro identifiers from #define statements placed at the top of the file. REGSEL and DATA are both port addresses for the sound card, respectively 0x388 and 0x389. The other two, SHORT and LONG are magic numbers fed to the WasteTime function. This is a function for delaying the CPU from further processing of the program by making it do specific code designed to waste time. The outp() function takes two parameters, the first is the port address, and the second is the value to be written. This is a non-ANSI function but is surprisingly the same and available in most compilers.

Unfortunately, the FM chip is slow. After writing the register number to the first port to select the register, we must wait about 2.3 microseconds. After writing to the second register to output a value, you must wait about 23 microseconds. To a modern processor, this is a long time! These delays are required because the chip is internally very slow; even the sluggish ISA bus on the PC is capable of feeding it data faster than the chip can process it.

To time the delays after writing to the FM ports, a delay function is used. The WasteTime() function will loop in code which reads the status port of the FM chip. We do not do anything with the status information; we're reading the port because it takes time:

```
static void WasteTime(word numreads)
{
  while (numreads--)
  {
```

```
inp(STATUS);        //reading the status port causes
    }               //a timed delay
}
```

Why not just add two numbers in a similar loop? Why port reads? There are two really good reasons: compiler independence and hardware independence. First, optimizing compilers are free to rewrite your code, in order to make it execute faster. If you simply add numbers together in a big loop, the compiler will often eliminate the loop. There goes your delay. As for the hardware problem, the end-user processor speed is never really known. But, a little trick can be exploited—the AT-bus runs at 8 MHz. Therefore each read or write using the bus will take at least 125 nanoseconds (Ns).

Determining the number of reads to cause a desired delay isn't nearly so simple. We resorted to the empirical method—trying and measuring. For 3.3 msecs, the loop needs to be executed 7 times, hence SHORT is defined as 7. For the LONG definition to supply 23 msecs, the loop is read 36 times.

Both of these functions, Write and WasteTime, are static, and therefore only available to the SBFM.CPP module. In a class, these functions would most certainly be made private to the class.

Is Sound Out There?

Before we get lulled away with the creation of sound, we need to check the computer to see if there is a sound card installed. This makes sense. A detection function determines furthermore whether or not an OPL-compatible FM chip is present. It does this by going directly to the hardware, not by asking the user or parsing the BLASTER environment variable. The detection function is required to return a Boolean value depending on whether the FM chip is present or not. There is no built-in Boolean type in Borland C++ 4.5 so we will include a header file at the top of the module which defines the boolean type and the value for false and true. (Future versions of ANSI C++ will define a built-in boolean type). All of our FM functions will begin with the prefix sbfm_, so our declaration looks like this:

```
boolean sbfm_PresenceTest()
{
```

The FM chip has two timers on it, which were intended by Yamaha to be hooked up to IRQ lines in the computer. Neither Adlib, nor Creative Labs, actually connected them to IRQ lines. But the terminology stems from this.

First, we reset one of these timers and start it ticking. Then we read the status port. If any bits are set right now, then there's definitely no FM chip present.

```
int res;

    Write(IRQ_TIMER_CNTRL, RESET_TIMER);    //reset timer
    Write(IRQ_TIMER_CNTRL, IRQ_ENABLE);     //enable timer IRQ
```

continued on next page

continued from previous page

```
    res = inp(STATUS);                     //get res after reset/before timeout

    Write(IRQ_TIMER_CNTRL, RESET_TIMER);  //reset timer

        //bit test :none of bits 5,6 or 7 should be set
    if((res&IRQ_BITMASK) != 0)  {
            return (false);    //if they are, then fail
            }
```

The identifier IRQ_TIMER_CNTRL is defined previously in the file as 4, the FM chip register number for the timer. Bits 5,6, and 7 of the STATUS port are examined to see if any are set via IRQ_BITMASK which is equal to 0xE0. STATUS is previously defined in the file as 0x388. Sharp readers may recognize this as the same port address as REGSEL. That's absolutely right. Input from the port indicates chip status while output to the same port selects a register for a subsequent operation.

Passing the first test, we start it ticking with a short countdown duration. We wait enough time to guarantee that the timer has timed out (run down):

```
Write(TIMER1, 0xff);                    //write low value to timer1
Write(IRQ_TIMER_CNTRL, STARTTIMER1);   //write timer1 start mask
WasteTime(TIMEOUT);                     //wait long enough for timer to expire
```

The WasteTime() function is passed the value of TIMEOUT, #defined earlier as 144. This is about 92 microseconds, plenty of time for our timer to count 0xff ticks.

Now, we read the status port again. This time, we should see an IRQ pending for this timer. If we do find it, then there is an FM chip present.

```
res = inp(STATUS);                     //get res after a timeout

Write(IRQ_TIMER_CNTRL, RESET_TIMER);   //reset timer

        //make sure IRQ masked bits are set to "timed out"
if ((res&IRQ_BITMASK) != IRQ_TIMEDOUT) {
            return(false);             //if not "timed out" fail
}

return(true);
            }
```

Note: Time-critical code like this is normally executed with the CPU's interrupt flag clear. Clearing the interrupt flag has the effect of disabling interrupts. This is done so that some hardware interrupt does not happen and steal some CPU time, thereby invalidating the test. To implement such control of the interrupt flag, we could wrap the code with one line assembler directive using the Borland C++ ASM keyword and the 8086 cli and sti instructions, or the enable and disable C functions. However, in practice, such interrupt problems are very rare. And also, in this particular case, we want the timer to expire. A hardware interruption which delays our immediate polling of the FM status does not invalidate our test, since that's what we want to happen.

The completed code of the sbfm_PresenceTest() function is in Listing 15-1.

Listing 15-1 The sbfm_PresenceTest() function

```
boolean sbfm_PresenceTest(void)
{
        int res;

        Write(IRQ_TIMER_CNTRL, RESET_TIMER);   //reset timer
        Write(IRQ_TIMER_CNTRL, IRQ_ENABLE);    //enable timer IRQ
        res = inp(STATUS);                     //get res after reset/before
                                               // timeout

        Write(IRQ_TIMER_CNTRL, RESET_TIMER);   //reset timer

           //bit test :none of bits 5,6 or 7 should be set
        if((res&IRQ_BITMASK) != 0)        {
                return (false);                //if they are, then fail
        }

        Write(TIMER1, 0xff);                   //write low value to timer1
        Write(IRQ_TIMER_CNTRL, STARTTIMER1);   //write timer1 start mask
        WasteTime(TIMEOUT);                    //wait long enough for timer
                                               // to expire
        res = inp(STATUS);                     //get res after a timeout

        Write(IRQ_TIMER_CNTRL, RESET_TIMER);   //reset timer

           //make sure IRQ masked bits are set to "timed out"
        if ((res&IRQ_BITMASK) != IRQ_TIMEDOUT) {
                return(false);                 //if not "timed out" fail
        }

        return(true);                          //it seems that an FM chip
                                               // is here

}
```

One of the things that might strike you as you look at the code is that there are a slew of capitalized identifiers used in this function. These are all defined at the top of the module. For your perusal, here are the defined identifiers from the SBFM.CPP module:

```
#define WAVESELECT_TEST    0x01   //1 per chip
#define TIMER1             0x02   //1 per chip (80  æsec resolution)
#define TIMER2             0x03   //1 per chip (320 æsec resolution)
#define IRQ_TIMER_CNTRL    0x04   //1 per chip
#define CSM_SEL            0x08   //1 per chip

#define SND_CHAR           0x20   //18 per chip (one per operator)
#define LEVEL_OUTPUT       0x40   //18 per chip (one per operator)
#define ATTACK_DECAY       0x60   //18 per chip (one per operator)
#define SUSTAIN_RELEASE    0x80   //18 per chip (one per operator)
#define FNUML              0xa0   //9 per chip (one per operator pair)
```

continued on next page

continued from previous page

```
#define KEYON_BLOCK_FNUMH   0xb0        //9 per chip (one per operator pair)
#define DRUMCONTROL         0xbd        //1 per chip
#define FEEDBACK_CON        0xc0        //9 per chip (one per operator pair)
#define WAVE_SELECT         0xe0        //18 per chip (one per operator)

#define STATUS              0x388       //read-only
#define REGSEL              0x388       //write-only
#define DATA                0x389       //write-only

#define SHORT               7           //approx 3.3 æsec delay
#define LONG                36          //approx 23 æsec delay
#define TIMEOUT             144         //approx 92 æsec delay

#define KEYON               0x20        //key on mask
#define STARTTIMER1         0x21        //start timer 1
#define WAVESEL             0x20        //enable wave select
#define RESET_TIMER         0x60        //timer reset
#define IRQ_ENABLE          0x80        //enable timer IRQ
#define KEYREL              0xdf        //key release mask
#define IRQ_BITMASK         0xe0        //for reading status
#define IRQ_TIMEDOUT        0xc0        //irq timer wound down

#define NUMVOICES           9           //9 2-operator channels
```

Initializing the FM Chip

After the detection function acknowledges the FM chip is present, the plan is to return the chip to an initialized state. The FM chip does not have a reset command, so we get to write one:

```
void sbfm_Reset(void)
{
```

Such a function stops all sound and sets the registers to some reasonable defaults. First, to stop the sound, all nine voices must be turned off. So, we go through a loop:

```
for (int channel=0;channel<NUMVOICES;channel++)   {
```

The organization of registers on the FM chip is easiest understood by using the following table as the base of operations:

```
static ofst_op1[] = {0x00, 0x01, 0x02, 0x08, 0x09, 0x0a, 0x10, 0x11, 0x12};
```

This table provides an offset register number for each of the nine voices, also referred to as channels. Each voice is composed of two operators, which can be thought of as the modulator and carrier. By adding three to each of the base values, the second operator array can be generated:

```
static ofst_op2[] = {0x03, 0x04, 0x05, 0x0b, 0x0c, 0x0d, 0x13, 0x14, 0x15};
```

These two arrays work in tandem such that an index into both arrays yields that voice's two operators. For example, the two base values for voice six are 0x0a and 0x0d

Table 15-2 ■ FM registers

Register Address (in hex)	Acts On	Attribute
20-35	Operator	Multiplier
40-55	Operator	Attenuation
60-75	Operator	Attack/Decay
80-95	Operator	Sustain/Release
A0-A8	Channel	Frequency (lower 8 bits)
B0-B8	Channel	Frequency (high 2 bits); Block number (octave); Key on
C0-C8	Channel	Stereo; Operator connection
E0-F5	Operator	Wave Select

since they are in the sixth element positions. The identification of the operator base value then makes it possible to alter its values for attack, decay, sustain, release, volume, vibrato, and other attributes. This is done by adding the attribute's register address to the channel operator's base value. Table 15-2 shows a partial list of the pertinent attribute registers for the FM chip. Notice that some registers modify the operator and some change the channel (therefore both operators are affected). As an example, suppose we want to address the sustain/release attribute of channel 2's carrier operator. Figure the base address as the channel - 1 + 3, then add the register number from the table for sustain/release, 80h, and arrive at the answer of 84h.

So, now, within the loop, several of the voice's characteristics are set to a startup value:

```
Write(LEVEL_OUTPUT + ofst_op1[channel], 0xff);
Write(LEVEL_OUTPUT + ofst_op2[channel], 0xff);
Write(ATTACK_DECAY + ofst_op1[channel], 0xff);
Write(ATTACK_DECAY + ofst_op2[channel], 0xff);
Write(SUSTAIN_RELEASE + ofst_op1[channel], 0x0f);
Write(SUSTAIN_RELEASE + ofst_op2[channel], 0x0f);
```

The volume for each voice is set, then the attack, decay, and release rates to super-fast, while sustain is set to 0. Any note still in progress will reach its end in no time at all (well, not quite literally).

The number which makes up the frequency spans two registers. More exactly, it spans one-and-one-half registers, the lower 8 bits into one register and the upper 4 bits in another. This frequency is used for both operators of the voice. Thus there is one set of frequency registers per voice. The other 4 bits of the high frequency register are used to turn the note on and to set an octave multiplier (also called a block). To make the carrier's frequency differ from the modulator's frequency, use different multipliers. The resulting frequency is therefore a formula involving the block value, the frequency

(12-bit value) and the multiplier. The following sets the block to 0 along with the upper 4 bits of the frequency, as well as turns the note off:

```
        Write(KEYON_BLOCK_FNUMH + channel, 0x00);
}
```

The loop repeats until all nine voices are finished. We're not done with sbfm_Reset(), however. Some odds and ends need to be fixed before we return from our function. In particular, the timer is reset and both rhythm and speech modes are turned off.

```
//this will set chip to 9 channel mode
Write(WAVESELECT_TEST, WAVESEL);              //enable wave select
Write(IRQ_TIMER_CNTRL, RESET_TIMER);
Write(CSM_SEL, 0x00);                         //clear Composite Speech Mode
  Write(DRUMCONTROL, 0x00);                   //clear drum mode
```

Listing 15-2 contains the finished code for the function.

Listing 15-2 The sbfm_Reset() function

```
void sbfm_Reset()
{
        //this loop keys off all channels
    for (int channel=0;channel<NUMVOICES;channel++) {
        Write(LEVEL_OUTPUT + ofst_op1[channel], 0xff);   //1st attenuate
        Write(LEVEL_OUTPUT + ofst_op2[channel], 0xff);   //channels volume

        Write(ATTACK_DECAY + ofst_op1[channel], 0xff);   //2nd accelerate
                                                         //attack,
        Write(ATTACK_DECAY + ofst_op2[channel], 0xff);   //decay, sustain, and
                                                         //release, this will
        Write(SUSTAIN_RELEASE + ofst_op1[channel], 0x0f); //quiet a channel
        Write(SUSTAIN_RELEASE + ofst_op2[channel], 0x0f); //down quickly

        Write(KEYON_BLOCK_FNUMH + channel, 0x00);        //3rd key release
                                                         //channel
    }


        //this will set chip to 9 channel mode
        Write(WAVESELECT_TEST, WAVESEL);                 //enable wave select
        Write(IRQ_TIMER_CNTRL, RESET_TIMER);             //reset/mask timer
        Write(CSM_SEL,  0x00);                           //clear Composite
                                                         //Speech Mode
        Write(DRUMCONTROLL,    0x00);                    //clear drum mode
}
```

Sounds and Silence

The next step in controlling the FM channels is the ability to turn them on and off. In sound chip lingo, a sound is keyed on when it is turned on, and turning it off is denoted as key release. These terms come from MIDI, where they are events, but they probably stem from the model of the piano keyboard. Before we can look at the procedure to key the channel, we need to look at the structure which will store all the sound characteristics.

Channel attributes are not readable from the FM chip. Thus, the programmer must keep track of the values written to the various voices. The sbfm_INST structure defines fields to hold the FM-instrument settings:

```
typedef struct {
        byte op1soundchar;
        byte op2soundchar;
        byte op1level_output;
        byte op2level_output;
        byte op1attack_decay;
        byte op2attack_decay;
        byte op1sustain_release;
        byte op2sustain_release;
        byte op1wave_select;
        byte op2wave_select;
        byte op1feedback_con;
} sbfm_INST;
```

Note there are two fields for every sound characteristic, each prefixed with one of two operators. There is only one feedback_con field since that information applies to how the two operators are connected.

To turn on the sound in a channel, we call the sbfm_KeyOn() function with three parameters: the channel number, a pointer to an instrument structure, and the frequency at which the sound should intone:

```
void sbfm_KeyOn(int channel, sbfm_INST *inst, word fnum)
{
```

First, the frequency is saved for later when the key is released. The block_fnumh array is declared as static at the top of the SBFM.CPP module. Both operators are then attenuated and the channel is turned off so that any snaps, crackles, or sputters will not occur as we write the registers with our instrument data.

```
block_fnumh[channel] = (byte)((fnum >> 8) | KEYON);
Write(LEVEL_OUTPUT + ofst_op1[channel], 0xff);      //attenuate this
Write(LEVEL_OUTPUT + ofst_op2[channel], 0xff);      //channel's volume
Write(KEYON_BLOCK_FNUMH + channel, 0x00);           //key release
```

Next, data from *inst* is transferred to the relative registers for the first operator.

```
Write(SND_CHAR        + ofst_op1[channel], inst->op1soundchar);
Write(LEVEL_OUTPUT    + ofst_op1[channel], inst->op1level_output);
Write(ATTACK_DECAY    + ofst_op1[channel], inst->op1attack_decay);
Write(SUSTAIN_RELEASE +ofst_op1[channel],  inst->op1sustain_release);
Write(WAVE_SELECT     + ofst_op1[channel], inst->op1wave_select);
```

The same transfer then happens for the channel's second operator.

```
Write(SND_CHAR            + ofst_op2[channel], inst->op2soundchar);
Write(LEVEL_OUTPUT        + ofst_op2[channel], inst->op2level_output);
Write(ATTACK_DECAY        + ofst_op2[channel], inst->op2attack_decay);
Write(SUSTAIN_RELEASE     + ofst_op2[channel], inst->op2sustain_release);
Write(WAVE_SELECT         + ofst_op2[channel], inst->op2wave_select);
```

The inividual operators are now set, so we write the channel fields.

```
Write(FEEDBACK_CON + channel, inst->op1feedback_con);
Write(FNUML + channel, (byte)fnum);
```

The lower 8 bits are written via a cast to the user type byte, which truncates the fnum argument. Finally, the last step is to key on the channel. Note that this is done last so noise is not heard; if we had keyed on the sound before making adjustments to the operator registers, unwanted noises might take place.

```
   Write(KEYON_BLOCK_FNUMH + channel, block_fnumh[channel] );
}
```

The previous value stored in block_fnumh is written out to key on the sound. The entire function is shown in Listing 15-3.

Listing 15-3 The sbfm_KeyOn() function

```
void sbfm_KeyOn(int channel, sbfm_INST *inst, word fnum)
{
   //store block_fnumh; we will need it for key release later
   block_fnumh[channel] = (byte)((fnum >> 8) | KEYON);

   //keyoff an instrument before programming the fm chip,
   //it helps minimize spurious sounds

   Write(LEVEL_OUTPUT + ofst_op1[channel], 0xff);   //attenuate
   Write(LEVEL_OUTPUT + ofst_op2[channel], 0xff);   //channels volume

   Write(KEYON_BLOCK_FNUMH + channel, 0x00);        //key release

   // Wait until you're done re-programming a channel before keying
   //it on. This helps to reduce spurious clicks, pops, and noises.

                            //re-program operator 1
   Write(SND_CHAR           + ofst_op1[channel], inst->op1soundchar);
   Write(LEVEL_OUTPUT       + ofst_op1[channel], inst->op1level_output);
   Write(ATTACK_DECAY       + ofst_op1[channel], inst->op1attack_decay);
   Write(SUSTAIN_RELEASE    + ofst_op1[channel], inst->op1sustain_release);
   Write(WAVE_SELECT        + ofst_op1[channel], inst->op1wave_select);

   //re-program operator 2
   Write(SND_CHAR           + ofst_op2[channel], inst->op2soundchar);
   Write(LEVEL_OUTPUT       + ofst_op2[channel], inst->op2level_output);
   Write(ATTACK_DECAY       + ofst_op2[channel], inst->op2attack_decay);
   Write(SUSTAIN_RELEASE    + ofst_op2[channel], inst->op2sustain_release);
```

```
Write(WAVE_SELECT          + ofst_op2[channel], inst->op2wave_select);

    //misc. characteristics
    Write(FEEDBACK_CON + channel, inst->op1feedback_con);
    Write(FNUML  + channel, (byte)fnum);

    //key it on
    Write(KEYON_BLOCK_FNUMH + channel, (byte)block_fnumh[channel]);

}
```

Shutting down a channel is pretty trivial. We just need to reset a bit in the FM chip.

```
void sbfm_KeyRelease(int channel)
{
    Write(KEYON_BLOCK_FNUMH + channel, block_fnumh[channel] & KEYREL);
}
```

This function alters the pitch of a sound which is already playing. Again, it's pretty simple.

```
void sbfm_KeyBend(int channel, word fnum)
{
    block_fnumh[channel] = (byte)((fnum >> 8) | KEYON);
    Write(FNUML + channel, (byte)fnum);
    Write(KEYON_BLOCK_FNUMH + channel, (byte)block_fnumh[channel] );
}
```

Flying Sounds

Now that we've got some decent low-level code up and running, we want a higher-level module which will be called by the rest of the application. In the appendix, this same module acts as an interface to DiamondWare's Sound ToolKit.

This module will be called SOUND.CPP. We'll discuss each of its functions in turn, beginning with sound_Init().

```
void sound_Init(void)
{
    if (sbfm_PresenceTest() == true)    {
        sbfm_Reset();
        initted = true;
    }
}
```

The *initted* variable is declared as user type boolean at the top of the file. Let's examine this trivial-looking function, because there are interesting points worth mentioning.

It begins with a call to our sbfm_PresenceTest(), from SBFM.CPP. Notice how we can tell what module the function is found in? The technique of using prefix mnemonics to identify files is especially useful in a program written by more than one programmer (and containing more than one module!). This same effect occurs when class functions are grouped in the same module since the object's type identifies the module.

Also, note our use of the Boolean variable, *initted*. This is set to true if, and only if, an FM chip is present in the machine. This variable later serves as a semaphore to verify that the FM chip is present and has been initialized.

```
void sound_Kill()
{
  initted = false;
  sbfm_Reset();
}
```

This function resets *initted*. This is important, as we'll soon see. But first, here's the structure to group together the various sound conditions which can exist in our simulator. It is self-evident from the code comments:

```
typedef struct {
        word rpm;           //rpm of engine (on or off)
        word tpos;          //throttle position
        word airspeed;
        boolean engine;     //true if engine running
        boolean airborne;   //true if the plane has taken off
        boolean stall;      //true if stall condition
        boolean brake;      //true if brake on
        boolean crash;      //true if plane is crashing
        boolean sound;      //true if sound is on
} sound_CNTRL;
```

The variable *airspeed* is the air speed. This structure then becomes our logical handle for the sound effects.

First let's design an additional sound of a switch being toggled. This is not part of our sound_CNTRL structure. We'll call PlaySwitch() from within the module whenever a state change indicates that a switch was thrown by the player (e.g., the brakes). Such a sound effect adds a nice touch.

```
static void PlaySwitch(void)
{
  sbfm_KeyOn(U1, &sfx[SWITCH].inst, 0x1d81);
  sbfm_KeyRelease(U1);
}
```

This function was declared with the keyword STATIC. That tells the compiler that only functions within SOUND.CPP will call it. The name PlaySwitch will not be visible to any module other than SOUND.CPP. If it can, the compiler will optimize the call to static functions by making them relative (near) calls. In a Sound Control class, such functions would be protected or private to achieve the same scope limitations.

Having defined the sound_CNTRL struct, we can use it immediately as a parameter to the sound_Update() function:

```
void sound_Update(sound_CNTRL *cntrl)
{
  if (initted == true) {          //Make sure only to update sounds
     UpdateCrash(cntrl);          //if the sound system has been
```

```
        UpdateEngine(cntrl);        //initialized
        UpdateStallB(cntrl);
        UpdateBrake(cntrl);
    }
}
```

When writing this module, we didn't know what assumptions we could make about the code which is calling us. For instance, would sound_Update() be called from some sort of timer interrupt handler? If so, then it's likely that it could be called before sound_Init(). Using the boolean, *initted,* prevents that problem if this module is reused in something other than our flight-simulator project.

There are four functions called from within the sound_Update() function. Each of them are declared static and take one parameter, a pointer to a sound_CNTRL structure. There are no coding abnormalities in these functions, the FM registers are manipulated to load instruments and key on the channel. The numbers used for data as frequency settings are from trial and error, tweak and adjustment. Feel free to mess with these values. The four functions are

1. UpdateCrash() If the flight-simulator code tells us that the player has crashed, we'll use five FM channels to cause a crashing sound effect. OK, OK, so it sounds like a colossal fizzle. Everyone knows what it means!

2. UpdateEngine() This function determines what the current engine noise should be, based on the sound_CNTRL struct. It remembers what it does from call to call and makes the appropriate FM calls to update the sound. The engine noise itself is composed of three separate FM noises. We deliberately leave one of them off when the engine is spinning but is turned "off." This models the real world in which a motor being spun by the propeller would make some noise, but not as much as when it's running under its own power.

3. UpdateStallB() This function turns the stall buzzer on when the flight simulator first tells us that the plane is stalling, and turns it off when (if) the plane recovers.

4. UpdateBrake() If the brake is turned applied or released, we make the switch noise.

Look at Listing 15-4 for complete details.

Listing 15-4 The sound_ Update functions

```
static void UpdateCrash(sound_CNTRL *cntrl)
{
        if (cntrl->crash == true)        {
                sbfm_KeyOn(U1, &sfx[CRASH].inst,  0x016b);
                sbfm_KeyOn(U2, &sfx[CRASH].inst,  0x01e5);
                sbfm_KeyOn(U3, &sfx[CRASH].inst,  0x0202);
                sbfm_KeyOn(U4, &sfx[CRASH].inst,  0x0120);
```

continued on next page

continued from previous page

```
                              sbfm_KeyOn(U5, &sfx[CRASH2].inst, 0x0141);

                              sbfm_KeyRelease(U1);
                              sbfm_KeyRelease(U2);
                              sbfm_KeyRelease(U3);
                              sbfm_KeyRelease(U4);
                              sbfm_KeyRelease(U5);
                  }
}


static void UpdateEngine(sound_CNTRL *cntrl)
{
          static boolean engstate=false;      //engine starts off
          static word lastrpm=0;
          dword fnum;

          if (cntrl->engine != engstate) {  //if the engine state has
                                            //changed
                  PlaySwitch();             //figure out if it has turned on
                                            //or off and turn its sound on or
                                            //off accordingly
                  if (engstate == false) {
                      //Turn part of the engine noise on
                      fnum = (dword)sfx[ENG3].minf;
                      fnum |= block[sfx[ENG3].block];
                      sbfm_KeyOn(E3, &sfx[ENG3].inst, (word)fnum);
                  }
                  else {
                      //Turn part of the engine noise off
                      sbfm_KeyRelease(E3);
                  }
                  engstate = cntrl->engine;
          }

          if (!cntrl->rpm && !lastrpm) {
                  //No sound is produced for this condition
          }
          else if (cntrl->rpm && !lastrpm) {
                  lastrpm = cntrl->rpm;

                  //Turn other part of the engine noise on
                  fnum = (dword)sfx[ENG1].minf;
                  fnum |= block[sfx[ENG1].block];
                  sbfm_KeyOn(E1, &sfx[ENG1].inst, (word)fnum);

                  fnum = (dword)sfx[ENG2].minf;
                  fnum |= block[sfx[ENG2].block];
                  sbfm_KeyOn(E2, &sfx[ENG2].inst, (word)fnum);
          }
          else if (cntrl->rpm && lastrpm) {
                  //Update the engine noise for a new rpm
```

```
                fnum = (dword)(sfx[ENG1].minf + (cntrl->
                            rpm/sfx[ENG1].scale));
                fnum |= block[sfx[ENG1].block];
                sbfm_KeyBend(E1, (word)fnum);

                fnum = (dword)(sfx[ENG2].minf + (cntrl->
                            rpm/sfx[ENG2].scale));
                fnum |= block[sfx[ENG2].block];
                sbfm_KeyBend(E2, (word)fnum);

                if (engstate == true) {
                        //update only if engine is running & has > 0 rpm
                        fnum = (dword)(sfx[ENG3].minf + (cntrl>
                                    rpm/sfx[ENG3].scale));
                        fnum |= block[sfx[ENG3].block];
                        sbfm_KeyBend(E3, (word)fnum);
                }
        }
        else  { //if (!cntrl->rpm && lastrpm)
                    lastrpm = cntrl->rpm;

                //Turn part of the engine noise off
                sbfm_KeyRelease(E1);
                sbfm_KeyRelease(E2);
        }
}


static void UpdateStallB(sound_CNTRL *cntrl)
{
        static boolean laststall = false;

        if ((cntrl->stall == false) && (laststall == false)) {
                //No action needed
        }
        else if ((cntrl->stall == true) && (laststall == false)) {
                //Turn buzzer on
                laststall = true;
                sbfm_KeyOn(STALL, &sfx[STALL].inst, 0x8fae);
        }
        else if ((cntrl->stall == true) && (laststall == true)) {
                //No action needed
        }
        else { //if ((cntrl->stall == false) && (laststall == true))
                //Turn buzzer off
                laststall = false;
                sbfm_KeyRelease(STALL);
        }
}


static void UpdateBrake(sound_CNTRL *cntrl)
```

continued on next page

continued from previous page

```
{
        static boolean brake = true;    //Plane starts with brakes on

        if (brake != cntrl->brake)      {
                brake = cntrl->brake;
                PlaySwitch();
        }

        if (brake != cntrl->brake)      {
                brake = cntrl->brake;
                PlaySwitch();
        }
}
```

Sounding Off

It isn't too terribly complicated to program the FM chip, but then again, it isn't too rewarding either. If you spend some effort on it as we did, the sound effects produced will be mediocre. Digitized sound effects provide maximum impact. On the other hand, many successful games of the past used FM effects; it's not completely worthless either.

The functions suggest classes for both managing the FM-chip registers and controlling the FM for the game as the logical sound-interface class. There are identifiable objects which naturally stand out for possible exploration as distinct classes: operators, channels (or voices), and instruments. We pointed out where static functions would be private or protected class members. The static variable members at the top of each update function could be made private class fields.

This has been the last piece of the puzzle in our quest to build a flight simulator. In the next chapter, we will fit all the pieces together.

CHAPTER 16

16

The Flight Simulator

The cleverest algorithms, the most optimized code, the best-looking graphics . . . are all useless unless they can be melded into a program. You now have an impressive repertoire of effects at your disposal. You know how to create 256-color VGA graphics on a PC-compatible microcomputer. You can decode PCX-format graphics files (and compress the data in them for later use). You can animate bitmaps. You've learned how to create images of three-dimensional objects using wireframe and polygon-fill techniques and how to manipulate those images to show how those objects would appear from any angle or distance. You can build a world and fill it with scenery. You can even perform rudimentary sound programming.

In this chapter, you're going to learn how to use these techniques in an application program. And not just any application, but the type of application to which such techniques are most frequently applied: a flight simulator. We're about to create a working flight simulator. Both the executable code and the source files for this flight simulator are available on the disk that came with this book, under the overall name FSIM.EXE. The first version of the program, called FOF.EXE (short for Flights of Fantasy), has been overhauled to incorporate the classes we created from the previous chapters. The full instructions for operating this program—that is, for flying the flight simulator—and for recompiling it under the Borland C++ compiler are in Appendix A of this book. But the story of how it works is in this chapter.

Interfacing to the View System

Any application can interface to the view system that we have created in this book and draw a view of a three-dimensional world. You need only follow these simple rules:

- Link the following modules to the application's code:

```
VIEW.CPP
POLY2.CPP
SCREENC.CPP
SCREEN.ASM
BRESNHAM.ASM
DRAWPOL2C.CPP
FIX.CPP
LOADPOLY.CPP
WORLD.CPP
POLYLIST.CPP
PALETTE.CPP
```

- You can also link in the PCX.CPP file, if you want to use the Pcx class to load a PCX format graphic file, and the INPUT.CPP file, if you want to use the input functions we used in this book. To use our sound effects, link in SOUND.CPP and SBFM.CPP.

- Create a world database using the format that we've described in this book.

- Write the application. It will need to initialize certain of the modules that contribute to the view system, and then it will need to make a call to the view system on each loop through the program's main event loop. Here is a skeleton program that initializes these modules:

```cpp
// The following files need to be included:

#include   <iostream.h>
#include   <dos.h>
#include   <bios.h>
#include   <conio.h>
#include   <stdlib.h>
#include   <math.h>
#include   "poly2.h"
#include   "view.h"
#include   "screen.h"
#include   "pcx.h"          // Optional

// The following constants are useful:

const XORIGIN=160;          // Virtual x screen origin
const YORIGIN=90;           // Virtual y screen origin
const WIND_X=16;            // Window upper lefthand x
const WIND_Y=15;            // Window upper lefthand y
```

```
const WIND_X2=303;          // Window lower righthand x
const WIND_Y2=153;          // Window lower righthand y
const FOCAL_DISTANCE=400;   // Viewer distance from screen
const GROUND=105;           // Ground color
const SKY=11;               // Sky color

// The following structures must be created:

view_type curview;          // Structure for view descriptor
Pcx background;             // PCX object (optional)
View winview;               // View object

void main(int argc,char* argv[])
{

  // Load background image in PCX format: (optional)

  if (background.load("bg.pcx")) {
          cerr << "Cannot load PCX file. \n"<< endl;
          exit(-1);
  }

  // Load world database:

  if( winview.SetWorld("world.wld") )   {
          cerr << "error loading world.wld" << endl;
          exit(-1);
  }
  // Create offscreen drawing buffer:

  unsigned char screen_buffer=new unsigned char[64000];

  // Save previous video mode:

  int oldmode=*(int *)MK_FP(0x40,0x49);

  // Set video to VGA mode 13h:

  setgmode(0x13);

  // Set initial position and orientation of view:
  curview.copx=0;
  curview.copy=-45;
  curview.copz=0;
  curview.xangle=0;
  curview.yangle=0;
  curview.zangle=0;

  // Set viewport parameters:

  winview.SetView(XORIGIN,YORIGIN,WIND_X,WIND_Y,WIND_X2,
                  WIND_Y2,FOCAL_DISTANCE,GROUND,SKY,
                  screen_buffer);
```

continued on next page

continued from previous page

```
    // Put background in screen buffer: (optional)

    for(long i=0; i<64000L; i++)
            screen_buffer[i]=background.image[i];
    putwindow(0,0,320,200,screen_buffer);

    // Display the current view:

    winview.Display(curview,1);

    // Put buffer contents on screen. (You may alter the
    // coordinates here to put as little or as much of the
    // buffer on the screen as you need.)

    putwindow(0,0,320,200,screen_buffer);

    //restore video mode and clean up memory
    setgmode(oldmode);
    if (screen_buffer)
            delete screen_buffer;
}
```

Animating the View

This puts a single static image on the display. It's up to you to do something with this image. The winview.Display() command will probably be in a loop, so that the parameters of the image can be updated between frames to create an animation.

The image can be changed between frames in two ways. You can change the fields of the *view_type* variable that is passed to winview.Display() so that the user's viewpoint on the world changes from frame to frame. For instance, if the view is initially placed at coordinates (0,0,0) at an orientation of (0,0,0), you can then cause the view to shoot forward down the world z axis by successively incrementing the z coordinate field of the *view_type* variable:

```
while (1) {
  winview.Display(curview,1);
  curview.copz++;
}
```

Movement along the other axes, or combinations of axes, is done the same way. Similarly, successively incrementing (or decrementing) any of the orientation fields—*xangle, yangle*, or *zangle*—would give the impression that the user is rotating in place. A slow rotation around the y axis, that is by steadily increasing the value of *yangle* from 0 to 255, will create rotation such as found when a movie camera pans the horizon. The movement of the view's orientation in the world can be used to create a cimematic fly over.

The second way to change the image between frames is to change the description of an object in the world database. Usually, you'll want to change it in one (or both) of two ways: making an object seem to move or making an object seem to rotate. To do the former, change the *x, y,* and/or *z* fields in the object's descriptor. To do the latter, change the *xangle, yangle,* or *zangle* fields in the object's descriptor. Thus, to make an object seem to rotate on its *x* axis, you would use a loop such as this:

```
while (1) {
  winview.Display(curview,1);
  Object *objptr = (winview.GetWorld()).GetObjectPtr(OBJNUM);
  objptr->xangle++;
}
```

This code assumes that the View class has been provided an access function to the world object and the Object class has made its *xangle* field accessible for external tampering. Animation information can be encapsulated into the Object class, such that the class stores movement data internally along with its position in the world. A semaphore in the class can be used to signal automation on or off. Each loop the object is checked for updating its position in the world, and a public method can be provided such as Animate(*x,y,z,xangle, yangle, zangle,* speed). This supplies a means for external manipulation of the type of motion.

By changing the view position or the world and calling winview.Display() each time to draw a new image of the world in the viewport, the screen will constantly be updated.The user will get the sense that the viewport really is looking into a real world—and that he or she is able to move through that world.

The final step is to connect the user to the world through some sort of input. This can be done via keyboard, joystick, mouse, or any type of input device. The changes in the view are then determined by the user's actions.

Now let's look at a real application, constructed precisely in this manner, that uses the view system: the *Build Your Own Flight Sim in C++,* version 2.0.

Flight Simulators

A flight simulator is a program that simulates the experience of flight. Most flight simulators are based on the performance of flying machines, such as airplanes, jets, helicopters, and spacecraft, though at least one flight simulator of a few years ago and today simulated the flight of a dragon. The spaceflight simulators, such as *Wing Commander* and *Tie Fighter,* are an immensely popular subgenre of flight simulation.

Although there are probably as many ways to build a flight simulator as there are to build a flying machine, most flight simulators look pretty much alike (though they vary widely in quality). We won't vary from the look of the standard flight simulator in this book, though this doesn't mean that the reader of this book need feel constrained to use the view system only in this manner. In fact, the view system presented in this book can be used to construct a nearly infinite variety of programs—not just flight simulators and not even just games.

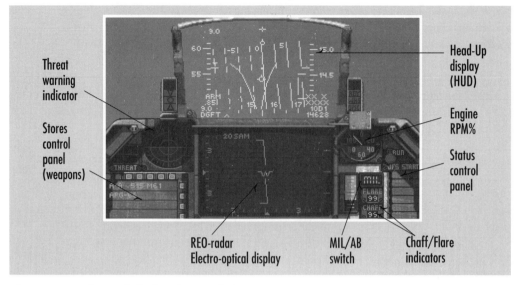

Figure 16-1 The cockpit view from *Falcon 3.0*

The standard flight simulator presents the armchair pilot with the view from the cockpit of an airplane. (The cockpit view of *Falcon* 3.0 is shown in Figure 16-1.) The control panel of the airplane is visible in the lower portion of the video display, while the majority of the screen is taken up with the out-the-window view. It is the out-the-window view that is produced by the view system. The control panel is then laid over the bottom of the viewport to produce the rest of the display.

The most common control device for a flight simulator is the joystick, because it resembles the actual controls of an airplane. However, the keyboard and mouse are also supported by most flight-simulator programs.

The Flight Model

The most important part of a flight simulator, except possibly for the view system, is the flight model. The flight model is the part of the flight simulator that stands between the user's input and the view system. It is the part that determines how an airplane would actually behave. Yet it is submerged so deeply beneath the surface of the simulator that many users may not be aware that it is there.

In the simplest sense, a flight simulator can be looked at as having three parts: user input, the flight model, and the view system. The reality is a little more complicated than this—actually, it's a *lot* more complicated than this—but it doesn't hurt to envision a flight simulator this way as we develop one.

We've already talked about input and the ways in which the actions of the joystick, keyboard, and mouse can be determined by the program code. We've spent many chapters developing a view system. All that remains in this chapter is for us to develop a flight model and meld it together with the other two parts of the program to form a full-fledged flight simulator. The flight model that we are using in this book, as well as much of the code, was originated by Mark Betz.

What does a flight model do? Based on user input, it determines what changes have taken place in the plane's control surfaces, the parts of the plane that determine how it flies. Based on these changes, it determines what changes have taken place in the airplane's position. Thus, we can pass the flight model the user's input and it will output the new position of the airplane. That's not *quite* how it will be done in our flight simulator, but it's close.

Before we talk further about the flight model, though, let's examine the thing to be modeled: airplanes and the way that they fly.

The Flight of an Airplane

We'll be honest here. The flight model used in this book is extremely simple, almost certainly simpler than that used in any commercial flight simulator available in the marketplace. Even so, it's going to stretch our ability to describe its workings in the space that we have available in this book. And the first thing we need to describe is the extremely simplified view of how an airplane flies that is the basis for this flight model.

Most people probably never worry about what makes an airplane fly—except in those tense moments when the plane hits an air pocket and begins lurching up and down as though it's suddenly forgotten whatever it was that was keeping it aloft. These moments notwithstanding, most of us are content to assume that some magic force is making the airplane fly.

Actually, there are four magic forces involved in the flight of an airplane, two of which keep it aloft and two of which try to knock it back to the ground again. Figure 16-2 shows these four forces—lift, gravity, thrust (or propulsion), and drag—at work. Each of these works in a different direction, and each is counterbalanced by one of the other forces. Lift, as you can see in Figure 16-2, pushes the airplane upward while gravity pulls it back down. Thrust pushes it forward while drag resists this forward motion.

When an airplane is in flight, the balance between these forces should be nearly perfect. Of course, if it were completely perfect, the airplane would simply stand still in the air, so we don't want it to be too perfect. (Since the interrelationship between these four forces is quite complex, this sort of perfect balance isn't even possible while the airplane is in the air, so it's a good thing that it isn't desirable.) By selectively

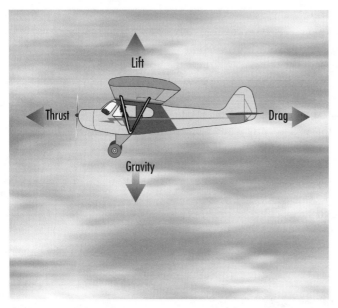

Figure 16-2 The four forces at work during an airplane fight

choosing which of these forces should be dominant at any given moment, we can make the airplane do what we want it to do. When lift is dominant over gravity, for instance, the airplane will go up; but when gravity is dominant over lift, the airplane goes down. Similarly, when thrust is dominant over drag, the airplane goes forward, but when drag is dominant over thrust, the airplane comes to a halt. (Only in a powerful headwind would the airplane actually go backward.) Balancing these forces, however, is no easy task. Thrust, for instance, is intimately associated with lift. Without thrust, there is no lift—which is why you can't make the plane stand still (relative to the air around it) without it falling out of the sky.

At this point, I should apologize to students of aerodynamics for the gross simplifications in this description. Anyone interested in knowing the full details on the subject should seek out a good text on aerodynamics. Alas, such texts are not easy to find and may require the resources of a good college bookstore or library.

Thrust

Let's look at how all of this works in practice. The first force that must come into play when flying an airplane is thrust. Thrust is generally created in one of two ways:

through the principle of reaction mass or through pressure differential. Let's look at these one at a time, starting with reaction mass.

Even if all you studied in college were nineteenth-century poets who used non-standard rhyme schemes, you probably have a vague recollection of Isaac Newton's First Law of Motion, usually restated as: "For every action, there is an equal and opposite reaction." This is why, when you fire a gun, you are propelled backward with the same force that propelled the bullet forward. (The reason you don't move as fast or as far as the bullet is that you're a lot larger than the bullet.) This tells us that we can start something moving in one direction by starting something else moving in the opposite direction. The something else that we move is called the reaction mass, because we're moving it in order to get a reaction.

In theory, for instance, we could propel a boat backward by placing a pile of stones on the deck and hurling them off the bow one by one. The stones would be the reaction mass. In practice this doesn't work very well because the stones are just too much smaller than the boat and the human arm isn't capable of applying all that much force to them. But it probably moves the boat a *little*. (See Figure 16-3.)

The most obvious application of reaction mass is in the rocket engine. Oxygen (or some similarly volatile substance) is heated to high temperatures inside a tank, causing it to expand explosively and escape through a hole located at one end of the tank. These atoms of oxygen (or whatever) serve as a reaction mass. Every time a hot atom shoots out of the hole, the tank itself (and anything that happens to be attached to it) is propelled in the opposite direction. Although an atom is substantially smaller than

Figure 16-3 Propelling a boat by throwing stones

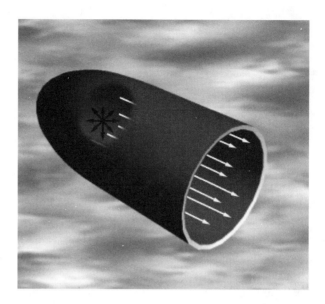

Figure 16-4 A rocket engine at work

the average rocket engine, enough of them shoot out of the engine at the same time, to create a powerful thrust. (See Figure 16-4.)

Jet planes use this same effect to achieve thrust. In fact, jet engines use oxygen for reaction mass just as a rocket engine does. The only real difference between a jet and a rocket is that jet engines heat oxygen from the air around them, while rocket engines carry their own oxygen supplies with them. (This allows rockets to boldly go where jet planes can't—into the airless void of space.)

Propeller-driven airplanes, which is what we are going to simulate in FSIM.EXE, rely more on pressure differential. The propellers are shaped in such a way that, as they rotate, air moves at a speed on one side of the propeller different from that on the other side. This creates more air pressure on one side of the propeller and this air pressure literally pushes the propeller, and the airplane attached to it, in the direction of the low pressure. Thus, the pressure differential produces thrust, as we see in Figure 16-5.

Drag is the countervailing force to thrust. Air doesn't necessarily like having things moving through it at a high speed, so it resists this motion. (Okay, this is blatant anthropomorphization of a substance that has nothing whatsoever resembling human motivation—but this is between friends, right?) This air resistance fights the motion of an aircraft, slowing it down. This drag becomes more and more significant as the craft moves faster and faster. It must be taken into account both in the physical design of the craft, which should minimize friction with the air, and in calculations of how much airspeed (speed relative to the air) will be produced by a given amount of thrust.

Propeller Blade

Figure 16-5 A propeller thrusts an airplane forward because the pressure to the front of the propeller is lower than the pressure behind

Thrust can make an aircraft fly all by itself, if there's enough of it. Aim a rocket at the sky, turn on the engine full blast, and it will shoot upward purely from the force of the reaction mass popping out of its rear end. Once it gets moving fast enough it can keep going on momentum alone, in the pure ballistic flight that we associate with bullets and ICBMs. This is how rockets and missiles fly. But airplanes use thrust mostly just to get moving. Flight is handled by a second force: lift.

Lift

Here's an experiment you can perform in the comfort of your own automobile, preferably after the rush hour and, more wisely, from the passenger's seat. Get on the freeway, drive at the speed limit, and hold your hand out the window—palm down. Now tilt the leading edge of your palm slightly into the wind. Suddenly your hand will be propelled upward; you'll have to fight to keep it down. Congratulations! You've just experienced lift!

There are a couple of reasons why objects such as your hand tend to move upward (or, under some conditions, downward) when air is rushing past them at a high speed. The most important one for our purposes is called the Bernoulli principle or airfoil effect. Like the thrust produced by a propeller, it results from differences in air pressure. (In fact, propellers are utilizing the Bernoulli principle, too.) When air pressure

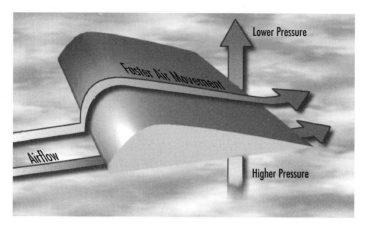

Figure 16-6 The pressure under the wing is higher than the pressure over it, which pushes the airplane into the air

gets higher on the underside of an object than on the upper side, the air literally pushes the object up.

Let's look at how this works in the case of an airplane. We've turned on the engine and the propellers are spinning, creating reaction mass that thrusts us forward. Air rushes past us both above and below. That air creates pressure, a force pressing directly against the wings and body of the plane. However, because it is passing both above and below the body of the plane, that force pushes both upward and downward at the same time. It would seem to cancel itself out. How then do we produce flight?

The shape of the wing is such that the air flows somewhat differently over the top than over the bottom, leaving a pocket of low pressure directly above the wing. Thus, the air pressure is greater beneath the wing than above it. (See Figure 16-6.) The faster the air moves past the wing, the greater the pressure differential. Once the air is rushing with sufficient speed over the wings to produce enough upward force—that is, lift—to overcome the gravity that is pulling the airplane down, it will actually begin to rise off the ground. We will have achieved flight!

Because lift results from the shape of the airplane and its wings, it is affected by the angle at which the airplane is oriented on its local x axis, known technically as the angle of attack. Tilting the front end of the plane upward, so that more of the underside of the body and wings is exposed to the onrushing air, increases lift and therefore altitude. Unfortunately, it also slows the airplane down, which decreases lift. Tilting back too much, therefore, can cause the airplane to stall and start falling out of the sky. (See Figure 16-7.)

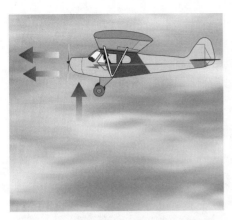

Figure 16-7 The angle of attack affects the degree of lift

(a) A small angle of attack produces a small amount of lift

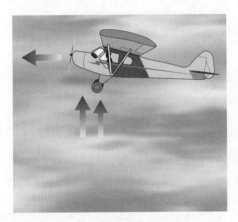

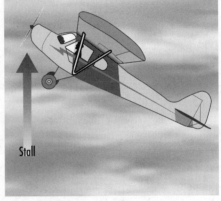

(b) A large angle of attack produces more lift

(c) Too large an angle of attack causes the plane to stall

Controlled Flight

Aerodynamic flight would be little more than an interesting curiosity were it not possible to *control* the way in which an airplane flies. We've figured out how to thrust an airplane forward and make it rise into the air, but now we need to control the amount of thrust that we produce and the amount of lift that results from that thrust. And, of course, we also need some way to control the direction in which we are flying, so that we can travel to the destination of our choice.

Controlling thrust is easy. Ultimately, thrust is produced by a fuel such as gasoline. This fuel is either burned to heat oxygen (in the case of a jet) or funneled into an engine to turn a propeller (in the case of a prop plane). Therefore the amount of thrust is roughly proportional to the amount of fuel flowing to the engine, which can be easily controlled with a throttle. Opening the throttle wide lets the maximum amount of fuel flow, producing the maximum amount of thrust. Pulling back on the throttle decreases the amount of fuel and therefore the amount of thrust.

This, in turn, can affect lift, though in a more complicated way than you might think. Since lift is created by the speed at which the plane is traveling through the air, it would make sense that pulling back on the throttle to reduce thrust would also reduce lift. This is true to some extent, but it isn't quite that simple. When the airplane slows down and loses lift, it starts to fall under the pull of gravity. But as it falls, it speeds up—which increases lift. Thus, getting an airplane to go back down after it is in the sky is not a trivial matter and requires some experience. Probably the single most difficult thing that a pilot has to do is to land a plane. Taking off and maneuvering while in the air are trivial by comparison.

Control Surfaces

To simplify these matters and to give us the added ability to steer, airplanes are given control surfaces. These are external features of the plane that can be manipulated via controls placed in the cockpit, effectively allowing the pilot to change the shape of the plane dynamically while flying in order to slow it down, speed it up, make it rise and fall, or steer it left or right.

The three major airplane control surfaces are the ailerons, the elevators, and the rudder. They are controlled from the cockpit by two controls: the stick (or joystick) and the pedals. When moved to the left or right, the stick controls the ailerons. When moved forward and back, the stick controls the elevators. The pedals control the rudder.

What do these control surfaces control? To explain that, we'll need some new terminology. Since an airplane moves in three dimensions, it is capable of rotating on all three of its local axes—the x, y, and z axes. These rotations have names. Rotation on the airplane's local x axis is called pitch, because it makes the craft pitch up and down from the viewpoint of the pilot in the cockpit. Rotation on the airplane's local z axis is called roll, because it makes the craft roll sideways from the viewpoint of the pilot. And rotation on the airplane's local y axis is called yaw, for no reason that I can figure out. (See Figure 16-8.)

The three main control surfaces control the airplane's rotation on these three axes: the ailerons control roll (z rotation); the elevators control pitch (x rotation); and the rudder controls yaw (y rotation). Thus, moving the stick left or right causes the airplane to roll left or right. This in turn causes the airplane to turn in the direction of the roll, making

Figure 16-8 The three rotations of an aircraft

(a) Pitch-rotation on the plane's local x axis

(b) Yaw-rotation on the plane's local y axis

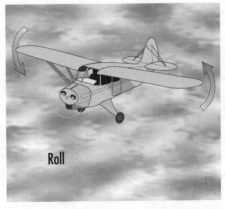

(c) Roll-rotation on the plane's local z axis

the stick into a kind of steering wheel. (Some planes actually use a wheel for this purpose.) Pulling the stick back (i.e., towards you) causes the airplane to pitch up (and climb or stall, depending on how far it pitches). Pushing it forward causes the airplane to pitch down (and lose altitude). Operating the pedals causes the airplane to yaw.

That's it for our description of how an airplane flies. It was an extremely simplified description, but so is the flight simulator that we are going to base on it. In the rest of this chapter, we'll show you how the flight simulator itself is constructed.

The AirCraft Class

The state of our imaginary airplane will be entirely described at any point in time by a structure that we will call the state vector. Everything that our program could possibly want to know about the airplane's position, orientation, motion, and control surfaces will be contained in this one comprehensive structure. This data, however, is not the only part of the airplane to be grouped together under one program element. Several functions are necessary to calculate updated flight statistics and run the flight model. This naturally extends itself to a class definition. Since we are inheriting an earlier version of the program which only described the data, we will inherit the data structure as a public base class and build our class around it. The disadvantage to this is that the data will not be encapsulated, and therefore vulnerable to external tampering. On the other hand, the advantage is that we can use functions already in place in version 1 and do not have to totally rewrite every function which accesses the data fields. The definition of the *state_vect* type, which is quite lengthy, is as follows:

```
struct state_vect
{
    int aileron_pos;       // aileron position -15 to 15
    int elevator_pos;      // elevator position -15 to 15
    int throttle_pos;      // throttle position 0 to 16
    int rudder_pos;        // rudder position -15 to 15
    boolean button1;       // stick buttons, true if pressed
    boolean button2;
    boolean ignition_on;   // ignition state on/off (true/false)
    boolean engine_on;     // engine running if true
    int rpm;               // rpm of engine
    byte fuel;             // gallons of fuel
    byte fuelConsump;      // fuel consumption in gallons/hr.
    int x_pos;             // current location on world-x
    int y_pos;             // current location on world-y
    int z_pos;             // current location on world-z
    double pitch;          // rotation about x 0 to 255
    double yaw;            // rotation about y 0 to 255
    double roll;          // rotation about z 0 to 255
    float h_speed;         // horizontal speed (airspeed, true)
    float v_speed;         // vertical speed for last time slice
    float delta_z;         // z distance travelled in last pass
    float efAOF;           // effective angle of flight
    float climbRate;       // rate of climb in feet per minute
    int altitude;          // altitude in feet
    boolean airborne;      // true if the plane has taken off
    boolean stall;         // true if stall condition
    boolean brake;         // true if brake on
    byte view_state;       // which way is the view pointing
    byte sound_chng;       // boolean true if sound on/off
                           //  state changed
};
```

The meaning of some of these fields should be clear from the comments. Others will become clear as we examine the flight-model code.

Some additional types have been defined to provide some continuity between the modules. In particular, *byte, word,* and *boolean* are defined in the TYPES.H header file. Care should be taken with using the boolean type since, in the future, it will be a C++ compiler built-in type.

With the data structure set, we can now build our class on top of it. The AirCraft class follows; we'll touch on the class functions throughout this chapter.

```
class AirCraft: public state_vect
{
private:
        void  CalcPowerDyn();
        void  CalcFlightDyn();
        float CalcTurnRate();
        void  CalcROC();
        void  ApplyRots();
protected:
        void  DoWalk();
public:
        inline boolean AnyButton()
            { return (button1 || button2) ; }

            // start up the aircraft model. This must be called at program
            // start-up
        boolean InitAircraft( int mode );

            // shut down the aircraft model. You have to call this one at
            // exit
            // If you don't, the very least that will happen is that the
            // sound  will stay on after the program terminates
        void Shutdown();

            // RunFModel() is called to iterate the flight model one step.
            // It is normally called once per frame, but will work
            // properly no matter how often you call it per frame (up to
            // some theoretical limit at which timer inaccuracy at low
            // microsecond counts screws up the delta rate calculations)
        void RunFModel();

        void ResetACState( );

        void LandAC( );

            // Called from GetControls() to remap surface deflection:
        void ReduceIndices();
            // change ignition to opposite state: off or on
        void ToggleIgnition();
        void ToggleBrakes();
};
```

Of course, the private functions are only accessible to the AirCraft class. There are no constructors or destructors, but InitAircraft() acts as the initializing function and Shutdown() parallels a destructor (but without deleting the aircraft from memory).

From Input to Flight Model

Although we've spoken of the input to a flight simulator as though it is conceptually separate from user input, in practice this isn't necessarily so. In the FSIM simulator, for instance, the flight simulation begins with the module that takes the user input. Just as we had a user-input class called EventManager way back in Chapter 5, we have a class called FControlManager, the flight control manager. The entry point to this module is a function (originally written by Mark Betz) called FControlManager::GetControls(). This function takes a single parameter: an AirCraft object. In return, it takes input from the user, converts that input into terms that make sense for the aircraft being modeled—motion on the flight stick, increased throttle, and so forth—and returns any changes to the AirCraft object's base state vector caused by this input.

Once GetControls() has been called to make any necessary changes to the state vector, the main flight-model module can be called. The entry point to the main flight model is a function (also originated by Mark Betz) called RunFModel(). This is a public member function of the AirCraft class. Based on information already in the state vector, this function (and the various subfunctions that it calls in turn) updates the state vector. For instance, if the state vector indicates that the aircraft is flying forward at a certain speed, RunFModel() updates the position of the craft along this line of flight (unless, of course, it finds that the line of flight has been changed since the last time the function was run).

Once both of these functions have been called, the view system can be invoked (using the updated position and orientation information from the state vector) to draw the out-the-window view from the cockpit of the plane. Then we loop to the beginning and start again.

Although this is simple conceptually, there's a lot going on in these two functions, GetControls() and RunFModel(). Most of the rest of this chapter will be spent looking at these functions—and the functions that they call—in detail.

The GetControls() Function

The complete text of the GetControls() function appears in Listing 16-1.

 Listing 16-1 The GetControls() function

```
void FControlManager::GetControls( AirCraft& AC )
```

```
{
  AC.button1 = false;              // reset both button flags
  AC.button2 = false;
  if (usingStick)                  // is the joystick in use?
          CalcStickControls( AC ); // yes, grab the control state
  else if (usingMouse)
          CalcMouseControls( AC );
  else
          CalcKeyControls(AC);     // no, get the keyboard controls
  CalcStndControls( AC );          // go get the standard controls

  CheckSndViewControls( AC );
  AC.aileron_pos = stickX;         // update the state vector
  AC.elevator_pos = stickY;        // with values calculated in
  AC.rudder_pos = rudderPos;       // the other functions
  AC.ReduceIndices( );             // remap the deflections
}
```

The FSIM simulator supports joystick, keyboard, and mouse input. When the program is first run, we'll ask the user which type of control he or she wishes to use and set the flags *usingStick* and *usingMouse* appropriately. (We'll see the code for this later in the chapter.) If the *usingStick* flag is nonzero, then the user wants joystick control. If the *usingMouse* flag is nonzero, then the user wants mouse control. If both the flags are zero, the user wants keyboard control. Of course, only some of the controls will vary according to this flag; others will always be performed through the keyboard. We'll call these the standard controls.

The GetControls() function starts out by setting the aircraft button states to false. If the joystick or mouse buttons (or for keyboard—the TAB or ENTER keys) are pressed they will be set in the appropriate function. The function checks to see if the user has requested joystick, mouse, or keyboard control. If the first, it calls the CalcStickControls() function, passing it the AirCraft object reference (which is in the parameter *AC*), to perform the necessary calculations for the joystick. Likewise, if mouse control is desired, the function calls CalcMouseControls() with *AC* passed as the parameter. If the third, it calls CalcKeyControls() to perform the necessary calculations for the keyboard. Then it calls CalcStndControls() to handle those controls that are always done through the keyboard.

Then it uses the information returned from these functions to update the state-vector positions of three control surfaces: the aileron, the elevator, and the rudder. Since *state_vect* is a public base class for AirCraft such access is permitted. Each of these surfaces has a center position, but can be deflected to either side of these positions. Therefore, we'll measure these positions on a scale of -15 to 15. Since the numbers returned from the earlier functions will be positive, we'll call the AirCraft function ReduceIndices() to adjust them to the proper scale. The text of this function appears in Listing 16-2.

Listing 16-2 The ReduceIndices() function

```
void AirCraft::ReduceIndices( )
{
  aileron_pos /= 7;                          // convert all to +/- 16
  if (aileron_pos > 15)
          aileron_pos = 15;
  else if (aileron_pos < -15)
          aileron_pos = -15;

  elevator_pos /= 7;
  if (elevator_pos > 15)
          elevator_pos = 15;
  else if (elevator_pos < -15)
          elevator_pos = -15;

  rudder_pos /= 7;
  if (rudder_pos > 15)
          rudder_pos = 15;
  else if (rudder_pos < -15)
          rudder_pos = -15;
}
```

That's the basic process involved in receiving input. However, we need to look at some of these functions in more detail. Let's start with the CalcStickControls() function, the text of which appears in Listing 16-3.

Listing 16-3 The CalcStickControls() function

```
void FControlManager::CalcStickControls( AirCraft& AC )
{
  word tempX, tempY;

  tempX = ReadStickPosit(0);               // get current x and y axes
  tempY = ReadStickPosit(1);               // position

     // map the ideal x,y axis range to reality, then assign the result
     // to stickX and stickY.
  tempX = tempX * (25500 / (xmax - xmin));
  stickX = tempX/100;
  tempY = tempY * (25500 / (ymax - ymin));
  stickY = tempY/100;

  if (stickX > xcent)                       // map X 0..255 range to
          stickX = (stickX - xcent);   // -128..127 range
  else
          stickX = (-(xcent - stickX));

  if (stickY > ycent)                       // map Y 0..255 range to
```

```
            stickY = (stickY - ycent);   // -128..127 range
else
            stickY = (-(ycent - stickY));

stickX = (-stickX);                      // flip the values so that
stickY = (-stickY);                      // the control directions
                                         // make sense

if (stickX > 127) stickX = 127;          // bounds check the results
else if (stickX < -128) stickX = -128;
if (stickY > 127) stickY = 127;
else if (stickY < -128) stickY = -128;

if (Button1())                           // get the buttons states
        AC.button1 = true;               // and update the state vector
if (Button2())
        AC.button2 = true;
}
```

This function is called from GetControls(). It calculates the state of the flight controls that are mapped to the joystick when it is in use. This function is only called when the joystick is in use. The comments placed in this function pretty much tell the tale. The goal of the function is to get the position and button status from the joystick (which will be used by GetControls() to set the positions of the rudder, ailerons, and elevator); remap the position of the joystick to a -128 to 127 range (where 0 means that the joystick is perfectly centered); and set the joystick and button fields in the state vector to the appropriate values.

The FControlManager class has an altered EventManager class as its base. If you look at the original EventManager class in Chapter 5, we defined the fields *xcent*, *xmax*, etc. as private to the class. This was changed to protected in order to allow derived classes to access these values.

The actual reading of the stick and buttons is performed by the function ReadStickPosit(). This function reads the joystick port and calculates the stick axes position. The text of this function appears in Listing 16-4. It is similar to the joystick reading function that we created back in Chapter 5. (In fact, you might want to go back and reread that chapter if you're feeling a little shaky on the basics of reading a joystick.)

Listing 16-4 The ReadStickPosit() function

```
byte FControlManager::ReadStickPosit(int axisNum)
{
  dword elapsedTime;
  word bit16Time;

  asm {
            mov ax, axisNum           // load the axisnum
```

continued on next page

continued from previous page

```
            xor ah, ah                 // and then push it while timer turned on
            push ax
            cli                        // disable ints for accurate timing
    }
    timer1->timerOn();                 // start the timer
    asm {
            pop bx                     // this is the axisnum mask

            // read the value of the selected axis by nudging the game port,
            // which sets the four lower bits of the status byte to 1. Exit
            // as soon as the bit for the selected axis resets

            xor ax, ax                 // out anything to port 0x201 and the
            mov dx, gamePort           // axis bits (low nibble) get set to 1
            out dx, al                 // time to reset indicates position
            xor cx, cx                 // we'll time out after 65535 loops
    }
    readloop1:
    asm {
            in al, dx                  // get the byte from the game port
            test al, bl                // test it against the axis mask
            loopne readloop1           // if it's still set loop
            xor ax, ax                 // clear ax in case this was a time_out
            jcxz done                  // did we time-out? if yes exit, ax == 0
    }
    elapsedTime = timer1->timerOff();
    bit16Time = ( word )elapsedTime;
    asm {
            sti
            // now read the joystick port repeatedly until the other 3 axis
            // timers run down. This is MANDATORY.
            mov dx, gamePort
            xor cx, cx
            mov bl, activeAxisMask     // mask for all active axes
    }
    readloop2:
    asm {
            in al, dx                  // same basic operation as in
            test al, bl                // readloop1
            loopne readloop2
            mov bx, bit16Time;         // get elapsed time into bx
            mov cl, 4                  // style x,y values, i.e. 0-255
            shr bx, cl
            mov ax, bx                 // final result in AX
            xor ah, ah                 // don't need the high byte
    }
    done:
    return(_AL);
}
```

This function uses a Borland C++ convention that we haven't used in any of the earlier functions in this book: the *asm* directive. This allows assembly language instruc-

tions to be embedded directly into C++ code. The statement or block of statements within curly brackets that follows the *asm* directive should be written in 80x86 assembly language rather than in C++. This allows us to selectively optimize parts of our code in assembly language or to access low-level functions without introducing a complete assembler module. C++ variables may be accessed from the *asm* code directly, by name. The compiler will substitute the proper addressing mode for accessing the memory location where the value of that variable is stored. Also note that normal C++ style comments using two forward slashes can be used within an *asm* block instead of the assembly language semicolon.

As you'll recall from Chapter 5, the trick to reading the gameport is to output a value—any value—through port 0201H. This tells the gameport that we want to read the joystick. We then read the value at this same port, checking the bit in the byte that we receive that corresponds to the joystick axis (horizontal or vertical) that we wish to read, waiting for it to become 0. The longer it takes to return to 0, the further the stick has been pushed to the right. (To determine specific values for specific positions on the axis we must calibrate the joystick during program initialization.)

The code in the ReadStickPosit() function does all this and more. The main difference between this and our readstick function is that ReadStickPosit() also sets a timer (about which we'll have more to say in a moment). This timer is used instead of the CX register count to provide accuracy for the resulting measurements of stick movement on the axes. It returns the stick timing as a number from 0 to 255.

Mouse input is imitative of the CalcStickControls() with the *x* and *y* positions being supplied by the relpos() function from Chapter 5. Control of the plane with the mouse is difficult—there should be some kind of stabilizer for mouse users by which the flight controls automatically center themselves. This will be left up to future flying enthusiasts.

The last method of controlling the plane is through the keyboard's arrow keys. If the user has requested keyboard input instead of joystick/mouse input, GetControls() calls the function CalcKeyControls(), the text of which is in Listing 16-5. It checks the state of all the flight control keys, and adjusts the values which would normally be mapped to a joystick. GetControls() only calls this function if both joystick and mouse are not being used.

Listing 16-5 The CalcKeyControls() function

```
void FControlManager::CalcKeyControls(AirCraft& AC)
{
  if (_keydown[LEFT_ARROW]) {
        // adjust the control position
        stickX += stick_sens;
        if (stickX > 127)
                stickX = 127;
        _keydown[LEFT_ARROW] = false;
```

continued on next page

continued from previous page

```
        }
        else if (_keydown[RIGHT_ARROW]) {
                stickX -= stick_sens;
                if (stickX < -128)
                        stickX = -128;
                _keydown[RIGHT_ARROW] = false;
        }
        else
                stickX = 0;
        if (_keydown[UP_ARROW]) {
                stickY += stick_sens;
                if (stickY > 127)
                        stickY = 127;
                _keydown[UP_ARROW] = false;
        }
        else if (_keydown[DOWN_ARROW]) {
                stickY -= stick_sens;
                if (stickY < -128)
                        stickY = -128;
                _keydown[DOWN_ARROW] = false;
        }
        else
                stickY = 0;
        if( _keydown[ENTER] ) {
                AC.button1 = true;
                _keydown[ENTER] = false;
        }
        if( _keydown[TABKEY] ) {
                AC.button2 = true;
                _keydown[TABKEY] = false;
        }
}
```

At first glance, there looks to be no input in this function. It simply appears to be checking values of an array. But where did this array come from and how does it get set? They came from a second function, never explicitly called in this function (or any of the others that we will be tracking) named New09Handler(). The workings of this function are effectively invisible to the rest of our program because it is interrupt-driven.

When a key on the PC keyboard is pressed, it triggers a signal called an interrupt that causes the CPU to begin executing a subroutine in the computer's memory called the keyboard handler. Since the PC is capable of generating quite a few different interrupts, this particular interrupt is identified as int 09. During the initialization of our program, however, we will slip a new int 09 handler into place, so that it can perform the keyboard handling that our flight simulator requires. The New09Handler() is that keyboard handler.

The New09Handler() grabs scan codes and updates the boolean state data. The boolean state array is updated on the press of any relevant key. Note that the array elements stay true until read by GetControls() or one of its subsidary functions. The code is in Listing 16-6.

Listing 16-6 The New09Handler() function

```
void interrupt New09Handler(...)
{
  byte code;
  if (KeyWaiting())        {          // make sure something in port
        code = inportb(kbd_data);      // grab the scan code
        keypressed = true;             // returned by KeyPressed()
        if( code < 128 )
                _keydown[code] = true;
  }
  Old09Handler();                      // chain the old interrupt
  *nextBiosChar = biosBufOfs;          // make sure the bios keyboard
  *lastBiosChar = biosBufOfs;          // buffer stays empty
}
```

When a keyboard interrupt is executed, the CPU port that we have labeled with the constant *kbd_data* contains the scan code of the key that has been pressed. (For a discussion of scan codes, see Chapter 5.) The value returned from reading the keyboard port directly is 1 byte where the first bit (0x80) signifies that the key has been pressed (0) or released (1). The lower 7 bits make up the scan code for the key. Thus, if the scancode for the [TAB] key is 15 (0x0f), a code of 15 returned from reading the keyboard port means the [TAB] key is pressed down, while a code of 143 (0x8f) signifies that the [TAB] key has been released. The New09Handler() checks if the code is less than 128; this is equivalent to qualifying only those codes without the high bit set. It then calls the regular BIOS keyboard handler function, which will not detect the key press because we've already read the scan code out of the port. Note that this function also sets a flag called keypressed so that other functions will know that a keyboard event has taken place. For details on which keys control which functions of the airplane, see Appendix A.

The CalcKeyControls() function checks to see if any keys were pressed that relate to joystick functions. If so, it sets the same variables that are set by the CalcStickControls() function, to make it look as though the joystick has been moved. The constants LEFT_ARROW, RIGHT_ARROW, etc. used as indices into the *_keydown* array have all been declared in EVNTMGR2.H and set equal to the appropriate scan code for that key.

Finally, in GetControls(), after polling the appropriate input device, we call the CalcStndControls() function, which checks for keys that don't relate to joystick movements. The text of this function appears in Listing 16-7.

Listing 16-7 The CalcStndControls() function

```
void FControlManager::CalcStndControls( AirCraft& AC )
{
  if (_keydown[KEY_GT]) {
         rudderPos += rudder_sens;
         if (rudderPos > 127)
                  rudderPos = 127;
         _keydown[KEY_GT] = false;
  }
  else if (_keydown[KEY_LT]) {
         rudderPos -= rudder_sens;
         if (rudderPos < -128)
                  rudderPos = -128;
         _keydown[KEY_LT] = false;
  }
  else
           rudderPos = 0;
  if ((_keydown[PAD_PLUS]) && (AC.throttle_pos < 15)) {
         AC.throttle_pos++;
         _keydown[PAD_PLUS] = false;
  }
  else if ((_keydown[PAD_MINUS]) && (AC.throttle_pos > 0)) {
         AC.throttle_pos--;
         _keydown[PAD_MINUS] = false;
  }
  if (_keydown[KEY_I]) {
         if (AC.ignition_on)
                  AC.ignition_on = false;
         else
                  AC.ignition_on = true;
         _keydown[KEY_I] = false;
  }
  if (_keydown[KEY_B]) {
         if (AC.brake)
                  AC.brake = false;
         else
                  AC.brake = true;
         _keydown[KEY_B] = false;
         }
  }
}
```

The controls monitored by this function operate the rudder (KEY_GT < and KEY_LT >), the throttle (PAD_PLUS and PAD_MINUS), the ignition (KEY_I), and the brake (KEY_B). The function checks the appropriate keys, and then sets the flags in the

AirCraft object that monitors the appropriate controls. It resets the _keydown_ array element to false, so that subsequent visits to the function do not cause false triggers.

That gets us through the input functions that we'll need during one loop of the flight simulator animation. Now, we can reveal the constructor code to the FControlManager:

```
FControlManager::FControlManager():EventManager()
{
  usingMouse =
  usingStick = false;
  for(int ii = 0; ii < 128; _keydown[ii++] = false) ;
  stick_sens = 15;                   // arbitrary value for control sensitivity
  rudder_sens = 15;
  keypressed = 0;
  activeAxisMask = joydetect();
}
```

The private fields of FControlManager are initated, as well as the global _keydown_ array and *activeAxisMask* variable. The joydetect() function has been added to the assembly I/O file. This new file with the joydetect() function has been renamed to MIO2.ASM and its header file to MIO2.H. We'll see the destructor for the FControlManager class later, after we have covered the int 9 installation process.

Now we need to call the AirCraft::RunFModel() function to see what our flight model makes of these changes to the control surfaces and other state vector parameters. The text of the RunFModel() function appears in Listing 16-8.

Listing 16-8 The RunFModel() function

```
void AirCraft::RunFModel( )
{
  float tmpX, tmpY, tmpZ;          // these are used later to preserve
  float newX, newY, newZ;          // position values during conversion
  static float collectX;           // accumulators for delta changes in
  static float collectY;           // x, y, and z world coords; adjusts
  static float collectZ;           // for rounding errors

#ifndef __TIMEROFF__               // this block controls whether the
  loopTime = timer1->timerOff();   // timer is in use for flight
  timer1->timerOn();               // calculations...
  if (!(loopTime /= 1000)) loopTime = 1;
  AddFrameTime();
#else                              // ...or running at LOOP ms for debugging
  loopTime = LOOP;                 // purposes
#endif

#ifdef __BUTTONBRK__               // this block allows a "break on button"
  if (button1)
```

continued on next page

continued from previous page

```
        loopTime = loopTime;         // SET BREAKPOINT HERE FOR BREAK
#endif                               // ON BUTTON 1 PRESS

    // these five calls update all current aircraft parameters
    // based on the input from the last pass through the control loop
    // The order in which they are called is critical

  if (opMode == WALK)
        DoWalk();                    // traverse the world
  else {
        CalcPowerDyn();              // calculate the power dynamics
        CalcFlightDyn();             // calculate the flight dynamics
  }

  InertialDamp();                    // apply simulated inertial damping
  CalcROC( );                        // find the current rates of change
  ApplyRots( );                      // apply them to current rotations

  // The rest of this function calculates the new aircraft position
  // start the position calculation assuming a point at x = 0, y = 0,
  // z = distance travelled in the last time increment, assuming that
  // each coordinate in 3D-space is equivalent to 1 foot

  tmpX = 0;                          // using temps because we need the
  tmpY = 0;                          // original data for the next loop
  tmpZ = delta_z;

    // note that the order of these rotations is significant
    // rotate the point in Z
  newX = (tmpX * cos(Rads(roll))) - (tmpY * sin(Rads(roll)));
  newY = (tmpX * sin(Rads(roll))) + (tmpY * cos(Rads(roll)));
  tmpX = newX;
  tmpY = newY;

    // rotate the point in x
  newY = (tmpY * cos(efAOF)) - (tmpZ * sin(efAOF));
  newZ = (tmpY * sin(efAOF)) + (tmpZ * cos(efAOF));
  tmpY = newY;
  tmpZ = newZ;

  efAOF = Degs(efAOF);

  // rotate the point in y
  newX = (tmpZ * sin(Rads(yaw))) + (tmpX * cos(Rads(yaw)));
  newZ = (tmpZ * cos(Rads(yaw))) - (tmpX * sin(Rads(yaw)));
  tmpX = newX;
  tmpZ = newZ;

    // translate the rotated point back to where it should be relative to
    // the last position (remember, the starting point for the rotations
    // is an imaginary point at world center)
```

```
collectX += newX;
if ((collectX > 1) || (collectX < -1))        {
          x_pos -= collectX;
          collectX = 0;
}
collectY += newY;
if ((collectY > 1) || (collectY < -1))        {
          y_pos -= collectY;
          collectY = 0;
}
collectZ += newZ;
if ((collectZ > 1) || (collectZ < -1)) {
          z_pos += collectZ;
          collectZ = 0;
 }

altitude = -(y_pos - SEA_LVL_Y);

    // set the airborne flag when we first take off
if ((!airborne) && (altitude))
          airborne = true;
}
```

This is a great deal more complex than the GetControls() function. It begins by calling a timer object to determine how much time has passed since the last frame of animation and records the result in the *loopTime* long integer variable. Then it starts the timer again. The timer functions are in the HTIMER.CPP module. In this file, the HTimer class is defined. The HTimer objects allow events to be timed to within a resolution of one microsecond. We don't need quite that fine a resolution here, so the first thing that RunFModel() does with the *loopTime* variable is to divide it by 1,000 to produce a millisecond resolution. The value of *loopTime* will be used again and again in the functions that follow, in order to determine how much time has passed since the previous frame. This information, in turn, will be used to determine how much the world of the simulator has changed since the last frame. If we did not perform these calculations, the simulator would run at a different speed on different machines. The aircraft would shoot across the skies on fast 486s but crawl on slow 286s. This way, the animation becomes smoother—i.e., is sliced into more and more frames—without becoming faster. The AddFrameTime() function, which is called after the *loopTime* variable has been set, is used to record the frame rate, so that it can be printed out later for debugging purposes.

Then we update the state vector (the base class to the RunFModel() function) to reflect any changes that have occurred since the previous frame of the animation. Next, a series of calculations determine what the new physical position of the aircraft will be, based on the state vector values. Finally, if the plane has reached flight altitude for the first time, a flag is set to indicate that the craft is now airborne. This allows certain controls to operate that could not operate if the craft were sitting on the ground. (For instance, it is impossible to bank the plane while it is on the ground.)

When debugging the FSIM program, if __TIMEROFF__ is defined at the top of the AIRCRAFT.CPP module, then this function sets the *loopTime* variable to LOOP ms, else it uses the timer1 object to time the running of the flight model. The *loopTime* variable is set on entry to this module with the number of elapsed ms since the last call, and then used throughout the module for calculations of rate of change parameters. Defining __TIMEROFF__ effectively sets the performance of the system to match a 486. This lets you step through the flight model and get a nice, smooth change in the variables you're watching. Otherwise the timer continues to run while you're staring at the debugger screen.

The RunFModel() function calls five functions, four of which are AirCraft member functions that update state-vector and global fields: CalcPowerDyn(), CalcFlightDyn(), InertialDamp(), CalcROC(), and ApplyRots(). These functions must be called in the order just listed, since there is a dependency on the fields being adjusted. This is noted in the comments throughout AIRCRAFT.CPP. To understand how the flight model works, we'll have to examine these five functions one at a time, starting with the CalcPowerDyn() function which appears in Listing 16-9. This function adjusts the engine RPM for the current iteration of the flight model. It also toggles the *engine_on* in response to changes in the *ignition_on* parameter.

Listing 16-9 The CalcPowerDyn() function

```
void AirCraft::CalcPowerDyn(  )
{
  if ( ignition_on ) {                              // is the ignition on?
            if (! engine_on)                        // yes, engine running?
                    engine_on = true;               // no, turn it on

    // increment or decrement the rpm if it is less than or greater than
    // nominal for the throttle setting
            if (rpm < (375 + (throttle_pos * 117)))
                    rpm += loopTime * .5;
            if (rpm > (375 + (throttle_pos * 117)))
                    rpm -= loopTime * .5;
  }
  else {                                            // no, ignition is off
            if (engine_on)                          // is the engine running?
                    engine_on = false;              // yes, shut it off
            if(rpm)                                 // rpm > 0 ?
                    rpm -= (int)(loopTime / 2);     // yes, decrement it
  }
  if (rpm < 0)                                      // make sure it doesn't
          rpm = 0;                                  // end up negative
}
```

This function first checks to see if the GetControls() function received a command requesting the engine be turned off. If so, it resets the appropriate flags in the state vector structure. If the throttle and ignition settings have been changed since the last loop, it resets the engine appropriately, changing its RPMs or shutting it on or off. (Negative RPMs are checked for and eliminated if found, since they aren't possible.)

Next comes the CalcFlightDyn() function, in Listing 16-10. This function calculates the flight dynamics for the current pass through the flight model. It does not attempt to model actual aerodynamic parameters. Rather, it is constructed of equations developed to produce a reasonable range of values for parameters like lift, speed, horizontal acceleration, vertical acceleration, etc.

Listing 16-10 The CalcFlightDyn() function

```
void AirCraft:: CalcFlightDyn( )
{
  float iSpeed;                        // speed ideally produced by x rpm
  float lSpeed;                        // modified speed for lift calc.
  float hAccel;                        // horizontal acceleration (thrust)
  float lVeloc;                        // vertical velocity from lift
  float gVeloc;                        // vertical velocity from gravity
  float AOA;                           // angle of attack

  iSpeed = rpm / 17.5;                 // calc speed from rpm
  iSpeed += (pitch * 1.5);             // modify speed by pitch

  hAccel = ((rpm * (iSpeed - h_speed)) / 10000);
  hAccel /= 1000;
  hAccel *= loopTime;

  if ((brake) && (!airborne)) {
          if (h_speed > 0)             // brake above 0 m.p.h.
              h_speed -= 1;
          else
              h_speed = 0;             // settle speed at 0 m.p.h.
  }
  else
          h_speed += hAccel;           // accelerate normally

  lSpeed = (h_speed / 65) - 1;         // force speed to range -1..1
  if (lSpeed > 1) lSpeed = 1;          // truncate it at +1
  lVeloc = Degs(atan(lSpeed));         // lift curve: L = arctan(V)
  lVeloc += 45;                        // force lift to range 0..90
  lVeloc /= 5.29;                      // shift to range 0..~17
  lVeloc *= (-(pitch * .157) + 1);     // multiply by pitch modifier
  lVeloc /= 1000;                      // time slice
  lVeloc *= loopTime;

  gVeloc = loopTime * (GRAV_C / 1000); // grav. constant this loop
  v_speed = gVeloc + lVeloc;           // sum up the vertical velocity
  if ((!airborne) && (v_speed < 0))    // v_speed = 0 at ground level
          v_speed = 0;
```

continued on next page

continued from previous page

```
climbRate = v_speed/loopTime;           // save the value in feet/min.
climbRate *= 60000L;

delta_z = h_speed * 5280;               // expand speed to feet/hr
delta_z /= 3600000L;                    // get feet/millisecond
delta_z *= loopTime;                    // z distance travelled

if (delta_z)                            // find effective angle of flight
        efAOF = -(atan(v_speed / delta_z));
else
        efAOF = -(atan(v_speed));       // atan() returns radians

AOA = Degs(efAOF);                      // convert to degrees

// handle a stalling condition

if (((pitch < AOA) && (AOA < 0)) && (h_speed < 40)) {
        if ((pitch - AOA) < -20)
            stall = true;
}
if (stall) {
        if (pitch > 30)
            stall = false;
        else
            pitch++;
}
}
```

This is where the flight modeling begins in earnest. At the beginning of the function, floating-point variables are created for the speed, acceleration, lift, and angle of attack of the aircraft.

Initially, the speed is calculated based on the current engine RPMs. This is modified according to the airplane's pitch, which will determine the angle at which it is moving through the air and thus the amount of drag from air resistance. As we saw a moment ago, the variable *loopTime* contains the number of milliseconds that have passed since the last frame of animation was drawn and the last flight model calculations performed. The acceleration of the craft per millisecond is calculated next and multiplied by this value, giving the distance that we have traveled since the last frame, which is stored in hAccel.

If the airbrake is on and the craft is in the air, it is slowed down by a unit—i.e., the *hSpeed* field of our AirCraft class is decremented. It is not allowed to become negative, however, since airplanes don't fly backwards. If the brake isn't on, the acceleration value is added to the *hSpeed* field.

The lift speed is then calculated. The amount of downward gravitational acceleration since the last frame is also calculated and added to the amount of lift since the last frame. (The gravitational constant, contained in GRAV_C, is negative, so this is effectively a subtraction.) The sum is the amount of change in the aircraft's vertical position since the last frame—i.e., the vertical speed, which is contained in *vSpeed*. This is used to calculate the airplane's climb rate.

Next, the angle of attack is calculated and finally, we check to see if the aircraft's angle of flight is such that it is in danger of stalling, in which case the appropriate flags are set.

In order to get the proper rotation rates on our aircraft, we need to simulate the effect of inertia (the tendency of an object in motion to remain in motion that we mentioned earlier) on the rotation of the craft. This is done in the function InertialDamp() (Listing 16-11). The inertia simulation is fairly crude but gives the interested reader a basis for writing his or her own code to approximate the actual rotation of an airplane. You can see its effects now in the momentum when the aircraft is rolled.

Listing 16-11 The InertialDamp() function

```
void near InertialDamp()
{
        // simulates inertial damping of angular velocities
  if (deltaVect.dPitch) {
        deltaVect.dPitch -= deltaVect.dPitch / 10;
        if ( ((deltaVect.dPitch > 0) && (deltaVect.dPitch < .01 )) ||
                ((deltaVect.dPitch < 0) && (deltaVect.dPitch > -.01 )) )
                deltaVect.dPitch = 0;
  }
  if (deltaVect.dYaw) {
        deltaVect.dYaw -= deltaVect.dYaw / 10;
        if ( ((deltaVect.dYaw > 0) && (deltaVect.dYaw < .01 )) ||
                ((deltaVect.dYaw < 0) && (deltaVect.dYaw > -.01 )) )
                deltaVect.dYaw = 0;
  }
  if (deltaVect.dRoll) {
        deltaVect.dRoll -= deltaVect.dRoll / 10;
        if ( ((deltaVect.dRoll > 0) && (deltaVect.dRoll < .01 )) ||
                ((deltaVect.dRoll < 0) && (deltaVect.dRoll > -.01 )) )
                deltaVect.dRoll = 0;
  }
}
```

The InertialDamp() function is not a member of the AirCraft object class and uses a global variable, *deltaVect*, to store its values from frame to frame.

The final flight-model function is CalcROC() (Listing 16-12). This function in turn calls the CalcTurnRate() function (Listing 16-13). The CalcROC() function finds the current rate of change for aircraft motion in the three axes, based on control-surface deflection, airspeed, and elapsed time.

Listing 16-12 The CalcROC() function

```
void AirCraft::CalcROC( )
{
  float torque;

    // load deltaVect struct with delta change values for roll, pitch, and
    // yaw based on control position and airspeed
    if (airborne)   {
        if (aileron_pos != 0)   {
                torque = ((h_speed * aileron_pos) / 10000);
                if (deltaVect.dRoll != (torque * loopTime))
                        deltaVect.dRoll += torque * 6; // *8
        }
  }
  if ( elevator_pos != 0 )      {
            torque = ((h_speed * elevator_pos) / 10000);
            if ((!airborne) && (torque > 0))
                    torque = 0;
            if (deltaVect.dPitch != (torque * loopTime))
                    deltaVect.dPitch += torque * 1.5;      //* 4
  }
  if (h_speed)   {
            torque = 0.0;
  if (rudder_pos != 0)
            torque = -((h_speed * rudder_pos) / 10000);
            torque += CalcTurnRate( );
            if (deltaVect.dYaw != (torque * loopTime))
                    deltaVect.dYaw += torque * 1.5;    // *8
  }
}
```

Listing 16-13 The CalcTurnRate() function

```
// FLIGHT MODEL STEP 4
float AirCraft::CalcTurnRate(   )
{
  float torque = 0.0;

  if ((roll > 0) && (roll <= 90))
          torque = (roll * .00050);                // (.00026)
  else if ((roll < 0) && (roll >= -90))
          torque = (roll * .00050);
  return( torque );
}
```

ROC stands for Rate Of Change. These two functions determine the rate at which the orientation of the craft is changing. The CalcTurnRate() function is called from CalcROC() to calculate the current turn rate based on roll.

Finally, to cause the craft to rotate, we call the ApplyRots() function (Listing 16-14).

This function applies the current angular rates of change to the current aircraft rotations, and checks for special case conditions such as pitch exceeding +/-90 degrees.

Listing 16-14 The ApplyRots() function

```
void AirCraft::ApplyRots( )
{
          // transform pitch into components of yaw and pitch based on roll
  roll += deltaVect.dRoll;
  yaw += deltaVect.dYaw;
  pitch += (deltaVect.dPitch * cos(Rads(roll)));
  yaw += -(deltaVect.dPitch * sin(Rads(roll)));

          // handle bounds checking on roll and yaw at 180 or -180
  if (roll > 180)
          roll = -180 + (roll - 180);
  else if (roll < -180)
          roll = 180 + (roll - -180);
  if (yaw > 180)
          yaw = -180 + (yaw - 180);
  else if (yaw < -180)
          yaw = 180 + (yaw - -180);

    // handle special case when aircraft pitch passes the vertical
  if ((pitch > 90) || (pitch < -90))        {
          if (roll >= 0)
                    roll -= 180;
                    else if (roll < 0)
                    roll += 180;
          if (yaw >= 0)
                    yaw -= 180;
          else if (yaw < 0)
                    yaw += 180;
          if (pitch > 0)
                      pitch = (180 - pitch);
          else if (pitch < 0)
                      pitch = (-180 - pitch);
  }
    // dampen everything out to 0 if they get close enough

  if ((pitch > -.5) && (pitch < .5))
          pitch = 0;
  if ((roll > -.5) && (roll < .5))
          roll = 0;
  if ((yaw > -.5) && (yaw < .5))
          yaw = 0;

}
```

The orientation of the aircraft is handled in an interesting manner in this simulator. Although a standard 360-degree system is in use, the aircraft rotation on the yaw and roll axes is actually measured in a range of -180 to +180. This is done only as a matter of preference. Even odder, the pitch axis is measured from -90 to +90. When it passes outside of this range, it is immediately mapped back into this range and one of the other axes is adjusted to compensate for the remapping. For instance, if the plane pitches back until it is pointing straight up, it will have a pitch value of +90. But if it then goes further and begins rolling over onto its back, the pitch value will be reset to +89 and the yaw value rotated 180 degrees to indicate that the airplane is now pointing in the opposite direction. The ApplyRots() function performs this remapping. It watches for values on the roll, yaw, and pitch axes that fall out of the ranges appropriate to each and performs the appropriate wraparounds and other adjustments.

All that remains in the flight modeling at this point is to determine where the airplane is located within the world space. Assuming that one world coordinate is equal to one foot in the virtual world, the RunFModel() function calculates the new position of the craft. The technique used here is based on the same three-dimensional rotation equations that we studied earlier. Basically, the point at which the plane was located at the time of the last frame of animation is assumed to be the world origin and the airplane is rotated around this position by its yaw, pitch, and roll values, then moved along the z axis by the distance that it has traveled since the last frame. Finally, it is translated back to its original position plus the change that has just been added to it.

That's it for the flight model. We now need a frame program from which to call both the flight model and the view system. That's the role of the FSMAIN.CPP module. The main() function from this module, which is also the main() function of our flight simulator, appears in Listing 16-15.

Listing 16-15 The main() function

```
void main( int argc, char* argv[])
{
  window(1,1,80,25);                    // conio.h: set a text window
  clrscr();                             // conio.h: clear the screen
  textcolor(7);                         // conio.h: set the text color
  oldVmode = *(byte *)MK_FP(0x40,0x49); // store the text mode
  opMode = FLIGHT;                      // assume normal operating mode
  ParseCLP( argc, argv );               // parse command line args
  if (opMode == HELP) {                 // if this is a help run
          DisplayHelp();                // then display the command
          exit(0);                      // list and exit
  }
  if (opMode == VERSION) {
          DisplayVersion();
          exit(0);
   }
  StartUp();
  steward.GetControls(theUserPlane);    // input.cpp: run one control pass
                                        // to initialize the AirCraft fields
```

```
        // *** main flight loop ***

while(!steward.Exit())  {

        steward.GetControls(theUserPlane);
        theUserPlane.RunFModel();
        SoundCheck(theUserPlane);
        GroundApproach();
        if (!UpdateView( theUserPlane ))           // make the next frame
                Terminate("View switch file or memory
                    error","UpdateView()");
        if (opMode != DEBUG)                        // if not debugging...
                blitscreen( bkground.Image() );     // display the new frame
        else                                        // else if debugging...
                VectorDump();                        // do the screen dump
}
checkpt = 4;                                        // update progress flag
Terminate("Normal program termination", "main()");
}
```

The first part of this function determines whether we've typed any command-line options. This enables us to put the program in a special debugging mode. In this mode, instead of displaying a cockpit view, the program will produce a changing readout of the values of variables. We used this mode to help in debugging it. However, we've left it in so that you can see it in operation. For full instructions on how to use the debugging mode, see the flight-simulator instructions in Appendix A. Alternatively, there are command-line options that will print out all of the available command-line options (the HELP option), will print out which version of the program this is (the VERSION option), and will draw frames without the airplane present (the WALK option).

The GetControls() function is called twice in main(). The first time it is used to initalize any fields in the AirCraft object. The FControlManager declared globally at the top of the FMAIN.CPP module is called *steward*, while the AirCraft object is declared globally as *theUserPlane*.

Both the HELP and the VERSION options cause the program to terminate early. If neither of these is chosen, the StartUp() function (Listing 16-16) is called which initalizes the major comoponents of the program: its internal systems for input, video and sound, as well as the object components which make up the flight model simulator.

Listing 16-16 The StartUp() function

```
void StartUp()
{
  CPU_386 = detect386();           // check for 386 processor
  if (!detectvga())
          Terminate( "No VGA/analog color monitor detected", "main()");
  steward.InitControls();                 // input.cpp: initialize controls
```

continued on next page

continued from previous page

```
checkpt = 1;
clrscr();                              // conio.h: clear the text screen
if ((opMode == FLIGHT) || (opMode == WALK))  { // if not debugging or
                                             // walking...
          setgmode( 0x13 );
          ClrPalette( 0, 256 );
          if (opMode == FLIGHT)
                  if ( !DoTitleScreen() )
                          Terminate( "error loading title image",
                                     "DoTitleScreen()");
}
if ( !InitView( &bkground, opMode ))
        Terminate( "Graphics/View system init failed", "main()" );
checkpt = 2;
if ( !theUserPlane.InitAircraft( opMode ))
        Terminate( "Aircraft initialization failed", "main()" );
checkpt = 3;
}
```

This function performs miscellaneous initialization, including setting the value of certain flags that will be important later in the program and printing a title screen. It starts by looking for a VGA monitor; if it doesn't find one, it aborts, since VGA is required for this program. This task is performed by the detectvga() function from the SCREEN.ASM module, which appears in Listing 16-17.

This function returns true if a VGA card is installed in the system, the VGA card is the active adapter, and the system has an analog color monitor.

Listing 16-17 The detectvga() function

```
; extern "C" boolean detectvga()

_detectvga      PROC
  push     bx
  mov      ax, 1a00h          ; bios function 1ah, subfunction 00h
  int      10h
  cmp      al, 1ah            ; if al = 1ah VGA card installed
  jne      no_vga             ; else exit through no_vga
  cmp      bl, 08h            ; bl = 08h means VGA active and color mon.
  jne      no_vga             ; else exit through no_vga
  mov      ax, 1              ; set return value to boolean true
  jmp      vga_done           ; exit
no_vga:
  xor      ax, ax             ; set return value to boolean false
vga_done:
         pop      bx
         ret
_detectvga      ENDP
```

Then StartUp() calls steward.InitControls() to (surprise!) initialize the aircraft controls. The InitControls() function must be called before putting the video card into graphics mode since it uses console text output to ask the user if they want to use the mouse, calibration of the joystick, etc. The InitControls() function is located in the INPUT.CPP module, and appears in Listing 16-18.

Listing 16-18 The InitControls() function

```
int FControlManager::InitControls()
{
  if (( timer1 = new HTimer() ) != NULL ) {
          if (activeAxisMask != 0) {                // is there at least
                                                    // 1 active
                                                    // joystick?
                  if (UseStick()) {                 // yes, do they want
                                                    // to use it?
                          Calibrate();              // yes, go calibrate it
                          usingStick = true;        // set the stick-in-
                                                    // use flag
                  }                                 // no, don't use the
                                                    // stick
          }                                         // no, there is no
                                                    // joystick
          if((usingStick==false) && hasMouse) {     // if mouse driver
                                                    // is present
                  while(AnyPress());
                  if( UseMouse())
                          usingMouse = true;
          }
          Old09Handler = getvect(9);    // hook keyboard hardware interrupt
                                        // vector
          setvect(9, New09Handler);
          return( 1 );
  }
  return 0;
}
```

This function creates the HTimer for the input module. (This is the same name, *timer1,* as the timer in the aircraft module. They are distinct objects, however, since both are declared as static and therefore local to their respective modules.) It then checks the activeAxisMask to see if there's a joystick attached to the user's machine. This was set in the FControlManager's constructor in the call to joydetect(). If there's a joystick, it calls UseStick() (Listing 16-19) to prompt the user to see if she or he wants to use it. UseMouse() and UseStick() both call YesNo() (also Listing 16-19) since they are so similar. If the joystick is being used, it calls Calibrate() (Listing 16-20) to walk the user through a calibration routine. (See Listing 15-21.) Our simpler method for calibrating the joystick from Chapter 5 could not be used since the HTimer object was needed for measurement, but feel free to refer to that chapter for an explanation of joystick calibration.

Listing 16-19 The UseStick(), UseMouse(), and YesNo() functions

```
boolean FControlManager::UseStick()
{
  return YesNo(
          "=> A joystick has been detected... do you wish to use it? (Yy/Nn)");
}

boolean FControlManager::UseMouse()
{
  return YesNo(
          "=> A mouse has been detected... do you wish to use it? (Yy/Nn)");

}

boolean FControlManager::YesNo(char *st)
{
  cout<<st<<endl;
  char ch = 0;
  while (ch ++ 0)
{
          ch = getch();
          if ((ch == 0x59) || (ch == 0x79))
                  return(true);
          else if ((ch == 0x4e) || (ch == 0x6e))
                  break;
          else
                  ch = 0;
  }
  return false;
}
```

 Listing 16-20 The Calibrate() function

```
void FControlManager::Calibrate()
{
  word tempX, tempY;

  clrscr();
  cout << "——————— Calibrating Joystick ———————" << endl;
  cout << "\nMove joystick to upper left corner, then press a button..." <<
  endl;
  while( ! EitherButton()) {
          xmin = ReadStickPosit(JOY_X);
          ymin = ReadStickPosit(JOY_Y);
  }
  delay(50);
  while( EitherButton() );
```

```
cout << "\nMove joystick to lower right corner, then press a button.."
    << endl;
while( ! EitherButton()) {
        xmax = ReadStickPosit(JOY_X);
        ymax = ReadStickPosit(JOY_Y);
}
delay(50);
while( EitherButton() );
cout << "\nCenter the joystick, then press a button..." << endl;
while( ! EitherButton()) {
        tempX = ReadStickPosit(JOY_X);
        tempY = ReadStickPosit(JOY_Y);
}
tempX = tempX * (25500 / (xmax - xmin));
xcent = tempX/100;
tempY = tempY * (25500 / (ymax - ymin));
ycent = tempY/100;
cout << "\n...calibration complete." << endl;
}
```

The InitControls() function then puts the new keyboard handler in place, after which it returns to the StartUp() function. The keyboard handler is safely installed by using the setvect() function after storing the original interrupt handler as returned from the getvect() function. We restore this older interrupt vector when our program terminates. This is performed automatically in the FControlManager destructor (Listing 16-21).

Listing 16-21 FControlManager destructor

```
FControlManager::~FControlManager()
{
  if(Old09Handler != NULL)
          setvect(9, Old09Handler);
  if (timer1 != NULL)
          delete timer1;
}
```

Note, too, that the timer is deleted to cleanup our memory allocation.

Returning from FControlManager::InitControls(), StartUp() clears the screen, puts the VGA in graphics mode, and calls the DoTitleScreen() function to output the title screen, which is stored on the disk as a PCX file. (See Listing 16-22.) This stays on the display until either a button is pushed or a timer runs down.

Listing 16-22 The DoTitleScreen() function

```
boolean DoTitleScreen()
{
  boolean result = true;
```

continued on next page

continued from previous page

```
   HTimer pixTimer;

   if (bkground.load("title.pcx"))
            result = false;
   if (result)        {
            putwindow( 0, 0, 320, 200, bkground.Image() );
            fadepalin( 0, 256, bkground.Palette() );
            pixTimer.timerOn();
            while ( ! steward.AnyPress())  {
                    if (pixTimer.getElapsed() > 10000000L)
                            break;
             }
            fadepalout( 0, 256 );
            ClrPalette( 0, 256 );
            ClearScr( 0 );
    }
   return( result );
}
```

The StartUp() function then performs initialization on the view system and the flight model. To do this, it calls two functions, appropriately named InitView() and InitAircraft(). These two can be seen in Listings 16-23 and 16-24, respectively.

Listing 16-23 The InitView() function

```
boolean InitView( Pcx* theBGround, int mode)
{
   boolean result = false;

   // load the world from the file:
   if( ! winview.SetWorld("byofs2.wld") )  {
            bkGround = theBGround;
            degree_mul = NUMBER_OF_DEGREES;
            degree_mul /= 360;
            current_view = 5;
            opMode = mode;
            if (SetUpACDisplay())
                    result = true;
   }
   return(result);
}
```

This function is called to initialize the view system. It's found in VIEWCNTL.CPP. The pointer to a Pcx object is passed from StartUp(), and is the same object used to load the title screen at the beginning of the program. Since we never deal with more than one PCX at a time we create a single Pcx object in main() and pass it to other parts of the program as required.

Listing 16-24 The InitAircraft() function

```
boolean AirCraft::InitAircraft( int mode )
{
  boolean result = true;

  loopTime = 0;

  if (( timer1 = new HTimer()) == NULL )
            result = false;
  else {
            ResetACState();        // Set the starting aircraft state
            timer1->timerOn();     // Don't want 0 on first pass
            frmWrap = false;       // Flag used by frame rate accumulator
  }
  opMode = mode;
  return( result );
}
```

Now all of the initialization is out of the way, also call the GetControls() function once to initialize the AirCraft's state vector. Once that's done, we enter the main flight-simulator loop. This loop begins with calls to steward.GetControls() and theUser-Plane.RunFModel() functions.

Now there are a couple of details we have to take care of. First, we need to check to see if there have been any changes in those things in the program that generate sound, so that we can change our sound output accordingly. This is the job of the Sound-Check() function, which appears in Listing 16-25. This does little else but tell the sound_CNTRL structure member that there is not a crash in progress. It then calls ExtractSoundData() which transfers fields from the state vector to the sound_CNTRL structure (see Listing 16-26).

 Listing 16-25 The SoundCheck() function

```
void SoundCheck(AirCraft &svct)
{
  sound_CNTRL cntrl;
  cntrl.crash = false;
  ExtractSoundData(cntrl,svct);
}
```

Listing 16-26 The ExtractSoundData() function

```
static void ExtractSoundData(sound_CNTRL& cntrl, AirCraft& ac)
{
```

continued on next page

continued from previous page

```
if(ac.sound_chng == true)        {
        sound_on = sound_on?false:true;
        ac.sound_chng = false;
        if( sound_on)
                sound_Init();
        else
                sound_Kill();
}
if( sound_on) {
        cntrl.rpm       =       (word)ac.rpm;
        cntrl.tpos      =       (word)ac.throttle_pos;
        cntrl.airspeed  =       (word)ac.h_speed;
        cntrl.engine    =       ac.engine_on;
        cntrl.airborne  =       ac.airborne;
        cntrl.stall     =       ac.stall;
        cntrl.brake     =       ac.brake;
        sound_Update(&cntrl);
}
}
```

The *AirCraft* field *sound_chng* is tested to determine if the sound should be toggled on or off. If the sound is being toggled on, sound_Init() is called. Conversely, sound_Kill() is called. The *sound_on* variable is a local static flag to store the sound's current state.

We need to see if we're approaching too closely to the ground. Assuming the aircraft has already taken off, this results either in a landing (if our approach is slow enough and at the correct angle) or a crash (if not!). This is done by the function Ground-Approach(), shown in Listing 16-27.

Listing 16-27 The GroundApproach() function

```
void GroundApproach()
{
  // handle approaching the ground
  if (opMode == FLIGHT)   {
      if ( (theUserPlane.airborne) && (theUserPlane.altitude <= 0)) {
          if ( ((theUserPlane.pitch > 10) ||  (theUserPlane.pitch < -10)) ||
               ((theUserPlane.roll > 10)  ||  (theUserPlane.roll < -10)) ) {
                ShowCrash();
                theUserPlane.ResetACState();
                SoundCheck(theUserPlane);
                delay(200);
                while( !steward.AnyPress() );    // input.cpp
          }
          else

                theUserPlane.LandAC();    // aircraft.cpp
      }
  }
}
```

Now it's time to translate all of this aircraft information into view information, so that we can draw it on the display. This is a little complicated. So, naturally, an entire function is devoted to it. This function is called to update the offscreen image buffer with the current aircraft instrument display and view overlay. It also checks for changes in sound state and toggles sound on or off in response. See the UpdateView() function in Listing 16-28.

 Listing 16-28 The UpdateView() function

```
boolean UpdateView( const AirCraft& AC )
{
  boolean result = false;

  ViewShift( AC );
  // stuff the struct we'll send to the view system
  MapAngles();
  curview.copx = AC.x_pos;
  curview.copy = AC.y_pos;
  curview.copz = AC.z_pos;

  if (ViewCheck( AC.view_state )) {
          result = true;
          winview.Display( curview, 1);
          if (opMode != WALK) {
                  ctransput( bkGround->Cimage(), bkGround->Image() );
                  if (current_view == 0)
                          UpdateInstruments( AC );
          }
  }
  return(result);
}
```

This function first calls the ViewShift() function (see Listing 16-29) to check which direction we are currently looking toward out of the cockpit and adjusts the view variables for front, back, right, or left views. Then it calls MapAngles() (see Listing 16-30) to convert the rotation system of the AirCraft to the 256-degree system used by the view system. The fields of a *view_type* variable are set to the appropriate position values and the view system is called to draw the out-the-window view. The ctransput() function (appearing in the SCREEN.ASM module and in Listing 16-31) is called to decompress the PCX image of the instrument panel over the view, then UpdateInstruments() (see Listing 16-32) is called to draw the current instrument settings on the instrument panel. Then the main loop copies the entire contents of the screen buffer to the video display.

Listing 16-29 The ViewShift() function

```
static void ViewShift( const AirCraft& AC )
{
```

continued on next page

continued from previous page

```
acPitch = AC.pitch;
acYaw = AC.yaw;
acRoll = AC.roll;

acYaw += view_ofs;
switch (current_view) {
        case 1:
        {
                int temp=acRoll;
                acRoll=acPitch;
                acPitch=-temp;
                break;
        }
        case 2:
                acPitch=-(acPitch);
                acRoll=-(acRoll);
                break;
        case 3:
        {
                int temp=acRoll;
                acRoll=-(acPitch);
                acPitch=temp;
                break;
        }
}

        // handle bounds checking on roll and yaw at 180 or -180
if (acRoll > 180)
        acRoll = -180 + (acRoll - 180);
else if (acRoll < -180)
        acRoll = 180 + (acRoll - -180);
if (acYaw > 180)
        acYaw = -180 + (acYaw - 180);
else if (acYaw < -180)
        acYaw = 180 + (acYaw - -180);

        // handle special case when aircraft pitch passes the vertical
if ((acPitch > 90) || (acPitch < -90))            {
        if (acRoll >= 0)
                acRoll -= 180;
        else if (acRoll < 0)
                acRoll += 180;
        if (acYaw >= 0)
                acYaw -= 180;
        else if (acYaw < 0)
                acYaw += 180;
        if (acPitch > 0)
                acPitch = (180 - acPitch);
        else if (acPitch < 0)
                acPitch = (-180 - acPitch);
}
}
```

This function performs a final rotation on the view angles to get the proper viewing direction from the cockpit. Note that the rotation values in the AirCraft's state vector are assigned to the file scope variables *acPitch*, *acRoll*, and *acYaw*. Final view calculation is done using these variables so that no changes have to be made to the actual AirCraft object.

Listing 16-30 The MapAngles() function

```
static void near MapAngles()
{

    if (acPitch < 0)                // requires conversion if negative
       acPitch += 360;
    acPitch *= degree_mul;
    if (acRoll < 0)
       acRoll += 360;
    acRoll *= degree_mul;
    if (acYaw < 0)
       acYaw += 360;
    acYaw *= degree_mul;

    // stuff the rotations fields of the struct we'll be passing to the
    // 3D view generation system
    curview.xangle = floor(acPitch);
    curview.yangle = floor(acYaw);
    curview.zangle = floor(acRoll);
}
```

The MapAngles() function changes the rotation system being used from the 180 to -180 range in the flight model to the rotation range in NUMBER_OF_DEGREES (FIX.H) used in the view system. The value of *degree_mul* is given by NUMBER_OF_DEGREES/360, and is calculated once in InitAircraft().

Listing 16-31 The ctransput() function

```
; void ctransput( void far* sbuffer, void far* dbuffer);
; NOTE: assumes a 64000 byte 320 x 200 image

_ctransput PROC
  ARG   sbuffer:DWORD, dbuffer:DWORD
  push  bp
  mov   bp,sp
  push  bx
  push  cx
  push  es
  push  ds
  push  di
  push  si
```

continued on next page

continued from previous page

```
      les   di, dbuffer            ; Point ES:DI at destination buffer
      lds   si, sbuffer            ; Point DS:SI at source buffer
      mov   bx,0
      mov   ah,0                   ; Be sure AH is clean
      cld
looptop:
      mov   al,BYTE PTR [ds:si]    ; Get runlength byte
      and   al,128                 ; Repeat run or random run?
      jz    randrun                ; If random run, skip ahead
      mov   al,BYTE PTR [ds:si]    ; Else get runlength byte again
      and   al,127                 ; Remove high bit of count
      inc   si                     ; Point to repeat value
      mov   ah,0
      add   bx,ax                  ; Count pixels in BX
      inc   si                     ; Point to next runlength byte
      mov   ah,0
      add   di,ax                  ; Move destination pointer past
                                   ; zero pixels

      jmp   endloop
randrun:                           ; Handle random run
      mov   al,BYTE PTR [ds:si]    ; Get runlength in AL
      mov   ah,0
      add   bx,ax                  ; Count pixels in BX
      mov   cl,al                  ; Get repeat count in CX
      mov   ch,0
      inc   si                     ; Point to first byte of run
      shr   cx,1                   ; Divide runlength by 2
      jz    randrun2               ; If zero, skip ahead
      rep   movsw                  ; Otherwise, move run of pixels
randrun2:
      jnc   endloop                ; Jump ahead if even
      movsb                        ; Else move the odd byte
endloop:
      cmp   bx,64000               ; Have we done all 64000?
      jb    looptop                ; If not, go to top of loop
done:
      pop   si
      pop   di
      pop   ds
      pop   es
      pop   cx
      pop   bx
      pop   bp
      ret
_ctransput ENDP
```

Listing 16-32 The UpdateInstruments() function

```
static void UpdateInstruments( const AirCraft & AC )
{
  int direction;
```

```
theKphDial->Set( AC.h_speed );
theRpmGauge->Set( AC.rpm );
theFuelGauge->Set( AC.fuel );
theAltimeter->Set(AC.altitude);
direction = floor(AC.yaw);
if ( direction < 0)
        direction += 360;
if (direction)
        direction = 360 - direction;
theCompass->Set( direction );

theSlipGauge->Set( -(AC.aileron_pos / 2) );  // slip gauge shows
                                             // controls

theIgnitionSwitch->Set( AC.ignition_on );
if ((AC.brake) && (current_view == 0))
        Line(23,161,23,157,12);
else
        Line(23,161,23,157,8);
}
}
```

The most important of these functions is the UpdateInstruments() function. This draws the various instruments on the cockpit control panel—altimeter, speedometer, fuel gauge, etc.—with their settings adjusted for the current values in the state vector. Each of these is an instance of the various instrument classes defined in the GAUGES.CPP module. (Definitions are in GAUGES.H.) In order to use these instrument objects to set the visible instrument on the screen, the object need merely be invoked with the proper setting as a parameter—and it will set itself. Since the ctransput() function has decompressed the cockpit control panel graphic from the memory buffer where it is stored on the screen, each gauge object only has to draw its own form in the appropriate place on the control panel.

And we're done, except for moving the contents of the offscreen drawing buffer into video RAM, which the main() function now proceeds to do by calling the blitscreen() function. The main() loop will continue executing until the Exit() function returns true, which will be done when the user presses the (Esc) key.

We've skimmed over a lot of the details here, but this is a complicated program. There's enough information in this chapter to give you a start either on modifying our program or on building a similar program of your own that uses a view system identical or similar to the one presented here.

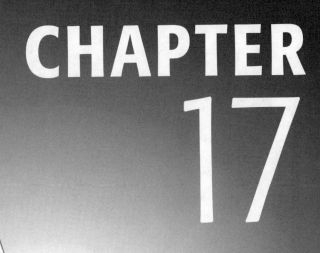

CHAPTER
17

17

The Three-Dimensional Future

How much will the flight simulators of tomorrow resemble the flight simulators of today? Will three-dimensional animators continue to think in terms of polygon-fill graphics of the sort that we've discussed in this book? Or are there bigger and better things on the horizon?

If there's one thing that's guaranteed in the fast-moving world of microcomputers, it's that everything will get bigger and better, not to mention faster. So, yes, the flight simulators of tomorrow will be quite different from the flight simulators of today.

In what ways will they be different? It's possible to make some predictions about that. Most of the techniques that will be used in tomorrow's flight simulators are already known today, and in some cases are already in use. The problem with most of these alternative techniques is that they are substantially slower than polygon-fill graphics. But, as PCs become faster, this factor will grow less important. The realism of these techniques will ultimately win out over their relative sluggishness. Thus, a quantitative increase in processing power will be translated into a qualitative improvement in graphic realism.

In this chapter we'll survey some of these alternatives to polygon-fill graphics and consider how they work.

3D Accelerators

The first type item to consider is not an alternative to polygon-fill graphics, but an improvement to how that graphic is implemented. Instead of writing a book full of routines to transform, shade, and paint the polygon, why not let hardware do it? 3D accelerator cards are video cards that include specific chips to perform such tasks as matrix mathematics, perspective texture mapping, automatic Gouraud shading, anti-aliasing, and Z-buffer sorting/clipping. Most of these cards are fully compatible with normal VGA modes and many include advanced special effects like fogging effects and mapping video on curved objects for use by the programmer/developer. The market for these cards today is very similar to the market for sound cards when they were first introduced. These 3D accelerator cards are not yet considered to be necessary for the home multimedia PC, because there are only a few software companies to write games for them and the price is anywhere from $100 to $250 higher than a high-end SVGA card. Gradually, as more of these cards are introduced and improved, the prices will come down and they will be accepted by the mass market, which will make more software companies interested in developing for them.

There is no standard for 3D accelerator cards, so the method of describing a polygon changes from one board to another. Some only work with triangles (so all polygons have to be broken down into triangle components). Most come with a prepared API library or driver by which to take advantage of the 3D chip set. Since the design of the terrain and objects in the world become increasingly complex, it is important that the data can be extracted from current 3D modeling tools (e.g., Autodesk's *3D Studio MAX,* MacroMedia's *Extreme 3D,* and Caligari's *trueSpace2*). Often programming development time must be set aside for filtering and/or massaging data files from one format to another.

The ATI Graphics Pro Turbo and Matrox MGA Impression Plus were early out on the market with 3D boards. More recently, Creative Labs' 3D Blaster and the Diamond Edge 3D entered into the fray. Undoubtedly more are on their way. (At this time, Western Digital and 3DO have announced development of similar boards.) Be prepared for comparing graphics performance in terms of frame rates and polygons per second!

Polygon Smoothing

In Chapter 12, we investigated three methods of providing more realistic shading to polygons. We used light sourcing in the final flight simulator, but no amount of light sourcing can turn a polygon-fill object into a completely realistic representation of an actual object. What's needed is a combination of the effects explored in Chapter 12, light sourcing, Gouraud shading, and texture mapping. Gouraud shading, as you might recall, helps to disguise the sharp edges of polygons so that they appear to be curved. Another popular technique similar to Gouraud shading is Phong shading. The Phong shading uses a strategy like Gouraud to interpolate colors between two edges of the polygon, but the calculation is more complex.

We saw how the color interpolation of these shading techniques require a great many computations and are therefore quite slow. However, these techniques have gained ground and are used in one form or another in several three-dimensional games on the market such as *Magic Carpet* and *Relentless*. The results produced by these polygon-smoothing techniques are a dramatic improvement over the polygon-fill techniques we've used in this book. Will it be possible in the future to use them in a flight simulator? Almost certainly. In fact, versions of these techniques have already found their way into several recent flight simulators, *Flight Unlimited*, a foremost example.

Ray Tracing

One of the most realistic of all the techniques currently in use for rendering three-dimensional graphics on a computer screen is also one of the simplest. Unfortunately, it's one of the most time-consuming as well. That technique is ray tracing.

You've probably heard of it. Ray tracing has enjoyed tremendously good press in recent years among computer-graphics aficionados, and with good reason. Ray-traced images can be startlingly realistic, often eerily so. Fantasy universes can come alive in a ray-traced picture to a much greater degree than in any motion picture. (As ray-tracing techniques find their way into the cinematic special effects arsenal, though, this distinction may cease to exist.)

How does ray tracing work? It's remarkably simple. (See Figure 17-1) A ray tracer treats the video display of the computer as a window into an imaginary world and each pixel on that display as a ray of light shining through that window into the eye of the viewer. One by one, each of those rays of light (one for each pixel) is traced backwards, from the viewer's eye into the world inside the computer, and the intersections of that ray with objects in that world are noted. If the ray passes through the world without intersecting an object, the pixel is assigned a background color, often black. If it intersects the surface of an object, the intensity of all light sources falling on that surface is calculated and the pixel is assigned the combined color of those light sources minus any colors absorbed by the surface. If the surface is reflective, the angle of incidence of the ray against the surface is calculated and the reflected ray is traced until it intersects a second surface (at which point the surface calculations are performed) or passes out of the world (and the pixel is assigned the background color). If the second surface is also reflective, the process is repeated, ad infinitum (or until the recursive depth of the tracer is reached). As each pixel is assigned a color, a bitmap is created and either displayed on the monitor or output to a file on the disk—usually both.

Although the description in the previous paragraph skimps on some details, that's really just about all there is to ray tracing. Conceptually, ray tracing is probably the

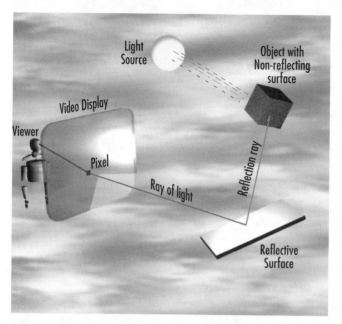

Figure 17-1 Ray tracing involves following a ray of light through a pixel on the video display and into a mathematically described world inside the computer

simplest graphics rendering technique ever developed. But tracing all of those rays takes time. A typical full-screen ray trace may take anywhere from half an hour to several days, depending on the complexity of the scene being rendered. The more objects in the scene, the longer it takes to determine if a ray intersects any of them and the longer the trace requires.

Implementing a Ray Tracer

You may want to consult other sources before you try to write a ray tracer—several of the books in Appendix B cover the topic—but it's not difficult to describe how a naive ray tracer might be constructed. (A naive ray tracer is one in which no attempt has been made to optimize the tracing process through clever algorithms.)

The world inside the ray tracer might be nothing more than an array of structured object definitions. These definitions could take different kinds of objects into account. Thus, some objects might be constructed of polygons while others might be constructed of spheres or curved surfaces. The object definitions would identify the type of object and the parameters specific to that type. Polygons would have lists of vertices, spheres would have a diameter, and so forth. Objects would also be defined by certain properties—reflectiveness, color, smoothness, and so on.

Tracing a ray would be a matter of calculating the angle of the ray and treating it as a line that can intersect these objects. For each type of object, a different kind of calculation can be used to test for an intersection between this line and the object's surface. Determining intersections with polygons, for instance, would be a matter of testing the equation of the line against the equation of the polygon's surface. Determining intersections with spheres would be a matter of testing the equation of the line against the equation of the sphere. Once an intersection is identified, the color of the pixel can be determined as described above.

This process is simple, but it's slow, at least if there are more than a few objects in the list. There are lots of ways of speeding it up, though. Large objects made up of vast numbers of polygons, for instance, can be surrounded by an invisible bounding cube, a simple predefined shape that delimits the outer reaches of the object. (See Figure 17-2.) Before testing the ray for intersections with all of the polygons in the object, the ray can be tested for an intersection with the bounding cube. If there is no intersection, then there's no point in testing against the individual polygons. Such techniques can save significant amounts of ray-tracing time.

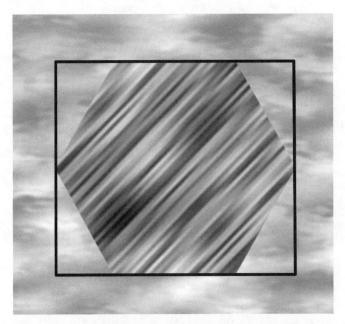

Figure 17-2 An object constructed out of polygons and surrounded by a bounding cube (depicted here as a two-dimensional bounding rectangle)

Bitmapped Animation

So, is it possible to produce real-time animation with ray-tracing techniques? Not now and probably not for a while to come. Even with clever optimizations, ray tracing just takes too darned long to perform. About the only way it would be feasible at present would be to build a custom animation computer with hundreds of thousands of parallel CPUs, so that each pixel on the screen could have its own processor assigned to trace rays through it. With all pixels thus being traced simultaneously, real-time ray tracing just might be possible. Such a custom animation computer would probably be fabulously expensive, but perhaps not beyond the means of some Hollywood studio interested in speeding up the process of computerized special effects (with an eye on possible video game spin-offs).

Yet there *is* a way that we can have ray-traced animation on current generation microcomputers. It isn't slow, it isn't fabulously expensive, and it's actually being used in computer programs that are available as you read these words. It's called bitmapped 3D animation, and it has become popular largely as the result of a series of space games published by Origin Systems, Inc.

The principle behind bitmapped 3D is this: you don't build images on the fly, while the program is running. You build them in advance, store them in memory, and copy them to the video display in real-time. We've talked at some length about bitmapped techniques in earlier chapters of this book, but we've ignored their application to three-dimensional animation in favor of polygon-fill techniques. However, it's time to pull them out of the closet and take a look at them again.

If you've ever played the *Wing Commander* games from Origin Systems, you've seen bitmapped 3D in action. (The most recent version is *Wing Commander III*.) These games are space-combat simulators, in which spaceships maneuver about in real-time on the video display. At their best, the spaceship images can look nearly photographic, but they are not photographs. They are ray traces. Not real-time ray traces, though. They are images that were ray traced while the game was being developed, and then saved as bitmaps. These bitmaps are animated while the program is running.

Yet these bitmaps behave much like polygon-fill images. They can be rotated and scaled, moved around on the screen on all three coordinate axes. How is this possible?

Let's look at that question in some detail. In order to store all of the images necessary to depict a single spaceship being rotated to all possible angles at all possible distances, a huge amount of RAM would have to be used. But the original *Wing Commander* game ran on microcomputers with only 640K of RAM, so this is clearly not what is happening in these games. Apparently, the *Wing Commander* graphics are a clever combination of stored bitmaps and graphic images created on the fly.

I am not privy to the programming secrets of the people who created *Wing Commander*, but I can guess some of the basic techniques. As you watch the game you can see that the rotation of the spaceships isn't especially smooth, certainly not as smooth as it would if the game used polygon-fill techniques (though the bitmap techniques make up for this through sheer realism). This means that the objects haven't been rotated to all possible angles, but probably only increments of about 30 degrees on each axis. Even so, that's a lot of images, especially if all three axes are used. But it isn't necessary to store images of a bitmap rotating on its z axis, because z-axis rotations don't bring any new information into the picture. These rotations can be calculated on the fly by rotating each pixel around the center of the image mathematically. The calculations for doing this are fairly slow, but there are no doubt techniques that can be used to speed them up. In fact, many of the techniques described in this book for rotating vertices are probably at work here, in somewhat modified form.

Rotations on the z axis can be calculated while the game is running, but rotations on the x and y axes cannot, at least not in all situations. Thus, these rotations would need to be performed while the advance is taking place and stored for later animation. Assuming 30-degree increments of rotation on the x and y axes, only 12 images would need to be stored for each axis. But because rotations can be performed on the two axes simultaneously, the images for both x- and y-axis rotations that need to be stored equal 12 times 12, or 144. That's still a lot of bitmaps, but the number is becoming manageable. And there are techniques that can prune this list still further. For instance, if the object being rotated is bilaterally symmetric—that is, if its left side looks like its right side—then a 30-degree, y-axis rotation will be the mirror image of a 330-degree, y-axis rotation, so there's no need to store both of them. One can be created by reversing the other (i.e., copying the pixels to the screen in the opposite order on each scan line). That means that only 6 y-axis rotations need be stored, for a total of 72 images instead of 144. There may be other tricks that can cut down on the number of images as well, particularly if the object exhibits other useful symmetries.

Even when we've taken rotations into account, though, it remains necessary to scale the images so that these same rotations can be depicted at a variety of distances. It would surely be impossible to store all of these images in memory not just once but several dozen times, for each distance from which we wish to view them. Fortunately, there are methods for scaling a bitmap to make it grow larger and smaller, as though the image were coming closer or receding into the distance. The simplest is to add and subtract pixels while the image is being drawn. Removing every other pixel, in both the horizontal and vertical dimensions, makes the image seem twice as far away. Doubling every pixel makes the images seem half as far away. Of course, this has the unfortunate side effect of making the image seem strangely blocky, but anybody who's ever had a close encounter with a *Wing Commander* spaceship knows that this is precisely what happens in that game.

The ray-tracing method is put to a different use in 3D maze games, the most popular being *Doom* and *DOOM II* by ID Software. In these games, the ray-tracing engine is made into a demon, which is an interrupt-driven process constantly being checked and given a slice of the processing time. Similar to *Wing Commander*, the game uses a limited set of views of the major characters in the game. These are stored as a sequence of sprite animations. Since the screen will only draw things that are in the viewing volume, a sequence of rays are cast at a fixed angle from the left side to the right side, and the intersecting background, wall, and/or sprite are projected onto their offscreen buffer. This idea of tracing rays to identify the objects within a viewing volume (viewing volume was discussed in Chapter 13) can be used in other 3D based programs.

Do-It-Yourself Bitmaps

Since bitmapped 3D requires powerful image-creation techniques such as ray tracing, you might think that they would be beyond your means. But all you need to get started with bitmapped 3D is a ray tracer, a little imagination, and the time for experimentation.

Where are you going to get a ray tracer? There are a number of commercial ray tracers on the market, but they tend to be expensive, often costing thousands of dollars. On the other hand, there are also public-domain ray tracers available, which won't cost you a cent. The best, and most popular, of these is the Persistence of Vision (POV) ray tracer, which is available for download from several commercial information services, as well as a number of local BBSs. It can also be purchased as part of the books *Ray Tracing Creations* and *Ray Tracing Worlds,* both from Waite Group Press.

Although free, POV is a remarkably powerful program. The main difference between POV and a commercial ray tracer is not in the quality of the images, which are often quite stunning, but in the lack of a slick interactive interface for creating three-dimensional scenes. With POV, images are created by editing an ASCII text file, just as they are in the programs we've presented in this book. POV boasts a surprisingly subtle scene-description language that can create a wide variety of objects and put them together in elaborate settings. The program is currently in its third version. A number of POV images are available through public-domain software channels. These range from pictures of fish descending marble staircases to jade tigers having encounters with purple snails. What all of these images have in common is that they look far more vivid and realistic than any computer-scanned photograph possibly could.

We don't have space in this book to discuss three-dimensional bitmapped techniques in any more detail than we've gone into here. But if you want to explore this important aspect of 3D programming on your own, I suggest you obtain a copy of POV and experiment with it. (The program is available for the IBM PC, Apple Macintosh, and Commodore Amiga computers.) Create a small object and learn how to save images of it to the disk. (POV comes with a documentation file explaining how to do these things, but *Ray Tracing Creations* also offers invaluable tips on such matters.) Build a library of bitmaps showing the object rotated at 30-degree increments on its y axis, then write a bitmap display routine (using the techniques we showed you earlier in this book) to display these images in sequence on the screen. Presto! Instant ray-traced animation! In real time, too.

The Ultimate Flight Simulator

What will the ultimate flight simulator be like? That's impossible to say. It may use techniques similar to the ray-tracing techniques we described earlier in this chapter, or it may use some completely new algorithm for generating images. The output device on which these images are shown may be a computer screen, a pair of 3D goggles that clamp to the user's face, or a jack that inserts directly into a hole in the back of the user's neck.

One thing's for sure, though. As computers get faster and more powerful, and as three-dimensional graphics techniques become more and more realistic, piloting a flight simulator will become more and more like piloting a real airplane, until the two experiences may be virtually—pun intended—indistinguishable. Armchair pilots won't have to be jealous of real pilots anymore, because they'll be able to do everything that the real ones can do—and a few things that they wouldn't dare to do.

Now that you know a thing or two about writing flight simulators yourself, go try out these techniques on your own computer. Maybe you'll become the programmer who invents the techniques that power the flight simulators of tomorrow.

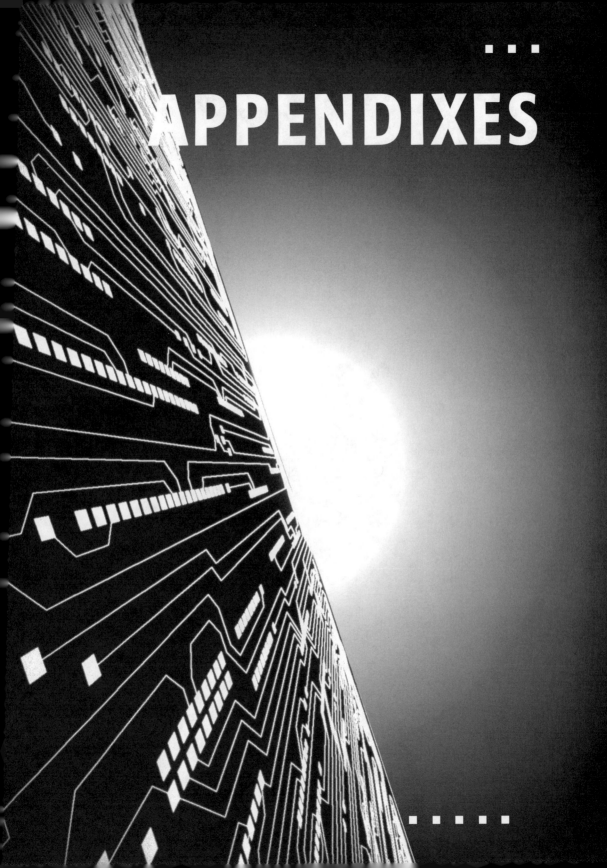

... **APPENDIXES**

......

A

Flying the *Build Your Own Flight Sim in C++* Flight Simulator

The instructions for using the *Build Your Own Flight Sim in C++* flight simulator are quite simple. Unlike big-budget flight simulators—*Falcon* 3.0, for instance, or Microsoft's *Flight Simulator*—FSIM has relatively few options. There are no combat missions or Head Up Displays (HUDs). After all, it is intended as much for demonstrating the principles of flight-simulator programming as it is to provide the armchair pilot with hours and hours of vicarious flying experience. Still, I'd like to think that it's fun to fly and that once you get in the air you'll want to spend a few hours circling around the tiny world of this flight sim, getting acquainted with the scenery. Once you've finished reading this entire book (which you may already have done before you began reading this appendix) and learned how all of the graphic tricks are performed, you may want to spend a few more hours in the cockpit, watching those tricks in action.

The airplane being simulated in the FSIM is a World War I-era biplane. It isn't any particular model of biplane; just think of it as a generic craft of the period. Still, Mark

Betz has modeled the cockpit graphics after genuine cockpits of the era (while taking a few liberties that aficionados of early manned flight will doubtlessly notice and quite possibly tell me about).

To boot the program from DOS, change to the directory where the executable file is stored and type the following at the DOS command prompt:

```
FSIM
```

FSIM will also run under Microsoft Windows. If you'd prefer this option, the file FSIM.ICO (included in the FSIM directory) should be placed in the same directory with the file FSIM.EXE, so that the program can have its own Windows icon.

The FSIM command can optionally be followed by a space and one of several command-line arguments, which are listed in Table A-1. (These arguments are explained in greater detail later in this appendix.) Note that if you forget any of these prompts or the controls for the simulator itself, you can invoke the simulator with the command:

```
FSIM H
```

or

```
FSIM ?
```

to activate help mode. This will cause a help screen listing the command prompts and control keys to be printed. The program will then abort.

If you have a joystick plugged into your machine, you'll be asked if you wish to use it. If you type Y (for "Yes"), the program will step you through a joystick calibration routine similar to the one discussed in Chapter 5. If you type N (for "No"), the program will check to see if you have a mouse connected to your machine. If you do, it will ask you if you want to use the mouse.

Once you're into the program proper (assuming you haven't activated any special modes using one of the command line arguments), you'll see the title screen. Press any key to continue or wait a few seconds for the program to continue on its own. You'll then find yourself in the cockpit of the generic *Build Your Own Flight Sim in C++* biplane, staring out a window above a control panel covered with dials, lights, and switches. (See Figure A-1.)

TABLE A-1 ■ Command-line arguments

Each of these arguments follows the name of the program (FSIM) on the command line and must be preceded by a slash(/):

H, h, or ?	Display a help screen
D or d	Enable debugging dump mode
W or w	Enable world traverse mode
V or v	Display program version

Figure A-1 The cockpit of the *Build Your Own Flight Sim in C++* biplane

Here's a quick rundown on what these dials, lights, and switches do.

- The reddish light on the left-hand side of the panel with the letters *BRK* beneath it is the brake light. It indicates whether or not the wheel brakes are currently turned on.

- Below the brake light is the compass. It rotates as you turn the aircraft, with the letters *S, E, N,* and *W* indicating headings of South, East, North, and West, respectively.

- To the right of the brake light is the fuel gauge. In the current version of the FSIM, it is inoperative; it was thrown in mostly for show (and to allow future expansion). You can fly indefinitely without running out of fuel.

- To the right of the fuel gauge is the altimeter, which tells you how high above sea level you are flying. It conveniently starts at zero when you are sitting on the landing field and will move clockwise as you climb.

- To the right of the altimeter is the airspeed indicator, with your airspeed marked off in miles per hour (MPH). As you go faster, it will move clockwise.

- Below the altimeter and airspeed indicator is the slip gauge, which shows your angle of bank (i.e., your orientation on your local z axis, as described in Chapter 16). Although the information provided by a real slip gauge is complex, this one simply follows your joystick motion. After watching it for a while during flight, you should be able to tell how the position of the ball in the slip gauge corresponds to your current angle of bank (z-axis rotation).

- To the right of the airspeed indicator is the RPM indicator or tachometer. It indicates how many revolutions per minute (RPMs) your engine is currently making. Roughly speaking, the more RPMs you rev the engine up to, the faster you will go, though you will notice a lag between increased RPMs and increased speed.

- Below the tachometer are three switches. The two on the left don't do anything and are there just for show. The one on the right turns on your engine; that is, when you activate your engine (which you'll learn how to do in a moment), this switch will go down. In effect, it is an engine indicator. When it is down, your engine is on; when it is up, your engine is off.

- Above and to the right of the engine switch is the real engine indicator. When this small light comes on, your engine will be on. When it goes off, your engine will be off. (You'll also hear an engine noise when your engine is on.)

The basic flight controls are listed in Table A-2. Using these controls, you should be able to take off, climb, turn, and even look out the four sides of your craft.

Let's step through a short flight with the FSIM. This walkthrough (or flythrough) will get you off the ground; figuring out what to do then—like how to land your plane—is up to you.

Before you even leave the landing field, press the [F1], [F2], [F3], and [F4] keys in any order to take a look around your craft. Each key lets you look in a different direction, as described in Table A-2. Notice that the control panel is only visible in the front view; you'll see other parts of your craft to the side and back. (You can still fly while looking to the sides, even work the controls; you just can't see the instruments.)

Now return to the front view by pressing [F1] and press the [B] key. (It doesn't matter whether you press [F] or have the [CAPS-LOCK] key on when you do this, since the FSIM recognizes both lowercase and uppercase control keys.) The brake light will go off, indicating that your wheel brakes are no longer on. Start your engine by pressing [I] (for Ignition). You'll hear the sound of your engine revving up and see your tachometer start to move clockwise. Rev your engine to about 15 or 20 RPMs by tapping (or holding down) the [+] key. After a few seconds, your airspeed gauge will start moving clockwise and your craft will begin taxiing forward.

When you reach about 80 MPH, press the [ ] key and keep on pressing it (or pull back on the joystick) until you start to climb. Now you're in the air!

What do you do next? That's up to you. Play with the controls until you get the hang of flying the aircraft. (If you frequently fly microcomputer flight simulators, you shouldn't have much trouble. If you're a real-life pilot, it might take a moment for you to adjust to some of the simplified aerodynamic assumptions built into the flight model, but if you don't expect too much realism, you should be okay.) Once you figure out what you're doing, take a look around. Enjoy the scenery. Remember that you have four views that you can examine that scenery from. The scenery database included on

> ## Table A-2 ■ Flight controls for the *Build Your Own Flight Sim in C++* flight simulator
>
> **Engine controls:**
> I or i   Toggle ignition/engine on and off
> +/-   Increase/decrease throttle setting
> (On numeric keypad)
>
> **Aircraft controls:**
> Pitch up: Pull joystick back or press ⬇
> Pitch down: Push joystick or press ⬆
> Left roll: Push joystick left or press ⬅
> Right roll: Push joystick right or press ➡
> Rudder: < or > key
> Brake: B or b
>
> **View controls:**
> F1   Look forward
> F2   Look right
> F3   Look behind
> F4   Look left
>
> **Sound control:**
> S or s   Toggle sound on/off

the disk is relatively small, but has a few surprises in it (not all of them realistic). Most of all, enjoy your flight!

When you get tired of looking around, hit the Y key and you'll drop back to DOS or Windows, whichever you booted the program from. Next time you run the program, you might try some of the special command-line options that are included. The special debug mode, for instance, fills the screen with a dump of the variables used in the flight model, as described in Chapter 16, so that you can see how they change with your input. The version-number mode simply tells you which version of the program you are using. The world traverse mode is intended for debugging scenery databases; it allows you to move around using an extremely simplified flight model, in which you climb and turn using the cursor arrows and accelerate and decelerate using the + and - keys. I don't recommend using this mode for your initial exploration of the FSIM world; it takes a lot of the fun out of it.

You'll notice that the scenery database used in the *Build Your Own Flight Sim in C++* flight simulator is small. You can fly off the edge of it quite easily. And what will happen when you do? You'll wrap around to the opposite side of the world. You may even be flying along through perfectly open space, then suddenly find yourself heading directly toward a mountain—or inside of one! In a commercial flight simulator, this problem would be avoided by loading a new scenery database when the user reaches the edge of the current one, but this is a no-frills, single-database simulator.

Have fun! Although it simulates an aspect of the real world, the FSIM is above all a game—a game that you are encouraged to examine, alter, and learn from, to your heart's content.

Bibliography

Books on Three-Dimensional Animation

Adams, Lee, *High Performance CAD Graphics in C,* Windcrest, Blue Ridge Summit, Pennsylvania, 1989.

———, *High Performance Graphics in C: Animation and Simulation,* Windcrest, Blue Ridge Summit, Pennsylvania, 1988.

Artwick, Bruce A., *Applied Concepts in Microcomputer Graphics,* Prentice-Hall, Englewood Cliffs, New Jersey, 1984.

Berger, Marc, *Computer Graphics with Pascal,* Benjamin Cummings, Menlo Park, California, 1986.

Foley, J.D., and A. Van Dam, *Fundamentals of Interactive Computer Graphics Second Edition,* Addison-Wesley, New York, 1990.

Giloi, Wolfgang K., *Interactive Computer Graphics: Data Structures, Algorithms, Languages,* Prentice-Hall, Englewood Cliffs, New Jersey, 1978.

Harrington, Steven, *Computer Graphics: A Programming Approach,* McGraw-Hill Inc., New York, 1987.

Hearn, Donald, and M. Pauline Baker, *Computer Graphics Second Edition*, Prentice-Hall, Englewood Cliffs, New Jersey, 1994.

Hyman, Michael, *Advanced IBM PC Graphics: State of the Art*, Brady, New York, 1985.

LaMothe, André, *Black Art of 3D Game Programming*, Waite Group Press, Corte Madera, California, 1995.

Lampton, Christopher, *Gardens of Imagination*, Waite Group Press, Corte Madera, California, 1994.

Rankin, John. R., *Computer Graphics Software Construction*, Prentice-Hall, Englewood Cliffs, New Jersey, 1989.

Stevens, Roger T., *Graphics Programming in C*, M&T Publishing Inc., Redwood City, California, 1988.

Sugiyama, Marc B., and Christopher D. Metcalf, *Learning C: Programming Graphics on the Amiga and Atari ST*, Compute Books, Greensboro, North Carolina, 1987.

Vince John, *3-D Computer Animation*, Addison-Wesley, New York, 1992.

Watt, Alan, *Fundamentals of Interactive Computer Graphics*, Addison-Wesley, New York, 1989.

Books on IBM-PC/VGA Graphics Programming

Ferraro, Richard F., *Programmer's Guide to the EGA and VGA Cards*, Addison-Wesley, New York, 1988.

Rimmer, Steve, *Bit-Mapped Graphics*, McGraw-Hill, New York, 1990.

General Programming Texts

Eckel, Bruce, *Using C++*, Osborne-McGraw Hill, New York, 1989.

Lafore, Robert, *Object-Oriented Programming in Turbo C++ Second Edition*, Waite Group Press, Corte Madera, California, 1991.

Prata, Stephen, *C++ Primer Plus Second Edition*, Waite Group Press, Corte Madera, California, 1995.

Swan, Tom, *Mastering Turbo Assembler*, Hayden, Indianapolis, Indiana, 1989.

Adding Music to the Flight Simulator

In the chapter on sound programming (Chapter 15), there was a strong case made for using digital for producing sound effects and FM for generating music. The programming involved in creating music generation involves using a timer to update a musical queue. Such a programming task was seen as beyond the scope of a book on flight simulators, since we were concerned with imitating as closely as possible the dynamics that occur when you fly an airplane. We do realize, however, that many people have used the first edition of the book to teach themselves the basics of 3D programming, and are not as interested in simulating an airplane. Some game programmers want to build spaceships (which don't need lift or drag) and fly through galaxies accompanied by a slick 12-bar theme song. For those aficionados, and for the hobbyists who just love to explore the many facets of programming, we present code here which will produce an accompanying musical theme.

To write the low-level code that could account for the many differences of sound cards on the market today would require a lot of research and a bottle of aspirin. The programmer needs to construct a generic interface that can be used no matter which sound card is present in the user's machine. This involves research to find out what sound cards are available on the market and how each of them operates. (The aspirins are for the headaches that occur when you have to test your code on the sound cards that you don't own.)

One solution to this problem is to use a programming tool library. In this appendix, we'll show you how to use DiamondWare's Sound ToolKit to make the flight simulator sound even better, and we'll add some music (by David Schultz), too! The sound library which we'll use is the Diamond Sound Toolkit, available from DiamondWare. DiamondWare's STK supports MIDI music played through the FM chip, and 16 channels of digitized sounds. It can also auto-detect the port, DMA, and IRQ settings used by the sound card. This is a shareware product and should be registered with DiamondWare at 2095 N. Alma School Rd., Suite 12-288, Chandler, AZ 85224. All of the code for this version of the program can be located in the FSIM_STKSOUND directory (and its subdirectories) on the distribution CD.

The remainder of this chapter shows you how to put DiamondWare's Sound ToolKit into the flight simulator. We're going to design the code to fit the same API as the FM module; thus this code will plug into the FSIM without any other changes. For a complete tutorial, guide, and reference to the STK, please read STKMAN.DOC, included with the shareware distribution.

We'll present sound_Init() first, and then sound_Update() because you're already familiar with them from our FM implementation.

```
dov.baseport = (word)-1;
dov.digdma   = (word)-1;
dov.digirq   = (word)-1;
```

These three lines initialize a struct required by the auto-detect function, below. In this case, we want to auto-detect port, DMA, and IRQ, without any manual overrides.

```
if (dws_DetectHardWare(&dov, &dres)) {
   ...
}
else {
   err_Display(dws_ErrNo(), err_DWS);
}
```

The first thing to notice about this sequence of code is that the return value of dws_DetectHardWare() is compared to 0. Like most functions in the STK, it returns 0 if there is an error. We should not encounter an error in this auto-detect function (failure to find a sound board installed is not an error). dws_DetectHardWare() takes two pointer parameters: The first is a pointer to dov, the dws_DETECTOVERRIDES structure which contains the parameters set in the lines above; the second points to the dws_DETECTRESULTS struct dres, which will be filled in during the call. Later, dws_Init() will need these auto-detect results.

Now we want to initialize the STK. The following lines specify how we want it set up and should be self-explanatory from the comments.

```
ideal.musictyp  = 1;        //OPL2 FM music
ideal.digtyp    = 8;        //8-bit
ideal.digrate   = 11000;    //11kHz
ideal.dignvoices = 16;      //16 channels
```

```
ideal.dignchan   = 1;              //mono

if (dws_Init(&dres, &ideal)) {
```

This function call works the same way as dws_DetectHardWare(); it returns nonzero if everything worked. In this case, it uses the dws_IDEAL struct we just initialized, and the results of the auto-detect to set up the sound board (and the STK) properly.

```
initted = true;

atexit(Kill);

LoadIt("music\\moon2.dwm",    &song);
LoadIt("sound\\starter.dwd",  &starter);
LoadIt("sound\\swtch.dwd",    &swtch);
LoadIt("sound\\wind.dwd",     &windorg);
LoadIt("sound\\stallbuz.dwd", &stallbuz);
LoadIt("sound\\plane.dwd",    &planeorg);
LoadIt("sound\\plane.dwd",    &plane1);
LoadIt("sound\\plane.dwd",    &plane2);
LoadIt("sound\\brake.dwd",    &brake);
LoadIt("sound\\landing.dwd",  &landing);
LoadIt("sound\\crash.dwd",    &crash);
```

We're just loading the song and sounds we'll need later.

```
//starter is too loud, make it more quiet
if (!dwdsp_ChngVol(starter, starter, 160))   {
  err_Display(dwdsp_ErrNo(), err_DWDSP);
}
```

DWDSP.C is a module which performs DSP on DWD-format sound effects. There are two functions: one to change the volume of a sound, and the other to change its pitch. Here, we're just changing the volume to compensate for an effect recorded louder than we'd like.

The FSIM itself will change volume and pitch to more accurately reproduce sounds made by the airplane in flight. You might want to pause reading here and run FSIM-STK.EXE now to hear what I'm talking about!

```
mplay.track = song;      //pointer to .DWM music file
mplay.count = 0;         //number of repeats; 0=infinite

if (!dws_MPlay(&mplay))
```

This function call to dws_MPlay() plays our music, in infinite repeat.

```
if (!dws_XMusic(190))
```

This call will lower the music volume setting in the hardware mixer; if there's no mixer, volume will be controlled in software.

Now, for sound_Update():

```
if (dres.capability & dws_capability_DIG) {
  //Only do Updates if digitized sound is available
```

When we called dws_DetectHardWare() (during sound_Init()), it filled in the dws_DETECTRESULTS struct. There's a lot of information in there, including the capabilities of the sound board installed in the machine. The conditional above is checking to see if the sound board can play digitized sounds. If not, let's not bother with anything else; the music will keep playing without our help. Fortunately, most cards support digitized sound playback.

```
if (cntrl->sound == false)   {
  dws_XMaster(0);
}
else    {
  dws_XMaster(242);
}
```

The sound field of the cntrl structure tells us whether the FSIM wants sound/music to play at the moment. If not, we'll turn the master volume down to 0.

```
UpdateEngine(cntrl);
UpdateBrake(cntrl);
UpdateLanding(cntrl);
UpdateStallB(cntrl);
UpdateCrash(cntrl);
UpdateWind(cntrl);
UpdateSwitches(cntrl);
```

This updates the individual sounds, just as we did for FM.

We'll leave UpdateEngine() and UpdateWind() for last, since they're the most complex. First, let's take a look at UpdateBrake().

```
dplay.snd      = brake;        //set up ptr to snd
dplay.count    = 1;            //set up for 1 rep
dplay.priority = 3000;         //give it a priority
dplay.presnd   = 0;            //start it immediatly

if ((lastbrake == false)   &&  //brake was just hit
    (cntrl->brake == true) &&
    (cntrl->airborne == false))  //while plane on ground
{
```

Flight simulators, like most interactive entertainment programs, are state-driven. What the player is doing now, and what he was doing last update, determines how the program should react. This function is responsible for playing a brake-squeal noise. We want to make sure that we only play it once, that it's played when on the ground, etc.

```
if (!dws_DPlay(&dplay))      {   //play a brake noise
    err_Display(dws_ErrNo(), err_DWS);
}

soundplayed = true;              //mark sound as played
```

```
}

if (    (soundplayed == true) &&       //sound was played and
        (    (cntrl->airspeed == 0)  ||   //plane has stopped or
             (cntrl->brake _== false)||   //brake has turned off or
             (cntrl->airborne == true)  )  //plane went airborne
    )
```

This conditional expression merely determines when it's time to stop the brake-noise sound.

```
{
    if (!dws_DDiscardAO(dplay.snd)) //stop any landing noises
```

The dws_DDiscardAO() function stops all occurrences of the brake noise. We're not starting multiple instances of brake-noise in FSIM, but the function works equally well for one instance as for 16.

UpdateLanding(), UpdateStallB(), UpdateCrash(), and UpdateSwitches() are all variations of their FM-version functions, similar to the changes above to UpdateBrake() from its Chapter 15 version. But now we want to take a look at UpdateEngine(). We're going to skip the glue logic where it determines the current and last state, turns on the starter noise, etc., and jump right to the hard part.

Unlike most sound effects, the engine noise is a short sound which is endlessly repeated. It's short to save on memory, but also because it wouldn't sound much better if it was longer. But it's not just an infinite repeat, like our music. We are constantly changing its volume and pitch to respond to the conditions of the airplane. Therefore, we'll want to change these each time the sound is played.

DiamondWare's Sound ToolKit provides a mechanism, called sequencing, for playing one sound back-to-back after another. It's sequencing, not simple looping, that we need here. Think of sequencing as manual looping, only you have the opportunity to change the sound between iterations.

There's one more complication, and then we'll dive into the code. Since sound_Update() is not interrupt-driven, we don't know how much time will elapse between calls. On slower machines, we may not be called again until the playing sound and the one sequenced after it are both finished!

To combat this problem, we keep a counter variable. If the engine sound ever dies out—both the active sound and the one on-deck are done—we increment the counter. When we play each sound, we repeat it as specified by the counter. Thus, on slower machines, we loop each sound several times, insuring that (once we adjust), we never skip or gap.

```
if (!dws_DSoundStatus(presndnum, &result))
```

This call will tell us whether the specified sound is playing, and whether there's another sequenced after it. The address of result is passed to dws_DSoundStatus() to set various status flags.

```
if ((soundplayed == true) &&                          //engine sound has
    (!(result & dws_DSOUNDSTATUSPLAYING)))   {   //run out and died
        count++;                              //play it longer next time
}
```

Note how we wait until the sound drops out before incrementing the count. We're
dynamically tuning our application to the user's machine, without making assumptions
in advance. This is a very good habit to get into.

Next, the result is tested to determine if the sound is not playing, or playing and not
sequenced.

```
if (!(result & dws_DSOUNDSTATUSSEQUENCED))   { //engine sound is
                                               //waiting for a sequence
```

Once we get inside the if clause bracket, we will need to sequence a sound. Because of
the relatively few times this happens, there will not be any extra time spent scaling vol-
ume/pitch on a sound and then not using it.

If a sound is currently sequenced, that means that one is playing, too. In this case,
we do nothing until next time. Otherwise:

```
if (lastrpm != cntrl->rpm)        {            //check to see if pitch
                                               //needs updating
  /*
    . Sequence another of the previous sound; if we spend
    . too much time doing DSP this will play; if we finish in time
    . the new sound will replace it.
  */
  dplay.count = count;

  if (!dws_DPlay(&dplay))
```

We're assuming for now that, since there's no sound sequenced currently, the currently
playing sound could expire immediately. Therefore, we play another instance of it; it
may not be the pitch and volume we want right now, but it will at least prevent sound
dropout.

Then we set up to create the next sound in the sequence to play. We have two sound
pointers, which are swapped here.

```
dplay.snd = plane2;               //use as place holder
plane2 = plane1;                  //swap pointers around
plane1 = dplay.snd;
```

Note that plane.dwd is the biggest possible size we will need it to be (lowest frequency). If you attempt to do anything but shorten the sound you will need to allocate
more memory.

```
newlen  = srclen;                 //size of sound
newlen -= cntrl->rpm / 3;         //the more rpm's the shorter
                                  //the sound will be
if (!dwdsp_ChngLen(plane1, planeorg, newlen))
```

If we take a sound and change its length, the perceived frequency of the new sound is inversely proportional to the new length; short lengths will sound high. For engine/propeller noise, the original is the lowest we'll ever need, so we'll always want to make it higher in pitch to correspond to higher RPMs. This is good from a programming standpoint, because we'll know that the resultant sound can never exceed the size of the original, and hence we can allocate buffers early.

```
volume   = cntrl->tpos;              //vary engine loudness based
                                     //on throttle position
volume *= 8;                         //scale by some factor
volume += 128;                       //add a minimum volume
```

Whereas pitch varies with RPMs, volume varies with throttle position. Obviously this is quite oversimplified from reality, but it works well enough for our purposes.

```
if (!dwdsp_ChngVol(plane1, plane1, volume))      {
   err_Display(dwdsp_ErrNo(), err_DWDSP);
}
```

Unlike pitch change, volume can be changed in place; that is the destination buffer can be the same as the source buffer. If you understand this, then UpdateWind() falls quickly into place.

DiamondWare's Sound ToolKit is well suited to games; with the included DSP code, it's also suited to flight simulators, auto-racing games, and other applications which must simulate engine noise. Let's take a look at this DSP. There are two functions we've been using; one to change volume and one to change pitch. Since volume is simpler, we'll look at it first.

It turns out that, to change the volume of a digitized sound, you need only to multiply each sample by a factor. If this is greater than one, then the sound will get louder, otherwise the sound will get softer.

When making sounds louder, you have to be careful to clip at the limit of the dynamic range of the playback hardware; since DWD files used signed bytes for data, this means you must clip all overflows to 127, and all underflows to -128.

There are a few issues imposed by the DWD file header; we'll point those out as we look at the code.

```
if (!CheckDWDHdr(srcdwd)) {
   errnum = dwdsp_NOTADWD;
   return(0);
}
```

It's always a good idea to validate your parameters to see if they're within the specifications of the function. In this case, we want to see if the buffer we were passed contains a .DWD file (we can determine this by checking some data in the header which is constant for all .DWD files—this was an important consideration in the design of the file format).

```
if (srcdwd != desdwd)              //if the source is different from
{                                  //the destination copy the header
  CopyDWDHdr(srcdwd, desdwd);
}
```

This function can change the volume within a buffer, or it can create the new sound in a different buffer. No assumptions are made as to which the user will choose. Like CheckDWD() above, the details within CopyDWDHdr() aren't really important to this discussion. You can easily check out DWDSP.C if you're curious.

Next, we'll build a look-up table custom-tailored for the specified volume. It allows us to convert each sample with a single array-indexing operation, instead of a multiply, a compare, a conditional branch, and possibly a load operation.

Since we're building the table using only fixed-point arithmetic, we'll handle positive and negative values differently. The code is otherwise straightforward.

```
for (loop=0;loop<HALFTABLE;loop++) {
  /* Postive numbers */
  volume = (int32)loop;
  tblidx = loop;

  tmp = ((volume * (int32)vollev) / dwdsp_IDENTITY);

  if (tmp > MAXPOSVOL)
  {
    tmp = MAXPOSVOL;              //clip if it exceeds the
  }                              //dynamic range

  table[tblidx] = (byte)tmp;

  /* Negative numbers */
  volume = MAXNEGVOL + (int32)loop;
  tblidx = (word)(HALFTABLE + loop);

  tmp = ((volume * (int32)vollev) / dwdsp_IDENTITY);

  if (tmp < MAXNEGVOL)
  {
    tmp = MAXNEGVOL;             //clip if it exceeds the
  }                              //dynamic range

  table[tblidx] = (byte)tmp;
}
```

The work loop is very simple, as I promised above. Each sample in the original is used as an index into the table we just built.

```
for (buffidx=min;buffidx<max;buffidx++) {      //convert sound
  dd->data[(word)buffidx] = table[ds->data[(word)buffidx]];
}
```

The rest is an extra step, required to keep the DWD header up-to-date. One field in the header specifies the maximum dynamic range used by the sound. Since we've just changed that, we should correct the header as well.

```
tmp = ((ds->hdr.maxsample * vollev) / dwdsp_IDENTITY); //Set max sample

if (tmp > MAXPOSVOL) {
  tmp = MAXPOSVOL;
}

dd->hdr.maxsample = tmp;
```

Now, let's take a look at dwdsp_ChngLen(). As mentioned earlier, length and pitch are integrally related. Changing the length can be accomplished simply. If we want to make a sound longer than it was, we can repeat some or all samples several times. If we want to make it shorter, we can omit some samples. This may sound too simple to work, but it actually works passably well!

```
lcm = LCM(srclen, deslen);
```

We need the Least Common Multiple later. Check out the LCM() function; it's some interesting code, though outside the scope of this discussion.

```
dd->hdr.length = deslen;        //set destination DWD data length
```

Go through source DWD, and either duplicate or remove samples in order to pitch shift a sound. It's not as mathematically correct as the real technique, but it's much faster. Note in the following loop that the use of floating-point operations has more to do with readability than performance, except on Pentium processors! A technique akin to Bresenham's line could quickly convert this to integer math.

```
for (x=0;x<deslen;x++)
{
  tmp = ((double)x * (double)lcm) / (double)deslen;
  interpidx = (dword)tmp;

  tmp = ((double)interpidx * (double)srclen) / (double)lcm;
  interpsmp = (dword)tmp;

  desdata[(word)x] = srcdata[(word)interpsmp];
}
```

The work-loop of pitch change is surprisingly simple. The entire desdata buffer array is assigned a srcdata sample from the computed index interpsmp. The arithmetic determines which source sample is closest.

That's it! It was pretty straightforward to convert to the use of the STK. Now we have the FSIM playing several digitized sound effects plus music.

Possible improvements from here would be: 1) you could make a better model for throttle and RPM affecting volume of engine noise. Clearly in the real world, throttle affects volume, but RPM affects it more. You could also model wind noise better, higher speeds probably mean higher frequency wind noise. 2) You could reduce the memory footprint of the sounds, by dynamically loading many of them on an as-needed basis.

Index

& address operator, 15, 88
& bitwise AND operator, 130-131, 141
&& logical AND operator, 130
* dereference operator, 15-17, 62
- unary minus operator, 180
. dot operator, 88
0x prefix (hex), 14
3D accelerators, 598
3D animation, 5, 602-604
3D coordinates, 34-36
3D space, 216-219
16-color mode, 9-10, 19, 60
256-color mode, 9-10, 19, 60, 69-70, 82
386 processor, 304-305
| bitwise OR operator, 130-132
|| logical OR operator, 130

A

address, memory, 14-15, 62-64
address operator (&), 15, 88
address, pixel, 31-34
ailerons, 558, 563, 565
AirCraft class, 560-562
algebra. *See* math
algorithms
    Bresenham's, 176-178, 183, 261, 266,
        416-423
    Painter's, 322-333, 336-337, 344, 346
    polygon-drawing, 261
    Sutherland-Hodgman, 364-366
    Z-Buffer, 333-335
aliasing, graphics, 181
aliasing, sound, 524-525
ambient light, 396-398, 403-404, 409, 478
AND operator (&), 130-131, 141
AND operator (&&), 130
angle of attack, 556, 576-577

angle of bank, 609
animation, 103-110, 122
    bitmapped, 602-604
    books on, 613-614
    cube, 241-244
    and math, 25
    real-time, 167-168
    speed, 119-120
    view, 548-549
    Walkman, 116-122, 154-162
antialiasing, 181
argv parameter, 92, 288
Artwick, Bruce, 3-4, 613
ASCII code, 145
ASCII descriptors, 284-285
asm directive, 566-567
assembler directives, 61
    ARG, 66, 68, 74, 142
    asm, 566-567
    ENDP, 61, 65
    EQU, 74
    LOCAL, 185
    PROC, 61
assembly language, 21, 61-67
assembly language instructions. *See* instructions
assignment operator override, 373-376
assignment statement, 41
attack, angle of, 556, 576-577
AX (AH/AL) register, 62, 68-69
axis, 29-31, 35

B

backface removal, 281-284, 322, 338, 340, 346,
    473-474
    See also hidden surface removal
background color, 73
background, save/restore, 107-108, 110, 120
bank, angle of, 609

Books have a substantial influence on the destruction of the forests of the Earth. For example, it takes 17 trees to produce one ton of paper. A first printing of 30,000 copies of a typical 480-page book consumes 108,000 pounds of paper, which will require 918 trees!

Waite Group Press™ is against the clear-cutting of forests and supports reforestation of the Pacific Northwest of the United States and Canada, where most of this paper comes from. As a publisher with several hundred thousand books sold each year, we feel an obligation to give back to the planet. We will therefore support organizations which seek to preserve the forests of planet Earth.

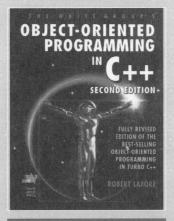

SOFTWARE LICENSE AGREEMENT

This is a legal agreement between you, the end user and purchaser, and The Waite Group®, Inc., and the authors of the programs contained in the disk. By opening the sealed disk package, you are agreeing to be bound by the terms of this Agreement. If you do not agree with the terms of this Agreement, promptly return the unopened disk package and the accompanying items (including the related book and other written material) to the place you obtained them for a refund.

SOFTWARE LICENSE

1.   The Waite Group, Inc. grants you the right to use one copy of the enclosed software programs (the programs) on a single computer system (whether a single CPU, part of a licensed network, or a terminal connected to a single CPU). Each concurrent user of the program must have exclusive use of the related Waite Group, Inc. written materials.

2.   The program, including the copyrights in each program, is owned by the respective author and the copyright in the entire work is owned by The Waite Group, Inc. and they are therefore protected under the copyright laws of the United States and other nations, under international treaties. You may make only one copy of the disk containing the programs exclusively for backup or archival purposes, or you may transfer the programs to one hard disk drive, using the original for backup or archival purposes. You may make no other copies of the programs, and you may make no copies of all or any part of the related Waite Group, Inc. written materials.

3.   You may not rent or lease the programs, but you may transfer ownership of the programs and related written materials (including any and all updates and earlier versions) if you keep no copies of either, and if you make sure the transferee agrees to the terms of this license.

4.   You may not decompile, reverse engineer, disassemble, copy, create a derivative work, or otherwise use the programs except as stated in this Agreement.

GOVERNING LAW

This Agreement is governed by the laws of the State of California.

LIMITED WARRANTY

The following warranties shall be effective for 90 days from the date of purchase: (i) The Waite Group, Inc. warrants the enclosed disk to be free of defects in materials and workmanship under normal use; and (ii) The Waite Group, Inc. warrants that the programs, unless modified by the purchaser, will substantially perform the functions described in the documentation provided by The Waite Group, Inc. when operated on the designated hardware and operating system. The Waite Group, Inc. does not warrant that the programs will meet purchaser's requirements or that operation of a program will be uninterrupted or error-free. The program warranty does not cover any program that has been altered or changed in any way by anyone other than The Waite Group, Inc. The Waite Group, Inc. is not responsible for problems caused by changes in the operating characteristics of computer hardware or computer operating systems that are made after the release of the programs, nor for problems in the interaction of the programs with each other or other software.

THESE WARRANTIES ARE EXCLUSIVE AND IN LIEU OF ALL OTHER WARRANTIES OF MERCHANTABILITY OR FITNESS FOR A PARTICULAR PURPOSE OR OF ANY OTHER WARRANTY, WHETHER EXPRESS OR IMPLIED.

EXCLUSIVE REMEDY

The Waite Group, Inc. will replace any defective disk without charge if the defective disk is returned to The Waite Group, Inc. within 90 days from date of purchase.

This is Purchaser's sole and exclusive remedy for any breach of warranty or claim for contract, tort, or damages.

LIMITATION OF LIABILITY

THE WAITE GROUP, INC. AND THE AUTHORS OF THE PROGRAMS SHALL NOT IN ANY CASE BE LIABLE FOR SPECIAL, INCIDENTAL, CONSEQUENTIAL, INDIRECT, OR OTHER SIMILAR DAMAGES ARISING FROM ANY BREACH OF THESE WARRANTIES EVEN IF THE WAITE GROUP, INC. OR ITS AGENT HAS BEEN ADVISED OF THE POSSIBILITY OF SUCH DAMAGES.

THE LIABILITY FOR DAMAGES OF THE WAITE GROUP, INC. AND THE AUTHORS OF THE PROGRAMS UNDER THIS AGREEMENT SHALL IN NO EVENT EXCEED THE PURCHASE PRICE PAID.

COMPLETE AGREEMENT

This Agreement constitutes the complete agreement between The Waite Group, Inc. and the authors of the programs, and you, the purchaser.

Some states do not allow the exclusion or limitation of implied warranties or liability for incidental or consequential damages, so the above exclusions or limitations may not apply to you. This limited warranty gives you specific legal rights; you may have others, which vary from state to state.

SATISFACTION REPORT CARD

Please fill out this card if you wish to know of future updates to
Build Your Own Flight Sim in C++, or to receive our catalog.

Name: _____ Last Name: _____

et Address: _____

: _____ State: _____ Zip: _____

ail Address _____

time Telephone: (   ) _____

e product was acquired: Month _____ Day _____ Year _____ Your Occupation: _____

erall, how would you rate *Build Your Own Flight Sim in C++*?

☐ Excellent   ☐ Very Good   ☐ Good
☐ Fair   ☐ Below Average   ☐ Poor

at did you like MOST about this book? _____

_____

_____

at did you like LEAST about this book? _____

_____

_____

ease describe any problems you may have encountered with
stalling or using the disk: _____

_____

_____

ow did you use this book (problem-solver, tutorial, reference...)?

_____

hat is your level of computer expertise?

☐ New   ☐ Dabbler   ☐ Hacker
☐ Power User   ☐ Programmer   ☐ Experienced Professional

hat computer languages are you familiar with? _____

_____

lease describe your computer hardware:

Computer _____ Hard disk _____

.25" Disk drives _____ 3.5" Disk drives _____

ideo card _____ Monitor _____

rinter _____ Peripherals _____

ound board _____ CD ROM _____

Where did you buy this book?

☐ Bookstore (name): _____
☐ Discount store (name): _____
☐ Computer store (name): _____
☐ Catalog (name): _____
☐ Direct from WGP   ☐ Other _____

What price did you pay for this book? _____

What influenced your purchase of this book?

☐ Recommendation   ☐ Advertisement
☐ Magazine review   ☐ Store display
☐ Mailing   ☐ Book's format
☐ Reputation of Waite Group Press ☐ Other

How many computer books do you buy each year? _____

How many other Waite Group books do you own? _____

What is your favorite Waite Group book? _____

_____

Is there any program or subject you would like to see Waite
Group Press cover in a similar approach? _____

_____

Additional comments? _____

_____

_____

Please send to: **Waite Group Press**
                   200 Tamal Plaza
                   Corte Madera, CA 94925

☐ **Check here for a free Waite Group catalog**

BEFORE YOU OPEN THE DISK OR CD-ROM PACKAGE ON THE FACING PAGE, CAREFULLY READ THE LICENSE AGREEMENT.

Opening this package indicates that you agree to abide by the license agreement found in the back of this book. If you do not agree with it, promptly return the unopened disk package (including the related book) to the place you obtained them for a refund.